Cosmic Connections

Cosmic Connections

POETRY IN THE AGE OF DISENCHANTMENT

Charles Taylor

THE BELKNAP PRESS OF HARVARD UNIVERSITY PRESS

Cambridge, Massachusetts, and London, England

2024

Library of Congress Cataloging-in-Publication Data

Names: Taylor, Charles, 1931– author.
Title: Cosmic connections : poetry in the age of disenchantment /
Charles Taylor.
Description: Cambridge, Massachusetts ; London, England :
The Belknap Press of Harvard University Press, 2024. |
Includes bibliographical references and index. | English,
with quotations in German and French.
Identifiers: LCCN 2023058564 | ISBN 9780674296084 (cloth)
Subjects: LCSH: Poetry, Modern—18th century—History and criticism. |
Poetry, Modern—19th century—History and criticism. |
Poetry, Modern—20th century—History and criticism. |
Romanticism. | Literature—Philosophy. | Poetry.
Classification: LCC PN1241 .T39 2024 | DDC 809.1/033—
dc23/eng/20240202
LC record available at https://lccn.loc.gov/2023058564

To Aube

CONTENTS

PREFACE

What is this book all about? This may seem a strange question to ask before the book has properly begun. The answer an author might be tempted to give is just: read and see for yourself. But it could nevertheless help the reader if I set out the context in which the developments I describe in the book took place.

The short answer to the question I raised in the previous paragraph could be: the book is about (what I see as) the human need for cosmic connection; by "connection" I mean not just any mode of awareness of the surrounding world, but one shot through with joy, significance, inspiration. My hypothesis is that the desire for this connection is a human constant, felt by (at least some) people in all ages and phases of human history, but that the forms this desire takes have been very different in the succeeding phases and stages of this history.

And what has also been different has been the name for what we seek connection to. "Cosmos" is an older word. Today people talk about our alienation from Nature, from the natural world, from "wilderness" (Thoreau's "wildness"), from the environment which we have been treating as a mere instrument, where it should really be a source of spiritual nourishment.

In this book, I want to look at the last two centuries or so, starting from the shift in literary and artistic sensibility that we tend to sum up with the term "Romanticism," in all its varied forms. I have chosen this shift because it corresponds to a moment when the previously viable form of cosmic connection became unviable.

In this earlier mode, cosmic connection involved the invocation of orders structuring the cosmos which distinguished higher from lower realities, self-realizing orders on the model of Platonic forms; schemes like Lovejoy's Great Chain of Being, or the Kabbalah, which defined the higher reality powering the merely visible / tangible world we live in.

Starting in the seventeenth century, belief in these orders had been steadily undermined, under the growing influence of modern science, principally the Galilean-Newtonian natural science foregrounding the laws of material reality.

The Romantic period, beginning in Germany in the 1790s, was the moment in which the drive to cosmic connection started to take another form. This book begins with an attempt to characterize this form, in which works of art take on a crucial role. I will be mainly concerned with some poets of this period. Their works bypass the philosophical objections to the belief in cosmic orders but generate in the reader the felt sense of a reality higher and deeper than the everyday world around us.

There are parallel movements in the music and visual art of the time, but I will speak mainly in this book about poetry.

The shift from cosmic orders to those invoked by some poets of the period (for instance, Wordsworth or Hölderlin) involved what I call an "epistemic retreat." They generate a powerful experiential sense of cosmic order but stop short of affirming the reality of these orders in the objective world beyond human experience.

As the nineteenth century passes, and the scientific picture of the universe reveals an immensely enlarged timescale and truly cataclysmic cosmic transformations, even the *experience* of continuing order loses its force, and the aspiration to cosmic connection shifts to the time dimension, and involves larger shapes and patterns in time, and access to what I will call "higher times." I will start to examine this changeover through the work of Baudelaire.

But some of the most significant poetry invoking higher times comes with early twentieth-century "modernism" (Eliot) and continues in the work of Czesław Miłosz.

The book ends with Chapters 15 and 16. Chapter 16 attempts to look up and out from the last two centuries, and see what can be said about the perennial longing for cosmic connection, in its changing forms.

Chapter 15 is an excursus, which attempts a (too ambitious?) sketch of the history of ethical growth, drawing on the felt connections in the time dimension discussed in the previous two chapters on Eliot and Miłosz.

Cosmic Connections

PART I

Chapter One

"TRANSLATION" AND THE "SUBTLER LANGUAGES"

I

1

In my earlier book, I tried to work out the relevance today of the theory of language which was developed among the German Romantics in the 1790s.[1] In this book, I want to explore the understanding of poetics which was implicit in (indeed, central to) this theory of language, and then see some of the consequences which flowed from this in the poetry of the last two centuries.

In this book, I shall be speaking a lot about "the Romantic era." So first of all, a word about what I mean by this term. I am at first mainly concentrating on German writers of the 1790s, because I think that this generation brought about a veritable revolution in our understanding of language, art, and our relation to Nature. This is not to scant or neglect other national literatures of the period: obviously, English, French, Italian,

1. Charles Taylor, *The Language Animal: The Full Shape of the Human Linguistic Capacity* (Cambridge, MA: Belknap Press of Harvard University Press, 2016).

and other European writers contributed to the Romantic transformation in thought and sensibility. In addition, a fuller account would not confine itself to literature and poetry, but also look at music, painting, and other arts. (And I will not be able to resist certain digressions and side glances as the argument unfolds.) But I think that the German writers of this period, centering their attention mainly on poetry (*Dichtung,* understood in a broad sense), worked out some key ideas, which later spread to other nations and their literatures. The best-known channels of this spread were, first, Germaine de Staël's *De L'Allemagne,* which helped introduce the thinking of Kant and the Romantics to France; and Coleridge's *Biographia Literaria,* which did the same for the English world, influencing both Carlyle and Emerson. The interesting point is that this (originally German) outlook came to be seen by some as articulating the theory that underlies the already existing practice of English writers of the Romantic period.

But even though the strand of Romanticism I'm looking at here was influential outside of Germany, it was not the only way of articulating the broad stream of thought and sensibility we associate with the term "Romantic." Ideally, the discussion of the strand I'm following here should be placed within a general portrait of the many facets and forms of this Europe-wide movement, but I can't do justice to this task here, although I will attempt to make connections, at least to English and French poets.

But there is no doubt that my port of entry into the world of Romantic art leads into the German thinkers of the 1790s. And this being so, it might help to articulate some of the thinking of this generation, which brought together not only philosophers, like Fichte, Schelling, and Hegel, but also poets and theorists of literature, like Schiller, the brothers A. W. and Friedrich Schlegel, Hölderlin, Novalis, and others. These all built on the thought and creations of major figures of the time who themselves refused the label "Romantic," most notably Kant and Goethe.

2

The new Romantic outlook   The new thinking of the 1790s was framed in two registers, as it were, philosophy on one hand, and new understandings of poetry, on the other. Moreover, although poets and philosophers were in close contact and exchange, they ended up having a rather different take on this complex of ideas, so it might help to explicate separately what came from the two sources.

The thinkers of the Romantic generation were a very diverse lot, and had a lot of quarrels and disagreements, but there were common themes and notions. I will try to set out their philosophical outlook, but this will be my reconstruction, which I hope captures its general shape and spirit. I will do this, with perhaps unbearable terseness, in seven interlocking theses.

The first is (1) that, inspired by Goethe, they embraced a Spinoza-derived pantheism. Literal readers of Spinoza might be horrified because this vision completely separated the seventeenth-century thinker from his Cartesian roots. Nature was not to be understood mechanistically. It was more like a living organism. In other words, the Romantics were rebelling against a dead, mechanical view of Nature. And they were also rebelling against mind-body dualism, and against a purely instrumental approach to nature. They rejected the one-sided emphasis on (a) the modes of discipline controlling impulses, particularly erotic; especially (b) disciplines aimed exclusively at efficacious control over the environment. They also wanted to dissipate (c) guilt over disturbing, especially erotic, impulses which upset (a) and (b). They longed for a unification of self, unity with our emotions, with nature in us, and with nature as a whole. In this regard, one of their primary sources of inspiration was Goethe (who was nevertheless uncomfortable with their more rebellious stances).

Then (2) our soul communicates with this whole, with Nature. Nature resonates in us, and we intensify this through expression, art.

But (3) our whole idea of Nature has undergone a modern shift. It isn't just a static set, or ordered cosmos, of beautiful forms; rather it is striving, developing; Nature is producing higher and higher forms. Spinoza's *natura naturans* [nature doing as nature does] is seen as in motion, unfolding, seeking its adequate form.

Moreover (4), this is what we also are doing. We are striving to discover our true form through creative expression, moving stage by stage. This type of development might be called "expressive-historical": at each stage we try to realize, that is, give expression to our potential; and this realization makes manifest how we fall short, and what further changes are necessary. Indeed, it is this new anthropology of serial self-discovery which lies behind the new view of nature as development (and perhaps vice versa).

(5) The two lines of expressive-historical development, of the cosmos and humans, respectively, are interlinked. Nature or cosmos can't reach its final form without our realizing ours. That is because the successive stages of the cosmos need continually advancing consciousness, of which humans are the locus.

This shows that our "normal," common sense of our predicament, the notion that the human subject stands apart from, and over against, the world of nature, is only part of the truth. On a deeper level, we discover that Nature is not static, but comes to its fullest realization along with, and through, our own self-realization as rational and free beings. This opens a new path to discovery; not just that of external observation, which issues in science, but also that of internal exploration (see Novalis). There is an important path to truth through the articulation of personal experience, of our emotions, which we explore through art, or poetry in the widest sense. In this search, imagination plays a crucial role.[2]

This notion of expression connects up to a new ideal of (6) freedom, as full self-realization; this goes beyond the notion of negative freedom, freedom from, which is one of the prominent modern understandings of the concept. It also includes, while going beyond, the new understanding of freedom as autonomy, which was both an ethical and political ideal. Kant is the great articulator of this ideal, followed by Fichte. But within the new anthropology of humans as self-developing, autonomy has to include full self-realization.

Points (3) and (4), together with (5) and (6), suggest (7) the ideal of the perfect reconciling of freedom and unity with nature, within and without. The progress to this is then envisaged through a narrative of his-

---

2. For an interesting discussion of what this involves, see Paul Ricoeur's lecture on imagination (as yet unpublished). Starting from the Kantian distinction between "productive" and "reproductive" imagination, Ricoeur shows how the former is not simply a possible source of error (as Hume thought), but can be an essential source of discovery, of new and more fruitful paradigms. See also Paul Ricoeur, *La Métaphore vive* (Paris: Seuil, 1975).

tory, the so-called *exzentrische Bahn* [spiral path], whereby we leave an initial state of harmonious unity between humans and nature, pass through a period of their opposition, as we develop our reason and increase our autonomy, to return to a higher unity. (This goal was often tersely defined as combining Fichte and Spinoza.) Hölderlin makes this point in his *Hyperion Fragment,* as does Schiller in his *Letters on the Aesthetic Education of Man.*[3]

But is the end attainable? Perhaps not. This gives a place to (8) Irony: the road to (7) may never be completed; we may always strive, suffer distance. Ironic expression, however, manifests the gap, and shows what we strive for.[4] There is one vision, espoused by some in the generation of the 1790s, which looks forward to no fully satisfactory end, but expects (and even rejoices in) perpetual challenge and change.

So we develop as Nature develops, and indeed, our proper development matches that of nature, brings it to consciousness, and unites it with freedom. In fact, as we saw, we partake in the development of nature, which requires conscious expression to realize its end. We are the locus where Nature becomes aware of itself. Many of the writers of the 1790s shared the view, later articulated by Schelling (and in a more rationalist form by Hegel), that the full realization of Nature requires the conscious expression which only Spirit can give it. Art (or philosophy) and Nature come into unison because they come to fulfillment together.

We find our own goals in Nature, which must thus be correctly read. But since our spiral path has taken us away from the immediate unity with nature, we can no longer read it easily. What Romantic art, Poetry, strives to do is recover an adequate reading, and this would of necessity mean the creation of a mode of symbolic access.

3. Friedrich Hölderlin, *Fragment von Hyperion* (Berlin: Aufbau Verlag, 1989); Friedrich Schiller, *On the Aesthetic Education of Man in a Series of Letters,* ed. and trans. Elizabeth M. Wilkinson and L. A. Willoughby (Oxford: Clarendon, 1967).

4. See also Robert Richards, *The Romantic Conception of Life* (Chicago: University of Chicago Press, 2002); and Fred Beiser, *The Romantic Imperative: The Concept of Early German Romanticism* (Cambridge, MA: Harvard University Press, 2006).

But before I explain this term, we should be clear that this whole spiral path was not yet seen as completed. The final reconciling steps were still a forward-looking agenda.

Before we examine this, let us look at the other sources of ideas which circulated among these thinkers.[5]

3

***Schiller's* Aesthetic Education**   I have given above the full, heavy-duty philosophical theory of the German 1790s. But there were other, less elaborate versions of the story of progress through loss, and eventual synthesis on a higher level: Schiller's theory, for instance, as developed in the essay *On the Aesthetic Education of Humanity*. The full development of humanity requires a provisional separation in human beings of the drive to rational control (*Formtrieb*), on one hand, and that to emotional fulfillment (*Stofftrieb*), on the other; it requires that the latter undergo over many centuries the severe tutelage of the first; until one comes to a point where the two can come together in harmony, in the drive to play (*Spieltrieb*), the aesthetic drive which allows all our powers to work in harmony, and thus give us real freedom (14th Letter). It is this drive which allows us to recognize and rejoice in beauty. This represents our ultimate fulfillment. "Der Mensch spielt nur, wo er in voller Bedeutung des Wortes Mensch ist, und er is nur ganz Mensch, wo er spielt" [Man only plays when he is in the fullest sense of the word a human being, and he is only fully a human being when he plays] (15th Letter).[6]

This development, through rigorous enforced discipline to a higher, harmonious unity, is Schiller's version of the Romantic generation's spiral path.[7] And it too was understood as yet to be achieved; indeed, it was not yet fully clear what this harmonious reconciliation would amount to.

---

5. For a fuller portrait of what I call the "Romantic generation" of the 1790s, see the remarkable and lively description of Andrea Wulf, *Magnificent Rebels: The First Romantics* (New York: Knopf, 2022).

6. Schiller, *Aesthetic Education of Man*, 107.

7. Schiller, *Aesthetic Education of Man*.

4

The historical sources of the Romantic outlook   Now along with this unprecedented (and very modern) outlook just described, the Romantic generation also drew on certain theories of the High Renaissance which were recovered and given a new meaning at this time.

One set of theories concerned a language which was anchored in the cosmos. This was behind a recurring idea in the medieval and early modern period: that of a language of insight. What would this be like? It would be a language in which the terms weren't just arbitrarily applied to what they designate but would be somehow uniquely right or appropriate to the things they named. They would be appropriate because they would reveal something of the nature of the objects designated. We might say that the right language would satisfy the demands of Plato's Cratylus: a word would figure what it designates.

The notion that the perfect language had already existed in Paradise was encouraged by a passage in Genesis: "So from the soil Yahweh God fashioned all the wild beasts of the field and all the birds of heaven. These he brought to the man to see what he would call them; each one was to bear the name the man would give it."[8] This seemed to suggest a superiority of the language Adam invented; the names he chose were those that things ought to bear. Or as the archangel Gabriel was said to have remarked to John Dee: in the primal language of Adam, "every word signifieth the quiddity of the substance."[9]

Now this revelatory rightness could itself be understood in different ways. On the simplest level, we can understand the Cratylist hypothesis as realized when the word, or phonetic element, qua sound mimics the object, which is plainly the case for words like "cuckoo" or (when the reference is to cats) "meow." But the revelation concerned could be understood on a deeper level, as showing something of the inherent nature of the object.

---

8. Genesis 2:19 (New Revised Standard Version, Catholic Edition, National Council of Churches).

9. Umberto Eco, *The Search for the Perfect Language* (Oxford: Blackwell, 1995), 185.

The notion of inherent nature owes a lot to the inheritance from Greek philosophy, in particular to the Forms of Plato and Aristotle. But this basic scheme comes to be applied in a host of different ways in the subsequent tradition, and surfaces in different forms in the medieval and early modern periods. The basic feature of this scheme, which one already sees in Plato, is the notion of a self-realizing order. This is what Plato presents in the *Republic:* the things we see about us in the world are in each case striving to realize the Idea or archetype to which they belong; and the cosmic order in which these things have their place is itself given its shape by the architectonic Idea, that of the Good.

Following Plato himself in the *Timaeus,* this was taken up by Christian theology, with the Ideas being the thoughts of God that he carries into effect in creating the world. In either variant, the cosmos and all it contains is to be understood as the realization of a plan which presides over its unfolding. This basic scheme was carried forward into Neoplatonism, but here the unfolding plan was understood as a kind of emanation from the One, rather than a creation ex nihilo.

The nature of this plan will then be variously described, as for instance in the works of Pseudo-Dionysius the Areopagite; and it finds application in such continuing schemes as the Great Chain of Being, described by Arthur Lovejoy.[10] The "principle of Plenitude," which Lovejoy identifies, follows from the premise that the plan is a perfect one, from which no possible degree of perfection can be omitted.

But the notion of a divine plan can be conceived in other ways. In the numerological Kabbalah, for instance, starting from the fact that in Hebrew numbers are indicated by letters, each word can be assigned a number by summing its letters. This allows us to uncover a mystic relation between words with different meanings but the same number. The serpent of Moses can be seen as a prefiguration of the Messiah, because both sum to the number 358.[11] In turn, the whole of Creation can be understood as having been put together by God from certain foundational letters.

10. Arthur O. Lovejoy, *The Great Chain of Being* (New York: Harper Torchbook, 1960).

11. Eco, *Perfect Language,* 28.

The basic notion of the cosmos as the realization of a plan can allow for other links of affinity, as with the Renaissance theory of the Correspondences: the king in the kingdom corresponds to the lion among animals, the eagle among birds, the dolphin among fish, because in each domain we are dealing with the supreme, ruling being. An analogous set of links underlies the notion of Creation as a Book containing signs.

Another influential source of ideas of order and affinity between things during the Renaissance was the Hermetic tradition, supposedly based on the thought of Hermes Trismegistus, an ancient Egyptian sage. Celestial bodies influence things on earth, and there exist relations of sympathy between the macrocosm and the human microcosm, and between heavenly and earthly beings. We can trace these links by recognizing the "signatures" in material things which are marks of the heavenly bodies, according to the theories of Paracelsus.[12] The seventeenth-century mystic Jakob Böhme took over this term and saw "signatures" in things as the key to reading the *Natursprache* [the speech of nature]: the language in which Adam had named the animals and other creatures at the beginning.[13]

These links were considered of the greatest importance for Renaissance thinkers because they were not only theoretically relevant. Knowing the sympathies between higher and lower can enable us to harness these astral powers to change things—for example, through alchemy. Hermetic and Kabbalistic research was at first interwoven with what later separated out as orthodox post-Galilean natural science. But beyond that, and inseparably linked with these instrumental capacities, was the ethical importance of grasping the language of insight and the order it reveals. Understanding the order gives us the pattern of life which we were meant to realize; and since to grasp this pattern is to love it, as Plato argued in relation to the Idea of the Good, seeing the pattern at once tells us what we ought to be and awakens in us the desire to realize it.

This ethical relevance emerges clearly from one of the most important Renaissance theories for the whole Romantic period—namely, the

12. Eco, *Perfect Language*, 118. See also Frances Yates, *Giordano Bruno and the Hermetic Tradition* (London: Routledge, 1964).

13. Eco, *Perfect Language*, 182–183.

notion that the human being is a microcosm, in which the order of the cosmos is repeated in miniature. This parallelism could be taken in two ways: either it invites us to seek the structures of the larger order by delving into our own nature, or it tells us that we can't fully understand ourselves, our goals, or the meanings which are crucial to us without a grasp of the cosmic order. Most often, both takes were combined: we need to understand the larger order to know ourselves, but we explore this order through the hints that we find in ourselves. "Nach innen geht der geheimnisvollen Weg" [Inwards runs the path full of mystery], as Novalis put it.[14]

The notion of a language of insight is one which would somehow reveal all these links, connections, and affinities; those between things, like "correspondences" and "signatures," and those linking us as microcosms to the greater cosmos. Why was it deemed important for us to attain—we should properly say "recover"—this language of insight? We have to see this in the light of the spiral understanding of history mentioned above. We were originally in touch with all these—now hidden—connections, but without fully understanding what this involved. We became alienated from them in the course of our development as rational and free beings, because this progression undermines and ultimately dissolves our original inarticulate sense of cosmic orders. Our freedom required that we develop the powers of abstract reasoning, which objectifies our world, and obscures some of its meanings for us. This enabled us to develop a consciousness of radical autonomy, reaching its fullest development in Kant and Fichte. We had thus initially to break off.

But our complete fulfillment comes in a recovery of this contact on a higher level, integrating our gains of reason and freedom. This completes our self-realization. Recovering the language of insight isn't just adding to our dispassionate knowledge: it also reconnects us to the cosmos, and this realizes our essential purpose. The microcosm connects once more to the macrocosm which it ought perfectly to reflect.

The Romantic appropriation of these Renaissance theories moves the emphasis away from knowledge (scientia, epistêmê), in the sense of a

14. Novalis, "Blüthenstaub," 22, in *Schriften: Die Werke Friedrich von Hardenbergs* (Stuttgart: Kohlhammer, 1960), 2:419. See also the illuminating discussion in Albert Béguin, *L'Âme romantique et le Rêve* (Paris: José Corti, 1991).

clear, self-conscious (or self-aware) grasp of reality; it moves it away also from the kind of knowledge which enables control; it focuses rather on the experience of connection, and the empowerment this brings: not a power over things, but one of self-realization.

If we just considered this borrowing from the past, it might look as though the Romantics were simply the irrationalist reactionaries they are sometimes portrayed as, that their goal was to restore the status quo ante the Enlightenment. But this would be to forget the crucial notion of the spiral history. The order we strive to connect with was not already there in its fullness. It is something yet to be realized, and partly through our efforts (points (3) to (6) above). And among the gains involved in its realization are freedom and reason. Their appropriation of Renaissance theories didn't involve a simple return, but a reappropriation with a difference.

First of all, they didn't simply reject the modern understanding of language, as an instrument whereby we encode and communicate information, and in the process increase our control over nature.[15] Rather they espoused what I want to call the "dual-language thesis." Language can be simply an instrument to encode information, describing the reality which already lies open before us, and communicating the information to others. But there are levels of language which do something much more, where our expressions bring about the revelation-and-connection the language of insight yields. This distinction between a higher, creative and a lower, merely instrumental language is one of the continuing legacies of the Romantic period. The Romantic theory applies to this higher level; it doesn't describe the whole.

5

But secondly, the way in which this higher language is thought to function marks it off very clearly from its Renaissance forebears. In order to clarify this, we have to get further insight into the Romantic notion of the Symbol (confusingly also referred to by some writers as "allegory," although the concept clearly contrasts with the usual use of this latter

---

15. In the terms of *The Language Animal,* this is the "Hobbes-Locke-Condillac" (HLC) theory. The theory elaborated in the 1790s, by contrast, I called the "Hamann-Herder-Humboldt" (HHH) theory.

term). How can the infinite be brought to the surface, to *Erscheinung* [appearance]? asks A. W. Schlegel. "Nur symbolisch, in Bildern und Zeichen" [Only symbolically, in pictures and signs], he answers. Poetry is what achieves this: "Dichten [. . .] ist nichts anderes als ein ewig Symbolisieren; wir suchen entweder für etwas Geistiges eine äussere Hülle oder wir beziehen ein Äusseres auf ein unsichtbares Inneres" [Poetry . . . is nothing but a perpetual creation of symbols; we either seek for something spiritual an external mantle or we relate something external to an invisible inner reality].[16]

We need to remark on two related features of this kind of disclosure.[17] First, it is defined in terms of the indispensability of mediation: in this, it partakes of the nature of metaphor, where we cast light on one matter through invoking another. We say of the politician: "He plays his cards close to his chest," characterizing his underhand and uncommunicative way of operating (the target) through an expression drawn from poker (the source of the metaphor).

But with the politician, we could have found some other way of describing his deplorable behavior, dispensing with the metaphor (albeit forgoing some rhetorical effect). While what Schlegel wants to claim for the symbol is that here A can only be disclosed through B ("Nur symbolisch, in Bildern und Zeichen"), Ricoeur has analyzed this kind of speech using the same term.[18] An example he gives is a conception of sin which is inseparable from a notion of impurity or defilement. Our grasp of this leans on, while going beyond, our ordinary understanding of dirt and soiling. Another example is our moral concept of "integrity." This is distinct from the wholeness, as against brokenness, of the objects we deal with, distinct even from the smooth combined function of our faculties, but we access this moral notion through these more familiar objects and experiences. Another famous example in the philosophical tradition is Plato's notion of the harmonious soul of the just person, distinct from, but accessed through, the musical experience.

16. August Wilhelm von Schlegel, *Kunstlehre* (Stuttgart: Kohlhammer, 1964), 81–82.

17. Here I am calling on my discussion in Taylor, *Language Animal*, ch. 5.

18.. See Paul Ricoeur, "Le symbole donne à penser," *Esprit*, n.s., no. 275 (7/8) (1959): 60–76, http://www.jstor.org/stable/24254991.

Now as I argued in *The Language Animal,* this kind of metaphor-type reference can be said to "figure" its object, in the sense that it offers some idea of the shape or nature of this latter. The source offers a way of conceiving the target. This gives us some clue as to what a "language of insight" might consist in. A key to understanding the poetics of this generation of the 1790s lies here: that they saw the poem, or work of art in general, as functioning like a symbol in the above sense. The work reveals to us, brings us into contact with, a deeper reality which would otherwise remain beyond our ken.

I am drawing on an analogy between different types of metaphor-like, A-through-B structures of description to explicate the Romantic notion of the work of art: the ordinary metaphor (the politician "playing his cards"), the symbol-concept (sin, or integrity), and a poem (let's take an English example, Wordsworth's "Tintern Abbey").

The first, the ordinary metaphor, can go dead. To be alive a metaphor must constantly draw on the source; you need to have a lively sense of source and target. But many ordinary metaphors survive as descriptive terms because they get associated, say, with a pattern of behavior which can be grasped independent of source.

Thus the politician who "plays his cards close to his chest": this couldn't have got started, and have the obvious aptness it has, without people being aware of poker (or at least some similar card game). But after a time, a certain cagey way of speaking, a certain prevarication in replying to questions, a certain fishy look in his eye, and so on can suffice to call up (or call down) this (negative) description of a politician. Once this independence of source occurs, it is possible to lose track altogether of the original source, and still use the expression, as we see, for instance with terms like "flash in the pan."[19]

Something like this can happen to our deeper metaphors, with stronger moral relevance, like sin and integrity. How many people think of brokenness when they judge one person as having integrity, and another as lacking it? It's hard to say: maybe there's always a sense of the person having a certain wholeness, a certain unity with self, a certain solidity,

---

19. See my discussion of this in Taylor, *Language Animal,* ch. 5.

which the dishonest person, "speaking out of both sides of his mouth," lacks. But it can be very tacit and implicit, not focal.

Something like this may happen with "sin," but it is less likely; and it couldn't happen with "impurity," for instance; although very often (ritual) impurity is sharply distinguished from sin. But certainly, a lively sense of the source may fade, and the term maintain something like its previous extension via a set of rules, a list of "sins," a pattern of behavior, so that very pious people, and those who reject religion altogether, can use the term to talk about (anyway, what seem to be) the same things.

But here another feature, or dimension, of such symbols enters in. I argued that strong ethical insights are grounded in what I called "felt intuitions."[20] Someone couldn't be said to have a moral conviction about universal human rights, for instance, if she wasn't prone on the appropriate occasions to experience them, to feel them as inspiring (hearing the choral movement of Beethoven's Ninth Symphony), and their flagrant violation as appalling. This doesn't stop other people from considering them overblown, ideological fantasies, identifying them simply via a code (say, the United Nations' Universal Declaration of Human Rights).[21] And this kind of communication across a moral gap is obviously the case with "sin."

But the communication is obviously limited; when it comes to radical reform of our notions of sin, or human rights, the appeal is necessarily to strongly felt intuitions. (Consider the statement in the New Testament that not what goes into a person, but what comes out of her "defiles" a person.) And something similar goes for a person who wants to reject the notion of sin altogether: "A sense of sin is crippling; what humans need is a strong sense of their own goodness." Only here the felt intuition about sin is negative, and the value of one's own goodness is positive. (And then there will also be people who think that one of these doesn't exclude the other [the biblical view, for instance], but that involves

20. Taylor, *Language Animal*, ch. 6.

21. Worse, some people may see the demand for universal equal rights as a mortal threat to their identity: e.g., US Republican voters with (often unadmitted) sympathy with white superiority, responding to the scarcely veiled appeal of Donald Trump to uphold "law and order."

a redefinition of both, which insight calls on a different set of felt intuitions.)

So both ordinary, everyday metaphors, like the politician playing his cards close to his chest, and morally charged ones, like sin or integrity, can go "dead," in the sense that they can take on a meaning independent of their source, in a pattern of "external" behavior. But for the morally charged, something of the semantic force is lost, namely, what under-lies—or rather inspires—proposed revisions.

Codes can be modified simply with arguments about consistency, and valid generalization from accepted cases (Weber's "rationalization"), but they can also be changed from a renewed sense of their "spirit," grounded in felt intuitions. (Talmudic argument, careful, text-based disputes about right judgments, is an obvious example of such dual-sourced thinking.)

The deeper level is obviously the one on which the original semantic intuition, launching a term like "sin," is to be found. And this is the level on which the poetic intuitions of the Romantic period are to be found, following the analogy I have tried to draw between these and mor-ally charged semantic innovations. The poetic work, or some part of it, is being analogized here to the descriptive term. Both open us to new insight.

But a disanalogy also exists. The poetic work cannot go "dead," in the same sense. Otherwise put, for the poem or work of art to go "dead" is for it to lose its deeper meaning, to no longer say anything to us. It can't have an afterlife, like a "dead" metaphor, allowing for a meaningful ex-change of descriptions through its "corpse." Whatever assertive sentences can be found in the work, and argued about or exchanged ("Beauty is Truth and Truth Beauty"), will not capture the core insight of the work. It is in the nature of subtler languages that they remain dependent on their original matrix in this way.

Let's look at a passage from "Tintern Abbey":

> And I have felt
> A presence that disturbs me with the joy
> Of elevated thoughts; a sense sublime
> Of something far more deeply interfused,
> Whose dwelling is the light of setting suns,

And the round ocean and the living air,
And the blue sky, and in the mind of man;
A motion and a spirit, that impels
All thinking things, all objects of thought,
And rolls through all things. (93–102)[22]

To let oneself be carried by this passage is to experience a strong sense of connection, far from clearly defined (I'll come to this in a moment), but deeply felt; a connection not static, but which flows through us and our world. The expression I've just used covers two kinds of experience, which in reality can fade into each other. The "felt intuition of connection" can mean the intuition that there is such a strong connection, which is ethically important (like our other moral convictions); or it can mean that we directly feel the connection. There is a spectrum between these two. With Wordsworth, we are closer to the first pole, but Hölderlin, as we will see below, seems to approach the second.

Off this spectrum altogether is the case where I just think some theory about connection, but without feeling it as these lines bring you to. And (unless this is all total illusion) to feel the connection in this way is to strengthen it, to enter into it more fully. So some reality which before was at best on the edge of awareness is manifested and at the same time intensified.

If the poem goes "dead," if it no longer speaks to us, the intuition it opens disappears with it. The work of art as "symbol" is like the symbol-concept ("integrity" or "sin") in that it opens a new avenue of insight. But if the avenue closes (the poem goes dead), it leaves no semantic residue, as the symbol-concept does (e.g., "sin" as a mere pattern of rule-governed behavior). That is because the work of art yields not just a (potentially dispassionate) insight, but a strong experience of connection, or more generally, it transforms our relation to the situation it figures for us.

---

22. William Wordsworth, "Lines Written a Few Miles above Tintern Abbey, on Revisiting the Banks of the Wye during a Tour, July 13, 1798," in *Lyrical Ballads and Other Poems, 1797–1800*, ed. James Butler and Karen Green (Ithaca, NY: Cornell University Press, 1991), 118–119.

6

But a language which "figures" in this metaphor-like sense also has limitations. It lacks the clarity and finality of the ordinary declarative proposition in "literal" terms. Figuring is one way of showing what something is like. But by definition the target is also unlike the source. Politics is not poker. Sin is not ordinary dirt. The soul is not an orchestra. Figuring can give insight, but it always leaves something more to be said, more about what features the object has and what features it doesn't. That is why it lacks the finality and clarity that ordinary prose can attain.

So for exact descriptions, as in science for instance, metaphor has to be used sparingly or not at all. Which is why the founders of the Hobbes-Locke-Condillac (HLC) theory, Hobbes and Locke for instance, fulminated so loudly against tropes and figures of speech.[23] The earlier understanding of the universe as the locus of "signs" was ridiculed and set aside by the thinkers propounding the HLC. For them, language was essentially an instrument by which we could control our imagination and build a responsible and reliable picture of the world which lies before us.

Words function in this task essentially as arbitrary signs, as Locke made clear; they are "unmotivated," to use the language of Saussure.[24] That is to say, certain concepts ("signifieds") are hammered out to fit a predisclosed reality, and vocables ("signifiers") are attached to them. I say the signs are essentially arbitrary, because while vocables can be found which in some way suggest or mirror the reality described (like "cuckoo"), this plays no role in the process. The development of a descriptive language can quite well proceed (and has proceeded) without any attention to this.

This double side to a language of insight, that it is revealing, and yet incomplete and inexact, was the source of some tension in the generation of the 1790s between philosophers and poets. For Hegel it should ultimately be possible to say everything in the language of reason ["Vernunft"], which is beyond that of *Vorstellung* ["representation," which

23. See the writings of Hobbes and Locke on metaphor.

24. John Locke, "Essay on Human Understanding Book III," in *The Selected Political Writings of John Locke,* ed. Paul E. Sigmund (New York: W. W. Norton, 2005), 195–198.

incorporates some element of what I'm calling "figuring"]. Of course, Hegel recognized that in earlier times this wasn't possible, but history leads to a point where a final, clear articulation will be possible in philosophy (and is being realized in his philosophy). But Novalis, the Schlegels, and others didn't agree. (Schelling came down at different moments on both sides of this question.)

As Friedrich Schlegel put it, what we need is a new mythology. We modern poets need something to do for us what the older mythology did for the writers of the ancient world. This modern mythology will be based on "Idealism"; Schlegel means here the philosophy developed beyond Kant through Fichte to Schelling. But this does not render mythology otiose. It is not enough to assert the essential connections, we have also to be able to figure them: to make visible and sensible how everything hangs together.

> Einen großen Vorzug hat die Mythologie. Was sonst das Bewußt-
> sein ewig flieht, ist hier dennoch sinnlich geistig zu schauen,
> und festgehalten, wie die Seele in dem umgebenden Leibe, durch
> den sie in unser Auge schimmert, zu unserem Ohre spricht.[25]

> [Mythology has a great superiority. What consciousness usually
> shuns is here nonetheless to be seen, spiritually and sensibly,
> and grasped, as the soul in its surrounding body shines out for
> us, and speaks to our ears.]

This reservation about the self-sufficiency of philosophy is itself inspired by a feature of the philosophical theory I tried to outline above. It is ultimately not just a matter of learning about the inner connections in things and between us and things; we need the kind of knowledge which reconnects us, and this requires more than just knowing about the links; we need to be reconnected—in the way that "Tintern Abbey" opens for us. Reconnection has to be experienced. We have to be able to "grasp it spiritually and sensibly." We have to be put in its presence.

The central notion here is that this is what revelation through the work of art as "symbol" does. It doesn't just inform you about the links in and

---

25. Friedrich Schlegel, *Gespräch über die Poesie* (Stuttgart: J. B Metzlersche Verlags-buchhandlung, 1968), 318.

with the cosmos. It makes them palpable for you in a way which moves you and hence restores your link to them. Philosophy can perhaps tell you how things relate, but only *Dichtung,* Poetry, Poesie (in a broad sense which includes other arts) can recover relation.

So we can see that this is not just a return to Renaissance theory. Then the idea was that we had lost the key to interpret reality and had to recover it. To recover it would be automatically to be drawn toward it; we couldn't see the order without loving it, being inspired by it; as we saw above that Plato claimed about the Idea of the Good, which we cannot see and be indifferent to. In a sense the Romantic vision is a return to that notion of a reality which couldn't leave us indifferent.

But note the change: this return to vision / connection is something we are now called upon to produce. We have to create (*poesis, Dichtung*) something, a work of art, which will bring this about. This is a crucial shift, which comes about fully in the line of development of modern culture. It is anything but a reactionary return.

But we can also see how the very idea of a language which gives insight into things seemed weird and incomprehensible to the early modern theorists of the HLC. If we think of our lexicon as consisting of words introduced one by one to name the things we perceive, then it is hard to imagine how the sounds we coin can give an insight into their designata (apart perhaps from the exceptional but trivial case of onomatopoeia). But it is clear that the forms of perfect language envisaged in the Renaissance and before, based as they were on the idea that the cosmos was the realization of a plan, claimed to offer insight not into individual items, but into the connections that linked them to each other and to the whole, whether through the correspondences, or Kabbalistic numerology, or the signatures in things. And this also helps us understand the crucial ethical importance placed on recovering this insight, which alone would show us how to live in tune with this order, and—crucially—at the same time, empower us to do so.

So it is unsurprising that the theories of this range were very popular with the Romantics. One of their ways of protesting against the reduced condition of language as purely instrumental was to invoke the Kabbalah. The Schlegels and Novalis mention it. Nor did it die with them, because in the last century, Benjamin, following them, also invokes it. Novalis in turn invokes the *signatura rerum*.

Just what is going on here? On one level, we might think that they are just underscoring the importance of symbolic access, and more generally of access to A through B, because this indeed involves figuring. In other words, symbols fit the specifications of the original Adamic language. They are the right terms, because they reveal (disclose) what they're about. To use them is to have insight, and if you put anything else in their place, you lose the insight. For example, to return to symbol-concepts, some facet of our moral life shows up in the language of elevation: we talk of "higher" modes of life; and in some American dialects, inferior people are referred to as "low life." No other expressions have equivalent force.

Nor is this kind of indirect access confined to speech. We can see it in works of art more generally. A kind of courage and determination shines through Beethoven's Fifth Symphony as it does nowhere else. And we can see something similar in the enacted meanings of behavior: the particular swagger which emerges in this gang which is evolving a new kind of machismo says it as nothing else can—because the expressive-enactive gesture is also far from the "arbitrarily imposed" sign; it also discloses its meaning.

But clearly the Romantics had a stronger thesis than this. They wanted to claim not just that A-through-B structures play a big role in language, but also that signs really do inhere in things, and that we have lost the capacity to read them. This means that seeing the signs correctly is re-connecting; and that this makes a real difference; an ethical difference, in that it constitutes an important human realization. This needs further explanation.

7

But before going on to elaborate on this point, I would like to make a step sideways. I have been talking about the outlook of the German Romantic generation of the 1790s. But there were other variants of a spiral view of history, where an earlier form of wholeness was lost, only to be recovered on a higher level in the contemporary world. For the Germans, the earlier wholeness was that of the ancient Greeks—although Novalis places it in the Middle Ages in his "Die Christenheit oder Europa." For the younger (and more radical) Wordsworth, the earlier point of reference was the age of Milton. As Paul Bénichou describes it, the crucial background to the Romantic generation in France was the loss of authority of the Catholic Church and its clerical spokesmen during the Enlightenment era of Voltaire and Diderot, who in turn lost credit through the catastrophe of the Revolution and empire. What emerged from the wreckage was the ideal of the Romantic poet as a kind of magus, an inspiring prophet in an age of confusion and gloom.[26] (But this authority in its turn collapsed later on.)

And running alongside these national variants was a generalized consciousness among educated people that an earlier period of community and a traditional way of life, involving a certain stable relation to what we now call the environment, was being sapped in several ways at once: through the growth of cities, with the resulting atomization theorized a century later by Simmel; through industrialization which created greater and greater urban environments of unprecedented ugliness and inexpressive of any human meanings; through a more and more "economic" (i.e., instrumental) management of rural estates, geared to increasing wealth, not to fostering community or doing justice to the beauties of Nature.[27] The old ways were also being sapped by the advance of certain technologies—for instance, railways—and the resulting speed of travel and communication.

All this was lived by many people with a sense of loss, and with a corresponding aspiration to recover a contact with nature which the large-scale, successful application of instrumental reason was destroying. This sense of loss, and longing to recover the link to nature, was a central aspiration of the Romantic period, and remains powerful today.

Underlying the different national understandings of loss, and recovery on a higher level, were deep and powerful templates of the European understanding of history, as M. H. Abrams has convincingly argued: the history implicit in Christianity—Creation, then Fall, then Redemption

26. Paul Bénichou, *Le Sacre de l'Écrivain* (Paris: Gallimard, 1971); Paul Bénichou, *Le Temps des Prophètes* (Paris: Gallimard, 1973).

27. Jonathan Bate, *The Song of the Earth* (Cambridge, MA: Harvard University Press, 2000), has a chapter on the novels of Jane Austen, and their reflection of the tension between two philosophies of estate management, conservative and "improving."

at a higher level; and also this story as filtered through the Neoplatonic doctrine of emanation and the return to unity.[28]

II

1

In the previous section, I tried to show that, for all their invocation of the theories of the Renaissance, the generation of the 1790s was not simply proposing a return to the mental horizon of the earlier epoch. This was because the reconnection they wanted to encompass was to be brought about by their own creative action, through poetry (in the wider sense) or *Dichtung*. But the creative action there envisaged, the elaboration of myth through poetry, was both indispensable, and epistemically limited, since it could not aspire to the clarity and finality of philosophy.

The same double feature of poetic creation, its indispensability to effect connection, and its epistemic limitation, comes to light if we approach their poetics from another angle, and this is what I want to do now. This will bring out other facets of their doctrine which will help to understand its subsequent effects on poetic practice.

For the Romantics our power of symbolic disclosure was ontically grounded, as we saw. It was derivative from the signs and symbols which were already there in the universe, the creation of God, or Spirit, or Nature. Since Hamann is in a sense the origin point of this whole outlook, its original inspirer, we can take the formulations from him. "Jede Erscheinung der Natur war ein Wort—das Zeichen, Sinnbild und Unterpfand einer neuen, geheimen, unaussprechlichen, aber desto innigern Bereinigung, Mittheilung und Gemeinschaft göttlicher Energien und Ideen" [Every appearance of Nature was a Word—a sign, symbol and pledge of a new, secret, inexpressible but all the more inward clarification, communication and community of divine energies and Ideas].[29] The inspiration was the Kabbalistic tradition, the understanding of the

---

28. M. H. Abrams, *Natural Supernaturalism* (New York: W. W. Norton, 1971).

29. Johann Georg Hamann, "Ritter von Rosencreuz," in *Sämtliche Werke* (Vienna: Verlag Herder, 1951), 3:32.

universe as a body of signs, which, drawing on Plotinus' emanationism, was mediated by Augustine, by Pseudo-Dionysius, through the theories of the High Renaissance, the Correspondences, Paracelsus' signatures, then later Jakob Böhme, to the eighteenth century. Hamann and others speak of the Kabbalah. Novalis was excited by Böhme, by Plotinus.

This is exactly what can create the illusion that they are simply reactionaries, trying to turn the clock back before disenchantment. There is a borrowing here. But there is an important difference.

As I explained above, premodern views of what I have called "ontic logos" took the universe as manifestation of an Idea, plan, or purpose. In one image, it was to be read like a text; in another, its elements refer us to each other, according to the Correspondences defined by the master Idea. These connections are hard to read, partly because our fallen condition makes us dim and uncomprehending; but (in some versions) also because the Fall has affected the world itself. In other words, it is not just that our eyes are dim, but the text itself is damaged. A further possibility opened by this view was that the recovery of our eyesight could help restore the text.

All this the Romantics took over. Hamann speaks of the original creation as one which has suffered damage through our Fall. "Noch war keine Creatur, wider ihren Willen, der Eitelkeit und Knechtschaft des vergänglichen Systems unterworfen, worunter sie gegenwärtig gähnt, seufzet und verstummt" [As yet no creature had been subjected, against its will, to the vanity and servitude of the transitory system, under which it presently yawns, sighs, and falls silent].[30] The difference comes in how they conceived our access to this order of signs.

On the original view, our access might indeed be imperfect, because of our inadequacy and the distortions in nature, but what it was to grasp this order could be understood on a straight correspondence view of truth. There is a code which underlies the connections. Understanding the text is grasping the code. To speak of the world as made up of signs was to suppose that there was a meaning for each element, as with words

---

30. Hamann, "Ritter von Rosencreuz," 32. See also Johann Georg Hamann, "Aesthetica in nuce," in *Sämtliche Werke,* 2:206.

in a lexicon, or expressions in a cipher. Knowing this is, as it were, making the same connection in our minds as holds in reality.

Hamann presents a rather different view. The way that we can appropriate the signs of nature is not by registering them in our minds—that is, coming to have knowledge of them according to the ordinary correspondence-theory view of knowledge. Rather we come to grasp them by re-creating, reexpressing them. The word Hamann uses for this is "translation." Our response to God's signs in the world is to translate them into our own. And this, indeed, is how human language originates. This translation is human language: "Reden ist übersetzen" [To speak is to translate].[31] The symbolic relation, with the distance it implies between two domains, between the A and the B through which it appears, applies not only to the things in the world, but also to the relation between our signs and those of nature or God. ("Translation" becomes a key term, which recurs with, inter alia, Novalis and Benjamin.)[32]

Why this change, and what does it mean? First, why? We can see it in the light of the whole movement of modern culture, toward interiorization, or anthropocentrism. One facet of this emerges in the central place of freedom. Humans have to take the initiative themselves to find and define their basic goals rather than simply reading them off some larger authoritative social or cosmic order. Another facet was the new understanding of what it was to lead one's life according to nature. Where this term evoked a hierarchic order in the traditional view derived from the ancients, either an order in the cosmos, or a ranking of human purposes, or both in relation; in the modern invocation we see developing in the eighteenth century—in such forms as moral sense theory, and the cult of sentiment, culminating perhaps in Rousseau—we are appealing to a voice within us.

The Romantics belonged to these two streams of anthropocentrism, freedom and the voice of nature within. Indeed, what they were striving to do was to bring them together, because contemporary versions were pulling them apart, while the Romantics were highly sensitive to the af-

31. Hamann, "Aesthetica in nuce," 199.

32. See an interesting recent book: Alexander Stern, *The Fall of Language* (Cambridge, MA: Harvard University Press, 2019).

finities between them. Moreover, they saw their task as reconciling them in a new unity.

Their protest was against the understandings of freedom and a life according to nature which were elaborated at their most extreme in the naturalist Enlightenment—say, with Helvétius, Holbach, and Bentham—but which were also present in a milder form, in, say, Voltaire.

A certain conception of freedom emerges from Locke among others, in which we stress the right and competence of the individual to direct his own life, and to exercise control over the world around him. In its most debased form—with Helvétius, for instance—this seemed to be demanding freedom for desire but had no place for freedom from desire. The human subject was elided with its desires. There were two ways of feeling unease at this. One focused on the fact that this view had no place for higher aspirations, even aspirations beyond life and human flourishing; the other was to attack the naturalist view for its "heteronomy." It made humans the servants of desire, incapable of judging or choosing their goals from a more radical standpoint.

This critique develops into a notion of freedom as self-determination, giving the law to oneself, elaborated by Rousseau and then in its most imposing statement by Kant. It was then pushed to its most far-reaching and ambitious form by Fichte, for whom the self-determination of the subject was ontologically ultimate.

The Romantic generation in Germany were heirs to this critique and were all deeply influenced by Fichte. But they were also critical of it because the aspiration to be in tune with nature also was important for them. Here their critique of the standard Enlightenment view was that life according to nature was interpreted as the application of instrumental reason to fulfill human needs. It made us split reason from nature, and treat the latter, both within and around us, as a domain to be worked on and manipulated instrumentally. They yearned for reunion—within ourselves, between reason and desire, between ourselves and the larger world of nature, and between individuals in society. This criticism, that Reason divides us from Nature, was directed also against Kant and the critics of Enlightenment naturalism, perhaps even more clearly against Kant, because the division was all the sharper in his philosophy. So Fichte couldn't satisfy them either.

They wanted to marry his philosophy with a vision of humans and nature as united, which placed us not over against a refractory nature, trying to submit it to the dictates of reason, but rather as part of a larger stream of life. Spinoza, as somewhat idiosyncratically read by Goethe, was often taken as the philosophical exponent of this view. As I indicated above, one way of describing their goal was: to unite Fichte and Spinoza.

It was out of this search for unity with the current of nature that they turned back and drew on the earlier theories of ontic logos, of the world as the locus of living purpose, speaking to us in signs. But it was as heirs of modern anthropocentrism that they reconceived what it was to get back in tune with this current. We do not just register, we re-create the meaning of things, and in doing so draw on our own characteristic powers, those of symbolic disclosure (or Poetry). We don't simply receive the answer but collaborate in defining it. Here we see the trace of the modern centrality of freedom. It is a variant different from that which defines autonomy in opposition to everything else, God and cosmos, but it is nevertheless a conception of freedom.

What distinguishes us from the animals, Hamann says, is freedom, which means the right to collaborate in defining ourselves. "Zur Freyheit gehören aber nicht nur unbestimmte Kräfte sondern auch das republikanische Vorrecht zu ihrer Bestimmung mitwirken zu können" [To freedom belong not only indeterminate powers, but also the republican prerogative to collaborate in determining their destiny].[33] This is what underlies the new conception of what it means to grasp the signs of nature and bring ourselves into alignment with them, not simply as registering their meaning and conforming to them, but as collaborative reexpression. This is what is conveyed in the notion that our understanding them is a translation. Hamann offers a new take on the much cited story from Genesis to underscore the human contribution. He speaks of when "GOTT sie (die Thiere) zu dem Menschen brachte, daß er sähe, wie er sie nennte; denn wie der Mensch sie nennen würde, so sollten sie heißen" [God brought them (the animals) before the human

---

33. Johann Georg Hamann, "Philologische Einfälle und Zweifel," in *Sämtliche Werke*, 3:38.

being in order to see what names he gave them; for how he named them is how they should be called].[34]

It is in virtue of the same idea that, in both art and the elaboration of language, the Romantics rejected simple imitation as our model. When we imitate, we do so in a creative, transforming fashion; we are "selbst-tätig" [self-acting, self-sustaining] in our mimesis, as A. W. Schlegel says.[35]

What is the significance of this for the Romantic theory of the symbolic? I want to mention three things. First: Symbolic disclosure involves a distance, a mediation, an acceding to A through B. Now we can see that this distance is not just to be understood negatively, a fruit of our incapacity, a look "through a glass darkly." It also has its positive meaning. Our translation is not just an imperfect approximation to the meaning; it is also our contribution to the collaborative work of reestablishing contact, communion between ourselves and the world.

Second: I used the word "communication." "Communication" often crops up in Romantic writings. In the quotation I cited above, where Hamann says that in the beginning every appearance of nature is a word, this is described as a "Zeichen, Sinnbild und Unterpfand einer neuen, geheimen, unaussprechlichen, aber desto innigern Bereinigung, Mitthei-lung und Gemeinschaft göttlicher Energien und Ideen" [sign, symbol and pledge of a new, secret, inexpressible but all the more inward clari-fication, communication and community of divine energies and Ideas].[36]

This picture of eschatology in images of communication is echoed by Novalis in his picture of the "goldene Zukunft aller Dinge" [a golden future of all things]: as an age when "Menschen, Tiere, Pflanzen, Steine und Gestirne, Flammen, Töne, Farben . . . wie ein Geschlecht handeln und sprechen" [humans, animals, plants, stones and stars, flames, tones, colors . . . act and speak as one species].[37] We can feel here the full eth-ical force of the Romantic drive to poetic expression.

34. Hamann, "Aesthetica in nuce," 206.

35. August Wilhelm von Schlegel, "Briefe über Poesie," in *August Wilhelm Schlegel: Kritische Schriften und Briefe,* ed. Edgar Lohner (Stuttgart: Kohlhammer, 1962), 141–180.

36. Hamann, "Ritter von Rosencreuz," 32.

37. Novalis, "Heinrich von Ofterdingen–Materialien," in *Werke,* ed. Gerhard Schulz (Munich: Verlag C. H. Beck, 2013), 289. See also Novalis, "Fragmente," in *Werke,* 401: "71.

The Romantics were indeed moving toward and finally embracing a dialogical view of language, which we see later fully developed in Humboldt. Hamann's peculiar position on the origin of language reflects this. Herder wrote his famous "Ursprung" essay critical of the "orthodox" theory of Süssmilch and others, that language was taught to humans by God. He presents it as a human potentiality, which we develop ourselves. Hamann, while unable to accept the rather simplistic picture offered by Süssmilch of God as a language instructor, nevertheless was uneasy with Herder's formulations. God didn't teach us language in the way we teach each other. But on the other hand, our language is a response to God's, the language of signs in the world. We don't develop language fully on our own, as the mainline Enlightenment theory had it, and as Herder seemed to be saying in his own way. Our language is already a reply to a message addressed to us, a reply which consists of a translation. Language is thus in its very origin dialogical and continues to develop in exchange between human beings.

In a sense, the whole Romantic "take" on freedom is hospitable to a dialogical conception. Freedom is not deriving everything out of oneself, out of the Ego in Fichtean terms; it is a collaborative response, saying one's piece in a conversation. That's why Romantic eschatology points toward a universal communion.

Third: A new understanding of the nature of poetic language arises from this, which still shapes our outlook today. As Earl Wasserman has argued, the Romantic period saw a profound shift away from a millennial outlook which saw the Chain of Being, and divine history, and ancient mythology, as treasuries of common reference points, on which poetry, and painting, could draw.[38] This corresponded to a view of this order as reflecting a unitary set of meanings which could be publicly registered and recorded.[39]

Alles, was wir erfahren ist eine *Mittheilung*. So ist die Welt in der Tat eine *Mittheilung*— Offenbarung des Geistes." [All that we experience is a *communication*. So too is the World actually a *communication*—the revelation of mind.]

38. Earl R. Wasserman, *The Subtler Language: Critical Readings of Neoclassical Poems* (Baltimore: Johns Hopkins University Press, 1959).

39. "In varying degrees, ranging from conviction to faith, to passive submission, man accepted, to name but a few, the Christian interpretation of history, the sacramentalism

The dissolution of this publicly accessible field of references brought us to an age in which each poet may struggle to create his own language, virtually his own mythology, if we take Blake as an example, or we refer to the aspirations that Friedrich Schlegel defined for his age, which I mentioned in the previous section. The poet may find himself struggling to create his own field of references, even as he is invoking them. Hölderlin's gods, Rilke's angels, Yeats' Byzantium belong to no publicly recognized story or doctrine, although they draw on certain of the resonances that formerly established stories and doctrines have left behind. These are the "subtler languages" of Wasserman's title.[40]

What helped to make the earlier public languages unavailable was the complex process that has been described as disenchantment, and particularly one facet of this, namely the sharp separation of subject and object, championed in paradigmatic form by Descartes. Outside of the thinking subject, the whole fabric of the material world was seen as inert, not expressive of anything, nor the site of human meanings of any kind, and certainly not ones of crucial significance to ethical life. This outlook becomes more and more entrenched in Western modernity because it is linked to a practical stance which is basically instrumentalist; we seek out the efficient causal relations in our world with the aim of discovering handles which will enable us to realize our purposes. We practice what Scheler called *Leistungswissen* (understanding, which brings control).

The world is no longer seen as the site of spirit and magic forces, but the universe comes to be understood in terms of laws defined purely by efficient causation. At the same time, traditional views of the cosmos and history were overturned by new discoveries: for instance, of a new unsuspected hemisphere, as well as by familiarity with other peoples, with their own mythologies and understanding of their past.

---

of nature, the Great Chain of Being, the analogy of the various planes of creation, the conception of man as microcosm, and, in the literary area, the doctrine of the genres." Wasserman, *Subtler Language,* 11. There is a clear overlap between this list and that of the Renaissance theories the Romantics looked to; but what is crucial is the change in register which "subtler languages" introduced.

40. I have discussed this at greater length in Charles Taylor, *Sources of the Self: The Making of Modern Identity* (Cambridge, MA: Harvard University Press, 1989); and in Charles Taylor, *A Secular Age* (Cambridge, MA: Belknap Press of Harvard University Press, 2007).

But this is just the negative side; there is also a positive facet, as I argued above: the developing anthropocentric understanding of freedom, and the scope of human action, both instrumental in the natural world, and creative in the structures of the social world, as political structures are progressively disembedded from the cosmos, and referred to human action in history.[41]

The Romantic movement, in many countries, while often aligning itself with the new aspiration to political freedom, rejected utterly this sharp separation of spirit and matter.

2

Wasserman's illuminating discussion shows the contrast between "classical" poetry and that of the Romantic epoch. He takes, as his examples of the first, two poems of the seventeenth and eighteenth centuries, Denham's "Cooper's Hill," and Pope's "Windsor Forest." Both rely heavily on a long-standing metaphysical view, expressed in the term *concordia discors*: every harmonious thing is constituted by opposites coming together.[42] This is true of music, but also of the polity. Indeed, the unity and coherence of the universe, and of each of its parts, is grounded in the harmonious and reconciling combination or opposed forces or elements.

In Denham's poem, the doctrine of *concordia discors* not only gives the work its sense, but is also incorporated in the poem's structure, logic, rhetoric, syntax, and melody. Indeed, the concept helps shape the heroic couplet, and the division of each line into hemistichs; the harmoniously balanced couplet, using parallelism, antithesis, and inversion, not only illustrates the doctrine but constitutes the inherent condition of his "subtler language."[43] The linguistic organization embodies the structural pattern of balanced oppositions.[44]

And this is as it should be; the poem makes order appear, makes it shine through, be apparent through what the poet describes, landscape or social world. And what we are dealing with is a feature of the order of

41. I have discussed this more fully in Taylor, *Secular Age*, ch. 3.
42. Wasserman, *Subtler Language*, 53.
43. Wasserman, *Subtler Language*, 82.
44. Wasserman, *Subtler Language*, 84–85.

things which we not only should know about, but which can move us to conform to it. This much continues through the epochal change which comes with the Romantic era.

Similarly, Pope makes this order of harmony-through-difference shine through his description of Windsor Forest. But this wood also stands as a synecdoche for England, and England in turn for the world as well.

Neoclassical art is not creating, but finding the inherent order, through a system of similitudes.[45] Poetry holds a mirror to Nature, but what it reflects is deep Nature, the underlying pattern, not the surface appearance. All this changes, however, with the fading of these millennial notions of order: "By the end of the 18th Century—and ever since—the poet has been required to conceive his own structure of order, his own more-than-linguistic syntax, and so to engage that structure that the poetic act is creative both of a cosmic system and of the poem made possible by that system."[46]

Ancient mythology sinks to the level of allegory. In itself, it carries no more felt depths. These stories were given depth formerly against the background of the standing notions of order, articulated for early modern Europe in classical works, like Ovid's *Metamorphoses.* When these latter lose their force, poets have to present a new background of order to give them sense, as Keats does in *Endymion* with his own, revised mythology. "The nineteenth century mythological poem is internally constitutive of the myth that makes possible its own existence as a poem."[47]

The descriptive-moral poem of Denham and Pope falls apart; it becomes the description of some landscape "with the addition of such embellishments as may be supplied by historical retrospection, or incidental meditation," as Dr. Johnson put it; merely "moralizing descriptions," in Coleridge's words.[48]

---

45. Wasserman, *Subtler Language,* 123.

46. Wasserman, *Subtler Language,* 172.

47. Wasserman, *Subtler Language,* 175.

48. Wasserman, *Subtler Language,* 183. Wasserman makes the point that Shaftesbury, with his notion of beauty as ineffable harmony, was already partway along the road to the new era, which explains the high regard Romantics had for him. Wasserman, *Subtler Language,* 180–184.

Wasserman completes his account in this chapter (chapter 3) with a reference to Wordsworth's "Tintern Abbey," which I invoked above. Talking of Wordsworth's faith in "some spirit deeply interfused," he says: "No longer can a poem be conceived of as a reflection or imitation of an autonomous order outside itself."[49] And he concludes his discussion with Yeats' "conviction that the world was now but a bundle of fragments."[50]

But here I would like to part company with him. If "Tintern Abbey" as poetry works for someone then they are convinced that they are connecting to an "autonomous order," which connection has deep significance for them. That is why they are moved. But there is a difference with earlier ages. There one could say that I am moved because I am convinced of this order (Great Chain, or *concordia discors,* or whatever). These two phases can be distinguished. But the reader of Wordsworth is convinced through being moved. This may seem an epistemically perilous concession to my emotional response. I will hold this point and deal with it later. But for the moment, we just note the difference from poetry which invokes traditionally established orders.

Which brings us to the first big difference between the two eras: the fragmentary nature of order or pattern invoked in poetry of the last two centuries. The skeptic wants to ask Wordsworth: "Tell us more about this spirit which rolls through all things." This is the general difference, of which the possible separation of factual belief from emotional or imperative significance is just one case. Although Romantic thinkers and writers were inspired by traditional doctrines, about languages of insight, or humans as microcosm, they couldn't say that much about how the features of the traditional view could be recaptured in the new context. And where they tried it was often in the language of myth. Novalis is a striking example.

The second feature, closely related to the first, was that the realities invoked were frequently puzzling and paradoxical: Hölderlin's "gods" for instance, who required the "feeling hearts" of humans to fulfill their function. The terms used often took their meaning in part from traditional

49. Wasserman, *Subtler Language,* 186.
50. Wasserman, *Subtler Language,* 179–180.

orders, as with Hölderlin here, or Rilke's "angels," but then departed radically from their traditional sense.

So we frequently find in post-Romantic poetry the invocation of what look like cosmic orders which make something like an ethical demand on us, for (re)connection, or in some other ways (which I'll try to enumerate later). But these are presented fragmentarily, and often enigmatically. We might be tempted to deal with these invocations by cramming them into previously familiar categories: either see them as muddled invocations of traditional, complete and coherent orders (e.g., theistic or pantheistic religion); or treat them as simply reflecting positive reactions, of pleasure or excitement, which throw up the illusion that something is being affirmed. But the first reading fails to recognize what is peculiar to them; and the second totally ignores the phenomenology, which sees the poem as offering a vision inspiring, and moving us to ethical commitment. "Du musst dein Leben ändern" [You must change your life] is the call which Rilke hears from the Torso of Apollo.

And we are not yet fully clear about what Romantic poetry is telling us. What relation do their insights have to philosophy? Simon Jarvis has admirably clarified this issue.[51] We have to avoid two unsatisfactory notions of what philosophical poetry could be. Jarvis' reflections on the possible relations of poetry to philosophy take us beyond the choice between (1) seeing poetry as a potentially decorative and pleasing presentation of a philosophical doctrine already elaborated elsewhere, on one hand, and (2) elevating it to the status of a direct route to philosophic truth, independent of ratiocination and argument, on the other. (1) denies that poetry can be a source of deep insight; (2) fails to see that it convinces through the force of the experience of connection, which is very different from conviction gained through the force of argument. This

51. See Simon Jarvis, *Wordsworth's Philosophic Song* (Cambridge: Cambridge University Press, 2007). I came across this book late in the process of drafting, but I would have greatly benefited from reading it earlier. Jarvis' book is a marvelous example of how much our understanding can be increased by breaking through some too widely accepted dichotomies, not just (1) versus (2), but science versus "ideology," economic versus ritual exchange, cognition versus feeling, consciousness versus bodily engagement, and more. Among the things recovered here is the importance of what I will call the "interspace," the locus of potentially transforming experience.

means that by its very nature, poetic insight will often be incomplete, tentative, and enigmatic (which is not to say that philosophical argument,
which aims at clarity and certainty, will not frequently fail to encompass
these in its own way); but it also means that serious philosophy cannot
afford to ignore poetic insight.

The orders invoked in the subtler languages of the last centuries do
indeed make claims, but they are of another kind, and on another basis
than the older doctrines of cosmic order. Compared to these the new
invoked orders seem incomplete, lacking explicitness, tentative, or provisional. But in the new predicament, where direct, exact, nonsymbolic
or nonmythical mirroring of the order is ruled out, and we can only
create "translations," the old kind of completeness and explicitness is
unattainable.

I want to return to the issue of the validity of these claims below, in
Chapter 2.

3

I hope that the parallelism stands out between Hamann's view of poetic
language as "translation," and Wasserman's notion of "subtler languages,"
at least as I want to read it. Both register a loss: of the earlier confidence
that we could grasp and define the cosmic orders which tell us how to
live. The sense that we can have immediate intuitive knowledge of these
orders has been sapped. This is the shift which has often been described
as a "disenchantment" of the world, and was experienced by the Romantic
generation as a loss. But they both propose poetry as a way of filling the
gap; more exactly a way of recovering the lost connection in a new form:
what will sometimes be understood later as a way of "reenchanting the
world." In both views, disenchantment opens a new field of human initiative, which *Dichtung* responds to.

But to see this, we have to make a clear distinction between the visions of Romantic poetry and the earlier notions of order which were
supposedly grounded in philosophical, metaphysical, or theological arguments. Even after the earlier theological-cosmological doctrines have
utterly lost universal acceptance and quasi-unchallengeable status, people
still hold underlying accounts of our place in the universe which claim
to explain our experience of the world and of art; some will be theolog-

ical, others based in natural science, others again appealing to a life force, or a Schopenhauerian Will.

The questions that these underlying, or etiological, stories try to answer are perfectly legitimate, and people will always go on trying to answer them. But it is also clear that the "translation" of insight in the subtler languages of Romantic poetry, and the recovered connection (and thus resonance) these languages bring about, doesn't—by its very nature can't—answer them. Their claim to insight and connection has to stand or fall on the force of the experience they make possible. The underlying stories, in contrast, rely on arguments which invoke realities—God, a life force—which transcend experience.

The important point to grasp is that these two formulations of insight or knowledge are in continuing relation to each other: the underlying accounts can make sense of and justify the poetic insights (or undermine and refute them); while the experience which inspires the insights is something the underlying doctrines cannot ignore. There is a basic difference here, but also a continuing exchange.[52] The difference explains the numerous crossovers we see in the nineteenth century and today, where people of very different outlooks can be moved by the same works.

Before raising the understandable skeptical objections which can be made to insights convincing through the force of experience, we should note another major difference from poetry and art of previous epochs.

52. This interchange is reflected in the different modes of origin of Romantic works, their different ways of finding their final shape. At one extreme we have Wordsworth in our example above, where the underlying story is merely hinted at through the experience of reconnection. (Wordsworth, pressed by Coleridge, felt called upon to articulate more of the underlying story in his long and uncompleted work *The Recluse,* but this goal remained unaccomplished.) On the other hand, a poetic work can also owe a lot to a new, untraditional underlying story. An example in the German world would be Novalis, who draws heavily on the new picture elaborated by Hamann, as we saw above. An English example could be Blake, whose work, in more than one medium, often takes the form of the creation of a new mythology or theology. And to jump outside literature for a minute, we can cite the way in which Schopenhauer's metaphysics informs Wagner's music, and its leitmotive. Of course, the distinctions here between different modes of origin are far from sharply bounded.

The notion of poetry as spawning an unending series of subtler languages, as resisting any new publicly established references, is a consequence that can be drawn out of the Romantic idea of symbolic disclosure, with another plausible assumption.

Disclosing the world of the "invisible," or the "spiritual," is never a matter of registering the connections of this world, but of retranslating them in "images and signs," to return to the Schlegel sentence with which we started. In making this world understandable, we collaborate and contribute something. We only need to add that we are different from each other, that there is more than one way of collaborating and contributing, and subtler languages come to seem our only recourse. Already the Romantic, "symbolic" theory of poetry is an account of how these can arise. Indeed, it is an exhortation to fresh coinage to return fullness to a desiccated world. Add a premise about human diversity, and you eliminate the perspective that sees this new coinage simply becoming another established public language.

This conclusion wasn't drawn right away. Here is the young Friedrich Schlegel, describing the phenomenon: "Aus dem Innern herausarbeiten das alles muss der moderne Dichter, und viele haben es herrlich getan, aber bis jetzt nur jeder allein, jedes Werk wie eine neue Schöpfung von vorn an aus Nichts" [The modern poet must create all these things from within himself, and many have done it splendidly; up to now, however, each poet separately and each work from its very beginning, like a new creation out of nothing].[53] The "up to now" betrays the hope that a *neue Mythologie* [new mythology] can rectify this state of dispersion. But the makings were there in the very Romantic celebration of diversity to recognize that plurality is inescapable, not only a lack but also a richness. And the whole Romantic theory of the symbol has to be understood in this double perspective. On one hand, it is a response to disenchantment, flattening: a loss of vision. It is a work carried out in *dürftiger Zeit* [meager time]. The distance of the symbol is partly loss. But on the other side, it

---

53. Schlegel, *Gespräch über die Poesie,* 312; Friedrich Schlegel, *Dialogue on Poetry and Literary Aphorisms,* trans. Ernst Behler and Roman Struc (University Park: Pennsylvania State University Press, 1968), 81.

is an affirmation of our power, of our unelidable collaborative role in the re-creation of meaning and communion. In both facets it is essentially modern: it starts from disenchantment and gives an essential place to human freedom and creativity.

4

There was a Hegelian version of this story of separation/alienation and return, which was uncompromisingly rationalist, and saw the whole development of reality as aiming to provide the conditions for Spirit, which was destined to be both rationally self-conscious and free. We can take up the (early) Schelling version, or that proposed by Schlegel; in these, the understanding of reality comes in art, or in a philosophy which is highly dependent on art. Let us take account of the crucial change which Hamann made in our understanding of what it is to grasp, or come in contact with, the Plan; that is, that we do it not through identifying the connections in the code (signatures, Kabbalistic numbers, correspondences), but through a kind of "translation." Human language, and thus artistic creation, is something very different from the language in things—that is, the universe as a manifestation of the Plan. But this language/creation can to some extent bridge the gap, can offer approximations of what the universe reveals. This is the best we can do.

But it is crucial. We recall that (for the Romantics as for those in earlier ages) recovering some contact with the Plan is of the first importance for human beings. This both reveals to us what it is to live up to our highest potential and empowers us to do so. Offering our "translations" is now our only way of recovering this contact.

We can see the two crucial amendments to the tradition of languages of reality (or insight into reality) which the Romantics made pull in the same direction: (1) On the ontological level, the Plan is no longer seen on the Platonic model as laid out in Ideas of perfection existing in eternity, but is rather understood as a direction of growth, toward which reality is tending; and (2) on the epistemological level, our grasp of the Plan is also incapable of matching it exactly, but rather constitutes a kind of translation in our terms of its thrust. This opens onto an era of subtler languages and the corresponding ontic indeterminacy.

Our artistic (or philosophical) creations can be the locus of what I want to call "epiphanies," which both (partially) reveal the Plan / direction of things and put us in empowering contact with it. Or viewed from another angle, a work of art can have a "transfiguration effect" on some scene, by which a deeper order becomes visible, or shines through. This is similar to what the neoclassical authors we cited above, Denham and Pope, bring about except that the order is much more ontologically fragile. (And also more experientially fragile, with consequences I will discuss later.)

(3) To this we should add a third amendment which concerns the notion of the human being as microcosm. This invites us to seek the key to the cosmos within ourselves. But for the Romantics this was no longer understood as a search in the fullness of rational clarity. On the contrary, the search within is carried out in the night (Novalis), in depths which are largely unconscious, where certain hints come in dreams, or in flashes of insights whose bases are shrouded in darkness.[54]

It took a while for the limitations of the subtler languages to be fully appreciated. As we have just seen, F. Schlegel still hoped for a new common "mythology." But the legacy of the Romantic period is this understanding of epiphanies that involve something like a double approximation to a possible Plan or thrust of things (that is, both a revelation of this Plan and an empowering contact with it). Later the notion that our epiphanies can contribute to repairing the (damaged) order (Novalis) may be dropped or reinterpreted. Later again, it may seem less certain, even impossible that we could grasp the whole Plan or thrust of things; we can only hope for partial aperçus, a momentary grasp of something bigger, of a fuller context of whatever is the object of our attention. But the notion of a revealing-connecting-empowering epiphany remains.

What also remains is a thesis about language. As I mentioned earlier, there are uses / forms of language which can serve to objectify and also on occasion manipulate the things around us. But this is the dead, uncreative side of language. Then there are the forms which are the sites of epiphanies. These constitute language as living, revivifying.

---

54. See Béguin, *L'Âme romantique*.

Epiphanies in this sense don't just add to our knowledge, they inspire us; catching a glimpse of these connections powerfully moves us; the current between us and Nature flows once more. We are in the domain of resonance. I will expand on this in a minute.

So a crucial distinction comes to the fore, between ordinary, flat, instrumental language which designates different objects, and combines these designata into accurate portraits of things and events, all of which serves the purpose of controlling and manipulating things (following the prescriptions of the HLC), on one hand; and on the other, truly insightful speech, which reveals the very nature of things and restores contact with them. Epiphanic languages give us a sense that we are called; we receive a call. There is someone or something out there.

My claim is that this distinction between dead, "blind" uses of language, and truly revelatory, insightful ones which restore contact, continues after the Romantic period, and up to our time, even though many features of the Romantics' view of the world, of literature, of the current which passes between us and the world, have been abandoned or greatly modified.

5

Before proceeding, I want to clarify a misunderstanding which may arise. Jarvis' remarks quoted above about the nature of Wordsworth's "philosophic song" helped us to distinguish two ways that poetry could be philosophical.[55] The first was (1) where a philosophical doctrine was presented in verse (which presentation can be more than merely decorative and pleasing, as I unfairly hinted above). The second is (2) where poetry can be "epiphanic," in the above sense, when it yields a powerful experience of (re)connection. The presence of (2) is essential to the force of certain Romantic works, like those of "Tintern Abbey," and certain poems of Hölderlin, which I'll discuss in Chapter 4. But this doesn't mean that a lot of their poetry doesn't realize (1).

55. "I yearn towards some philosophic Song / Of truth that cherishes our daily life" (bk. 1, 229–230). William Wordsworth, *The Thirteen-Book "Prelude,"* ed. Mark L. Reed (Ithaca, NY: Cornell University Press, 1991), 112.

In fact, much of Wordsworth's poetry is "descriptive" (function 1), rather than "performative"—bringing about connection. In fact, some description may be essential, providing the context to the epiphanic or performative passages. We can see this with our paradigm example from "Tintern Abbey."

Here is the longer passage, which starts from a description of the author's earlier communion with nature:

> The sounding cataract
> Haunted me like a passion: the tall rock,
> The mountain, and the deep and gloomy wood,
> Their colours and their forms, were then to me
> An appetite; a feeling and a love,
> That had no need of a remoter charm,
> By thought supplied, nor any interest
> Unborrowed from the eye.—That time is past,
> And all its aching joys are now no more,
> And all its dizzy raptures. Not for this
> Faint I, nor mourn nor murmur; other gifts
> Have followed; for such loss, I would believe,
> Abundant recompense. For I have learned
> To look on nature, not as in the hour
> Of thoughtless youth, but hearing oftentimes
> The still, sad music of humanity,
> Nor harsh nor grating, though of ample power
> To chasten and subdue. And I have felt . . . (77–94)[56]

Clearly this description of the relation to nature in earlier times is the essential context for the powerful reconnective passage which follows. The reconnective vision realized here takes off from the background of loss which enframes it, and constitutes its condition, glancingly evoked by the reference to "the still, sad music of humanity."[57]

Of course, this description shouldn't be called "theoretical," but there are many passages of what we can call (movingly and convincingly) stated

56. Wordsworth, "Tintern Abbey," 118–119.
57. Wordsworth, "Tintern Abbey," 118.

theory (e.g., in "Intimations of Immortality" and many other places). It is in the very nature of Wordsworth's poetry, and the mutual relation of passages of types (1) and (2), that it is very difficult to draw a line between the two. But what can be said, I believe, is that without the epiphanic force which breaks out in his work, his poetry would not have the power for us that it has.[58] We can see the same pattern here which was implicit in the Romantic notion of the symbol, the same combination of creation and discovery. Something we make, the work, brings it about that a reality normally hidden appears. Or from another angle, the work realizes a (re)connection which we now see to be in the nature of things.

A similar duality attends Wordsworth's conception of "Imagination." For Wordsworth, imagination is the power which enables us to create, and yet he can speak of it as a "sudden gift, / Gift of imagination's holy power."[59] A similar duality attends Wordsworth's notion of "spots of time," which in memory can restore to us the power to create, at moments when we are

> . . . depressed
> By false opinion and contentious thought,
> Or aught of heavier or more deadly weight,
> In trivial occupations, and the round
> Of ordinary intercourse
> . . .
> This efficacious spirit lurks
> among those passages of life that give
> Profoundest knowledge to what point, and how
> The mind is lord and master—outward sense
> The obedient servant of her will. (Book 9, 258–266)[60]

58. See, for instance, the passage on climbing Snowdon in Wordsworth, *"Prelude,"* bk. 1.

59. William Wordsworth, "St. Paul's," in *The Tuft of Primroses with Other Late Poems for the Recluse,* ed. Joseph F. Kishel (Ithaca, NY: Cornell University Press, 1986), 59, quoted in Jarvis, *Wordsworth's Philosophic Song,* 216. I have greatly benefited from Jarvis' discussion in the concluding chapter of his book.

60. Wordsworth, *"Prelude,"* 301.

This can sound almost like a statement of philosophical idealism, unless one takes account of the intertwined nature of poetry as both creation and revelation. If Wordsworth's poetry combines both "descriptive" and "epiphanic" passages (with admittedly a fuzzy line between them), later on modes of poetic practice develop where the "epiphanic" is all-pervasive. This happens in a number of different languages, but at different times and through different stages.

More generally, we can remark that this epiphanic or connective dimension arises earlier in German and English poetry than it does in French. The Romantic generation of the 1820s—Hugo, Vigny, Lamartine—remain more within the descriptive, constative. Lamartine has some moving and convincing statements of theory: for example, this passage setting out his view of the earlier insightful languages of the cosmos, which we humans have lost (and a similar glance backward was essential to the birth of German Romanticism, as we have seen).

He speaks here of an angel who early on falls into the human realm:

> Il parla des humains ce sublime langage
> Où chaque verbe était la chose avec l'image,
> Langage où l'univers semblait se révéler,
> Où c'était définir et peindre que parler,
> Car l'homme n'avait pas encor, dans son trouble,
> Brouillé ce grand miroir où Dieu l'avait fait lire,
> Et, semant au hasard ses débris en tout lieu,
> Mis son verbe terni sur le verbe de Dieu.[61]

> [He spoke the sublime language of humans,
> Where each word revealed the thing with its image;
> A language where the universe seemed to reveal itself,
> Where to speak was to define and depict.
> Because man had not yet in his inner trouble
> darkened the great mirror that God had let him read.
> And sowing at random the shards of his thoughts
> Imposed his tarnished words on the Word of God.]

61. Alphonse de Lamartine, "La Chute d'un Ange," quoted in Paul Bénichou, *Les Mages Romantiques* (Paris: Gallimard, 1988), 103.

A slightly later generation moves in the epiphanic direction: Nerval, and then Baudelaire and Mallarmé. It is this move I want to trace in this book, always recognizing that this is but one of the many tracks to follow among the supernovae of new poetic forms which has succeeded the Romantic era.

6

A note on "disenchantment"   It might help here to clarify the uses of the term "disenchantment," which was invoked at the beginning of Section II.3 as one of the forces undermining the credibility of traditional cosmic orders.

A short definition of this term would point to the decline of magic, and the associated beliefs throughout the early modern period. And indeed, the term was introduced into sociological-historical thinking by Weber, and his term *Entzauberung* could be more literally translated "demagification" (*Zauber* being the German term for "magic").

But less tersely, we could point to the decline of belief in spirits, like the spirits of the woods which were thought to threaten crops and animals; of objects and substances (e.g., potions or relics), whose benign or malign effects were conceived more widely than could be explained by their physical constitution (e.g., relics which could cure any malady), or more narrowly (like love potions—not aphrodisiacs, but the kind of drink which bound Tristan and Isolde forever); and the like.[62]

---

62. Later on, we find the word used in a much broader sense, embracing the decline in belief in God, or in religion in general. But this is clearly a distinct concept from the one I'm invoking, and of much more recent coinage. Unfortunately, Weber sometimes encouraged this confusion. In fact, the disenchantment which undermined the belief in cosmic orders through the seventeenth and eighteenth centuries did not offer support for atheism; on the contrary, one of its driving forces was the spread of more stringent forms of Christianity (mainly but not exclusively Protestant) which saw magic as a threat to the faith. Another was, of course, the rise of post-Galilean natural science, which could only undermine faith in relics and potions. To put it briefly, this science only allows what we might call "mechanistic" explanation. But it was only meant to apply to the material cosmos, not to the actions of the Creator. As a matter of fact, in the wake of Newtonian science, there are attempts (Boyle, Paley) to prove from the complexity, intricacy, and benignity of the material cosmos the necessity of positing an all-powerful and benevolent Creator. The error of fusing these two concepts has been

What have the drivers been of this process of "disenchantment" of the world; or the "decline of magic"? Of course, many factors play a role: there was a growing sense of the importance of individual freedom, of respecting the capacity of individual human beings to judge important issues. This entailed giving less importance to inherited social forms, which authoritatively attributed certain roles to individuals based on the nature of things. But the most important driver came from the successes of the new post-Galilean sciences. These were successes in solving certain intractable puzzles arising in Aristotelian accounts (e.g., what keeps the cannon ball moving after it leaves the cannon?—a great mystery on the Aristotelian assumption that continued movement requires a continuing mover; but the problem disappears on the inertial assumption that only changes in velocity need explanation).

But they were also successes in offering new forms of technological control of bodies and the world, which were celebrated by Bacon. So much so that the word "science" undergoes a mutation, where it comes more and more to mean "physical" sciences, with a strong mathematical component; and the new word "scientist" refers to practitioners of this kind of science. (So that even studies which can't attain this degree of rigor are anxious to take over the word; for example "social science.")

The new science involves a focus on matter, in the sense the word has in the ancient distinction form-matter. The form shapes the matter, on the ancient Platonic-Aristotelian understanding; that is, form draws matter toward the shape it defines; matter is made to aim at, and eventually realize, the form.

The new post-Galilean science of nature sidelines Form in this sense, as irrelevant, and looks for regularities, for efficient causal relations, in the world of matter. It is clear that this outlook doesn't have much place for Renaissance concepts of order, which have the Platonic feature that they try to shape material reality to conform to them, so that deviations from them call forth movements to restore their proper shape. For instance, inversions of hierarchical order in society trigger countermove-

---

eloquently demonstrated by Hans Joas in his *Die Macht des Heiligen*. See Hans Joas, *The Power of the Sacred,* trans. Alex Skinner (Oxford: Oxford University Press, 2021).

ments, or further disturbances which undermine them (see the cosmic responses to Duncan's murder in *Macbeth*).

It is very understandable that the continuing and growing successes of the new post-Galilean sciences more and more undercut the credibility of these traditional and early Renaissance doctrines.

Disenchantment driven by this scientism is closely related to the process I described in *A Secular Age* as the replacement of the "porous" selves by "buffered" selves. According primacy to efficient causal relations forces us to understand mind-body relations as holding between clearly distinct entities: the "mind" as a kind of "internal" space, and the "external" world of space in the ordinary sense. We are induced into a Cartesian-Lockean picture, whereby the "mind" receives input from the "world," on the basis of which it erects its portrait or map of this world, while at the same time learning to effect its internally generated purposes in this world.

These clearly distinct entities don't seem to allow for the kind of felt link or connection which is supposedly invoked in and by a poem like Wordsworth's "Tintern Abbey." The felt link to an "external" object must be the result of its causal action on my senses, or receptors. There is no place for any other kind of relation, involving a supposedly more intimate connection.

Does this mean that the revelations conjured by Romantic poetry are simply illusions? Unsubstantial fantasies? That would be too quick a conclusion. It is not clear that all facets of human life can be understood within the terms set by natural science. Those who believe that all human action and feeling can be explained reductively in terms of a mechanistic physiology are happy to embrace this conclusion. But it is far from being established that animate beings can be exhaustively understood in such reductive terms; and in human life phenomena like value, morality, ethics, and the love of art itself seem to require explorations which can only be carried out in vocabularies which are validated or not in hermeneutic terms, where progress involves making the best sense we can of actions and emotions.

I will return to these issues in Chapter 2.

Chapter Two

EPISTEMIC ISSUES

|

1

So we can see two great ontological shifts involved in the Romantics' taking up of earlier theories of a language which reveals the nature of things. The first was made right at the beginning with Hamann's "Reden ist übersetzen": we have no direct contact with the archetypes; we can't map them in an accurate dictionary. The second followed (one might think) almost inevitably from this first step. If we have no direct contact with the language of things, if we have to derive our own translations, then we are engaged via the "subtler languages" which each poet must invent or transpose to create his or her work; and this divergence of languages is the greater in that each arises from hints originating in a personal experience which may be hard to communicate to others. The ontic status of the realities invoked, be it the great force which "rolls through all things" of Wordsworth, or Hölderlin's "gods," or Rilke's "angels," remains irremediably indeterminate. Should these terms be taken literally? Does this question even have a clear sense?

The crucial shift in the understanding of what it is to grasp the order in the cosmos can be put in this way: in the traditional version, understanding would take the form of a code in which elements could be assigned meanings which were independently identifiable. The meaning of Moses' serpent is given in the Kabbalistic number—358—which underlies its creation (and hence its link with the Messiah is revealed); the meaning of the eagle is given in its role of embodying the supreme, ruling element in its domain, that of birds (even as lions do among animals, dolphins among fishes, kings in kingdoms). But the meaning of a symbol (in the sense of A. W. Schlegel or Ricoeur) can't be independently accessed; it has to be recognized in the symbol itself. This means two things: negatively, that its meaning can never be definitively disclosed— there is an uncertainty, an incompleteness in the "translation," a possibility of its being improved on, of making a better translation. This possibility can never be totally fulfilled, foreclosing all future attempts to improve on it. The meaning of a symbol is thus never totally and definitively delineated. But at the same time, positively, it lends the symbol a kind of depth, or "semi-transparency."[1] The meaning appears in the symbol; we see it "through" the symbol.[2] And this meaning resonates in us.

This is true whether the symbol is some reality that is serving as such (soiling in relation to sin, unbrokenness in relation to integrity), or consists in a work of art.

But from the standpoint of the post-Cartesian, sharp separation of mind and matter, the supposed "insights" of Romantic poetry must be judged to be merely in the eye of the beholder, or in other terms, simply "subjective." (This connects to the second way of not taking the claim to

1. See Iain McGilchrist, *The Master and His Emissary* (New Haven, CT: Yale University Press, 2009).

2. This "seeing through" is what underlies the power of a portrayal of some everyday reality in art, say, in a poem of painting, to alter our perception of this reality in the everyday. See Maurice Merleau-Ponty, "Cezanne's Doubt," in *Sense and Non-sense*, trans. Hubert L. Dreyfus and Patricia Allen Dreyfus (Chicago: Northwestern University Press, 1964), 9–25.

order seriously, which I enumerated above: seeing it as a simple positive reaction without epistemic content.)

Many of our contemporaries take this stance. Romantic poetry tells us something about the psychology of the poet, but nothing at all about the world this poet responds to. It reveals something about the (creator's or reader's) psychology, but nothing ontological about what exists in the world. The opposition seems clear, but perhaps there is undistributed middle here. I'd like to explore further what's at stake in this debunking claim.

There are purely psychological meanings: I like roses, not peonies. This could easily change, you could even work on me to change it, *but:* we all agree that there is no right and wrong here; you couldn't validly *convince* me to change my mind.

Contrast life meanings: I need air, water, food. This is not just a fact about me; all humans do. And it is not just a fact about humans; animals do. Moreover, even if I took it into my head to believe that I don't need these things, I would just be wrong, demonstrably wrong. (And you would hope to convince me, before I died of my illusion.)

We might see this difference in kind of meaning as one of location. Liking roses is just in me, whereas these biological needs are facts about the space between animal and ecological niche. But there is also another difference. The biological meanings are decidable through hard natural science; the likes and dislikes aren't; they are human meanings.

Now the question: Are there human meanings which are founded on facts about the interspace between human beings and their ecological niche, comparably "objective" to the facts which found life meanings, but different from these? There seem to be: for instance, the joy we take in spring, in life, in nature; our sense of being (more than biologically) fed by the life around us.

But can we define the need / meaning here more fully? This is something we might try to do with the term "resonance": some movement of sympathy between us and our niche. This term is central to the interesting, and (to me) persuasive theory of the good life recently proposed by Hartmut Rosa. His contention is that a full life is impossible without a relation of resonance between self and world. Here is one characterization of this relation:

> In this mode (sc of resonance) the subject experiences the
> world. . . . as "answering", responding and carrying. The connec-
> tion here is of an intrinsic nature and meaning, not causal and
> instrumental, but constitutive. In this mode, the subject is ca-
> pable of "appropriating" the world in a manner that transforms
> the self's essence through "connection" (*Anverwandlung* instead
> of simple instrumental *Aneignung*). Thus, the mode of resonance
> can be defined as a mode in which the self is moved, touched,
> "meant to be" or "addressed", but also feels capable of reaching
> out and touching or moving the external world.[3]

This theory is of particular interest to me, in that it obviously finds its
origin in the Romantic era; we can see the concern of Romantic poets
with "reconnection" continuing and being expanded in a full-fledged
theory of resonance.

Resonance arises in the case of this passage from Wordsworth through
the connection and interweaving of a movement in the world with the
poet's act of creation. If we look at the passage we've been examining as
a simple description, it seems to pick out a process, "a motion and a
spirit . . . which rolls through all things." But what is going on here is
very far from what happens when an observer notes a movement in the
scene he observes. The poet is not a simple observer; he connects with
the scene. The connection comes about through an interweaving of the
experience of reception, on one hand—as the light from the sun strikes
the river and fields below and this comes to the poet's eyes—with the
poet's act of expression which acknowledges and intensifies the reception, casting it in the process as part of this larger motion, on the other.
The act of expression brings to light this larger motion; reception and
expression have to come together in a harmony. This is resonance—or
at least what it means in this "axis of resonance" [*Resonanzachse*], to
use Rosa's term.[4]

3. Hartmut Rosa, "Resonance—towards a New Conception of the Good Life" (unpublished manuscript, 2013), 2–3.

4. Hartmut Rosa, *Resonance: A Sociology of Our Relationship to the World,* trans.
James Wagner (Cambridge, UK: Polity, 2019).

But this crucial role of expression will inevitably raise doubts and questions: How do we establish this or other claims about our essential needs, or the essential constituents of a good life?

The traditional way of doing this was by making ontological claims about the universe—for instance, the Great Chain of Being; or God, who has created a world of signs; there is a language here, which we have to connect to. This lies in the realm of what I called earlier underlying doctrine. But the attempt to demonstrate, to everyone's satisfaction, something along this avenue seems blocked. Although some people may understand and accept our theological arguments (to take one example), among humans in general, basic outlooks are, it seems irremediably, diverse.

Is there, however, another way to proceed, which doesn't immediately involve such ontic claims, even though our ultimate explanation of our experience might require some such claims?

Otherwise put, can we establish some claims to human meaning here, so that there would be a right and wrong, founded and unfounded, without in the first instance making an ontic claim about Nature?

Let's look at certain Romantic poets, such as Hölderlin: he speaks of *Dichtung* (which for Hölderlin brings to light, and connects us to, a movement in Nature; which in turn involves an intensification of life); this shows us a meaning of these movements in Nature, and of our connection with them, which makes a claim on us. There is a strong evaluation here: not to see / feel this is to be missing something true and important. Now this can't be shown biologically as with life meaning. However, like life meaning it is situated in the "interspace."

This is the undistributed middle, between the "ontological" and the "psychological"—at least until we can achieve a deeper explanation, which might involve ontic claims about Nature; or we might settle on a reductive account, which would simply show this sense to be a reflex of the biological, or the psychological, that is, generated within the individual, even though present perhaps in all (like disgust at certain substances).

Are Wordsworth and Hölderlin bringing to light something in Nature, and in our relation to Nature, which we should all recognize, some more intensely vivifying meaning? (Even though each of us may offer another interpretation of it or find something similar in somewhat different objects.) This is indeed a claim which people make on behalf of certain forms of art, whether or not they evoke resonance with Nature; music, for instance, even though we differ about what music we are moved by. We deal here with a human meaning which we consider founded but couldn't ground biologically. (Or at least, not with our present biology.)

Let's make a grid with four quadrants. On the horizontal, we have human versus biological meanings; on the vertical, we have grounded (strong evaluation) versus ungrounded (weak evaluation):

	Human	*Biological*
Strong	Beethoven, Médecins sans frontières	Air, water
Weak	Roses v. peonies	Ice cream

In the lower right quadrant we have biological meanings which are just matters of individual psychology, like: I like strawberry ice cream, and you like vanilla. In the upper right, we have grounded biological meanings. In the lower left we have weak human meanings, roses versus peonies.

Question: Is there anything in the upper left quadrant?

Normally, we would concede that great music has a meaning which is in some way grounded; also another example: some lives are very meaningful, like dedicating one's medical skills to helping people through Médecins sans frontières. But we have trouble saying what makes it the case that these are meaningful, a problem which doesn't arise with biological needs, like air and water. Should that bother us?

The question of this discussion amounts to this: Is recognizing and connecting with a movement in Nature, as with Wordsworth and Hölderlin, up there in the upper left quadrant, or does it fall into the lower left quadrant? This comes down to an issue of the good life, this central ethical notion. Is the connection that our two poets are pointing to and (claim to be) bringing about a crucial component of a full human life?

The sense of heightened meaning we experience in reading Romantic poetry involves some notion of my realizing an important potential, which is a constituent of a full human life, of a meaningful life, one worth living. It belongs to "ethics" in an important but often neglected sense, where this term designates the attempt to enumerate the crucial components of a fulfilled, or fully realized, human life.

So there is a strong evaluation underlying the experience here: not responding in this way is missing something important in the range of potentialities for a full life. It's similar to the experience of great art, hearing Beethoven's late quartets, or seeing *King Lear*. But is this intuition valid?

Note that objectivity, groundedness, strong evaluation can go along with variation. To say Beethoven's last quartets are great music is not to say that people who are deeply moved by something else are misguided. The shape of meaning in music can be complex and varied. Something similar is true of meaningful lives: Médecins sans frontières is not the only such career.

But also in the upper left are moral judgments, like: all humans have a right to life. There we don't allow for variation of positions: we rightly reject the idea that only superior people deserve to live. Lots of people, even those who would banish great art and meaningful lives from the upper left quadrant, want to plead for the groundedness of ethics.[5] But often one can question the arguments they offer to back this up: for instance, utilitarian and Kantian theories.

I said above that meaningfulness judgments can admit of variation, although not all do. There is another distinction which is orthogonal to the two mapped in this quadrant; that is, meanings which are (with exceptions) invariably experienced, versus those which only some people have. Example: nausea. Not everybody likes ice cream, but all humans experience nausea before excrement (unless they have undergone special training). But still nausea belongs in the lower right quadrant. It is something generated by our biological makeup, and happens to be universal, but there are no grounds which might figure in an argument to this effect. You couldn't convince someone not to be nauseated.

5. But of course, there are subjectivists in morals as well; see John Mackie's "error theory," in John L. Mackie, *Ethics: Inventing Right and Wrong* (London: Penguin, 1977).

So the issue is about the Wordsworth-Hölderlin idea, the alleged connectedness with the movement in Nature: Is it properly in the upper left quadrant? Or just the lower left? Is there some revivifying, intense meaning here, which is really there, but has no biological grounding (that is, grounding in biological science, as we presently understand it)?

2

This invocation of essential human meanings is one way of challenging the simple distinction ontological versus psychological. Indeed, the above discussion shows an indeterminacy in our original way of putting this question: ontological or psychological? The criterion of the "ontological" might be: grounded in something quite independent of human beings, something which would exist in the world even if humans disappeared. We spoke above of facts about the "interspace" between humans and the world, such as needing food (biological or life meanings), or sensing a deep connection with Nature (human meanings). Let's call these "human-related" realities, because they wouldn't exist if there were no more humans.

Now most underlying stories appeal to realities which are not human-related: God, Life Force, the Schopenhauerian Will, and so on. But when we ask our question of human meanings, we are clearly dealing with matters which are human-related. They exist only in the interspace defined by humans and their niche in the world. So if we read "ontological" as human-unrelated, then these meanings have to be "psychological." But this term often carries the implication: depending on the variations of individual psychology—that is, belonging in the lower left quadrant. Combining the restrictive readings of the two terms entirely screens out the upper left quadrant. In order to ask the crucial question here, we have either to expand "ontological" to include this quadrant or expand "psychological" to allow it to cover both left quadrants.

We can see how the question, Ontological or psychological? still lacks precision. On a restrictive reading of each term, it prevents us from asking the really important question, about the status of meanings in the upper left quadrant. These are experienced as having validity independently of how we happen to feel, that is they are lived as strong evaluations. Can we allow into our ontology a kind of objective validity which can't be backed up biologically, or more generally, in terms of natural science? Many thinkers, who take a reductive stance to explanation, want to say no. But our actual human experience inescapably treats these meanings as objective. Moral right or wrong, great art, wonder at Nature, these don't come across to us as matters of shifting taste.

The unclarity around this dichotomy, ontological or psychological, also obscures the fact that there are two issues here. One concerns the account underlying our experience, which unquestionably involves human-unrelated realities; the other concerns the experiences themselves, their objective validity or lack thereof. The subtler languages of Romantic poetry make claims in this second domain. True, there will be references to a force "rolling through all things" (Wordsworth), or to "gods" (Hölderlin), and the claim that reconnection to these is an essential fulfillment of human life must entail that the connection is not simply illusory, which in turn must be grounded in some truth about the human-unrelated world.

Taking Wordsworth's passage as an example, one can say that, since the experience is one of a new (or restored) connection that the poem brings about, the work must not only release a potentiality in us to feel this connection, but also one in the world to offer this connection, which has just been strengthened and intensified in the utterance of this poem. For otherwise the difference it makes would lie purely in our psychological response.[6] This involves ontic commitments, but the poem itself may and often does leave uncertain what these commitments are.

This, of course, says nothing about what any given poet believed or would accept as an underlying story. In many cases, the poet might not even make a distinction between poetic force and underlying truth; but if pressed, might accept that the first should be taken as a first approximation, or manifestation, of the second (Wordsworth, Hopkins). In this they would not be followed by their more skeptical admirers, who would

6. See the interesting discussion of "ergetic knowledge" and its relation to magic in John Milbank, "Religion, Science and Magic: Rewriting the Agenda," in *After Science and Religion: Rewriting the Agenda,* ed. Peter Harrison and John Milbank (Cambridge: Cambridge University Press, 2022), 75–143.

however enthusiastically recognize the revealing, even reconnecting power of their work.

The above discussion shows another possible blind spot (or another way of revealing the same blind spot) in the original distinction (or at least in the way it's often taken). It's not just a matter of forgetting the upper left quadrant. It is also the fact that our convictions about matters in this quadrant can have two sources or can be of two types. We respond to the poetry of Hölderlin or Wordsworth with a conviction that there is a crucial human fulfillment or realization in recognizing our relation to Nature and recovering it. But this conviction is different from beliefs we might have about a possible underlying story. It is grounded in the power of the experience, whereas the underlying story has to draw on beliefs about the universe, God, the Life Force, or human depth psychology, or whatever, which have other grounds, other sources, other bases. Subtler languages in the post-Romantic period usually bespeak their own limitations; the implicit metaphysic is either too sketchy and partial (Wordsworth's "force"), or too paradoxical (Hölderlin's "gods"), or is from the very beginning presented as tentative (Keats' "Beauty," as we will see in Chapter 6). That is why they can enjoy a certain independence from convictions about underlying realities, and why people of such different theological and anthropological persuasions could share a sense of the revealing power of Wordsworth's poetry.[7]

One might be tempted to say: the conviction this poetry commands is purely aesthetic, as against the intellectually grounded theories of theology or anthropology. But this isn't quite right, because intellectual reflection, in criticism for instance, can alter, refine, develop the actual experience. What is crucial is the grounding in this experience.

Perhaps we can recur to a distinction crucial to Kant, between the phenomena and noumena. However ill-adapted this is applied to our

---

7. This underlies the important difference between the mature Hegel and the rest of the Romantic generation of the 1790s, which he grew up with and then repudiated. Hegel believed that he was offering a fully adequate underlying story, fully grounded in reason. He refused to be satisfied with a partly "symbolic" account through art, which even his close colleague Schelling thought unavoidable. Accounts in terms of art or "religion" have to be *aufgehoben* [sublated] in a fully conceptual medium.

perception of our everyday world, I think it might be illuminating here.[8] Phenomena (*Erscheinungen,* appearances) are realities as they enter our experience; noumena (*Dingen-an-sich,* things in themselves) are these realities as they exist without relation to us. What I've called here "underlying stories" plainly have to invoke "noumena"; while the sense of reconnection revealed and strengthened by a work of art is rather "phenomenal." Indeed, what I've called "interspaces" are by their very nature "phenomenal."

3

A crucial question which arises in the above discussion concerns the status and nature of what I've been calling the interspace, the space of interaction between us and our world. Does it constitute an object domain which needs to be examined on its own terms? What underlies the posing of the dichotomous question, ontological or psychological? The assumption is that the phenomena of interaction can be accounted for by putting together what we learn about two object domains separately, the universe (in its relevant aspects), and human being (or organism).

We can see that this works fine for the upper right quadrant, where we are dealing with objectively established life meanings. Human beings need air, water, nourishment to survive. We can work out exactly what kind of food they require by putting together what we know about the substances the organism needs, on one hand, and the potential sources of these substances that the world around us offers, on the other. Different sciences may be needed in each domain, but they are all what we recognize in the post-Galilean era as natural sciences.

But does this work for the other quadrants? Probably it does for the lower right one, where we note our taste preferences; for instance, I prefer vanilla to strawberry ice cream. I don't know how to explain this, but we can think of cases where we account for our tastes in a fashion similar to the one we apply to the upper right quadrant. Consider the explanation sometimes offered for the widespread human craving for sweet things.

8. And I think it badly distorts the issues here. See Hubert Dreyfus and Charles Taylor, *Retrieving Realism* (Cambridge, MA: Harvard University Press, 2015).

The speculation is that, during the early evolutionary stages of *Homo sapiens,* as we struggled with the bleak conditions of the retreating ice age, we needed a large intake of sugar. The result was the evolution of a human type which had this (to us now) fatal craving, which we have to combat. This is an interactive explanation, in the sense that we are tracing the consequences for our present state to past interactions with the environment, but it involves our putting together facts gleaned from each domain separately. This is in fact the structure of many explanations in evolutionary psychology: for example, the supposed different nature of the sex drive in men and women.

But this combination of findings from two distinct domains breaks down in the upper left quadrant. When it comes to human meanings, like our aspiration to solidarity with others, or our desire (central to the Romantics) to reconnect with the natural world around us, this way of proceeding won't work. There is no internal, intraorganismic account possible of the desire, even one causally explained by past interactions, as there is in the case of the sweets we crave; because we can't specify what the desire is for just by naming a clearly identifiable object (sugar-filled foods). We have to understand what it means to reconnect with nature, or to be in real solidarity with our fellows. In this upper left realm of human meanings, there is an inescapable hermeneutic dimension involved, with the consequent possibility of endless interpretive dispute.

This means that we have to recognize the interspace as a third object domain, which has to be examined on its own, as a whole, and can't be broken down into the two domains we recognize in the life meanings of the upper right quadrant, organism and universe, the findings about which we simply combine. What is at stake in the upper left can only be specified from the relationship of human agent to world. It is here that the phenomena of resonance appear.[9]

---

9. One could argue that Wordsworth himself was quite clear that he was concerned with what I've been calling the "interspace":

> For the discerning intellect of Man,
> When wedded to this goodly universe
> In love and holy passion, shall find these
> A simple produce of the common day.

The failure to recognize the interspace as a third, irreducible domain is what underlies the dichotomous question, ontological or psychological? The distinction here is in fact threefold.

Recognizing this is extremely important for another crucial issue—if I can introduce a digression here: that of understanding the human past. Our attitude in the modern world toward earlier societies who saw themselves as living in an enchanted universe, where animals have souls, and sacred spaces emanate power, is generally one of dismissive condescension. These poor people were just deluded, projecting all sorts of wild features onto a dead, neutral universe. Once we grasp the independent status of the interspace, we can see that this condescension is misplaced.

We will not be ready to accept these earlier world views as literal truths, but we can now recognize them as earlier attempts to grapple with issues that we are not that good at dealing with, the more so in that many of us want to deny that they exist. From the standpoint of this discussion, we should rather be examining these earlier outlooks for insights which we could translate into our own terms. We badly need a lesson in humility.[10]

4

We could restate the argument of the previous pages in another, terser fashion. The claim that I feel in a work like "Tintern Abbey" could be analytically set out in two (inseparable) facets: (a) that it reconnects me to a larger order and (b) that it realizes a crucial potentiality in me as a human being. The first reaction of a post-Cartesian mind, following the model of natural science, is to check the first facet: Is there an actual connection being realized, whatever its meaning for me? The assumption here is that we can answer this by examining agent and environment separately in order to determine their actual relation (as we did in the ex-

---

Wordsworth's claim was that "individual mind" and "external world" were "fitted to" each other, and "they with blended might / Accomplish" a new "creation." William Wordsworth, "The Recluse," quoted in M. H. Abrams, *Natural Supernaturalism* (New York: W. W. Norton, 1971), 27.

10. My discussion here has been greatly helped by reading Rosa's latest book. See Rosa, *Resonance,* chs. 5, 8.

planation of our addiction to sugar in terms of the early experience of evolving hominids).

I have been arguing here that there are reasons why this approach cannot work when it comes to our response to works of art. We can only explore this if we approach it through the second facet, which is what I have been doing here, and will continue later in this chapter.

5

So the introduction of subtler languages, which I have claimed was implicit in Hamann's opening move, the affirmation that "Reden ist übersetzen" (to speak is to translate), involves a profound change in our understanding of art. Whereas previously, poets and artists in general drew on (what were seen as) ontically firm realities, as described by history, theology, philosophy (with its pictures of cosmic order, the Great Chain of Being, etc.), the new languages invoke entities whose ontic status is not clear. Earlier works invoked simply what was understood as a firm underlying account. This clarity about ontic status applies also to painting and literature invoking classical mythology, not that it was accepted literally, but in that its fictional, and perhaps allegorical, status was fully clear.

Now we have entities (Wordsworth's "spirit," Hölderlin's "gods," Rilke's "angels") which lack this clear status. The distinction was not evident at once but came over time to be recognized. Wordsworth's spirit was (anyway, some of the time) seen by him as a first approximation of an eventual underlying account, a sort of implicit and provisional metaphysic. But it gradually came to be realized that the entities invoked had force independent of their redemption in an underlying story, and even for people who couldn't envisage accepting any such story (e.g., an atheist George Eliot who was moved by Wordsworth's poetry). And today, Rilke can be recognized as a great poet even by those who never envisage giving a coherent, ontically grounded account of his "angels."[11]

11. But prior to a recognition of the difference between symbol and underlying story, Wordsworth's poetry faced a formidable obstacle. His poetry could easily be condemned by orthodox Christians as heretical, even pantheistic. See Stephen Gill, *William Wordsworth: A Life* (Oxford: Oxford University Press, 1989), 308–309.

And in fact, the founding generation of German Romanticism, that of the 1790s, philosophers and poets alike, shared (or at least tried to hammer out together) a unified theory, englobing both philosophy and poetics (which I tried to sketch in Section I.2 above). This was prior to the intrusion of a self-consciousness about subtler languages, and hence of a distinction between truth of underlying account, on one hand, and the efficacy of the symbol, on the other.[12]

So how are subtler languages validated, if not alethically through a correspondence theory of truth? Here we come to one of the important contributions of the Romantic era to modern culture. The notion of the symbol, as I've tried to expound it following Schlegel, and in our time Ricoeur, has this crucial property, that the work of art as symbol gives us access to a certain experience of meaning. Certain "interspaces"—that is, human agents in situations—carry meanings which can only take shape for us, and hence fully enter our experience, thanks to their articulation in a work of art.

There is an analogy here with a distinction between different "semantic logics" which I discussed in *The Language Animal*.[13] According to one logic, the "designative" one, a word can be introduced to give a name to a certain object which we have noticed. We come across a new species of rodent and give it its scientific designation. But another logic is evident in our development of new vocabulary for human meanings. Certain terms, like "indignation" (as against just anger), and "joy" (as distinct from just happiness), or "meaningfulness" (describing a life path, distinct from other kinds of positive assessment, like financially rewarding, interesting, stress-free, etc.), make possible the experience of

---

12. Both Schelling and Hegel tried to give a full philosophical expression to this unified view. In Hegel's case, there is some distinction between philosophy and poetry, but only as different levels of absolute spirit. The truth is conveyed by art, religion, and philosophy, in ascending order of adequacy.

And of course, even those who abandoned the philosophical route continued to be drawn to some underlying story—for instance, in the intuition that we cannot understand our own nature (or "destiny" [*Bestimmung*]) without grasping the order of the cosmos, but they are aware how provisional and underdefined this intuition is.

13. Charles Taylor, *The Language Animal: The Full Shape of the Human Linguistic Capacity* (Cambridge, MA: Belknap Press of Harvard University Press, 2016), ch. 6.

meaning. Without them, there may be a felt pressure to articulate something important, but the meaning only takes its full shape with their articulation. These terms interpret, articulate what that felt pressure was about; they give the experience form. This is what I called the "constitutive" semantic logic.[14]

We can see this if we think of cases of self-correction, such as, for instance, when I come to see that my anger at your action was not really indignation—that is, morally motivated—but that what really disturbed me was that it made me and my inaction in that situation look bad. In such cases, my feelings re-gestalt, or perhaps become conflicted where they weren't before. Moreover, in my immaturity, I may not even have realized that we are capable of this kind of self-deception. Seeing my response under the new description allows me to experience it in a new way. I may previously have had some inkling of this at the edge of consciousness, but applying the description allows the experience of appalled self-correction its full force.

Turning from the first-person perspective of self-correction, and focusing on whole cultures of lived meanings, we can see how these are only made possible by the skein of appropriate terms:

- moral terms, which allow us to capture what is not just more intensely desired, but seen as worthy to be desired;

- emotional distinctions which rely on moral terms, like anger versus indignation;

- the languages of honor, pride, and shame;

- the discrimination of some lives as worthwhile, and hence the language of "ethics," in the sense mentioned in Section I.1 above.

Without some terms here to discriminate meanings, or situations in their meaning ("interspaces"), we wouldn't be able to experience the meanings.

---

14. This "constitutive" link between word and reality is what underlies Walter Benjamin's concept of the Name, which clearly owes a lot to the innovations of the Romantic period. See the interesting work of Alexander Stern, *The Fall of Language* (Cambridge, MA: Harvard University Press, 2019).

The right descriptive term, in the designative logic, is the one contributing to a correct description of an independent object. We often need such words in order to grasp, for instance, some pattern in the field we are studying; and here there is some analogy to the way a redescription of our emotional state reorders this state. But the crucial difference is that what the new terms reveal in the realm of independent objects was there already, regardless of how we saw them, while the experience of meaning is really altered. This is why we speak of a "constitutive" force of words here.

The work of art as symbol participates in this constitutive logic. It opens for us a new field of meaning, by giving shape to it. But the work can do something more than the introduction of a new term does, which enables us to recognize a new meaning, or shade of meaning. The work can help realize a powerful experience of fulfillment. That is why the revelation here is also an experience; an experience of connection with the meaning, and of a connection which empowers. We need a compound term here, like "revelation-empowerment-connection," to capture this. And it is this triple enablement which validates the subtler languages, rather than the correspondence of their terms to some underlying reality. Such a correspondence is not excluded, but if it exists it is distinct from the enablement.

We can see a certain coherence between the innovations of the Romantic generation: the revelatory power of the symbol, the link between revelation and connection, acknowledging a new status for subtler languages, and recognizing the new constitutive logic, all belong together and make sense of each other. And that is also why, as I mentioned above, the new distinctions between languages were not immediately recognized. It took time for the differences to come fully into view. Indeed, they have not yet entirely done so.

6

But there is another important distinction between epiphanic works of art and underlying accounts. The latter are couched in theories, and their virtue, when they succeed in hitting their target, is to be true. The former, on the other hand, bring about a powerful effect, giving us a convincing experience of connection. Of course, in being convinced we are taking on certain ontic commitments. Wordsworth must have held that something in the nature of things lay behind this sense of a force running through all things. Without offering a theory, he assumes that certain things are true of the cosmos. But the work of art—in this it is analogous to a ritual— produces an effect, and it does so in the here and now.

Underlying theory and work relate differently to time. If our theory about the cosmos (explaining why this experience is possible) is true now, then it is always so. But the poem which so moves and convinces us now offers no certainty that it will always do so in the future. If at some future time it fails (and our theory is true), the fault will not lie with the cosmos, but in us: we are distracted, the cares of the world press us too closely, we have become hardened and insensitive. Wordsworth himself in "Tintern Abbey" sees his vision as a return at a higher level of the "aching joys" and "dizzy raptures" of his youth, after a period in which he has often been

> In darkness and amid the many shapes
> Of joyless daylight; when the fretful stir
> Unprofitable, and the fever of the world,
> Have hung upon the beatings of my heart. (52–55)[15]

So the claims implicit in certain works to bring about a meaningful connection with a larger order are essentially fragile, and that in a double sense. They are open to refutation by a "debunking" account; and even if fully validated by a timelessly true underlying theory, there is no guarantee that the connection can be recovered at will.

7

The shift from the traditional context of poetry, anchored in accepted underlying stories, like *concordia discors,* or the Great Chain of Being, on one hand, to the post-Romantic predicament, on the other, brings about an "epistemic retreat." Earlier writers and thinkers asserted their notions of cosmic orders as fundamental truths; but their post-Romantic

15. William Wordsworth, "Lines Written a Few Miles above Tintern Abbey, on Revisiting the Banks of the Wye during a Tour, July 13, 1798," in *Lyrical Ballads and Other Poems, 1797–1800,* ed. James Butler and Karen Green (Ithaca, NY: Cornell University Press, 1991), 117.

successors could only claim to characterize the interspace. In a variety of ways, this retreat continues, and reaches its ultimate point with some "symbolist" poets and writers of the late nineteenth century who renounced all claims to characterize reality and identified the goal of poetry with the creation of certain positive experiences.

II

1

To the bundle of changes described in the previous paragraph, we should add another, which is also tightly connected to them: the exploration of new meanings, previously uncharted. The early modern period operated with the notion that there was a recognized catalogue of emotions, which had its source in ancient philosophy, in particular the Stoics. Although differences were expressed, and new ones might be added (as Descartes did with "admiration" in his treatise on the emotions), the understanding was that one could draw up such a catalogue.

On a parallel track, lyric poetry could operate with a vocabulary of situations: wooing, unrequited love, a sense of loss at love which fades; on this changes and variations could be run. We can see one connection with the package above, when we note that something like the designative logic was assumed: the predicaments are there, the poets described / expressed them, noted perhaps subtle features of them previously undescribed, but dealt with perennial objects.

(The exception to this perhaps was religious experience; the late medieval and early modern "mystics" definitely charted new territory.[16])

16. See Michel de Certeau, *La Fable Mystique: XVIe–XVIIe Siècle* (Paris: Gallimard, 1982), for the circumstances surrounding the introduction of this term. Among these writers and searchers—Meister Eckhardt, Teresa of Avila, John of the Cross—one does indeed find a language which is searching, often apophatically, teetering on the brink of sense, in short, way outside the usual "boxes." "Entréme donde no supé / y quedéme no sabiendo, / toda ciencia transcendiendo" [I entered where I did not know / and remained not knowing / all thought transcending]. San Juan de la Cruz, quoted in Reginald Gibbons, *How Poems Think* (Chicago: University of Chicago Press, 2015), 89.

But first of all we need to enlarge our palette of examples. And thus also the scope of what I have been calling "(re)connection."

In the above, I have been concentrating on the theory of German Romantic poetry—even though I paradoxically started with a more familiar work by Wordsworth: but Chapter 4 will look at the work of Hölderlin and Novalis. The reconnection which the Romantic work, as symbol, brings about with these three authors was with the whole order, a force or movement running through all things. But the recovery of contact can also be of more immediate scope: with or through a given scene, for instance.[17] Or it can be the recovery of a sense of "being at home" in a given region, or landscape; or it can be seen as the breaking through of a sort of veil, cast by our dualist-instrumental stance, which prevents us from finding the words which reconnect us with the inner nature of things, as we will find later with Hopkins, and then in a different way with Rilke, followed by Heidegger.[18]

But Romantic "connection" is even more polymorphous than this. It can also involve a new reading of ourselves through nature. A paradigm example of this comes in Goethe's "Wanderers Nachtlied," perhaps the most famous poem in the German language:

> Über allen Gipfeln ist Ruh
> In allen Wipfeln, fühlest du
> Kaum einen Hauch
> Die Vögelein schweigen im Walde
> Warte nur; balde
> Ruhest du auch.[19]

17. See Simon Jarvis, *Wordsworth's Philosophic Song* (Cambridge: Cambridge University Press, 2007), 216–223.

18. Jonathan Bate, *The Song of the Earth* (Cambridge, MA: Harvard University Press, 2000). See esp. ch. 6. This book offers an illuminating discussion of the relation between the Romantic rejection of the modern Mind / Body split, and the concerns of ecological recovery. Indeed, poetry is seen as having a crucial role in this recovery. Hence Bate's important concept of "ecopoetics" (75).

19. Johann Wolfgang von Goethe, "Wanderers Nachtlied," in *Werke* (Leipzig: Insel Verlag, 1986), 1:64.

[Over every mountaintop
Lies peace,
In every tree-top
You scarcely feel
A breath of wind;
The little birds are hushed in the wood.
Wait, soon you too
Will be at peace.][20]

Goethe is of course an outlier from the Romantics. He shares a view of the whole of Nature of which we are a part; a view also of Nature as organic development. He was in many ways an inspiration for the Romantics who espoused this understanding; but he was without sympathy for the Kantian and even less Fichtean philosophies which constituted the other pole which the Romantics were trying to reconcile and synthesize. And he was no friend of schemes to revolutionize society and usher in a new age. But his poetry invokes resonance in its own way and opens what can be called epiphanies.

Take my reaction (not only mine) to this poem. "Balde / Ruhest du auch." There is a kind of rest / peace which I long for. I still don't fully understand it, but now I have some sense of it. Where did I get it? From Goethe. Yes, true, but incomplete. Goethe's poem makes for me the connection between this longed-for peace and the hushed stillness of the forest / mountain. He makes it that my sense of this stillness opens my aspiration to this deeper peace. (And perhaps I might experience something like this on my own, later, as I wander in the forest.)

The poem has expanded my semantics of aspiration. It now includes this *Ruh.* (Works of art often bring about such expansion; Chopin's *Fantaisie-Impromptu* opens me to an unnameable longing.) But Goethe expands my world by connecting my language of aspiration with something like the language of things; the language seen / felt / heard in the forest / mountain.

In reading this poem, I come to see or sense this deeper repose in and through the stillness of the forest. Of course, this seeing-in was not simply

---

20. Johann Wolfgang von Goethe, "Wanderers Nachtlied," in *The Book of Lieder,* trans. Richard Stokes (London: Faber and Faber, 2005).

invented by Goethe; it belongs to poetry, and art in general throughout the ages, to portray our joys and longings through a scene, described or depicted. But with this poem we are on the brink of a new phenomenon which the Romantic turn made possible. Formerly, the human meanings thus conveyed had recognizable names and status in human life: jubilation, longing, melancholy, sense of loss. But Goethe's *Ruh* here can't quite be placed in the catalogue of recognized meanings. Is it the repose after death? The repose of inner harmony? The repose of a fulfilled life? Perhaps it is none of the above. We aren't told; the full story is somewhere between us and the forest; it calls for further exploration.

There is thus something not traditionally familiar in Goethe's invocation of a kind of peace which isn't just familiar repose. It does indeed have some affinities to deep religious or spiritual or mystic experience, but now appears in a purely immanent setting, which makes sense rather on Goethe's nontranscendental understanding of Nature.

There is an obvious analogy between this kind of newness, in relation to established catalogues and distinctions, and the newness of subtler languages, in relation to traditional views of order. In order to see what's different here, we have to stand back a little and see how these felt experiences were new. It is a commonplace to see the Romantics as moving from an old to a new focus of concern: from poetry and art in general as aiming at mimesis to a new focus on expression of feeling.[21] Think of Wordsworth's invocation of "powerful feeling," or of poetry as "emotion recollected in tranquility."

The focus on expression makes sense in relation to the Sturm und Drang period, which sought to liberate art from the shackles of a Taste which was under the hegemony of Morality and Order (as the Stürmer und Dränger saw it). This reading also connects to new accounts of the origin of language in expressive cries.[22] These eighteenth-century theo-

21. See M. H. Abrams, *The Mirror and the Lamp* (Oxford: Oxford University Press, 1953). This is a very rich and complex book, which itself can't be reduced to the formula of expression replacing mimesis, but that is often how it has been taken.

22. This was very widespread and influential, but it wasn't only accepted by those who wanted to recover and rehabilitate emotional expression from its marginalization by rationalist thought. Even figures who prized the development of reason adopted it, such as Condillac.

ries also saw a common origin in the cry for both spoken language and music. I shall return to music later.

There is some truth in this notion, that Romanticism was concerned with liberation from restrictive form, because Romantic poets sometimes saw themselves as freeing poetry from outmoded "classical" forms which inhibited the expression of spontaneous feeling. But there is a fatal confusion around the notion of "expression" here.

There is an ordinary use of the term "expression of feeling," which would cover things like shaking my fist in anger, my body drooping in sadness, my sighs and languorous glances toward the beloved, and the like. We could extend these to verbal expressions, like my complaints at the beloved's neglect of me, or my making declarations to her; or even telling my sad story to a sympathetic friend.

But the sense in which lyric poetry has given "expression" to love (with Petrarch's sonnets to Laura), or sadness and loss (Gray's "Elegy Written in a Country Churchyard"), or a longing for God (St. John of the Cross, George Herbert) is different. What brings poetry beyond any of these ordinary uses of the term is precisely what one might call, in a very general sense, form: its sound, the music it creates, the interplay of striking images, and more.[23] What does this do?

It doesn't just report, provide information. In this pedestrian sense mimesis has never been the issue. Rather it evokes for us, gives us a vivid sense of what it is like to be in the situation of the lover, the bereaved, the devout seeker for God. Or otherwise put, it invokes the intentional object of the emotion. Because even to describe, let alone to evoke powerfully, this kind of feeling—as against one of discomfort, or unease—is to characterize what it is about. It is the man pining after this woman,

---

23. I will return to this issue of the interplay of images, or better, the force field they create between them, below when I talk about Keats. But in passing, one should perhaps see here what Novalis was driving at in the famous and much misunderstood passage of his *Monolog*: "One can only be astonished by the ridiculous, mistaken belief that we are talking for the sake of objects. Nobody seems to understand that language is unique because it cares only about itself." John Neubauer, *The Emancipation of Music from Language* (New Haven, CT: Yale University Press, 1986), 200. This does indeed sound absurd if we talk about ordinary descriptive language, but referring to the higher language of poetry, it begins to make sense.

the person mourning the lost loved one, the seeker reaching out for God, that we have to invoke.

In terms of our discussion above, it is a certain kind and quality of interspace which the lyric poem presents to us, draws us sympathetically into, makes us feel; not just the inner state of the agent. Or rather, the only way to get at this inner state is through dwelling in the interspace.

In great art, there is a further dimension to this presentation. We are made to feel not only this interspace, but what we might call its value. In the case of the three examples just cited, this value will be emphatically affirmed in the presentation. (Affirmed in the poetic work, that is; the reader / hearer may differ.) The love affirmed as good, the mourning as over a loss of what gave life meaning, the seeking as of ultimate significance. But a work of art can also invoke a bad person, or a trivialized life. For instance, the very unconvincingness of Iago's explanations of why he wants to harm Othello gives us an insight into the vertigo of evil, of destruction for its own sake, and we shudder at it. The life of Willy Loman at the end of Miller's play *Death of a Salesman* appears as distressingly empty. The best art always has this depth dimension.

So the intentional object which such works opens us to carries a human (meta-biological) meaning which is strongly valued. It belongs in the upper left quadrant of the table presented earlier. It has ethical significance for us.

We can see from this that the new situation of the poet, no longer able (or willing) to draw on established orders, doctrines, categories, was bound to carry new meanings, if only those intrinsic to the new predicament of disenchantment: from a feeling of bereavement and despair at what was lost, to a sense of excitement and resolve at the new powers and challenges.

If we think of what might be the original experience which inspired this poem, it would be something like this: the deep, uncanny hush in the forest—even the "Vögelein schweigen" [the birds fall silent]—is suddenly the model for a deep repose of the spirit that I have been longing for without recognizing it. For the moment my experience of the hush in the forest is at the same time an experience of this spiritual repose. I am experiencing a condition of the forest as a state of my spiritual being.

This is the kind of (re)connection with the cosmos which this poem brings about; not a link to a larger and continuing order, as with William Wordsworth, but a momentary identity of a condition of my world and my spiritual state. Or we might also say that this condition of repose is common to subject and forest, that it links the two, that this single state unites subject and world, that it holds both in agent and around him/her.[24]

We see once again here how this kind of reading of one's spiritual/psychological state through the cosmos, just as much as Wordsworth's reconnection to cosmic order, cannot but seem illusory to a contemporary mindset dominated by natural science, with its clear separation of mind and world linked by causal relations.

So inevitably this mindset tends to see poetry as dealing with emotions, our inner world; but in nonliteral description. It cannot be true literally that human subject and forest share the same state. This must be a metaphoric, or an "as if," description. Poets have "license" to operate in this way. What you really meant was that the experience in the mountain "felt like" something shared by you and forest. But this was just an image, not the perception of a real identity, or an intense connection which defies and momentarily overcomes the localizing inner-outer distinction, deemed universal and inescapable.

In a sense, we all agree that language here is being used in some exceptional way, defying its everyday logic in our disenchanted world; where we differ is in holding that these uses can convey some insight into the reality of how we relate to the world.

Once again, the difference lies in some underlying story, either one which allows for real moral exploration through deeply felt insight, or one which sees all this exploration as purely "subjective."

2

We can find analogies to the changes in poetics in the slow discovery in the eighteenth century of the immense potentialities of music, in particular of pure instrumental music (not accompanying voice as in song,

---

24. Another example of a condition gathering together agent, subject of feeling, and world: Caspar David Friedrich. And then, later on we see a similar fusion of state of subject and world in Poe's "Fall of the House of Usher." Except that here it is even more weird.

opera, liturgy). Although I will mainly be dealing with the changes in poetry in this book, it's obvious that similar, or connected, transformations came about in other artistic media: in music and the visual arts,
for instance.

At first, instrumental music on its own was classed by many as a minor
art, offering pleasant sensations, or provoking agreeable reactions. But
by the end, in the great compositions of the classical period, and even
further in the works of Beethoven and Schubert, it came to be seen as a
way of exploring the most profound truths.[25]

One stage on the road was the view that music can express and evoke
affect, and this also draws strength from the theories of the origin of
language in expressive cries, cited above. But this theory generated *apo-
riai,* analogous to those mentioned above in relation to poetry. How did
we move from the expressive cry to music as we know it? Did music try
to imitate these cries? But imitate how? Surely music like poetry takes a
step away from the immediate uttering of feeling. The very nature of art
requires some *mise en forme.* And also: How could this understanding
of music find a place for instrumental music, as against song?

What the great compositions at the end of the eighteenth century
showed is that music has a power, analogous to poetry, of placing us in
an interspace, that of an emotion with its intentional object, a felt experience with the depth dimension of value.[26] This is the truth behind the
affect theory, which is distortedly oversimplified by saying that it expresses and evokes the emotion, and even more by saying that it imi-
tates it. It rather draws us, in a uniquely powerful way, into the interspace
where that emotion dwells.[27]

25. I have learned a great deal from the study of Neubauer, *Emancipation of Music.*

26. For an excellent and very detailed account of musical meaning, see Roger
Scruton, *The Aesthetic of Music* (Oxford: Clarendon, 1997).

27. One of the earliest, most acute critics to recognize the importance of Beethoven's
symphonic music stresses the importance of the difference—and distance—that artistic
form demands from what we ordinarily speak of as emotional expression. For all its
emotional intensity, Beethoven's music possesses "sobriety." "He separates the self from
the inner realm of sounds." He combines emotional intensity with inner detachment.
This shows how the artistic form demands not just distance from the emotion-interspace
concerned, but a quite different kind of intense involvement with it. See Neubauer,
Emancipation of Music, 206.

And this is something which becomes more strikingly evident, in music as in the case of poetry, when the emotion and interspace is in an important respect new, outside the recognized gamut of feeling. The original affect theory of the early eighteenth century took it for granted that the catalogue of affects was a familiar one, constituting a bounded domain, even though attempts to chart this domain never got very far. In fact, this had been a common assumption for centuries, accepted by the Stoics, for instance, and later by Descartes and others, in spite of the fact that the catalogues proposed differed.

But some may balk at the word "interspace" here; surely music can just inculcate a mood. We are sad, depressed, worried, and then we hear a gay polka and this mood lifts; we are carried along with it to a happier, lighter one. This is certainly true of some kinds of music, including what we often call "mood music." They are infectious, they carry us along with them. "Interspace," as I use it here, implies that there is some intentional object which in virtue of its meaning for us calls forth the emotion. But a mood, recurring here to Heidegger's distinction, is more like a background tone to all the feelings you are now having. It may actually foster some and discourage others: you wake up in an anxious mood, and worries about X and Y impinge; a serene mood, and you aren't bothered by these things. But the mood is not a feeling directed to a definite object.

If all music were mood music, then we could collapse the intentional dimension, and just think of its causal effect on us; the polka has the same effect as a pill might have done; I feel better, lighter, relieved, even gay. Such effects can be pleasant or unpleasant (say the music is somber, insistent, overpowering). But to enjoy music is to find the effect agreeable.[28]

---

28. This understanding of music, which collapses intentionality and meaning, is what underlies the reductive accounts of our musical experience, such as Steven Pinker's "music is auditory cheesecake." See Steven Pinker, *The Blank Slate: The Modern Denial of Human Nature* (New York: Viking, 2002), 534. What this theory overlooks is that, with a great Beethoven symphony, for instance, I experience a revelation / connection with a strongly valued human meaning (table, upper left quadrant); whereas the cheesecake, as an object of desire, the potential cause of a pleasurable taste experience, has a contingent meaning (table, lower left quadrant).

But this cannot be an adequate account of the music we most admire, which strongly moves us. What may give the reductive story some plausibility is that the object may be very indefinite, even enigmatic, especially once we try to characterize it, or put words to it. Hearing Chopin's *Fantaisie-Impromptu,* I have a powerful sense of longing, but I can't say for what; hearing Beethoven's *Coriolan* Overture, a sense of resoluteness before fateful events (but I'm helped here by the name), but no more.

And with longer works—symphonies, sonatas, quartets, for example—another dimension is added. The musical idea which provoked the feeling undergoes development, encounters others, creates tensions and resolves them. There is also exploration, an unfolding of potential.

The indefiniteness is what may give some credit to the notion that music works on us simply by inculcating moods. But the indefiniteness is of another kind: there is an object which rightly calls forth the response we feel, only we can't say what it is.

Instead of "mood," we might say "atmosphere." A musical work can draw us into an imagined space with a certain atmosphere. "Mood" and "atmosphere" come at the phenomenon from different directions. I attribute the mood to a subject, to me for instance; but it colors my world. We attribute the atmosphere to the world, but the attribution says a lot about how it strikes me.

To move to another medium, the sight of a landscape can also draw us into an atmosphere in a similar way. Only music is more insistent; it really penetrates us (Herder), draws us in strongly. It "gets to" me, or as we say in Quebecois, "Ça vient me chercher."

Roger Scruton has a good account of how this happens.[29] Our response to music is something like a sympathetic reaction to the feeling of another, say, a friend experiencing joy or pain. Seeing this joy or pain recruits our feelings. And so does music. But the response here goes beyond feeling; we want to respond bodily, move with the music, one

---

Things are in fact more complicated. The cheesecake, as part of a larger constellation, can take on a deeper meaning. Say I am seeking the good life, which as a hedonist I define as one crammed with pleasurable experiences. Or more plausibly, I find that sharing high-quality meals intensifies the pleasure of friendship. But cheesecake alone can't cut it.

29. See Scruton, *Aesthetics of Music,* ch. 11.

might almost say, dance. Scruton speaks of "our experience in the concert hall, which is itself a kind of truncated dance. When we listen we may tap our feet and sway subliminally, our whole being is absorbed by the movement of the music, moves with it, compelled by incipient gestures of imitation."[30]

Of course, most of us in the audience are inhibited, but the pianist, the more flamboyant conductors: they enact or embody the music. They couldn't perform as well without this. We are all recruited into the music as a response; to what? To the interspace of human meaning which the music is exploring.

It may help here to bring out a certain polysemy in the terms "meaning" and "meaningful." We often use the latter term to mean something like "significant"; a pianist might say that her profession was more meaningful to her than, say, the fact that she was born in a certain city. But when we say that a word has "meaning," we have to go further; there must be an answer to the question, what the meaning is: we point to an object, or we give an explanation.

There is no doubt that music is meaningful (significant) in the first sense. Music resonates in us, but some moves us at a deeper level. A work by Beethoven or Mozart enters us at a depth incomparable to the gay polka. But is it possible to attribute "meaning" to music in another way? Not "meaning," in the sense of the lived human significance of an intentional object, but rather in a sense analogous to what we attribute to language: this would be to say that the music invokes, makes us live vicariously and in imagination in the lived meaning. We are saying that music has the power to place before us, to draw us into, the lived meaning. It can be a medium of presentation and communication, analogous to language, even though very different.

Saying this gives rise to lots of confusion. When one says "language," one is taken to be saying "description," "representation." But music doesn't do this, except in very marginal cases, where, for instance, the trilling of a flute is supposed to invoke birdsong. But this is to take too limited a view of the human linguistic capacity. We language animals also gesture, we "act out," for example our virtues or styles of self-presentation,

---

30. Scruton, *Aesthetics of Music*, 355–356.

as well as find words for them and describe them—and this is rarely just a matter of realizing in practice what is already fully defined in theory; we also create our relations through discourse.[31] Music is another one of these paralinguistic practices, not wholly separable from others (dance, song, ritual).

A full account of musical meaning, its genesis and forms, is probably beyond our capacity (although a very interesting account of what it means is presented by Scruton).[32] But clearly the existing repertoire for instrumental music in Western civilization (which is, of course, in constant development) draws heavily on "embedded" uses of music, in liturgy, song, opera. But this doesn't mean that instrumental musical meanings just arise by association (like the case where I might say, "Ah, that melody, that reminds me of the summer we spent together by the sea"). Because when the libretto was set to music, the sense was that this music was "right" for it.

The "semanticization" (Adorno's *Semantisierung*) comes about this way: First in the various "embedded" forms—song, opera, liturgy, dances, marches—the music is chosen for its felt affinity to the embedding, words, or ceremony. Then this first semanticization is modified and developed by music which intends to say something. So Beethoven feels the influence of French Revolutionary music, and this is part of what fed into the *Eroica*.[33] This material is worked over through sonata form with its development, tensions, resolutions, to say something much more complex about Bonaparte, reflecting Beethoven's complex and conflicted feelings. This is turn leaves a semantic legacy, ready to be worked over by others, and so on.

These new creations could be grasped by listeners, helped sometimes by hints, like titles (*Eroica*), names to movements ("Marcia funebre"), words (in the Ninth Symphony).

This semanticization through "embedded" forms like liturgy and opera should not be thought of as arbitrary, as arising through mere habitual association. The musical setting is felt to be right, and to enhance, to

31. See Taylor, *Language Animal*.
32. Scruton, *Aesthetics of Music*.
33. Cf. Maynard Solomon, *Beethoven* (New York: Schirmer Books, 1977), 138.

confer greater power on the libretto, or ceremony: see the "Ode to Joy" in Beethoven's Ninth Symphony, or Bach's Mass in B Minor on the prayer "Kyrie Eleison." In some cases, the music elevates the original verbal composition to an entirely new level: for instance, Beaumarchais' late ancien régime play *La folle journée* taken up by Da Ponte and Mozart into *Le nozze di Figaro.*

There is perhaps a more general lesson to be drawn about the semanticization of different media from this case. Some forms of art which we now see as distinct and separate emerged together in human history. The odes of Pindar, which can be transcribed and classified as "poetry," figured in and emerged from choral performances in which the words were sung and danced to.[34] There were felt affinities between words, music, and choreography, and these can be built on and modified with a continuing sense of appropriateness, analogous to the way (to extend Scruton's example) we feel that the movements of a flamboyant conductor express an affinity to the symphony the orchestra is performing.

Perhaps one can speculate further and postulate additional affinities between movements and rhythms in nature and those sung and danced by humans (as we see, for instance, in Vedic thought), further developing the possibilities for the "semanticization" of these media.[35]

In the course of history, arts separate, take on autonomy, which closes one source of semanticization, but opens others. Something like this seems to have happened with European music in the Romantic period. And this doesn't seem to me a mere coincidence. The new modes of creation of musical meaning arose to meet a need for new explorations.

And so with Beethoven's great symphonies: the *Eroica*, the Fifth, and the Choral Symphony, not to speak of his late quartets; we are obviously

34. These are among the original models which fed into the ever-extending concept of "lyric" in modern Western poetry. See Virginia Jackson, "Lyric," in *The Princeton Encyclopedia of Poetry and Poetics*, 4th ed. (Princeton, NJ: Princeton University Press, 2012), 826–834. Also see Gibbons, *How Poems Think*, 52.

35. See David Shulman, who speaks of the concept of *dhvanana* [reverberation] in David Shulman, *More than Real: A History of the Imagination in South India* (Cambridge, MA: Harvard University Press, 2012), 70. See also his statement on Vedic thought: "We could propose that imagination is a specialized mode of listening to the still undefined vibrations that underlie all phenomena" (168).

in a different creative space. The interspaces were new, and hard to define exactly. But plainly, the music had (has) the power to draw us into such spaces and open us to new existential possibilities. After this transition, of course, we begin to see / hear earlier music in a new way.[36]

I mentioned above Chopin's *Fantaisie-Impromptu,* as an example of a work whose effect I tried to describe as a powerful sense of longing, whose object remains undefined. One can try to say more about it, but in the process we would perforce have recourse to metaphor, and this may be hard to understand by those who don't share the experience.

If we are looking for an analogue in visual art in the period, the painting of Caspar David Friedrich comes to mind, whose landscapes, of forest, mountain, seashore, invoke a powerful atmosphere which we struggle to articulate.[37]

Like in the case of poetry, but even more so, it becomes impossible in these other two media to render the exact shape of the interspace in ordinary descriptive prose. As we move over from description to the force fields of art, the "language" changes so profoundly that equivalences cannot be found. This gives a new sense of Kant's notion of an "aesthetic idea," which cannot be fully rendered in concepts, but continually provokes new attempts to do so. And thanks to Schopenhauer, Wagner, and Benedetto Croce, this untranslatability has come to be widely recognized.

This new grasp of the languages of art, as well as its ability to say unprecedented things, is part of the great break the Romantics brought about. It is deeply connected to the other break mentioned in Section I.1, which opened through a subtler language a new domain of what might be called

36. This, of course, is a crucial point. We can find lots of precedents in earlier poetry and music for inventivity and exploration beyond or outside the "box" set by the established cosmology, theology, and psychology. But what changed was the whole context of understanding of what artistic creation was doing, which came to be no longer containable within these earlier frameworks. And this whole liminal understanding didn't change overnight. Wordsworth, for instance, probably didn't understand it as we do today. But once the change occurs, we understand earlier creations in a new light. The important change is in the understanding of what artistic creation involves.

37. Charles Rosen and Henri Zerner, *Romanticism and Realism: The Mythology of Nineteenth-Century Art* (New York: Norton, 1984), ch. 2.

implicit provisional metaphysics, which self-consciously withheld a claim to be the final underlying story.

Poetry draws here closer to music—or what music is already becoming—anticipating Walter Pater's wish.[38]

And when music and lyric combine in the Lied, the full innovative potential of both arts is intensified, as Schubert's *Winterreise* reveals in all its enigmatic force. Who is the speaker? Why is he fleeing? And above all, what drives him ever forward?

3

It would help to spell out a little further what is involved in Pater's famous dictum about other arts "approaching the condition of music." Because it is obvious that poetry has often been fused with music—and the farther we go back, the more prominent this fusion is, as we just noted in connection with Pindar above.

This condition I take to be what I have just been discussing: music can place us in an interspace, and "atmosphere," whose nature can't be (fully) rendered in linguistic assertions. This is what is meant by the term "untranslatable." A lot can be said by composers, critics, musicologists to help us "get" what is going on in a given piece, but this discourse never amounts to "translation" in the above sense.

I tried to describe earlier the effect of "reconnection" which "Tintern Abbey" can open for the reader, but this is the discourse of commentary, pointing the reader in a certain direction. What is the nature of the "connection"? That is something which only the reader / hearer who "gets" Wordsworth can know. No additional such assertions can make up the gap, only at best nudge us further toward a vantage point whence the experience can open for us.

38. Moving along what we might call "Pater's vector," approaching the condition of music, has occurred in all arts in the last century and a half. Works evoke meanings, while being less and less forthcoming about their intentional object. If clarity about the intentional object is a goal of mimesis, then this vector involves a retreat of mimesis. Moving along this vector—to abstract art, twelve-tone music, enigmatic poetry— downgrades mimesis more and more in favor of enigmatic evocation. Even radically innovative poets can find their favorite forms broken in order to move further along the vector. Mallarmé: "On a touché au vers."

But what this shows is that poetry is already—or at least can be—very much like music. What lies then in this Paterian concept of "approaching music"?

Poetry affects us, moves us, on many levels. We might analytically distinguish three. There is (1) first of all the "music" of speech as sound, and its rhythms, meters, as well as its periods, and recurrences: rhyme, alliteration, assonance, and so on. We could speak of "word music"; then there is (2) a music of thoughts, or images, which is carried by the semantic force of the words used, or other words they remind us of, and their multiple associations, in their combination and mutual impact. Let's say: "image music." Then (3) a poem often is an assertion or series of assertions.

Of course, the contribution of each of these can't be separated, but we can have some sense of it, if we try some variations on the words or sounds, images, and see how they alter, improve, or weaken the overall effect—as indeed the poet herself may have done in composing it.

All poetry functions on these three levels, but the relative importance of each may vary considerably. A couple of examples of all three in combination might help. First, from Shakespeare, a model for many Romantic writers, from *The Tempest*:

> Full fathom five thy father lies
> Of his bones is coral made
> Those are pearls that were his eyes;
> Nothing of him that doth fade,
> But doth suffer a sea change
> Into something rich and strange. (400–405)[39]

An assertion here is made, about the "sea change." But our sense of what this is is greatly enriched by musics (1) and (2), of words and images. It is also rendered somewhat enigmatic: it is no minor matter, but a global change of some kind which hints at magic, mystery, enigma.[40] The enigma

---

39. William Shakespeare, *The Tempest*, act 2, scene 2, in *The Norton Shakespeare* (New York: W. W. Norton, 1997), 3067.

40. Thus in cultures where Shakespeare is taught in school, the expression "sea change" can become current in conversation, with the sense of something global, mysterious, alluring.

here can't be dispelled by further assertions. There is something "untranslatable" here.

Another example, one of my favorites: the sonnet "El Desdichado" of Nerval. Here is the octave:

> Je suis le Ténébreux,—le Veuf,—l'Inconsolé,
> Le Prince d'Aquitaine à la Tour abolie:
> Ma seule Étoile est morte,—et mon luth constellé
> Porte le Soleil noir de la Mélancholie.
>
> Dans la nuit du Tombeau, toi qui m'as consolé,
> Rends-moi le Pausilippe et la mer d'Italie,
> La fleur qui plaisait tant à mon Coeur désolé.
> Et la treille où le Pampre à la Rose s'allie.[41]
>
> [I am the shadowed—the bereaved—the unconsoled,
> The Aquitanian prince of the stricken tower:
> My one *star*'s dead, and my constellated lute
> Bears the *Black Sun* of *Melancholia*.
>
> You who consoled me, in the tombstone night,
> Bring back my Posilipo, the Italian sea,
> The *flower* that so pleased my wasted heart,
> And the arbor where the vine and rose agree.][42]

There are assertions here, and an imperative (second quatrain) whose content is described. But you need to look up a number of recondite references in order to see exactly what is being asserted / demanded here. I often have looked them up, but then I forget half of them; but the sonnet nevertheless powerfully moves me. My sense of it is largely carried by the two musics (1) and (2).

---

41. Gérard de Nerval, "El Desdichado," in *Les Chimères* (Paris: J. Corti, 1962), 9.

42. Gérard de Nerval, "El Desdichado," trans. Peter Jay, in *The Chimeras* (London: Anvil, 1984), 15.

At the other extreme, we have neoclassical poetry, the object of a strong negative reaction by many Romantics. Here (3) the assertions dominate. Not that Alexander Pope is unaware of the musics, at least of (1) [but how can he have been unaware of (2)?], because he stipulates "the sound must seem an echo to the sense." But these musics clearly play a subordinate role. We are very far from "full fathom five," where they play an essential role in our understanding of the "sea change"; and also from "El Desdichado," where the "sound" (including both musics) gives the "sense" so powerfully, we almost don't need to look up the references (but of course, they do add something important).

All this gives us the background to understand Pater's prediction / demand; which we can understand in the light of two contexts. The first is Romantic poetry as a reaction to and against neoclassicism. This meant that the sound and image musics recovered their full importance, and in this way poetry could be seen to (re)approach the condition of music. But the second context was the exploration of hitherto unidentified meanings which—I want to argue—has been central to post-Romantic art. This has intensified the dimension of the enigmatic, the untranslatable, in whatever is asserted in poetry (and in the plastic arts, depicted), entailing a correspondingly greater weight attaching to the music-analogues in these different media.[43]

4

This is the place to say a word about the multiple meanings, and evolution, of the term "symbol." This played an important part in the evolution of German Romanticism, as we saw in our discussion at the beginning of this chapter. There I distinguished two forms, the symbol concept, and the work of art as symbol, which both have the property that they open access for us to certain (alleged) realities. These have to be distinguished from the term as it is often used in ordinary speech, where the maple leaf (or maple leaf flag) is taken as a symbol of Canada, or Marianne as representing France, and a lion as the symbol of courage, or a fox of craftiness, and the like. These, unlike the Romantic notion, or that of Ricoeur, are

---

43. But I have some criticisms to make of how Pater understands the approach to music, which I will discuss in the "Note on 'Symbolism.'"

tacked onto already recognized realities, as handy tools of reference, in virtue of historical connections or alleged similarity.

But we should also note that the Romantic notion also underwent an important development in the nineteenth century, connected to the evolution of the Paterian trend just discussed in the previous section. "Symbolist" becomes a description for a kind of poetry, for instance in France at the end of the nineteenth century, and in Russia at the beginning of the twentieth century. This is a poetry which prolongs and extends Baudelaire's famous phrase a "forest of symbols," where the surrounding world is made to embody human meanings of an unprecedented, often enigmatic kind, ungrounded in familiar notions of cosmic order. Mallarmé was an important influence here, with his famous slogan: "Peindre non la chose, mais l'effet qu'elle produit" [To paint not the thing, but the effect it produces].[44] I will discuss this in Chapter 12.

44. Translated by Thom K. Sliwowski.

Chapter Three

AN EPOCHAL CHANGE

I

I have been dealing in this book with the original launching pad of German Romanticism in the generation of the 1790s in Jena and Berlin. There was much that was peculiar to that generation and that didn't travel elsewhere or to other times. In particular, the background in German Idealism, and the fascination with Renaissance theories of the cosmos and language. Not that these themes don't continue to figure, but others also enter.

But what remains as a crucial power of poetry is the ability to capture the meaning of an interspace—the situation of a human being before a given scene, in relation to nature, or even, more generally in relation to time and the world—in such a way as to encompass and convey a powerful sense of its meaning for our purposes, our fulfillment, or our destiny. This meaning may be evident in the light of an already felt lack or need; or it may totally surprise us and transform our outlook. But the revelatory and connecting power of poetry is the continuing thread that I want to trace here.

Let me try once more to define the difference between the orders re-vealed by subtler languages, and the traditional cosmologies which clas-sical poetry tried to "mirror." Seen as attempts at philosophy, the first could be classed as "implicit, provisional (or tentative) metaphysics," compared to the express finality and completeness of established cosmol-ogies. But perhaps the term "metaphysic" implies a similarity which doesn't exist, and "implicit" or "provisional" suggests wrongly that they are destined to grow into full-fledged cosmologies. But in fact they have a different kind of basis; the "transfiguration effects" of post-Romantic art convince us through moving us; whereas a cosmology has also to be based on other kinds of reasoning, bringing in considerations from sci-ence and history. These epiphanic invocations of order are like flashes of insight which are incomplete, and, in the nature of things, ultimately uncompletable, no matter how much they may be further elaborated.

They are frequently also fragmentary, and indeed, vary greatly in the degree of definition of the vision they offer—all the way down to a song like Louis Armstrong's "What a Wonderful World," where all we are told about the lyrical subject's vision is that it calls forth this outburst, but you have a strong sense that he sees something here, and are moved by it. (But a concentration on this end of the spectrum can, falsely, give comfort to a reductive account which treats our responses to art as varieties of subjec-tive feeling, situated in the lower left quadrant of the table in Chapter 2.)

These invocations can never enjoy the status of firm, indubitable truths. But what one can claim is that any underlying theory has to take account of the fragmentary insights they offer. They are part of the "phenomena" which any "noumenal" account must explain. Our being moved by works of art in this way is a fact of experience, which can't be simply ignored.

II

It might help to offer a synoptic view of the epochal change I've been describing. The Romantic poets I have been talking about reacted to the fading of solidly accepted metaphysico-moral cosmic orders with a sense of loss. They sought to recover contact with a deeper order in things. In this they were inspired by the earlier notions of order but were aware that they couldn't recover them through a clear theoretical vision. Their response was to attempt to recover contact through "symbols," which offered "translations" of this deeper order. But the orders to which they felt reconnected were in the nature of things defined in fragmentary and incomplete fashion, accessed as they were through the constitutive semantic logic of the symbol.

And by the same token, the meanings of the interspaces they explored were often unprecedented. It is one thing to interpret one's life through the established categories of a long and firmly established view (like *concordia discors*); quite another to grope toward a new and fragmentary meaning of life. In particular, the sense of disorientation, of a vitally important search after one is not sure what, occupies more and more of the scene. Schubert's *Winterreise* offers a striking example.

And before we widen the discussion beyond the boundaries of early German Romanticism, perhaps it might help to gather together some of the themes treated above, in another way, from a new starting point.

Starting from something that "everyone knows": Romantic poets aimed at the expression of strongly experienced feeling, and this forced them to burst the limitations of classical style.[1] The focus was "inward," on our feelings and reaction to things, rather than "outward," on the realities that surround us. This shift seems to be conveyed by Schiller in his famous contrast between "naïve" and "sentimental" poetry.

The "naïve" poet, paradigmatically represented by the ancients, strives to portray the objects in Nature. By contrast, "Der sentimentalische Dichter *reflektiert* über den Eindruck, den die Gegenstände auf ihn machen, und nur auf jene Reflektion ist die Rührung gegründet, in die er selbst versetzt wird und uns versetzt. Der Gegenstand wird hier auf eine Idee bezogen, und nur auf dieser Beziehung beruht seine dichterische Kraft."[2] [The sentimental poet *reflects* on the impression that objects

---

1. "All good poetry is the spontaneous overflow of powerful feelings." William Wordsworth, preface to *Lyrical Ballads and Other Poems, 1797–1800*, ed. James Butler and Karen Green (Ithaca, NY: Cornell University Press, 1991), 3.

2. Friedrich Schiller, "Über naive und sentimentalische Dichtung," in *Sämtliche Werke* (Munich: Carl Hanserverlag, 1967), 5:720.

make on him, and how it moves him is grounded only on this reflection, in which he repositions himself and in which he will reposition us. The object is here elevated to an idea, and his poetic force lies only in this relation.][3] The sentimental poet concentrates on "die Rührung," the meaning of the situation, how it moves us.

This is not untrue, but it leaves out a lot. First, "expression" means more than giving vent to, or describing, our feelings. The striking power of art is that it can place you, sometimes imaginatively, sometimes really, in the situation which has this meaning and inspires these feelings; it enables you to experience at least what this is like (see Chapter 2, Section I).

Second, what is remarkable about the Romantic period is that this *mise en situation* enables us to experience and grasp hitherto unexplored, unidentified meanings, such as Goethe's *Ruh* or the sense of connection in "Tintern Abbey."

Third, some of these experiences present themselves as transformative, in an ethically important way; that is, they help to realize crucial human potentials. They can transform how we live a situation. For instance:

Goethe identifying *Ruh* in the mountain forest (1);

Reconnecting us to Nature or the cosmos (Wordsworth,
    Hölderlin) (2).

This second category can take two forms: (a) just articulating the reconnection, which strengthens and affirms it; and (b) doing this through offering some description of what we are connected to (like Wordsworth's "motion" which "impels").

These two (or three) are very important, but there are other understandings in our post-Romantic age of what the poem, or work of art, as symbol, is bringing about. We can also see the work (3) as bringing to light the inner flow, or rhythm in things, the *dhvanana* [reverberation] in Vedic thought that I invoked earlier, as described by David Shulman.[4]

3. Translated by Thom K. Sliwowski.

4. David Shulman, *More than Real: A History of the Imagination in South India* (Cambridge, MA: Harvard University Press, 2012).

Making these manifest enhances or intensifies them, and in this way realizes more fully their potential.

These categories don't mark strict and fast distinctions; rather they fade into each other, as we see with (2a) and (2b), reconnecting to forces in nature, as against also offering some description of them. But the emphasis can shift from one work to the other: in one case, restoring the link, in the other bringing to light the inner nature of something. When this latter is at stake, I shall borrow from Hopkins his eloquent word "inscape." The idea that making the inscape of something manifest intensifies it and realizes its potential is reminiscent of the traditional notion, reinvoked by Novalis, that our laying bare the underlying order in things helps to restore this order to its pristine form. I will argue that an analogous notion can be found in Keats.

And paradoxically, what I'm calling (re)connecting here may include the failure to connect. Romantic art as a response to the loss of cosmic orders begets the aspiration to reconnect, and this issues in visions of what an ethically fulfilling connection might be, even when this seems beyond our grasp. These visions are in the register of irremediable loss (for example, of unfragmented ancient Greek polis [Hölderlin], or medieval wholeness [Novalis' *Die Christenheit oder Europa*]), or of unattainable aspirations (e.g., to full creativity [Keats' "Nightingale"]).

And besides the above, I will discuss other ways in which Romantic works can be ethically transformative:

> Enabling us to live humanly in time and the cosmos (Baudelaire).
>
> Showing the world as "radiant," suggesting an opening to "higher times" (Mallarmé, Rilke, Eliot, Miłosz).
>
> And there are still other ways which I won't be able to deal with here, for instance: opening new ways of freedom and self-assertion (Byron).

I want to look at some of these in the following chapters. But it is already clear that the issues involved may not be that raised by the quotes from Wordsworth and Hölderlin with which my discussion began—namely, revealing and recovering contact with a force running through all things. I think they all involve (re)connection in some way, because what is at stake is an alienation from, or a sensed alienness in, our world, a loss of resonance with it (if we choose as our guiding thread Hartmut Rosa's theory of "resonance").[5] The lost contact may be felt as with Nature, or with a meaningful cosmos, or the human predicament more generally, or with our life in time, but there is always a loss of full attunement. "(Re)connection" may be my (misleading, unsatisfactory) generic term, but it has many species and varieties.

If we take into account that Romantic poetry arises in a sense in response to disenchantment, we might describe all these attempts at reconnection as phenomenologies of reenchantment.

III

However, before embarking on this, I want to recall to mind the issue around the third claim above, that among the experiences that the work of art enables are some which are transformative, which realize crucial human potentials. In this, they are—or at least appear to be—analogous to rituals. I made this point in the table in Chapter 2, in relation to the four quadrants in which our meanings can be classed. Do the meanings we experience through poetry, those of (re)connection, or of a deep kind of repose and peace (Goethe's *Ruh*), have their place alongside moral and ethical demands?

Or, more radically, are these experiences illusory? Is there no real connection manifested and strengthened in "Tintern Abbey"? Is the sense of *Ruh* not an indication of a profound potential, but just a shadow cast by buried childhood memories? And the claim here that there is something more involves its own kind of connection, because it entails that we come to understand ourselves at a deeper level through this immersion in the mountain forest.

The experience as lived carries this claim with it. And this is because it is one of joy, and not just pleasure. You experience joy when you learn, or are reminded of something positive, which has strong ethical or spir-

5. See Hartmut Rosa, *Resonance: A Sociology of Our Relationship to the World,* trans. James Wagner (Cambridge, UK: Polity, 2019).

itual significance, whereas intense pleasure tends to enfold you even more in yourself. This can also be positive, integrative, and you "enjoy" it, but it's not "joy." Now pre-1800, the spiritual significance of the reconnections which can bring joy—to God, to the Great Chain in the cosmos— were defined by long-established doctrines. One might doubt or reject these, but the shape of things they defined was (supposedly) clear.

But in the Romantic epoch and since, a poem like "Tintern Abbey" might open me, and seem to connect me to a force "running through all things," but this has nothing like the clear definition offered by earlier established doctrines—though we might ultimately hope to link it, and even explain it, by reference to one such doctrine (as Wordsworth seems to have done in later life, in relation to orthodox Christianity).

So if one is tempted to doubt all notions of a higher, not immediately visible order, these doubts can only be intensified by the fluidity and uncertainty of the claim.

Now there is no doubt that the claim originates in, and relies principally on, the force of the experience, which awakens a felt intuition. I argued above that this does not mean that our positive reaction is merely "subjective" or "psychological." It could be opening us to an "ontological" ethical truth, anchored in the interspace, as it claims. But is this all that can be said to make it plausible?

Emphatically not. I propose to examine this issue from the angle of our human experience of nature in the post-Romantic era. This I will attempt in Chapter 5. But first it might help to introduce a couple of examples from German literature, to place alongside the example of Wordsworth we have been examining here.

PART II

Chapter Four

HÖLDERLIN, NOVALIS

I

First, I want to look at the ways that the poetic tradition has diversified. The starting point of the "poetic tradition," as I am trying to expound it, is the generation of the 1790s in Germany. What was elaborated there was the basic idea of two kinds of language, or uses of language: a dead, instrumental one, and a living, disclosive, epiphanic one.

This starts off in close symbiosis with a unified theory, englobing philosophy and poetics, that was worked out, and in broad lines more or less accepted, by this generation, which included Hölderlin, Novalis, the Schlegels, Schiller, Schelling, and the young Hegel: both Nature and human beings are in development; both these developments are linked—our destiny is to grasp and give expression to the development of Nature, and indeed, this grasp completes that development by bringing it to consciousness. What we are destined for is a condition of harmony and resonance with Nature. And according to the spiral-path understanding of history, we humans had a version of this harmony earlier, but it was implicit and unreflected; our development as humans required that we abandon this earlier state in order to become fully rational and conscious beings, which will permit a return to harmony at a higher level.

So the earliest developments of the two-language hypothesis assumed something like this background. In the English case, the philosophical framework was missing until introduced later by Coleridge, but there were strong analogies. In particular, the notion that the modern development of rationality and instrumental reason has alienated us both from our own emotional nature and from the Nature we live in (Blake, Wordsworth), and the concomitant idea that repairing the internal division and overcoming the division with Nature are indissolubly linked. Our destiny is to heal both these rifts together. Indeed, repairing these two divisions also involves restoring harmony in a third domain, between human beings in society. The new age will bring a triple restoration of harmony: within each of us, with Nature, and within society.

Now there were two forms or structures that we identified in the first two chapters, within which our resonant connection with Nature can be expressed, one with a wider focus, including our relation to the cosmos, and one with a narrower one, centering on some epiphanic symbol.

A paradigm example of the second comes in Goethe's "Wanderers Nachtlied," as I explained in Chapter 2, Section II.1. In this we widen or deepen our grasp of meanings, through some phenomenon of nature as a symbol.

Through the first, we reestablish our connection with Nature or the cosmos.

II

Hölderlin   As an example of the wider focus, let's look at Hölderlin. He was very much of the generation of the 1790s, and spent some time in Jena, which was one of the crucial centers where philosophers and poets came together to elaborate the outlook of this group. Indeed, he coined a term to describe the spiral movement away from an original unreflected unity, through the division occasioned by the development of reason and freedom, to the higher harmonious synthesis of rational freedom and nature. He described this as an *ekzentrische Bahn* [spiral path].

He, together with many young Germans of his time, sees the original unity as having existed in Greek antiquity, and the higher unity as a task for his own generation. In both cases, the unity is triplex: between reason and feeling, between humans and Nature, and within society. But a crucial role in both these triplexes is played by the gods (mythically understood). In Greece, the gods were the powers underlying Nature; and their cult was the basis of unity in the polis. The intervening period, in which we break with Nature without and become divided from our nature within, and society becomes the scene of opposing interests and will, is one where the gods withdraw. The new era can only be one in which the gods return, are recognized and honored in Nature, and their renewed cult unifies society.

But Hölderlin's gods are rather strange beings. I have said that they "withdraw" in the interim period between the two triple unities, but it might be more accurate to say they go into abeyance. Because they need us to be fully themselves:

> Denn weil
> Die Seeligsten nichts fühlen von selbst,
> muss wohl, wenn solches zu sagen
> Erlaubt ist, in der Götter Nahmen
> Theilnehmend fühlen ein Andrer,
> Den brauchen sie.[1]

> [For since
> The most Blessed in themselves feel nothing
> Another, if to say such a thing is
> Permitted, must, I suppose,
> Vicariously feel in the name of the gods.][2]

1. Friedrich Hölderlin, "Der Rhein," in *Sämtliche Werke* (Stuttgart: Kohlhammer, 1965), 2:152.

2. Friedrich Hölderlin, "The Rhine," in *Poems and Fragments,* trans. Michael Hamburger (London: Anvil, 1994), 437.

Or from "Der Archipelagus":

> Es ruhn die Himmlischen gern am fühlenden Herzen.[3]

> [For the Heavenly like to repose on a human heart that can
>   feel them.][4]

> Immer bedürfen ja, wie Heroen den Kranz, die geweihten
> Elemente zum Ruhme das Herz der fühlenden Menschen.[5]

> [Always, as heroes need garlands, the hallowed elements likewise
> Need the hearts of us men to feel and to mirror their glory.][6]

This dependence of the divine on us humans is certainly enigmatic. But I think we can make at least some sense of it in terms of my discussion in Chapter 1. The deliverances, or felt connections, of Romantic poetry concern the interspace between humans and their world. They make no claims about "noumenal" or human-independent reality. Hölderlin here seems to be endorsing this view: what we can say about the action of the gods is limited by the ways in which they touch our "feeling hearts."

But even by the standards of the mythologies that other poets and thinkers of the time had recourse to—Novalis, and the Schlegels, for instance—this was strikingly enigmatic: gods who cannot feel without our participation? What are they, then, when we don't play our role? Mere forces of Nature?

I spoke in Chapter 1 of the essential fragility of the epiphanies which works of art bring about. To revert to the example of Wordsworth: even though he must have felt that the force he sensed looking down at the Wye near Tintern Abbey was part of the nature of things, which any adequate underlying story would have to explain, and thus ratify, he could never be sure that he could recapture this vision at will, which in

---

3. Friedrich Hölderlin, "Der Archipelagus," in *Sämtliche Werke*, 2:114.
4. Friedrich Hölderlin, "The Archipelago," in *Poems and Fragments*, 231.
5. Hölderlin, "Der Archipelagus," 2:109.
6. Hölderlin, "Archipelago," 219.

fact he had lost for a number of years. The conditions in himself might be lacking; he might not be up to it.

With Hölderlin, by contrast, the underlying fragility goes deeper. If the gods without us cannot feel, then presumably they cannot act either. Our feelings of joyful response to their action are not only a condition of our *awareness* of this beneficent intervention in our lives, but more radically, of this intervention itself, of there being divine *agents* at all.

This might explain the extremely tentative tone of Hölderlin's expressed hope of a return of the gods; or as David Constantine puts it, of his alternation of such hopes with expressions of doubt and despair. The convincing portraits of the gods uniting with humans lie in the past, as in "Der Archipelagus" and certain passages of "Brod und Wein." When it comes to the future, passages of hope and confidence alternate with expressions of despair and anticipations of impotence.[7]

Now the recovery of triple unity must have appeared more and more as mission impossible, as the hopes raised by the French Revolution were dashed, first in the Terror, and then under the empire of Napoleon; and beyond the political obstacles, the reintroduction of a cult of the gods hardly seemed in the cards (but perhaps a remythologized Christianity might serve the purpose). So what could a poet do? "Wozu Dichter in dürftiger Zeit?" [And who wants poets at all in lean years?][8]

One thing the poet can do is make us see/feel the connectedness of things under the aegis of a "Deity," whose vision constitutes and reinforces our reconnection. Wordsworth, as we saw, does something similar. But he does this by expressing with conviction and force his belief that such a link exists. Let's look at the larger passage from which the quote in Chapter 1 was excerpted:

> For I have learned
> To look on nature, not as in the hour
> of thoughtless youth; but hearing oftentimes
> The still, sad music of humanity,
> Nor harsh nor grating, though of ample power

---

7. David Constantine, *Hölderlin* (Oxford: Clarendon, 1990), ch. 8.
8. Friedrich Hölderlin, "Bread und Wine," in *Poems and Fragments*, 271.

To chasten and subdue. And I have felt
A presence that disturbs me with the joy
Of elevated thoughts; a sense sublime
Of something far more deeply interfused,
Whose dwelling is the light of setting suns,
And the round ocean and the living air,
And the blue sky, and in the mind of man;
A motion and a spirit, that impels
All thinking things, all objects of all thought,
And rolls through all things. (88–102)[9]

Hölderlin by contrast will invoke a scene, which draws the reader (at least this reader) into an intuition of connectedness. The connections are not just being described; they are being made in the scene itself. Take the opening lines of "Heimkunft":

1.

Drinn in den Alpen ists noch Nacht und Wolke,
    Freudiges dichtend, sie deckt drinnen das gähnende Thal.
Dahin, dort toset und stürzt die scherzende Bergluft
    Schroff durch Tannen herab glänzet und schwindet ein Stral.
Langsam eilt und kämpft das freudigschauernde Chaos,
    Jung an Gestalt, doch stark, feiert es liebenden Streit,
Unter den Felsen, es gährt und wankt in den ewigen Schranken,
    Denn bacchantischer zieht drinnen der Morgen herauf.
Denn es wächst unendlicher dort das Jahr und die heiligen
    Stunden, die Tage, sie sind kühner geordnet, gemischt.
Dennoch market die Zeit der Gewittervogel und zwischen
    Bergen, hoch in der Luft weilt er und rufet der Tag.
Jetzt auch wachet und schaut in der Tiefe drinnen das Dörflein
    Furchtlos, Hohem vertraut, unter den Gipfeln hinauf.

9. William Wordsworth, "Lines Written a Few Miles above Tintern Abbey, on Revisiting the Banks of the Wye during a Tour, July 13, 1798," in *Lyrical Ballads and Other Poems, 1797–1800*, ed. James Butler and Karen Green (Ithaca, NY: Cornell University Press, 1991), 118–119.

Wachstum ahnend, denn schon, wie Blitze, fallen die alten
    Wasserquellen, der Grund unter den Stürzenden dampft,
Echo tönet umher, und die unermessliche Werkstatt
    Reget bei Tag und Nacht, Gaben versendend, den Arm.

2.

Ruhig glänzen indeß die silbernen Höhen darüber,
    Voll mit Rosen ist schon droben der leuchtende Schnee.
Und noch höher hinauf wohnt über dem Lichte der reine
    Seelige Gott vom Spiel heiliger Stralen erfreut.
Stille wohnt er allein und hell erscheinet sein Antliz,
    Der ätherische scheint Leben zu geben geneigt,
Freude zu schaffen, mit uns, wie oft, wenn, kundig des Maases,
    Kundig der Athmenden auch zögernd und schonend der Gott.
Wohlgediegenes Glük den Städten und Häußern und milde
    Reegen, zu öffnen das Land, brütende Wolken, und euch,
Trauteste Lüfte dann, euch, sanfte Frühlinge, sendet,
    Und mit langsamer Hand Traurige wieder erfreut,
Wenn er die Zeiten erneut, der Schöpferische, die stillen
    Herzen der alternden Menschen erfrischt und ergreifft,
Und hinab in die Tiefe wirkt, und öffnet und aufhellt,
    Wie ers liebet, und jezt wieder ein Leben beginnt,
Anmuth blühet, wie einst, und gegenwärtiger Geist kömmt,
    Und ein freudiger Muth wieder die Fittige schwellt.

3.

Vieles sprach ich zu ihm, denn, was auch Dichtende sinnen
    Oder singen, es gilt meistens den Engeln und ihm;
Vieles bat ich, zu lieb dem Vaterlande, damit nicht
    Ungebeten uns einst plözlich befiele der Geist;
Vieles für euch auch, die im Vaterlande besorgt sind,
    Denen der heilige Dank lächelnd die Flüchtlinge bringt,
Landesleute! für euch, indessen wiegte der See mich,
    Und der Ruderer saß ruhig und lobte die Fahrt.
Weit in des Sees Ebene wars Ein freudiges Wallen
    Unter den Seegeln und jezt blühet und hellet die Stadt

Dort in der Frühe sich auf, wohl her von schattigen Alpen
    Kommt geleitet und ruht nun in dem Hafen das Schiff.
Warm ist das Ufer hier und freundlich offene Thale,
    Schön von Pfaden erhellt grünen und schimmern mich an.
Gärten stehen gesellt und die glänzende Knospe beginnt schon,
    Und des Vogels Gesang ladet den Wanderer ein.
Alles scheinet vertraut, der vorübereilende Gruß auch
    Scheint von Freunden, es scheint jegliche Miene verwandt.

4.

Freilich wohl! das Geburtsland ists, der Boden der Heimath,
    Was du suchest, es ist nahe, begegnet dir schon.[10]

[1.

There in the Alps a gleaming night still delays and, composing
    Portents of gladness, the cloud covers a valley agape.
This way, that way roars and rushes the breeze of the mountains,
    Teasing, sheer through the firs falls a bright beam, and is lost.
Slowly it hurries and wars, this Chaos trembling with pleasure,
    Young in appearance, but strong, celebrates here amid rocks
Loving discord, and seethes, shakes in its bounds that are timeless,
    For more bacchantically now morning approaches within.
For more endlessly there the year expands, and the holy
    Hours and the days in there more boldly are ordered and mixed.
Yet the bird of thunder marks and observes the time, and
    High in the air, between peaks, hangs and calls out a new day.
Now, deep inside, the small village also awakens and fearless
    Looks at the summits around, long now familiar with height;
Growth it foreknows, for already ancient torrents like lightning
    Crash, and the ground below steams with the spray of their fall.
Echo sounds all around and, measureless, tireless the workshop,
    Sending out gifts, is astir, active by day and by night.

---

10. Friedrich Hölderlin, "Heimkunft," in *Sämtliche Werke*, 2:100–101.

2.

Quiet, meanwhile, above, the silvery peaks lie aglitter,
    Full of roses up there, flushed with dawn's rays, lies the snow.
Even higher, beyond the light, does the pure, never clouded
    God have his dwelling, whom beams, holy, make glad with
      their play.
Silent, alone he dwells, and bright his countenance shines now,
    He, the aethereal one, seems kindly, disposed to give life,
Generate joys, with us men, as often when, knowing the measure,
    Knowing those who draw breath, hesitant, sparing the God.
Send well-allotted fortune both to the cities and houses,
    Showers to open the land, gentle, and you, brooding clouds,
You, then, most dearly loved breezes, followed by temperate
  springtime,
    And with a slow hand once more gladdens us mortals grown sad,
When he renews the seasons, he, the creative, and quickness,
    Moves once again those hearts weary and numb with old age,
Works on the lowest depths to open them up and to brighten
    All, as he loves to do; so now does life bud anew,
Beauty abounds, as before, and spirit is present, returned now,
    And a joyful zest urges furled wings to unfold.

3.

Much I said to him; for whatever the poets may ponder,
    Sing, it mostly concerns either the angels or him.
Much I besought, on my country's behalf, lest unbidden one day the
    Spirit should suddenly come, take us by storm unprepared;
Much, too, for your sake to whom, though troubled now in our
  country,
    Holy gratitude brings fugitives back with a smile,
Fellow Germans, for your sake! Meanwhile the lake gently rocked me,
    Calmly the boatman sat, praising the weather, the breeze.
Out on the level lake one impulse of joy had enlivened
    All the sails, and at last, there in a new day's first hour

Brightening, the town unfurls, and safely conveyed from the
  shadows
    Cast by the Alps, now the boat glides to its morning and rests.
Warm the shore is here, and valleys open in welcome,
    Pleasantly lit by paths, greenly allure me and gleam.
Gardens, forgathered, lie here and already the dew-laden bud breaks
    And a bird's early song welcomes the traveller home.
All seems familiar; even the word or the nod caught in passing
    Seems like a friend's, every face looks like a relative's face.

                                4.

And no wonder! Your native country and soil you are walking,
    What you seek, it is near, now comes to meet you half-way.][11]

The mountain scene at dawn is full of energy and movement, breaking
through the night and clouds which have covered the valley. Winds roar;
bacchantic chaos boils (*gährt*). A sunbeam breaks clear through the pines
into the yawning valley. But all this restless movement hides, feeds, and
protects the peaceful village below, orders its time, its days and hours.
The village awakens, fed and protected. *Äther* gives Light and Life, sparing
us, gives gifts.

   This drawing together into a single scene, a single connected action, is
the work of Poetry (*Dichtung*). But we sense that it is not just the work of
the poet (*Dichter*); it comes together through the joint action of *Dichter*
and scene. The coming together of connected movements in the poem
meets, meshes with, draws out a coming together in reality, a link made in
the world described. Line 2 already tells us this, where it says of the *Wolke*
[cloud], "freudiges dichtend" [composing portents of gladness].[12]

   The poem unifies the different actions, of wind, rushing water, light,
and unites them in their purpose of protecting, ordering, feeding the

---

11. Friedrich Hölderlin, "Homecoming," in *Poems and Fragments*, 275–277.

12. Richard Unger, *Hölderlin's Major Poetry: The Dialectics of Unity* (Bloomington:
Indiana University Press, 1975), 87–88, points out this fusion of the movements of Nature and the process of composition; he points out the similarities to passages of Shelley's "Mont Blanc," noticed earlier by Earl Wasserman.

small village. But this is not felt as an arbitrarily selected and imposed ordering, but as a unity inherent in the reality itself.

We have here the same double movement which I described in Chapter 2 in connection with Wordsworth's "Tintern Abbey": on one hand, the multiplex awe-inspiring scene strikes the poet; on the other, the poet responds by taking it in through an act of interpretation which is the poem.

The *Dichtung* makes palpable this common action, because it creates and sustains a sense of the immense distances between sky and earth, between bacchantic action and peaceful hours in the village; but also their connection, affinity, their drawing each other into a whole.

Is this just a conceit? But it claims to be something more; and you feel it, for instance, in the instantaneous spanning of huge distances, in the beam breaking precipitously through the trees ("Schroff durch Tannen glänzet und schwindet ein Stral" [Teasing, sheer through the firs falls a bright beam, and is lost]), in the eagle spanning immense distance ("Dennoch market die Zeit der Gewittervogel und zwischen / Bergen, hoch in der Luft weilt er und rufet der Tag" [Yet the bird of thunder marks and observes the time, and / High in the air, between peaks, hangs and calls out a new day]). Immense action in sky, winds, mountain, waters, all comes together to protect and nourish the *Dörflein* [small village].

We feel that this is not just a matter of a blind contingent concatenation of processes, which happen to work for fuller life in the *Dörflein*, and which are being presented, cast as self-sustaining system. Rather it feels that *Dichtung* is revealing, making plain such a system, with its own inner necessity. And this revelation brings joy, invites (re)connection; and this is something which is a crucial realization of potential for us.

This conviction holds in what I called in Chapter 2 an "interspace," which is a joint creation of poet and scene, but which doesn't offer an underlying story which would validate it objectively.

What underlies and sustains this system? A god, in this case *Vater Aether.*

> Ruhig glänzen indeß die silbernen Höhen darüber,
> Voll mit Rosen ist schon der leuchtende Schnee.
> Und noch höher hinauf wohnt über dem Lichte der reine
> Seelige Gott vom Spiel heiliger Stralen erfreut.

Stille wohnt er allein und hell erscheinet sein Antlitz,
   Der ätherische scheint Leben zu geben geneigt,
Freude uns zu schaffen, mit uns, wie oft, kundig des Maases,
   Kundig der Athmenden auch zögernd und schonend der Gott
Wohlgediegenes Glük den Städten und Häusern und milde
   Reegen, zu öffnen das Land, brütende Wolken, und euch
Trauteste Lüfte dann, euch, sanfte Frühlinge, sendet . . . [13]

[Quiet, meanwhile, above, the silvery peaks lie aglitter,
   Full of roses up there, flushed with dawn's rays, lies
     the snow.
Even higher, beyond the light, does the pure, never clouded
   God have his dwelling, whom beams, holy, make glad with their
     play.
Silent, alone he dwells, and bright his countenance shines now,
   He, the aethereal one, seems kindly, disposed to give life,
Generate joys, with us men, as often when, knowing the measure,
   Knowing those who draw breath, hesitant, sparing the God
Sends well-allotted fortune both to the cities and houses,
   Showers to open the land, gentle, and you, brooding clouds,
You, then, most dearly loved breezes, followed by temperate
   springtime . . .][14]

(Hölderlin's Pindaric style, with its (to us) unfamiliar word order, is, in a way I am far from fully understanding, a great help to his knitting of distances and disparate things; to feel / sense the movement, the interconnectedness between the constituents of this dynamic, self-sustaining constellation.)

But of course, we are not back in old notions of order. These gods need the connection to work, connection with the *fühlendes Herz des Menschen* [the feeling hearts of humans]. Without this, it's not clear what their status and action is; they become recessive.

13. Hölderlin, "Heimkunft," 100–101.
14. Hölderlin, "Homecoming," 275–277.

Does that mean that you are already convinced of the whole of Hölderlin's strange theology? No, to be moved by the poetry isn't necessarily to adopt the whole outlook. To think this follows is not to take account of the new status of the subtler languages. Whereas a classical poem, like those of Pope and Denham discussed in Chapter 1, could make us discern a deeper pattern in things, a pattern already ratified by established tradition and near-universal acceptance, but which needs discernment to grasp in the world around us, Romantic poems can make us sense a new, as yet unratified pattern, which may also appear fragmentary and enigmatic. So we don't immediately accept the full mythology Hölderlin offers. But his poetry speaks so directly and powerfully to us (or is it just me?) that one can't help thinking that it has something important to tell about our world and the resonance we seek within it, even if we have to transpose it to another metaphysical register.

See also "Wie wenn am Feiertage," which stresses the poet's task of making the underlying agency of Nature evident:

> Wie wenn am Feiertage, das Feld zu sehen
> Ein Landmann geht, des Morgens, wenn
> Aus heißer Nacht die kühlenden Blitze fielen
> Die ganze Zeit und fern noch tönet der Donner,
> In sein Gestade wieder tritt der Strom,
> Und frisch der Boden grünt
> Und von des Himmels erfreuendem Regen
> Der Weinstock trauft und glänzend
> In stiller Sonne stehn die Bäume des Haines:

> So stehn sie unter günstiger Witterung
> Sie die kein Meister allein, die wunderbar
> Allgegenwärtig erzieht in leichtem Umfangen
> Die mächtige, die göttlichschöne Natur.
> Drum wenn zu schlafen sie scheint zu Zeiten des Jahrs
> Am Himmel oder unter den Pflanzen oder den Völkern
> So trauert der Dichter Angesicht auch,
> Sie scheinen allein zu seyn, doch ahnen sie immer.
> Denn ahnend ruhet sie selbst auch.

Jezt aber tagts! Ich harrt und sah es kommen,
Und was ich sah, das Heilige sei mein Wort.
Denn sie, sie selbst, die älter denn die Zeiten
Und über die Götter des Abends und Orients ist,
Die Natur ist jezt mit Waffenklang erwacht,
Und hoch vom Aether bis zum Abgrund nieder
Nach vestem Geseze, wie einst, aus heiligem Chaos gezeugt,
Fühlt neu die Begeisterung sich,
Die Allerschaffende wieder.[15]

[As on a holiday, to see the field
A countryman goes out, at morning, when
Out of hot night the cooling flashes had fallen
For hours on end, and thunder still rumbles afar,
The river enters its banks once more,
New verdure sprouts from the soil,
And with the gladdening rain of heaven
The grapevine drips, and gleaming
In tranquil sunlight stand the trees of the grove:

So now in favorable weather they stand
Whom no mere master teaches, but in
A light embrace, miraculously omnipresent,
God-like in power and beauty, Nature brings up.
So when she seems to be sleeping at times of the year
Up in the sky or among plants or the peoples,
The poets' faces likewise are sad,
They seem to be alone, but are always diving,
For divining too she herself is at rest.

But now day breaks! I waited and saw it come,
And what I saw, the hallowed, my word shall convey,

---

15. Friedrich Hölderlin, "Wie wenn am Feiertage . . . ," in *Sämtliche Werke*, 2:122.

> For she, she herself, who is older than the ages
> And higher than the gods of Orient and Occident,
> Nature has now awoken amid the clang of arms,
> And from high Aether down to the low abyss,
> According to fixed law, begotten, as in the past, on holy Chaos,
> Delight, the all-creative,
> Delights in self-renewal.][16]

In the reappearance of the trees, standing and gleaming, after the night and storm, we sense the force which brings them there and sustains them. As the poem continues, we see that the task of poets is to divine (*ahnen*) and make manifest this force.

The notion that the scene is a coworker with the poet in the creation of the poem (when the god and the feeling heart of humans combine) opens a new potential seam of poetic exploration. It can be expressed in the thought that the flow, the movement in the poem matches in some way, and connects up with a similar flow in reality; and that this is an important part of the reconnection the poem brings about. Something like this is at work in Hopkins' notion of an "inscape" in some particular reality, which the poet brings to light. I want to return to Hopkins in Chapter 7.

But besides a poetry of present experience, Hölderlin also created one of yearning for a lost past, the age of ancient Greece. He gives us such a vivid sense of what it is (was) to live in a world where the gods are present, that we have an acute awareness of what is lost.

The opening lines of "Archipelagus" (1–85) offer a portrait of the Aegean (imagined, Hölderlin was never there), sunlit, with its islands, in a continuing, revivifying exchange with the surrounding lands: these send up rainclouds, to descend far away on the "stormdrunk forests," whose waters return through rivers to their place of origin; all this under the aegis of the sea-god (Poseidon), and *Vater Aether*. The whole passage is in the form of an address to the sea-god, starting with the question:

> Kehren die Kraniche wieder zu dir, und suchen zu deinen
> Ufern wieder die Schiffe den Lauf? umathmen erwünschte
> Lüfte dir die berühigte Fluth, und sonnet der Delphin,

---

16. Friedrich Hölderlin, "As on a Holiday . . . ," in *Poems and Fragments*, 395.

Aus der Tiefe gelokt, am neuen den Rüken?
Blüht Ionien? Ists die Zeit? Denn immer in Frühling,
Wenn den lebenden sich das Herz erneut und die erste
Liebe den Menschen erwacht und goldener Zeiten Erinnerung,
Komm' ich zu dir und grüß' in deiner Stille dich, Alter!

Immer, Gewaltiger! lebst du noch und ruhest im Schatten
Deiner Berge, wie sonst; mit Jünglingsarmen umfängst du
Noch dein liebliches Land, und deiner Töchter, o Vater!
Deiner Inseln ist noch, der blühenden, keine verloren.
Kreta steht und Salamis grünt, umdämmert von Lorbeern,
Rings von Stralen umblüht, erhebt zur Stunde des Aufgangs
Delos ihr begeistertes Haupt, und Tenos und Chios
Haben der purpurnen Früchte genug, von trunkenen Hügeln
Quillt der Cypriertrank, und von Kalauria fallen
Silberne Bäche, wie einst, in die alten Wasser des Vaters.
Alle leben sie noch, die Heroënmütter, die Inseln,
Blühend von Jahr zu Jahr, und wenn zu Zeiten, vom Abgrund
Losgelassen, die Flamme der Nacht, das untre Gewitter,
Eine der holden ergriff, und die Sterbende dir in den Schoos sank,
Göttlicher! du, du dauertest aus, denn über den dunkeln
Tiefen ist manches schon dir auf und untergegangen.

Auch die Himmlischen, sie, die Kräfte der Höhe, die stillen,
Die den heiteren Tag und süßen Schlummer und Ahnung
Fernher bringen über das Haupt der fühlenden Menschen
Aus der Fülle der Macht, auch sie, die alten Gespielen,
Wohnen, wie einst, mit dir, und oft am dämmernden Abend,
Wenn von Asiens Bergen herein das heilige Mondlicht
Kömmt und die Sterne
Droben, ihr Nachtgesang, im liebenden Busen dir wieder.
Wenn die allverklärende dann, die Sonne des Tages,
Sie, des Orients Kind, die Wunderthätige, da ist,
Dann die Lebenden all' im goldenen Traume beginnen,
Den die Dichtende stets des Morgens ihnen bereitet,

Dir, dem trauernden Gott, dir sendet sie froheren Zauber,
Und ihr eigen freundliches Licht ist selber so schön nicht
Denn das Liebeszeichen, der Kranz, den immer, wie vormals,
Deiner gedenk, doch sie um die graue Loke dir windet.
Und umfängt der Aether dich nicht, und kehren die Wolken,
Deine Boten, von ihm mit dem Göttergeschenke, dem Strale
Aus der Höhe dir nicht? dann sendest du über das Land sie,
Daß am heißen Gestad die gewittertrunkenen Wälder
Rauschen und woogen mit dir, daß bald, dem wandernden Sohn
    gleich,
Wenn der Vater ihn ruft, mit den tausend Bächen Mäander
Seinen Irren enteilt und aus der Ebne Kayster
Dir entgegenfrohlokt, und der Erstgeborne, der Alte,
Der zu lange sich barg, dein majestätischer Nil izt
Hochherschreitend aus fernem Gebirg, wie im Klange der Waffen,
Siegreich kömmt, und die offenen Arme der sehnende reichet.[17]

[Are the cranes returning to you, and the mercantile vessels
Making again for your shores? Do breezes longed for and prayed for
Blow for you round the quieter flood and, lured from beneath it,
Does the dolphin now warm his back in a new year's gathering
    radiance?
Is Ionia in flower? Is it the season? For always in springtime
When the hearts of the living renew themselves, the first love of
Human kind, reawakened, stirs and the golden age is remembered,
You, old Sea-God, I visit and you I greet in your stillness.

Even now you live on and, mighty as ever, untroubled
Rest in the shade of our mountains; with arms ever youthful
Still embrace your beautiful land, and still of your daughters, O Father,
Of your islands, the flowering, not one has been taken.
Crete remains, and Salamis lies in a dark-green twilight of laurels,
In a ring of blossoming beams even now at the hour of sunrise
Delos lifts her ecstatic head, and Tenos and Chios

17. Hölderlin, "Der Archipelagus," 107–108.

Still have plenty of purple fruit, and the Cyprian liquor
Gushes from drunken hillsides while from Calauria the silver
Brooks cascade, as before, into the Father's old vastness.
Every one of them lives, those mothers of heroes, the islands,
Flowering year after year, and if at times the subterranean
Thunder, the flame of Night, let loose from the primal abysses,
Seized on one of the dear isles and, dying, she sank in your waters,
You, divine one, endured, for much already has risen,
Much gone down for you here above your deeper foundations.

     And the heavenly, too, the powers up above us, the silent,
Who from afar bring the cloudless day, delicious sleep and
     forebodings
Down to the heads of sentient mortals, bestowing
Gifts in their fullness and might, they too, your playmates as ever,
Dwell with you as before, and often in evening's glimmer
When from Asia's mountains the holy moonlight comes drifting
In and the stars comingle and meet in your billows,
With a heavenly brightness you shine, and just as they circle
So do your waters turn, and the theme of your brothers, their
     night song
Vibrant up there, re-echoes lovingly here in your bosom.
When the all-transfiguring, then, she, the child of the Orient,
Miracle-worker, the sun of our day-time, is present,
All that's alive in a golden dream recommences,
Golden dream the poetic one grants us anew every morning,
Then to you, the sorrowing god, she will send a still gladder
     enchantment,
And her own beneficent light is not equal in beauty
To the token of love, the wreath, which even now and as ever
Mindful of you, she winds round your locks that are greying.
Does not Aether enfold you, too, and your heralds, the clouds, do
They not return to you with his gift, the divine, with the rays that
Come from above? And then you scatter them over the country
So that drunken with thunderstorms woods on the sweltering
     coastline

Heave and roar as you do, and soon like a boy playing truant,
Hearing his father call out, with his thousand sources Meander
Hurries back from his wanderings and from his lowlands Kayster
Cheering rushes towards you, and even the first-born, that old one
Who too long lay hidden, your Nile, the imperious, majestic,
Haughtily striding down from the distant peaks, as though
  armed with
Clanging weapons, victorious arrives, and longs to enfold you.][18]

The questions open the floodgates of nostalgia for a bygone age, in which the fullness of connection between gods and humans, humans and nature, citizen and society, was a living presence. The movements of nature continue, but the connections are all broken. In that sense, the answer to the questions is affirmative, but their human meaning is lost.

Dennoch einsam dünkest du dir; in schweigender Nacht hört
Deine Weheklage der Fels, und öfters entflieht dir
Zürnend von Sterblichen weg die geflügelte Wooge zum Himmel,
Denn es leben mit dir die edlen Lieblinge nimmer,
Die dich geehrt, die einst mit den Schönen Tempeln und Städten
Deine Gestade bekränzt, und immer suchen und missen,
Immer bedürfen ja, wie Heroën den Kranz, die geweihten
Elemente zum Ruhme das Herz der fühlenden Menschen.[19]

[Yet you think yourself lonely; at night in the silence the rock
  hears
Your repeated lament, and often, winged in their anger,
Up to heaven away from mortals your waves will escape you.
For no longer they live beside you, these noble beloved ones
Who revered you, who once with beautiful temples and cities
Wreathed your shores; and always they seek it and miss it,
Always, as heroes need garlands, the hallowed elements likewise
Need the hearts of us men to feel and to mirror their glory.][20]

18. Hölderlin, "Archipelago," 217–219.
19. Hölderlin, "Der Archipelagus," 108–109.
20. Hölderlin, "Archipelago," 219.

But the portrait of that age awakens a longing for a time when the sea and the islands, and their life-giving exchange, could appear in full daylight in a space where gods and humans meet; where the return of the Nile waters from their sources in the mountains can take this form:

> Und der Erstgeborene, der Alte,
> Der zu lange sich barg, dein majestätiger Nil itzt
> Hochherschreitend aus fernem Gebirg, wie im Klage der Waffen,
> Siegreich kömmt, und die offenen Arme der sehnende reichet.[21]

> [And even the first-born, that old one
> Who too long lay hidden, your Nile, the imperious, majestic,
> Haughtily striding down from the distant peaks, as though armed with
> Clanging weapons, victorious arrives, and longs to enfold you.][22]

Through these two avenues—nostalgia for what is lost, intimations of what is still there, and could perhaps return—Hölderlin tries to make manifest the hidden connections in our world. In "Brod und Wein," the two modes of approach combine. Night and the moon draw us on, "gönnen das stromende Wort" [grant the onrushing word] (stanza 2); "Göttliches Feuer auch treibet, bei Tag und bei Nacht, Aufzubrechen" [Divine fire strives by night and by day to break out] (stanza 3; translation altered). Something must be said, articulated. But where to find it? Where to go?

> Drum an den Isthmos komm! Forthin, wo das offene Meer rauscht
>   Am Parnaß und der Schnee delphische Felsen umgläntzt,
> Dort ins Land des Olymps, dort auf die Höhe Cithärons,
>   Unter die Fichten dort, unter die Trauben, von wo
> Thebe drunten und Ismenos rauscht im Lande des Kadmos.
>   Dorther kommt und zurük deutet der kommende Gott.[23]

> [Off to Isthmus, then! To land where wide open the sea roars
>   Near Parnassus and snow glistens on Delphian rocks;

21. Hölderlin, "Der Archipelagus," 108.
22. Hölderlin, "Archipelago," 219.
23. Friedrich Hölderlin, "Brod und Wein," in *Sämtliche Werke*, 2:96.

Off to Olympian regions, up to the heights of Cithaeron,
    Up to the pine-trees there, up to the grapes, from which rush
Thebe down there and Ismenos, loud in the country of Cadmus:
    Thence has come and back there points the god who's to come.][24]

Then stanza 4 begins: "Seeliges Griechenland!" [Blessed land of the Greeks!]. The cry "Vater Aether" [father aether] comes down and gathers us together in the day.

Vater! Heiter! Und hallt, so weit es gehet, das uralt
    Zeichen, von Eltern geerbt, treffend und schaffend hinab.
Denn so kehren die Himmlischen ein, tiefschütternd gelangt, so
Aus den Schatten herab unter die Menschen ihr Tag.[25]

[Father! Clear light! and long resounding it travels, the ancient
    Sign handed down, and far, striking, creating, rings out.
So do the Heavenly enter, shaking the deepest foundations,
    Only so from the gloom down to mankind comes their Day.][26]

In stanza 5, we learn how the different gods come, slowly, and after much human suffering are eventually recognized and named: "Nun müßen dafür Worte, wie Blümen, entstehn." Now we must find words [like flowers leaping alive] for this new experience. So humans built "Tempel und Städte, / Fest und edel" [temples and cities, / Noble and firm].[27] But where are they now (stanza 6)?

Thebe welkt und Athen; rauschen die Waffen nicht mehr
In Olympia, nicht die goldnen Wagen des Kampfspiels,
    Und bekranzten sich denn nimmer die Schiffe Korinths?

[Athens is withered and Thebes; now do no weapons ring out
In Olympia, nor now those chariots, all golden in games there,
    And no longer are wreaths hung on Corinthians ships?]

---

24. Hölderlin, "Bread and Wine," 265.
25. Hölderlin, "Brod und Wein," 96.
26. Hölderlin, "Bread and Wine," 267.
27. Hölderlin, "Brod und Wein," 96; Hölderlin, "Bread and Wine," 267.

Once more, the questioning look into the past, that must be in vain. Stanza 7 begins:

> Aber Freund! Wir kommen zu spät. Zwar leben die Götter
> Aber über dem Haupt droben in anderer Welt.[28]

> [But, my friend, we have come too late. Though the gods are living,
> Over our heads they live, up in a different world.][29]

And the question returns: *Wozu Dichter in dürftiger Zeit?*

We are divided: within ourselves (reason versus feeling), from Nature around us, and from each other. The way back to unity is to connect again with the force which runs through everything: *Eins und Alles*. But the connection needs to be made by whole communities, who bring this force down, or from the margins, or out of hiddenness into the fullness of light and presence; through their celebrations, and their architecture, and their ritual and whole way of life. As the Greeks did.

But it seems that we aren't (yet) strong enough. *Vater Aether* can only be brought into action by the *fühlendes Herz des Menschen*. They have to respond to him, but this means also naming him. Poetry can show this response, "naming" it, articulating it. "Denn wir sind herzlos, Schatten, bis unser / Vater Aether erkannt jeden und allen gehört" [For we are heartless, mere shadows, until our / Father Aether, made known, recognized, fathers us all].[30] But we are left with some signs. Bread and wine; rites given by the *Syrier* [Syrian], son of the Highest (Christ or Dionysius?). And we also have poets.

Of these two avenues of approach, discerning the ordering power in our contemporary world, and looking back with nostalgia at a past in which it was beautifully manifest, there is no doubt where the preponderance lies with Hölderlin. The moments of present discernment are more than balanced by expressions of loss and despair, or at best uncertainty about our fate in the present world, whereas the portraits of an-

---

28. Hölderlin, "Brod und Wein," 97.
29. Hölderlin, "Bread and Wine," 268.
30. Hölderlin, "Brod und Wein," 97; Hölderlin, "Bread and Wine," 268.

cient Greece glow with a powerful longing. This is evident from the way in which "Brod und Wein" unfolds. Stanza 4 starts with the affirmation "Seeliges Griechenland!" but then turns quickly to a cry of bereavement:

> Aber die Thronen, wo? Die Tempel, und wo die Gefäße?
> Wo mit Nektar gefüllt, Göttern zu Lust der Gesang?

> [But the thrones, where are they? Where are the temples, the vessels,
> Where to delight the gods, brim-full with nectar, the songs?]

The glowing account of stanza 5 is followed in the middle of stanza 6 by

> Aber wo sind sie? Wo blühn die Bekannten, die Kronen des Festes?[31]

> [Only where are they? Where thrive these famed ones, the festival's
> garlands?][32]

And continued by the lines beginning "Thebe welkt" [Thebes withers] quoted above.

The major convincing power of Hölderlin's poetry lies in the register of nostalgia and longing. But as Constantine remarks, it is so powerful in this register that it draws us almost irresistibly into his vision.[33]

This introduces us to a different modality of Romantic sense of cosmic connection. There are works which affirm this connection, like "Tintern Abbey," and (more hesitantly) the works of Hölderlin above. But there are also those where the connection is powerfully evoked as failed, even unattainable, as a magnificent achievement in the conditional mood, in the register of "if only." These are by no means rare.

And there are many types. What renders the connection unattainable may be deemed some feature of human nature itself, or it may be a more contingent failure on the part of our present generation. Or it may be the nature of time. And there may be mixed modes, in which unattainability

---

31. Hölderlin, "Brod und Wein," 96.
32. Hölderlin, "Bread and Wine," 269.
33. See Constantine, *Hölderlin*.

is an ultimate flaw in a convincingly realized connection. We will see (lots) more of this later.

The tension of not being able to return perhaps awakened in Hölderlin another longing: to join the *Hen kai Pan,* the *Eins und Alles,* by self-annihilation, melting into it. Perhaps this is what Empedocles meant to him. This aspiration will return with other poets in this tradition.

III

Novalis' magical idealism   Novalis works out Hamann's crucial idea, that speech is translation, but builds into it his own conception of an original condition from which we have fallen, but which can be recovered. In this he is very influenced, as the whole Romantic generation was, by Kantian-Fichtean idealism. But he is far from being a disciple of Fichte, even though one of the labels he gives his theory is "magical idealism." In fact, the Fichtean influence is ultimately contained by Hamann's basic idea: in speaking, we are trying to grasp an original which is independent of us; there is something here that we have to get right.

But, and here the idealism enters, our getting it right also transforms it. The world as we know it is fallen, out of shape, in some sense broken. The world is a kind of language, but lacunary and distorted. What we have to get right is the original, of which it is a damaged and unfaithful rendition. And our discovery of this proper original version helps to reinstate it, to make the world once more a faithful expression of it. This transformative power is the "magical" dimension of Novalis' thought. The world responds to the recognition of its true nature by coming closer to this true nature.

Novalis is in many ways an orthodox Christian. He speaks of our original unspoiled condition as a golden age, and of our eschaton as a return to a renewed golden age. This is not a biblical term, but our departure from the original can be understood in biblical terms, as the result of sin, and our return is placed ultimately in a Christian framework. Certainly "magical" idealism can sound as though this return is something we bring about, but our ability to do so is placed in a larger theological context of a restored life beyond death.

Readers of Rilke, who then plunge into Novalis, will be again and again struck by the resonances. In a way what Rilke did was to transpose Novalis—and his key images of inwardness, death, and night—quite out of his Christian framework, where the crucial transcendent figure is not God in heaven, but the *Doppelbereich* [dual realm] through which the angel moves freely.

> Ist denn das Weltall nicht in uns? Die Tiefen unseres Geistes kennen wir nicht—Nach innen geht die geheimnisvolle Weg. In uns, oder nirgends ist die Ewigkeit mit ihren Welten—die Vergangenheit und die Zukunft.[34]
>
> Die Außenwelt ist die Schattenwelt—Sie wirft ihren Schatten in das Lichtreich. Jetzt scheints uns freylich innerlich so dunkel, einsam, gestaltlos—Aber wie ganz anderes wird es uns dünken—wenn diese Verfinsterung vorbey, und der Schattenkörper hinweggerückt ist—Wir werden mehr genießen als je, denn unser Geist hat entbehrt.[35]

[For is the whole universe not *in us*? We don't know the depths of our spirit—Inward goes the way full of mystery. In us, or nowhere is eternity with its worlds—the past and the future.

The outer world is a world of shadows—it throws its shadows onto the realm of light. Now we must admit everything inner seems to us so dark, lonely, shapeless—But how different will it appear to us—when this darkening is over, and the body of shadows has been shunted aside—We shall enjoy more things than ever before, for our spirit has been in need.]

---

34. Compare Rainer Maria Rilke, *The Poetry of Rilke*, trans. Edward Snow (New York: North Point, 2009), 323. "Siebte Duineser Elegie": "Nirgends, Geliebte, wird Welt sein als innen" ["Seventh Duino Elegy": "Nowhere, love, will World exist but within"].

35. Novalis, "Blüthenstaub," 22, in *Schriften: Die Werke Friedrich von Hardenbergs* (Stuttgart: Kohlhammer, 1960), 2:419.

Der Sitz der Seele ist da, wo sich Innenwelt und Aussenwelt sich
berühren. Wo sie sich durchdringen—ist er in jedem Punkte
der Durchdringung.[36]

[The site of the soul is there, where inner- and outer-world
touch each other. Where they interfuse, this site is in every
point of this fusion.]

As I hinted above, "magical idealism," the idea that we can restore things
to their original form by recognizing what this form is, seems to attribute
excessive powers to language. And in a sense it does, but not in the way
we readers of Fichte easily assume. We have to remember that reality itself
is language. "Alles, was wir erfahren ist eine *Mittheilung*. So ist die Welt in
der That eine *Mittheilung*—Offenbarung des Geistes." [Everything that
we experience is a *communication*. Hence the world in fact is a communication: a disclosure of Mind.][37] Novalis returns to the age-old theory that
the creation is made up of signs, which have to be interpreted.

But this is made difficult, because the power of the original form lies
latent and imprisoned in the distorted reality. The magic consists in this,
that our recognition of the real, full, undistorted form releases its power,
and this power is what restores reality to its pristine shape. There is no
sense of a "triumph of the will" here. Our task is not to will, but to discern the true shape.

Wir sind auf einer <u>Mission</u>. Zur Bildung der Erde sind wir
berufen.[38]

[We are on a <u>mission</u>. We are called to the formation of the
world.]

Or as the teacher in *Die Lehrlinge zu Saïs* puts it: "Ein Verkündiger der
Natur zu sein, ist ein schönes und heiliges Amt" [To announce *the* true
form of Nature is a beautiful and holy office].[39] Put negatively, our inca-

36. Novalis, "Blüthenstaub," 20, p. 418.
37. Novalis, "Fragmente," in *Schriften,* 2:594.
38. Novalis, "Blüthenstaub," 32, p. 426.
39. Novalis, *Die Lehrlinge zu Saïs,* in *Schriften,* 2:107. Note the resonance in Rilke:
"Da ist keine Stelle, die nicht trüge den Ton Verkündigung" (Siebente Duineser Elegie)

pacity to discern the true signs is blocking the return of things to their proper form. So later in the same work, the *tausendfaltigen Naturen* [thousandfold natures] in their *wunderbaren Gespräch* [miraculous conversation] complain of how they are prevented from returning to their proper unity by the blindness of humans.[40]

Now we are here in Hamann territory: to describe our world is to translate. Only Novalis wants to insist that there are better and worse translations. The best are not literal. Translations which change the reality (in the direction of its real, underlying nature) are better, as when we give a new formulation to the idea behind a work. And the best of all which are available to us are the mythic. Here Novalis follows a widely held doctrine of his generation, which I discussed in Chapter 1. We come closest to the underlying reality not through philosophical concepts, but through stories, myths, fables (*Märchen*)—of the kind which he attempts in *Heinrich von Ofterdingen*. The mythological translation lays bare the underlying ideal.

It is clear that the task of discerning-and-thus-transforming reality is a long and arduous one, and comes about in several stages. So we move from an account of things in which there seems to be little or no order, and everything happens by chance (the realm of *Unregel*), to accounts in terms of arbitrary action (*Willkürregel*), to those evoking lucky chance (*Zufallsregel*), and finally we see in events a *Wunderregel*, the way things are guided by God. Each step builds on the understanding and hence transformation wrought in the previous one.

Another image that Novalis invokes to describe this progress is drawn from mathematics. Enriching our grasp of things involves raising them to a higher power.

The word that Novalis often uses for this progression in understanding and transformation is *romantisierung*.

"Inward goes the secret path": for Novalis, this is not only true in the case of us seekers after knowledge, who have to turn inward. It is also

["Annunciation / would echo everywhere" (Seventh Duino Elegy)] (Rilke, *Poetry of Rilke,* 321). The resonance with the original Annunciation, of Gabriel to Mary, is central to both these uses of the word.

40. Novalis, *Die Lehrlinge zu Saïs*, 1:95.

true cosmically: the key to the outer reality around us is to be found deep
below in the bowels of the earth. Here Novalis drew on his profession as
mining engineer. In the mineral realm, we find hieroglyphs of inorganic
nature. Through them we become capable of understanding what we observe on the surface.

But the analogy between what is inner and what is underground goes
further. It extends to the grave, and hence death. And so we understand
life through death.

> Der Tod ist eine Selbstbesiegung—die, wie alle Selbstüber-
> windung,
>> eine neue, leichtere Existenz verschafft.[41]

> [Death is a victory over self—which, like all self-overcoming,
> brings about a new lighter existence.]

> Leben ist der Anfang des Todes. Das Leben ist um des Todes
> willen.
>> Der Tod ist Endigung und Anfang zugleich. Scheidung und
> nähere Selbstverbindung zugleich. Durch den Tod wird die
> Reduktion vollendet.[42]

> [Life is the beginning of death. Life is for the sake of death.
>> Death is at once an ending and a beginning. Separation and
> nearer self-relation alike. Through death Reduction comes to
> completion.][43]

From death we turn to night, darkness. As we turn from outer experience inward in order to question our everyday understanding of things,
and then turn to the deep mine shafts to grasp things on the surface of
the earth; and then to death, and the completed life which has departed
in order to grasp what this life amounted to, so, in the same way, we turn
from daylight vision to night and darkness to grasp the ultimate significance of everything.

---

41. Novalis, "Blüthenstaub," 11, p. 414.
42. Novalis, "Blüthenstaub," 15, p. 416.
43. Again, there are clear echoes in Rilke.

Novalis' great poem *Hymnen an die Nacht* opens by singing the joys
of daylight existence, the

> Wundererscheinungen des verbreiteten Raums, das allerfreuliche
> Licht—mit seinen Farben, seinen Strahlen und Wogen; seiner
> milden Allgegenwart, als weckender Tag. Wie des Lebens in-
> nerste Seele atmet es der rastlosen Gestirne Riesenwelt, und
> schwimmt tanzen in seiner blauen Flut—atmet es der funkelnde,
> ewigrunde Stein, die sinnige, saugende Pflanze, und das wilde,
> brennende, vielgestaltete Tier.[44]

> [The wondrous shows of the widespread space around, the
> all-joyous light, with its colours, its rays and undulations, its
> gentle omnipresence in the form of the wakening day. The
> giant world of the unresting constellations inhales it as the
> innermost soul of life, and floats dancing in its azure flood; the
> sparkling, ever-tranquil stone, the thoughtful, inhibiting
> plant, and the wild, burning multiform beast inhales it.][45]

Here, in this hymn to Light, are all the joys of fullness of presence, all
the riches of daylight experience.

What does night have to offer which can compare? Precisely, the distance, the long perspective, what was irremediably blocked by presence,
fullness, richness of experience. In the dark, for the first time, we see the
stars. And

> Himmlischer, als jene blitzenden Sterne, dünken uns die un-
> endlichen Augen, die die Nacht in uns geöffnet. Weiter sehen
> sie, als die blässesten jener zahllose Heere—unbedürftig des
> Lichts durchschauen sie die Tiefen eines liebenden Gemüts—
> was einen höheren Raum mit unsäglicher Wohllust füllt.[46]

> [More heavenly than those glittering stars we hold the eternal
> eyes which the Night has opened within us. Farther they see

44. Novalis, "Hymnen an die Nacht," in *Schriften*, 1:131.

45. Novalis, *Hymns to the Night and Spiritual Songs*, trans. George Macdonald (Maid-
stone, Kent, UK: Crescent, 2010), 17–18.

46. Novalis, "Hymnen an die Nacht," 132.

than the palest of these countless hosts. Needing no aid from the
Light, they penetrate the depths of a loving soul that fills a
loftier region with bliss ineffable.]

And, as a result, "wie arm und kindisch dünkt mir das Licht nun" [how
poor and childish a thing seems to me now the Light].[47]

Just as the full significance of life is only visible after death has put an
end to it, so the full significance of daylight joys only comes in the emptiness of the dark; and most poignantly of all for Novalis, the full depth
of his love for his departed fiancée only came in the experience at her
graveside which he recounts in the third hymn. On this Novalis built a
Christian-inspired eschatology of death as the portal to the afterlife.

All this is not easy to follow. One has the feeling that Novalis has the
tendency to chase hares in a number of different directions, without necessarily knowing that they will contribute to the same coherent picture.
So he classes translations, in ascending order: *grammatisch, verändernd,
mythisch* [grammatical, transforming, mythic]. This culminates in the
crucial role of *Märchen,* a major doctrine of his. But then beyond this he
also ranks understandings by the mathematical concept of power; then
again there is a ranking by nature of *Regel: Unregel, Willkürregel, Zufallsregel,* and then *Wunderregel* [absence of rule, arbitrary rule, contingent
rule, and then miraculous rule].[48]

Presumably, these rankings can be aligned with one another? But also,
his characterizations of the coming golden age in terms of language are
not, on the face of it, consistent. The main line seems to be that in the
end, all the deep expressions of language incorporated in things will be
understood, and hence the things themselves will reach their highest
form. This assumes one language underlying reality. But at another point,
he speaks of the eschaton as one of everything, "Menschen, Tiere,
Pflanzen, Steine und Gestirne, Töne, Farben [. . .] wie ein Geschlecht
handeln und sprechen"[49] [humans, animals, plants, stones and stars,
notes, colors . . . acting and speaking as one Genus], as though in our present fallen state different things had different languages, a kind of
cosmic Babel effect, which the Golden Age has to overcome.

47. Novalis, *Hymns to the Night,* 37–38.
48. Novalis, "Blüthenstaub," 68, p. 439.
49. Novalis, "Heinrich von Ofterdingen," in *Schriften,* 1:347.

Chapter Five

NATURE, HISTORY

I

In the first chapters, I have mainly focused on the way certain poets of the Romantic period create a powerful sense of connection to cosmic orders. These are modeled on the traditional notion of such orders, but the poets I have been discussing stop short of a claim to define these orders as they exist in nature, independently of us, poets and readers. That would require a convincing underlying story, which has yet to be provided.

My examples are drawn from English and German literature, most prominently Wordsworth and Hölderlin, but the underlying theory has been drawn from the generation of the 1790s in Germany, the poets and thinkers of German Romanticism, Hamann and the group centered on Jena and Berlin, including Schelling, Hölderlin, and A. W. and Friedrich Schlegel.

I also mentioned another mode of connection to nature implicit in a poem by Goethe, which reads our deep aspiration to *Ruh* through the mountain forest, but I want to concentrate here on the link to cosmic orders.

What does reconnection do? Take Wordsworth and Hölderlin. We are now linked to this wider space, in the sense that there is a flow between us. This in some sense nourishes us. How nourish? We are part of a wider life, and this fulfills some need / aspiration in us; at least we experience it thus. I am trying to interpret the experience that, for example, the poetry of Wordsworth and Hölderlin brings on, and is meant to bring on, in the reader.

When we read the lines from "Tintern Abbey" about "a sense sublime / Of something far more deeply interfused, / Whose dwelling is the light of setting suns, / And the round ocean and the living air, / And the blue sky, and in the mind of man: / A motion and a spirit, that impels / All thinking things, all objects of all thought, / And rolls through all things," we are not just noting that we humans exist in a larger context, even one which nourishes and sustains us. These lines bring on (what is felt as) an experience of this "motion" and this "spirit" which passes through our world and into us. This goes beyond, for instance, an experience of awe in the presence of a magnificent landscape, because what Wordsworth calls forth is our life now lived in a wider frame, whose constituent inner movements are felt as at one with ours.

A similar point can be made in connection with Hölderlin: for instance, the description of the mountain scene in "Heimkunft"; or, in another key, the nostalgic recall of the way the cycle of sea, cloud, rain, and rivers was (supposedly) lived by ancient Greeks, through their relation to the god Poseidon.

Because this connection is partly defined in terms of our experience, we can say that the poetry which reveals it (as a potentiality which already existed) also brings it about or realizes it.

The understanding here of cosmic order, and of our access to it, differs from but is essentially related to theories of such orders, and of their relation to language, which were dominant in the late Renaissance. These were essential points of reference for the German Romantics, as I outlined at the beginning of Chapter 1.

Crucial in this context was, for instance, the notion of an ideal language whose terms would figure or capture the essence of the realities they designate, such as the "Adamic" language, or the Creation considered as a book which communicated a message alongside the Bible, and conveying the same content. The ideal language would lay before us how these realities relate to each other and form a cosmic order, variously conceived in terms of Lovejoy's "principle of plenitude," or Paracelsus' "signatures," the Hermetic theories, or the Kabbalah, to mention some of the best-known examples.

Notions of this order were essential reference points for the philosophical outlook underlying German Romanticism. But at the same time, these thinkers recognized that the whole outlook was losing credibility in the face of the steady advance of a "disenchanted" view of the world, encouraged among other factors by the growing achievements of post-Galilean natural science, which reinterpreted the physical world in terms of inert matter.

In Chapter 1, we saw that the response, in the form proposed by Hamann, was a sort of strategic retreat, an admission that we couldn't directly read and reproduce God's language, but only offer our, fallible and approximate, "translations" of it. The retreat involved reducing our epistemic claim: the "translation" can't be guaranteed to reproduce the full force of the original. But this retreat was at the same time an assertion of the enhanced importance of human creativity in the activity of translation—an assertion very much in tune with this new outlook. The retreat carried with it a claim to a greater role in defining the outlook we live by.

But the recovery of connection to cosmic order inevitably involved a very different experience from that of the late Renaissance. It was not just that the description of order was tentative in the absence of an underlying story. It was also that the whole context had changed. Between, say, 1500 and 1800, the whole outlook, and deeper, the whole experience of the world in Europe, underwent a profound change. At the popular level, outside of elite circles, its inhabitants lived in an "enchanted" universe, peopled with spirits and moral forces inherent in things, like relics and other sacred objects.[1] The intellectual elites, however, also understood

1. I am using "enchantment" and its antonym in a narrow sense, related to a world in which such "magic" forces were salient. "Disenchantment" therefore designates the fading of this kind of experience, and the slide toward a sense of the physical world as

their world in terms of the theories of the late Renaissance. These two life contexts coexisted, often without a sense of mutual opposition.

But the Reformation, with its new understanding of the value of ordinary life in this world, tended to create a distance from the enchanted context; and the anxieties it generated about each person's individual salvation profoundly undermined trust in our felt relation to God and his world. And on top of this, the advance of scientific, mechanistic accounts of things, and the resultant technology (e.g., watches) further sapped confidence in the felt meaning of things.

As Mark Vernon put it:

> Life during the Middle Ages was experienced very differently from now, and that's hardly a surprise. Most people lived closer to the land, and closer to the divine, and, experientially speaking, closer to the planets and stars as their influence washed over Earth. If, today, it's easy to feel like an onlooker on life, peering out from an island of awareness somewhere inside your head, the mediaeval person must have felt like an immersed participant whose life was naturally involved with the seasons, the saints and the skies.[2]

For the "mediaeval mind . . . everything was an intermingling of surface and depth," of physical realities and their deeper meanings.[3]

Once this outlook passes, and we live most of the time in a physical world of inert matter, the experience of connection that we see re-created by Wordsworth and Hölderlin has to be very different. It is not just that it is more tentative in its description, it is also, precisely in being exceptional, very much tied to its particular locus.

Of course, the assumption of both Wordsworth and Hölderlin was that the order they discern exists and operates everywhere. Wordsworth sees "a motion and a spirit, that impels / All thinking things, all objects of all

---

constituted by inert matter. I don't want to extend this term to cover a decline of religious belief and practice, which Weber unfortunately did. This decline comes later and is a distinct development of its own.

2. Mark Vernon, *A Secret History of Christianity* (Alresford, Hampshire, UK: John Hunt, 2019), 149.

3. Vernon, *Secret History*, 145.

thought, / And rolls through all things." But it wasn't visible, discernable everywhere. On the contrary, the vision was tied to a particular place and a privileged moment: such moments which at their most intense and powerful Wordsworth called "spots of time." They occur at rare vantage points in the vast extension of space-time, from which, for a moment, the larger order shows up.

The onward march of scientific culture and technological control has rendered this experience more fragile, easier to dismiss when the vision has passed. And it should not surprise that such visions into what lies underneath the surface of things become rarer as the century unfolds. I will take this up later, along with the greater focus on issues of recon-nection in relation to time.

II

But the most important change wrought by the Romantic period is not the epistemic one, that affirmations about the shape of order become more tentative, and arise only in certain places; nor is it the loss of the detailed descriptions which earlier notions of order gave us—like, for in-stance, the Kabbalah's allocation of numbers to specific realities in virtue of the Hebrew letters spelling their names, which allows us to track the affinities between them. The big shift is in the nature of the relationship, what reconnection does for us.

In the era where the traditional cosmic orders reigned unchallenged, the important intellectual achievement consisted in our grasping a vi-sion of hierarchical order, which in turn inspired us to embrace certain ultimate values; but, in the Romantic period, the important goal was to gain a sense of connection which was life-enhancing; or to use the term of Hartmut Rosa invoked earlier, a connection which was "resonant."

III

But at this point we need to return to where we left the discussion at the end of Chapter 1. There I raised the question: How seriously should we take the alleged experience of reconnection? To answer this, we need to

ask: How does this fit with what we know about our common experience of nature in the post-Romantic age? Because in our time, what our
forebears might have thought of as our relation to the Cosmos now arises
for us as our place and stance in Nature.

We need to examine from other angles our human relation to Nature,
or more broadly, to our whole environment, natural and human built.
Let's imagine a nightmare science fiction scenario: we live in a concrete
jungle, or an environment consisting entirely of airport lounges (*non-
lieux*, in Augé's expression, *Nicht-Orte*, no-places). We would find Shakespeare, Goethe, Keats, Hölderlin, not to speak of Pink Floyd recordings,
all the more indispensable; we would cling to them like shipwrecked
sailors to floating spars. But would that be enough, so we wouldn't
need to ask for anything else? Certainly not. And of course, in these no-
places, we might still have our relation to loved ones. Would we then
have enough? Again not.

We need a relation to the world, the universe, to things, forests, fields,
mountains, seas, analogous to that we have to human beings we love and
works of art; where we feel ourselves addressed, and called upon to
answer.

So how to explore this? There are two possible directions: the first
would look at our behavior, including our stated longings, even those we
fail to act on. I'm trying here to identify certain experiences, widely sought
after, and see what they could mean. Two dimensions seem to emerge
from our experiences and longings or desires: a spatial and a temporal
one. In the first, our behavior shows an evident need to connect with organic nature, with life, vegetable and animal. We see this in tourism,
visiting parks, trips to the country, seeking beautiful spots; or just in
making gardens. We are kin to what we see, feel and experience in life
and nature. And we seem to need this contact to feel the fullness of life in
ourselves.

As far as stated longings are concerned, we find, in several stages over
the last centuries, a sense of loss arising over a felt lack of the contact with
nature enjoyed in the recent past, only to see this supposedly bereft era
becoming the standard for a later sense of loss of the same kind. In Jane
Austen's era, a new kind of landowner was identified and pilloried in her
novels, who only wanted to make profitable "improvements" on their

estates; but this era became in turn the object of nostalgia later in the nineteenth century, when economic "development" had been pushed even further; and this process has been repeated many times since.[4] We may be tempted to caricature this recurring nostalgia, and dismiss it from serious consideration; but above and beyond the illusions it betrays, there is clearly a continuing aspiration here which, illusory or not, has to be taken seriously as telling us something about (at least many) human beings.

The second dimension is time. In relation to the first, the spatial dimension, the sense is that human life has grown out of, and still feeds off, this milieu of life. But the temporal dimension includes more than this; it includes our history, our development, the story of what we have become. Hence the fascination for history; and tourism again attests to this: we go to visit the sites where important things have happened; we seek great buildings which belong to earlier epochs.

And particularly churches, mosques, temples, sites of pilgrimage. Partly because these are important definers of earlier periods; but also perhaps because human beings have always had a sense of the greater spatial and temporal order in which they fit, and the great religious buildings reflect the different takes on this throughout history, including many with a transcendent perspective.

What is (are) the desires and longings that move us in these two dimensions? In the first, we seem to want to have a deep connection with the larger milieu of life. In the second, we seek a connection across time, analogous to each individual's seeking in memory and story the sense of his/her own life. Speculating on what lies deeper behind this, we could think that there is an aspiration to eternity, as gathered time. And this perhaps also powers our desire not to be forgotten, that our story be told. (And there may also be some aspiration like what Benjamin invokes when he speaks of "redeeming the past.")

We might think that the longing in the first dimension is just biological. And indeed, there is some of this. We go out into nature, breathe fresh air, relax, soak in the sun and breeze, imbibe vitamin D, feel safe

---

4. See Jonathan Bate, *The Song of the Earth* (Cambridge, MA: Harvard University Press, 2000), ch. 1.

and unhurried. All this could be part of a doctor's prescription for a holiday. The doctor's reasons may have been simply biological. But it seems to me that an important dimension of the need is metabiological. We could have clean air and pure water, lots of relaxing time, in our spaceships. We might even play movies of gardens, or unspoiled wilderness, but this wouldn't be an adequate substitute for *being there*, being among flowers, trees, at the edge of the forest.

And when we look at the temporal dimension, the need is obviously metabiological. The lift we get passes through the sense we are making of all this, even of unknown ruins as our imagination swirls around a form of life deep in the past.

But on reflection, this is also true of the first dimension. We grasp the sun, fields, forests as the larger life we aspire to belong to. In both cases, we are fed by our surroundings, temporal and spatial; but the feeding is made deeper, more intense, more palpable when we see the meaning in it; which comes to us largely through beauty.

Jonathan Bate, in a remarkable book, shows how living in a civilization which more and more emphasizes and entrenches a Cartesian mind-body dualism, and in the same spirit, a Baconian instrumental-technological stance to Nature, awakens a strong need to recover contact with nature. So in the heart of the modern city, inspired by Olmstead, we install great parks; and following Muir, we try to set aside wilderness areas where people can hike in primeval terrain. But this need also has consequences for art: we might see what Bate calls our eco-poetry as "imaginary parks in which we may breathe an air that is not toxic and accommodate ourselves to a mode of dwelling that is not alienated."[5]

We can situate the beginnings of this sense of alienation in England in the early nineteenth century. Even the wider public, which had no knowledge of what was going on in philosophical circles in Jena and Berlin, or of the critique of the radical Fichtean notion of freedom, and of its destructive consequences for our communion with nature, could note the growth and impersonality of cities, the growing strength of an "improving" economic drive in country estates and industrial towns, and feel troubled at the loss of a traditional way of life and of a new alien-

---

5. Bate, *Song of the Earth*, 64.

ation from nature. The obvious parallel between high-level German thought and widespread English popular sentiment is great enough that some thinkers at the time (e.g., Coleridge), and many later, saw in the first a philosophical account of the rise of the second.

And, as a technological, instrumentally rational economy has come to dominate our society, more and more parts of the world have experienced similar feelings of alienation.

This brought on a growing awareness that we are nourished in a sense by nature surrounding us. Which is why we compensate for our urban environments, which tame and subordinate nature, and hold it at a distance, by parks, gardens, suburbs where there are trees, open light, fresh air; and also by going to the country, trekking through wilderness, going to sun and seaside.

The nourishment is not only physical, but also for the spirit. We feel cramped in, alienated, without this contact. But this need is diffuse, not focused, its nature not fully grasped by most of us most of the time. Just fulfilling this diffuse need is highly beneficial.[6] However, there are moments where, through articulation in a work of art, we can concentrate and thus intensify the effect: some painting gives us an acute sense of the light over a scene, or a poem intensely concentrates how a given scene, or being in a certain space, moves us. And there is a certain joy which comes from articulating this experience. This joy, the sense of how important it is, how essential a human fulfillment it is, all come together. The diffuse feeling can be brushed off as just subjective but the concentration is a heightening awareness and a sharpening of focus, and the joy which accompanies it demonstrates how much this articulation is a realization of our nature as human beings, or to use an Aristotelian expression, the human Form.[7]

---

6. See Lucy Jones, *Losing Eden* (London: Penguin Random House, 2020). Jones lays out the very neglected but immense advantages for human health and morale of contact with nature.

7. This brings us back to the discussion of "ethics" in Chapter 2 as the attempt to identify the fulfillments essential to our nature as humans. We will return to this topic in later chapters.

But is this heightened, concentrated awareness not just itself a "subjective feeling"? We might imagine, ultimately, coming to this conclusion in the eventual underlying story we adopt. But this seems highly implausible. Because what is proper to the experience which this poetry makes possible is that we sense ourselves as receiving nurture. Bate gives a number of examples, among others, from Wordsworth and Keats.[8] In particular, in "To Autumn" Keats takes us deep within the experience of the fully ripened season—especially in the final stanza, which points beyond this season to the yearly round.

We can articulate this as a more intense sense of this space enclosing us, defining this relation of nurture from our world. The poetry which articulates this and makes us feel palpably what we owe to this field, these woods, these hills, brings out the connection and intensifies it. This poetry is like a ritual which makes the connection more powerful.

This kind of intensification of our experience of nature, of need and reception, is related to but different from the modes of cosmic connection we discussed earlier in this chapter. It differs from, say, Wordsworth's invocation of a force running through all things, and from Hölderlin's recognition of the Gods at work in the world surrounding us. And this in two related ways.

First, the intensified experience may offer no general picture of our relation to the cosmos, it may offer no concept describing this relation— like "force" or "god"; and second, it articulates and transforms this particular experience, what we live in our immediate surroundings. It carries the "epistemic retreat" much farther than any of the other forms of (re)connection. And with the steady advance in the retreat from the other forms, this may become the main reason that we still are moved by "Tintern Abbey."

Of course, there is no sharp boundary between these two, more a continuous scale of possible articulations; but we need to recognize the more immediate end of the scale. In Chapter 6 I will give further examples from Keats of such intensification of our lived situation.

This experience is closer to another kind of cosmic connection which I introduced above with Goethe's "Wanderers Nachtlied," where Goethe

8. Chs. 3 and 4 in Bate, *Song of the Earth*, 74, 93, 103–104.

reads a new and deeper form of *Ruh* [rest], hitherto unrecognized, in the mountain forest. This insight too arises out of an immediate situation (whether lived or imagined). But it is still very different because what is given articulation here is a new human possibility, a form of experience which can in principle be recovered and deepened on a future occasion ("Balde / Ruhest du auch").

(I've been discussing post-Romantic poetry in this chapter; but in some sense humans have always been aware of and concerned with their relation to the cosmos, and the forces within it. In earlier times, our connection to these was established through ritual invocations of the spirits of the woods, or of the deer, of mountains or rivers. Who knows what underlying story is ultimately right here but perhaps, as language animals, we need to articulate this; it is a crucial fulfillment to live this connection more intensely by articulating it.)

We could complement these reflections by looking to the temporal dimension, where hermeneutic works, like Robert Pogue Harrison's on forests, for instance, show the way they connect us to the remote past.[9] These works try to lay out the temporal meanings that monuments, gardens, forests have for human beings, and to explain somewhat why people turn again and again to wilderness, for instance.

Forests are highly significant, as Harrison has shown. They have always represented the opposite of civility, and order. (This is certainly true of our Western civilization, where the etymology behind the distinction between civilized and savage refers us to cities and forests.) The latter are seen as spaces of disorder and the absence of boundaries. But they also are our point of origin, our beginning, what we have awakened out of, developed from.

Perhaps we still need them, like sleep. We have to reconnect with them, plunge into them again and again. Thoreau: "In Wildness is the preservation of the world."[10]

---

9. Robert Pogue Harrison, *Forests: The Shadow of Civilization* (Chicago: University of Chicago Press, 1992).

10. Quoted in Roderick Nash, *Wilderness and the American Mind* (New Haven, CT: Yale University Press, 2014), ch. 3. See also the "Explanatory Note: Emerson and Transcendentalism" in this volume.

What are the hungers to connect with the whole of time; why do the forests where we originated, which we have emerged from, fascinate us? Why do we still need them in our world, so that the prospect of a total and irreversible deforestation fills us with a powerful anguish?

We can speculate: perhaps (a) it's because we always understand ourselves in biography, in how we came to be what we are now. There is no instant, achronical self-understanding. But, one might object, the forests were a long time ago.

So perhaps (b) it's because we all have to emerge from the primitive, each one in his/her own life, so we need to see what this means.

And perhaps besides, (c) the emergence has involved loss as well as gain, so we have constantly to revisit this past to redeem what is still imprisoned there.

In any case, we humans have emerged on our planet, and out of its nourishing environment, first nourishing life in general, and then our lives. We inhabit time, and we know that we have come about through an immense evolution over time. We want to know this story; as language animals we have an urge, feel a necessity to know this story, not just each of our own biographies, but also the shared history of our nation and mankind. That's why people go on tours to recover some contact with the past; we go to important centers to visit the monuments and churches, and many of us go on wilderness tours to recover contact with the remote past. We feel anguish at the thought that the wilderness forests out of which we grew might be entirely destroyed.

So once again, we can think of Thoreau; and also of attempts at recovering the Primitive in works like Stravinsky's *Le Sacre du Printemps*.

But then perhaps (d) we need a biography which coheres, where the past is not lost. So Proust. Perhaps this is also because we need to access the eternal dimension, a gathered eternity.

Can we put together these two lines of inquiry: discerning what we long for and why, and then looking at the post-Romantic poetic developments to get further, deeper insight into this why, into the meanings resonance has for us? That is the hope underlying this discussion.

In fact, to understand our relation to nature and time, we need a multiavenue approach, incorporating (1) what we do, (2) our ordinary expressions of what these activities do for us (e.g., "renewing," "recharging our batteries"), and (3) our dissatisfactions at everyday life (for instance, at lived time which is monotonous and fragmented). To these we should add a fourth avenue: following the poetic discoveries / inventions of epiphanic languages, which have come in the wake of the Romantic period.

A really adequate inquiry would explore all these avenues, to take them as complementary perspectives on what we want to define and articulate. The complementary relation might be described in this way: the study of our desires and behavior gives some idea of what in our world we seek to relate to, while the various forms of poetic response which we see emerging from the Romantic period offer insights into what these relations mean to us.

Of course, this book won't come even close to meeting this standard. I shall be focusing on the fourth avenue. But I will try not to lose sight of the other three.

IV

I'd like to take a brief forward look, anticipating (some of) the metabiological needs we experience, and the ways in which poetry in the post-Romantic period tries to meet them. I have been talking a great deal about different ways of "reconnecting" with the cosmos. This turns out to encompass rather different kinds of connection.

On one hand, there is the form we find in Wordsworth, which offers some description of the powers or forces in the cosmos with which we feel once more linked, beyond the objectifying vision wrought by disenchantment. But there is another kind of link, where we can come to read our own deepest longings through the cosmos—Goethe's *Ruh* as felt in the mountain forest. This might be seen as another mode of "reconnection." And the same goes for the poetry (and other arts) which articulates and intensifies our need for nourishment by the natural world which surrounds us. (And this need is also met by activities which we don't usually think of as art—for instance, gardening.)

And beyond these, there are quite different understandings of reconnection, and of what we reconnect to, corresponding to the very different

notions of the lack, the separation. There is, for instance, Hopkins' invocation of "inscape," the inner form shaping individual beings.

This is in some ways akin to Rilke's striving to close the gap by insti-
tuting a *Weltinnenraum* [interior world], an aspiration which he felt was
realized in his *Duino Elegies;* and then there are post-Symbolist attempts
to connect to a bigger order which emerge early in the twentieth century
in early modernist English literature, with Eliot, Pound, and Joyce.

But these later explorations are also fed by attempts to recover humanly bearable, even spiritually nourishing forms of lived time, which I
want to discuss starting with a chapter on Baudelaire (Chapter 10); and
this chapter will also try to describe the context that Baudelaire lived in
and Bergson helped clarify. For disenchantment not only undermines
traditional modes of resonance with the world surrounding us—we might
say in the spatial dimension; it also threatens the forms of resonance that
belong to us as temporal beings.

Then "Symbolism" (e.g., Verlaine, Rimbaud, Valéry), which drew inspiration from Baudelaire and Mallarmé, involved an epistemic retreat
from the early Romantics. In a sense, they (Wordsworth and Hölderlin,
for example) offer us pictures of cosmic order similar to the traditional
pre-Enlightenment ones. Their epistemic retreat comes in the fact that
their poetry offers the experience of order without claiming the confirmation of its truth that an underlying story (theistic or other) would give
it. The symbolists retreat further, in that their symbols are much more
indefinite and suggestive; they invoke different things to different people;
and at the limit they lack alethic content altogether; only the power of
their emotional impact seems to count, for Pater, for instance: "To burn
always with this hard gem-like flame, to maintain this ecstasy, is success
in life."[11]

I think of Eliot as a "postsymbolist," because he finds a way, in *The
Waste Land,* to assemble a picture of the human condition—that is, our
dire predicament and ways in which we might transcend it—through a
concatenation of fragments, which made a huge impact in spite of (or
because of?) its contradictory ending. Fragments do more than stave off

11. Quoted in Denis Donoghue, *Walter Pater: Lover of Strange Souls* (New York:
Knopf, 1995), 14.

ruin; they can also situate and orient us in our troubled history. And Eliot's later poetry retains a lot from the earlier work and builds on it to lead us toward an underlying story with a long tradition behind it.

The way the different "fragments," or references, combine, illuminate, or challenge and transform each other is crucial to this poetics, which in a quite different way, and to other purposes, was practiced by Pound.

But there can be, and I would argue, has been, a further step toward a minimalism of overt doctrine. This would attempt to orient us in our present conflicted predicament, laying bare the present evil, while also identifying sources of hope, and possible avenues of transformation.

Chapter Six

SHELLEY, KEATS (AFTER WORDSWORTH)

I

As the parallels noted above between Wordsworth and Hölderlin indicate, there were analogies between the "Romantic" poets of the two nations, even though the elaborate German philosophical-aesthetic theory played no role in the English case at the beginning. And even after it was introduced to the anglophone world by Coleridge, it took some time for its influence to be felt.

But we should take a look at other English poets of the Romantic period, in order to see how some analogous formative ideas were worked out differently.

Let us first look at Shelley: he seems to believe in a power underlying all, like that developing in Nature for the (implicit and tentative) German Romantic "metaphysic," and (more pertinently) like that supposed by Wordsworth, and arguably Blake. But this power is not benign. Unlike Hölderlin's gods, it is not friendly to humans and their feeling hearts.

Shelley's "Mont Blanc" invokes a power which resembles in some ways the *Vater Aether* of "Heimkunft," but it is utterly indifferent to us.[1] It is in a sense beyond good and evil.[2] This is the conclusion the poet draws, feels he cannot but draw, as he contemplates the great mountain. The glaciers, the rivers that flow from them, the storm winds which blow wreak destruction, but also help nourish life in the valley below (for instance, in lines 117–126); unlike the *Vater Aether* in "Heimkunft," whose titanic action seems directed only to the latter goal. But when Shelley lifts his eyes to contemplate the summit, he sees it as "far, far above, piercing the infinite sky," "still snowy and serene," although surrounded by an "uninhabitable desert" (lines 60–62).[3]

Here dwells the power which shapes both reality and thought. "The secret strength of things / Which governs thought, and to the infinite dome / Of heaven is a law, inhabits Thee!" (lines 139–141). This Power produces all the movement and the clashes of the world around us; but in itself "Power dwells apart in its tranquility / Remote, serene, and inaccessible" (lines 96–97). This power, for Shelley, remains "through time and change unquenchably the same."[4]

Thus we find in Shelley a vision analogous to that in German Romanticism (and Wordsworth), except that the power running through all things is not benign. It is unconcerned for us. It is inconceivable that we might establish a relation to it, similar to the one Hölderlin posits between his gods and our "feeling hearts." This by itself renders impossible the goal of a harmonious fusion between humans and Nature. In both England and Germany Romanticism arises against a background of felt

1. See Richard Unger, *Hölderlin's Major Poetry: The Dialectics of Unity* (Bloomington: Indiana University Press, 1975), 87. Unger makes this point: "A poet is here transforming the described landscape into poetic myth through interpretive language.... Here it serves to indicate that the poet [in each case] is interested in problems of poetic composition and that the scene is interpreted in terms of poetic process." I would add that in Hölderlin's case, the idea is also more radical: the suggestion is that the scene's self-composition inspires and leads the poet. Unger, like me, has drawn on the valuable work of Earl R. Wasserman, *The Subtler Language: Critical Readings of Neoclassical Poems* (Baltimore: Johns Hopkins University Press, 1959).

2. I have drawn a great deal on Wasserman's work here.

3. Percy Bysshe Shelley, "Mont Blanc," in *Poems* (Harmondsworth, UK: Penguin, 1956), 77.

4. Wasserman, *Subtler Language*, 235.

alienation from Nature; Shelley's identification of a Power shaping Nature which is utterly indifferent seems to make this alienation impossible to overcome—at least in the terms familiar to German poets of that epoch.

But the battle against our separation from Nature in fact can take different forms.

All Romantics shared a sense that the reigning morality, and/or understandings of freedom and reason, with their implicit controlling, manipulative stance toward our emotions and the world around us, constituted a kind of alienation from Nature, within and without, repressing spontaneous feeling and aspirations, as well as a deeper communication with the natural world. These two dimensions of alienation were linked and had to be overcome together. The two go together, because the stance of separation, which objectifies my emotional nature, also objectifies the world outside. The sympathetic current between us and nature cannot but be broken by this stance.

But within this agreement, there is a (sometimes) subtle difference of emphasis: between those who primarily strive to overcome both divisions by reconnecting with Nature; and those who strive primarily to throw off the inner yoke of disengaged reason, or the moral-religious condemnation of our inner nature. Most German Romantics, and also Wordsworth, are in the first category. But Byron is emphatically in the second category. He offered the exciting prospect of an utter freedom from the trammels of established social morality, both in his art and in his life.

This doesn't stop him from his own kind of radical political rebellion against established power, which took the form of participation in the Greek struggle for independence from the Ottomans, of which he was an early casualty.[5]

Blake, for his part, seems to take a third road; he looks forward to an apocalyptic eschatology, in which humans are united in a harmonious brotherhood, inspired by Christianity (as he understood it). But

---

5. Isaiah Berlin, in his interesting study *The Roots of Romanticism* (London: Chatto and Windus, 1999), gives its full due to the Byronic strain in Romanticism, but perhaps he goes too far in appearing to make this the essential form of Romanticism, which was in fact a much more varied and multiform movement, with many internal conflicts and incompatibilities.

this requires an utter break with the established moral and political order.[6]

Now Shelley's posit of an indifferent Power fails to overcome alienation on the first construal; but it can liberate us from an oppressive, self-denying moral-religious code—analogously to the later aspiration of Nietzsche to take us "beyond good and evil."

But there is another reason why we might think that a return to unity with nature is ultimately beyond us, and this is one which Shelley shares with Keats. We see this in Shelley's "Adonais," and in some powerful poems of Keats which focus, sometimes narrowly, on the ecstatic moment. First, let's look at "Adonais," a lament for Keats.

> The One remains, the many change and pass;
> Heaven's light forever shines, Earth's shadows fly;
> Life, like a dome of many-coloured glass,
> Stains the white radiance of eternity,
> Until Death tramples it to fragments—Die,
> If thou wouldst be with that which thou dost seek!
> Follow where all is fled!—Rome's azure sky,
> Flowers, ruins, statues, music, words, are weak
> The glory they transfuse with fitting truth to speak.[7]

The aporia here comes from our being time-bound creatures. If this condition is an ultimate bar to achieving unity with Nature, then this goal is unattainable, at least in our life here.

II

I want to look at this aporia as it arises for Keats, and this for more than one reason, but principally because Keats is at the origin of important new forms of Romantic poetry.

6. See Northrop Frye, *Fearful Symmetry: A Study of William Blake* (Princeton, NJ: Princeton University Press, 1947).

7. Percy Bysshe Shelley, "Adonais," in *Poems*, 269.

Although the philosophical context was very different, and in the English case not as fully elaborated, there are important analogies between the "implicit metaphysic" of Keats and that of the poets of the Romantic generation in Germany.

First, the famous statement of equivalence, "Beauty is Truth and Truth Beauty," was much more than a throwaway flourish. Beauty and Truth come into existence together. Art raises the object to a new unity and intensity, which constitutes Beauty. But this is not something which just exists in the mind of the artist (or reader); it has reality, and hence Truth, even though this reality is partly brought to fruition by artistic (re)creation.

Keats puts it: There are "things real—things semireal—and no things." Things real include "Sun Moon & Stars and passages of Shakespeare"; the semireal include "Love, and Clouds &c which require a greeting of the Spirit to make them wholly exist," whereas "Nothings are made Great and dignified by an ardent pursuit."[8] The first category are there independently of us; the third have their status (being Great and dignified) conferred on them by our stance toward them (ardent pursuit). But in the case of the semireal, they are not simply made so by us, although they need the transfiguration in art to achieve their fullness. This transfiguration brings the object to its full unity and intensity, purifies it, as it were, of ancillary matter. "The excellence of every Art is its intensity, capable of making all disagreeables evaporate, from their being in close relation to Beauty and Truth."[9]

This intense unity has a basis in reality independent of us, even though it attains fullness only in artistic re-creation. This re-creation constitutes Beauty, but this Beauty is True to the nature of the object.

In the terms of our earlier discussion, Beauty and Truth are not fully independent realities; they are human meanings which exist in the interspace between humans and their world. They become fully themselves only through us, but there are objectively right and wrong, or better and worse, re-creations. The better ones correspond to a real potential in

8. Walter Jackson Bate, *John Keats* (Cambridge, MA: Harvard University Press, 1983), 241.

9. Bate, *John Keats*, 243.

things. Referring back to the table in Chapter 2, they belong in the upper left quadrant.

Keats' extraordinary power to create such intense unities can be illustrated from what is perhaps his most famous poem, the "Ode to a Nightingale." Two oft-quoted stanzas are worth repeating here:

2.

O, for a draught of vintage that hath been
 Cool'd a long age in the deep-delved earth,
Tasting of Flora and the country green.
 Dance, and Provençal song, and sunburnt mirth!
O for a beaker full of the warm South,
 Full of the true, the blushful Hippocrene,
  With beaded bubbles winking at the brim,
   And purple-stained mouth;
 That I might drink, and leave the world unseen.
  And fade away into the forest dim.

[. . .]

5.

I cannot see what flowers are at my feet,
 Nor what soft incense hangs upon the boughs,
But, in embalmed darkness, guess each sweet
 Wherewith the seasonable month endows
The grass, the thicket, and the fruit-tree wild;
 White hawthorn, and the pastoral eglantine;
  Fast-fading violets cover'd up in leaves;
   And mid-May's eldest child,
 The coming musk-rose. Full of dewy wine,
  The murmurous haunt of flies on summer eves.[10]

10. John Keats, "Ode to a Nightingale," in *Selected Poetry* (Oxford: Oxford University Press, 1997), 175–176.

It is hard to describe this, but what we see / feel here in each of these stanzas is a fusion of some of the most moving features into a more intense image. The constellation of these features carries us in each case into the interspace they relate to (quaffing the wine in the warm South, feeling the full force and meaning of the summer night). But this is only possible because of Keats' uncanny ability to get inside these experiences, to capture the embodied, even sensual feel of being there. Each stanza flows from one mode of intense bodily contact to another, linking them together into a single powerful sense of presence, of absorbed enclosure in a peak experience. The flow from one point of contact to another seems to come from the experience itself, following its own inner movement.

Of course, we know that this experience only comes to full expression in the verse, its music of sound and images, but we sense that this brings out a movement in the experience itself. (This reminds us of the thoughts of Sanskrit grammarians, that language is first heard in things, really via the intermediate case of music.[11])

These reflections send us back to the discussion of Chapter 2, Section II.3, where the work manages to make manifest the inner rhythm of a thing (here an interspace); and analogously to Novalis, this manifestation brings its object to the perfection which Keats calls "Beauty."

These stanzas constitute a paradigm case of the potentiality of poetry I mentioned in Chapter 3, to concentrate and intensify our sense of nurture by the surrounding world of nature.

It is worth examining a bit more closely the relationship between felt experience and poetic evocation. The features mentioned in each stanza are among those which give the respective experiences their power. But the effect of the poetry, invoking one on top of the other, is to intensify this power and the joy which it brings. This intensification is a process

---

11. See David Shulman, *More than Real: A History of the Imagination in South India* (Cambridge, MA: Harvard University Press, 2012), 168. Shulman mentions the Sanskrit grammarians' notion that "imagination is a specialized mode of listening to the still undefined vibrations that underlie all phenomena." These vibrations, I would want to add, bring us close to music. They are part of what is captured in, say, Beethoven's *Pastoral*. See also Simon Jarvis, *Wordsworth's Philosophic Song* (Cambridge: Cambridge University Press, 2007).

in time (with poetry, unlike painting, it cannot be otherwise). So the constellation is also a concatenation. There is a flow here. But my claim is that the flow in the poetic description matches the flow in the lived experience.

In stanza 2, the experience is not actual, the description is drawn from the past: I am offered a beaker of wine, which I am told was cooled in the earth, redolent of its origins in Provence, and now I experience the beaded bubbles, the stained mouth. Thus concentrated, the experience intensifies in memory.

In stanza 5, the experience is felt as present: the surroundings which I cannot see, but I gradually pick out by smelling the flowers. The sense of being enfolded in a summer garden each time intensifies, and then I add on top of these another feature, in another modality, the murmurous sound of the flies, typical of summer. One flow captures the other and gives it the saliency and intensified consciousness that poetry can bring.

We are coming here again to a relation which was implicit in Hölderlin's idea of a poem coauthored by scene and artist. We can say that the poet is responding to the inner shape of the experience. We are on the road to recognizing the importance of inscapes.

But I still feel that I haven't really brought out what is remarkable in these passages: in each case we have a set of pleasurable experiences which, co-occurring, erupt into a sense of joy. This is expressed in, and at the same time produced by, the force of the poetry. There is a magic here which I can't fully fathom.

What results is a powerful unity of an experience which, though it unfolded in time, stands out as a single, undivided moment, a duration without succession. But above all, we have two passages where, in the light of our discussion in Chapter 5, an experience of being nourished by our natural surroundings is raised to an ever-higher power as it unfolds for us facet by facet. This is particularly true of the second, related in stanza 5.

So art reveals something in the world, and at the same time connects us to this something, which is intensely meaningful for us, "a joy forever" (*Endymion*). In our current terms, we "resonate" with our world.

We are converging on an outlook very similar to that of the Romantic generation in Germany, but without the philosophical background

("Spinoza," Kant, Fichte), and without the background of premodern notions of a language in things. There is even an analogy between Keats' notion of the "semireal" and the views of, for instance, Novalis, that poetic insight not only reconnects us to the order of meaning in things, but also corrects and completes this order.

Secondly and not surprisingly, Keats is aware of the whole drift of poetry in his age toward an exploration of personal experience. This was partly rendered inevitable, because of a widespread reaction to, or at least desire to complement, the disenchanted scientific view of the world. Keats cannot simply accept the latter's "unweaving the rainbow" any more than could Blake. And this reaction was widespread among the German Romantics.

This exploration of experience is reflected, among many other places, in the work of Wordsworth, whom Keats greatly admired (although he was also critical of the older poet); as well as in the growing stress on the importance of originality in their day. This contrast between earlier and contemporary art was given expression in Germany, among other places in Schiller's famous distinction between "naïve" and "sentimental" poetry.[12]

III

But it seems clear that Keats takes a step further in epistemic retreat in relation to the German Romantics, and even to Wordsworth. We see this in the value he places on what he calls the "Negative Capability," "that is, when man is capable of being in uncertainties, Mysteries, doubts, without any irritable reaching after fact & reason. Shakespeare did this." This distances Keats from Wordsworth, whom, for all his admiration of the older poet, he nevertheless faulted for launching too quickly into the "wordsworthian or egotistical sublime."[13] What this lapidary judgment

12. See Chapter 3.

13. Susan Wolfson, *A Greeting of the Spirit: Selected Poetry of John Keats with Commentary* (Cambridge, MA: Harvard University Press, 2022), 14, 22. See n. 13. But, as Wolfson comments, Keats may have been unfair to Wordsworth, who showed some

seems to condemn is the endorsement of any picture of cosmic order, however tentative.

Rather, what the poet should (must) seek in the stressful ignorance of Negative Capability is "Soul Making." With a "sharpened vision into the heart and nature of Man," we see that "the world is full of Misery and heart-break, Pain, Sickness and Oppression."[14] This opens to a labyrinth of dark Passages. And one sees the world as vale of "Soul Making." Dogmas and Superstitions are no help.

There is a truth here, but it is not the truth *of* or *about* some independent object that the poet seeks to discover; rather, it is the truth *to* the poet's deepest potentiality. What seems to bring us farther on the road to Soul Making is contact with beauty: which puts the celebrated bidirectional equivalence of the two at the end of the "Ode on a Grecian Urn" in a new light. "Beauty is Truth and Truth Beauty . . ."

I V

The break with the past created a certain tension for Keats, because of his deep investment in "classical" models, Spenser, and even more, Shakespeare and Milton. He wanted to continue their profound explorations into the universe and the human condition, and the articulation of personal experience threatened to divert us from these into

---

awareness of the problems and uncertainties attending his sense of the cosmos, as we see in the passage of "Tintern Abbey," where he avows the fragility and momentary nature of his vision, invoking

> that blessed mood,
> In which the burden of the mystery,
> In which the heavy and the weary weight
> Of all this unintelligible world,
> Is lightened. (38–42)

William Wordsworth, "Lines Written a Few Miles above Tintern Abbey, on Revisiting the Banks of the Wye during a Tour, July 13, 1798," in *Lyrical Ballads and Other Poems, 1797–1800,* ed. James Butler and Karen Green (Ithaca, NY: Cornell University Press, 1991).

14. John Keats to J. H. Reynolds, May 3, 1818, in *Letters of John Keats* (London: Oxford University Press, 1970), 95.

"dark passages." We have no option but to explore these, but here "we are in a Mist."[15]

Once again we recognize a phenomenon which was more fully theorized in the German context. But there the dilemma was (perhaps too easily) resolved by the theory of the "spiral path" (*exzentrische Bahn*). True, modern subjectivism makes us lose something of the direct contact with Nature, while at the same time opening the path to freedom. But unity with Nature and freedom can (supposedly) be reconciled on a higher level in our day, through art (or in some cases, philosophy).

And there is a third analogy with the German scene: it is clear that Keats has his own version of the two contrasting languages, the merely instrumental one of the everyday world as against the languages of art which realize the Beauty which is Truth.

V

We have traveled a long way from the notion of a language of things in early modern Europe. Though references to this tradition are still rife among the German Romantics, Keats makes no mention of it (to my knowledge). It is not just that there are no more attributions of meaning to particular phenomena, such as: this flower refers to that planet (because it has the planet's "signature" within it); or the Kabbalistic number of the Messiah is 358; or the eagle is the dominant being in the realm of birds. The very ideas of systematic order which give all these attributions their sense seem to have disappeared. Each of Keats' "semireal" things is transmuted for itself by transfiguring art; and although they may function as Schlegelian "symbols" defining a direction of aspiration (like the nightingale), they are no longer placed in a system.

Thus the double-sided resonance between us and the cosmos loses its systematic character, which it still had with the German Romantics; partly because of their inheritance from the theories of a cosmic language; partly because of their embrace of the Romantic metaphysic, where the realization of the potential of the cosmos includes and requires a realization

15. Bate, *John Keats*, 333–334.

of our potential. This was strengthened by their relation to philosophy, particularly Schelling (who also is basic to Hegel), and more particularly in his notion of *Naturphilosophie*.

Now with Keats by contrast, the relation is with particular things, or features. The bilateral resonance now isn't grounded in a systematic view of the cosmos and our relation to it, as with Hölderlin and Novalis, or even Goethe's much looser system. Rather it is something that resides in the interspace (on the left side of the table in Chapter 2). It resides in the fact that our artistic creation or portrayal resonates with meaning for us; confers on some object intense meaning for us; or better, makes manifest in this object its meaning, like Keats' Beauty.

But the resonance is not unidirectional, because the Beauty corresponds to a Truth. It is an objective fact, at least about the interspace, that this object carries for us that meaning (it's in the upper left quadrant of the table).

This disembedding from a wider philosophical view connects to a source of great concern for Keats: questions about this intense beauty and its place in human life. This revealing / realizing the beauty of things in the concentrated-and-intensified rendering of experience, which brings about a profound connection with them, almost a fusion, was in one way his first and strongest instinct as a poet. This instinct was given full rein in one of the earlier works (although "early" has an unusual sense in a career so soon cut short), in the long poem *Endymion*. Here he seems to find the path to ultimate fulfillment through erotic love, carried to its highest point where the beloved is the goddess Diana-Cynthia. In this Love, earthly and heavenly beauty are fused. This poem, as many of Keats' richest and lushest works, is cast in the images of classical mythology.

But he came to feel that this poetry of beauty and fusion was inadequate, radically incomplete; and this in several interconnected ways. On the first, most obvious level, beauty can't swallow or wipe out suffering, change, loss, not to speak of the ultimate decay of beauty; it can't prevent even the cloying of this intense fusion through the inexorable advance of time; or guarantee the experience against being relegated by some new powerful impressions—in the way, for instance, that overwhelming good news can often wipe out chagrin over some minor setback. The poet of beauty-fusion can't just ignore this.

In addition, Keats always had sympathy with the forces of reform in his day, with the cause of liberty and equality, but he came to feel more and more strongly that in a world "full of Misery and Heartbreak, Pain, Sickness and Oppression," there is an obligation to act.[16] In the "Fall of Hyperion," the priestess Moneta tells the poet that only those can climb to the altar of prophetic knowledge

> To whom the miseries of the world
> Are misery and will not let them rest. (148–149)[17]

That is the moral issue, but there are others which we can call ethical, to do with the good life. The world which is often called a "vale of tears" must be seen, Keats thought, as a "vale of Soul Making," as we have just seen.[18] What has one to face in order to rise to this challenge? Keats was a great admirer of Shakespeare, and in particular of the climax of *King Lear*: Lear has lost everything, throne, family, love; he experiences desolation; we are quite outside the realm of beauty; and still there is something ethically admirable in his "ripeness is all." We have to confront the suffering of the world to go beyond being mere "Intelligences . . . atoms of perception," and become "Souls," who possess "the sense of identity."[19]

Ultimately, we have to come to the realization that suffering, the negative, is inextricably linked with the power to create Beauty.

Or we can come at these issues again from another angle; not so much ethical as what we could call religious. As Keats puts it: We need "a system of salvation which does not affront our reason and humanity."[20] By which he means something different from (what he understands as) the orthodox Christian revelation. But what does "salvation" mean here? Perhaps something like the highest fulfillment that human beings can

16. Sidney Colvin, *John Keats: His Life and Poetry, His Friends, Critics, and After-Fame* (London: Macmillan, 1923), 448–449. Nicholas Roe, *John Keats and the Culture of Dissent* (Oxford: Oxford University Press, 1997), makes clear how much throughout his life Keats was committed to the liberal-egalitarian stream in English politics.

17. John Keats, "The Fall of Hyperion," in *Selected Poetry*, 183.

18. Bate, *John Keats*, 482.

19. Andrew Motion, *Keats: A Biography* (London: Faber and Faber, 1997), 377–378.

20. Helen Vendler, *The Odes of John Keats* (Cambridge, MA: Harvard University Press, 1983), 63.

attain, which they might carry into immortality, if that exists. He seems to be hinting at a condition where we would no longer simply recognize the inescapability of suffering but be fully reconciled to it.

This whole range of issues was the more unavoidable for Keats because, as we saw, his most cherished models, the writers who kindled his desire to be a poet, were the great classics, especially Shakespeare and Milton, who grappled directly with these questions.

These considerations helped transform his sense of his vocation as a poet. He grew beyond the fusion of Love and Beauty in *Endymion* and attempted a richer perspective in other major works, most notably the two fragments on Hyperion. But he also tried to work out these deeper issues in his great series of odes of 1819.[21]

VI

Take the "Nightingale" ode again: I'd like to attempt a reading of this poem through the lens of the German Romantics. This is in a sense inappropriate, but it might bring out something interesting. Stanzas 2 and 5 bring us into the very heart of the respective experiences, which are brought to their Truth in Beauty.

Through creating this constellation, we connect to a deeper Truth. This truth, at least in the first instance, isn't about the universe *an sich,* but about the interspace. It is part of our ethical fulfillment as humans to relate to the world in this way—namely, that we can catch glimpses of and through that experience fully, and thus realize (at least for now) such a connection; one central to our ethical self-realization.

Of course, there must be something true of the universe *an sich,* which together with something about us, gives the connection this significance. But this is in the nature of an underlying story. Now with the poem we are at the stage of sensing the charge of this interspace.

The joy at this connection is the consequence / reflection of its ethical importance.

21. I owe a great deal to the brilliant study of the odes and their interconnections by Helen Vendler, *The Odes of John Keats* (Cambridge, MA: Harvard University Press, 1983).

Realizing this, formulating it in song, bringing this about, is "singing," in the meaning of the poem. The Nightingale is the symbol of this, as the silent night forest is of Goethe's *Ruh*.[22]

But there's the rub. We hit an ethical limit. The Nightingale is constantly, uninterruptedly, immortally—that is, undyingly—song, whereas the poet has to fall off from this pitch, and eventually die. The Nightingale is beyond the world where we know "the weariness, the fever and the fret . . . where youth grows pale and spectre-thin and dies" (stanza 3).

Singing is the poet's vocation; but he can't be fully, totally in it. She must leave the poet behind. "Away! Away!" begins stanza 4. But the only way to join her is to die. The longing to follow becomes a longing to die.

> Darkling, I listen; and, for many a time
>   I have been half in love with easeful Death,
> Call'd him soft names in many a mused rhyme,
>   To take into the air my quiet breath;
> Now more than ever seems it rich to die,
>   To cease upon the midnight with no pain,
>   While thou are pouring forth thy soul abroad
>   In such an ecstasy!
> Still wouldst thou sing, and I have ears in vain—
>   To thy high requiem become a sod.[23]

But this desire can only be ambivalent. Death also would separate me from her: "To thy high requiem become a sod." In fact, "I have been half in love with easeful Death"; that is, not totally.

So I cannot follow.

The same incompatibility can be seen from another angle, visible in the unfolding of the poem itself. The most intense realizations of beauty, stanzas 2 and 5, transfigure moments of embodied experience, which only living beings can enjoy. Transience is built into them.

22. In fact, the Nightingale as a symbol of the poet's creation resembles more what I called in Chapter 1 an "external" symbol, as the lion is of courage, for instance. But the idealized nightingale, capable of unceasing song, is what suggests the impossible feat of a poetic perpetually in the ecstasy of creation.

23. Keats, "Ode to a Nightingale," 176.

Once I recognize this limit, it seems that I can only have what communion I enjoy with the Nightingale in a trancelike condition, which seems the antechamber of death, drinking hemlock and sinking Lethe-wards (stanza 1). So that I can only coincide for the moment with the bird through a special state, trancelike, in darkness. In this darkness, I once more exercise song.

But then, I have to recognize the separation poet / bird. After stanza 6, the poet stands in a new relation to this immortal bird: one of longing and resignation. Quite outside the momentary identity, I slide from the standpoint of yearned-for identity to one of survey of the perennial human condition, from which I see the Nightingale as a transcendent presence, consoling humanity from above (stanza 7); heard by emperor and clown, and touching the heart of Ruth amid the alien corn. And charming magic casements, in faery lands forlorn.

Then this last word breaks the spell of longed-for identification. Now the bird departs in a quite everyday sense. She flies off out of earshot. I wake from my trancelike state. "Fled is that music:—Do I wake or sleep?" (stanza 8).

But why is there an aporia here? Why <u>should</u> I be able to follow the Nightingale? Because as a symbol, like Goethe's *Ruh*, she manifests my inescapable aspiration as a poet, to sing, manifesting Beauty and Truth—in short, transfiguring song. And as we saw in Chapter 5, the transfiguring art of this new age is very ontologically fragile. But it is also experientially fragile; in another mood, in another situation, I would be incapable of bringing about this epiphany. And experiential fragility underscores ontological uncertainty, in a way it didn't in an earlier epoch of established theological and cosmic orders.

But to overcome experiential fragility, I would have to freeze ordinary life; never have to stop, cope with everyday life, with illness, incapacity, the drudgery of every day. But the only way to do this would be not to live as we animals do. So already to enter into communion with this muse, I have to sink into some death-resembling torpor: It's as though I had drunk hemlock and sunk "Lethe-wards." The summer vintage of stanza 2 should enable me "to leave the world unseen, / And with thee fade away into the forest dim." But of course, that cannot be; the bird lives forever in ecstatic song. I would fly away with her and cannot.

VII

The "Ode on a Grecian Urn" gives us a similar or connected dilemma or impossibility. What is depicted on the urn is in its own way timeless, or eternal. Not the eternity of undying life, like the bird, but the time-lessness of stasis. Stanza 2: the fair youth cannot leave off song, the trees will never be bare. The boughs and the youth are "happy" in their immunity to change. But they are totally out of lived time; they cannot ever be lived.

Stanza 5: Cold Pastoral! We will grow old, but you (the Urn) won't. But you leave us a message: Beauty is truth and truth is beauty . . .[24]

The very intensity of the epiphany / contact / resonance which the Nightingale, or Grecian urn, affords means that the experience cannot survive our continued existence in a world of change, decay, passing time. One could say: the recovered unity is incompatible with lived time.

The "Nightingale" operates like one of the *via negativa* poems which I mentioned in connection with Hölderlin. In Hölderlin's case, I am thinking of the sense one has reading "Bread and Wine" that we could never establish the firm and full relation with our "gods" that the Greeks enjoyed with theirs, but that this constitutes the ideal. In rela-tion to Keats, the very power of the poetry, the singular success of the poet's "song," suggests another step higher, to unceasing "song," which cannot be taken.

But why take the impossibility of this step as a loss, as against a natural limit to human life? Perhaps because the transfiguration which poetry achieves of the "semireal," into a more intense existence, was linked in Keats' mind with eternity. The transfigured realities belong there, where we mortals cannot follow them. Unless . . . Unless there is something like survival beyond the grave. Keats seems to have envisaged this pos-sibility, although it is unclear (at least to me) whether he ever em-braced it. But it is clear why the transient vision of something eternal should suggest this further stage as a consummation devoutly to be wished.

Did Keats ever resolve the tension here between poetic creation and ordinary human life? Helen Vendler thinks he did, in his last great

24. John Keats, "Ode on a Grecian Urn," in *Selected Poetry*, 177–178.

ode, "To Autumn," and in one sense she is certainly right.[25] As I said in discussing this ode in Chapter 5, Keats makes us feel this declining season as a moment of fullness in the year, and at the same time as part of a recurring cycle ever renewing itself. He makes us see the present season not so much as part of a cosmic order, like Wordsworth and Hölderlin, but as a moment in a continuing pattern in time. And this answers our need for a nourishing contact with the natural world.

We will see in later chapters how cosmic (re)connections can come about through patterns of lived time, as well as through continuing orders.

But the reigning atmosphere of the ode "To Autumn" doesn't seem to allow of poetic experience of the same intensity that we find in the "Nightingale" ode.

VIII

The felt incompatibility between song and the transience of life that defined this earlier poem is one source of the oft-returning temptation toward annihilation that we see in other poets of this age.

The same powerful sense of incompatibility is conveyed in Shelley's lament for Keats, "Adonais," quoted above:

> Heaven's light forever shines, Earth's shadows fly;
> Life, like a dome of many-coloured glass,
> Stains the white radiance of eternity,
> Until Death tramples it to fragments—Die,
> If thou wouldst be with that which thou dost seek!

And perhaps also in Hölderlin's figure of Empedocles (as I suggested in Chapter 4). The issues of lived time, of how to make it humanly bearable, will return again in our post-Romantic era, both in the sphere of philosophical thought (Bergson, Heidegger, Benjamin) and in poetry (see Chapter 10), as will the issue of how to reconcile lived time with the aspiration to eternity (Proust can be seen as opening a way to this end).

25. John Keats, "To Autumn," in *Selected Poetry*, 212–213. See also Vendler, *Odes of John Keats*, ch. 7. "To Autumn" certainly gives us a vision of what reconciliation might feel like, but could or did the author really feel / live this reconciliation?

One is reminded of the phrase from Nietzsche: "Alle Lust will Ewigkeit" [All joy wants eternity].

IX

I think there are parallels to the themes I've been discussing here in the work of Leopardi.

He adopted a similar "two-language" theory, but it had a quite different basis (see his "To the Moon"). His version of the contrast between languages distinguishes "termini" and "parole." The former are handy terms in the language of designation-manipulation; but "parole" have a richer history of resonances; they connect us to the past. We are no longer living the naked present, as it were.

But in Leopardi, resonance is linked to an almost Dionysian loss of self. The yearning beyond life seems there. His great poem "L'infinito" ends in something approaching joy at oblivion. In fact, this poem has many features which recall Keats—in particular, the way it brings us deeper and deeper into the experience it figures.

> Sempre caro mi fu quest'ermo colle,
> E questa siepe, che da tanta parte
> Dell'ultimo orizzonte il guardo esclude.
> Ma sedendo e mirando, interminati
> Spazi di là da quella, e sovrumani
> Silenzi, e profondissima quiete
> Io nel pensier mi fingo, ove per poco
> Il cor non si spaura. E come il vento
> Odo stormir tra queste piante, io quello
> Infinito silenzio e questa voce
> Vo comparando: e mi sovvien l'eterno,
> E le morte stagioni, et la presente
> E viva, e il suon di lei. Cosi tra questa
> Immensità s'annega il pensier mio:
> E il naufragar m'è dolce in questo mare.[26]

26. Giacomo Leopardi, "L'infinto," in *Versi del Conto Giacomo Leopardi* (Bologna: Stamperia delle Muse, 1826), 7.

[I've always loved this lonesome hill
And this hedge that hides
The entire horizon, almost from sight.
But sitting here in a daydream I picture
The boundless spaces away out there, silences
Deeper than human silence, an infathomable hush
In which my heart is hardly a beat
From fear. And hearing the wind
Rush rustling through these bushes,
I pit its speech against infinite silence–
And a notion of eternity floats to mind,
And the dead seasons, and the season
Beating here and now, and the sound of it. So
In this immensity my thoughts all drown.][27]

X

Before passing on to the rather different concerns of Baudelaire, I would like to return briefly to a distinction I invoked again at the beginning of this chapter (see also Chapter 2, Section II.1), between two forms of our resonant connection with nature. One, exemplified by Goethe's invocation of *Ruh*, finds in Nature or the cosmos an epiphanic symbol which allows us to sense, become aware of an important human meaning—in this case, something we long for or strive after. But the experience in the mountain forest doesn't actually deliver what we long for.

In the second, exemplified by Hölderlin, and Wordsworth, the revelation of our longing for connection partly realizes or restores this connection.

We can see the interplay between these two facets running through the foregoing discussion of English poets. What also emerged, in Chapter 2, and in a number of (perhaps too cursory) side references, was a partial analogy to music in the Romantic period. The analogy is clearer

---

27. Giacomo Leopardi, "L'infinto," in *Selected Poems,* trans. Eamon Grennan (Princeton, NJ: Princeton University Press, 1997), 3.

when it comes to the second form, and the example I would cite here is Beethoven's *Pastoral* Symphony. Clearly, part of what underlay its creation was a longing for connection. The first movement, both the music and the title Beethoven gave it (as well as the composer's remarks to friends at the time), show his sense that this recovered presence in the countryside gives us something we need / crave, a kind of *ressourcement* [healing, revitalization].[28] The symphony, perhaps particularly the slow movement, here makes us sense / feel the meaning, in this case the hunger / need being filled. In terms of the major question posed in Chapter 5, what to make of this kind of need / craving, in which "quadrant" to place it, and the two approaches proposed for dealing with it, this symphony should be put alongside our behavior in seeking the countryside, as offering a key to its explanation.

This distinction between the two forms of resonance seems clear enough. But now, what about Keats' "Nightingale" poem? The Nightingale herself does something like the mountain forest for Goethe: she fixes, she is a symbol for ecstatic artistic creation. But much of the poem operates more like the *Pastoral:* stanzas 2 and 5 give us intense images of how our world, cultural (draught of vintage) and natural (murmurous haunt of flies), feeds us, spiritually, and therefore intensifies this feeding. The Ruth stanza puts us into the kind of eternity where we survey before us the whole passage of time (close to the Platonic stasis eternity of the urn). Other stanzas introduce us into the bower / dream / near-sleep, which is the antechamber to these experiences.

The great ode "To Autumn" also shows the parallel to the *Pastoral.* The disanalogy comes to light when we consider other great Beethoven symphonies, for instance the Fifth and the Ninth. Here profound human meanings are opened and articulated for us. But the epiphanic symbol resides here much more in the work itself, without clear, focused reference to Nature or the Cosmos (although cosmic forces are invoked in the first and second movements of the Ninth). But of course, before the Romantic period, and since, much poetry functioned as symbol in this way as well.

28. See Lewis Lockwood, *Beethoven's Symphonies: An Artistic Vision* (New York: Norton, 2015), 121–124. Translated by Thom K. Sliwowski.

PART III

Chapter Seven

HOPKINS, INSCAPE AND AFTER

I

Gerard Manley Hopkins extends the scope of Romantic poetry, as I've been describing it, by developing a new mode or form of—or perhaps a new route to—(re)connection. This is to capture and present to us the inner force which shapes a given particular being, which Hopkins describes as its "inscape" (see Chapter 3, Section II).

For this, he uses the full range of fused, multilevel poetry that we saw in Chapter 2, Section II.3: incorporating the "music" of speech or sound, the "music" of thoughts or images, and the assertions made. But the special feature of Hopkins' writing is that he renders the rhythms of the being itself through the "sprung rhythm" of the verse.

Sprung rhythm takes up the stress and intonation of human speech, as moved by the target being; it captures its inner rhythm by matching it; but at the same time it keeps to the meter and repeating periods of the chosen verse form. The contrapuntal marriage of these two is what constitutes a Hopkins poem in sprung rhythm. These two facets are essential: the first to capture the inscape of the target being, the second to raise it to the heightened language of poetry with the intensity of feeling it releases.[1]

> I caught this morning morning's minion, kingdom
>> of daylight's dauphin, dapple-dawn-drawn falcon, in his riding
>> Of the rolling level underneath him steady air, and striding
> High there, how he wrung upon the rein of a wimpling wing
> In his ecstasy!, then off, off forth on swing,
>> As a skate's heel sweeps smooth on a bow-bend; the hurl and
>> gliding
>> Rebuffed the big wind. My heart in hiding
> Stirred for a bird—the achieve of, the mastery of the thing![2]

The Windhover (a local name for a kestrel) is introduced as the "dauphin" (as it were, crown prince) of the kingdom of the morning, drawn forth by the dappled dawn, and then riding high, alternating hovering and swooping, in spite of the shifts of wind. It rides these like a skilled chevalier rides a powerful horse: "the hurl and gliding / Rebuffed the big wind." You can feel the inner power of this bird.

Hopkins has a philosophical account of what an inscape is, and it is very much an underlying story. It is a very old, traditional account, drawn from ancient and medieval philosophy. In medieval terms, Hopkins is a passionate "realist"; he believes that things are as they are because they are shaped to conform to their Idea or Form. If this Platonic-Aristotelian doctrine is true then the distinctions we mark in our language are really there in reality—hence "realism." The rival view held that the distinctions we mark depend on the names we give things: hence "nominalism"; on this latter view, we are ultimately unconstrained by allegedly "essential" differences.

But Hopkins went beyond standard medieval realism. Besides the shaping force of the general Form, each particular thing has its own force

---

1. See James I. Wimsatt, *Hopkins's Poetics of Speech Sound: Sprung Rhythm, Lettering, Inscape* (Toronto: University of Toronto Press, 2006), ch. 1.

2. Gerard Manley Hopkins, "The Windhover," in *The Poems of Gerard Manley Hopkins* (New York: Oxford University Press, 1956), 73.

which maintains it in its "thisness" (*haecceitas*). This was the doctrine of the Oxford scholar John Duns Scotus, who inspired Hopkins. What the "Windhover" poem captures is the driving inscape of *this* falcon.

So this leads us back to a very traditional underlying story; but what makes a Hopkins poem undeniably "post-Romantic" is that we got there not through scholastic argument but through a poem which makes us *feel* the inscape of the bird, respond to its constitutive inner rhythm. We are reconnecting with a medieval doctrine, with ancient roots, via a <u>felt</u> connection, that the poetry brings about in us.

Now the underlying story that Hopkins recurs to is not only philosophical; he is also an orthodox Christian, a Catholic. The sonnet "As kingfishers catch fire" starts as an emphatic statement of the "thisness" of each being in its octave,

> As kingfishers catch fire, dragonflies draw flame;
> > As tumbled over rim in roundy wells
> > Stones ring; like each tucked string tells, each hung bell's
> Bow swung finds tongue to fling out broad its name;
> Each mortal thing does one thing and the same:
> > Deals out that being indoors each one dwells;
> > Selves—goes itself; *myself* it speaks and spells,
> Crying *What I do is me; for that I came.*

And then he turns in the sestet to what he sees as the underlying theological reality underpinning these:

> I say more: the just man justices;
> > Keeps grace: that keeps all his goings graces;
> Acts in God's eye what in God's eye he is—
> > Christ. For Christ plays in ten thousand places,
> Lovely in limbs, and lovely in eyes not his
> > To the Father through the features of men's faces.[3]

---

3. Gerard Manley Hopkins, "As kingfishers catch fire," in *Gerard Manley Hopkins* (New York: Oxford University Press, 1986), 129.

II

What Hopkins celebrates in the inscapes of things is ultimately God's creative power. But there are disturbing dimensions to this. Sometimes this
power is presented as peaceful and benign, as in "Pied Beauty"; "Glory
be to God for dappled things." But the Nature that issues from the hands
of God can also be violent and destructive; and is portrayed as such in
"The Wreck of the *Deutschland*."

The *Deutschland* was a German ship sailing with emigrants from
Bremen to America. Among these were some Catholic nuns fleeing from
the persecutions of Bismarck's anti-Catholic Kulturkampf. It was caught
in a violent storm and came to grief in the Thames estuary on December 7,
1875, with many lives lost, including those of the emigrating nuns.

Such events are inevitable, and life must come to an end (stanza 11).
Hopkins sees this end in the light of Christ's Passion, his self-giving for
the salvation of the world. And what he singles out in this story of the
wreck is the stance and words of one of the nuns:

> She to the black-about air, to the breaker, the thickly
> Falling flakes, to the throng that catches and quails
>   Was calling "O Christ, Christ, come quickly".
> The cross to her she calls Christ to her, christens her wild-worst
>   Best. (Stanza 24)[4]

The nun seeks in her death to become part of Christ's saving death. She
wants to give it, and not simply undergo it. The poem as a whole sets this
self-giving alongside Hopkins' own radical decision to take up his Jesuit
vocation.

> The frown of his face
> Before me, the hurtle of hell
> Behind, where, where was a, where was a place?
>   I whirled out wings that spell
> And fled with a fling of the heart to the heart of the Host.
> My heart, but you were dove-winged, I can tell,

---

4. Gerard Manley Hopkins, "The Wreck of the *Deutschland*," in *Poems*, 63.

> Carrier-witted, I am bold to boast,
>   To flash from the flame to the flame then, tower from the grace
>   to the grace. (Stanza 3)[5]

God creates a world whose vocation is to be saved by Christ, each creature in its own way, after its own fashion.

Hopkins' novel and frame-breaking poetry, building on the Romantics, became a path back to the original faith which he saw England first, and then the modern world, as having deserted.

III

But it is not just that the poetry leads us back to the theology. It also leads to the struggles against the loss and distance which the fallen world imposes on us in our search for faith. The analogy between Romantic poetry and the striving of the "mystics," mentioned in Chapter 2, Section II.1, approaches fusion here.

To return to my discussion in Chapter 3, Hopkins' invocation of the inscapes in things enables him to live in a wider frame, along with the kestrel, kingfishers catching fire, and each mortal thing. But this wider space for him was fundamentally that of God's grace, moving to redeem the world. And this involves, even demands such a radical transformation of human life, desire, aspiration, that we cannot live in it without an insistent sense of how greatly we fall short.

There are bound to be moments of distance, self-division, even despair.

We are led in Hopkins' case to the "dark sonnets" of his Dublin years. Any faith in far-reaching transformation is bound to encounter moments of lost intensity, when fatigue sets in, the vision weakens, and the banal facets of everyday life occlude it. Moreover, a far-reaching faith strives for deepening of the vision, which is often only possible at the cost of confusion, a loss of orientation, as the shallower insights are shed. But in Hopkins' case, his vulnerability to such moments of loss

5. Hopkins, "Wreck of the *Deutschland*," 56.

and confusion was the greater because he was exploring the new avenue
toward faith—alongside theology, philosophy, and traditional forms
of devotion—which post-Romantic poetics had opened for him.

In the "dark sonnets," Hopkins struggles with this distance and loss,
and an almost overwhelming sense of abandonment; resisting it:

> Not, I'll not, carrion comfort, Despair, not feast on thee;
> Not untwist—slack they may be—these last strands of man
> In me or, most weary, cry *I can no more* . . .

Or exploring it:

> I wake and feel the fell of dark, not day.
> What hours, O what black hours we have spent
> This night! What sight you, heart, saw: ways you went!
> And more must, in yet longer light's delay.
>   With witness I speak this. But where I say
> Hours I mean years, mean life. And my lament
> Is cries countless, cries like dead letters sent
> To dearest him that lives alas! Away

> I am gall, I am heartburn. God's most deep decree
> Bitter would have me taste; my taste was me;
> Bones built in me, flesh filled, blood brimmed the curse.
>   Selfyeast of spirit a dull dough sours. I see
> The lost are like this, and their scourge to be
> As I am mine, their sweating selves; but worse.

And then at moments breaking through:

> Man, how fast his firedint, / his mark on mind, is gone
> Both are in an unfathomable, / all is in an enormous dark
> Drowned. O pity and indig / nation! Manshape, that shone
> Sheer off, disseveral, a star, / death blots black out; nor mark
>   Is any of him at all so stark
> But vastness blurs and time / beats level. Enough! The Resurrection,
> A heart's clarion! Away grief's gasping, / joyless days, dejection.
>   Across my foundering deck shone

A beacon, an eternal beam. / Flesh fade, and mortal trash
Fall to the residuary worm; / world's wildfire, leave but ash:
  In a flash, at a trumpet crash,
I am all at once what Christ is, / since he was what I am, and
This Jack, Joke, poor potsherd, / patch, matchwood, immortal
  diamond,
  Is immortal diamond.[6]

The analogy with those whom the Renaissance called "mystics" stands out: for instance, with St. John of the Cross, and "la noche oscura del alma."[7]

IV

What I want to explore further here is why Hopkins' opening up and articulation of an inscape, like that of the Windhover, can release a joy in the reader / hearer. This will help cast light on the question, implicit in Chapter 1, how any kind of (re)connection with Nature, or the cosmos, can matter so much to us. But here I want to narrow my examination to the Hopkins inscape.

The human being is a rational animal: this involves a mind which can map reality, but much else besides. The (episodically) conscious human being also senses, perceives, experiences pain / pleasure, is happy / sad, lives through moods, feels sympathy / antipathy, feels at home or alienated.

We need a concept here like Maurice Merleau-Ponty's *chair* [flesh], which can play two roles: both an object of experience (as I examine, say, a wound in my foot) and also that through which we experience objects (my hand as I explore the wound).

What I'm calling "mapping" is concerned with describing correctly. Describing involves a mode of (mostly linguistic) expression. It is concerned with grasping certain bounded and reliable nuggets of information; and

6. Gerard Manley Hopkins, "That Nature Is a Heraclitean Fire and of the Comfort of the Resurrection," in *Poems*, 105.

7. See Michel de Certeau, *La Fable Mystique: XVIe–XVIIe Siècle* (Paris: Gallimard, 1982).

also with assembling them in a bigger picture. But there are other facets of the total relation of flesh to world. These are shaped by, and can be captured in, a range of other expressions, which include but also go beyond the linguistic.

Thus when we want to understand what it is actually to be there (*Dasein*, in Heidegger's term), in the world, encountering things—moreover, as whole beings, who also feel, sense, are moved on many levels—we can see that much more is involved than mapping.

To describe reality, we extract information; by "information" I mean what we can capture in propositions, where we attribute some property to some referent object. Information is what can be taken away from the encounter, the "takeaway" message.

Western epistemology has tended to sideline much of what happens in our encounter with things to concentrate on the "takeaway" message, whether this is expressed in terms of "aesthesis" (Aristotle), "ideas" (Descartes and Locke), "impression" (Hume), "intuition" (*Anschauung*, Kant), or "sense data" (logical empiricists).

Much of modern Western philosophy in the epistemological tradition, which starts from Descartes, has been exclusively concerned with how we take in information, to the point where the encounter of agent and world has been conceived exclusively as a process of such taking-in. The Cartesian-Lockean "idea" is seen as an element of information which strikes the senses and is recorded; almost as though the mind were a camera, which can carry away copies of the external world. Hume's main word for the elements of experience, "impressions," derives from the same picture. Mind meets world and interiorizes copies of it. The two meet, and the boundary between them is where this taking-in happens.

This simplified view of the encounter survives the demise of Cartesian dualism, and the sidelining of immaterial mind. The mechanistic successors of Cartesianism perpetuate the same basic error. Now the mind is seen in mechanistic terms, very often identified with the brain, and frequently understood as operating like a computer. The "input" to this machine is taken from the external world, and then processed. Mind meets world, as a calculating machine taking in bits of information from a material world, also understood mechanistically.

The basic Cartesian ontology, that there are two kinds of being (substance), immaterial minds and material beings, is modified by suppressing the first kind, and replacing it with another class of material beings, capable of computation. Apart from this, much carries over from the earlier mind-affirming theory to the later materialist one.[8]

What both these construals have in common is that they make no place for the kind of living, experiencing beings that we are. This is what Merleau-Ponty articulated very forcefully in his later work, with the concept of *chair* [flesh].[9] The flesh-and-blood human being is what makes the Cartesian scenario impossible, of a pure mind meeting and taking in features of the material world. The human agent is neither, or if one likes, both. It is an object in the world, but also an agent of experience.

The human being perceives and takes in the world, but she is also part of the world which she comes to grasp. Moreover, her ability to grasp things takes continuous account of her own action. She wants to examine some scene or object more closely, and so she moves so as to get a clear "take" on it. Her continuing, ever-renewed orientation in space is an essential capacity underlying her perception.

The human agent is why there is no clear boundary between pure mind and pure matter; or in mechanistic terms, between inert objects and those which compute. The computing machine is "in" its surroundings; the human agent "inhabits" its world. This is the sense of Merleau-Ponty's *chair*.[10]

But the actual, "fleshly" encounter of agent and world involves more; we meet a particular object in a particular situation, and it impinges on us, or resonates in us, or makes an impression on us, in a certain way. This encounter may be the occasion of our extracting information in the above sense. But this is not because it simply and invariably *consists* in this. Its serving this purpose requires that it be *used* in this way,

8. See Hubert L. Dreyfus, *What Computers Can't Do* (New York: Harper and Row, 1972); and Hubert Dreyfus and Charles Taylor, *Retrieving Realism* (Cambridge, MA: Harvard University Press, 2015).

9. See Maurice Merleau-Ponty, *Le Visible et l'Invisible* (Paris: Gallimard, 1964); and Maurice Merleau-Ponty, *L'Œil et l'Esprit* (Paris: Gallimard, 1964).

10. Merleau-Ponty, *L'Œil et l'Esprit*, 9.

approached with this end in view. We do this by ignoring much of the experience (the buzzing of the flies on the window, the sunlight on the lawn outside); and zeroing in on what we want to know, measuring what is relevant, noting the signs of what we want to establish, asking the relevant questions, and so on.

In short, taking in information is not coterminous with experience; it is one of the things we do, the ways we stand toward and treat experience.

Moreover, it has been a crucial human goal since the very outset. Our ancestors, who examined the ground to see when the deer had passed and in what direction, engaged in it; and it has become all the more prestigious with the growth of civilization and the set of activities we call "science." But however important, it is just one of the things we do; it is the product of one possible stance to the world, among others.

Not seeing this is the crucial founding error of the epistemological tradition descending from Descartes. Various features of our developing modern culture have favored this. Besides the growth and increasing importance of science, the development of linear perspective in Renaissance art may also have contributed to this one-sided take on "experience."[11]

And then there is the primacy of the eye, of the theoretical stance (θεωρειν) since the Greeks which has also fed this hegemony of mapping, and this has intensified since the early modern period, what Heidegger calls "the Age of the World Picture."[12] The supposed advantage (undoubted advantage for mapping) of this stance is that information becomes "disentrammeled from our turbid selves."[13] Vision can put things at a distance. Seeing a whole landscape can give us a sense of dominance, of holding at a distance, can still or sideline our reactions of resonance.

One of the interesting and challenging aspects of Merleau-Ponty's *L'Œil et l'Esprit* is that he uses precisely this modality of vision to show

11. See William Poteat, "Paul Cézanne and the Numinous Power of the Real," in *Recovering the Personal: The Philosophical Anthropology of William H. Poteat*, ed. Dale W. Cannon and Ronald L. Hall (Lanham, MD: Lexington, 2016), 276.

12. Martin Heidegger, "Die Zeit des Weltbildes," in *Holzwege* (Frankfurt am Main: Klostermann, 1972).

13. Poteat, "Paul Cézanne," 277.

how the epistemological polarity mind / world is indefensible even here. One of the examples he uses in this work, which reflects where and when it was written, in the last autumn of his life, in the South of France, Cézanne country, is this:

> Quand je vois à travers l'épaisseur de l'eau le carrelage au fond de la piscine, je ne le vois pas malgré l'eau, les reflets, je le vois justement à travers eux, par eux. S'il n'y avait pas ces distortions, ces zébrures du soleil, si je voyais sans cette chair la géométrie du carrelage, c'est alors que je cesserais de le voir comme il est, où il est, savoir plus loin que tout lieu identique. L'eau elle-même, la puissance aqueuse, l'élément sirupeux et miroitant, je ne peux pas dire qu'elle soit *dans* l'espace: elle n'est pas ailleurs, mais elle n'est pas dans la piscine. Elle l'habite, elle s'y matérialise, elle n'y est pas contenue.[14]

> [When through the water's thickness I see the tiling at the bottom of a pool, I do not see it *despite* the water and the reflections there; I see it through them and because of them. If there were no distortion, no ripples of sunlight, if it were without this flesh that I saw the geometry of the tiles, then I would cease to see it *as* it is and where it is—which is to say, beyond any identical, specific place. I cannot say that the water itself—the aqueous power, the syrupy and shimmering element—is *in* space; all this is not somewhere else either, but it is not in the pool. It inhabits it, it materializes itself there, yet it is not contained there.][15]

One could use, interrogate this experience, through examination and measurement, and discover that such and such a volume of water is to be found in a pool of such and such dimensions; to extract, in other words, clear, bounded, reliable information. But the experience itself is far from being "of" bounded objects in the objective relation of container / contained. In the experience itself, the things are not clearly separated; the water "inhabits" the pool, "materializes itself there," but

14. Merleau-Ponty, *L'Œil et l'Esprit,* 70–71.

15. Maurice Merleau-Ponty, "Eye and Mind," in *The Primacy of Perception and Other Essays on Phenomenological Psychology, the Philosophy of Art, History and Politics* (Evanston, IL: Northwestern Un3iversity Press, 1964), 182.

each of these elements speaks of the other, refers to the other, can't be neatly separated from it.

This interlacing or mutual reference is what Merleau-Ponty wants to bring out, because his subject here is painting, Cézanne; and "c'est cette animation interne, ce rayonnement du visible que le peintre cherche sous les noms de profondeur, d'espace, de couleur" [this internal animation, this radiation of the visible is what the painter seeks under the name of depth, of space, of color].[16]

So the focus on information casts much of what happens in our actual experience into darkness. We rush by it, in our thrust to acquire and use information.

This falsifies the total encounter of world with embodied intelligence. Much of this can't be said, but "shows itself," to use Wittgenstein's expression.

Once we cast off the distorting Cartesian spectacles, we can become aware of the host of ways in which an object hits us, affects us, works on us. This oak for instance, which stands in the nearby wood, which I am now entering: it overshadows me, looms over me, its unmistakably shaped leaves strike me, even thrill me; its symbolism in history, Druidism, resonates somewhere in me; the color of the leaves arouses something in me. The oak also bespeaks a vast stretch of time, behind and ahead. And so on.

We can think of all this as extra "information"; this time "subjective," the way we respond or react or feel before the object. All information would be neatly sorted into objective (about the object), or "subjective" (about us and our reactions). But this sharp dualist divide is not true to experience, to what it is to live in the world. Through the way we live / experience the object, we also contact something in it, as well as in ourselves. The truths I enumerate in the previous paragraphs are truths about the "interspace": not truths about the "world" only, beyond us, nor truths about ourselves, in abstraction from the world we perceive and experience. True, we can abstract facts merely about us: "I feel good when I stand under an oak." But as we live these contacts, they reveal things about the object as well; only not things about the object as it is in itself—though the standard units of information are often framed as

16. Merleau-Ponty, *L'Œil et l'Esprit*, 71; Merleau-Ponty, "Eye and Mind," 182.

"objective." Rather, interspatial realities reveal the object as it comes across to us, as we live it, as it reverberates in us, and so on.

Exploring the interface: how the tree strikes us, looms before us, its colors reverberate in us; how it culturally evokes something for us; the fears and awe it may inspire, partly from its overweaning presence, partly from its reminiscence of barbaric cultural practices (human sacrifice; even more, think of the powerful effect on European artists of African masks). All these offer ways of penetrating into the object, plumbing its depths. Not the depths as they "objectively" are, *an sich,* as it were; but the depths as they are sensed as connected, as opening to us.

Sometimes artists betray this kind of revelation in their descriptions of what they are doing. Mallarmé: "Peindre non la chose, mais l'effet qu'elle produit" [To paint not the thing, but the effect it produces]. This sounds like: turn inward and see how it makes you feel. But in reality he is doing something much deeper (see Chapter 12).

The "intentional objects" of this kind of take are features of the en-counter with the object, even though we may be aware that their accu-racy is not guaranteed in the way that "objective" research (much less science) prescribes.

Poetry goes beyond epistemically driven prose, generated by the information-extracting stance. Some poetry concentrates on and artic-ulates how we feel before a certain scene. This is perennial; it goes back far, to well before the Romantic era.

Take Gray's "Elegy Written in a Country Churchyard," whose opening lines,

> The curfew tolls the knell of parting day,
>   The lowing herd wind slowly o'er the lea
> The plowman homeward plods his weary way,
>   And leaves the world to darkness and to me.
> Now fades the glimmering landscape on the sight,
>   And all the air a solemn stillness holds,
> Save where the beetle wheels his droning flight,
>   And drowsy tinklings lull the distant folds;[17]

---

17. Thomas Gray, "Elegy Written in a Country Churchyard," in *Thomas Gray's Selected Poems* (New York: Harper and Brothers, 1876), 25–26.

create the crepuscular atmosphere that his reflections on life, death, and remembrance call for.

And much poetry since the Romantic period does something not too different. Some of Rilke's poetry can illustrate this; all the better, because there are no general reflections on life, of the kind Gray offers. Rilke doesn't communicate his response in any other way except by the detail he picks out. There is no "commentary." For instance, "Herbsttag":

> Herr: es is Zeit. Der Sommer war sehr groß.
> Leg deinen Schatten auf die Sonnenuhren,
> und auf den Fluren laß die Winde los.

> Befiehl den letzten Früchten voll zu sein;
> gib ihnen noch zwei südlichere Tage,
> dränge sie zur Vollendung hin und jage
> die letzte Süße in den schweren Wein.

> Wer jetzt kein Haus hat, baut sich keiner mehr.
> Wer jetzt allein ist, wird es lange bleiben,
> wird wachen, lesen, lange Briefe schreiben
> und wird in den Alleen hin und her
> unruhig wandern, wenn die Blätter treiben.[18]

> [Lord, it is time. Our summer was superb.
> Lay your shadows on the sundials,
> And in the meadows let winds go free.

> Command the last fruits to be full;
> Give them only two more southern days,
> urge them on to completion and chase
> the last sweetness into the heavy wine.

18. Rainer Maria Rilke, "Herbsttag," in *Sämtliche Werke* (Frankfurt am Main: Insel Verlag, 1962), 1:398.

Whoever has no house will never build one now.
Whoever is alone will long remain so,
Will stay awake, read books, write long letters
And wander restless back and forth
Along the tree-lined streets, as the leaves drift down.][19]

These lines create, make palpable a certain feeling. A season is over, the summer which was full of a sense of joy in things. This is gone, and there is a certain apprehension of loss, deprivation. But this mingles with the background, implicit awareness that this is a regular occurrence, part of the yin and yang of life; so there is a soothing feeling around the recognition of this change / loss. This is part of the order of things; the heart also rejoices at its familiarity. The experience is bittersweet; it is happy / sad. It is comforting in its being the way things are.

These poems, one pre-, one post-Romantic, both draw on the penumbra of experience which surrounds whatever information one might be taking in on this autumn day. The role of this penumbra is a constant in the poetry of any age.

These examples might suggest a view of the relation of science and poetry, in terms of two different stances we can take to the world: on one hand, the stance of information extraction, which culminates in science; on the other, a stance in which we articulate our feelings in response to this world, which can easily continue into and merge with emotion-tinged reflections on human life and fate.

But the stance we find in much post-Romantic poetry is distinct from either of these. It is concerned with something different, more, in this manifold surrounding experience.

Hopkins' capture of the inscape is a case in point. Poetry goes beyond creating a mood, an atmosphere of feeling, and claims to give access to the inner force in a thing, not by describing it, but by making it palpable. Poetry enters a new terrain.

It is clear that this involves a break with the primacy of mapping. Articulating the inscape of the windhover is not capturing a "takeaway" message. It is articulating the way the rhythm of that being resonates in

19. Rainer Maria Rilke, "Autumn Day," in *The Poetry of Rilke,* trans. Edward Snow (New York: North Point, 2009), 83.

us. It can't be detached from this experience. It can only be communicated to us as something we feel, and/or could feel more intensely were we to see the bird up there riding on the wind. The transaction with nature can't be "normalized" into the standard information-gathering form.

But the "feeling" involved here is not the subjective reaction called up in us by the scene. It is feeling as a mode of perception, in this case, of the "inscape."

We can see why the encounter with the falcon, though it can be accounted for philosophically in general terms (medieval "realism," in Scotus' version), is in itself an encounter with an individual, in its "thisness"; why the philosophical realist explanation must be in his version, invoking *haecceitas*.

We can gesture toward this particularity with the aid of a concept of twentieth-century analytic philosophy: "knowledge by acquaintance," as against "knowledge by description"; or we can invoke languages where the distinction is still in ordinary vocabulary, and say that this is a matter of *connaître*, or *kennen*, rather than of *savoir*, or *wissen*.

And we will see others who try to explore the depths of the object (or the world) through articulating the "interspace" (from Rilke, Rodin, Cézanne).

But just as the Cartesian agent seeking information doesn't define the nature of the contact of mind and world, and this seeking doesn't even occur in many such encounters, so Hopkins' articulation of the inscape isn't an invariant feature of all encounters—far from it. The Cartesian lives his experience of the surrounding world through one purpose; Hopkins lives his through another. But the parallel between the two straddles big differences in the nature of the experience. The Cartesian has to exercise strict control to extract his "clear and distinct" units of information; he holds the experience at a distance, as it were. Hopkins has to let the full, multifaceted encounter happen, to let it wash over him, to allow the inscape insight to emerge.

But does this help explain the joy we experience at the articulation of inscape, which was our original question? Perhaps.

Is it the joy at uncovering the hidden underpinnings of our acquisition of knowledge (information), which are buried in our everyday practical consciousness?

Answer (1): Aristotle says humans desire to know. There is a great satisfaction for us in knowing, even (useless) knowledge. So why shouldn't there be greater satisfaction in uncovering the hidden basement, the lost underpinnings of this crucial capacity? Is it strange that we rejoice in it?

This answer brings us close to the satisfaction we have when these underpinnings are recovered by philosophy—for example, phenomenology (Heidegger brings *Dichten* and *Denken* [poetizing and thinking] close together).

I noted in Chapter 1, and at other points in this study, how post-Romantic poetry is a response to modern, particularly post-Enlightenment, disenchantment, in a broad sense. This broad sense covers more than the removal of magic forces and powers from the world (the original etymological sense of *Entzauberung*); it also can extend to a picture of the universe as the realm of mechanical causation, without intrinsic human meaning. Much of this poetry, and art in general, can be seen as an attempt to "reenchant" the cosmos.

But our discussion of post-Cartesian epistemology uncovers another deep source of dissatisfaction, not now concerning the world, but rather ourselves. Are we just minds, or computing mechanisms, taking in information? Are we not also incarnate beings, beings of "flesh" in Merleau-Ponty's sense? "Immersed" in our world, "dwelling" in it? Is the Cartesian-or-mechanist picture not a desiccated, etiolated view of what we are?

These two causes of discontent, a flattened world and an etiolated agent, are obviously closely related intellectually and spiritually, but we can distinguish two dimensions of dissatisfaction which they engender. If we focus on the second dimension, on ourselves, we can perhaps understand how a description of what it is to live as an incarnate agent can unleash a satisfaction, even a joy, akin to other ways in which a misrecognized identity can flourish once it gains an adequate articulation.

Seen in this perspective we can attribute the joy we feel in hearing, reading, seeing some contemporary art, and also in coming across certain philosophical articulations (such as those of Merleau-Ponty), to our sense of liberation at the recovery of our identities as incarnate knowers.

Answer (2): there is some great satisfaction at coming back into communion, resonance with the universe / cosmos. So inscapes are analogous to the kinds of reconnections which Hölderlin and Wordsworth bring to light and bring about.

Here we are looking at the first dimension of dissatisfaction, our response to a flattened world.

Are these answers combinable? Are they facets of the same answer?

V

Perhaps we can approach this question from another angle.

"Mapping," as I said above, is concerned with describing correctly. Describing involves a mode of (mostly linguistic) expression. But there are other facets of the total relation of flesh to world. These are shaped by, and can be captured in, a range of other expressions, which go beyond the linguistic.

For instance, early societies often expressed / defined their relationship to the cosmos (including spirits / gods) in ritual; this could be collective dance and music.

The whole predicament, which ritual reacts to while projecting an interpretation onto it, may also be made sense of in descriptions; these may also later be seen as proto-attempts at what becomes science. "Myth" is what we call them now.[20]

Here—in both of these media—we see the constitutive dimension of language (in the widest sense) at work.[21] But this power of language / expression to define our situation was not seen as arbitrary, as just invented / made; it was experienced as correct, as called for.

The sense that we have to get and set things right is still with us, but it now tends to be distinguished between different dimensions—for ex-

---

20. I have drawn here on the very illuminating work of Merlin Donald. See Merlin Donald, *Origin of the Modern Mind: Three Stages in the Evolution of Culture and Cognition* (Cambridge, MA: Harvard University Press, 1993); and Merlin Donald, *A Mind So Rare: The Evolution of Human Consciousness* (New York: Norton, 2002).

21. I am invoking here my thesis in *The Language Animal* that spoken / written language cannot be properly understood if we dissociate it from other human expressive activities, or symbolic forms.

ample, the aesthetic versus the moral or religious. These, of course, can be related, as in the Platonic doctrine that the Good, the True, and the Beautiful coincide. Classical poetry makes manifest the true, and also good, cosmic order, in such a way as to move and inspire us.

Romantic art has loosened the connection to cosmic claims, in the sense of my "underlying stories." But it explores our relations to the cosmos, through constitutive expression which carries conviction with it. This expression, and the relation it constitutively establishes, is seen as correct. The true and the beautiful once more coincide. This expression and the relation it establishes realize a crucial human potential.

This is a "true" (essential) potential of the interspace. This is made so in virtue of how things are in the cosmos and us, but we can be uncertain about this while putting faith in what is revealed about the interspace. Or we can consider all this as pleasing illusion; that option is also open.

There are biological flows between us and the (time-space) cosmos; but there are also metabiological flows. Art reveals some of these latter; on the face of it, they claim to be as "real" in their way as the biological are in their own fashion.

For instance, metabiological reality is about what really constitutes human flourishing, as against what only seems to be such flourishing.

And in fact, Romanticism was not the source of the dissociation of the three "transcendentals," the True, the Good and the Beautiful, which was a central dogma of Western civilization before the modern period (and for many people, also after). The Romantics were rather reacting to a deeper split which arises out of certain facets of the Enlightenment. Those trends which made modern mechanistic science, stemming from Galileo, the road to knowledge, threatened to dislodge first the beautiful (now understood as the "aesthetic"), and later even the morally good from their high normative status, and relegate them to the subjective reactions of individuals. From this relegation, normativity could be saved either by counting (what's morally good is what fulfills the greatest number of people's desires), or through a priori reason (only universal maxims can be acted on).

A main line of Romantic thinking was concerned rather with restoring the link between the three, admittedly on a more fragile basis.

To take a different and anti-Romantic stance to the dissociation of the three, we might look at Flaubert.

In describing the limited, stupid, and illusion-drenched world (for instance, in *Madame Bovary*), he claims truth, and also "beauty" (for his portrayal, not the reality); but most emphatically not goodness. We can understand the claim to truth, but whence that to beauty? Platonically, we can understand the claim to the Good, if the portrayal made the true human potential shine through the failed life of the protagonist. But his message seems to be that the person couldn't do better; she is insensitive to real beauty, the beauty in her portrayal. Indeed, beauty can't be in this way of living, only in the (disengaged) portrayal.

So where is the beauty? In the art with which the situation is rendered. We can take, for instance, the famous scene where her lover seduces her, and their conversation runs in parallel to the public function outside. What is remarkable here is the way in which the real nature of the relationship is revealed indirectly in this juxtaposition, contrasting with the blindness of the protagonist. The real, illusion-filled relation to her world and human potential is rendered in this—poetic juxtaposition of images. This is the beauty in the novel.

And it is true that there is genuine art in the fashioning of this portrayal. But why beauty? I think we might explain the experience underlying this claim through the power of art to present what we usually experience as a disturbing, distressing, even frightening reality as an independent order we can contemplate unperturbed; rather like the Aristotelian concept of tragedy, where the frightening and distressing destruction of the flawed hero can be presented purged of (overwhelming) pity and fear, presented as an independent order, which is just the way things are. Art can lift us to a realm of such undisturbed contemplation.

Something analogous is what Flaubert achieves in this novel in relation to the way of the human world (but without the awe-provoking greatness of the classical hero), captured as just the way things are with flawed humanity, a portrayal which releases us from the distress and pity we might experience through involuntary sympathy with ordinary human beings.

I am *not* saying that Flaubert is looking *de haut en bas* with contempt at his protagonist. He is believed to have said on some occasion: "Madame Bovary, c'est moi." The portrayal of tawdry, deluded humanity is also drawn from within. It couldn't be as effective if it were not.

Something similar is brought about by Zola in *L'assommoir*: the distance from the distressing happenings in the novel is achieved and rendered through some beautiful passages, of streets, of fog and lights, of the large apartment building which almost plays the role of a character in the story. But the distancing effect is now rationalized as "naturalism," a scientific grasp of the way things are in the terrible conditions of working-class life. Art is here in the service of science. We have a picture of appalling human destruction, an important component of which is self-destruction.

But this objectified world can call for another sort of engagement, the commitment to policies which would do away with the conditions which produce such destruction. Sympathy is not the issue, even though we may feel sympathy for Gervaise.

If we look at Flaubert in these terms, then his oeuvre offers two quite different kinds of beauty: the deflationary but purgatorial (*Madame Bovary* and *L'Éducation Sentimentale*), on one hand, and the archaic scenes of high and violent deeds in striking decor (*Salammbô*), on the other.[22]

It goes without saying that only the second form has any relation to Romanticism. In the first, the "Romantic" is rather identified with Emma Bovary's contemptible and tawdry emotions (prefiguring Eliot?).

(Contrast this with another kind of distancing through art: the way that Baudelaire lifts us out of Spleen, the all-pervasive paralyzing force of *acēdia*, through the music of words-and-images. Here there is a transfiguration of the ugly into a new kind of beauty, as will be seen in Chapter 10.)

What light does this discussion of Flaubert cast on the question above about the source of joy at the articulation of inscapes? It is clear that Flaubert inaugurates a new relationship between truth and beauty. Beauty is linked to truth, but this lies in the (utterly deflationary) portrayal of the truth, not the reality itself (leave aside the archaic high deeds of *Salammbô*, which was perhaps conceived as a mere fantasy by Flaubert, for all his

---

22. The deflationary is a necessary but not sufficient condition for the purgatorial.

claims to meticulous scholarship). On the contemporary relation to beauty, we are on a path which reaches some of its most powerful expressions in the twentieth century—for instance, in the works of Samuel Beckett.

Hopkins, by contrast, is on to a vindication of some analogue of the original Platonic relation: goodness and beauty reside in reality itself, not just in its portrayal. The joy stems from the recovery of what seemed a precious but endangered connection. And indeed, these two relations between truth and beauty coexist and cannot but be in relation, in a state of mutual reference, in modern culture, and sometimes in the same writers. Beckett's sources in rich Joycean language reflect this (sometimes underground) connection—as though only the descent into maximum disconnection can legitimize a return to ontic beauty.

In another way, the tense but ineliminable relation between the two stances is central to the poetry of Miłosz (Chapter 14).

Wider Spaces of Meaning

The discussion of Hopkins' work is a good place to mark a distinction between the Romantic invocations of cosmic order and another experience which may seem similar but is in reality quite distinct.

The distinction can be blurred because there are in fact common features. They both put us in what we can call a wider space of meaning.

We normally live in a mental / emotional frame which is narrowly centered on us; on me and the things that matter to me, including close relations. But we can occasionally reach / leap beyond this, and live, really live, in a much bigger space; that is, feel this as our primary locus, of which the me-focus region is just a small province. While the dangers, concerns, worries which define this province are still there, they are no longer the main matters, no longer fill the whole horizon.

To live in this wider frame is to experience this shift in center: we no longer live by our own particular needs, desires, goals; there is a certain ethic which defines this space, from which we would cut ourselves off if we globally assumed the objectifying-instrumental stance to the world which cannot recognize the kind of fulfillment / nourishment which is offered here. To enter this space is to take as our center not only our own needs / wants, but also the ethos of the larger space. It involves a decentering and recentering. This is what the space requires of us.

Now being reconnected through poetry to a palpable sense of cosmic order is, indeed, one way of living in a wider space. But there is another way, which has different, even contrasting features.

Take for example the experience described in Dostoyevsky's *Brothers Karamazov* which Staretz Zossima ascribes to his deceased brother

Markel: "All around me there has been such divine glory: birds, trees, meadows, sky, and I alone have lived in disgrace, I alone have dishonoured it all, completely ignoring its beauty and glory."[1] Here the sense of the larger world doesn't really have the characteristics of a cosmic order, but rather an overpowering sense of its central meaning; here, joy. And at the same time, its revelation is not something which the agent as poet brings about. Of course, the description the author gives helps define the experience, but it breaks in on him / her unbidden.

True, the vision is precious, and the agent strives to retain it, not to let it slip away; perhaps through prayer, or meditation, or concentrated attention. But unlike the visions of order by Wordsworth or Hölderlin, the sense of a larger space is not something that is conjured by poetry.

At the same time, this wider space requires something of us. It asks that we respond to it with joy. So Markel reproaches himself for his past blindness, which ignored and disvalued this glory. "Birds of God, birds of joy, you must forgive me too, for against you too I have sinned."

When his mother remonstrates with him, "You take too many sins on yourself," he replies: "But dear mother, . . . I am crying from joy, not from grief; I want to be guilty before them, only I cannot explain it to you, for I do not know how to love them. Let me be culpable before all, and then all will forgive me, and that will be paradise. Am I not in paradise now?"[2]

There is an analogy, but also an obvious difference, between what Dostoyevsky is describing here, and the invocations of Wordsworth and Hölderlin. Something which we can only describe with a term like "transcendence" enters here: something which takes us beyond the cosmos or universe (and the cosmos is the universe considered as a morally relevant order).

We can recognize here a certain analogy to visionary experiences which we often classify as "religious," even "mystical." The "wider space" is filled with a force of deep spiritual significance; of agape, for instance, or *karuna*.

There remains, indeed, an analogy with poetic reconnections here, but there are important distinctive features which separate the two con-

1. Fyodor Dostoyevsky, *The Brothers Karamazov*, trans. David McDuff (London: Penguin, 2003), 375.

2. Dostoyevsky, *Brothers Karamazov*, 375.

texts. The "wider" frame in the "religious" (for example, Christian or Buddhist) contexts involves such a radical transformation of action and motivation, that one cannot be aware, even fleetingly, of living in it without a vivid sense of our inability to do so fully, and of the tension between call and response. Now the vision invoked by much Romantic poetry is also at odds with the dominant ethos of our civilization, which adopts an objectifying, instrumental stance to nature; but it is possible to abandon this stance, as many readers of Romantic poetry do, without radically changing one's life (although actually following through on the ecological consequences of such a conversion requires more strenuous action). The call to change is less radical, less far-reaching, less urgent and insistent.

On the other hand, a wide range of people with very different outlooks can and do resonate with the poetry of Wordsworth and Hölderlin; whereas skeptical detachment can very well be the response to the Buddha and Simone Weil and even Dostoyevsky.

Hopkins' work is an obvious place to mark this distinction, because he is a rare figure, both cosmic poet and religious visionary. In the first capacity, he brings to light underlying forces in nature; while the acute sense of falling short, which belongs to the second identity, is evident in certain of his poems of despair. Like the work of the early Romantics, his poetry effects a reconnection with nature, but this only yields a vision of cosmic order when subsumed in his philosophical-theological underlying story.

Another example of transcendence in this sense: the vision presented in the Buddha's "Fire Sermon"; not, of course, in relation to the Buddha himself, but as it comes across to the *bhikkus* he is addressing: the gestalt shift of experiencing the central personal attribute of desire as pain inflicted on one; as burning; where the proper response is taking refuge in a dispassionate stance.

Another example, Weil:

> Dieu a créé par amour, pour l'amour. Dieu n'a pas créé autre chose que l'amour et les moyens de l'amour. Il a créé toutes les formes de l'amour. Il a créé des êtres capables d'amour à toutes les distances possibles. Lui-même est allé, parce que nul autre ne pouvait le faire, à la distance maximum, la distance infinie.

Cette distance infinie entre Dieu et Dieu, déchirement suprême, douleur dont aucune autre n'approche, merveille de
l'amour, c'est la crucifixion. Rien ne peut être plus loin de Dieu
que ce qui a été fait malédiction.

Ce déchirement par-dessus lequel l'amour suprême met
le lien de la suprême union résonne perpétuellement à travers
l'univers, au fond du silence, comme deux notes séparées et
fondues, comme une harmonie pure et déchirante. C'est la
parole de Dieu. La création toute entière n'en est que la vibration. Quand la musique humaine dans sa plus grande
pureté nous perce l'âme, c'est cela que nous entendons à
travers elle. Quand nous avons appris à entendre le silence,
c'est cela que nous saisissons, plus distinctement, à travers
lui.[3]

[God created through love and for love. God did not create
anything except love itself, and the means to love. He created
love in all its forms. He created beings capable of love from
all possible distances. Because no other could do it, he
himself went to the greatest possible distance, the infinite
distance. This infinite distance between God and God, this
supreme tearing apart, this agony beyond all others, this
marvel of love, is the crucifixion. Nothing can be further
from God than that which has been made accursed.

This tearing apart, over which supreme love places the
bond of supreme union, echoes perpetually across the universe in the midst of the silence, like two notes, separate yet
melting into one, like pure and heart-rending harmony. This
is the Word of God. The whole creation is nothing but its vibration. When human music in its highest purity pierces our
soul, this is what we hear through it. When we have learned
to hear the silence, this is what we grasp more distinctly
through it.][4]

3. Simone Weil, "Attente de Dieu," in Œuvres (Paris: Gallimard, 1999), 697.
4. Simone Weil, Waiting for God, trans. Emma Craufurd (New York: Harper and Row,
1951), 123–124.

The early Romantics whom I have been describing here, with the exception of Hopkins, are very cosmic-centered, concerned with its order and potential disorder. This is even true of Novalis. But this is not to say that they wanted to deny the transcendent in the sense invoked here. Shelley and Byron certainly did. Keats seems less sure; but for Wordsworth, for instance, an orthodox form of Christianity offered an underlying story to the cosmos he invoked, and something similar can be said about Novalis. But as the century unfolds, the poetry of cosmic connection moves farther away from religion and the transcendent, as we will see with Rilke.

And this coincides with the disappearance of poetry invoking this kind of cosmic order; whereas the sense of transcendence breaking in through the secure wall of ordinary experience continues, as the quote from Weil attests.

On the contrary, the connection to transcendence becomes even more important in the present secular age, where more and more people are engaged in searching for a spiritual / religious path.

But later on, after Baudelaire, when the search for reconnection explored by poets turns from cosmic order to time and history (see Chapter 9), the relations between the cosmic and transcendence become more complex and interwoven. They come to turn on issues about "higher times" (see Chapter 11).

In anticipation of this discussion, I want to recur to the first distinction I mentioned above between Hopkins and the earlier Romantics, on one hand, and the experience described in Dostoyevsky's *Brothers,* on the other.

Earlier Romantic poetry had a ritual-like nature. I am referring here to the way in which Wordsworth's poetic formulation brings on—one might say releases—the sense we feel of a "force running through all things"; or the way the opening stanzas of Hölderlin's "Heimkunft" create the sense that what is described there is a joint creation of the poet and the scene he is trying to portray; or again, how the order Hölderlin invokes in the Aegean in the opening stanzas of "Archipelago" becomes vivid for us through the poetry.

There is a parallel here with Hopkins: the invocation of the kestrel through the sprung rhythm of his "Windhover" makes palpable the inscape of the bird.

When we compare these with the way a larger order breaks into the consciousness of Markel in the *Brothers Karamazov*, it seems that the order of causation is reversed. Far from the order being invoked in the portrayal, it is seen as breaking through unbidden and unsuspected, and is thus at first bewildering—an experience in search of a description. These can, of course, be found, and the appropriate response identified: in this case, Markel's heartfelt expression of apology and gratitude to the "birds of joy."

We will see this phenomenon later when we look at writers' break-in experiences nearer the end of the nineteenth century and into the twentieth century; and here the accounts which make sense of them will be in terms of higher times. And this will in turn make possible a new poetry of invocation in the temporal dimension.

One of the threads I am trying to follow in this book is the evolution of the human longing for reconnection, first to cosmic orders, traditionally conceived, and later, to the order of Nature which modern science has helped define for us; along with this, I want to trace the media in which reconnection has been sought in literature, starting with the Romantic poetry of the nineteenth century, and turning toward hybrid forms of writing, informed by science. All the while, spiritual traditions nourished by different visions of transcendence have been continued, modified, and added to. These two histories have been related in complex ways; but it would not help to lose sight of the difference between them. Hence the present note.

This is the more important for me because I nourish another perhaps impossible ambition: I would like to cast light on the continuities and differences between the different modes and conceptions of cosmic connection throughout human history, including the special forms that we find in early tribal religions, which are so hard to understand for those immersed in contemporary global civilization.

Chapter Eight

RILKE

I

There is an interesting relationship between the notion of "inscape" which we explored in connection with Gerard Manley Hopkins, on one hand, and the development of Rilke's poetry, on the other. Not that there was any question of influence: Hopkins' work wasn't published until near the end of Rilke's life. The connection is rather one of overlapping concerns.

From relatively early on, Rilke sees his task as a poet, and indeed the task of human beings, one could say the purpose of our lives, as discerning the meaning of things, the world, the cosmos. In other terms, closing a gap, of understanding, of communication, between us and the surrounding world.

In his monograph of 1902 about the painters' collective in Worpswede, where he stayed on several occasions (and met the woman who would become his wife), there is the following passage:

Denn gestehen wir es nur: die Landschaft ist ein Fremdes für uns und man ist furchtbar allein unter Bäumen, die blühen, und

unter Bächen, die vorübergehen. Allein mit einem toten Menschen, ist man lange nicht so preisgegeben wie allein mit Bäumen.
Denn so geheimnisvoll der Tod sein mag, geheimnisvoller ist das
Leben, das nicht unser Leben ist, das nicht an uns teilnimmt und,
gleichsam ohne uns zu sehen, seine Feste feiert, denen wir mit
einer gewissen Verlegenheit, wie zufällig gekommenen Gäste, die
eine andere Sprache sprechen, zusehen.[1]

[For let us admit it: landscape is something foreign for us, and
we are afraid when alone among trees which are flowering, and
streams which rush by. Even when alone with a dead human
do we not feel so exposed as we do when we are alone among
trees. Because, mysterious as death is, still more mysterious is
life that is not ours; life which does not participate in ours, and,
without noticing us, celebrates its own feasts, while we look on
with a certain embarrassment, like guests arriving by accident
who speak another language.]

But for Rilke this condition of distance, of separation, was not just taken
as a fact, but rather as a separation which must be overcome, a secret
which must be learned. We sense this already in an early poem from a
collection of the late 1890s:

> Vor lauter Lauschen und Staunen sei still,
> Du mein tieftiefes Leben;
> Daß du weißt, was der Wind dir will,
> Eh noch die Birken beben.
>
>
> Und wenn dir einmal das Schweigen sprach,
> Laß deine Sinne besiegen.
> Jedem Hauch gieb dich, gieb nach,
> Er wird dich lieben und wiegen.

1. Rainer Maria Rilke, "Worpswede," in *Werke* (Leipzig: Insel Verlag, 1978), 3:393–394,
quoted in Käte Hamburger, *Rilke: Eine Einführung* (Stuttgart: Ernst Klett Verlag,
1976), 18.

Und dann meine Seele sei weit, sei weit,
Daß dir das Leben gelinge.
Breite dich wie ein Feierkleid
Über die sinnenden Dinge.²

[Stand still, listening in astonishment,
You my deepest life,
That you may know what the wind wants from you
Before even the birches shake.

And when on occasion silence spoke to you,
Let your senses be overcome.
To each breath, give yourself, give way,
It will love you and cradle you.

And then my soul, reach out, reach out,
So that your life be fulfilled
Spread yourself like a ceremonial garment
Over the thought-filled things.]³

One might say, this was his vocation as a poet. As he put it in a letter to one of his patrons, the Princess von Thurn und Taxis, in a letter of 1912: "Ich . . . wünsche mir so viel Fassung in mein Herz, solchen Gegenständen gegenüber dazusein, still, aufmerksam, als ein Seiendes, Schauendes, Um-sich-nicht-Besorgtes" [I . . . wish for such an openness in my heart that I'd be able to stand before such objects, and be still, looking attentively, unconcerned with myself].³ *Schauen* [to look] is the key verb here; for Rilke, at this time, it describes the kind of absorbed, attentive observation out of which a poem emerges (later he will modify this view).

2. Rainer Maria Rilke, "Vor lauter Lauschen," in *Werke*, 1:154.

3. Rainer Maria Rilke, "Briefe an die Fürstin von Thurn und Taxis. 13 November 1912," in *Briefwechsel: Rainer Maria Rilke und Marie von Thurn und Taxis* (Zurich: Niehans and Rokitansky, 1951), 228–229.

In a sense this penetration of the secret of things was not for Rilke just a personal vocation, but a charge laid on us humans by our world. We will see this with his use of the word *Auftrag* [vocation] later on in the *Duino Elegies*.

The major issue of the Romantics returns: our being cut off from the world, cosmos, Nature, and our striving to recover the contact; but this arises in a new way. Whereas with the early Romantics, there was some notion of the order from which we are estranged, with which we want to reconnect—a force running through all things (Wordsworth), the gods who dwelt with humans in the Greek polis (Hölderlin), the restored golden age (Novalis)—with Rilke, what comes first is the sense of distance and foreignness. Out of the struggle to overcome this, he first comes to work out some kind of sense of the larger order in which we humans fit. We can see from this how far we have traveled from the initial fading of cosmic orders to which the Romantics responded because this increasing distance was the precondition for our standing before the world as an alien realm, one where we don't know the language.[4]

We observe the outside of things, as it were, we feel ourselves moved, we sense the beginnings of a response in ourselves, but we don't know what gives the world this power to move us. We have to dive deeper into reality. Or the space of outer reality must become one with the space within.

This goal of going through the barrier, closing the distance, recovering to full awareness the inner being of reality, runs through his career, but it was understood rather differently in the different phases of his work. To give a sense of this development, I would like to outline three such conceptions, from the early years, from a middle phase, and from the final crowning achievement of his work, respectively.

II

The early phase finds its fullest expression in the *Buch der Stunden* [Book of Hours]. The source of inspiration, what calls forth writing, is given the name "God"; and his searching is cast as entries in a monk's book of

---

4. There is perhaps also an echo here of Novalis' description of the golden age as one in which humans, animals, and things can really speak to each other.

hourly prayers. More specifically, he casts himself as a Russian Orthodox monk. This fancy was inspired by Lou Andreas-Salomé, under whose strong influence he thought and wrote at this period (late 1890s), and reflected their somewhat illusory idea that Russian peasants don't suffer from the self-division and alienation of Western culture. The "prayers" are a kind of attempt to break through:

> Du, Nachbar Gott, wenn ich dich manchesmal
> In langer Nacht mit harten Klopfen störe,—
> So ists, weil ich dich selten atmen höre
> Und weiß: Du bist allein im Saal.[5]

> [You, neighbor God, if sometimes in the long night
> I rouse you with my loud pounding,—
> It's only that I so seldom hear you breathing
> And know: you're in that huge room alone.][6]

The wall separating monk from God is made of images; and the images stand before like names. But when the light goes on within me, the glare that reflects from these prevents me seeing you.

This could invoke an experience of a real believer, but the monk's "God" in these poems is far from the God of Abraham, as other poems make clear—for example, the one which starts: "What will you do, God, when I die?"[7] The relation is better expressed in this poem:

> Ich kreise um Gott, um den uralten Turm,
> und ich kreise jahrtausendelang;
> und ich weiß noch nicht: bin ich ein Falke, ein Sturm
> oder ein großer Gesang.[8]

> [I circle around God, around the age-old tower;
> I've been circling for millennia

5. Rainer Maria Rilke, "Du, Nachbar Gott," in *Werke*, 1:255.

6. Rainer Maria Rilke, "You, neighbor God," in *The Poetry of Rilke*, trans. Edward Snow (New York: North Point, 2009), 11.

7. Rainer Maria Rilke, "What will you do, God, when I die?," in *Poetry*, 27.

8. Rainer Maria Rilke, "You, neighbor God," in *Poetry*, 11.

And still don't know: am I a falcon, a storm,
Or a sovereign song.][9]

But the inseparability between poet and God is well expressed in this:

Lösch mir die Augen aus: ich kann dich sehn:
Wirf mir die Ohren zu: ich kann dich hören
Und ohne Füße kann ich zu dir gehen,
und ohne Mund noch kann ich dich beschwören.
Brich mir die Arme ab, ich fasse dich
Mit meinem Herzen wie mit einer Hand,
halt mir das Herz zu, und mein Hirn wird schlagen,
und wirfst du in mein Hirn den Brand,
so wird ich dich auf meinem Blute tragen.[10]

[Put my eyes out: I can see you,
and my ears shut, I can hear you,
and without feet I can walk toward you,
and without a mouth I can still beseech you.
Break my arms off, with my heart
I will grasp you as with a hand,
Tear my heart out and my brain will beat,
And if you put a torch to my brain
I will bear you through all my blood.][11]

And this poem expresses a continuing human aspiration for Rilke:

O Herr, gieb jedem seinen eigenen Tod.
Das Sterben, das aus jenem Leben geht,
darin er Liebe hatte, Sinn und Not.[12]

---

9. Rainer Maria Rilke, "I live my life in widening circles," in *Poetry*, 7.
10. Rainer Maria Rilke, "Lösch mir die Augen aus," in *Werke*, 1:313.
11. Rainer Maria Rilke, "Put my eyes out," in *Poetry*, 35.
12. Rainer Maria Rilke, "O Herr, gieb jedem seinen eigenen Tod," in *Werke*, 1:347.

[O Lord, give us each our own death. Grant us
The dying that comes forth from that life in which
We knew love, grappled with meaning, felt need.][13]

|||

In the later 1890s, when Rilke began his stay at the Worpswede colony of artists, and began to familiarize himself with visual art, painting, and sculpture, a new conception of his own task began, which reached further definition in the early years of the new century, when he went to work for and with Rodin.

In the light of this new conception, we can understand why Rodin was such an inspiration and pathfinder for Rilke in the early 1900s; why Rilke so eagerly accepted the otherwise onerous and unrewarding post as his secretary.

Rodin's work had a great impact on the world at the turn of the century. The sculpture of the human form has always conveyed something of the stance, aspiration, feeling of the subject. But Rodin greatly increased and widened the human strivings, longings, sufferings which sculpture can invoke. Rilke saw how Rodin treated hands, often "no bigger than my little finger, but filled with a life that makes one's heart pound . . . each a feeling, each a bit of love, devotion, kindness, searching."[14] Each hand is not merely a sentence in the narrative of the body, but its own landscape, complete.

In fact, Rodin often didn't start from a wholly resolved idea, but explored the matter before him; he began to shape it, and some meaningful form emerged. He often didn't wait for overall inspiration of work when shaping what was meant to be a part of it.[15] He moved intuitively.

The effect of Rodin's sculpture came not only from the form, but also from the material itself. To take the most famous case, the massiveness

13. Rainer Maria Rilke, "O Lord, give us each our own death," in *Poetry,* 47.

14. Rachel Corbett, *You Must Change Your Life: The Story of Rainer Maria Rilke and Auguste Rodin* (New York: Norton, 2016), 87.

15. Corbett, *You Must Change Your Life,* 91–92.

of the *Thinker* lends a depth and weight to the contemplation thus bodied forth (Heidegger's "earth," as well as "world," figures here). Form and matter together conjured something of the order of an "inscape" in Hopkins' sense.

Rodin's influence lies behind a new phase in Rilke's writing, the one which finds expression in his *Neue Gedichte*. The aim in this collection was to offer an objective description of some person, object, or scene, without invoking his own subjective reactions. In this he was inspired by Rodin's advice and practice.

As Rilke put it, he is recording "non des sentiments, mais des choses que j'avais senties" [not my feelings, but things I had felt].[16] He is trying to grasp the essence of the phenomena he describes: these are very varied. Some are about people, some concern objects; some characterize events or emotions, or moods or situations. And so it is hard to identify a formula which covers all the 178 poems in the two collections.

Of events he describes their essential inner meaning (although for biblical scenes, this is often very different from what the sources assert). But when his target is a thing or person, he often captures it by reading it through some appropriately related object or process, and / or by identifying its inner movements, or thoughts.

Thus in the very first poem in the first collection, "Früher Apollo," he invokes the early spring sunshine through the still-bare branches to convey how "der Glanz / aller Gedichte uns fast tödlich träfe" [the splendor / of all poems strikes us with almost lethal force], and how the god's song seems to come to him, infused through his smile.[17]

Apollo is, of course, the god of poets, and this poem cannot but send us to the first poem of the second collection, "Archaïscher Torso Apollos," a statue of the god which has lost its head and much else, but which nevertheless makes us feel its glance and smile: "Denn da ist keine Stelle, / die dich nicht sieht. Du mußt dein Leben ändern." [For there is no place / that does not see you. You must change your life.][18]

16. Quoted in Rainer Maria Rilke, *Rilke: New Poems,* trans. Joseph Cadora (Port Townsend, WA: Copper Canyon, 2016).

17. Rainer Maria Rilke, "Früher Apollo," in *Werke,* 1:481.

18. Rainer Maria Rilke, "Archaïscher Torso Apollos," in *Werke,* 1:557.

The question can't but arise: Is this injunction aimed especially at poets? The mutilation of the founding god calls perhaps for new creations by his devotees.

In "Römische Sarkophage," we find also the revealing analogous process, followed by the inner reciprocal movements:

> Was aber hindert uns zu glauben, daß
> (so wie wir hingestellt sind und verteilt)
> Nicht eine kleine Zeit nur Drang und Haß
> Und dies Verwirrende in uns verweilt,
>
> wie einst in dem verzierten Sarkophag
> bei Ringen, Götterbildern, Gläsern, Bändern,
> in langsam sich verzehrenden Gewändern
> ein langsam Aufgelöstes lag—
>
> bis es die unbekannten Munde schluckten,
> die niemals reden (wo besteht und denkt
> ein Hirn, um ihrer einst sich zu bedienen?)
>
> Da wurde von den alten Aquädukten
> ewiges Wasser in sie eingelenkt—:
> das spiegelt jetzt und geht und glänzt in ihnen.[19]
>
> [But what prevents us from believing
> (the way we're set down here and put in place)
> that only for a short time rage and hate
> and this confusion live in us.
>
> just as once this ornate sarcophagus
> among ribbons, rings, images of gods
> in slowly disintegrating veils and garments
> something lay slowly decomposing—

19. Rainer Maria Rilke, "Römische Sarkophage," in *Werke*, 1:509–510.

till it was swallowed by those unknown mouths
that never speak. (Where does a brain
wait and think that one day will employ them?)

then from the ancient aqueducts
eternal water was channeled into them—:
where it shimmers now and laps and gleams.][20]

The sarcophagus is read through the human experience of deep emotional conflict and stress, which gradually subsides, calmed by a long process in time, represented by the slow decay of the bodies they contain; and what is left is a gentle equilibrium of two reciprocal movements, water flows in and down through them and collects below, so that it shines and mirrors them back upward.

In his poems about cathedrals (reminiscent of a visit he made to Chartres with Rodin)—"L'Ange du Méridien," "Die Kathedrale," "Das Portal"—Rilke captures the relation of the huge stone monuments to their more humble surroundings in dramatic terms. These poems carry the strong suggestion that the religion they serve is fading. But in the poem that immediately follows, "The Rose Window," filling the eye of a cat below, is recognized as having once seized "ein Herz und rissen es in Gott hinein" [a heart and carried it up to God].[21]

But perhaps the most famous result of this new direction was Rilke's "Panther." This was the product of what in the fashion of the time was called *Einfühlung,* or "empathy." And in this case, it meant opening oneself to the Panther's way of experiencing his plight, as Rilke observed the caged animal in the Jardin des Plantes in Paris.

> Sein Blick ist vom Vorübergehn der Stäbe
> So müd geworden, daß er nichts mehr hält.
> Ihm ist, als ob es tausend Stäbe gäbe
> Und hinter tausend Stäbe keine Welt.

---

20. Rainer Maria Rilke, "Roman Sarcophagi," in *Poetry,* 155.
21. Rainer Maria Rilke, "Die Fensterrose," in *Werke,* 1:501.

Der weiche Gang geschmeidig starker Schritte
Der sich im allerkleinsten Kreise dreht,
ist wie ein Tanz von Kraft um eine Mitte.
In der betäubt ein großer Wille steht.

Nur manchmal schiebt der Vorhang der Pupille
Sich lautlos auf—. Dann geht ein Bild hinein,
geht durch der Glieder angespannte Stille—
und hört im Herzen auf zu sein.[22]

[His gaze has from the passing of the bars
become so tired that it holds nothing anymore.
It seems to him there are a thousand bars
and behind a thousand bars no world.

The supple pace of powerful soft strides,
turning in the very smallest circle,
is like a dance of strength around a center
in which a mighty will stands numbed.

Only at times the curtain of the pupils
soundlessly slides open—. Then an image enters,
glides through the limbs' taught stillness—
dives into the heart and dies.][23]

The "inscape" here is captured by "empathy" in the strictest sense, by an attempt to see / feel the world from the panther's point of view. This is something that can't be realized with all the "objects" which this work attempts to capture.

22. Rainer Maria Rilke, "Der Panther," in *Werke*, 1:505.
23. Rainer Maria Rilke, "The Panther," in *Poetry*, 147.

I V

However, an approach of this kind, exploring individual objects one by one, cannot really achieve the goals which Rilke set himself.

The intuition grows in him that this kind of indirect probing—taking up some independent object or event and exploring its inner nature—cannot bring about the kind of connection he seeks.

But at the end of this decade, and partly by working through his experiences of abandonment and lack of meaning in Paris—a working through which was importantly realized in *The Notebooks of Malte Laurids Brigge*—he comes to a new understanding of the nature of the task.[24]

This he works out, painfully, and in very difficult circumstances, through the drafting of the *Duino Elegies,* which occupied him through the whole decade 1912–1922; and this was in large part a time of the war, which made the Austrian citizen Rilke an enemy alien in his beloved Paris, and during which he spent some time in military service—an occupation more alien to Rilke's nature is difficult to imagine.

At the beginning of this decade, the work on the *Elegies* was slow and Rilke's sense of distance from his goal was at times very powerful, as we can see in this poem from the beginning months of the war (August–September 1914):[25]

---

24. Rilke's understanding of his experience in Paris, which is the basis of his "novel," presented as an autobiographical work by a young Dane, was deeply influenced by the French poets he read and admired: chiefly Baudelaire, but also Mallarmé and Verlaine. I will discuss Baudelaire's experience of Paris, as both challenge and opportunity; the challenge being the threatened onset of "Spleen" in the contemporary expanding, self-transforming, potentially shapeless urban scene. A question arises about Rilke's relation to these French poets, out of whose work "symbolism" emerges; and in the case of Verlaine, we have a paradigmatic practitioner. Why did Rilke not follow their practice? In his *Neue Gedichte* phase, the answer is obvious: symbolists wanted to bring poetry close to music (Pater), whereas Rilke's model was sculpture. But this doesn't explain why he never was drawn into this movement, for all his admiration of the French practitioners (after the war, he translated Valéry). See the interesting discussions on this in Charlie Louth, *Rilke: The Life of the Work* (New York: Oxford University Press, 2020), 106, 112–113. I have learned a great deal from this work.

25. See Hamburger, *Rilke,* 86–90.

Ausgesetzt auf den Bergen des Herzens. Siehe, wie klein dort,
Siehe: die letzte Ortschaft der Worte, und höher,
aber wie klein auch noch ein letztes Gehöft von Gefühl. Erkennst du's?
Ausgesetzt auf den Bergen des Herzens. Steingrund
Unter den Händen. Hier blüht wohl
Einiges auf; aus stummen Absturz
Blüht ein singender Kraut singend hervor.
Aber der Wissende? Ach, der zu wissen began
Und schweigt nun, ausgesetzt auf den Bergen des Herzens.

Da geht wohl, heilen Bewußtseins,
manches umher, manches gesicherte Bergtier,
wechselt und weilt. Und der große geborgene Vogel
kreist um der Gipfel reine Verweigerung—. Aber
ungeborgen, hier auf den Bergen des Herzens . . . [26]

[Abandoned on the mountains of the heart. Look, how small there,
look: the last village of words, and higher
but how small too, still one last farmstead of feeling. Do you
    see it?
abandoned on the mountains of the heart. Rockground
under the hands. Here, granted,
some things do flourish; out of mute downthrust
an unknowing herb breaks forth singing.
but the one who knows? Ah, who began knowing
and now keeps silent, abandoned on the mountain of the heart.

True, many an unhurt consciousness roams here,
many, so many sure mountain animals
change fields and stay. And the great sheltered bird
circles the peaks' pure refusal.—But
unsheltered, here on the mountain of the heart . . .][27]

---

26. Rainer Maria Rilke, "Ausgesetzt auf den Bergen des Herzens," in *Werke*, 2:94.
27. Rainer Maria Rilke, "Abandoned on the mountains of the heart," in *Poetry*, 147.

The poet sees himself abandoned in this mountain landscape of the heart; the last line adds: unprotected in this desolate landscape. He can't connect to it; can't find the words to make this stony ground less than alien. He looks way back behind and under him and sees the last refuge of words, the last hut of feeling. Up here the unknowing plants are connected, one comes forth singing; and confident mountain animals move around. And the great bird who circles the mountain is also described as "protected." But the one who knows? He began to know but has now (at this abandoned height) fallen silent.

This poem reflects the unfulfilled longing that more and more troubled Rilke. But at the same time, another poem expressed his conception of what it would be to fulfill it.

> Es winkt zu Fühlung fast aus allen Dingen,
> aus jeder Wendung weht es her: Gedenk!
> Ein Tag, an dem wir fremd vorübergingen,
> entschließt im künftigen sich zu Geschenk.
>
> Wer rechnet unseren Ertrag? Wer trennt
> Uns von den alten, vergangenen Jahren?
> Was haben wir seit Anbeginn erfahren.
> Als daß sich ein im anderen erkennt?
>
> Als daß an uns Gleichgültiges erwarmt?
> O Haus, o Wiesenhang, o Abendlicht
> Auf einmal bringt du's beinah zum Gesicht
> Und stehst an uns, umarmend und umarmt.
>
> Durch alle Wesen reicht der *eine* Raum
> Weltinnenraum. Die Vögel fliegen still
> Durch uns hindurch. O, der ich wachsen will,
> ich seh hinaus, und *in* mir wächst der Baum.
>
> Ich sorge mich, und in mir steht das Haus,
> ich hüte mich, und in mir ist die Hut.

Geliebter, der ich wurde: an mir ruht
der Schönen Schöpfung Bild und weint sich aus.[28]

[It beckons to feel from almost all things,
From every turn it blows: Remember!
A day when we passed as strangers,
decides to give a present to the future.

Who calculates our gain? Who separates us from the old, the
   past years?
What have we learned since the beginning
Than that one recognizes oneself in the other?

Than that what is indifferent in us warns?
O House, O meadow slope, O evening light,
Suddenly you almost bring it to clear *sight,*
And stand by us, embracing and embraced.

Through all beings ranges a single space,
World-inner-space. The birds fly silently
Through us. O, as I want to grow
I look outside me, and *in* me the tree grows.

I care and in me stands the house.
I protect myself and in me is the protection.
Beloved that I became: on me rests
The image of a beautiful creation,
And weeps itself out.]

But how to move from the condition depicted in the first poem ("Ausge-setzt") to that invoked here, where inner and outer merge into a single space?

---

28. Rainer Maria Rilke, "Es winkt zu Fühlung fast aus allen Dingen," in *Werke,* 2:92.

Before turning to look at the *Elegies,* we should note a shift in his sense of what is required to attain his goal. Earlier, in the quote cited from his letter to the Princess of Thurn und Taxis, he speaks of his goal as achieving a special kind of "looking" (*Schauen*). But now the connection comes to be understood primarily in terms of feeling. Already in "Ausgesetzt," he spoke not only of an "Ortschaft der Worte" [village of words] being left far behind, but also of a "Gehöft der Gefühl" [farmstead of feeling] back down there. This new emphasis is given even more importance in the *Weltinnenraum* [world-inner-space] poem just quoted. And another poem of this period, "Wendung," reaches a verdict about "sein fühlbares Herz" [his feelable heart], "daß es der Liebe nicht habe" [that it had no love].[29]

The striking—and puzzling—notion of a *Weltinnenraum* already announces a crucial thesis which is given full expression in the *Duino Elegies,* completed only after the war. But in this same prewar period the image of an external reality contained within consciousness is balanced by the counterimage of a forest pond (*Waldteich*), which mirrors events in the stormy outer world in its still surface.[30] Nevertheless, it is clear that Rilke is looking for a deeper, more intensely felt reconnection with the world than the brilliant descriptions and invocations of the *Neue Gedichte* can provide.

Yet another poem of this period expresses a sense that he is moving toward his goal:

Fortschritt
Und wieder lauscht mein tiefes Leben lauter
Als ob es jetzt in breitern Ufern ginge.
Immer verwandter werden mir die Dinge
Und alle Bilder immer angeschauter.
Dem namenlose fühl ich mich vertrauter:
Mit meinem Sinne, wie mit Vögeln, reiche
Ich in die windigen Himmel aus der Eiche,
und in der abgebrochenen Tag der Teiche
sinkt, wie auf Fischen stehend, mein Gefühl.[31]

29. Rainer Maria Rilke, "Wendung," in *Werke,* 2:82. See also Rainer Maria Rilke, "Turning," in *Poetry,* 525.

30. Hamburger, *Rilke,* 95.

31. Rainer Maria Rilke, "Fortschritt," in *Werke,* 1:402.

[Progress

And again my deep life rushes louder,

as if moved now between steeper banks.

Objects grow ever more akin to me,

all images more intensely seen.

I've become more at home amid the nameless:

With my senses, as with birds, I reach up

into the windy heavens from the oak,

and in the small ponds' broken-off day

my feeling sinks, as if it stood on fishes.][32]

There is a powerful sense that from within himself, with his feelings, he can actually touch the external realities which move him. He has moved from his goal in the *Neue Gedichte* toward a deeper, more immediate contact with the world. One might say: closer to his goal in the *Book of Hours,* except that the contact sought now is more immediate; it is captured in the strange concept of *Weltinnenraum,* a kind of fusion of external and internal space; something which it is hard to make sense of.

Another statement of this contact: "Die Geheimnisse der Dingen verschmelzen in seinem [the artist's] Innerem mit seinen eigenen tiefsten Empfindungen und werden ihm, so als ob es eigene Sehnsüchte wären laut" [The secrets of things fuse within (the artist) with his own deepest feelings and thus become for him as though his own longings were expressed out loud].[33]

It almost seems that in these last two poems, "Es winkt zu Fühlung" and "Fortschritt," the goal was already reached. The very notion of a *Weltinnenraum* seems to suppose that it is, that there is an inner space which can reach out and incorporate what is out there. But Rilke isn't satisfied. Perhaps one can understand this sense of incompleteness with the question: What if this sense of connection was illusory? Surely, there has to be some confirmation from the world.

32. Rainer Maria Rilke, "Progress," in *Poetry,* 93.
33. Louth, *Rilke,* 46.

This is what I believe Rilke sought, and (to his satisfaction) found in the completed *Duino Elegies*.

VI

I want now to try to penetrate what Rilke thought was the successful achievement of his goal in the climax to the *Elegies*. These accord a crucial place to the figure of the angel. It's not necessary to posit that or in what way Rilke really believed in such beings. But the nature of the angel supposes an idea of the cosmos. It is a cosmos, in which besides the realm of the living, there is a realm of the dead, alongside the first, and communicating with it. The particular power of the angel is that he / it can see the whole and follow things which pass from one realm to the other. As will become more evident as the *Elegies* unfold, for Rilke grasping and bringing inward the meaning of things means grasping them in this whole order, not just singly as with the *Dinggedichte* (the poems of his earlier phase, like "The Panther").

The idea that we live not only in a cosmos of the living, but in a *Doppelbereich* [dual realm], which also includes the realm of the dead, goes along with the idea that our death is not simply a negation of our lives, but is a "fruit" of the life; our whole life builds toward this. The terrible thing about *Großstädte* (e.g., Paris) is that they rob people of "their own" death; we die en masse and in special places for leaving the world, like hospitals. (This contrasts with Malte's grandfather, who died "his" own death.)

One of the difficulties of the human condition is that we start off not seeing clearly our goal as human beings: understanding the cosmos, bringing together inner and outer space into a *Weltinnenraum*. We only feel it vaguely, without being able to make clearer what it involves. We are bemused, like Rilke before the language of trees at Worpswede; only mostly, we don't even guess at our real vocation.

Language, or better *Deutung* [interpretation], is what confuses us. Unlike animals (Eighth Elegy), we are aware of the world, which means that we have given an interpretation to it, which claims to be right, and which therefore excludes others; and we are confused, misled by our own interpretations, blinded to what is valid in other interpretations. In this, we are unlike animals, who live without interpretation in the undivided world. They can just go straight ahead and live, without even raising the question how. "Und die findigen Tiere merken es schon,/ daß wir nicht sehr verläßlich zu Haus sind/ in der gedeuteten Welt" [And the sly animals see at once,/ how little at home we are/ in the interpreted world].[34] And so animals go right into their death without even seeing it beforehand. They live in the *Doppelbereich* [dual realm]. But most of us do not; and even those who do, do so only part of the time.

> Mit allen Augen sieht die Kreatur
> das Offene. Nur unser Augen sind
> wie umgekehrt und ganz um sie gestellt
> als Fallen, rings um ihren freien Ausgang.
>
> [. . .]
> das freie Tier
> hat seinen Untergang stets hinter sich
> und vor sich Gott, und wenn es geht, so gehts
> in Ewigkeit, so wie die Brunnen gehen.[35]
>
> [With all their eyes, the animal world
> beholds the Open. Only ours
> are as it were inverted and set all around it
> like traps at the doors to freedom.
>
> [. . .]
> The free animal has its demise
> perpetually behind it and always before it
> God, and when it moves, it moves into eternity,
> the way brooks and running streams move.][36]

But we can't do this. We haven't got "den reinen Raum vor uns, in den die Blumen/ unendlich aufgehn. Immer ist es Welt" [the pure space ahead

34. Rainer Maria Rilke, "Die Erste Elegie," in *Werke,* 1:685; Rainer Maria Rilke, "The First Elegy," in *Poetry,* 283.

35. Rainer Maria Rilke, "Die Achte Elegie," in *Werke,* 1:714.

36. Rainer Maria Rilke, "The Eighth Elegy," in *Poetry,* 326–327.

of us into which flowers / endlessly open. What we have is World]. What Rilke means by *Welt* here is the world as (fallibly, and mostly mis)interpreted by us. This is opposed to *Erde* [Earth]—Rilke is plainly one of Heidegger's sources for his similar distinction. We live in a *Welt,* and "niemals Nirgends ohne Nicht: das Reine, / Unüberwachte, das man atmet und / unendlich *weiß* und nicht begehrt" [never Nowhere without negation: / that pure unguarded element one breathes / and *knows* endlessly and never craves]. But whatever has this power to go straight ahead, not to be confused and delayed by multiple possible interpretations, is to be praised. Not just animals, but also young children, before we make them into beings like us. And also potentially lovers, except that they end up blocking the vision for each other, so that they return to World.[37] The First Elegy begins with the cry:

> Wer, wenn ich schriee, hörte mich denn aus der Engeln
> Ordnungen? Und gesetzt selbst, es nähme
> einer mich plötzlich ans Herz: ich verginge von seinem
> stärkeren Dasein. Denn das Schöne ist nichts
> als des Schrecklichen Anfang, den wir noch grade ertragen,
> [. . .]
> Ein jeder Engel ist schrecklich.
> Und so verhalt ich mich denn und verschlucke den Lockruf
> dunkelen Schluchzens.[38]

> [Who if I cried out, would hear me among the Angels'
> Orders? and even if one of them pressed me
> suddenly to his heart: I'd be consumed
> in his more potent being. For beauty is nothing
> but the beginning of terror, which we can still barely endure,
> [. . .]
> Every angel is terrifying.
> And so I grip myself and choke down that call note
> of dark sobbing.][39]

37. Rilke, "Die Achte Elegie," 714; Rilke, "Eighth Elegy," 326–327.
38. Rilke, "Die Erste Elegie," 685.
39. Rilke, "First Elegy," 283.

Why do I want to cry to the angel? Because he / it alone can grasp the whole, which I strive to understand, to grasp the "inscape" of. But this is also something terrifying, because grasping this involves accepting death into the picture, the other realm, which seems to (and in a sense does really) negate life. So the beginning of the Second Elegy repeats the point: "Ein jeder Engel ist schrecklich" [Every angel is terrifying].[40]

Here we see a crucial, structuring thesis which underlies the *Duino Elegies,* and indeed is crucial to Rilke's outlook. We (at least most of us moderns) have trouble accepting loss and death: the ultimate loss. We are held back from throwing ourselves into a full-hearted life project, because this must at some point encounter incapacity or death, and we are shaken by this into uncertainty or irresolution. The exceptions are the rare beings who can carry their project right into and through death, or other insuperable obstacles. We will see two types who exhibit such ultimate resolve in the course of this first elegy.

First, only those who love unrequitedly escape this, and Rilke seems to think that these are always female. But this brings us back to the First Elegy, where Rilke identifies those who can go straight ahead in full unity with themselves, like animals, as first, "die Liebenden" [the women who loved]; "lange / noch nicht unsterblich genug ist ihr berühmtes Gefühl" [their prodigious feeling still lacks an undying fame].[41] And the abandoned ones are even more to be admired. (Gaspara Stampa is mentioned here.) And secondly, he cites heroes who go to early death:

> es erhält sich der Held, selbst der Untergang war ihm
> nur ein Vorwand, zu sein: seine letzte Geburt.[42]

> [the hero lives on, even his downfall
> was only a pretext for attained existence: his ultimate birth.][43]

40. Rainer Maria Rilke, "Die Zweite Elegie," in *Werke,* 1:685; Rainer Maria Rilke, "The Second Elegy," in *Poetry,* 291.

41. Rilke, "First Elegy," 283; Rilke, "Die Erste Elegie," 685.

42. Rainer Maria Rilke, *The Poetry of Rilke,* trans. Edward Snow (New York: North Point, 2009), 284.

43. Rilke, *Poetry of Rilke,* 285.

What's striking about them is that they don't rely on anyone else, and don't depend on how others react to them. Speaking of the unrequited lovers, Rilke asks:

> Sollen nicht endlich uns die ältesten Schmerzen
> fruchtbarer werden? Ist es nicht Zeit, daß wir liebend
> uns vom Geliebten befreien und es bebend bestehen:
> wie der Pfeil die Sehne besteht, um gesammelt im Absprung
> *mehr* zu sein als er selbst. Denn Bleiben ist nirgends.

> [Isn't it time these most ancient sorrows
> at last bore fruit? Time we tenderly detached ourselves
> from the loved one and, trembling, stood free:
> the way the arrow, suddenly all vector, survives the string
> to be *more* than itself. For abiding is nowhere.][44]

In this context, we can better understand the original reading of the biblical story of the prodigal son at the end of his *Malte* novel: he leaves not because he is thoughtless and unconcerned about his father, but because being loved shackles you, prevents you from carrying out your vocation. And that's the strength that we also see in women who love unrequited and permanently.

All these beings who can move straight ahead like this have a certain solidity, an inner consistency which we ordinary humans lack in the divisions and uncertainties of our "interpreted world."

Rilke's stance toward death is the context in which we can understand his rejection of Christianity. Both views have some place for continuing existence beyond death, but Christianity conceives this as eternal *life*; and this for Rilke is a snare and a delusion.

The Christian faith points to an increased potentiality of the afterlife (resurrection); whereas the Rilkean sees a loss:[45]

44. Rilke, "Die Erste Elegie," 687; Rilke, "First Elegy," 284–285.

45. Of course, Rilke, like many of his (and our) contemporaries, took the Nietzschean view that Christianity denigrates our rich embodied existence here in favor of an unfleshly etiolated existence in the afterlife, but it should be clear to everyone, from the often bitter disputes between Christians, that there is no single agreed reading of the faith.

Freilich ist es seltsam, die Erde nicht mehr zu bewohnen,
kaum erlernte Gebräuche nicht mehr zu üben,
Rosen, und andern eigens versprechenden Dingen
Nicht die Bedeutung menschlicher Zukunft zu geben;
Das, was man war in unendlich ängstlichen Händen,
nicht mehr zu sein, und selbst den eigenen Namen
wegzulassen wie ein zerbrochenes Spielzeug.
Seltsam die Wünsche nicht weiterzuwünschen. Seltsam,
alles, was sich bezog, so lose im Raume
flattern zu sehen. Und das Totsein ist mühsam
und voller Nachholn, daß man allmählich ein wenig
Ewigkeit spürt.—Aber Lebendige machen
alle den Fehler, daß sie zu stark unterscheiden.
Engel (sagt man) wußten oft nicht, ob sie unter
Lebenden gehn oder Toten. Die ewige Strömung
reißt durch beide Bereiche alle Alter
immer mit sich und übertönt sie in beiden.[46]

[Granted, it's strange to dwell on earth no more,
to cease observing customs barely learned,
not to give roses and other things of such promise
a meaning in some human future;
to stop being what one was in endlessly anxious hands,
and ignore even one's own name like a broken toy.
Strange, not to go on wishing one's wishes. Strange,
to see all that was once so interconnected
drifting in space. And death exacts a labor,
a long finishing of things half-done, before
one has that first feeling of eternity.—But the living
all make the same mistake: they distinguish too sharply.
Angels (it's said) often don't know whether they're moving
   among
the living or the dead. The eternal current

46. Rilke, "Die Erste Elegie," 688.

sweeps all the ages with it through both kingdoms
forever and drowns their voices in both.][47]

And yet, there is some analogy between the Christian and the Rilkean
outlook. There is a Rilkean piety:

> Stimmen, Stimmen. Höre, mein Herz, wie sonst nur
> Heilige hörten: daß sie der riesige Ruf
> Aufhob vom Boden; sie aber knieten,
> Unmögliche, und achtetens nicht:
> *So* waren sie hörend. Nicht daß du *Gottes* ertrügest
> Die Stimme, bei weitem. Aber das Wehende höre,
> die ununterbrochene Nachricht, die aus Stille sich bildet.
> Es rauscht jetzt von jungen Toten zu dir.[48]

> [Voices, voices. Listen, my heart, the way
> only saints have listened till now, as that vast call
> lifted them from the ground; while they kept on kneeling
> and noticed nothing, those impossible ones:
> listeners fully absorbed. Not that you could bear
> *God's* voice—not at all. But listen to the wind's breathing,
> the unbroken news that takes shape out of silence.
> It's rustling toward you now from all the youthful dead.][49]

So, taking full account of the heroic lives, what can we average, timid beings do? Who can help us? Not angels, not beasts, because of our interpreted world. So we turn to hints of meaning we have experienced: some
tree on a hill-slope, the fidelity of an old habit; or we turn to the ways in
which we have been moved, the ways we have felt addressed by the world:

> O und die Nacht, die Nacht, wenn der Wind voller Weltraum
> uns am Angesicht zehrt—, wem bliebe sie nicht, die ersehnte,
> sanft enttäuschende, welche dem einzelnen Herzen mühsam
>   bevorsteht.

47. Rilke, "First Elegy," 287.
48. Rilke, "Die Erste Elegie," 687.
49. Rilke, "First Elegy," 285.

[. . .]
Weißt du es *noch* nicht? Wirf aus den Armen die Leere
zu den Räumen hinzu, die wir atmen; vielleicht daß die Vögel
die erweiterte Luft fühlen mit innigerm Flug.[50]

[O and the night, the night, when the wind full of worldspace
gnaws at our faces—, for whom *won't* the night be there,
desired, softly disappointing, setting hard tasks
for the single heart.

[. . .]
You *still* don't see? Fling the emptiness in your arms
out into the spaces we breathe; perhaps the birds
will feel the increase of air with more passionate flight.][51]

(And perhaps we have a hint here of a limit-transcending act which can
unite us to the whole: an anticipation of the Seventh Elegy?) But in any
case, these moments call us.

Ja, die Frühlinge brauchten dich wohl. Es muteten manche
Sterne zu dir, daß du sie spürtest. Es hob
sich eine Woge heran im Vergangenen, oder
da du vorüberkamst am geöffneten Fenster,
gab eine Geige sich hin.[52]

[Yes, the Springs needed you. Many a star was waiting
for your eyes only. A wave swelled toward you
out of the past, or as you walked by the open window
a violin inside surrendered itself.][53]

50. Rilke, *Poetry of Rilke,* 282.
51. Rilke, *Poetry of Rilke,* 283.
52. Rilke, "Die Erste Elegie," 685.
53. Rilke, "First Elegy," 282.

(To sum up the assertion here, we could say: Yes, the springs needed you. And many stars made the demand on you, that you sense them.)

And then the crucial words: "Das alles war Auftrag. / Aber bewältig-test du's?" [All that was your charge. / But were you strong enough?][54] Here is the task laid on us; our *Auftrag;* our vocation, but we don't know what to do about it. No one can help, it seems. Not angels, not beasts, not others. Some just know (heroes, unrequited lovers), but we others seem lost.

V I

The Second Elegy deepens the sense of the ontological insecurity of or-dinary, nonheroic humans, but the inevitable consequence of this is an existential insecurity. Ordinary lovers in a happy relationship can feel the same sense of fuller existence that the unrequited have. But this is tem-porary. Lovers promise eternity, but they cannot really sustain this, and the result is that we feel our transience.

> Liebende, euch, ihr in einander Genügten,
> frag ich nach uns. Ihr greift euch. Habt Ihr Beweise?
> [. . .]
> euch frag nach uns. Ich weiß,
> ihr berührt euch so selig, weil die Liebkosung verhält,
> weil die Stelle nicht schwindet, die ihr, Zärtliche,
> zudeckt; weil ihr darunter das reine
> Dauern verspürt. So versprecht ihr euch Ewigkeit fast
> Von der Umarmung. Und doch, wenn ihr der ersten
> Blicke Schrecken besteht und die Sehnsucht am Fenster,
> und der ersten gemeinsangen Gang, *ein* Mal durch den Garten:
> Liebende, *seid* ihrs dann noch? Wenn ihr einer dem anderen
> Euch an dem Mund hebt und ansetzt—: Getränk an Getränk:
> O wie entgeht dann der Trinkende seltsam der Handlung.[55]

54. Rilke, "Die Erste Elegie," 685; Rilke, "First Elegy," 282.
55. Rilke, "Die Zweite Elegie," 691.

[Lovers, secure in one another, I ask you
about us. You hold each other. Have you assurances?
[. . .]
I ask *you* about *us*. I know
you touch so fervently because the caress protects,
because the place you cover, O tender ones,
doesn't vanish; because, underneath, you feel
pure permanence. Thus your embraces almost promise you
eternity. And yet, when you've passed the terror
of the first look, and the long yearning at the window,
and the first walk—the *one* walk—together through the garden:
lovers, *have* you survived? When you lift yourselves
each to the other's lips and kiss—: drink unto drink:
O how strangely then the drinker slips from the deed.][56]

And the consequence of this inconstancy is that we have so little subsistence, that we hardly endure.

Denn wir, wo wir fühlen, verflüchtigen: ach wir
Atmen uns aus und dahin; von Holzglut zu Holzglut
Geben wir schwächeren Geruch. Da sagt uns wohl einer:
ja, du gehst mir im Blut, dieses Zimmer, der Frühling
füllt sich mit dir . . . Was hilfts, er kann uns nicht halten,
wir schwinden in ihm und um ihn. Und jene, die schön sind,
o wer hält sie zurück? Unaufhörlich steht Anschein
auf an ihrer Gesicht und geht fort. Wie Tau von dem Frühgras
hebt sich das Unsre von uns, wie die Hitze von einem
heißen Gericht. O Lächeln, wohin? O Aufschaun:
neue, warme, entgehende Welle des Herzens—;
weh mir: wir *sinds* doch. Schmeckt denn der Weltraum,
in dem wir uns lösen, nach uns? Fangen die Engel
wirklich nur Ihriges auf, ihnen Entströmtes,
oder ist manchmal, wie aus Versehen, ein wenig
unseres Wesen dabei? Sind wir in ihre
Züge soviel nur gemischt wie das Vage in die Gesichter

56. Rilke, "Second Elegy," 293–295.

Schwangeren frauen)? Sie merken es nicht in dem Wirbel
Ihrer Rückkehr zu sich. (Wie sollen sie's merken)[57]

[For our part, when we feel, we evaporate; ah, we breathe
ourselves out and away; from ember to ember
we give off a fainter scent. True, someone may tell us:
you're in my blood, this room, the Spring itself
is full of you . . . but why? He can't hold us,
we vanish in and around him. And the beautiful ones,
ah, who holds *them* back? Appearance ceaselessly
flares in their faces and vanishes. Like dew from the morning grass
what's ours rises from us, the way heat lifts
from a steaming dish. O smile, going where? O spurned look:
new, warm, departing surge of the heart—;
alas, we *are* the surge. Then does the cosmic space
that we dissolve in taste of us? Do the Angels
recapture only what's theirs, their ceaseless streamings,
or sometimes, as if by accident, does a bit of ours
get mixed in? Are we blended in their features
like the slight vagueness that complicates the looks
of pregnant women? Unnoticed by them as they
swirl back into themselves. (How *could* they notice?)][58]

To gather the full force of this last reference to the angels in this passage,
we should cite the one that immediately precedes it, in which these terrifying creatures are described:

Frühe Geglückte, ihr Verwöhnten der Schöpfung,
Höhenzüge, morgenrötliche Grate
aller Erschaffung—Pollen der glühende Gottheit,
Gelenke des Lichtes, Gänge, Treppen Throne,
Räume aus Wesen, Schilde aus Wonne, Tumulte

---

57. Rilke, "Die Zweite Elegie," 689–690.
58. Rilke, "Second Elegy," 291–293.

Stürmisch entzückten Gefühls und plötzlich, einzeln
Spiegel: die die entströmte eigene Schönheit
wiederschöpfen zurück in das eigene Antlitz.[59]

[Favored first prodigies, creation's darlings,
mountain ranges, peaks, dawn-red ridges
of all genesis,—pollen of a flowering godhead,
links of light, corridors, stairways, thrones,
spaces of being, shields of rapture, torrents
Of unchecked ecstatic feeling and then suddenly, singly,
Mirrors: scooping their outstreamed beauty back
Into their peerless faces.][60]

Lovers may think that their passionately given love will endure, but this is an illusion. As for sexual desire, the Third Elegy tells us how much this carries us away from our vocation.

Heroes and unrequited lovers are like the animals described in the Eighth Elegy. They go straight forward into the Open; because they do not see death as a boundary, their *Untergang* [demise] is behind them; whereas we ordinary mortals foresee it. What stops us from being like them is our *gedeutete Welt* [interpreted world].

Our praise song doesn't shut out death, but exists somehow in the *Doppelbereich*. This is perhaps not so clear in the Seventh and Ninth Elegies. But it is what (some) *Sonnets to Orpheus* bring out, especially 1 through 8.

A condition of fullness of life, real *Dasein,* is that we live fully and without reservation in the *Doppelbereich,* not shying away from the boundary we pass through in dying.

But poetry which fully realizes its vocation of saying / praising the earth is another such way of living the *Doppelbereich,* alongside heroic sacrifice of the young and unrequited love. It is a poetry of life which fully

59. Rilke, "Die Zweite Elegie," 689.
60. Rilke, "Second Elegy," 291.

embraces the afterlife, the beyond-life. And that is what it means to say
that it is the poetry of Orpheus, of the god who has moved between the
two realms.

So the (re)connection which poetry can effect, and which brings enhanced life for Rilke, is subtly but importantly different from the kind
we see with the early Romantics, Wordsworth and Hölderlin. It is not
recovering a sense of an enduring cosmic order which makes the difference; just coming to know that there is such a *Doppelbereich* isn't the crucial step. Rather it is taking a stand which embraces the whole realm, of
life and death together, without the all-too-human reservation, and even
the dread and recoil that most of us feel.

What also emerges in the Second Elegy is the connection between our
ordinary way of evading and ignoring our mortality, and a kind of ontological insecurity: we evaporate with time; the question is raised whether
the world's space in which we live, move, and have our being retains a
taste of us. Our impression is rather that

> Alles ist einig, uns zu verschweigen, halb als
> Schande vielleicht und halb als unsägliche Hoffnung.[61]

> [And it all conspires to keep quiet about us,
> Half out of shame perhaps, half from some secret hope.][62]

The "unsayable hope" points perhaps to the possibility that we might
really take up our vocation (our *Auftrag*) in the world. But it seems that
our temptation to shy away from death is a source of fragility for our lives
and projects. In the language of a later, post–Second World War philosophy, it undermines our power to take firm existential decisions, which
in turn fragilizes our existence.

Is this true of the human condition in general? Or is it a malady peculiar to modernity? In the last two stanzas of this elegy, Rilke seems to
opt for the second hypothesis. He looks backward to Greek civilization

---

61. Rilke, "Die Zweite Elegie," 690.
62. Rilke, "Second Elegy," 293.

and sees how they were able to live their lives independently of their relation to the ultimate realities, there understood as the Gods. If we look
at Attic tombs, we see how the relation between humans was portrayed
in their gestures.

> Diese Beherrschten wußten damit: so weit sind wirs,
> *dieses* ist unser, uns *so* zu berühren, stärker
> stemmen die Götter uns an.[63]

> [Those self-mastered ones knew: *this* far we can go,
> this much is *ours,* to touch *this way;* the gods press down
> on us more forcefully.][64]

What they could do, are we incapable of it?

> Fänden auch wir ein reines, verhaltenes, schmales
> Menschliches, einen unseren Streifen Fruchtlands
> zwischen Strom und Gestein. Denn das eigene Herz übersteigt
>   uns
> noch immer wie jene. Und wir können ihm nicht mehr
> nachshaun in Bilder, die es besänftigen, noch in
> göttliche Körper, in denen es größer sich mäßigt.[65]

> [If only we too could find a pure, carved-out, narrow
> human place, our own small strip of fertile soil
> between stream and stone. For even now our heart
> transcends us, just as it did those others. And no longer
> can we gaze after it into images that soothe it, or
> into godlike bodies where it finds a higher restraint.][66]

63. Rilke, *Poetry of Rilke,* 294.
64. Rilke, *Poetry of Rilke,* 295.
65. Rilke, "Die Zweite Elegie," 694.
66. Rilke, "Second Elegy," 295.

VII

I now would like to move to what I see as Rilke's triumphant completion of the project of the *Elegies;* how he managed to confirm (to his satisfaction) his project of reconnection. And I want to move directly to this climax, in the Seventh and Ninth Elegies, bypassing (regretfully) four elegies which are very rich in their own right:

The Third, the exploration, influenced by Freud, of our deep (male) sexual instincts with the hidden guilty river-god of the blood;

The Fourth, which starts: "O Bäume Lebens, O wann winterlich?" [O tree of life, how long till winter?]. In contrast to this winter form, we must confess that we suffer the alternation of flowering and withering:

> Blühn und verdorrn ist uns zugleich bewußt.
> Und irgendwo gehen Löwen noch und wissen,
> solang sie herrlich sind, von keiner Ohnmacht.[67]

> [Blooming makes us think: fading.
> and somewhere out there lions still roam,
> unmindful, in their great splendor, of any weakness.][68]

In the Fifth, the negative is stressed, and the saltimbanques are taken as an image of empty, inauthentic lives; and in the Sixth, the image of the fig tree, which goes right to the stage of fruit bearing, skipping the preliminary of flowering, serves as another occasion to evoke the hero who goes straight to the consummation of his life in death. The Seventh starts with an invocation of wooing, but negatively:

> Werbung nicht mehr, nicht Werbung, entwachsene Stimme,
> sei deines Schreies Natur.[69]

> [No longer, voice. No longer let a wooing shape your cry.
> You're beyond it.][70]

67. Rainer Maria Rilke, "Die Vierte Elegie," in *Werke,* 1:697.
68. Rainer Maria Rilke, "The Fourth Elegy," in *Poems,* 303.
69. Rainer Maria Rilke, "Die Siebente Elegie," in *Werke,* 1:709.
70. Rainer Maria Rilke, "The Seventh Elegy," in *Poems,* 321.

But, as though triggered by the very mention of wooing, and thus mating, there follows an immense outburst of joy, and rapturous descriptions of the world in the returning spring and summer:

O und der Frühling begriffe—da ist keine Stelle,
die nicht trüge den Ton Verkündigung. Erst jenen kleinen
fragende Auflaut, den mit steigender Stille
weithin umschweigt ein reiner, bejahender Tag.
Dann die Stufen hinan, Ruf-Stufen hinan zum geträumten
Tempel der Zukunft—; dann der Triller, Fontäne,
die zu dem drängenden Strahl schon das Fallen zuvornimmt
im versprechenden Spiel . . . Und vor sich, den Sommer.

Nicht nur die morgen alle des Sommers—, nicht nur
Wie sie wandeln in der Tag und strahlen vor Anfang,
Nicht nur die Tage, die zart sind um Blumen, und oben,
um die gestalteten Bäume, stark und gewältig.
Nicht nur die Andacht dieser entfalteten Kräfte,
nicht nur die Wege, nicht nur die Wiesen im Abend,
nicht nur, nach späten Gewitter, die atmenden Klarsein,
nicht nur der nahenden Schlaf und ein Ahnen, abends . . .
Sondern die Nächte! Sondern die hohen, des Sommers,
Nächte, sondern die Sterne, die Sterne der Erde.
O einst tot zu sein und sie wissen unendlich,
alle die Sterne: denn wie, wie, wie sie vergessen![71]

[O and the Spring would understand—, annunciation
would echo everywhere. First those small
questioning notes, which a clear confident day
would surround with heightening silence.
Then up the calls, up their flight of steps, to the dreamt-of
temple of the future—; then the trill, that fountain,

---

71. Rilke, "Die Siebente Elegie," 709–710. This is one of those moments chez Rilke which most evoke Novalis.

whose jet ascends through its own falling as in a union
of promise and play . . . And up ahead, Summer.

Not just all summer's dawns—, not just
how they change into day and glisten with genesis.
Not just the days, which are mild around flowers, and above,
around the full-formed trees, forceful and strong.
Not just the calm reverence in these outspread powers,
not just the paths, not just the meadows as evening deepens,
not just, after late thunderstorms, the pulsing clarity,
not just the approach of sleep and, at twilight, a premonition . . .
but the nights! All those towering summer nights!
and the stars, the stars of earth.
O to be dead one day and then know them forever,
all the stars: for how, how, how, to forget them!][72]

Then the cry: "Hiersein is herrlich" [To be here is glorious].

The crucial point of our vocation is seen as realized: the gap between inner and outer is closed. "Nirgends, Geliebte, wird Welt sein, als innen" [Nowhere, Love, will World exist but within].[73] We have reached an inner understanding of the meanings, the "inscapes," of things in our world. But this is not just the carrying out of our task (*Auftrag*). In the Ninth Elegy, Rilke tells us,

—Und diese, von Hingang
Lebenden Dinge verstehn, daß du sie rühmst; vergänglich,
traun sie ein Rettendes uns, den Vergänglichsten, zu.
Wollen, wir sollen sie ganz im unsichtbaren Herzen verwandeln
in—o unendlich—in uns! Wer wir am Ende auch seien.[74]

[—And these things
That live on departure know that you praise them; transient,
They look to us, the *most* transient, to save them.

72. Rilke, "Seventh Elegy," 321.
73. Rilke, "Die Siebente Elegie," 711; Rilke, "Seventh Elegy," 323.
74. Rainer Maria Rilke, "Die Neunte Elegie," in *Werke*, 1:719.

They want us to change them utterly, in our invisible hearts,
into—O endlessly!—*us!* Whoever, finally, we may be.][75]

Our grasp of things, being inner, is also invisible, in the sense that it is not a feature of the commonly accessible world we observe.[76]

We reach our completion in our full and adequate vision of things; but they too reach their fullness only in this vision.

Both poet and world need each other to reach the fullness of their being. Rilke's poetry makes not only a claim about the interspace, but about the cosmos as well, because the connection between poet and world in a *Weltinnenraum* raises both to an enhanced existence, a higher and fuller mode of being.

We are transitory, doomed to pass. And we sense this. "Unser / Leben geht hin mit Verwandlung" [Our / life is spent in changing].[77] But there are moments, as with the "Mädchen" invoked in this passage, when

> Denn eine Stunde war jeder, vielleicht nicht
> ganz eine Stunde, ein mit den Maßen der Zeit kaum
> Meßliches zwischen zwei Weilen—, da sie ein Dasein
> hatte. Alles. Die Adern voll Dasein.[78]

> [There was an hour for each of you,
> Perhaps not even an hour, but between two intervals
> A space scarcely measured by the rules of time—,
> When you *existed*. Completely. Veins filled with existence.][79]

---

75. Rainer Maria Rilke, "The Ninth Elegy," in *Poems,* 335.

76. As Rilke famously said, "Wir sind die Bienen des Unsichtbaren. Wir trinken unablässig den Honig des Sichtbaren um ihn in den großen Bienenkorb des Unsichtbaren anzuhäufen." [We are the bees of the invisible. We drink incessantly the honey of the visible, in order to carry it into the giant beehive of the invisible.] Rainer Maria Rilke, "Notes to 'Duino Elegies,'" in *Poems,* 70.

77. Rilke, *Poetry of Rilke,* 322, 323.

78. Rilke, "Die Siebente Elegie," 711.

79. Rilke, "Seventh Elegy," 323.

"Dasein" means here the fullness of existence, the state in which we know that "Hiersein ist herrlich."[80] In these moments we reach the inner certainty, unity, self-consistency which the First Elegy attributed to heroes and unrequited lovers. We are beyond the fragile, fleeting condition that the Second Elegy ascribed to us, where the "taste" of us gradually disappears from the space we inhabited. The "unsägliche Hoffnung" [unsayable hope] of that elegy is now not only said, but realized.

And something similar is true of the things in our world. Their existence too is raised to a higher power.

> Erde, ist es nicht dies, was du willst: *unsichtbar*
> In uns erstehen? Ist es dein Traum nicht.
> Einmal unsichtbar zu sein?—Erde! Unsichtbar!
> Was, wenn Verwandlung nicht, ist dein drängender Auftrag?[81]

> [Earth, isn't this what you want: to arise
> in us *invisibly?* Isn't it your dream
> to be invisible someday? Earth! Invisible!
> What, if not transformation, is your urgent charge?][82]

A call to which the poet replies:

> Erde, du liebe, ich will. O glaub, es bedürfte
> Nicht eine Frühlinge mehr, mich zu dir zu gewinnen—*einer*
> Ach, ein einziger ist schon dem Blute zuviel.
> Namenlos bin ich zu dir entschlossen, von weit her.
> Immer warst du im Recht, und dein heiliger Einfall
> ist der vertraulicher Tod.

> Siehe, ich lebe. Woraus? Weder Kindheit noch Zukunft
> werden weniger . . . Überzähliges Dasein
> Entspringt mir in Herzen.[83]

80. See Rilke, "Die Siebente Elegie," 322. "Gesang ist Dasein."
81. Rilke, "Die Neunte Elegie," 721.
82. Rilke, "Ninth Elegy," 337.
83. Rilke, "Die Neunte Elegie," 721.

[Earth, my darling, I will! Oh believe me,
you need no more of your Springs to win me—, *one,*
just one, is already too much for my blood.
Namelessly I'm wed to you forever.
You have always been right, and your most sacred tenet
is Death the intimate Friend.

Look, I am living. On what? Neither childhood nor future
grows less . . . Overabundant existence
wells up in my heart.][84]

But here, we have to pause and take in what has changed since the First Elegy. It's as though we had already realized the vocation (*Auftrag*) which that elegy gave us. And this is reflected in our stance toward the Angel. There we tremulously considered appealing to angels to help us, but refrained because we thought they would never listen, and besides being close to them frightened us ("Ein jeder Engel ist schrecklich" [Every angel is terrifying]).

Now the Seventh Elegy begins with an injunction: "Werbung nicht mehr, entwachsene Stimme, / sei deines Schreies Natur" [Wooing, not wooing, be the nature of thy cry].[85]

Who are we enjoined not to woo? It turns out to be the angel (here a single addressee). "Glaub *nicht,* daß ich werbe, Engel" [*Don't* think that I'm wooing you, angel]. "Wie ein gestreckter Arm ist mein Rufen" [My call is like a stretched out arm]. "Wie Abwehr und Warnung" [Warning you off].[86]

There is a 180-degree turn. In the First Elegy, the poet asks if he dare appeal to the angel for help. Now his cry is meant to warn him off. What has happened?

One of the key changes is that the operation of bringing things within, of creating the *Weltinnenraum,* has been reconceived as a two- (or even many-)staged process. To bring things inward is to articulate

84. Rilke, "Ninth Elegy," 337.
85. Rilke, "Die Siebente Elegie," 709.
86. Rilke, "Die Siebente Elegie," 713.

their significance for us. Discovering this significance (and we ought to be able to put this in the plural and speak of their "meanings" for us) is one aspect of our vocation (*Auftrag*), and that is why this discovery is deeply satisfying for us, why the things in question really speak to us, to our *fühlbares Herz* [feeling heart].

But in the earlier poetry, this operation of bringing within was understood as taking place (or failing to take place) between the poet and a certain scene. Now it is understood as realized also through the whole gamut of the creations of a culture. Through cathedrals, for instance. Following Rodin, we can see cathedrals as setting forth the shape of the cosmos in time and space, in relation to God. Take Chartres, which the poet calls to the attention of the angel, lest he underestimate us ("Chartres war groß" [Chartres was great]).[87] The whole sweep of time, from Creation to the last judgment, is portrayed in the stained-glass windows, in all its historical meanings for us; at the same time, the various forces for good or evil are there for us in the statues, either of saints, of animals, or of the gargoyles. The massive internal space as well, which is meant to harbor a presence of God, itself understood as an impossible goal, but which is adumbrated as an aspiration by the immense height of the nave; while at the same time, the high columns invoke the forests of our cultural / religious history; and we could go on. And obviously, cathedrals are not the only form of meaningful architecture, which in some way expresses and makes apparent a way of life.

And equally obviously, architecture is not alone among the means of expression of human meanings. There is music as well, which the poet also draws to the attention of the angel.

> Musik
> [...]
>   Du Sprache wo Sprachen
> enden. Du Zeit,
> die senkrecht steht auf der Richtung vergehender Herzen.

---

87. Rilke, "Die Siebente Elegie," 712.

Gefühle zu wem? O du der Gefühle
Wandlung in was?—in hörbare Landschaft.[88]

[Music:
[...]
    You language where languages
end. You time
standing straight up on the path of vanishing hearts.
Feelings ... for whom? O you the mutation
Of feelings ... into what?—: into audible landscape.][89]

And not to be neglected when talking of Rilke, there are the instruments of everyday life, furniture, utensils, and the like, which have often been designed to manifest the way of life they facilitate, but which now in the industrial age are more and more mass-produced, made often of nondescript materials, like plastic; thereby losing their expressive function.

These are the *erlebbare* [livable] things, of which he will speak in the Ninth Elegy.

This loss is part of a development which Rilke views as the most dangerous and damaging for the culture of his age. Indeed, the reason why it is very clear that Rilke counts all of the above as one crucial phase in bringing our world within is that he apprehends that his world is either destroying or forgetting these first-level expressions:

Weite Speicher der Kraft schafft sich der Zeitgeist, gestaltlos
Wie der Spannende Drang. den er aus allem gewinnt.
Tempel kennt er nicht mehr. Diese, des Herzens, Verschwendung,
sparen wir heimlicher ein. Ja, wo noch eins übersteht,
ein einst gebetetes Ding, ein gedientes, geknietes—,
hält es sich, so wie es ist, schon ins Unsichtbare hin.
Viele gewahrens nicht mehr, doch ohne den Vorteil,
daß sie's nun *innerlich* bauen, mit Pfeilern und Statuen, größer![90]

---

88. Rainer Maria Rilke, "An die Musik," in *Werke*, 2:111.

89. Rainer Maria Rilke, "To Music," in *Poems*, 549.

90. Rilke, "Die Siebente Elegie," 711. See this theme developed in *Sonnets to Orpheus* I.18, I.22, I.23, II.10.

[The Zeitgeist is stockpiling vast reservoirs of power, formless
as the stretched tension it gathers from everything.
It no longer recognizes temples. Furtively we hoard
what the heart once lavished. Where one of them still survives,
A thing once prayed to, knelt before, revered—,
It's already reaching out, secretly, into the invisible.
Many no longer see it, yet forgo the advantage
Of building it *within* now, with pillars and statues, greater!][91]

All of this makes the second phase of "inwarding" all the more important. That is the phase invoked in the last two lines; and it seems that it
is reserved for poetry. This is the one art among all the others that can
preserve what is expressed in them, because (perhaps) it can render
the vision they express more fully articulate, more fully "inward," just
because its medium, language, is the "innermost" one, and the most
consciously articulate. So it always has a crucial role to play in inter-
preting the more "external" articulations, of, say, architecture and
music; but today it has the even more urgent and indispensable one of
remembering these meanings. The forms which once stood there,
"und bog / Sterne zu sich aus gesicherten Himmeln" [and bent stars
toward them from the secure heavens], have to be rescued through
the more intense inwardness of poetry, now that they have been destroyed, or become unrecognizable.[92]

The crucial place of poetry here, as a more intense phase of rendering
inward, can answer an objection that many may have felt a few paragraphs back. How can Rilke invoke Chartres, whose expressed meanings are quintessentially Christian, when his outlook sharply departs
from the Christian one? His notion of death and life after death is ex-
pressly understood as a rejection of the Christian idea of "eternal life."
The answer here is that the poetic articulation of these great historical
expressions enjoys the right and duty to depart from the original outlook they manifested. We can already see this in his "Russian" phase,

91. Rilke, "Seventh Elegy," 323.
92. Rilke, "Die Siebente Elegie," 712.

where, influenced by Lou Andreas-Salomé, he tried to reinterpret the peasant Orthodox piety which fascinated them both in terms which were clearly nontheistic.[93]

The great monuments of Christian civilization can, and (Rilke would add) must, be reinterpreted in the light of his cosmology of the *Doppelbereich* (double realm, of both living and dead) if our world is to be creatively brought within, and hence shown in all its glory.

My use of this word here reflects the interpretation I give to the phrase "Hiersein ist herrlich." This word we usually translate as "glorious"; but the word is often used as a rather indefinite, even colorless term of praise, for which we could substitute "wonderful," "great," and a host of other terms of hefty approval. But I believe it has to be taken with the full weight of its theological origins, where it refers to a deeper, more powerful illumination of the divine, which is invoked in the New Testament account of the Transfiguration. The German term translates the Hebrew *kâvôd*, Greek *doxa*, Latin *gloria*.

So I would argue that "Hiersein ist herrlich" doesn't just say something about how we feel—"It's great to be here"—but bespeaks an illumination of the world, the cosmos, that poetry brings about when it gives full expression to it; or otherwise put, when the cosmos and our grasp of it come together within; or, put still another way, when the *Weltinnenraum* is fully realized.

In fact, the second and third stanzas of the Seventh Elegy carry a strong sense of a vision of light, an illumination; indeed, this passage is

---

93. The *Elegies* are full of theological language borrowed from Christianity: *Herrlichkeit, Verkündigung, Verwandlung, Preisen* [glory, annunciation, transformation, praise]. But Rilke saw very clearly the incompatibility between his view and orthodox Christianity. His notion of life after death is quite different from Christian "eternal life." The dead, to play their role, have to be stripped of personality, and be beyond love of any kind. But despite the differences, there are parallels; and these can help explain the fascination for Russian Orthodoxy of his earlier years, which Lou Andreas-Salomé inspired in him. The guiding idea here was that earlier phases of human culture had an intuition of our vocation to unity with the world which later, "modern" phases had lost sight of. This was, of course, a key idea of the Romantic period.

reminiscent of the opening passages of Novalis' *Hymnen an die Nacht;* and also perhaps of Hölderlin's "Brod und Wein."[94]

One of Rilke's key words for bringing the visible into internal space is "saying."

> Aber weil Hiersein viel ist, und weil uns scheinbar
> Alles das Hiesige braucht, dieses Schwindende, das
> Seltsame uns angeht. Uns die Schwindesten. *Ein* Mal
> Jedes nur *ein* Mal. *Ein* Mal und nichtmehr. Und wir auch
> *Ein* Mal. Nie wieder. Aber dieses
> *ein* Mal gewesen zu sein, wenn auch nur *ein* Mal:
> *irdisch* gewesen zu sein, scheint nicht wiederrufbar
>
>
> Und so drängen wir uns und wollen es leisten,
> wollens enthalten in unsern einfachen Händen,
> im überfüllteren Blick und im sprachlosen Herzen.[95]
>
>
> [But because *life* here compels us, and because everything here
> Seems to need us, all this fleetingness
> that strangely entreats us. Us, the *most* fleeting . . .
> *once* for each thing, only once. Once and no more. And we, too,
> only once. Never again. But to have been
> *once,* even though only once:
> This having been *earthly* seemed lasting, beyond repeal.
>
>
> And so we press on and try to achieve it,
> try to contain it in our simple hands,
> in our brimming look, our voiceless heart.][96]

---

94. Early in the decade of gestation of the *Elegies,* Rilke began to read Hölderlin, under the guidance of Norbert von Hellingrath, no less; see Louth, *Rilke,* 302–313.

95. Rilke, "Die Neunte Elegie," 717.

96. Rilke, "Ninth Elegy," 333.

How can we answer this call?

> Bringt doch der Wanderer auch vom Hange des Bergrands
> Nicht eine Hand voll Erde ins Tal, die Allen unsägliche, sondern
> Ein erworbenes Wort, reines, den gelben und blaun
> Enzian. Sind wir vielleicht *hier,* um zu sagen: Haus,
> Brücke, Brunnen, Tor, Krug, Obstbaum, Fenster,—
> höchstens, Säule, Turm . . . aber zu sagen, verstehs,
> oh zu sagen *so,* wie selber die Dingen niemals
> innig meinten zu sein.[97]

> [The traveler doesn't return to the valley from the mountainside
> with a handful of sod, around which all stand mute,
> but with a word he's won, a pure word, the yellow and the blue
> gentian. What if we're only *here* to say: *house,*
> *bridge, fountain, gate, jug, fruit tree, window,—*
> at most: *column, tower* . . . but for *saying,* understand,
> oh for such saying as the things themselves
> never dreamt so intensely to be.][98]

All these things have a human meaning and use, and when we articulate them we further define and reaffirm this meaning. They are the *erlebbar* [livable] things, those we live in and by, which I referred to above.

We see here that it is not just the massive creations of high culture—the temples, cathedrals, paintings, literature of our culture—that give expression to our grasp of the cosmos and the divine; the things which underpin and make possible our everyday lives do as well. The meanings they have for us taken together help constitute our sense of who we are and where we stand in the universe.

Take another example that Rilke mentions immediately after the list just cited: a threshold (*Schwelle*). Rilke imagines a threshold to their dwelling that two lovers pass over as they come and go; and indeed this

97. Rilke, "Die Neunte Elegie," 718.
98. Rilke, "Ninth Elegy," 335.

same threshold will see many couples walking over it, and wearing it down. The threshold and its meaning as a place of passage are closely woven in the meaning of their relationship for the couple, and this connects to how they understand what a good life together consists in, and thus helps constitute their whole understanding of life.

But all this is under threat, as we also saw in the Seventh Elegy:

> *Hier* ist des *Säglichen* Zeit, *hier* seine Heimat.
> Sprich und bekenn. Mehr als je
> fallen die Dinge dahin, die erlebbaren, denn
> was sie erdrängend ersetzt, ist ein Tun ohne Bild.[99]

> [*Here* is the time for the sayable, *here* is its home.
> Speak and attest. More than ever
> the things we can live with are falling away,
> and ousting them, filling their place: an act without image.][100]

This last expression points to action without any sense of the human meanings which are at stake in it. This is the degradation which the Seventh Elegy foresaw. As the new mass-produced instruments we operate with more and more lose their power to express meanings, these latter disappear from our consciousness. Until the point comes where all that counts is instrumental efficacy.

What can combat this is poetic "saying," invoking the skein of meanings which surround our dealings with *Haus, Brücke, Brunnen, Tor, Krug, Obstbaum, Fenster, Säule, Turm* [house, bridge, fountain, portal, jug, fruit tree, window, column, tower]. (We can already discern here the Rilkean background to Heidegger's notion of the "Thing.")

This "saying" has become not only possible, but imperative in our age of mass production; today, we would say: the age of plastic containers (at least Rilke was spared this).

In the Ninth Elegy, Rilke gives us new terms to describe what is meant by bringing things inward. We praise things (*Preisen, Rühmen*), the things

99. Rilke, "Die Neunte Elegie," 718.
100. Rilke, "Ninth Elegy," 335.

we live through and by, the *erlebbar* things. In doing this we raise them to a higher power, to a higher space. This is how we rescue them, perishable beings, even though we are among the most perishable.

But how does praising accomplish this? What does "praising" mean here? I can praise someone or something by heaping up positive descriptions so as to give a favorable picture. But this I can do insincerely; and it is not clear how I can bridge the gap with the cosmos just by this kind of positive description. So what is *Rühmen, Preisen,* for Rilke? It can't be just saying laudatory things; these have to be drawn out of us by a powerful vision of reality.

But nor can the vision be there quite independently of the praising. It's not like the case where I enter a room, and then give a report, positive or negative, of what I see.

For, as we have just seen, the merging of inner and outer space is not just our vocation (*Auftrag*), but also that of the world. To be here is glorious; but only because (and when) we perceive the glory of the *erlebbare* world, the world in its human meaning, which our praising brings to completion. So, as with the case of the early Romantics, the vision comes to fullness only with the poetic expression, but it comes with a force of conviction which can't be gainsaid. We feel it is drawn out of us by the marvels it articulates. "O staune, Engel. [. . .] Mein Atem reicht für die Rühmung nicht aus" [Be astounded, Angel. . . . My breath isn't big enough for all the praising which is called for]; and especially, for our great human achievements: Chartres, music.[101]

Can we say something more about this powerful vision? Perhaps something like this: that the whole, including us humans and the (double-realmed) world, is united, forms a coherent unity; and that this unity is magnificent, inspiring. Before we grasp this, we feel the gap, the lack, the breaks and mutual oppositions, the separation of our vision and reality.

But all along, human culture—art, music, literature, architecture, down to everyday objects of use—has been preparing us to see and respond to this unity. There lacks only the expression of the vision in the most inward and self-transparent medium, which is language, and crucially, a form of language which can respond to the magnificent and inspiring

101. Rilke, "Die Siebente Elegie," 712.

with praise. And this is poetry: and not just any poetry, but that which celebrates the vision of this unity.

The long, lonely, and often despairing struggle to complete the *Elegies*, begun in 1912, and only finished in 1922, was a search for the poem which would close the circuit, and bring the unity to light.

Put differently, much of human art and culture has been an implicit celebration of the vision that the earth, as well as ourselves, is calling for *Verwandlung*. We could translate this last word as "Transformation"; but might we render *Verwandlung* as "Transfiguration"? Because in the light of this unified whole, the parts stand out as praiseworthy; they command praise.

We take things from our everyday lives, our special creations, the seasons, and a host of other things that we live by and in and transfigure them in the light of the whole.[102]

We might sum the foregoing discussion up by asking and answering the question: What has changed between Rilke's writing of the poem on the *Weltinnenraum* in 1914, and the completion of the *Elegies* almost a decade later? We might put it this way: the *Weltinnenraum*, the coming together of inner and outer space, was in 1914 still an aspiration. The *Elegies*, particularly the Seventh and Ninth, realize this aspiration. Why? Because our full articulation of the human meanings of the things in our earth, in the most transparent medium of poetry, fulfills our vocation (*Auftrag*), and in the same act the "desire" of the earth ("*to rise in us unseen*"). Our aspiration is ratified.

But how to justify this startling claim? Whence comes the ratifying move on the part of the earth? In the fact that the response of the earth to *this* praise is to shine in glory. It is the sense that this move is now occurring which infuses passages in the Seventh and Ninth Elegies with exaltation. In finding at last a fully adequate expression of this exaltation, Rilke brings his decade-long search to a successful conclusion—and his career as a poet to a new height.[103]

---

102. It is clear that Rilke's use of *Ding* [thing] here is an important source for the notion of *Ding* in Heidegger's work after the *Kehre*.

103. I think that my account of the climax of the *Elegies* has affinities with the interesting and powerful take of Mark S. Burrows, "The Poet Alone Unites the World," in *Literature and Theology* 29, no. 4 (2015): 415–430, although our underlying explanations differ.

VIII

So praise rises from seeing ourselves connected to the whole. But this whole is the *Doppelbereich,* including the living and the dead. Rilke was resolved to hold life open to death.[104] What does this mean? How does it affect the above account? Death, for Rilke, as we saw in the First Elegy in Section V above, meant no longer dwelling in the world, no longer having a human future, "und selbst den eigenen Namen / wegzulassen wie ein zerbrochenes Spielzeug" [even to let go one's name like a broken toy]. "Und das Totsein ist mühsam / und voller Nachholn, daß man allmählich ein wenig / Ewigkeit spürt" [And death is wearisome and full of catching up, before one senses a bit of eternity].[105]

So it sounds like death is a condition in which nothing further happens, no changes occur, except that you gradually lose your particularities, your individual personality, and your name becomes like a broken toy, abandoned. Also, at the end of the Tenth Elegy, after the Lament (*Klage*) leads the newly dead arrival through certain fields, explaining about the realm of the dead, she gets to a point where he has to go on alone. They stand at the foot of the mountain:

> Und da umarmt sie ihn, weinend.
> Einsam steigt er dahin, in die Berge des Ur-Leids,
> Und nicht einmal sein Schritt klingt aus dem tonlosen Los.[106]

> [And she embraces him there, weeping.
> He climbs on alone, into the mountains of primeval grief.
> And no step echoes back from that soundless fate.][107]

So the whole order with which we must find unity which rejoices us is a *Doppelbereich,* and includes death. This is what we have to accept; and this is very difficult for us. We are for the most part fearful, disturbed

---

104. "The resolve grew up more and more, within my deepest feelings, to hold life open to *death*"; from a letter by Rilke to Nanny von Escher, quoted in Rainer Maria Rilke, *The Sonnets to Orpheus,* trans. Stephen Mitchell (New York: Simon and Schuster, 1985), 160.

105. Rilke, "Die Zweite Elegie," 688.

106. Rainer Maria Rilke, "Die Zehnte Elegie," in *Werke,* 1:725.

107. Rainer Maria Rilke, "The Tenth Elegy," in *Poems,* 345.

before the prospect of death; or at least we moderns, contemporaries, are unsettled by it, as I explained above (Section V). We see death as the very negation of life. We can't see it as a continuation, a completion of our existence. And so we can't go forward, unchecked, into the Open as animals do, "like fountains."

And this incapacity lends a certain fragility, an insecure hold on being, to our lives, which Rilke invokes in his Second Elegy.

For Rilke, however, death doesn't put an end to the vision. In the Seventh Elegy, after the invocation of Night, and stars, "O einst tot sein, und sie wissen unendlich, / alle die Sterne: Denn wie, wie, wie sie vergessen!" [O, to be dead one day and then know them forever, / and the stars, for how, how, how to forget them!][108] Divested of human personality, and of the distractions of embodied existence, with its changing events and new desires and aspirations, a pure contemplation is possible uninterrupted. And it is because something of this can get through to us, the living, even in our distracted condition, that we are able to see, fitfully, through poetry, how it all fits together.[109]

The decade-long struggle, through multiple obstacles, including the First World War, with the division of Europe and his own forced mobilization, was Rilke's crowning attempt to articulate this poetic vision in his *Duino Elegies,* and also to some degree in the postwar *Sonnets to Orpheus.* These came on him, in a sudden rush of inspiration, along with the completion of the *Elegies.* Indeed, the first of the two cycles of sonnets preceded, and one might even think enabled, the drafting which brought the *Elegies* to completion.

IX

We already saw how Rilke finds a special place for those rare human beings who, like animals, go forward unaffected by the prospect of death: heroes who gladly face early death, lovers who nourish a lifetime of un-

---

108. Rilke, "Die Siebente Elegie," 710; Rilke, "Seventh Elegy," 323. A passage which reminds one again of Novalis, *Hymnen an die Nacht.*

109. See extract from Rilke's letter to Countess Mirbach in Rilke, *Sonnets to Orpheus,* 161–162.

requited love. This suggests a counterpart in the realm of poetry; one which yields a vision of life untroubled and unimpeded by the boundary with death. This is what Rilke set out to accomplish and felt he had triumphantly achieved, a song of praise (*Preisen*).

It follows that for Rilke, our full capacity to Praise can only be realized if we take account of the standpoint of the dead. The medium of *Preisen* is *Gesang* [song]. Thus the voice which most fully carries this song would have to be that of the god Orpheus, who moves in both realms, that of the living and that of the dead.

And the sonnet is the medium. As its name suggests, it is a poetic form which asks to be heard, and not only read on the page. These two modes of reception are essential to all poetry, but in the sonnet the musical dimension becomes the most important avenue to the message.

So a praise-song from both sides, that of the dead, as well as the living. They call on Orpheus, the singer-god who moves between the two realms. Hence the *Sonnets to Orpheus*. There are two series, one written before the completion of the *Elegies,* and one after. The first of the early series begins:

> Da stieg ein Baum. O reine Übersteigung
> O Orpheus singt! O. hoher Baum im Ohr!
> Und alles schwieg. Doch selbst in der Verschweigung
> ging neuer Anfang, Wink und Wandlung vor.[110]

> [A tree arose. O pure transcendence!
> O Orpheus sings! O tall tree within the ear!
> And all was silent. Yes in that silence
> Pulsed a new genesis, new signaling, new change.][111]

Ein Baum im Ohr: We are in the realm of hearing, a realm not of space, but of time. And just as inner and outer reality came together in the *Weltinnenraum,* so they now meet in this new stretch of time. And the beasts of the forest are drawn to the call, and assemble silently, stilling

---

110. Rainer Maria Rilke, "Sonette an Orpheus I.1," in *Werke,* 1:731.
111. Rainer Maria Rilke, "Sonnets to Orpheus I.1," in *Poems,* 350.

their cries and roars, in the new temple of hearing. We, like the beasts, learn a new song:

> Gesang, wie du ihn lehrst ist nicht Begehr,
> nicht Werbung um ein endlich noch Erreichtes;
> Gesang ist Dasein.[112]

> [Singing, as you teach it, is not desire,
> nor the courting of some end to be attained.
> Singing is being.][113]

Dasein, which, we have learned in the *Elegies,* is the fullness of existence. And then the poem goes on:

> Für den Gott ein Leichtes.
> Wann aber *sind* wir. Und wann wendet *er*

> an unser Sein die Erde und die Sterne?
> Das *ists* nicht, Junglich, daß du liebst, wenn auch
> Die Stimme dann den Mund dir aufstößt,—lerne

> vergessen daß du aufsangst. Das verrint.
> In Wahrheit singen, ist ein andrer Hauch.
> Ein Hauch um nichts, Ein Wehn im Gott. Ein Wind.[114]

> [Easy, for a god
> But for us, when *are* we? And when does *he*

> cast all the earth and stars upon our lives?
> It's *not,* youth, when you're in love, even
> If then your voice forces open your mouth;—

112. Rilke, *Poetry of Rilke,* 350–351.
113. Rilke, *Poetry of Rilke,* 354–355.
114. Rilke, "Sonette an Orpheus I.3," in *Werke,* 732.

Learn to forget these songs. They elapse.
True singing is a different breath
A breath serving nothing. A gust in God. A wind.][115]

Part I, Sonnet 8:

Nur im Raum der Rühmung darf die Klage
gehen, die Nymphe der geweinten Quells.
wachend über unsern Niederschlage
Dass es klar sei an demselben Fels.

[. . .]
Aber plötzlich schräg und ungeübt,
hält sie doch ein Sternbild unsrer Stimme
in den Himmel, den ihr Hauch nicht trübt.[116]

[Only in the realm of Praise may Lament
range, the nymph of the tear-fed stream,
watching over our cascade to ensure
that it strikes clearly on the same rock.

[. . .]
Yet suddenly, unpracticed though she is,
She lifts a constellation of our voice
Into skies not clouded by her breath.][117]

The first sonnet tells how the "space of praise" mutates through music into a stretch of time; this eighth one shows how the long time of suffering (*das alte Schlimme*) is transposed by the Lament into a constellation, standing there, "untroubled by her breath."

115. Rilke, "Sonnets to Orpheus I.3," in *Poems*, 355.
116. Rilke, "Sonette an Orpheus I.8," in *Werke*, 735–736.
117. Rilke, "Sonnets to Orpheus I.8," in *Poems*, 365.

Part I, Sonnet 9:

> Erst in dem Doppelbereich
> werden die Stimmen
> ewig und mild.[118]

> [Only in the double realm
> do the voices become
> eternal and mild.][119]

In reality, the *Sonnets* explore the ways that space and time mutate into each other and are inextricably related. In I.3, our passion-driven songs fade before "ein Hauch um Nichts"; in I.8, our long suffering reaches the repose of a constellation. In I.22, we are seen as "Treibenden," but only "Verweilende" can initiate us. But at the same time, Orpheus is a god of the ever changing.

I've dipped into this very rich work because the sonnets extend the vision of the *Elegies* in a host of new directions and offer their own original views on our present condition, but I can't take things further now. I would just like to set out one further sonnet, which I find profoundly moving. Part II, Sonnet 21:

> Singe die Gärten, mein Herz, die du nicht kennst; wie in Glas
> eingegossene Gärten, klar, unerreichbar.
> Wasser und Rosen von Isphahan oder Schiras,
> singe sie selig, preise sie, keinem vergleichbar.

> Zeige, mein Herz, daß du sie niemals entbehrst.
> Daß sie dich meinen, ihre reifenden Feigen.
> Daß du mit ihren, zwischen den blühigen Zweigen
> Wie zum Gesicht gesteigerten Lüften verkehrst.

> Meide den Irrtum, daß es Entbehrungen gebe
> Für den geschehnen Entschluß, diesen: zu sein!
> Seidener Faden, kamst du hinein ins Gewebe.

118. Rilke, "Sonette an Orpheus I.9," in *Werke*, 736.
119. Rilke, "Sonnets to Orpheus I.9," in *Poems*, 367.

Welchem der Bilder du auch im Innern geeinst bist
(sei es selbst ein Moment aus dem Leben der Pein),
fühl, daß der ganze, der rühmliche Teppe gemeint ist.[120]

[Sing the gardens, my heart, those you never knew; gardens
As if poured into glass: bright, unattainable.
Waters and roses of Isfahan or Shiraz,
Sing them blissfully, praise them, beyond compare.

Show, my heart, that you *aren't* without them.
That when their figs ripen, they have *you* in mind.
That when their winds grow almost visible
Amid the flowering branches, it's *you* they embrace.

Avoid this error: that so many chances die
when one choice is made: to be!
Silk thread, you were drawn into the fabric

Whatever single image you made yourself part of
(be it even a scene from a life of torment),
Feel how the whole carpet is meant, its glorious weave.][121]

X

Such is my interpretation of Rilke's *Duino Elegies*. I have to admit that there are still problems raised by this reading.

One which arises from my interpretation: Doesn't all this talk of earth wanting to be raised by our bringing it inward to a higher realization sound terribly idealist? But for all the echoes of Novalis that we find in Rilke, there is no question of "magical idealism" here. The nonhuman

120. Rilke, "Sonette an Orpheus II.21," in *Werke*, 765.
121. Rilke, "Sonnets to Orpheus II.21," in *Poems*, 445.

universe is not transformed. What is raised to a higher power is the world as we live by and in it.

But what does Rilke mean in the passages where he says things like: the earth wants "*unsichtbar*/ In uns erstehen" [to arise/ in us *invisibly*]? Is he attributing mental states to some super-entity called "earth"? Clearly not. We can perhaps get closer to his claim if we formulate it this way: the reason why the whole reality exists, englobing both universe and us, as well as the *Doppelbereich* which includes living and dead, is in order to bring about this juncture between reality and vision.

But what could convince us of this? It can only be that, when we break through all the barriers, and draw on the lived meanings that the things of the earth have for us, we transpose them in the transparent medium of poetry; then the realities of earth and sky show up in all their glory (*Herrlichkeit*), and in response we experience a heightening, a fullness of existence ("die Adern voll Dasein," like the "Mädchen" of the Seventh Elegy, stanza 4). Further than that, explanation cannot venture.

Rilke and Visual Art

This is perhaps the place to note the importance of visual art for Rilke. Worpswede, where he lived for a time at the beginning of the century, was a colony of artists, and it is here that he met his wife. He worked with Rodin as his secretary for a number of years in the 1900s and published a book about the sculptor.

His response to Cézanne is particularly revealing about what he drew from painting. When Rilke remarked about a portrait of Mme. Cézanne that "all the parts seemed to know about each other," he seemed to be on to one of the crucial features of the painter's way of proceeding, which has often been commented on.[1]

Cézanne portrayed his human subjects in the same way as he did natural objects. As noted by Merleau-Ponty and others: "He desired an ardent connection between [nature and human beings], a deep concordance so that the picture, despite fragmentary handling, would reveal a superior essence."[2] This is an almost pantheist dimension of Cézanne's work.[3]

The epoch of Rilke, straddling the nineteenth and twentieth centuries, was also a time of new departures in painting, which have some

1. See Paul Cézanne, *Finished Unfinished*, exhibition catalog (Zurich: Hatje Kantz, 2000), 136–137.

2. Cézanne, *Finished Unfinished*, 27.

3. Cézanne, *Finished Unfinished*, 202. What he showed was "the connection between human 'being' and the 'being' of the world."

similarity to the theme I've been following in this book, in that they seem to invoke unseen forces or orders in the cosmos.

An often-cited example was Monet, whose arresting studies of light, on haystacks, on flowers, on cathedral facades, were linked to his Buddhist convictions. Some postimpressionists, like Van Gogh, go beyond suggestion, and seem to be portraying the force fields emanating from the landscapes (and stars) they depicted.[4] But Rilke himself seems to have felt a strong affinity not to these, but rather to Cézanne. How to understand this?

We might try starting with Cézanne's debt to Pissarro. This calls for a description of what Pissarro achieved. As we look out over a rural scene, made up, say, of field and forest, our perception of its component parts is influenced, one might say shaped, by our grasp of the whole. This may easily escape us, because our interest is often getting some feature right, say an area of pasture, and our focus on this detail leads us to walk there, perhaps measure it. All this activity produces in the end an "objective," "accurate" description of the field, and we forget the whole process of learning, and read this in the light of the resulting "correct" mapping. The nature of the actual experience involved here is forgotten, buried under the useful knowledge acquired.

But suppose what we are interested in is precisely the experience. If so, what we need to bring out is the way in which our grasp of each detail of the scene is shaped by its relation to the whole. We could say that in experience the scene as a whole is inhabited by a force field uniting the parts. How can we bring this to consciousness? Perhaps through a painting which renders this field, which brings it to visible expression, where it can be recognized by others, precisely because it is a deeply tacit part of their experience. And this surging forth of the hitherto hidden in an expanded awareness can provoke a kind of joy at its sudden discovery.

"In ordinary life, we are immersed in things; our style of perceiving them does not exist independently of our body. The painting, however,

---

4. See Katharine Lochnan, ed., *Mystical Landscapes: From Vincent van Gogh to Emily Carr*, exhibition catalog for the Art Gallery of Ontario, the Musée d'Orsay, and the Musée de l'Orangerie (Toronto: Art Gallery of Ontario, 2016).

frees the painter's style from this confine, and makes it exist at a public level—as a possibility of experience for others."[5] (Paul Crowther, from whom this quote is taken, goes on to discuss Merleau-Ponty's point that we read the "invisible" [i.e., not directly presented] facets of things through the face they present to us. We can do this because we read them "through" our multiform capacities to handle them, deal with them, navigate through them.[6])

I think the above account, or something like it, describes Pissarro's achievement. And Cézanne builds on it, takes it farther. The difficulty lies in saying just what this further step involves. Perhaps we should better say: Cézanne tries to take this achievement farther, because he never seems to have been totally satisfied with the result. He described his method: "Je vois. Par taches." (I see. By spots.) This is highly misleading; it doesn't mean that he tried to build the picture element by element; this would have defeated the purpose. It rather means that successive dabs are meant to culminate in a sense of force field. One has to keep a voracity of eye, be restlessly active, in order to achieve this sense of the totality.[7] The totality is felt "all at once." This, it seems, is what Rilke was getting at in the remark I quoted above, that "all parts seem to know each other."[8]

Cézanne is in a sense postimpressionist in that he has abandoned the duality of drawing and painting; but his is a postimpressionism which rejects any form of subjectivism: what he is striving to articulate is not just his personal experience. His frequently repeated goal was to "remake Poussin from nature," in other words, return to the solidity and objectivity of the old Masters, "like the Venetians," but by a new route.[9] He tried, but frequently didn't manage to complete the effect; patches of white or inconsistencies in his landscapes seem to indicate that the work

5. Paul Crowther, *The Phenomenology of Modern Art* (London: Continuum, 2012), 55.

6. Crowther, *Phenomenology of Modern Art*, 238–240.

7. T. J. Clark, *If These Apples Should Fall: Cézanne and the Present* (London: Thames and Hudson, 2022).

8. Cézanne, *Finished Unfinished*, 136–137.

9. Cézanne, *Finished Unfinished*, 27, 37.

was unfinished—unless the point was to convey the sense of movement, becoming.

I've been looking at Cézanne as a continuator of Pissarro; but in what sense can he be seen as attempting something analogous to the poets I have been tracking here—namely, connecting to cosmic forces? This is very difficult to discern. But there are hints:

> About landscapes:
>
> Everything around us disperses, vanishes, doesn't it? Nature is always the same, but nothing remains of how it appears to us. Our art must convey the thrill of its permanence, with the elements and the appearances of all its changes. It must give us a taste of nature's eternity.[10]
>
> Yes, the earth here is always vibrating, it has a harshness that throws the light back and makes you blink, but you sense how it is always nuanced, full and soft. A rhythm inhabits it.[11]
>
> Look at this Sainte-Victoire. What energy, what imperious thirst for the sun, and what melancholy in the evening, when all that weight sinks back. . . . Those blocks were made of fire. There's still fire in them. During the day the shadows seem to recoil with a shudder, to be afraid of them.[12]

I don't know whether these quotes answer the question I put above. But maybe it's worth asking what made Rilke feel a strong affinity to Cézanne. Perhaps he saw the painter as striving to realize what we can call his (Rilke's) "elegies" moment, when his poetic descriptions of the universe and our sense of it met with a confirmation from the universe itself in an affirmation of the glory of our existence here: "Hiersein ist herrlich." Perhaps Cézanne never experienced such a moment; this would have consisted in a sense of certainty that he had brought to expression the full shape of the force field he was striving to render.

10. Cézanne, *Finished Unfinished*, 269.
11. Cézanne, *Finished Unfinished*, 352.
12. Cézanne, *Finished Unfinished*, 361.

Emerson and Transcendentalism

Ralph Waldo Emerson and the movement he launched, "Transcendentalism," inaugurated a new kind of individualism, distinct from the entrepreneurial form which was already powerful in American society, and from the "possessive" form which Brough Macpherson traced to Locke. The new doctrine was not only distinct from these, but highly critical of them. Transcendentalism is an individualism of spiritual search.

Emerson defended the "absolute independence and right" of every soul to "interpret for itself the meaning of life, untrammeled by tradition and conventions."[1]

The inspiration for this search comes most immediately from Nature. Looking at nature, the whole brings an exhilaration, in which all mean egotism vanishes: "I am the lover of uncontained and immortal beauty"; "nature always wears the color of the spirit."[2]

Nature moves us with its beauty, and this beauty manifests virtue. "Beauty is the mark God sets upon virtue." But beauty is but one expression: "God is the all-fair. Truth, and goodness, and beauty, are but different faces of the same All."[3] So we also learn from the lives of great teachers. Emerson looks for a "new Teacher, that . . . shall see the world to be the mirror of the soul, shall see the identity of the law of

---

1. Compare Robert A. Gross, *The Transcendentalists and Their World* (New York: Farrar, Straus and Giroux, 2021), 402.

2. Ralph Waldo Emerson, "Nature," in *Essays and Poems* (New York: Penguin Library of America, 1986), 10–11.

3. Emerson, "Nature," 19.

gravitation with purity of heart, and shall show that the Ought, that Duty, is one thing with Science, with Beauty, and with Joy."[4]

But if we can learn what a truly virtuous and spiritual life is through the example of great prophets and founders of religion, where would the place be for individualism? Emerson's answer is that an essential pre-condition for this learning is some intuition that each of us has come to within. And by intuition he means an insight which can't be adequately stated in unambiguously understandable speech. But an intuition "cannot be received at second hand. Truly speaking, it is not instruction, but prov-ocation, that I can receive from another soul. What he announces, I must find true in me, or wholly reject; and on his word, or as his second, be he who he may, I can accept nothing. On the contrary, the absence of this primary faith is the presence of degradation. As is the flood so is the ebb. Let this faith depart, and the very words it spake, and the things it made, become false and hurtful. Then falls the church, the state, art, letters, life."[5]

We humans all share the same nature, and that includes the capacity to see the truths about nature, virtue, and religion. In one place Emerson can even speak of an "over-soul," a love of the eternal and beautiful, which animates us all. This is the center of our moral world, but to be effective it has to be activated by each individual.[6]

> Let man, then, learn the revelation of all nature and all thought to his heart: this, namely: that the Highest dwells with him; that the sources of nature are in his own mind, if the sentiment of duty is there. But if he would know what the great God spea-keth, he must "go into his closet and shut the door," as Jesus said. God will not make himself manifest to cowards. He must greatly listen to himself, withdrawing himself from all the ac-cents of other men's devotion. Even their prayers are hurtful to him, until he have made his own. Our religion vulgarly stands on numbers of believers. Whenever the appeal is

---

4. Ralph Waldo Emerson, "The Divinity School Address," in *Essays and Poems,* 92.
5. Emerson, "Divinity School Address," 79.
6. Ralph Waldo Emerson, "The Over-soul," in *Essays and Poems,* 387.

made—no matter how indirectly—to numbers, proclamation
is then and there made, that religion is not.[7]

Emerson sees his doctrine as a species of idealism. The term "tran-
scendental" is drawn from Kant, "who replied to the skeptical philosophy
of Locke, which insisted that there was nothing in the intellect which was
not previously in the experience of the senses, by showing that there is
an important class of ideas, or imperative forms, which did not come by
experience, but through which experience was acquired; that these were
the intuitions of the mind itself; and he denominated them *Transcen-
dental* forms."[8]

Now clearly there is a debt here, not just to the German philosophy
which immediately preceded the Romantic period, but also to German
Romanticism itself; which Emerson learned of through Coleridge and
Carlyle, among others. And there does seem to be a certain affinity between the Romantic reconnection with cosmic order through poetry,
and Emerson's doctrine. And at one point Emerson says of Nature that
it exhibits a "serene order," which is "inviolable by us. It is, therefore, to
us, the present expositor of the divine mind. It is a fixed point whereby
we may measure our departure."[9]

But there are important differences.

If we take Hölderlin, for instance, there is a conception of the cosmic
order, on the model of premodern conceptions of such order; and the
Gods who figure in this order are those of the Community. Both these
features are far removed from Emerson's Transcendentalism. But there
remain affinities between the two. For Emerson, the beauty and order
in Nature invites a deep response in the soul, which if answered, would
bring about the fullest realization of our human potential, a quasi-
religious faith which would transform our lives.

There is some palpable resonance with the post-Romantic search for
(re)connection. And this individualist variant has been a fertile source
for American poetry, through Whitman and beyond.

7. Emerson, "Over-soul," 399.

8. Ralph Waldo Emerson, "The Transcendentalist," in *Essays and Poems*, 198.

9. Emerson, "Nature," 42.

Chapter Nine

EPISTEMIC RETREAT AND THE
NEW CENTRALITY OF TIME

I

A central theme of my discussion of post-Romantic poetry has been (re-) connection. The prefix "re" here reflects the sense of loss and then recovery. The loss came with the uncertainty about, and growing loss of confident contact with, traditional and Renaissance notions of cosmic order: the Great Chain of Being, the Creation as a communication from God, the Kabbalah, and the like.

This traditional cosmos was ordered with higher and lower levels. This hierarchy was seen as a scale of value, but not simply subjective. It was also a standard which exercises power to shape reality. So it is modeled on a Platonic Idea; it draws reality into conformity with it.

The order is also reflected in human society. This means that attempts to upset it, subvert it, will be resisted. So when Macbeth kills Duncan, horses rise against masters, because the upsetting of order in the society (regicide!) triggers off repercussions in the larger cosmos. This destructive move is self-subverting. This self-realizing power seems to be a feature of all Renaissance order concepts.

Even when we can't attempt subversion, the order tells us something about how elements influence each other, relate to each other. So the Kabbalah gives numbers to all realities based on the Hebrew letters which spell their names. This tells us conduits of sympathy. The same can be said of Paracelsian "signatures."

That is why it is important to search for and discover the original Adamic language, because this allows you to grasp the self-shaping force in each reality.

And a similar motivation underlies alchemical research; learning how to treat lower metals so that they turn into gold is learning how to elevate our lives (initially made up of lesser elements) to the highest form.

Orders are also present at all levels: so what the king is in the state "corresponds" to the lion among animals, the eagle among birds, the dolphin among fish.

And order in the whole cosmos matches order in the microcosm which is the human being. The cosmos calls on us to be similarly ordered, ruled by reason, not brute desire.

All these orders are thought to be unchanging and sempiternal. But the first big change comes with the Romantic era (period of "Raptures" for Miłosz). Not only do traditional orders get obscured, even fall into doubt; not only are new definitions of order proposed (even if under the sign of art-induced conviction—hence in many cases, ultimate uncertainty about the underlying story); but also a certain historical dimension enters. The ultimate proper order can be lost, and then regained; or even more radically, lost in an earlier version, and then recovered in a higher form. This was the standard German Romantic story of the *exzentrische Bahn* [spiral path]. But it was also implicit in Blake. (And it was also implicit in the Christian story of the Fall as a *felix culpa*.)

EXCURSUS 1

There is an important difference between Blake and the German Romantics: the *felix culpa* model had a distant civilizational influence on the Germans; but the Romantic generation thought out division and reuniting in terms of philosophy: Kant, Fichte, then the *Versöhnung* [reconciliation] projected by Schiller; whereas Blake's Fall and Redemption are a (highly unorthodox) reading of the biblical story.

But where they both agree is in opposing Descartes, Locke, and the objectifying stance to Nature these philosophers justified, which exalted post-Galilean natural science as the royal road to knowledge: "objectification" here means that one abstracts from all the human meanings of the surrounding world, and sees this as a set of inert objects and forces, without deeper meaning; fit objects for a natural science, which can enable control; the kind of science that Scheler called *Leistungswissen*. This stance was tersely expressed by a symbolist poet of the modernist era, W. B. Yeats:

> Locke fell into a swoon;
> The garden died;
> God took the spinning jenny
> Out of his side.[1]

Like Yeats later, all the Romantics passionately rejected this kind of reduction, and refused to see freedom in terms of control; for them freedom doesn't lie in control, but in a response to the meaning of things which unites us as embodied-reasoning beings.

(Re)covering unity with, or contact with, or felt connection with these orders both is brought about by poetry (or, more widely, art: e.g., both music and painting) and is a source of joy. We can speak of what is realized here as (i) communion or (ii) resonance in the sense of Hartmut Rosa.

In Chapters 1–6, we have several examples of poets, and a variety of modes of connection. There is (a) felt awareness of the force of the order in the world around us: William Wordsworth in "Tintern Abbey"; Hölderlin in "Heimkunft," "Archipelago," and so on; Novalis in *Hymnen an die Nacht*. Less obvious modes of connection are (b) "reading" our

---

1. William Butler Yeats, *The Collected Poems of W. B. Yeats* (New York: Macmillan, 1982), 240–241.

own feelings / aspirations "through" the landscape surrounding us (Goethe in the mountain forest), and (c) poetry which intensifies our experience of belonging to, and being nourished by, surrounding Nature (e.g., Keats' "Nightingale").

The difference between (a) and (c): with (a) we give some name / description to the order / force; while with (c) we don't, but the *relation* of communion / resonance is intensified, and this intensification is *felt,* but unlike with (a) and (b), there is no account offered of why and how this is brought about.

Then we go on to note different kinds of (a). First with Hopkins' "inscape": we sense the force shaping, affirming a given being (e.g., kestrel), and this in turn is read as one place where we come in touch with a reality universal in the cosmos: a cosmos made up of such individual beings who / which are actively realizing their own natures. The joy for Hopkins comes from his recognizing the ubiquity in the cosmos of such natures, read through an underlying philosophical story of medieval realism in Duns Scotus' form, and an underlying Christian theology of creation.

Then with Rilke we have another way of reading our original state of disconnect, which we are called upon to overcome: instead of a supposition of some underlying order in things, we have the sense of a barrier: we are not really managing to get through to what underlies and powers the beings which surround us. At first, God is postulated as this reality underlying the things we encounter; then there is a notion, borrowed from Novalis, that things have their own language, which we can't yet read / grasp. Then finally, in the *Elegies,* we see the realities of our world as putting an obligation on us (an *Auftrag*) to say / celebrate them. Success in this enterprise releases an immense joy.

Devising the language in which we can "say" them is our greatest fulfillment.

II

Let's pause here and ask: What is so good, even great, about such (re)connections? If we are thinking of the original premodern cosmic orders, the answer was obvious. The consciousness of, and sense of contact with, these orders quickens our sense of the good, or hierarchy of goods, that they embody. Our ethical being is enlivened, felt more powerfully, and hence also empowered. Feeling, sensing, being moved by the good in this way is understood as realizing more fully our human nature. Theologically, for those still within a Christian perspective, we participate somewhat in God's vision, when he "saw that it was good."

Something of this carries forward into the early Romantic invocations of order. So Hopkins is not just becoming conscious of an underlying causal force, but seeing / sensing the goodness in creation. But as we move on through the different forms of invocation in the Romantic period, this model is less and less applicable.

Take for instance (b) above, Goethe's rendering palpable a human fulfillment which is captured by *Ruh;* and also (c): obviously, as we saw in Chapter 5, poetry can intensify our sense of being nourished by Nature.

Clearly, I have been using the term "(re)connection" to characterize not a single goal, but rather an aspiration which can take a number of different forms. These have in common that they involve recovering contact with deeper forces or currents which are at work below / behind the immediately visible / tangible surface of things.

But as we go forward through the century, what I called in earlier chapters the "epistemic retreat" continues. This consisted at first in the implicit abandonment of claims about the "underlying story"; about, that is, the reality beyond our experience. The claim was about the "interspace" that the poem drew us into: the strong sense of being connected to a larger order. But with Goethe's experience in the mountain forest, the felt claim is not primarily about the world; rather what emerges is a deep and enigmatic inkling of a profound aspiration in us, toward (in some hard-to-fathom sense) *Ruh.*

And when we come to (c), the articulation of our need to be nourished by nature, the primacy of the self-reading is all the more evident. The "reading" of the surrounding world is more and more about us humans.

But it is still appropriate to speak of (re)connection here: what is coming to light here is our need to be closely related to the surrounding natural world. This need, this aspiration is ethical. It aims at what is felt to be a profound aspiration of human beings, inscribed one might say in their nature.

I'm using the word "ethical" here, in the sense in which it figures in a distinction commonly recognized in today's discussions in philosophy, whereby "morality" concerns justice between agents, or "what we owe each other" (T. M. Scanlon), and "ethics" defines the ends we seek, the fulfillments which our nature as human beings prescribes for us; we are here in Aristotelian, rather than Kantian, territory. (Although from an ethical perspective, the distinction lies between two departments of ethics, because creating just, mutually respectful relations constitutes an essential end for us.[2])

This raises an important issue: whether this aspiration to connection is not a human constant, and connection a perennial human possibility, albeit taking very different forms in different epochs and cultures. I want to look again at this question toward the end of this book.

But to return to the discussion of the preceding pages, all of the authors and works we've examined can be seen as identifying different forms of initial disconnection, then (re)connection, with the surrounding natural world. But the reconnection was to this world as it perennially is. Time entered into consideration because we may initially be disconnected and have to struggle to reconnect. But reconnection links us to contemporaneous, continuously existing orders; the link, one might say, is spatial; it connects us to a wider, cosmic space.

In contrast to this, there are modes of disconnection / reconnection which concern time as well as space, where the connection through time is crucial.

Now with hindsight it is clear that not all of these (purely "spatial") forms were destined to last. Works which invoke experiences like (b) (Goethe's reading a deep aspiration through the mountain forest) and like (c) (intensifying our feeling of being nourished by our natural surroundings), which are in their very nature indefinite, can probably still be produced. Certainly this is true of (c). But (a) makes much more definite claims, even if under the proviso I invoked at the beginning, that these

---

2. I am returning here to an issue which was raised in Chapter 2, section I.1, where I discussed what could validate the claim that a poem can reconnect us to a cosmic order.

are claims about what is *experienced,* rather than about what exists in the cosmos independent of us. They suppose a continuing order, or forces.

And in fact, from midcentury on, we have a decline even in such invocations of experienced orders—Rilke's *Doppelbereich* (Double realm of living and dead) is very different from the traditional cosmic order; and this comes along with a concentration on issues about time, restoring time.

What is going on here?

I don't want to imply that earlier in the Romantic period, writers and poets were not aware of issues around the evolution of species. On the contrary, from the very beginning writers and thinkers were interested not just in continuing orders, but also in the forces underlying life and development. Indeed, one of the most influential thinkers (for the Romantics) of this time tried to address this question. Linné gave a static classification of life-forms; but Goethe sees this as the work of a life force, driving each generation to beget the next one. We know this from within: this is the sexual drive.

But Goethe's "Metamorphosis" goes further. The image is partly borrowed from Ovid, who imagines transformation. So Goethe sees his force as not only driving living things to reproduce; it also underlies evolution, which produces new species, not limiting itself to perpetuating these species once they exist.[3]

But it wasn't until later in the nineteenth century that the fact of, and issues around, evolution began to drain the traditional standing orders of their hold on the human imagination.

In part, we see here a continuation of what I called above the "epistemic retreat," when invocations even of "experiential" orders become rarer, as do also, somewhat later, attempts to bring to light, or connect with, the inner sustaining force in things.

But something else is happening, which underlies the epistemic retreat: as I mentioned in Chapter 5, the sense of the real as the object of natural science hardens, in our civilization, and comes to dominate. This is a continuation of the movement which earlier put in doubt visions of

---

3. Heinrich Detering, "Kapitel V," in *Menschen im Weltgarten* (Göttingen: Wallstein Verlag, 2020).

cosmic order. Issues of evolution arise, undercutting notions of unchanging order.

But it took some time for the awareness of evolutionary change to undermine the sense of static order and replace it with our present ecological visions of an ever-changing (and now threatened) planetary Nature.

The last three centuries in Western civilization have seen a long slide toward an increasing focus on the bare materiality of things. This is what sapped the earlier belief in cosmic orders, to which the Romantic invocation of order in an interspace is a response.

In similar fashion, once it no longer can be taken for granted that material things in general reflect or participate in soul or spirit, the way is open for a new laying bare of an interiority in things: Hopkins, Dostoyevsky, Rilke.

This is a crucial part of what is new in the post-Romantic period. In the earlier "enchanted" world, every material thing is sustained by a skein of underlying forces: each material thing has its Form, among other forms; forest and field are the sites of spirits and forces. This background sustains everything. But the perceptions, or experiences of order, or underlying forces in the post-Romantic context are different: they are visible only at particular loci; or they are of particular realities. Wordsworth sees the order in / through the Wye valley; Hopkins grasps the inscape *of this kestrel*. The assumption in each case is that the order exists everywhere in nature, that all particular things have inscapes, but the poetry generates, releases a grasp of the order in a particular spot: Wye valley, mountain with falcon, sky, valley, Mediterranean around Salamis (the latter two here invoke Hölderlin).

One could argue: the general underlying sense that forces were everywhere had to recede for these particular revelations to emerge with the emphatic power that they have.

The unshaken confidence that cosmic orders are there, that moral forces operate everywhere, lends a quality to our ancestors' perceptions of woods, valley, fields, animals, which inhibits the kind of perception of the particular that the post-Romantic period generates. To the medieval mind, everything was treated as allegory: things were seen both in themselves and allegorically, both literally and as symbols. "Everything was an intermingling of surface and depth."[4] Body and soul share the same energy; the crucial term for their relation is *methexis* [participation].[5] The High Renaissance still operated in this world. Ficino is an example.

But the same fading of the earlier outlook which made the Romantic invocation of orders and forces possible continued unchecked, and eventually came totally to obliterate this past, rendering earlier invocations of allegory and participation less and less meaningful, even understandable.

This is not to say that everyone now agrees with the most hard-nosed believers in reductive scientific accounts of human life and action; far from it. But in the immanent frame which we now inhabit, the natural-scientific account of the universe is more or less universally shared, while deeper understandings of human meanings are contested. The epistemic retreat is a response to this situation.

III

But the impact of the expanding field of modern natural science on our visions of order has not only been negative. Granted, a feature of the classical to Renaissance orders disappears: the one which I described in the opening paragraphs above—namely, that the cosmos is ordered with higher and lower levels, and that this rank ordering is related to the hierarchy in the social order and the hierarchy of ethical actions. But the discoveries of science can also inspire a new sense of beauty and awe in the universe, as we see most strikingly in the work of Alexander von Humboldt in the nineteenth century.

Humboldt, starting with his exploratory journey in South America at the beginning of the nineteenth century, began to lay bare connections and analogies between plant and animal forms, and also between climatic phenomena in different regions, which he experienced, and led others by his writings to experience, as deeply moving, in a way analogous to the beauty of poetry. What disappears is a difference in rank; the most

---

4. Mark Vernon, *A Secret History of Christianity* (Alresford, Hampshire, UK: John Hunt, 2019), 143.

5. Vernon, *Secret History,* 147.

detailed specification of the smallest living creature, or geological phenomenon, can inspire us as much as large-scale and terrifying volcanic activity. If anything, the older rank order is replaced by the difference between the beauty of intricate design versus the sublime of the massive volcanic eruption. The emotion awakened in us differs, the quality of excitement is greatly intensified (see Humboldt's awe at the sight of Mount Chimborazo), but the ontological status is the same.

Now this leveling of ontological value differentiates the Humboldtian from the earlier Romantic invocations of underlying cosmic order, from Hölderlin to Rilke; and along with this comes another crucial distinction: the orders and connections which inspired Humboldt were not revealed by poetry, but by scientific observation and study; discovery may, indeed, inspire poetry, but doesn't emanate from it. According to Humboldt, the scientific vision of Nature he developed was already "poetic." He stands in what we may call a Goethean tradition (and indeed, the two maintained, in spite of the difference in age, and very rare moments together, an intense relation of mutual inspiration). Like his model, his work primarily reveals a profound aspiration in us, coupled with an enigmatic hint at the underlying forces in the natural world.

As Andrea Wulf shows in her very interesting book on Humboldt, he inspired a great number of thinkers of the first rank in the nineteenth century and beyond: among them, Thoreau, Haeckl, Marsh, Muir.[6] This tradition makes no concession to Cartesian-Baconian objectification of nature as mechanism, and everywhere these Humboldtians combat the destruction of forest and wilderness that this stance encourages, even though they push outward the corpus of scientific knowledge. As Thoreau put it, "In Wildness is the Preservation of the World."[7] And Muir was so moved by the majestic beauty of Yosemite that he dedicated himself to the protection of American wilderness—and convinced Theodore Roosevelt to take up the cause.[8]

6. Andrea Wulf, *The Invention of Nature: Alexander von Humboldt's New World* (New York: Knopf, 2016).

7. Quoted in Roderick Nash, *Wilderness and the American Mind* (New Haven, CT: Yale University Press, 2014), ch. 3.

8. Wulf, *Invention of Nature*, 331.

And there were, of course, other nineteenth-century figures, outside the Humboldtian ambit, like Chateaubriand, who inaugurated a similar stance of inspired awe before untamed nature.

IV

But the growth in scientific understanding of nature also explains, I would argue, the shift in our aspiration to reconnection with the cosmos from a focus on static orders to concerns about time. The natural-scientific account of the cosmos we now share, unlike its Newtonian predecessor, is anything but static order. From the Big Bang on, it is in continuous development, change, and when it comes to living beings, evolution. In the scientific account, *panta rhei*—everything flows, as Heraclitus put it. The Natural Science story is a long chain of change, development, evolution, destruction, and recombination of orders, transforming things every minute; there is no static point. In addition, the order of "Nature" on the planet itself is clearly not sempiternal; rather it is threatened by us.

And similarly, human history, from the extinction of the Neanderthals to the rise of the web, is constant, usually unforeseeable innovation.

This cannot be without effect on the earlier order-invoking powers of poetry.

So, perhaps partly in response to this, at the end of the nineteenth century, "symbolist" poetry (a trend which Yeats followed early in his career) brings a third phase of epistemic retreat: at its apogee it avoids any determinate existential claims, in any domain, although these can be replaced with powerful but indefinite suggestions.

EXCURSUS 2: INTO (NON)EXPLANATION

Many would want to explain this decline of claims—even just experiential—about universal cosmic orders, or against underlying forces active behind/beneath the visible, tangible, scientifically researchable surfaces of things, as a simple victory of Enlightenment and Reason. The forward march of scientific understanding has relegated all such unfounded imaginings to an unrecoverable past, as it dissipates the dreams of folklore and religion.

Well, that *could* be right. But its too-quick acceptance begs a deeper question: Where do all these imaginings come from? It seems that all human societies before the scientific age have seen the lives of human beings as in continuing interchange with cosmic interlocutors and forces: gods, spirits, the human dead, and so forth. And our present age is in no way unanimous in denying this—not to speak of the fact that many who reject the very idea of cosmic forces are moved to do so by their faith in a transcendent deity.

So we need to ask ourselves: Whence these perennial imaginings? Are they really just gratuitous inventions? For the moment, these are questions on which I am agnostic, if we're talking about sure, undeniable knowledge; but I have certain hunches, intuitions. This seems to me a more rational response than outright total denial.

But along with the decline of these incursions into inner or underlying "space" come a new range of issues about time. On one side, the new understanding of cosmic space-time which arises in the wake of post-Newtonian science provokes a new focus on its antonym, lived time. And this opens the way to issues about its nature (Bergson, Husserl, Heidegger, and phenomenology). And beyond that, burning questions arise about the conditions of bearable lived time; of resonance and the conditions thereof.

At a deeper level, issues of underlying order, of constancy, of connections and continuities over time, raise questions about possible overarching links between/across times. Hence higher times, patterns in time.

I will return to this after Chapter 10, on Baudelaire.

But what becomes of the desire for cosmic connection? Does it just disappear? No, rather it mutates. Minimally, the cosmic order we seek reconnection with is no longer unchanging, but evolving over time.

Or, more radically, what we seek to recover contact with is no longer a cosmos, but Nature; that is, the complex, interwoven, and vulnerable order of living beings on our planet. Many of us seek to recover a sense of belonging to, of membership in this larger order, to be nourished by it, and in solidarity with it, in the face of the terrible destruction which now threatens it.

That is why works of the category (c) above, which yield a sense of our being part of, and nourished by, Nature, are still important and sought after. Only poetry is no longer the only, or even the principal, vehicle of this sense today. Works of detailed description, or scientific accounts of underlying causes, can also transform our felt relation to the natural world; and perhaps more effectively than poetry can aspire to. Think of the work of Annie Dillard, for example.[9]

(And this drive to reconnect with Nature shows the long-term influence of a giant figure of the Romantic age, who nevertheless held aloof from the Romantic movement, i.e., Goethe, whose relation to Humboldt I discussed above.)

And the fading of static orders as poles of reconnection has not been accompanied by a decline in the experience of breaking through to wider spaces of transcendence. On the contrary, the decline of the "established" churches, uniting whole societies, characteristic of Christendom, has led to widespread spiritual / religious searching on a plurality of paths, characteristic of our secular age.

---

9. Compare Annie Dillard, *Pilgrim at Tinker Creek* (New York: Harper Perennial, 2013).

PART IV

Chapter Ten

BAUDELAIRE

|

The escape from spleen

1

In the previous chapters, I have been looking at the way post-Romantic poetry strives to reconnect with Nature, or the cosmos, or some phenomena in the world, understanding this connection as essential to human fulfillment. What is being defined and sought here is our proper relation to the spatiotemporal world. But there are other issues which concern more narrowly how we inhabit time, and which equally raise questions about our essential fulfillment as human beings. As we shall see, there are reasons why these should have come to the fore in the last two centuries. There is no better door to enter this area than the poetry of Baudelaire, and no better place than *Les Fleurs du Mal*, in its first section, "Spleen et Idéal." I want to talk here mostly about *Les Fleurs du Mal*; but there will be some side glances at other poetic works, and some insights drawn from the critical and autobiographical writings. We can start with these two key terms which make up the section title.

First "Idéal." What does this mean? This is one of the central Romantic longings which still beats in the heart of Baudelaire. It is a longing for a wholeness, a fullness, in which we would be brought to harmonious unity in being enraptured by beauty. In "I. Bénédiction," the opening poem of *Les Fleurs du Mal,* the poet, in the face of all obstacles and persecutions, wins through to a vision:

> "Soyez béni, mon Dieu, qui donnez la souffrance
> Comme un divin remède à nos impuretés
> Et comme la meilleure et la plus pure essence
> Qui prépare les forts aux saintes voluptés!
>
> Je sais que vous gardez une place au Poëte
> Dans les rangs bienheureux des saintes Légions,
> Et que vous l'invitez à l'éternelle fête
> Des Trônes, des Vertus, des Dominations.
>
> Je sais que la douleur est la noblesse unique
> Où ne mordront jamais la terre et les enfers,
> Et qu'il faut pour tresser ma couronne mystique
> Imposer tous les temps et tous les univers.
>
> Mais les bijoux perdus de l'antique Palmyre,
> Les métaux inconnus, les perles de la mer,
> Par votre main montés, ne pourront pas suffire
> À ce beau diadème éblouissant et clair;
>
> Car il ne sera fait que de pure lumière,
> Puisée au foyer saint des rayons primitifs,
> Et dont les yeux mortels, dans leur splendeur entière.
> Ne sont que des miroirs obscurcis et plaintifs!"[1]

1. Charles Baudelaire, "I. Bénédiction," in *Œuvres complètes* (Paris: Gallimard, 1975), 1:1.

["Be blessed, oh my God, who givest suffering
As the only divine remedy for our folly,
As the highest and purest essence preparing
The strong in spirit for ecstasies most holy.

I know that among the uplifted legions
Of saints, a place awaits the Poet's arrival,
And that among the Powers, Virtues, Dominations
He too is summoned to Heaven's festival.

I know that sorrow is the one human strength
On which neither earth nor hell can impose,
And that all the universe and all time's length
Must be wound into the mystic crown for my brows.

But all the treasury of buried Palmyra,
The earth's unknown metals, the sea's pearls,
Mounted on Thy hand, would be deemed an inferior
Glitter to his diadem that shines without jewels.

For Thou knowest it will be made of purest light
Drawn from the holy hearth of every primal ray,
To which all human eyes, if they were one bright
Eye, are only a tarnished mirror's fading day!"][2]

But we can already hear in the tone of longing in these lines that this magnificent consummation is felt as unattainable. And other poems of this first part only confirm this impression: like "XII. La Vie Antérieur," which starts:

J'ai longtemps habité sous de vastes portiques
Que les soleils marins teignaient de mille feux, (1–2)

---

2. Charles Baudelaire, "I. The Blessing," trans. David Paul, in *The Flowers of Evil*, ed. Marthiel Mathews and Jackson Mathews (New York: New Directions, 1962), 9–10.

[Long since, I lived beneath vast porticoes,
By many ocean-sunsets tinged and fired,]

and continues:

C'est là que j'ai vécu dans les voluptés calmes.
Au milieu de l'azur, des vagues, des splendeurs, (9–10)

[And there I lived amid voluptuous calms,
In splendours of blue sky, and wandering wave,]

and finishes:

Et dont l'unique soin était d'approfondir
Le secret douloureux qui me fait languir. (13–14)[3]

[the only care they had
To know what secret grief had made me sad.][4]

We can see that here is a dream from childhood, and "LXII. Moesta et errabunda" (last three stanzas) confirms this, invoking "le vert paradis des amours enfantines" [the green paradise of childhood loves], which lies behind us in our infancy.[5]

But it's a dream that cannot be realized. And the major obstacle is in us. This sense of the unrealizable Ideal Baudelaire inherits from earlier generations of French Romantic poets, first from the great hopes of a human life and society regenerated by poetic vision, in the 1820s and 1830s, articulated for instance in the works of Hugo and Lamartine, and then from the period of bitter disenchantment which followed through the reign of Louis-Philippe (whose slogan was "enrichissez-vous" [enrich yourselves]), the failure of the Revolution of 1848, and takeover of Louis Napoléon in the Third Empire.

3. Charles Baudelaire, "XII. La Vie anterieure," in *Œuvres complètes,* 1:17.
4. Charles Baudelaire, "XII. A Former Life," trans. F. P. Sturm, in *Flowers of Evil,* 20.
5. Baudelaire, "XII. La Vie anterieure," 80.

Baudelaire finds himself in this age of "disenchantment," as Paul Bénichou describes it, following Musset, Nerval, and Gautier.[6] Beauty was seen as this ideal of harmony and unity. And with Gautier, the closest of these precursors to Baudelaire, the solution eventually became to wall it off from the world of action, suffering, division. It becomes sculptural, perfect, moving in its own world, far from passion. It isn't an answer to this world, a resolution to division and passion. It is a safe realm far from them, shored up against them, a Parnassus. Gautier's work *Émaux et Camées* [Enamels and Cameos], as the title implies, was made up of carefully crafted works, like those of an expert jeweler. It is precisely not the lost childhood, but a very sophisticated and mature place of escape.

Baudelaire seems to speak of this in "XVII. La Beauté." Clearly he doesn't agree with Gautier, for all his admiration of him, and a sense of solidarity-friendship with him. But in this poem, there also is a menace. And this links up with "XXII. Hymne à la Beauté": "Viens-tu du ciel profond, ou sors-tu de l'abîme, / O Beauté" [Do you come from deep heaven, or emerge from the abyss, O Beauty].[7] This kind of beauty is one of the modes of fascination which both liberates us from Spleen, but also takes us farther away from the real Ideal, the real paradise; anchors us into the world of negation, to the "Satanic." It makes "l'univers moins hideux et les instants moins lourds" [the universe less hideous and the instants less heavy]; but it destroys as the candle does the insect that flies toward it, and makes the panting lover look like "un moribund caressant son tombeau" [a dying man caressing his tomb]. "De Satan ou de Dieu, qu'importe?" [From Satan or God, what's the difference?].[8] Here we see the profound ambivalence—more than ambivalence, the double-mindedness of Baudelaire: what he calls the two "postulates." But to see what all this means, we have first to turn to Spleen. What is this?

Spleen, ennui, is an extreme state of melancholy. It is not just a condition in which we feel our exile acutely, in which the things which surround us have no meaning, do not speak to us, in which we are far from sensing the higher love which we long to follow. Much worse befalls us.

6. Paul Bénichou, *L'École du désenchantement* (Paris: Gallimard, 1992).

7. Charles Baudelaire, "XXII. Hymne à la Beauté," in *Œuvres complètes*, 1:30.

8. Baudelaire, "XXII. Hymne à la Beauté," 30.

We begin to lose even the sense of what meaning and love might be. The very shape of what we're lacking disappears from the world; we lose sight of the very possibility. We suffer extreme deprivation but have lost a grasp on what it is we are missing. This brings no peace, but on the contrary the most profound form of despair, of numbness, and paralysis.

See this letter to his mother of 1857: "Un immense découragement, une sensation d'isolement insupportable, une peur perpétuelle d'un malheur vague, une défiance complète de mes forces, une absence totale de désirs, une impossibilité de trouver un amusement quelconque" [An immense discouragement, an unbearable feeling of isolation, the perpetual fear of a vague misfortune, a complete loss of confidence in my own strength, a total absence of desire, the impossibility of finding any form of amusement whatsoever].[9] Note that *malheur* is "vague": the distress even loses definition; and note the demobilization: "défiance complète de mes forces," and absence of desire.

One of the things which characterizes this despair is precisely this loss of power. It is as though we become paralyzed, incapable of acting. Like what you feel in very cold water. This is close to what was called *acēdia* in the religious tradition; it was precisely an extreme condition of the debility of sin. God gives us force. Following sin and the devil might borrow this force for a while, but in the end the distance from God undermines our strength. Our batteries run down. It is a consequence of distance from God, and also a state of sin. This doesn't mean that good, spiritual men might not encounter it, as a trial. But it has to be countered, fought against. The one thing you mustn't do is surrender to it. This would be fatal, like falling asleep in a snowbank. We'll see that Baudelaire also understands this in a theological dimension. He also portrays this condition as one of being hemmed in: *à l'étroit*. See "LXXXI. Spleen":

> Quand le ciel bas et lourd pèse comme un couvercle
> Sur l'esprit gémissant en proie aux longs ennuis,
> Et que de l'horizon embrassant tout le cercle
> Il nous verse un jour noir plus triste que les nuits;

9. Charles Baudelaire, "Lettre à Madame Aupick (sa mère). 30 décembre 1857," in *Correspondance générale* (Paris: L. Conrad, 1947), 108.

Quand la terre est changée en un cachot humide,
Où l'Espérance, comme une chauve-souris,
S'en va battant les murs de son aile timide
Et se cognant la tête à des plafonds pourris;

Quand la pluie étalant ses immense trainées
D'une vaste prison imite les barreaux,
Et qu'un people muet d'infâmes araignées
Vient tendre ses filets au fond de nos cerveaux,

Des cloches tout à coup sautent avec furie
Et lancent vers le ciel un affreux hurlement,
Ainsi que des esprits errants sans patrie
Qui se mettent à geindre opiniâtrement.

Et de longs corbillards, sans tambour ni musique,
Défilent lentement dans mon âme; L'Espoir,
Vaincu, pleure, et l'Angoisse atroce, despotique,
Sur mon crâne incliné plante son drapeau noir.[10]

[When the low heavy sky weighs like a lid
Upon the spirit aching for the light
And all the wide horizon's line is hid
By a black day sadder than any night;

When the changed earth is but a dungeon dank
Where batlike Hope goes blindly fluttering
And, striking wall and roof and mouldered plank,
Bruises his tender head and timid wing;

When like grim prison bars stretch down the thin,
Straight, rigid pillars of the endless rain,

10. Charles Baudelaire, "LXXXI. Spleen," in *Œuvres complètes*, 1:76.

And the dumb throngs of infamous spiders spin
Their meshes in the caverns of the brain,

Suddenly, bells leap forth into the air,
Hurling a hideous uproar to the sky
As 'twere a brand of homeless spirits who fare
Through the strange heavens, wailing stubbornly.

And hearses, without drum or instrument,
File slowly through my soul; crushed, sorrowful,
Weeps Hope, and Grief, fierce and omnipotent,
Plants his black banner on my drooping skull.][11]

Here are powerful images of enclosure, imprisonment, despair (*chauve-souris* [bat] of stanza 2, *vaste prison* [vast prison] of stanza 3, the final defeat of the last stanza). But for Baudelaire, Spleen is also perhaps primarily a malady of time: first of all, of a time which runs down, which never renews itself, as we see in "X. L'Ennemi":

Ô douleur! ô douleur! Le Temps mange la vie,
Et l'obscur Ennemi qui nous ronge le Coeur
Du sang que nous perdons croît et se fortifie![12]

[Time and nature sluice away our lives.
A virus eats the hear out of our sides,
digs in and multiplies on our lost blood.][13]

Or "XXX. De Profundis Clamavi":

J'implore ta pitié, Toi, l'unique que j'aime,
Du fond du gouffre obscure où mon coeur est tombé.
C'est un univers morne à l'horizon plombé,
Où nagent dans la nuit l'horreur et le blasphème;

---

11. Charles Baudelaire, "LXXXI. Spleen," trans. John Squire, in *Flowers of Evil*, 92–93.

12. Charles Baudelaire, "X. L'Ennemi," in *Œuvres complètes*, 1:16.

13. Charles Baudelaire, "X. The Ruined Garden," trans. Robert Lowell, in *Flowers of Evil*, 19.

Un soleil sans chaleur plane au-dessus six mois,
Et les six autres mois la nuit couvre la terre;
C'est un pays plus nu que la terre polaire;
Ni bêtes, ni ruisseaux, ni verdure, ni bois!

Or il n'est pas d'horreur au monde qui surpasse
La froide cruauté de ce soleil de glace
Et cette immense nuit semblable au vieux Chaos;

Je jalouse le sort des plus vils animaux
Qui peuvent se plonger dans un sommeil stupide,
Tant l'écheveau du temps lentement se dévide.[14]

[Have pity, You alone whom I adore
From down this black pit where my heart is sped,
A sombre universe ringed round with lead
Where fear and curses the long night explore.

Six months a cold sun hovers overhead;
The other six is night upon this land.
No beast; no stream; no wood; no leaves expand.
The desert Pole is not a waste so dead.

Now in the whole world there's no horror quite
So cold and cruel as this glacial sun,
So like old Chaos as this boundless night;

I envy the least animals that run,
Which can find respite in brute slumber drowned,
so slowly is the skein of time unwound.][15]

14. Charles Baudelaire, "XXXI. De Profundis Clamavi," in *Œuvres complètes*, 1:40.
15. Charles Baudelaire, "XXXI. De Profundis Clamavi," trans. Desmond Harmsworth, in *Flowers of Evil*, 40.

Once again, the poem finishes with an image of time running down, a spool which unravels: "Tant l'écheveau du temps lentement se dévide." Here there is also invocation of closed-in horizon, "horizon plombé," and also of cold, eternal winter, which paralyzes us; an image which recurs in "LXXXIII. Le Goût du Néant": "Et le Temps m'engloutit minute par minute, / Comme la neige immense un corps pris de roideur" [And time swallows me minute by minute, / As endless snow a stiffening corpse].[16] Spleen is here seen as a malady of time, of lived time. In a world without meaning, without even a trace of higher time, the moments of time are quite unconnected. Nothing builds up, no meaningful end is approached. One is, as it were, imprisoned in each moment, and yet it passes, and leaves one in another, similar one. Each moment passes, taking the force, the effort, the meaning one may have invested in it, without leaving anything. One is, as it were, bled by time. It "eats life." Or it thickens my prison: all I can remember is more and more such disconnected moments, which pile up on me; their cumulative effect is of being suffocated, buried. But buried in something cold; the corpse is stiffening.

This description of Spleen is also one of *acēdia:* endless repetition of moments but deprived of meaning. Lived time has meaning only when moments connect, the earlier calling forth the later; as do the successive moments of a story; or a melody, a symphony. The nadir of meaninglessness is where no moments bring us onto the next. The moments have no traction, they don't in any way send us on. They are inert, and in this they are all alike. Trapped in a time like this, we live and relive meaningless repetition.[17]

Memories are now a burden. "LXXIX. Spleen": "J'ai plus de souvenirs que si j'avais mille ans" [I have more memories than if I were a thousand years old].[18] So this disconnected time, which we can see as our being imprisoned in the moment, can also be grasped in a seemingly opposed

16. Charles Baudelaire, "LXXXIII. Le Goût du Néant," in *Œuvres complètes,* 1:76.

17. See Rowan Williams' account of St. Paul's notion of "flesh" as human life which is somehow "alienated," "not properly inhabited," cut off from the meaningful growth of "spirit." Rowan Williams, *Holy Living: The Christian Tradition for Today* (London: Bloomsbury, 2017), 14.

18. Charles Baudelaire, "LXXIX. Spleen," in *Œuvres complètes,* 1:75.

image, of time as seemingly endless, unchanging, as slowed down almost to stasis. (The paradox is merely apparent. In unconnected time, without narrative meaning, the past is lost, but also nothing happens. A world of *Langweiligkeit*; the German term captures it.)

> Rien n'égale en longueur les boiteuses journées,
> Quand sous les lourds flocons des neigeuses années
> L'ennui, fruit de la morne incuriosité
> Prend les proportions de l'immortalité.[19]

> [Nothing can equal those days for endlessness
> When in the winter's blizzardy caress
> Indifference expanding to Ennui
> Takes on the feel of immortality.][20]

Apt and powerful images. But what does poetry do? It begins to transform our experience. It articulates Spleen, and this is a first step toward reversing it. The feature of melancholy which makes it so difficult to counter is that the sufferer can't see any reason, any cause or occasion; it is nameless, faceless; one can see no ways of combating it. Baudelaire's poetry doesn't identify a cause, but his powerful images do give it a face. It makes Spleen appear as the meaning of things it invokes, closed spaces, imprisoned bats, winter, piles of accumulating snow. These operate as symbols in Schlegel's sense, through which we have access to this malady, an alternative to its invasive, all-infecting, and paralyzing presence.

But this very move counters Spleen. In the depths of ennui, we merely live it; we can see no meaning, we cannot encompass it as one condition among many. It rapidly fills the whole space, becomes the only possible meaning. So articulating it begins to give it a place, as one way among possible others. But what is more, making it show up through symbols reverses the splenetic situation, because now things are not utterly meaningless; some things have been made to speak.

19. Baudelaire, "LXXIX. Spleen," 1:75.
20. Charles Baudelaire, "LXXIX. Spleen," trans. Anthony Hecht, in *Flowers of Evil*, 91.

Put in another way, a condition which has just been lived, in which we have been totally immersed, as it were, which has been as close to us as our skin, so close that we cannot properly identify it, is now *mise en forme, mise en intrigue;* we give it a plot, a story, and in this way give it a dramatic shape. We can now see our life as a story, a drama, a struggle, with the dignity and deeper meaning which that has. Putting one's life in a story transforms one's stance to it. One relates to it no more just immediately, but also as something one can survey. Insofar as the story has a meaning, one's life partakes of meaning. This is part of the drive to self-narrative.

So this conferral of form, or emplotment, also involves our taking a distance from the all-invasive experience of Spleen; and through this it can also be a participation in meaning. This triple change is brought about through language, through articulation. But then this makes us aware of a fourth aspect of the change: the language and the story are ours; we take a standpoint through language which is ours, not mine, even if I say something new in it. It is a story which I could tell others. Indeed, in formulating it, I am normally addressing someone, telling it to someone. There can then develop kinds of writing, such as this type of lyric, which are more detached from the conversational situation. The implied author is not the "real" one; the poet may retreat from immediate communicability. But the poem's encapsulating, articulating this predicament well, and that means for a potential other, is inseparable from its being good poetry. Even the most hermetic poetry calls for a reader; and even if it has to create its readers over time itself. This is in the nature of poetry.

The poem invokes a certain mode of address; even if part of its point is to depart from this kind of communication, the evocation is essential to the poem, essential to give the departure the weight and meaning it has. For example, this is still the speech of an implied author. Seen from this fourth aspect, the move is from living immersed, overwhelmed by the condition, as close as our skin, which is a kind of ne plus ultra of subjective, first-person suffering of it; to a living it in/through our language, casting it into an act of communication, real or virtual.

But there is also a fifth aspect of this transformation. This is an articulation of spleen, but an articulation in poetry, and poetry with a form which brings it close to music. But music, as Augustine saw, is what best and most immediately knits time into meaningful shapes and connections. The very fact of composing (or reading) these poems gives lived time a shape, a meaning. Time is already connecting, renewing its energies, taking us away from the meaningless accumulation of indistinguishable instants.

So to return to "LXXXI. Spleen": The first stanza invokes "le ciel bas et lourd" [the sky low and heavy], and we have a sense of being enclosed: "bas"; of being weighed down: "lourd" comes here again. But on another level, we now see ennui emerging from the sky, the low-hanging sky; it is, in a sense, the meaning of this sky. We have been lifted into a different stance to it—the stance of the reader of the language of things.

Immediately follows another image. Now not one from the immediate experience, but an image of another kind of predicament which bespeaks ennui. The "cachot humide" [humid cell]. This itself speaks ennui like the sky. But now we have the ennui articulated by a short allegorical story: the "chauve-souris" [bat]. Then another statement of actual surroundings, which bespeaks ennui, followed by another image of a predicament, with another action described, this time allegorized to what goes on within.

Auerbach noted the use of language which shocks, which jars with the supposed dignity of the subject, and the still-classical declamability of the verse. Baudelaire writes like Racine, that is, with the same poetic forms; but he introduces common terms for lowly objects, like "couvercle" [lid], "cerveaux" [brains]; not to speak of the "chauve-souris," instead of *colombe* [the dove, symbol for hope]. This is a tour de force which is central to the project. These common things, in the case of "couvercle" something banal and utilitarian, are brought up into a world of things which speak. There is a kind of transfiguration.[21]

Then a further transformation. In the last two stanzas, the torpor is broken. We no longer simply have spleen as a standing condition, at the final point of congelation. But we have the diabolical action which brought it about. We live through the drama of being overcome by Spleen: the howling of bells, and the moaning of "esprits errants" [wandering

---

21. See Charles Baudelaire, "VIII. Le Couvercle," in *Œuvres complètes,* 1:141.

spirits]. There is a terrible outbreak of disorder. And then the final conquest, of majestic beauty.

This lowest now finds its place in lyric poetry. A new language was needed to release the revelation in the commonplace.

2

T. S. Eliot says of this transposition:

> It is not merely in the use of imagery of the common life, not merely in the use of imagery of the sordid life of a great metropolis, but in the elevation of such imagery to the first intensity— presenting it as it is, and yet making it represent much more than itself—that Baudelaire has created a mode of release and expression for other men.[22]

(And especially for Eliot.) This reversal of the hierarchy of references, bringing the commonplace, the ugly, the tawdry, to the highest intensity, previously reserved for the most noble realities, is one of Baudelaire's most important achievements, and goes beyond his Spleen poems. Perhaps his most famous work in this respect is "Une Charogne." Baudelaire's alchemy helps to dispel one of the salient negative features of modern life, one which Eliot comments on in another passage. Eliot wrote of this discovery,

> that the sort of material that I had, the sort of experience that an adolescent had had, in an industrial city in America, could be the material for poetry. . . . That, in fact, the business of the poet was to make poetry out of the unexplored resources of the unpoetical.[23]

What was this material? In fact, it was very unpromising. The modern urban landscape frequently contains neglected and run-down neighbor-

---

22. T. S. Eliot, "Baudelaire," in *Selected Prose of T. S. Eliot*, ed. Frank Kermode (New York: Harcourt Brace, 1975), 234.

23. T. S. Eliot, "What Dante Means to Me," in *To Criticize the Critic* (London: Faber and Faber, 1965), 126.

hoods, which in consequence have become squalid and ugly; it contains non-places (non-lieux), like vacant lots which are the site of a disordered collection of cast-off objects; we can encounter the sudden eruption in an older neighbourhood of buildings of an alien style (if of any recognizable style at all).[24] And the city also may contain large areas of factories, processing plants, refineries and the like, their buildings being often surrounded by disused machines and waste products. All this, for a temperament and sensibility nourished on the great classic sites of our civilization, Venice, Paris, London or for Americans Washington, brings on a potentially overpowering feeling of alienation, ennui, of the absence even negation of a strong life-orienting meaning.

In short, these surroundings are an important source of Spleen. Of course, Baudelaire didn't see many of these things, but he did live in Paris in the decades in which the Baron Haussmann destroyed big swathes of the medieval city in order to build his sweeping boulevards.

For Eliot, Baudelaire was the first in a line of poets which showed him how this new urban world could be opened up and transformed by poetry.

One poem, quoted by Eliot (*Fleurs du Mal,* "XCIII. Les Sept vieillards"), opens:

> Fourmillante cité, cité pleine de rêves,
> où le spectre en plein jour raccroche le passant. (1–2)

> [Ant-seething city, city full of dreams,
> Where ghosts by daylight tug the passer's sleeve.]

The speaker describes meeting in the street, one after the other, seven old men, who seem to radiate wickedness (*méchanceté*) and hostility; he is deeply shaken, even frightened, but also very conflicted, because at the same time, he cannot but feel "un frisson fraternel" [a fraternal shudder]

24. See Marc Augé, *Non-lieux: Introduction à une anthropologie de la surmodernité* (Paris: Le Seuil, 1992).

before these fellow humans. He struggles with and conjures these feelings through the verse, but remains deeply troubled:

> Je rentrai, je fermai ma porte, l'esprit fiévreux et trouble.
> Blessé par le mystère et par l'absurdité! (47–48)[25]

> [I locked my room, sick, fevered, chilled with fright:
> With all my spirit sorely hurt and troubled
> By so ridiculous and strange a sight.][26]

The reference to "un frisson fraternel" makes clear that part of what
disturbs the poet is the sense of a common humanity, which should inspire fellow feeling, but the sinister aspect of the seven old men overrides
this response. But in the next poem, "XCIV. Les Petites Vieilles," he gives
full rein to his compassion.

The poetry here brings about the same transformation that I remarked
on earlier in connection with the Spleen poems. Giving expression to the
original distressful emotions allows us to hold these at a distance, while
through the rhythm of the verse we begin to inhabit another quality of
time than the blocked sense of being enfolded in the ugly moment.

In other poems again, he utterly turns the tables, and invokes beyond
the pain the beauty and mystery of a scene. See, for instance, "CIV. Brumes
et Pluies":

> Ô fins d'automne, hivers, printemps trempés de boue,
> Endormeuses saisons! Je vous aime et voue loue
> D'envelopper ainsi mon cœur et mon cerveau
> D'un linceul vaporeux et d'un vague tombeau. (1–4)[27]

> [O ends of autumn, winters, springtimes deep in mud,
> Seasons of drowsiness,—my love and gratitude

---

25. Charles Baudelaire, "XCIII. Les Sept vieillards," in *Œuvres complètes*, 1:87.

26. Charles Baudelaire, "XCIII. The Seven Old Men," trans. Roy Campbell, in *Flowers of Evil*, 111–113.

27. Charles Baudelaire, "CIV. Brumes et Pluies," in *Œuvres complètes*, 1:100.

I give you, that have wrapped with mist my heart and brain
As with a shroud, and shut them in a tomb of rain.][28]

Or "CVI. Le Crépuscule du Matin":

C'est l'heure où l'essaim des rêves malfaisants
Tord sur leurs oreillers les bruns adolescents;
Où, comme un œil sanglant qui palpite et qui bouge,
La lampe sur le jour fait une tache rouge;
Où l'âme, sous le poids du corps revêche et lourd,
Imite les combats de la lampe et du jour.
Comme un visage en pleurs que les brises essuient,
L'air est plein du frisson des choses qui s'enfuient,
Et l'homme est las d'écrire et la femme d'aimer.[29]

[It was that hour of night when guilty dreams
Rise from brown, restless adolescents in swarms,
When, quaking and cringing like a blood-shot eye,
The lamp stains the coming day with its dye;
When under the body's reluctant, stubborn weight
The soul, like the lamp, renews its unequal fight;
When the air shivers as if to escape, to efface
Itself in furtive breezes drying a tear-stung face;
When woman is sick of love, as the writer of his work.][30]

This section of *Les Fleurs du Mal,* which he calls "Tableaux parisiens," touches more than the misfortunes of the Parisian world. He also invokes the depth and complexity of city scenes behind which we sense so many unseen lives struggling to realize their purposes, good or bad, confused or understood (see also "CII. Rêve parisien").

28. Charles Baudelaire, "CIV. Mists and Rains," trans. Edna St. Vincent Millay, in *Flowers of Evil,* 128.

29. Charles Baudelaire, "CVI. Le Crépuscule du Matin," in *Œuvres complètes,* 1:103.

30. Charles Baudelaire, "CVI. Morning Twilight," trans. David Paul, in *Flowers of Evil,* 131–132.

Eliot's early poetry exploits this Baudelairean breakthrough. We can see this in the first lines of "The Love Song of J. Alfred Prufrock":

> Let us go then you and I,
> When the evening is spread out against the sky
> Like a patient etherized upon a table;
> Let us go, through certain half-deserted streets,
> The muttering retreats
> Of restless nights in one-night cheap hotels
> And sawdust restaurants with oyster shells:
> Streets that follow like a tedious argument
> Of insidious intent
> To lead you to an overwhelming question . . .
> Oh, do not ask, "what is it"?
> Let us go and make our visit. (1–12)[31]

Here the first stanza gathers together details of the meaningless and sordid urban zones, a collection of non-places ("non-lieux" in Augé's sense), in that they fail to amount to a place in the full sense of a gathering point of common meaning, the "one-night cheap hotels" which are the scene of "restless nights." In a precipitate Auerbachian descent, we plunge from the evening sky to the patient "etherized upon a table." The iambic-dominated rhythm carries us through these sordid locations and events. Even the takedown of higher realities—implicit in the word "etherized," parodic for "ethereal"—doesn't stop and imprison us in the banal.

To grasp the meaning of our condition would involve asking "an overwhelming question." But this turns out later to have less than cosmic significance. Meanwhile, in a recurring background we have the repetition of what we suspect are trivial, empty conversations on great matters: "In the room the women come and go / Talking of Michelangelo." And all this is clearly a malady of time. For "indeed there will be time," but in which nothing significant will happen:

31. T. S. Eliot, "The Love Song of J. Alfred Prufrock," in *The Poems of T. S. Eliot,* ed. Christopher Ricks and Jim McCue (Baltimore: Johns Hopkins University Press, 2015), 1:5.

> Time for you and time for me,
> And time yet for a hundred indecisions,
> And for a hundred visions and revisions,
> Before the taking of a toast and tea. (31–34)[32]

3

Perhaps it might help here to summarize the five dimensions of the Spleen poems as preparation for a comparison between these and the "reconnecting" poetry of the English and German Romantics, of Hölderlin and Wordsworth. Baudelaire's poems capture Spleen, they capture its essence, but in an expression which brings it before us, makes it an object of contemplation.

The angle at which they capture Spleen, melancholia, is as a quality of lived time: endless repetition, identical repetition, without any meaning; not proceeding toward anything, and without a terminal point. (Benjamin picks this up, as we will see below.) Such a *mise en forme* shifts our relation to Spleen. Formerly, this sense of blocked, monotonous, unending repetition pressed in on us, hemmed us in, imprisoned us, dragged us into this unbearable mode of lived time. Now it is there, as an object of contemplation. We have taken a distance from it. We are liberated. The lock has been sprung.

There is an analogy to Schopenhauer's theory in *Die Welt als Wille und Vorstellung*. When we grasp the Will in a work of art, we take a distance from it. It no longer relentlessly drives us. We can contemplate it in a beautiful form. But how does poetry do this? How does it realize this new distance / disengagement / liberation? Not every kind of *mise à distance* does this. For instance, clinical descriptions grasp the condition as an object of study. We relate to the condition in a new way; "You're suffering from monotony depression syndrome." Though they may give us a certain distance from our condition, show us we aren't alone, such descriptions don't liberate in the same way. There is an exhilaration in liberation through poetry, which is lacking in clinical description.

32. Eliot, "Prufrock," 6.

What is the secret of the poem's power? The poem is an event, a passage. It links features, marks of the object, in this case, spleen. It links them in a quasi-musical chain. The poem-as-event has a rhythm, a beat, a tempo, or successive tempi. This re-creates for us an essence, an "inscape." How?

In the same way as we see in the "Nightingale" poem of Keats. The rhythmic flow between the features as recounted in the poem somehow encounters, meets, connects up with the flow between the features as we live it. We could say that there is a rhythmic flow in the object, but an ontic claim here would be unsubstantiated. The flow is in the object as we experience it, perhaps for the first time in this way when we read/hear the poem. The claim here is about the interspace. The poem liberates a potential here, which is precisely this link, this flow between the features. Of the draught of vintage, of summer in the garden. This moves, exhilarates us.

But with Spleen, we have not a cool draught of vintage or summer in the garden, but something ugly, which depresses our spirits. Whence the exhilaration here? We can get it in two steps:

1. We are now living the experience of Spleen in a new way, through the rhythm, flow of the captured inscape. But this is in itself a revolution in lived time, which temporarily overcomes and dissolves or supersedes the cramped, stopped up, obsessional repetition of the immediate lived experience of spleen. This *mise en abîme* works beyond spleen, as I argued above. Baudelaire raises the ugly, the sordid, the commonplace, to the "first intensity" (Eliot).

2. And this also presents spleen in a broader, human context; here of the need, one might say, the craving for meaning. But to complete our liberation, we have to find a meaningful movement or connection beyond ourselves, in the world of time-space. The essence of spleen is meaningless repetition; the paradox is that we are trapped in the moment, even though this moment is constantly changing; and even more paradoxi-

cally, these unconnected moments pile up, threaten to bury us. ("Et le temps m'engloutit minute par minute.")[33]

We need a meaningful connection in lived time which can last beyond this instant, even potentially for a lifetime. We need a connection to a larger pattern in time, with a positive meaning—or to put it more directly, one which brings exaltation. Through the Spleen verses, we have been freed to search for this; and Baudelaire finds it—for example, in "Le Cygne." (I will explain this later.)

Now the analogy to Hölderlin and Wordsworth becomes clear. "Heimkunft" and "Tintern Abbey" bring about an experience of connection, which carries conviction, and which is sensed as the realization of a crucial human potential, and hence as more than a personal reaction. Analogously, the Spleen poems bring about an experience of living in time, which carries the undeniable conviction that this is how we are supposed to live. In both cases, there is a ritual or performative dimension, something the poetry brings about, and at the same time the sense that this fills an essential need in human life; not a biological need, but a metabiological one. The proper shape of lived time is as essential to us as reconnection, but in its own dimension.

||

Cosmic versus lived time

1

It is not an accident that this need comes to light in the nineteenth century, for prior to this the very distinction between lived and "objective," or we might say "cosmic," time didn't exist. Augustine, in the *Confessions,* made the famous observation that when he just lived in time, it seemed quite clear to him, but once he tried to grasp it as an object of thought, it slipped

33. Baudelaire, "LXXXIII. Le Goût du Néant," 76.

away, since most of it—past and future—didn't exist. But he wasn't specifically talking about cosmic time. He neither saw the need, nor had the
means to make the clear distinction.

This possibility, as we understand it, comes with the development of
modern natural science. For Newton, time and space were unconnected
from what fills them. This is already clear with the spatial dimension.
Modern space is different from the older notion of place (topos, locus).
A place is identified by what fills it, exists in it. Places fit together in a
broader landscape. By contrast, a given volume of space is identified by
its abstract coordinates, and the same space can be filled by different objects; an analogous everyday example would be a garage which houses
first a truck, and then my Mercedes. But we usually think of the garage
as being at a place; we find it by its placement.

The same abstracting move involved in passing from places to spaces
was also carried out in relation to time. When Hamlet says, "The time is
out of joint / O cursed spite / That ever I was born to set it right," he is not
thinking of the abstract concept.[34] The "time" is defined by the (terrible)
conditions it manifests. Machiavelli's use of "i tempi" has the same, concrete sense.

But in relation to the cosmic time of physics, with its abstract coordinates, the understanding of lived time stands out as different.

Or it ought to. The problem was that much philosophy and science
tended to ignore this. We can think of (cosmic) time and space as infinitely divisible, or as falling into determinate, distinct units. So philosophy and psychology thought of perception (which happens in lived
time) as consisting of a series of impressions, of snapshots. What we get
in the nineteenth and twentieth centuries is a rebellion against this conception, which seems utterly alien to lived time.

But the same cultural and civilizational development which imposes
a distinction between cosmic and lived time puts obstacles in the way if
we want to focus on this latter. I mean here the greater and greater importance and prestige of the scientific-technological stance toward the
world. This stance is both objectifying (that is, unconcerned with human

34. William Shakespeare, *Hamlet,* act 2, scene 1, in *The Norton Shakespeare* (New
York: W. W. Norton, 1997), 1688.

meanings), and manipulative, concerned with control. From this point of view, time as a field of experience to be appreciated fades in favor of time as a resource to be managed.

And if viewed as a field of experience, it is seen through the lens of the anthropology implicit in the modern epistemological tradition which originates in Descartes. The human agent takes in information from the world, but this information comes in atomic bits as the agent takes note of the information impinging at a certain point in time-space. Described in the language of the Vienna circle in the 1920s, a paradigm case of a basic description—what they called a *Protocolsatz*—was, for instance, "red here now." But expressed in less bare atomic terms, might be, for instance, "this bird has wide wings." The assumption was that our basic time experience was of particulate moments, which only connect to other moments through the correlations in which—our experience shows— they invariably figure. Such a wide-winged bird may turn out to lay particular kinds of eggs, to live in a particular sort of habitat, to live on a special kind of prey: we have identified a new species. We build our outlook on the world through noticing such correlations, and concatenations, of phenomena.

But this makes certain assumptions about the human agent. First, its primary passivity; at base, its information is just received. Later, it may go in search of correlates, for instance, but at the beginning and throughout, new information just comes to us. Second, we assume atomicity: the information comes in particulate bits—or at least ought to: we may take in a clutch of new data at a single glance, but this is a way of taking in confused and unreliable data. Third, the end of this data collection is to build a reliable science; and fourth, one of the fruits of this science (and also a reliable criterion of such science) is that it enables us to control things in the world. In Scheler's term, it is a *Leistungswissen*.

Of course, along with this goes a susceptibility to see skepticism as a problem; what if observed correlations of the perceptible are misleading us about what lies behind and beneath perception? And, of course, we can be led to solve this problem by denying that there is anything "underneath and beyond" at all—as Hume solved the skeptical problem of identifying real as against apparent causation by defining the causal relation in terms of invariant correlation.

If this picture of the knowing subject defines our view of human agency, then the issue of different qualities of lived time can't even be stated. Our experience of the world comes in particulate features impinging at particular moments (passivity and atomicity). Any link between moments must be made by our own mental action of assembling the data into correlations. Any impression that they spontaneously connect themselves must be erroneous. Moreover, since building a reliable science, and in particular a *Leistungswissen,* requires that we objectify the phenomena, finding a source of meaning in their order of appearance is ruled out.

But what has this to do with the experience of Spleen as invoked by Baudelaire? The answer is: nothing. But that doesn't mean people who hold this view can't experience *acēdia,* even acutely; quite the contrary. They could fight against this; for instance, by trying to convince themselves that their lives have meaning. They just couldn't see any point in turning to poetry as the source or terrain of another time-experience.

This is analogous to the way that people who have been convinced that mechanistic materialism is irrefutably the truth of things couldn't turn to some spiritual or religious source to find meaning in their lives. In both these cases, only cosmic time, not lived time, would be relevant to their search.

In an era in which post-Galilean physical science is playing a bigger and bigger role in people's lives and exercising an increasing influence on their view of the world, it is not surprising that in reaction artists, poets, and musicians should seek to recover contact with the meaningful rhythms in things. And so it is not an accident that Baudelaire and Bergson belong to the same culture in overlapping centuries.

Or, to take the same point from another angle, it is not surprising that in this era, attempts should be made among philosophers to refute the post-Cartesian notion of the human subject. These attempts start much earlier, and in a sense go back to the seventeenth century, when this atomistic-objectifying view was first put forward. And a particularly important role in this refutation was played by Kant, even though his distinction between phenomena and things-in-themselves still is prisoner of this modern epistemology. But various commentators have recognized that this moment, around the turn of the nineteenth and twentieth centuries, saw a number of radical attempts to refute and replace the post-Cartesian outlook.

Bergson is one of the important figures in this movement. Time isn't lived in discrete units, but can only be captured as flow, durée. Husserl and Heidegger develop and alter this basic insight. The philosophico-scientific issue was how to rescue lived time from its scientistic distortion. The issues raised in Baudelaire's Spleen poems can't even be formulated if we fail to do this.

One of the major interpreters of Bergson, Frédéric Worms, speaks of "un moment 1900," when two rather different attempts, which have not had much contact with each other, were launched.[35] We can associate these with Husserl and Bergson respectively. Husserl's "phenomenology" was prolonged and transformed at another such "moment," close to the middle of the twentieth century, in the writings of Heidegger and Merleau-Ponty. Husserl's followers decisively reject the notion of a passive subject receiving and then working over information taken in from the world. The knowing agent is involved with the world, trying to realize his / her goals in it. In Merleau-Ponty's terms, the agent is "aux prises avec le monde." For Heidegger the objects of our world are not just there, but they figure as "vorhanden" or "zuhanden."

Bergson is offering a parallel refutation of the modern epistemological picture, but its key point of departure is that time and space are not envisaged in the same way. We can make sense of atomism for objects which appear in space. But time is very different. Time is "durée." Its moments flow into each other; to separate and isolate a moment is to denature the time in whose flow it falls. "La durée toute pure est la forme que prend la succession de nos états de conscience quand notre moi se laisse vivre, quand il s'abstient d'établir une séparation entre l'état présent et les états antérieurs" [Pure duration is the form taken by the succession of our states of consciousness when our self lets itself live, when it abstains from separating the present moment from past moments].[36]

---

35. Frédéric Worms, *Bergson ou les deux sens de la vie* (Paris: Presses Universitaires de France, 2004), 21.

36. Henri Bergson, *Essai sur les données immédiates de la conscience* (Paris: Presses Universitaires de France, 1927), 8. Translated by Thom K. Sliwowski.

Agents are ever active, even when they're sitting there, taking things in. Actions take time, they link times, past, present, and future. What holds the different stages in time together is action; thus we can say that what holds them together (in lived time) is the agent. To isolate a moment is to denature it; to make it no more a moment in the flow of time. Just like isolating a note from the whole melody in which it figures amounts to denaturing it. The note is now different, and the melody is no more.

Where atomism become possible is in space. Our grasp of space "consiste essentiellement dans l'intuition ou plutôt dans la conception d'un milieu vide homogène. Car il n'y a guère d'autre définition possible de l'espace" [consists essentially in the intuition or, rather, in the conception of an empty and homogenous medium. For there is no other possible definition of space].[37] We can see that in his concept of space, Bergson has borrowed from the model of the epistemological subject. This is because he holds that as living beings we need to project space, in order to effect changes in our surroundings to meet our needs. Developing an effective *Leistungswissen* is the most important step in such an enterprise.

This is not to say that Bergson would agree that this is the ultimate truth about the things which surround us in space; because in his view they also have their durée, only it is very different, and much less intensely unified than the one we have as humans.

But leaving this aside for a moment, we can see the significance of Bergson's work as lying in the rehabilitation of lived time as crucial for the realization of our nature. The real self can only get in touch with itself by overcoming the attempts to reify and separate off aspects of its lived being, which is durée.

We can understand now the title of this first, pathbreaking work of Bergson's. He is trying to define "les données immédiates de la conscience" [the immediate givens of consciousness].[38] Grasping time as a series of separable moments is possible, but it is not how time comes through to us immediately. First we experience time as flow; because we

37. Bergson, *Essai*, 10. Translated by Thom K. Sliwowski.
38. Translated by Thom K. Sliwowski.

are durée, that is, time as flow. On the other hand, space is at first blush the medium of separable objects. Only later can we see its deeper nature as another kind of durée. Clearly, Bergson's main goal here is to rescue our nature as durée from the occultation it suffers at our own hands, as we learn to operate as objectifying subjects of knowledge and control.

And clearly Bergson and Baudelaire are not living in different ages or on different planets. Lived time needs to be shaped by stories, narrative. For narrative, not all moments are of equal significance; there are, for instance, turning points, where crucial issues are decided (decisive battles are an example in history). But there are other ways in which some moments count more than others. Where higher times are recognized—for instance in our traditional civilization, God's eternity, as gathered time; and the time of origins, of the foundation of present reality—there are moments in ordinary time, which come closer to these. For instance, high feasts in the liturgical calendar, like Easter; or on a pilgrimage, we gradually approach a climax of higher time, as we advance to our goal. "Knots" of time accrete around these high moments. And something analogous happens with certain places: sites of great liturgical contact with the higher: Rome, Canterbury, Assisi; or Mecca, or Varanasi, and so on. Knots of time gather around them; and that's why they are sites of pilgrimage; and even ordinary tourists flock to them, savor them, feel something powerful there.

These time-gathering sites also gather people; they become *lieux de mémoire* [places of memory] for nations and civilizations.[39] An important question arises: Is there a need for new forms of gathered time, of contact across great gaps? Why does Proust's *À la Recherche du temps perdu* [*In Search of Lost Time*], which builds toward such a contact, speak to us so powerfully? But now the objectifying stance behind our notion of cosmic time not only distorts our understanding of lived time as a theory. The practice it encourages also contributes. Time as a resource needs to be managed, and this opens the prospect of organizing time, so that our activities can be more productive, and (instrumentally) rational. But to what extent do these "rational" organizings make our time unlivable, as with assembly lines, for instance? Baudelaire's plaidoyer for

39. See Pierre Nora, *Les Lieux de mémoire*, 3 vols. (Paris: Gallimard, 1984, 1986, 1992).

livable time can also be drawn on to criticize such rational organizings, as we see with Benjamin.

Baudelaire's Spleen comes out of a kind of dislocation of time, an endless time, a timeless time, dragging on without change or end. We are imprisoned in the momentary but borderless time which is incessantly repeated. This is the temporal equivalent of *non-lieux* [non-places]. Now this connects up to an important dimension of modern experience, as Benjamin shows in his comment on Baudelaire.[40] Workers on an assembly line, for instance, or in another way, compulsive gamblers, are reduced to this kind of time experience.[41] And Hartmut Rosa shows how this is a widespread experience in today's accelerated society, where imposing various kinds of alien time use, or time sequencing, on people is common: forcing people to work without regard for their bodily rhythms, for instance, or the rhythms inherent in the actions concerned.[42] This is bad but a quite different kind of bad from time uses that make action meaningless; like assembly lines where my movements are controlled by the machine, and where I just react, and can't act in pursuit of the ultimate goal. This involves the kind of compulsive identical repetition that Benjamin points to.[43]

That this latter is worse can be seen from the fact that if we are working together for some cause, working to produce some good quickly—build

40. Walter Benjamin, "Über einige Motive bei Baudelaire," in *Illuminationen* (Frankfurt: Suhrkamp, 1955).

41. Benjamin, "Über einige Motive bei Baudelaire," 208–209, 209–214.

42. Rosa argues that the overriding of bodily rhythms, or those of action, is an important cause of burnout. Hartmut Rosa, *Beschleunigung: Die Veränderung der Zeitstrukturen in der Moderne* (Frankfurt: Suhrkamp, 2005); Hartmut Rosa, *Social Acceleration: A New Theory of Modernity* (New York: Columbia University Press, 2013).

43. We can appreciate how much Bergson's theory anticipates social practice here. Think of the assembly line, for instance. In order to maximize production, we are led to objectify human action in time, divide it into action segments and rearrange these to get the maximum result in minimal time. In order to do this, we have to do what Bergson calls spatializing time, distinguishing segments and reordering them to maximum effect. But this means interrupting the flow of durée. And as Bergson says, we are led to take this objectifying stance ultimately by the demand on us to meet our vital needs.

a dam before the rains, for example—then we don't mind . . . neglect of our bodily rhythms—and perhaps even can take a certain turn on the assembly line. The importance of purpose here can be shown negatively in the cruel treatment of some prisoners, which consists in forcing them to dig holes and then fill them in again. Here we add a sense of futility to the imposition which disregards their own rhythms.

These impositions represent one way of ignoring, even crushing our lived time, which deprives it of what we crave in it; some sense of meaning or purpose. Something the same is evident in the imposition of abstract time on event time. Unfortunately, our epoch also has developed new forms of compulsive identical repetition, where the driver is not some external power, as in the assembly line, but internal, in our own addictions. We are kept chained by the feeling "just one more time, and . . ."

Casinos know how to organize the environment so that gamblers on slot machines get into the flow, where even catastrophic losses can't dislodge, but on the contrary intensify, the feeling of "just one more time." And Apple designs its machines to hook people, especially children, into the "one more time" flow. The lack of meaning can be felt here, often very strongly, when you stop, and sense: What have I been doing? And are overwhelmed by the sense of emptiness—which is one more reason to go on "just one more time."

But let's say you're a successful entrepreneur, and you manage to get a number of enterprises going and fulfill a number of purposes. You manage time, often micromanage it. So you have meaning. But there can still be something missing in your lived time, compared with those stretches where you are carried along, by a symphony or a sunset, or a story. The entrepreneur may have this, in a different compartment of his life; his leisure, cultural activities, family. Or you can get it gardening; you manage things, but you work alongside nature and its forces. Or the entrepreneur may have this at another level; through his whole life he is building some new community, achieving some moral goal, doing something he is called to do.

But in the absence of this overarching goal, both the imposed rhythm of the assembly line, or the prison colony; and the sense of power and efficacy that comes with great achievements of control, which are also control of time use; both these lack this sense that I am responding to the demands of reality; that I am led by something, discerning and expressing a demand of things; this the artist feels, for instance, or the gardener.

Lived time which follows a pattern in things; or a pattern in time itself. Here is a domain in which resonance resides, a *Resonanzachse,* in Rosa's sense.[44] The one whose meaning is found in control forgoes this resonance, makes the world and / or time go dumb.

Benjamin gives us a vocabulary to talk about what is lacking in compulsive identical (hence, non-Kierkegaardian) repetition: *Erfahrung* [deep experience]. The meaninglessly repeated episodes are *Erlebnisse* [shallow experiences], but they don't amount to meaningful experience (*Erfahrung*), and Rosa follows this usage. Fully meaningful experience would come to be in a lived time where we connect with a sense of the pattern in reality; where the unifying meaning given to our actions would not rely simply on the will, but on a recovered contact with a meaning in things.

Baudelaire's poems in *Les Fleurs du Mal* mainly make this show up as the contrast to our broken condition; but there are a few poems which give us a hint of what the positive experience might be based on. Benjamin sees "Les Correspondances" as one of these, where Baudelaire reaches back to one of the themes of the premodern languages of insight into reality, as we mentioned above. "Was Baudelaire mit den correspondances im Sinn hatte, kann als eine Erfahrung bezeichnet werden, die sich krisensicher zu etablieren sucht" [What Baudelaire had in mind with "correspondences" could be defined as an experience which seeks to establish itself fully, free of crisis]. And then he adds: "Möglich ist sie nur im Bereich des Kultischen" [This is only possible in the realm of the cultic].[45]

44. Hartmut Rosa, *Resonanz: Eine Soziologie der Weltbeziehung* (Berlin: Suhrkamp, 2016); Hartmut Rosa, *Resonance: A Sociology of Our Relationship to the World,* trans. James Wagner (Cambridge, UK: Polity, 2019).

45. Benjamin, "Über einige Motive bei Baudelaire," 215.

This reference to "cult" shows the negative side of Benjamin's reaction to this attempt to retain contact with cosmic order, in the face of modern conditions which make it less and less viable. His conception of Judaism, influenced by Hermann Cohen, had no place for cult.

But seen in the light of the patterns of reconnection I have been exploring in this book, he might rather have been calling attention to the way in which the post-Romantic epiphany doesn't just reveal a pattern in things but restores contact with it. In this it takes on something of the nature of ritual. The most important rituals in human history, early or contemporary, are what one might call "rituals of restoration": they are meant to reconnect to the powerful sources of strength and well-being, whether they be Roman sacrifices which aim to restore the *pax deorum* [peace of the gods] or contemporary celebrations which rededicate us to our essential common values.

This connects to Benjamin's discussion of Aura a little further on.[46] A truly auratic object cannot simply be a dead presence; it must look back at us. To see the Aura as "die einmalige Erscheinung einer Ferne" [the momentary appearance of something distant] has this for it, "den kultischen Charakter des Phänomens transparent zu machen" [it makes transparent the cultic character of the phenomenon].[47]

---

46. Benjamin, "Über einige Motive bei Baudelaire," 223.

47. Benjamin, "Über einige Motive bei Baudelaire," 224. This "looking back" has been identified as a crucial feature of icons in Eastern Orthodoxy; see the work of Jean-Luc Marion and Rowan Williams.

I would like to call into question Benjamin's too-rapid and too-simple dismissing of the aura, both in his Baudelaire essay, and in the "Work of Art in the Age of Mechanical Reproducibility." Is it really so clear that "reproducible" works—e.g., films—lack (in a meaningful sense) "aura"? Benjamin's move here was part of his "materialist" turn, which opened up very many important insights about art in our age, but these aren't dependent on the overhasty dismissal of much of our traditional language about art.

When it comes to the positions which were adopted in the name of this "materialism," there are good reasons not to see them as Benjamin's last word. The turn itself was part of a political shift (influenced by Brecht) by which Baudelaire put himself under the (loosely construed) influence of Bolshevism, and which was meant to open the path to effective political action. But the Bolshevik allegiance became more and more unsustainable, as the

III

Good and evil

1

So poetry can break the tyrannic hold of Spleen. But the break is only momentary. What stops us from sliding back? Can there be poetry which, as a "symbol" in the Schlegel-Ricoeur sense, opens a lived experience of the world and time which meets the demands of a full human life? This will be our recurring question in this chapter. But before we tackle it directly, we have to get some sense of the world in which this question can be posed for Baudelaire.

Now the world which *Les Fleurs du Mal* portrays for us is very dark. Eliot was right when he said that "Baudelaire has created a mode of release and expression *for other men*" (emphasis added).[48] Others, including Eliot himself, will turn this new potential to create a positive vision of a redeemed world, but not Baudelaire. In his poetry indeed, the sordid turns out to "represent much more than itself."[49] But what it often reveals is a world irremediably shot through with fallenness, with evil. In "CVI. Le Crépuscule du Matin," we get much more than the meaningless repetition of Spleen; there is a kind of story, of sequence; a world of suffering is laid out like a landscape, or as we might feel today, like a film sequence, as we move toward dawn. But it ends, not with release, but with a sense of impotence, and stoic acceptance.

> L'aurore grelotante en robe rose et verte
> S'avançait lentement sur la Seine déserte,
> Et le sombre Paris, en se frottant les yeux,
> Empoignant ses outils, vieillard laborieux. (25–28)[50]

Moscow government committed more and more horrifying acts, like the Moscow show trials, culminating in the Molotov-Ribbentrop Pact, and the joint Soviet-Nazi invasion of Poland which started the Second World War. His 1940 text "On the Concept of History" departs decisively from the "materialist" viewpoint.

48. Eliot, "Baudelaire," 234.
49. Eliot, "Baudelaire," 234.
50. Baudelaire, "CVI. Le Crépuscule du Matin," 1:103.

[Morning, shivering in her robe of rose and green,
Made her hesitant way along the deserted Seine,
While Paris, rubbing tired eyes in its dark,
Woke like an ancient drudge to another day's work.][51]

But we find with "LXXXVII. L'Irrémédiable" that we stand before an even
grander story, a cosmic story, which relates the fall of our world.

Une Idée, un Forme, un être
Parti de l'azur et tombé
Dans un Styx bourbeux and plombé
Où nul œil du Ciel ne pénètre;

Un Ange, imprudent voyageur
Qu'a tenté l'amour du difforme,
Au fond d'un cauchemar énorme
Se débattant comme un nageur. (1–8)

[A Dream, a Form, a Creature, late
Fallen from azure realms, and sped
Into some Styx of mud and lead
No eye from heaven can penetrate;

An angel, rash wanderer, who craves
To look upon deformity,
The vast nightmare's gulf to try
As swimmer struggling with the waves.]

He falls into a realm

Où veillent des monstres visqueux
Dont les larges yeux de phosphore
Font une nuit plus noire encore
Et ne rendent visibles qu'eux;

51. Baudelaire, "CVI. Morning Twilight," 132.

Un navire pris dans le pôle,
Comme en un piège de cristal,
Cherchant par quel détroit fatal
Il est tombé dans cette geôle;

Emblèmes nets, tableau parfait
D'une fortune irrémédiable,
Qui donne à penser que le Diable
Fait toujours bien tout ce qu'il fait! (21–32)

[Where clammy monsters guard the way,
Whose great eyes' phosphoric light
Makes even blacker still the night,
And nothing but themselves betray;

A vessel icebound at the pole,
As in a crystal trap secure,
Seeking the fatal aperture
By which it reached that prison goal:

Perfect emblems, clear and true,
Of irremediable Fate,
They make us think the Devil's hate
Does well whatever he will do!]

And then the reflection on this condition:

Tête à tête sombre et limpide
Qu'un cœur devenue son miroir!
Puits de Vérité, clair et noir,
Où Tremble une étoile livide,

Un phare ironique, infernal
Flambeau des grâces sataniques,

Soulagement et gloire uniques
—La conscience dans le Mal! (33–40)[52]

[The dialogue is dark and clear
When a heart becomes its mirror!
Black well of Truth, but none is clearer,
Where that livid star appears,

That ironic and primaeval
Beacon, torch of Satan's grace,
Our sole glory and our solace—
Consciousness in doing Evil!][53]

We have a story here, not a meaningless repetition, and so we escape Spleen, the depths of *acēdia*. But the story displays a world of impotence and repeated frustration, symbolized very tellingly by the image of the ship caught in polar ice, searching in vain for a way out. And yet there is an immense satisfaction, at once a relief and a sense of glory, in achieving this consciousness of evil.

2

We have now gone beyond showing the immediate meaning of surrounding things; we have brought to light the whole background story. What role does this play? For Baudelaire, it makes sense of it all. It is a piece of theory he has to adopt in order to make sense of the whole of moral experience. It tells us something about the relations between the different poems describing different experiences and allows them to make a certain kind of sense together. They make this sense, in other words, against the background of the explanatory story; and this structure allows him to achieve the articulations he does.

52. Charles Baudelaire, "LXXXVII. L'Irrémédiable," in *Œuvres complètes*, 1:98.
53. Charles Baudelaire, "LXXXVII. The Irremediable," trans. Henry Curwen, in *Flowers of Evil*, 98–100.

What is the explanatory story? The power of sin. Central to Baudelaire is a certain doctrine of Original Sin. But this wavers between a Christian and a gnostic or even Manichean story, with a side reference to
Hermes Trismegistus. (The poem "Au Lecteur" has a reference to "Satan
Trimégistre.") So he returns to the *idée catholique* [Catholic idea]. It is
partly that he finds the unbelieving story too shallow, too banal. There is
much greater and more frightening drama going on. Hugo is a major
target here, in spite of his great admiration for the poet. And George Sand
comes in for some rough treatment. But it is partly (perhaps mostly) also
his experience which is speaking here, particularly the sexual experience.
This has opened him to the attraction of evil, even the ugly.[54] "Tout enfant, j'ai senti dans mon coeur deux sentiments contradictoires, l'horreur
de la vie et l'extase de la vie" [Even as a child, I sensed in my heart two
contradictory feelings: a horror at life and at the same time, an ecstasy].

> Pour certains esprits plus curieux et plus blasés, la jouissance de
> la laideur provient d'un sentiment encore plus mystérieux, qui
> est la soif de l'inconnu, et le goût de l'horrible. C'est ce sentiment,
> dont chacun porte en soi le germe plus ou moins développé, qui
> précipite certain poétes dans les amphithéâtres et les cliniques,
> et les femmes aux exécutions publiques. Je plaindrais vivement
> qui ne comprendrait pas;—une harpe à qui il manquerait une
> corde grave![55]

> [For certain minds who are more curious and more blasé, the
> enjoyment of ugliness comes from a feeling which is even more
> mysterious, which is the thirst for the unknown and a taste for
> the horrible. It's the feeling, of which everyone carries the germ
> more or less developed, which pushes certain poets to amphi-
> theatres and clinics, and women to public executions. I would
> feel acute pity for anyone who couldn't understand this—a harp
> which was missing a deep chord.]

54. Charles Baudelaire, "Mon coeur mis à nu," in *Œuvres complètes,* 1:703.
55. Charles Baudelaire, "Maximes consolantes sur l'amour," in *Œuvres complètes,*
1:548–549.

Quand à la torture, elle est née de la partie infâme du coeur de l'homme, assoiffé de voluptés. Cruauté et volupté, sensations identiques, comme l'extrême chaud et l'extrême froid.[56]

[As for torture, it is born in the infamous part of the human heart, athirst for voluptuous pleasures: cruelty and the voluptuous, identical sensations, like extreme hot and extreme cold.]

He often finds people discussing various ideas of what the *plaisir d'amour* consists in to be "orduriers" [obscene] and "impudents utopistes" [impudent utopians]. "Moi, je dis: la volupté unique et suprême de l'amour gît dans la certitude de faire le mal.—Et l'homme et la femme savent de naissance que dans le mal se trouve toute volupté" [For myself, I say: that the unique and supreme voluptuousness of love lies in the certitude of committing evil—And men and women know from birth that all voluptuous pleasure comes from evil].[57]

We sink into sin and evil, because part of us loves it. Not all of us. There are "deux postulations":

Il y a dans tout homme, à toute heure, deux postulations simultanées, l'une vers Dieu, l'autre vers Satan. L'invocation à Dieu, ou spiritualité, est un désir de monter en grade; celle de Satan, ou animalité, est une joie de descendre. C'est à cette dernière que doivent être rapportées les amours pour les femmes et les conversations intimes avec les animaux, chiens, chats, etcetera.[58]

[There are in every human being, at every moment, two simultaneous postulations or fundamental tendencies, one to God, the other to Satan. The invocation of God, or spirituality, is the desire to rise to a higher level; that toward Satan or animality is a joy at sinking lower. This latter drive explains feelings of love for women, and intimate conversations with animals, dogs, cats, etcetera.]

56. Baudelaire, "Mon coeur mis à nu," 683.
57. Charles Baudelaire, "Fusées," in *Œuvres complètes*, 1:651–652.
58. Baudelaire, "Mon coeur mis à nu," 682–683.

Note the lining up of the oppositions God / Satan and spirituality / animality. And also the antifeminism. Here we see the gnostic or Manichean
side of Baudelaire's doctrine at its most flagrant.

So the picture is this: we long for the *Idéal*, which is paradise, and a
sense of which was there in infancy. This is more or less identified with
paradise in the religious tradition, full salvation. But this is not the whole
story. There also is the postulation toward Satan. And this too draws on
the energy of longing, but gives it a deviant direction. The love of evil is
the longing for God which has been highjacked, as it were. This is a
Platonic and Christian idea. Sexual desire is a "dépravation du sens de
l'infini" [depravation of the sense of the infinite].

There is a kind of inescapable mirage, where evil dresses itself in the
light of the Ideal, and draws us toward itself. But this cuts us off further
from the paradise, draws us down into matter, away from the spirit;
wherein we are ultimately enclosed, and hence see the paradise receding,
farther and farther; far from its warmth, we freeze into ennui. The attempted flights from ennui which take us into these false paradises just
aggravate the condition. "X. L'Ennemi":

> Ma jeunesse ne fut qu'un ténébreux orage,
> Traversé çà et là par de brillants soleils;

> [My youth was nothing but a dark, shadowy storm,
> Crossed here and there by brilliant sunlight]

My present condition results from this "ravage" (verse 3).[59]

59. It might help to place Baudelaire in the context of the evolution of French Romanticism. As I briefly mentioned above, there was a period when, like the German
movement of the 1790s, like the English with early Wordsworth, Shelley, and Keats,
French Romantics were aligned with the Left, and were enthusiastic in their hopes for
social transformation. This was particularly so in the early 1830s, in the wake of the July
Revolution. Hugo was the leading figure in this phase. But disillusionment set in as
political events unfolded, and a reaction ensued in which not only was the potential for
transformative politics put in doubt, but also the authenticity of the human commitment to transformation. Writers like Musset, Nerval, and Gauthier had already explored
this path, and Baudelaire is following in their footsteps. In view of Hugo's early promi-

The point of *Les Fleurs du Mal* is the exploration of this whole condition. A crucial point about this is that the human in this condition is not continually in a single disposition. The saint might be. But we "hommes moyens sensuels" [average sensual humans] are not. We are fascinated by sexual being in one phase, and then, feeling deeply the degradation later, say, the next morning, fall deeply into Spleen. The same will go in other departments. This human being will at moments long for release, then at other moments be excited by Satanism, and long to give himself to the devil utterly.[60] At other moments again, there will be a response of anger out of human dignity against God for having created this predicament; and thus a revolt against God: "CXXIV. Le Reniement de Saint Pierre" and "CXXV. Abel et Caïn." At other moments again, remorse and pity. And so on.

The point of *Les Fleurs du Mal* is to explore this whole gamut, to articulate this whole range of experience. Why? Because this entire range of experience is transfigured and made to speak. The spiritual depths or truth underlying it all is made to emerge into light, to show up.

In "Puisque réalisme il y a," there is a statement of transfiguration: "La Poésie est ce qu'il y a de plus réel, c'est ce qui n'est complètement vrai que dans *un autre monde*" [Poetry is what is most real, what is only completely real in *another world*].[61] But the transfiguration is clearly limited; the second clause all but takes back what the first clause asserts.

There may seem a paradox that showing our life in (frequently) an evil and sordid light may elevate us, overcome ennui, return something of the energy of the Ideal to us. But this is not so surprising. We suffer from the distance, the absence from our lives of the spiritual. The worst comes about when we not only draw away from it but begin to lose sight of it, begin to lose any knowledge of its existence. This is what is happening for Baudelaire in the modern secular consciousness of humans as good, as just requiring a reconstructed society, the liberal or democratic

---

nence, and his continuing commitment to a politics of transformation, we can see why he became representative of what Baudelaire saw as the illusion he must oppose. See Bénichou, *L'École du désenchantement*.

60. See "CXXVI. Les Litanies de Satan."

61. Charles Baudelaire, "Puisque réalisme il y a," in *Œuvres complètes,* 2:59.

dream. That's why he is often so hard on Hugo; why he turns against democracy after 1848. Why he so much swears by Joseph de Maistre. Why it is better to have de Sade than George Sand. What for others is an inspiring or at least consoling view of human potentiality, for Baudelaire is a further layer of opacity, of distance, of forgetfulness between us and the Ideal. All hope of returning to the real paradise, which in its deviant form consists of reveling in evil, in its true form in rising above evil; all hope of this is lost if evil itself is denied and lost sight of. So a recovery of a sharp sense of original sin is a relief, a liberation, a spiritual awakening and enlivening. It was the error of the eighteenth century to deny original sin. Nature only teaches crime. An infallible nature created parricide and anthropophagy. Rien que d'affreux.[62]

"XVIII. L'Idéal": We can't be satisfied with "beautés de vignettes" [the beauty of labels]; these are "pâles roses" [pale roses]. We need a view of humans which opens onto the full greatness of their embracing evil: Lady Macbeth, Michelangelo, Titans, Milton's Satan. So writing the book comes out of his gut. In his "Lettre à Ancelle" from February 18, 1866:

> Faut-il vous dire, à vous qui ne l'avez pas plus deviné que les autres, que dans ce livre *atroce* j'ai mis *tout mon coeur, toute ma tendresse, toute ma religion* (travestie), *toute ma haine*? Il est vrai que j'écrirai le contraire, que je jurerai mes grands dieux que c'est un livre *d'art pur,* de *singerie,* de *jonglerie,* et je mentirai comme un arracheur de dents.[63]

62. Was it so different with Calvinism and Jansenism? These people could only return to a lively sense of the goodness and mercy of God by making plain again how deep he was stooping to lift such depraved beings as themselves out of the mud. Take Jonathan Edwards describing in loving detail the damnation of lost souls. The message was: This is what we all deserve; our deserving this defines what we are. Now look at the love and mercy that God shows, in pardoning some of us. This was a release for his congregation (and undoubtedly also for him), because (a) it allowed their deep malaise about their own evil to surface and be faced, and (b) it made the love of God show up. Arminianism was still a cover-up, and it diminished the role of God. Of course, the (b) dimension with Baudelaire is not mercy and love of God. But it is that paradise can show up again, not reduced and banalized by Hugolian democracy.

63. Charles Baudelaire, "Lettre à Ancelle. 18 février 1866," in *Correspondance* (Paris: Gallimard, 1973), 2:610. Here we have a reference to what he had to say to avoid indict-

[Do I have to tell you, to you who hasn't any better got the point than the others, that in this *dreadful* book, I have put *my whole heart, all my tenderness, all my* disobeyed *religion, all my hatred*? It's true that I'll write the opposite, that I'll swear by the highest gods that it's a book of pure art, of monkey-tricks, of a juggler, and I'll lie like any tooth-puller.]

The book is analogous to what Bakhtin says about Dostoyevsky. It is mul-tivoiced. These are all human responses. Actually, there is a strong parallel to Dostoyevsky: they both stress the importance of recovering the human sense of existing in the dimension of good and evil. This means to grasp imaginatively what it is to be fascinated by evil. The loss of this dimension is a closing off from the spiritual, a way of masking the real options in an attempt to bring things under control. There is also a parallel to Nietzsche. Both have contempt for modern liberal cover-up.

3

But there is a more difficult issue. In the letter to Ancelle just quoted above, *Les Fleurs du Mal* is presented as a coherent whole. But in fact, the book, like its author, was profoundly divided. Let's return to "LXXXVII. L'Irrémédiable." Here there is a kind of triumphant synoptic consciousness, a total and cruel lucidity. There is something glorious and also soothing ("soulageant") about this, as verse 39 tells us. But there is also ambivalence. This is something which also partakes of Satan. What is it here that is wrong?

One thing which it seems to be is that this self-splitting, which brings reflection—"Tête-à-tête sombre et limpide / Qu'un coeur devenu son miroir" [a somber and limpid confrontation: a heart which has become its own mirror]—also paralyzes the will. One is lucid but absolutely not resisting. So the tête-à-tête is also "sombre"—or does this just refer to its content? I think not.

ment for publishing an obscene book, which, alas, he didn't avoid as things turned out. Distance between Baudelaire and *Les Fleurs du Mal*. Nature of a work of art. Author creates implied author, and protagonist. Here the same. But there is no doubt that the language chosen resonates with the author: the Christian.

This kind of impotent self-reflection is irony. So the last stanza speaks of "un phare ironique, infernal" [an ironic and infernal lighthouse].[64] This connection between irony, mirror and evil, destruction comes out in the previous poem, "LXXXIII. L'Héautontimorouménos."

> Ne suis-je pas un faux accord
> Dans la divine symphonie,
> Grâce à la vorace Ironie
> Qui me secoue et me mord?
>
>
> Elle est dans ma voix, la criarde!
> C'est tout mon sang, ce poison noir!
> Je suis le sinistre miroir
> Où la mégère se regarde.[65]
>
>
> [Am I not a jarring note
> In the heavenly symphony
> Since devouring Irony
> Gnaws me, shakes me by the throat?
>
>
> Hers is the shrillness in my voice;
> Through my blood her poisons race.
> I am the unholy mirror
> Where the shrew can watch her face.][66]

What does "irony" mean here? Not what Socrates was talking about, but a kind of irony of distance. One is drawn into an experience, on the path to being moved by it, but then one holds back; or better, one is held back; cannot enter fully and without qualification into it.[67]

---

64. Baudelaire, "LXXXVII. L'Irrémediable," 79.

65. Charles Baudelaire, "LXXXVI. L'Héautontimorouménos," in Œuvres complètes, 1:78.

66. Charles Baudelaire, "LXXXVI. The Heautontimoroumenos," trans. Naomi Lewis, in Flowers of Evil, 97–98.

67. Jean Starobinski, La Mélancholie au Miroir (Paris: Julliard, 1997). Starobinski points to the close connection in Baudelaire of the mirror with this stance of ironic

So there is ambivalence about this achievement, great and glorious as it is. Indeed, one might go further: Is the impotence of the will here not just a kind of null energy, or is it rather that there is some fascination here still with evil? The question can only be answered out of the resonances of the whole poem "L'Irrémédiable." But perhaps also we find a strong hint in verse 38: "flambeaux des grâces sataniques" [flames of satanic grace].[68] And in "XXII. Hymne à la Beauté," we find the notion that beauty can as much partake of the fascination (*engouement*) with evil as it can with the love of the spiritual and the good. Indeed, it is talked about here as though it was really on the side of evil. It is one of those mirages, which draws us on to escape Spleen, and excites us, but in the end brings us even farther into the desert.

Perhaps the notion is here that in bringing all the facets of the human condition, all the phases of our response to our predicament, to poetic expression, including those of false *engouement* themselves—for instance, sexual passion—beauty can just as much be the accomplice of evil as of good. What it always has is this power to render "l'univers moins hideux et les instants moins lourds" [the universe less hideous and the moments we live through less heavy]. (Note the term *lourd*, associated with Spleen.) But this can be in the service of fascination.

Then there is passage on *Beauté* in "Fusées": "Je ne conçois guère . . . un type de Beauté où il n'y ait du *Malheur* [. . .] Le plus parfait type de Beauté virile est *Satan*—à la manière de Milton." [I can't conceive of a type of beauty where there is no *misfortune* [. . .] The most perfect type of virile beauty is *Satan*—as Milton portrays him.][69] But we can say that there is a kind of contradiction at the heart of this collection. This is not just a display side by side of different modes of beauty we can enjoy; but the pursuit of one kind, the evil, can render one incapable of really

---

distance. The mirror can be a symbol of fidelity to reality; the mirror image gives it as it is. But the mirror is also "l'accessoire obligé de la coquetterie" [accessory of coquetry] and thus of a distance from reality that makes the full truth unreachable. "Je suis le sinistre miroir / Où la mégère me regarde" [I am the sinister mirror / In which the scowl sees me]. The "mégère" here is Medusa, which transfixes us in impotence.

68. Baudelaire, "LXXXVII. L'irrémédiable," 79.

69. Baudelaire, "Fusées," 657–658.

experiencing that of the mystic fulfillment we long for. That longing finds expression in a passage like this one:

> C'est cet admirable, cet immortel instinct du Beau qui nous fait considérer la terre et ses spectacles comme un aperçu, comme une correspondance du Ciel. La soif insatiable de tout ce qui est au-delà, et que révèle la vie, est la preuve la plus vivante de notre immortalité.
>
> C'est à la fois par la poésie et *à travers* la poésie, par et *à travers* la musique, que l'âme entrevoit les splendeurs situées derrière le tombeau; et quand un poème exquis amène les larmes au bord des yeux, ces larmes ne sont pas la preuve d'un excès de jouissance, elles sont bien plutôt le témoignage d'une mélancolie irritée, d'une postulation des nerfs, d'une nature exilée dans l'imparfait et qui voudrait s'emparer immédiatement, sur cette terre même, d'un paradis révélé.[70]

> [It's this admirable, immortal instinct for the Beautiful that makes us consider the earth and its spectacles as a glimpse, as a correspondence of Heaven. The insatiable thirst for all that lies beyond, and that life reveals is the most living proof of our immortality.
>
> It is both by poetry and *through* poetry, by and *through* music, that the soul glimpses the splendour beyond the grave; and when an exquisite poem brings tears to the edge of the eyes, these tears are not the proof of an excess of enjoyment, they are rather the testimony of an irritated melancholy, of a postulation of the nerves of a nature exiled in the imperfect and which would like to seize immediately, on this very earth, a revealed paradise.]

Or this:

> Il est des jours où l'homme s'éveille avec un génie jeune et vigoureux. Ses paupières à peine déchargées du sommeil qui les scellait, le monde extérieur s'offre à lui avec un relief puissant, une netteté de contours, une richesse de couleurs admirables. Le

---

70. Charles Baudelaire, "Études sur Poe," in *Œuvres complètes*, 2:334.

monde moral ouvre ses vastes perspectives, pleines de clartés nouvelles. L'homme gratifié de cette béatitude, malheureusement rare et passagère, se sent à la fois plus artiste et plus juste, plus noble, pour tout dire en un mot. Mais ce qu'il y a de plus singulier dans cet état exceptionnel de l'esprit et des sens, que je puis sans exagération appeler paradisiaque, si je le compare aux lourdes ténèbres de l'existence commune et journalière, c'est qu'il n'a été créé par aucune cause bien visible et facile à définir.[71]

[There are days when man awakens with a young, vigorous genius. His eyelids have barely been relieved of the sleep that sealed them, and the outside world presents itself to him with a powerful relief, a sharpness of outline, an admirable richness of colour. The moral world opens up its vast vistas, full of new clarity. The man graced with this bliss, unfortunately rare and fleeting, feels both more artistic and more just, more noble, to put it in a nutshell. But what is most singular about this exceptional state of mind and senses, which I can, without exaggeration, call paradisiacal, if I compare it to the heavy darkness of common, everyday, existence, is that it was not created by any visible, easily-defined cause.]

And Baudelaire goes on to recognize this state as a manifestation of the "volonté divine" [divine will]. So one can lay out the whole collection, showing the beauties of good and evil; but not be fully committed to them at once. Putting them all together bespeaks a stance of observation, rather than one of engagement. This finds expression in "LXXXVII. L'Irrémédiable": a distance is taken from the whole field and its contradictory directions of possible spiritual search. We lay these possibilities out in a tableau for a controlling synoptic eye. This couldn't be a way of knitting time together. The stance is one of noninvolvement, nonsympathy, but allowing for fascination. This is hardly the experience of the world and time which can make us immune to spleen, the kind of experience which we invoked at the beginning of Section I.3.

71. Charles Baudelaire, "Le Poème du Haschich," in *Œuvres complètes*, 1:401.

But the synoptic eye is also potentially an agent of control. Does Baudelaire's work also explore this alternative possibility? I think it does, but exploring it went in a certain way against the grain for him. Not necessarily control through a synoptic eye, but some kind of control seems very much an ideal of Charles Baudelaire the man.

IV

The attractions of control

1

We have just been looking at a source of deep division in Baudelaire, his affirmation of both "postulates," for God and for Satan, in spite of their incompatibility; presumably because both can hold at bay the spleen which he found really unbearable.

But there is another source of division, which is equally powerful, between what one might call elitism and (at risk of misunderstanding) "populism." I'm not talking here about political positions (though they might spill over into them), but rather about sources of inspiration for his poetry, and his ethical outlook.

There are perhaps two things here: his self-enclosure, one could say, monologism. This had two sides: (a) his sense of his own exceptionalism, the classical elitism of the Romantic, and scorn for the crowd. He took pride in not depending on the crowd, in hiding himself from them, making no appeal to them. Now this could be a stance of the Romantic figure in total bad faith, really appealing to sympathy, parading alienation, calling for attention. A sort of Werther or René. Baudelaire despises this. "Tous les élégiaques sont des canailles" [All elegiacs are scoundrels].[72] One of his reasons to look down on Hugo. This is a kind of pride: "Il faut tout dire, j'ai un orgueil qui me soutient et une haine sauvage contre les hommes. [...] Je veux que la foule me paie, il m'importe peu qu'elle me comprenne." [I must tell the whole truth, I

72. Georges Blin, *Le Sadisme de Baudelaire* (Paris: J. Corti, 1948), 25.

have a pride which supports me, and a savage hatred for humans. [. . .]
I want the crowd to give me something; that they understand me is
unimportant.][73] He didn't think himself "assez *bête* pour mériter le suffrage universel" [stupid enough to win universal suffrage].[74] He derived
"une jouissance de la haine" [enjoyment from hatred].[75]

He loved to "se glorifier dans le mépris" [take glory in scorn].[76] "Plus
je deviens malheureux, plus mon orgueil augmente" [The more I grow
unhappy, the more my pride grows].[77] This is prolonged by his reactionary views after 1848–1852: he was against liberalism, and universal
suffrage. And it fits with his rejection of any attempt to be useful for the
public. "Robespierre n'est estimable que parce qu'il a fait quelques belles
phrases" [Robespierre is only worthy of esteem because he made some
beautiful statements].[78] (b) The other facet is his despair of any real
human communion. Love can't seem to work. There is intense desire,
then recoil and disgust. Or else idealizing from a distance. Though he
seems to have hoped for some kind of companionship with Jeanne, really
his life is built on a Tower, which would be the locus of his poetic
creation.

> Dans l'amour, comme dans presque toutes les affaires humaines,
> l'entente cordiale est le résultat d'un malentendu. Ce malen-
> tendu, c'est le plaisir. . . . Le gouffre infranchissable, qui fait
> l'incommunicabilité, reste infranchi.[79]
>
> [In love, as in almost all human matters, cordial understanding
> is the result of a misunderstanding. This misunderstanding is
> pleasure itself. . . . The uncrossable gulf, which make commu-
> nication impossible, remains unbridged.]

73. Charles Baudelaire, "Lettre à Madame Aupick (sa mère). 11 octobre 1860," in *Correspondance générale*, 191–195.

74. Charles Baudelaire, "Lettre à Joséphin Soulary. 23 fêvrier 1860," in *Correspondance*, 1:680.

75. Massin, *Baudelaire*.

76. Blin, *Le Sadisme*, 24.

77. Blin, *Le Sadisme*, 27.

78. Baudelaire, "Mon coeur mis à nu," in *Œuvres complètes*, 1:680.

79. Baudelaire, "Mon coeur mis à nu," 695–696.

And,

> Épouvantable jeu où il faut que l'un des joueurs perde le gouver-
> nement de soi-même![80]

> [A terrible game where one of the players must lose self-
> control.][81]

"Qu'est-ce que l'amour? Le besoin de sortir de soi." [What is love? The
need to go beyond the self.][82] Baudelaire had a great need to get out of
himself but also an irresistible distrust (*méfiance*), a fear and recoil from
too close contact. The need:

- "Et quand je sens en moi quelque chose qui me soulève, que sais-je,
  un violent désir de tout embrasser, ou bien simplement un beau
  couchant à la fenêtre, *à qui le dire*?" [And when I feel in myself
  something which raises my spirits, like what? Say, a violent desire to
  embrace everything, or simply a beautiful sunset at the window, *to
  whom can I tell it*?][83]

- "Je n'ai jusqu'à présent joui de mes souvenirs que tout seul. Il faut en
  jouir à deux. Faire des jouissances du coeur une passion." [Up to
  now, I have enjoyed my memories alone. One should enjoy them
  together with another; make the joys of the heart a passion.][84]

- "Sentiment de *solitude*, dès mon enfance. Malgré la famille,—et au
  milieu des camarades, surtout,—sentiment de destinée éternelle-
  ment solitaire" [A feeling of *solitude*, beginning in childhood—and
  especially among comrades—the feeling of a destiny of eternal
  solitude].[85]

---

80. Baudelaire, "Fusées," 651.

81. See also in *Spleen de Paris* "XXVI. Les Yeux des Pauvres."

82. Baudelaire, "Mon coeur mis à nu," 692.

83. Charles Baudelaire, "Lettre à Madame Aupick (sa mère). 16 juillet 1839," in *Correspondance*, 75.

84. Charles Baudelaire, "Hygiène," in *Œuvres complètes*, 1:672. There is also a stronger
sexual reading of this sentence.

85. Baudelaire, "Mon coeur mis à nu," 680.

The last sentence of this quote begins to give the other side. Baudelaire distrusts this self-giving, and fears that it is incompatible with his vocation. The definition of love above from "Mon coeur mis à nu" continues: "L'homme est un animal adorateur. Adorer c'est se sacrifier et se prostituer." [The human being is an adoring animal. To adore is to sacrifice and prostitute oneself.][86] This last word isn't the crucial objection; Baudelaire uses it in a special sense, that of self-giving, which I'll come to in a minute. Rather it's "sacrifier," which is crucial here. Later he says: "Goût invincible de la prostitution dans le coeur de l'homme, d'où naît son horreur de la solitude.—Il veut être *deux*. L'homme de génie veut être un, donc solitaire. . . . C'est cette horreur de la solitude, le besoin d'oublier son moi dans la chair extérieure, que l'homme appelle noblement besoin d'aimer." [The invincible inclination to prostitution in the human heart, from which stems his horror at solitude—He wants to be two. The genius wants to be one, and so solitary. . . . It's this horror of solitude, the need to forget oneself in the flesh of another, which people call the need to love.][87]

Over against this, there is his love of *foules* [crowds], entering them, in a sense, giving himself to them. "Ce que les hommes nomment l'amour est bien petit, bien restreint et bien faible, comparé à cette ineffable orgie, à cette sainte prostitution de l'âme qui se donne toute entière, poésie et charité, à l'imprévu qui se montre, à l'inconnu qui passe" [What people call love is very small, very limited and weak, compared to that ineffable orgy, that holy prostitution of the soul, which gives itself utterly, poetry and charity, to the unforeseen which show up, the unknown person who passes].[88]

Note the strange use of "prostitution," as self-giving. "L'amour peut dériver d'un sentiment généreux: le goût de la prostitution; mais il est bientôt corrompu par le goût de la propriété" [Love can come from a generous feeling: the taste for prostitution; but very soon it is corrupted by the taste for property].[89] "L'être le plus prostitué, c'est l'être par excellence,

---

86. Baudelaire, "Mon coeur mis à nu," 692.

87. Baudelaire, "Mon coeur mis à nu," 700.

88. Charles Baudelaire, "XII. Les Foules," in *Œuvres complètes*, 1:291.

89. Baudelaire, "Fusées," 649.

c'est Dieu, puisqu'il est l'ami suprême pour chaque individu, puisqu'il est le réservoir commun, inépuisable de l'amour" [The most prostituted being, who is Being par excellence, is God, because he is the supreme friend for each individual, because he is the common and inexhaustible reservoir of love].[90]

This *bain de foule* is, of course, a very monological experience. We might even think it is voyeurism, although it aliments his transfiguration in poetry. But the *charité* is also really meant. "Car s'il est une place qu'ils [les poètes] dédaignent de visiter . . . c'est surtout la joie des riches. Cette turbulence dans le vide n'a rien qui les attire. Au contraire ils se sentent irrésistiblement entraînés vers tout ce qui est faible, ruiné, contristé, orphelin." [Because if there is one place which they [poets] scorn to visit . . . it's above all the joys of the rich. This turbulence in the void has nothing which attracts them. On the contrary they feel irresistibly drawn toward whatever is weak, ruined, saddened, orphaned.][91]

And, as Massin says, he never makes fun of those who suffer. He knows that laughter comes from a sense of superiority.[92]

But over against his undoubted compassion, and his love of contact with crowds, there stands his love of control, his belief in the will, his desire to control his own life by willing: even the belief that salvation comes through willing and hard work. He speaks in *Paradis artificiels* of "rédemption par le travail" [redemption through work] and "l'exercice assidu de la volonté" [the diligent exercise of the will].[93]

This goes along with the disdain for raw nature, the love of the artificial.[94]

90. Baudelaire, "Mon coeur mis à nu," 692.

91. Charles Baudelaire, "Les Veuves," in *Œuvres complètes*, 1:292.

92. Jean Massin, *Baudelaire: Entre Dieu et Satan* (Paris: Julliard, 1946), 317. "Cythère," "Cygne," "Les Petites Vieilles," "Femmes Damnées," and many "Tableaux parisiens." Massin makes a list of compassionate prose poems in *Spleen de Paris*: "Le Désespoir de la Vieille," "Le Fou et la Vénus," "La Femme sauvage et la Petite-Maîtresse," "Les Veuves," "Le Vieux Saltimbanque," "Le Gâteau," "Le Joujou du Pauvre," "Les Yeux des Pauvres," "La Fausse Monnaie," "Assommons les Pauvres!," "Mademoiselle Bistouri."

93. Charles Baudelaire, *Paradis artificiels,* in *Œuvres complètes*, 1:377–398.

94. Letter to Desnoyers on nature, in Massin, *Baudelaire*, 178–179.

He states in "Éloge du maquillage": "Tout ce qui est beau et noble est le résultat de la raison et du calcul" [Everything which is beautiful and noble is the result of reason and calculation]. "La vertu est artificielle, sur-naturelle" [Virtue is artificial and supernatural]. The same is true of beauty. "La mode est symptôme du goût de l'idéal surnageant dans le cer-veau humain au-dessus de tout ce que la vie naturelle y accumule de grossier, de terrestre et d'immonde" [Fashion is a symptom of the taste for the ideal surfacing in the human brain, over and above everything coarse, earthly, and filthy that natural life accumulates in it].[95]

Along with this goes his idealization of the dandy.[96] He seems to be deeply invested in this one. But is this called into question by his am-bivalence—for example, in "L'Irrémédiable"? Is the dandy ideal itself something ambivalent: a great response of the will and the aesthetic transforming power to the slow death which comes from the loss of the spiritual; while at the same time it partakes of that loss, becomes com-plicit with it, can even be fascinated by it?

Perhaps at some level, there is ambivalence, but his attachment to the ideal is very strong. The passage in "Fusées" X about *Beauté, Malheur,* and Satan mentions the dandy.

"Le Peintre de la vie moderne": "Le dandysme est un soleil couchant; comme l'astre qui décline, il est superbe, sans chaleur et plein de mélan-colie" [Dandyism is a setting sun; like the star which declines, it is su-perb, without heat and full of melancholy].[97] This is said in a tone of regret in the face of the rise of democracy. But is there any ambivalence about "sans chaleur" [without warmth] and melancholy?

"Le Dandy doit aspirer à être sublime sans interruption; il doit vivre et dormir devant un miroir" [The dandy must aspire to be sublime without interruption. He must live and sleep before a mirror].[98] This in-vocation of the mirror, what does it mean? This comes after the statement

95. Charles Baudelaire, "Éloge du maquillage," in *Œuvres complètes,* 2:714–718. Translated by Thom K. Sliwowski.

96. Massin, *Baudelaire,* 266–269.

97. Baudelaire, "Les Veuves," in *Œuvres complètes,* 712.

98. Baudelaire, "Mon coeur mis à nu," 678.

that we need God to tell us what our purpose is—that is, a statement of non-self-sufficiency.

He has banished "le végétal irrégulier" [the vegetal irregular]. What is the tone of this poem? It is beautiful, but is it also repellent? Utterly no movement, and no concern for us. The Ganges are "insouciants et taciturnes" [uncaring and taciturn]. And over all this "planait . . . un silence d'éternité" [there hovers a silence of eternity]. There seems something sinister, inhuman; and a fascination here with this inhumanity.[99]

All this attraction to self-control is shot through with ambiguity. Opposites meet: like the notion of God as engaged in "prostitution."

The ambiguity springs from the fact that Baudelaire is attracted in the religious dimension to both "postulations": the satanic, fascination with which can hold Spleen at bay, but also God, mercy, and solidarity which he cannot deny. And in the social dimension, his sources of inspiration are both elitist and "populist." I will return to these two-sided stances (really reflecting many-sidedness) at the end of the chapter.

V

The swan

1

But there is another way that Baudelaire explores to knit together a time no longer vulnerable to Spleen; and this is an intensification where the different moments come together in an accord, one might almost say, a solidarity. One is now no longer imprisoned in the passing single now, not because one has synoptically brought together a huge expanse by grasping it as one's object; but rather because one participates in this accord across the ages and differences, in which each resonates in the other. There is a proto-Proustian recovery of time.

Examples are "XCII. Le Cygne" and "VI. Les Phares."

99. Charles Baudelaire, "CII. Rêve parisien," in Œuvres complètes, 1:101.

XCII. Le Cygne.

Le Cygne
à Victor Hugo

I

Andromaque, je pense à vous! ce petit fleuve,
Pauvre et triste miroir où jadis resplendit
L'immense majesté de vos douleurs de veuve,
Ce Simoïs menteur qui par vos pleurs grandit,

A fécondé soudain ma mémoire fertile,
Comme je traversais le nouveau Carrousel.
Le vieux Paris n'est plus (la forme d'une ville
Change plus vite, hélas, que le cœur d'un mortel);

Je ne vois qu'en esprit tout ce camp de baraques,
Ces tas de chapiteaux ébauchés et de fûts,
Les herbes, les gros blocs verdis par l'eau des flaques,
Et, brillants aux carreaux, le bric-à-brac confus.

Là s'étalait jadis une ménagerie;
Là je vis, un matin, à l'heure où sous les cieux
Froids et clairs le Travail s'éveille, où la voirie
Pousse un sombre ouragan dans l'air silencieux,

Un cygne qui s'était évadé de sa cage,
Et, de ses pieds palmés frottant le pavé sec,
Sur le sol raboteux traînait son blanc plumage.
Près d'un ruisseau sans eau la bête ouvrant le bec

Baignait nerveusement ses ailes dans la poudre.
Et disait, le cœur plein de son beau lac natal:

"Eau, quand donc pleuvras-tu? quand tonneras-tu, foudre?"
Je vois ce malheureux, mythe étrange et fatal,

Vers le ciel quelquefois, comme l'homme d'Ovide,
Vers le ciel ironique et cruellement bleu,
Sur son cou convulsif tendant sa tête avide,
Comme s'il s'adressait des reproches à Dieu!

II

Paris change! mais rien dans ma mélancolie
N'a bougé! palais neufs, échafaudages, blocs,
Vieux faubourgs, tout pour moi devient allégorie,
Et mes chers souvenirs sont plus lourds que des rocs.

Aussi, devant ce Louvre une image m'opprime:
Je pense à mon grand cygne, avec ses gestes fous,
Comme les exilés, ridicule et sublime,
Et rongé d'un désir sans trêve! et puis à vous,

Andromaque, des bras d'un grand époux tombée,
Vil bétail, sous la main du superbe Pyrrhus,
Auprès d'un tombeau vide en extase courbée;
Veuve d'Hector, hélas! et femme d'Hélénus!

Je pense à la négresse, amaigrie et phthisique,
Piétinant dans la boue, et cherchant, l'oeil hagard,
Les cocotiers absents de la superbe Afrique
Derrière la muraille immense du brouillard;

À quiconque a perdu ce qui ne se retrouve
Jamais, jamais! à ceux qui s'abreuvent de pleurs
Et tètent la Douleur comme une bonne louve!
Aux maigres orphelins séchant comme des fleurs!

Ainsi dans la forêt où mon esprit s'exile

Un vieux Souvenir sonne à plein souffle du cor!

Je pense aux matelots oubliés dans une île,

Aux captifs, aux vaincus . . . à bien d'autres encor![100]

I

[Andromache, I think of you. The little stream,

A yellowing mirror that onetime beheld

The huge solemnity of your widow's grief,

(That other Simoïs your tears have swelled)

Suddenly flooded the memory's dark soil

As I was crossing the new *Place du Carrousel.*

The old Paris is gone (the face of a town

Is more changeable than the heart of moral man).

I see what seem the ghosts of these royal barracks,

The rough-hewn capitals, the columns waiting to crack,

Weeds, and the big rocks greened with standing water,

And at the window, a jumble of bric-à-brac

One time a menagerie was on display there,

And there I saw one morning at the hour

Of cold and clarity when Labor rises

And brooms make little cyclones of soot in the air

A swan that had escaped out of his cage,

And there, web-footed on the dry sidewalk,

Dragged his white plumes over the cobblestones,

Lifting his beak at the gutter as if to talk,

100. Charles Baudelaire, "XCII. Le Cygne," in *Œuvres complètes,* 1:85.

And bathing his wings in the sifting clay dust,
His heart full of some cool, remembered lake,
Said, "Water, when will you rain? Where is your thunder?"
I can see him now, straining his twitching neck

Skyward again and again, like the man in Ovid,
Toward an ironic heaven as blank as slate,
And trapped in a ruinous myth, he lifts his head
As if God were the object of his hate.

II

Paris changes, but nothing of my melancholy
Gives way. Foundations, scaffoldings, tackle and blocks,
And the old suburbs drift off into allegory,
While my frailest memories take on the weight of rocks.

And so at the Louvre one image weighs me down:
I think of my great swan, the imbecile strain
Of his head, noble and foolish as all the exiled,
Eaten by ceaseless needs—and once again

Of you, Andromache, from a great husband's arms
Fallen to the whip and mounted lust of Pyrrhus,
And slumped into a heap beside an empty tomb,
(Poor widow of Hector, and bride of Helenus)

And think of the consumptive negress, stamping
In mud, emaciate, and trying to see
The vanished coconuts of hidden Africa
Behind the thickening granite of the mist;

Of whoever has lost what cannot be found again,
Ever, ever; of those who lap up the tears

And nurse at the tears of that motherly she-wolf, Sorrow;
Of orphans drying like flowers in empty jars.

So in that forest where my mind is exiled
One memory sounds like the brass in the ancient war:
I think of sailors washed up on uncharted islands,
Of prisoners, the conquered, and more, so many more.][101]

Andromache is mourning in exile, over a river, Simoïs, "pauvre et triste miroir" [a poor and sad mirror], which can't capture the immense majesty she bears as the widow of Hector; in fact it is she who enlarges it with her tears. This triggers a recent memory of a walk through Paris, whose great past is also being swept away in the chaos of new construction. This awakens a feeling of exile, melancholy, approaching ennui. The third stanza stresses the absence of any overall meaning in this bustle, which produces just a disordered assemblage of objects. The portrayal of disorder reaches a climax in "bric-à-brac confus" [confused bric-à-brac] at the end of verse 12. The rhymes of "baraques" and "bric-à-brac" with "Andromaque" tie us to the original figure whose exile and mourning start this train of thought.

And the most poignant memory of the swan, lost, out of its element; it is surrounded only by puddles (*flaques*), a stream without water (*un ruisseau sans eau*). Its world has dried up, has lost its essential life-enhancing features.[102] The swan is exiled, "le coeur plein de son beau lac natal" [his heart full of some cool, remembered lake], turning in vain to "le ciel ironique et cruellement bleu" [toward an ironic heaven as blank as slate].

And then part II begins. "Paris change! mais rien dans ma mélancolie / N'a bougé!" [Paris changes, but nothing of my melancholy / gives way]. The reconstruction of Paris yields another image of melancholic time; one phase after another, but there is no meaning to the change, so it is as though nothing had happened; a kind of succession without

---

101. Charles Baudelaire, "XCII. The Swan," trans. Anthony Hecht, in *Flowers of Evil*, 109–111.

102. Starobinski, *La Mélancholie au Miroir*, 66.

meaning, but which is not a real connection with the past. The heaviness of the Spleen poems returns in verse 32: "Et mes chers souvenirs sont plus lourds que les rocs" [My dearest memories are heavier than rocks].

But then: "Tout pour moi devient allégorie" [Everything for me becomes allegory]. This is an important turning point. First, "becoming allegory" can be understood in two senses. Either a thinning out of the world: things lose their meaning and their substance, we can only give them meaning by seeing them as allegories. Or else, allegory in the rich sense, that besides their full existence, things show a deeper meaning. The first kind of allegory is just applied from outside by the desperate viewer; the second comes to us as a deeper vision. The first is a desperate maneuver within ennui, the second overcomes it.

And then a strange thing happens here. We start off with the first, and then the second takes over. Already above, in verse 24, the swan had become "mythe étrange et fatal" [strange and fatal myth]. And now we start thinking of the swan again with a sense of oppression: "une image m'opprime" [an image oppresses me]. But in the course of describing this a great reversal happens. Instead of petrification comes movement. "Je pense" [I think], repeated, moving from scene to scene, first from the swan, to Andromache; and then on from suffering being to suffering being, all suffering in exile. The movement comes alive, and these beings are in a sense resurrected, brought together, in one great company of compassion, which includes the swan, and also the author. The circle widens out, in the end has no exact limits: "à bien d'autres encor!" [to many others, too!]. (And we must include in their number Hugo, to whom the poem is dedicated, and who was then in exile in Jersey from the France of Napoleon III.)

Before the memories were "plus lourds que les rocs" [heavier than rocks]. Now "dans la forêt où mon esprit s'exile / Un vieux Souvenir sonne à plein souffle du cor!" [In the forest where my spirit lives its exile / An old memory sounds to the full a horn]. (Is it significant that "cor" is a palindrome of "roc"?) What is this change? We can think of it as all taking place within one traditional understanding of melancholy: the view that it takes two forms, the ecstasy of unitive intuition, but also the torpor of hebetude or ennui. Here we have shifted from the second to the first. The move comes with Andromache, now "auprès d'un tombeau vide en extase courbée" [and slumped into a heap [or, in ecstasy] beside an empty tomb]" (verse 39). (*Extase* means literally "sortir de soi" . . .)

But what does ecstasy mean, what does it here consist in? Another way of inhabiting time. Neither just the impotent loss of melancholy-ennui, nor the controlling overview-objectification. But a kind of accord, solidarity, sympathy, across the ages. Its only possible vehicle is compassionate identification; a compassion for suffering humanity, which includes the author. (Does this amount to what Benjamin calls for, a kind of rescuing [*retten*] of the past? It is anyway as though these people are alive again. In talking of Guys, Baudelaire talks of his "mémoire résurrectioniste, évocatrice, une mémoire qui dit à chaque chose: 'Lazare, lève-toi!'" [his evoking, resurrecting memory, which says to every thing: "Lazarus, come forth!"]).[103]

It is important to stress the time dimension. The poem comes together in the theme of exile. Part of what constitutes exile for the author, along with sin, and the reduction of ennui, is the inexorable passage of time as mere meaningless change; and this is intensified by the deconstruction-reconstruction of Paris by Haussmann under the Second Empire, which meant a loss of surroundings which were those of earlier meaning (see verse 7: "Le vieux Paris n'est plus" [The old Paris is no more]). The new stuff is itself temporary; or perhaps worse, it makes claim to monumental duration, as with Haussmann's creations. But there is something pathetic and infinitely sad about these modern imitations of the ancient monumental. The claim is to overarch time, to be still in contact with what was and what will be. But without rituals of recurrence, which bring key moments close together (e.g., pilgrimages, or parliaments) this can't be credible. It can't be made credible just on the basis of stone and form. The stone wears, and the style changes, and one has a sense of pathos, distance, yesterday's triumph. The depressing reminder of distance, on the way eventually to having the pleasing melancholy of a ruin.

Keeping this sense of a place as gathering times was easier when our worldview included multidimensional time. Cathedrals were time-gatherers, and part of their power for us today, beyond any faith commitment, comes from our remembering this. The totalizing hegemony

103. Charles Baudelaire, "Le Peintre de la vie moderne," in *Œuvres complètes*, 2:699.

of secular time threatens to carry away past moments of fullness, without hope of recurrence.

In thus striving to bring times together again, Baudelaire anticipates Proust.

A second important thing is that "tout pour moi devient allégorie" [everything for me becomes allegory]. Allegory is no longer confined to suitably noble objects. Andromache and the swan pass muster by old rules, but now it is also the bric-à-brac, the mud, disorder, new buildings: all of this becomes allegory, symbol, capable of showing forth something. Eliot's remark is also relevant here.[104]

Another crucial theme: barren dryness is then made fertile. Sorrow does this, and this triggers memory which carries us further. So stanza 1 and verse 5: Andromache's tears have increased the Simoïs; and this has "fécondé soudain ma mémoire fertile" [made fecund my fertile memory]. Sorrow and memory fertilize the barren wastes. How they do so, and the result, is evident in the climax of the poem, in the second to last stanza: "à ceux qui s'abreuvent de pleurs / Et tètent la Douleur comme une bonne louve"! [To those who water themselves with tears, / and suck Pain like a good she-wolf!] till finally memory sounds a horn (reminder of "Les Phares").

The move from part I to part II is marked by a change in tense; the events related in part I are conveyed in an array of past tenses; but "the present indicative of Part II imposes itself as the time of eternity, the time of salvation."[105] The stanza on Andromache makes her a statue outside of time. Suffering exiles across the ages are united in a company which spans the ages.

---

104. Paul Claudel said of Baudelaire's style that it was "un extraordinaire mélange du style racinien et du style journalistique de son temps" [an extraordinary mélange of Racine's style and the contemporary journalistic style of its time]. Quoted in Jacques Rivière, *Études* (Paris: Nouvelle Revue Française, 1911).

105. Victor Brombert, *The Hidden Reader: Stendhal, Balzac, Hugo, Baudelaire, Flaubert* (Cambridge, MA: Harvard University Press, 1988), 101. "Eternity" may not be the best word here; I will use it in another, more appropriate context in Chapter 11. But the objective solidarity which Baudelaire establishes between the exiles, widely separated as they are in time, does carry with it a sense of simultaneity.

VI. LES PHARES.

Rubens, fleuve d'oubli, jardin de la paresse,
Oreiller de chair fraîche où l'on ne peut aimer,
Mais où la vie afflue et s'agite sans cesse,
Comme l'air dans le ciel et la mer dans la mer;

Léonard de Vinci, miroir profond et sombre,
Où des anges charmants, avec un doux souris
Tout chargé de mystère, apparaissent à l'ombre
Des glaciers et des pins qui ferment leur pays;

Rembrandt, triste hôpital tout rempli des murmures,
Et d'un gran crucifix décoré seulement,
Où la prière en pleurs s'exhale des ordures,
Et d'un rayon d'hiver traversé brusquement;

Michel-Ange, lieu vague où l'on voit des Hercules
Se mêler à des Christs, et se lever tout droits
Des fantômes puissants qui dans les crépuscules
Déchirent leur suaire en étirant leurs doigts;

Colères de boxeur, impudences de faune,
Toi qui sus ramasser la beauté des goujats,
Grand cœur gonflé d'orgueil, homme débile et jaune,
Puget, mélancolique empereur des forçats;

Watteau, ce carnaval où bien des cœurs illustres,
Comme des papillons, errent en flamboyant,
Décors frais et légers éclairés par des lustres
Qui versent la folie à ce bal tournoyant;

Goya, cauchemar plein de choses inconnues,
De fœtus qu'on fait cuire au milieu des sabbats,

De vieilles au miroir et d'enfants toutes nues,
Pour tenter les démons ajustant bien leur bas;

Delacroix, lac de sang hanté des mauvais anges,
Ombragé par un bois de sapins toujours vert,
Où, sous un ciel chagrin, des fanfares étranges
Passent, comme un soupir étouffé de Weber;

Ces malédictions, ces blasphèmes, ces plaintes,
Ces extases, ces cris, ces pleurs ces *Te Deum,*
Sont un écho redit par mille labyrinthes;
C'est pour les cœurs mortels un divin opium!

C'est un cri répété par mille sentinelles,
Un ordre renvoyé par mille porte-voix;
C'est un phare allumé sur mille citadelles,
Un appel de chasseurs perdus dans les grands bois!

Car c'est vraiment, Seigneur, le meilleur témoignage
Que nous puissions donner de notre dignité
Que cet ardent sanglot qui roule d'âge en âge
Et vient mourir au bord de votre éternité![106]

[Rubens, garden of idleness watered by oblivion,
Where quick flesh pillows the impotence of dreams,
Where life's affluence writhes in eddying abandon
Like air in the air, or water in streams.

Leonardo da Vinci, deep mirror of darkness,
Where angels appear, their smiles charged with mystery
And tenderness, within the shadowy enclosures
Of pines and glaciers that shut in their country.

106. Charles Baudelaire, "VI. Les Phares," in *Œuvres complètes,* 1:13.

Rembrandt, tragic hospital re-echoing round a sigh;
A tall crucifix for only ornament
Traversed obliquely by a single wintry ray
Through which prayers rise, exhaling from excrement.

Michelangelo, no man's land where Hercules and Christ
Are one; where powerful phantoms in crowds
Erect themselves deliberately in darkening twilights,
With pressed, rigid fingers ripping open their shrouds.

Rage of the wrestler, impudence of the faun;
Puget, the convicts' melancholy emperor,
Caging the lion's pride in a weak, jaundiced man,
Deducing beauty from crime, vice and terror.

Watteau, carnival where many a distinguished soul
Flutters like a moth, lost in the brilliance
Of chandeliers shedding frivolity on the cool,
Clear decors enclosing the changed of the dance.

Goya, nightmare compact of things incredible:
Foetuses being fried for a witch's sabbath feast;
An old woman at a mirror, a little naked girl
Lowering an artful stocking to tempt a devil's lust.

Delacroix, blood lake haunted by evil angels
In the permanent green darkness of a forest of firs,
Where under a stricken sky a muffled sigh fills
The air like a faintly echoed fanfare of Weber's.

Such, O Lord, are the maledictions, the tears,
The ecstasies, the blasphemies, the cries of Te Deum
Re-echoing along labyrinthine corridors:
A dream for mortal hearts distilled from divine opium,

The watchword reiterated by sentinels
A thousand times, the message whispered from post to post,
A beacon burning on a thousand citadels,
A call of all the hunters lost in the great forest.

For is this not indeed, O Lord, the best witness
That our dignity can render to Your pity,
This tide of tears which age after age gathers
To fail and fall on the shore of Your eternity?][107]

Something similar, a coming together in the last three stanzas. The "écho redit par mille labyrinthes" [re-echoing along labyrinthine corridors], which is a "divin opium" [divine opium] for "cœurs mortels" [moral hearts]. Then we see all these cries coming together in solidarity: a cry repeated by sentinels, a light lit on a thousand citadels, "un appel de chasseurs perdus dans les grands bois!" [a call of all the hunters lost in the great forest]. A common striving, in pain and suffering, hence the "ardent sanglot qui roule d'âge en âge" [ardent sob which rolls from age to age]. This is the testimony of our dignity. Everything connects across history; time gathers.

The *sanglot* dies "au bord de votre éternité" [on the shore of Your eternity]. Is this a reproach to God for indifference? Or does it die because in God's eternity, as opposed to the gathered time of humans, we no longer want to sob? These poems open a new way of gathering time, or perhaps better, times, since the different happenings (or works in the case of "Les Phares") are separated sometimes far from each other. But it is not the gathering realized by an objectified tableau; rather the different times, events, works gather themselves by a kind of inner affinity. And this affinity is in turn based on the stance of the writer, no longer an objectifying observer: rather he is engaged; in the case of "Le Cygne," engaged in the stance of sympathy, and ultimately solidarity with all the exiles, captives, conquered, human and animal. "Le Cygne" shows another side to Baudelaire, which contradicts the drives toward solitude and control, which we discussed above, but which appears in a number

107. Charles Baudelaire, "VI. Beacons," trans. David Paul, in *Flowers of Evil*, 14–16.

of his poems—for instance, "Femmes Damnées," "Les Petites Vielles," some of *Spleen de Paris*—his sympathy for those who suffer. In the case of "Les Phares," it is an affinity-sympathy for all these artists.

These poems open a way of connecting times which is not imposed by a controlling consciousness, but which emerges from the moments or elements themselves. It is a way of living time(s) which is free from irony and ambivalence. This can resist much more effectively than the timeless objectifying grasp or the collapse into meaningless repetition which is the onset of spleen. They offer a connection to a larger pattern in time which can inspire, even exalt us, and put an end to spleen.

2

This invocation of and connection to a self-gathering pattern in time, which we see in the second half of "Le Cygne," needs a name; and I would like to propose "deep time."

What does it mean to attach the adjective "deep" to time? The explanation passes through our discourse about "deep" experience. There is a series of metaphors at work here, but they seem unavoidable. What we can immediately see and touch is on the "surface"; what lies "beneath" is what "underlies" this. What counts as deep in this context doesn't necessarily occur "lower" than us spatially; we have to go "deeper" to discover the life processes under the bark of a tree. So "depth" here has the antonym "surface" rather than "heights." "Depth" applied to experience concerns "underlying" conditions of our "immediate" perceptions, of which we are not necessarily aware.

This allows us to make sense of "deep time." Consider the following scene. I stand at the edge of the forest at dusk in late summer; I hear the wind shaking the branches as it moves through the trees; suddenly I feel a contact not just with this immediate scene, but with the whole cycle of the seasons, how the wind in winter sounds so muffled, because only the evergreens are responding, but this rich sound will recur, next year and in all subsequent years.

I am carried beyond the immediate experience to a sense of the whole cyclical movement of the seasons which is the condition of life on our planet. I am in touch with a movement at a much greater depth, and I rejoice at this connection.

I am not talking simply of my knowing the fact that this rustling of
the wind in the trees is part of a larger process; or even of my bringing
the fact to mind. Sensing the deeper process is something more; it involves being moved by this awareness, feeling joy at the contact. As far
as I can tell, a condition of my being moved by this underlying movement is that it has important human significance, which cannot be denied of this basic condition not just of my life, but of all the lives which
nourish me, biologically and spiritually.[108]

Does this apply to the connection that "Le Cygne" evokes between all
suffering exiles across history? Yes, because this consciousness of a
common undeserved fate can give me the courage to endure a condition
which might otherwise overwhelm me. This awareness creates a kind of
objective solidarity, not grounded in a common will, but in a deeply felt
common suffering. The sense of solidarity is realized in the poem, which
can (and in this case will) be read by (countless) others. Such poetry records a common heritage of humanity.

The sense of deep time which the poem evokes is a perfect antidote
to "spleen" as Baudelaire conceives it. The essence of spleen lies in the

108. This ever-renewed return of the seasons seems to deserve the Nietzschean title
"eternal return" (*ewige Wiederkunft des Gleichen*); except that this is notoriously seen as
a cause of despair for Nietzsche: "The life as you now live it and have lived it, you will
have to live once more and innumerable times more; and there will be nothing new in it,
but every pain and every joy and every thought and sigh and everything unutterably
small or great in your life will have to return to you, all in the same succession and sequence." The greatest weight, because if it were true of every action, it would "change
you as you are or perhaps crush you." Friedrich Nietzsche, *The Gay Science, with a Prelude in Rhymes and an Appendix of Songs,* trans. Walter Kaufmann (New York: Vintage
Books, 1974), 274.

But if you were ever able to affirm, give full value to your life, you would want to respond to this same prospect with the enthusiastic phrase: "You are a god and never have I
heard anything more divine" (Nietzsche, *Gay Science,* 273–274). This seems to confirm the
distinction I made in my text above: the continued repetition of a process with real human
significance evokes joy, while the endless recurrence of the meaningless is the heart of
spleen. The difference with Nietzsche seems to be that he thinks meaningfulness can be
conferred on an act by decision, an act of will. See the interesting discussion of this issue
in Humberto Beck, *The Moment of Rupture* (Philadelphia: University of Pennsylvania
Press, 2019), 39–45. I have learned a great deal from this very insightful book.

meaningless repetition of immediate surface experiences. To be lifted into a wide and deep pattern of objective solidarity takes me far beyond this.

VI

Baudelaire's modernity

1

But as often with Baudelaire, this sympathy-compassion is not unmixed. In the stance of "le flâneur," the observer drunk on customers and commodities, it goes along with a kind of excitement and jouissance which Baudelaire feels in observing modern life, the modern city, *la foule*. He describes this very well in his praise of Guys in "Le Peintre de la vie moderne." In a more general sense, much of this work is a self-portrait.

His passion, "c'est épouser la foule" [to marry the crowd]. "Pour le parfait flâneur, pour l'observateur passionné, c'est une immense jouissance que d'élire domicile dans le nombre, dans l'ondoyant, dans le mouvement, dans le fugitif et l'infini. Être hors de chez soi, et pourtant se sentir partout chez soi." [For the perfect flaneur, for the passionate observer, it is a moment of immense enjoyment to take up domicile in the number, in the fluctuating, in movement, in the fugitive and infinite. To be outside oneself and nevertheless everywhere at home.] "Prince qui jouit partout de son incognito" [Like a prince who enjoys being everywhere incognito].[109]

"L'amoureux de la vie universelle entre dans la foule comme dans un immense réservoir d'électricité. On peut aussi le comparer, lui, à un miroir aussi immense que cette foule." [The lover of universal life enters the crowd as into an immense reservoir of electricity. One could also compare him to a mirror as immense as this crowd.][110]

---

109. Baudelaire, "Le Peintre de la vie moderne," 691–692.

110. Baudelaire, "Le Peintre de la vie moderne," 692. Compare Charles Baudelaire, *Spleen de Paris*, "XII," *Œuvres complètes*, 1:291.

Guys seeks modernity, "de tirer l'éternel du transitoire" [to bring out
the eternal in the transitory]. "La modernité, c'est le transitoire, le fugitif,
le contingent, la moitié de l'art, dont l'autre moitié est l'éternel et
l'immuable" [Modernity is the transitory, the fugitive, the contingent,
which is half of art, of which the other half is the eternal and immutable].
The task of art is: "en extraire la beauté mystérieuse" [to bring out its mysterious beauty].[111]

The same idea occurs in "Salon de 1846."[112] "La beauté transitoire vient
des passions. Les milliers d'existences flottantes qui circulent dans les sou-
terrains d'une grande ville—Chaque époque a son port, son regard, son
geste." [Transitory beauty comes from the passions: thousands of mobile
beings who circulate in the underground spaces of a great city. Each has
its bearing, its look, its gestures.][113]

There is a heroism also in this modern life, as he says in the "Salon de
1846" passage. The minister in the chamber, the criminal on the scaffold.
"Il y a donc une beauté et un héroïsme moderne!" [There is thus a beauty
and a heroism in the modern age!][114] Whence this excitement? It is seeing
the human drama; the drama of good and evil, the drama of sin, seduction, of the fight against leveling (the dandy), of the continued battle
against "nature" (*maquillage*). Here there is a kind of excitement, which
doesn't have to spill over into compassion. (See *Spleen de Paris,* "XXXV.
Les Fenêtres.") The excitement is that the world, which threatens to go
dead, dry up, come to the stasis of meaningless which it has under ennui,
and to which it is helped by the rush toward disenchantment, the destruc-

111. Baudelaire, "Le Peintre de la vie moderne," 694, 695. In the chapter on Rilke and
in Section I.1 of this chapter, I mention the two features of modern big cities which
tended to repel or dismay post-Romantic poets, among others. One was the Simmel
factor, the multiplication of "shallow" functional relations, and the shrinking of more
intense many-sided ones, along with the constant changing of what was required to succeed, or even survive; the second was the ugliness and meaninglessness of many urban
landscapes, discussed in Section I.2 above. Baudelaire certainly felt the second, as evi-
denced by his reaction to Haussmann's destruction of the old Paris. But the first, far
from deterring him, was the source of excitement.

112. Charles Baudelaire, "Salon de 1846," in *Œuvres complètes,* 2:493–496.

113. Baudelaire, "Le Peintre de la vie moderne," 695–696.

114. Baudelaire, "Salon de 1846," 495.

tion of the past, the loss of awareness of evil, nevertheless is a source of meaning; the excitement is that this world takes on its meaning again. The great achievement of Guys was that he made this world come alive; he found the eternal in the transitory.

This is particularly important, since the modern world seems to have dedicated itself to the transitory; in its destruction of historical buildings, cities, in perpetually making itself over in the name of utility, the most humanly meaningless of categories. It is a triumph to bring out exactly the human-spiritual drama which is being played out in this frenetic change. "Il [Guys] a cherché partout la beauté passagère, fugace, de la vie présente, . . . la *modernité*. Souvent bizarre, violent, excessif, mais toujours poètique." [Guys has sought everywhere the fleeting, passing, beauty of our present life . . . *modernity*. This is often bizarre, violent, excessive, but is always poetic.][115]

There is an especial emphasis on these characteristics: bizarre, violent, excessive. Baudelaire thinks these are especially crucial to our age. Why? Because our age is the age of disenchantment, of failing meaning; and of rampant, because self-hidden, evil. And we can only bring out its meaning by portraying its drama of wildness, *démesure,* despair, and melancholy. And that's why the Romantic period has given such a place to these things. In his discussion of Banville, he gives a pencil sketch of this movement.[116] Beethoven started to "remuer les mondes de mélancolie et de désespoir" [set in motion the worlds of melancholy and despair]; then this was continued by Maturin, Byron, Poe.

> Ils ont projeté des rayons splendides, éblouissants sur le Lucifer latent qui est installé dans tout coeur humain. Je veux dire que l'art moderne a une tendance essentiellement démoniaque. Et il semble que cette part infernale de l'homme, . . . , augmente journellement.[117]

> [They projected splendid and dazzling rays of light on the latent Lucifer which has installed itself in every human heart. I

115. Baudelaire, "Le Peintre de la vie moderne," 724.
116. See Baudelaire, *Œuvres complètes,* 2:168.
117. Charles Baudelaire, *L'Art romantique,* in *Œuvres complètes,* 2:168.

mean that modern art has a tendency toward the essentially
demoniac. And it seems that this infernal part of humans
grows every day.]

Hence "XVIII. L'Idéal," with its invocation of Lady Macbeth; hence the
attack on George Sand, the invocation of de Maistre, the refusal to adopt
an optimistic view of human goodness. (We should also mention the
"Salon de 1846," "Qui dit Romantisme dit art moderne,—c'est-à-dire in-
timité, spiritualité, couleur, aspiration vers l'infini" [Who says Romanticism says modern art—that is: intimacy, spirituality, color, aspiration to
infinity].)[118] Hence also the fascination, shared with Poe, for the uncanny,
the monstrous, beings on the fringes of horror. And the tendency to see
modern cityscapes in these terms—for example, "XCII. Les Sept vieillards." Indeed, the love of such cityscapes in reality or fantasy—"Rêve
parisien." Dandyism is very much a move in this drama. It is a kind of
heroic reaction, holding out against the empty world and the masses.
But it can't amount to a resistance of real deeds, but only of self-presenting
dissent. The fight against triviality.[119]

Baudelaire evokes a great figure of the Romantic period: Chateaubriand, whose travels to the American wilderness, and discovery of the
Natchez tribe, seized the imagination of many in that period. He took
part in the resistance to triviality. Baudelaire sees in him a form of the
dandy: he cultivated the idea of beauty, in love above all with the distinction between higher and lower forms of life. This was a passion which
became a doctrine: dandyism expressed an ardent need to take an original stance, held within the external limits of propriety. It was "a sort of
cult of the self, which can consist with the search for happiness of another, of a woman, for example, which can even survive through all of
what are generally called illusions. It is the pleasure of astounding others,
and the proud satisfaction of never being astounded." Even if he suffers,
he smiles like the Spartan being bitten by a fox.[120]

118. Baudelaire, "Salon de 1846," 421.
119. See Baudelaire, "Le Peintre de la vie moderne," 709.
120. Baudelaire, "Le Peintre de la vie moderne," 710.

Like stoicism, dandyism requires tremendous discipline, and great will power. "Étrange spiritualisme! Perinde ac cadaver!"[121] This need to combat and destroy triviality. From this comes that haughty attitude of caste which can provoke others. In the transition period between aristocracy and democracy, there is an attempt to make a new aristocracy. In Baudelaire's view, "Le dandysme est le dernier éclat d'héroïsme dans les décadences; Le dandysme est un soleil couchant; comme l'astre qui décline, il est superbe, sans chaleur et plein de mélancolie." [Dandyism is the last brilliant moment of heroism in a decadent era. It is a setting sun; like the star which declines, it is superb, without heat and full of melancholy.] But the tide of democracy will drown them. "Le caractère de beauté d'un dandy consiste surtout dans l'air froid qui vient de l'inébranlable résolution de ne pas être ému" [The beauty of a dandy consists in his cool stance which comes from his unshakeable resolution to be unmoved].[122]

So as we see with the dandy and the flaneur, there are ways of living the ambivalence of our world where beauty mingles with the atrocious, and the decadent ("Hymne à la Beauté"), not just in the distancing, objectifying stance of "L'Irrémédiable," but also with a kind of rapt excitement. This can border on, be partly mingled with, the stance of sympathy-compassion as we saw above, but it can be enjoyed for itself. The goal is not here to reconnect time, but to live in the moment.

But then seemingly nonidentical with both the ways we identified above of reconnecting time—the objectifying-synoptic way of "L'Irrémédiable," and the solidarity-gathering mode of "Le Cygne"—there seem to be moments of grace where the poet comes close again to the sense of the original paradise.

In his writings about poetry and art, Baudelaire sometimes refers to such moments. For instance the "paradisiac" state he refers to in the opening of "Le Poème du Haschich."[123] Or,

---

121. Baudelaire, "Le Peintre de la vie moderne," 711. The Latin phrase is a Jesuit slogan, enjoining absolute obedience to superiors even to the point of death.

122. Baudelaire, "Le Peintre de la vie moderne," 712.

123. Baudelaire, "Le Poème du Haschich," 401–402.

Il y a des moments de l'existence où le temps et l'étendue sont plus profonds, et le sentiment de l'existence immensément aug-menté. . . . Dans certains états de l'âme presque surnaturels, la profondeur de la vie se révèle toute entière dans le spectacle, si ordinaire qu'il soit, qu'on a sous les yeux. Il en devient le symbole.[124]

[But there are moments in one's existence where time and space are deeper, and the feeling of existence [a reference to Rousseau?] is immensely increased. . . . In certain almost supernatural states of the soul, the depth of life is revealed in its entirety in the spectacle, however ordinary it might be, which we have before our eyes.]

In the hashish poem, Baudelaire speaks of these moments as like visita-tions of grace. And he expresses the same idea in his essay on Poe, where he talks of "ces états de santé poétique, si rares et si précieux qu'on pour-rait vraiment les considérer comme des grâces extérieures à l'homme et comme des visitations" [these states of poetic health, so rare and precious that one could really see in them states of grace external to the human, and as visitations].[125]

Something different is meant from the ordinary Christian theological notion of grace, because Baudelaire talks right in this passage on Poe, and elsewhere, about being able to control these moments, bring them on at will, by discipline and method. But this is something he more aspired to than achieved.

I don't know whether to connect these moments with a certain tone which appears in some of Baudelaire's poetry. Perhaps these moments of inspiration were what also underlay such breakthroughs as we seem to have in "XCII. Le Cygne." But there are poems, precisely the ones I mentioned at the beginning, where the original innocent paradise is in-voked directly, and not simply through its absence and opposite. Of course, it is also invoked as absent, but in the warmth of the language

124. Baudelaire, "Fusées," 658–659.
125. Charles Baudelaire, "Notes nouvelles sur Edgar Poe," in *Œuvres complètes*, 2:331.

we feel what it is, and not just what it's like to be exiled from it. For example, the last stanza of "I. Bénédiction."

2

There is another stance to the world and time which Baudelaire explores; this one from the standpoint of the end of life, of death. Baudelaire frequently writes out of a sense of readiness for death. The last section of *Les Fleurs du Mal* is titled "La Mort." "CXXVII. La Mort des Amants" bespeaks a calm sense that the lovers have lived. That's what life is about, and they've had it. "CXXVIII. La Mort des Pauvres" bespeaks the peace of rest at last, and an end to suffering, but here connected with the idea of a new life starting. There is something very moving about both these poems; but one feels their distance from the poet's depth feelings.

"CXXIX. La Mort des Artistes": it is hard to see what is being said here. Yes, there is a perpetual struggle to reach beauty; one can empty one's quiver without ever hitting it. But what exactly is hope here? Is the hope in eternity in the sense of remembrance by others, that one's reputation will live, or some survival in an afterlife? In either sense, this hope is perhaps strongly felt, but just as an offsetting consideration, not as a reconciliation with death.

"CXXX. La Fin de la Journée": There is here a real sense of repose from the agitation of life; but it is not just negative. A sense of release into something, into the essential, something higher. Something similar with "Recueillement," from the 1868 edition.[126] This is another synoptic view. But different from the type of "L'Irrémédiable"; not a synopsis which totally objectifies, that is, where the speaker stands outside, with a heroic consciousness of terrible inevitability. He stands outside the "multitude vile des mortels" [vile multitude of mortals] of verse 5. But there is another movement, which runs through his whole life coming to this end, like day ends in night; and this movement he takes on, he assumes; "il l'épouse." He brings his Pain to assume it. So there is a sense of connection with, of going along with the movement of life which was quite absent in "L'Irrémédiable." And this brings a sense of connection with the

126. Charles Baudelaire, "Recueillement," in *Œuvres complètes*, 1:140–141.

past, with "les défuntes Années" "en robes surannées" [the dead years in outdated clothes] (verses 9–10).

There is a delicious, a beautiful resignation, acceptance here, and this brings the connection, which gets deeper as the sonnet draws to a close. We can see the "défuntes Années," and also the "Soleil moribond" [dying sun]. But at the very end it is through a more inward sense, that we hear "la douce Nuit qui marche" [the soft night which advances]. The tone of acceptance is strengthened by the breaking in of the final élan even before the end of the second quatrain, in verse 8.

Whence the resignation, acceptance? Nothing is specifically said, but there is a tone of peace, rather than despair. The speaker must reason with his Pain, which is tempted to agitation before the prospect of the night: "Sois sage, ô ma Douleur, et tiens-toi plus tranquille" [Be wise, my pain, and keep calm and still]. But he reasons by reminding his Pain that it has wanted this end: "Tu réclamais le Soir" [You called for the evening].[127]

CXXVI. Le Voyage

I.

Pour l'enfant, amoureux de cartes et d'estampes,
L'univers est égal à son vaste appétit.
Ah! que le monde est grand à la clarté des lampes!
Aux yeux du souvenir que le monde est petit!

Un matin nous partons, le cerveau plein de flamme,
Le cœur gros de rancune et de désirs amers,
Et nous allons, suivant le rythme de la lame,
Berçant notre infini sur le fini des mers:

Les uns, joyeux de fuir une patrie infâme;
D'autres, l'horreur de leurs berceaux, et quelques-uns,
Astrologues noyés dans les yeux d'une femme,
La Circé tyrannique aux dangereux parfums.

127. Charles Baudelaire, "CXXIV. La Fin de la Journée," in Œuvres complètes, 1:128.

Pour n'être pas changés en bêtes, ils s'enivrent
D'espace et de lumière et de cieux embrasés;
La glace qui les mord, les soleils qui les cuivrent,
Effacent lentement la marque des baisers.

Mais les vrais voyageurs sont ceux-là seuls qui partent
Pour partir; cœurs légers, semblables aux ballons,
De leur fatalité jamais ils ne s'écartent,
Et sans savoir pourquoi, disent toujours: Allons!

Ceux-là, dont les désirs ont la forme des nues,
Et qui rêvent, ainsi qu'un conscrit le canon,
De vastes voluptés, changeantes, inconnues,
Et dont l'esprit humain n'a jamais su le nom!

II.

Nous imitons, horreur! la toupie et la boule
Dans leur valse et leurs bonds; même dans nos sommeils
La Curiosité nous tourmente et nous roule,
Comme un Ange cruel qui fouette des soleils.

Singulière fortune où le but se déplace,
Et, n'étant nulle part, peut être n'importe où!
Où l'Homme, dont jamais l'espérance n'est lasse,
Pour trouver le repos court toujours comme un fou!

Notre âme est un trois-mâts cherchant son Icarie;
Une voix retentit sur le pont: "Ouvre l'œil!"
Une voix de la hune, ardente et folle, crie:
"Amour . . . gloire . . . bonheur!" Enfer! c'est un écueil!

Chaque îlot signalé par l'homme de vigie
Est un Eldorado promis par le Destin;

L'Imagination qui dresse son orgie
Ne trouve qu'un récif aux clartés du matin.

Ô le pauvre amoureux des pays chimériques!
Faut-il le mettre aux fers, le jeter à la mer,
Ce matelot ivrogne, inventeur d'Amériques
Dont le mirage rend le gouffre plus amer?

Tel le vieux vagabond, piétinant dans la boue,
Rêve, le nez en l'air, de brillants paradis;
Son œil ensorcelé découvre une Capoue
Partout où la chandelle illumine un taudis.

III.

Étonnants voyageurs! quelles nobles histoires
Nous lisons dans vos yeux profonds comme les mers!
Montrez-nous les écrins de vos riches mémoires,
Ces bijoux merveilleux, faits d'astres et d'éthers.

Nous voulons voyager sans vapeur et sans voile!
Faites, pour égayer l'ennui de nos prisons,
Passer sur nos esprits, tendus comme une toile,
Vos souvenirs avec leurs cadres d'horizons.

Dites, qu'avez-vous vu?

IV.

"Nous avons vu des astres
Et des flots; nous avons vu des sables aussi;
Et, malgré bien des chocs et d'imprévus désastres,
Nous nous sommes souvent ennuyés, comme ici.

La gloire du soleil sur la mer violette,
La gloire des cités dans le soleil couchant,
Allumaient dans nos coeurs une ardeur inquiète
De plonger dans un ciel au reflet alléchant.

Les plus riches cités, les plus beaux paysages,
Jamais ne contenaient l'attrait mystérieux
De ceux que le hasard fait avec les nuages.
Et toujours le désir nous rendait soucieux!

—La jouissance ajoute au désir de la force.
Désir, vieil arbre à qui le plaisir sert d'engrais,
Cependant que grossit et durcit ton écorce,
Tes branches veulent voir le soleil de plus près!

Grandiras-tu toujours, grand arbre plus vivace
Que le cyprès?—Pourtant nous avons, avec soin,
Cueilli quelques croquis pour votre album vorace,
Frères qui trouvez beau tout ce qui vient de loin!

Nous avons salué des idoles à trompe;
Des trônes constellés de joyaux lumineux;
Des palais ouvragés dont la féerique pompe
Serait pour vos banquiers un rêve ruineux;

Des costumes qui sont pour les yeux une ivresse;
Des femmes dont les dents et les ongles sont teints,
Et des jongleurs savants que le serpent caresse."

V.

Et puis, et puis encore?

VI.

"Ô cerveaux enfantins!

Pour ne pas oublier la chose capitale,
Nous avons vu partout, et sans l'avoir cherché,
Du haut jusques en bas de l'échelle fatale,
Le spectacle ennuyeux de l'immortel péché:

La femme, esclave vile, orgueilleuse et stupide,
Sans rire s'adorant et s'aimant sans dégoût;
L'homme, tyran goulu, paillard, dur et cupide,
Esclave de l'esclave et ruisseau dans l'égout;

Le bourreau qui jouit, le martyr qui sanglote;
La fête qu'assaisonne et parfume le sang;
Le poison du pouvoir énervant le despote,
Et le peuple amoureux du fouet abrutissant;

Plusieurs religions semblables à la nôtre,
Toutes escaladant le ciel; la Sainteté,
Comme en un lit de plume un délicat se vautre,
Dans les clous et le crin cherchant la volupté;

L'Humanité bavarde, ivre de son génie,
Et, folle maintenant comme elle était jadis,
Criant à Dieu, dans sa furibonde agonie:
'Ô mon semblable, ô mon maître, je te maudis!'

Et les moins sots, hardis amants de la Démence,
Fuyant le grand troupeau parqué par le Destin,
Et se réfugiant dans l'opium immense!
—Tel est du globe entier l'éternel bulletin."

VII.

Amer savoir, celui qu'on tire du voyage!
Le monde, monotone et petit, aujourd'hui,
Hier, demain, toujours, nous fait voir notre image:
Une oasis d'horreur dans un désert d'ennui!

Faut-il partir? rester? Si tu peux rester, reste;
Pars, s'il le faut. L'un court, et l'autre se tapit
Pour tromper l'ennemi vigilant et funeste,
Le Temps! Il est, hélas! des coureurs sans répit,

Comme le Juif errant et comme les apôtres,
À qui rien ne suffit, ni wagon ni vaisseau,
Pour fuir ce rétiaire infâme: il en est d'autres
Qui savent le tuer sans quitter leur berceau.

Lorsque enfin il mettra le pied sur notre échine,
Nous pourrons espérer et crier: En avant!
De même qu'autrefois nous partions pour la Chine,
Les yeux fixés au large et les cheveux au vent,

Nous nous embarquerons sur la mer des Ténèbres
Avec le cœur joyeux d'un jeune passager.
Entendez-vous ces voix, charmantes et funèbres,
Qui chantent: "Par ici! vous qui voulez manger

Le Lotus parfumé! c'est ici qu'on vendange
Les fruits miraculeux dont votre cœur a faim;
Venez vous enivrer de la douceur étrange
De cette après-midi qui n'a jamais de fin!"

À l'accent familier nous devinons le spectre;
Nos Pylades là-bas tendent leurs bras vers nous.

"Pour rafraîchir ton cœur nage vers ton Électre!"
Dit celle dont jadis nous baisions les genoux.

VIII.

Ô Mort, vieux capitaine, il est temps! levons l'ancre!
Ce pays nous ennuie, ô Mort! Appareillons!
Si le ciel et la mer sont noirs comme de l'encre,
Nos cœurs que tu connais sont remplis de rayons!

Verse-nous ton poison pour qu'il nous réconforte!
Nous voulons, tant ce feu nous brûle le cerveau,
Plonger au fond du gouffre, Enfer ou Ciel, qu'importe?
Au fond de l'Inconnu pour trouver du nouveau![128]

[THE VOYAGE

I.

For the boy playing with his globe and stamps,
the world is equal to his appetite—
how grand the world in the blaze of the lamps,
how petty in tomorrow's small dry light!

One morning we lift anchor, full of brave
prejudices, prospects, ingenuity—
we swing with the velvet swell of the wave,
our infinite is rocked by the fixed sea.

Some wish to fly a cheapness they detest,
others, their cradles' terror—others stand
with their binoculars on a woman's breast,
reptilian Circe with her junk and wand.

---

128. Charles Baudelaire, "CXXVI. Le Voyage," in *Œuvres complètes*, 1:129–134.

Not to be turned to reptiles, such men daze
themselves with spaces, light, the burning sky;
cold toughens them, they bronze in the sun's blaze
and dry the sores of their debauchery.

But the true voyagers are those who move
simply to move—like lost balloons! Their heart
is some old motor thudding in one groove.
It says its single phrase, "Let us depart!"

They are like conscripts lusting for the guns;
our sciences have never learned to tag
their projects and designs—enormous, vague
hopes grease the wheels of these automatons!

II.

We imitate, oh horror! tops and bowls
in their eternal waltzing marathon;
even in sleep, our fever whips and rolls—
like a black angel flogging the brute sun.

Strange sport! where destination has no place
or name, and may be anywhere we choose—
where man, committed to his endless race,
runs like a madman diving for repose!

Our soul is a three-master seeking port;
a voice from starboard shouts, "We're at the dock!"
Another, more elated, cries from port,
"Here's dancing, gin and girls!" Balls! it's a rock!

The islands sighted by the lookout seem
the El Dorados promised us last night;

imagination wakes from its drugged dream,
sees only ledges in the morning light.

Poor lovers of exotic Indias,
shall we throw you in chains or in the sea?
Sailors discovering new Americas,
who drown in a mirage of agony!

The worn-out sponge, who scuffles through our slums
sees whiskey, paradise and liberty
wherever oil-lamps shine in furnished rooms—
we see Blue Grottoes, Caesar and Capri.

III.

Stunningly simple Tourists, your pursuit
is written in the tear-drops in your eyes!
Spread out the packing cases of your loot,
your azure sapphires made of seas and skies!

We want to break the boredom of our jails
and cross the oceans without oars or steam—
give us visions to stretch our minds like sails,
the blue, exotic shoreline of your dream!
Tell us, what have you seen?

IV.

     "We've seen the stars,
a wave or two—we've also seen some sand;
although we peer through telescopes and spars,
we're often deadly bored as you on land.

The shine of sunlight on the violet sea,
the roar of cities when the sun goes down;

these stir our hearts with restless energy;
we worship the Indian Ocean where we drown!

No old chateau or shrine besieged by crowds
of crippled pilgrims sets our souls on fire,
as these chance countries gathered from the clouds.
Our hearts are always anxious with desire.

(Desire, that great elm fertilized by lust,
gives its old body, when the heaven warms
its bark that winters and old age encrust;
green branches draw the sun into its arms.

Why are you always growing taller. Tree—
Oh longer-lived than cypress!) Yet we took
one or two sketches for your picture-book.
Brothers who sell your souls for novelty!

We have salaamed to pagan gods with horns,
entered shrines peopled by a galaxy
of Buddhas, Slavic saints, and unicorns,
so rich Rothschild must dream of bankruptcy!

Priests' robes that scattered solid golden flakes,
dancers with tattooed bellies and behinds,
charmers supported by braziers of snakes . . ."

V.

Yes, and what else?

VI.

Oh trivial, childish minds!
You've missed the more important things that we

were forced to learn against our will. We've been
from top to bottom of the ladder, and see
only the pageant of immortal sin:

there women, servile, peacock-tailed, and coarse,
marry for money, and love without disgust
horny, pot-bellied tyrants stuffed on lust,
slaves' slaves—the sewer in which their gutter pours!

old maids who weep, playboys who live each hour,
state banquets loaded with hot sauces, blood and trash,
ministers sterilized by dreams of power,
workers who love their brutalizing lash;

and everywhere religions like our own
all storming heaven, propped by saints who reign
like sybarites on beds of nails and frown—
all searching for some orgiastic pain!

Many, self-drunk, are lying in the mud—
mad now, as they have always been, they roll
in torment screaming to the throne of God:
"My image and my lord, I hate your soul!"

And others, dedicated without hope,
flee the dull herd—each locked in his own world
hides in his ivory-tower of art and dope—
this is the daily news from the whole world!

VII.

How sour the knowledge travellers bring away!
The world's monotonous and small; we see

ourselves today, tomorrow, yesterday,
an oasis of horror in sands of ennui!

Shall we move or rest? Rest, if you can rest;
move if you must. One runs, but others drop
and trick their vigilant antagonist.
Time is a runner who can never stop,

the Wandering Jew or Christ's Apostles. Yet
nothing's enough; no knife goes through the ribs
of this retarius throwing out his net;
others can kill and never leave their cribs.

And even when Time's heel is on our throat
we still can hope, still cry, "On, on, let's go!"
Just as we once took passage on the boat
for China, shivering as we felt the blow,

so we now set our sails for the Dead Sea,
light-hearted as the youngest voyager.
If you look seaward, Traveller, you will see
a spectre rise and hear it sing, "Stop, here,

and eat my lotus-flowers, here's where they're sold.
Here are the fabulous fruits; look, my boughs bend;
eat yourself sick on knowledge. Here we hold
time in our hands, it never has to end."

We know the accents of this ghost by heart;
our comrade spreads his arms across the seas;
"On, on, Orestes. Sail and feast your heart—
here's Clytemnestra." Once we kissed her knees.

VIII.

It's time. Old Captain, lift anchor, sink!
This country bores us, O Death! Let's set sail!
if now the sky and sea are black as ink
our hearts, as you must know, are filled with light.

Only when we drink poison are we well—
we want, this fire so burns our brain tissue,
to drown in the abyss—heaven or hell,
who cares? Through the unknown, we'll find the new.][129]

The voyage is life, and many of the images of the whole book recur, including childhood, memory, woman, ennui, *bourreau et martyr* [executioner and martyr], *infini, temps, mort,* and so forth, but in the register of the objectifying observer, who pitilessly recounts the illusions which drove us; we were agitated, active, always driven by hopes (verse 8: "berçant notre infini sur le fini des mers" [rocking our infinite on the finitude of the seas]). But these turn out to be illusions. "Et toujours le souci nous rendait soucieux" [And always worry made us more worried] (verse 68). Section VI of the poem then takes us through the full load of Baudelairean misanthropy, all the terrible things humans do.

Then VII: time is inexorable. But a meaningless time, "une oasis d'horreur dans un desert d'ennui! / Faut-il partir? Rester?" [an oasis of horror in a desert of boredom!] (verses 115–116). Then the resolution. This sounds like one of these forced self-decisions. Like the warrior, we will throw ourselves into a stance of being ready, motivated by the inclination to flee this world. "Ce pays nous ennuie, ô Mort! Appareillons!" [This country bores us, O Death! Let's set sail!] (verse 138).

But it is not clear whether we go to God or Satan. "De cette après-midi qui n'a jamais de fin" [this afternoon which never ends] (verse 132) sounds like paradise, but enframed in an ironic context. But then, "Nos cœurs que tu connais sont remplis de rayons!" [our hearts, as you must know,

129. Charles Baudelaire, "CXXVI. The Voyage," trans. Robert Lowell, in *Flowers of Evil*, 179–185.

are filled with light] (verse 140). But then again, we are about to "plonger au fond du gouffre, Enfer ou Ciel, qu'importe?" [dive into the abyss, Hell or Heaven, what's the difference?] (verse 143). And all we're sure to find is "du nouveau." It sounds pretty desperate.

Baudelaire often seemed ready for death. But maybe, although this was not necessarily his true and definitive position (as its situation at the end might imply), it was always in this mode of self-mobilized forced stance.[130]

3

But for all his novelty, and his disillusion with the world, Baudelaire feels his roots in the original Romantic attempt to recover, in a transformed mode, the earlier understandings of cosmic order. We see this first in "IV. Les Correspondances."

> La Nature est un temple où de vivants piliers
> Laisse parfois sortir de confuses paroles;
> L'homme y passé à travers un foret de symbols
> Qui l'observent avec des regards familiers.
>
>
> Comme de longs échos qui de loin se confondent
> Dans une ténébreuse et profonde unité,
> Vaste comme la nuit et comme la clarté,
> Les parfums, les couleurs et les sons se répondent.
>
>
> Il est des parfums frais comme des chairs d'enfants,
> Doux comme les hautbois, verts comme les prairies,
> —Et d'autres, corrompus, riches et tromphants,
>
>
> Ayant l'expansion des choses infinies,
> Comme l'ambre, le musc, le benjoin et l'encens
> Qui chantent les transports de l'esprit et des sens.[131]

130. Baudelaire, "CXXVI. Le Voyage," 129–134.
131. Charles Baudelaire, "Correspondances," in *Œuvres complètes*, 1:11.

[Nature is a temple whose living colonnades
Breathe forth a mystic speech in fitful sighs;
Man wanders among symbols in those glades
Where all things watch him with familiar eyes.

Like dwindling echoes gathered far away
Into a deep and thronging unison
Huge as the night or as the light of day,
All scents and sounds and colors meet as one.

Perfumes there are as sweet as the oboe's sound,
Green as the prairies, fresh as a child's caress,
—And there are others, rich, corrupt, profound

And of an infinite pervasiveness,
Like myrrh, or musk, or amber, that excite
The ecstasies of sense, the soul's delight.][132]

Baudelaire connected to these cosmic theories mainly through Hoff-mann, Poe, and also Toussenel. But like his predecessors', his under-standing of cosmic connections has been transposed and reinterpreted. Famously, the correspondences are now understood synesthetically: "Les parfums, le couleurs et les sons se respondent" [All scents and sounds and colors meet as one]. But, to recur to the discussion in Chapter 1, there is nothing here like the recovery of a fixed code: the forest of symbols is likened to "de longs échos qui de loin se confondent / Dans une téné-breuse et profonde unité" [Like dwindling echoes gathered far away / Into a deep and thronging unison].

Baudelaire bought deeply into this Romantic-modified theory of cosmic signs. In the notice on Hugo, he says:

Nous arrivons à cette vérité que tout est hiéroglyphique, et nous savons que les symboles ne sont obscurs que d'une manière rel-

132. Charles Baudelaire, "IV. Correspondences," trans. Richard Wilbur, in *Flowers of Evil*, 12.

ative, c'est-à-dire selon la pureté, la bonne volonté ou la clair-voyance native des âmes. Or qu'est-ce qu'un poète (je prends le mot dans son acception la plus large) qu'un traducteur, un déchiffreur.[133]

[We come to this truth: that everything is hieroglyphic; and we know that symbols are only relatively obscure, that is, in accordance with the purity, the good will, and the native clairvoyance of souls.]

Later he speaks of metaphors and comparisons "puisées dans l'inépuisable fonds de l'universelle analogie" [brought up from the inexhaustible depths of the universal analogy].[134]

Imagination is "la plus scientifique des facultés, parce que seule elle comprend *l'analogie universelle,* ou ce qu'une religion mystique ap-pelle la *correspondance*" [the most scientific of faculties, because it alone understands the *universal analogy,* or what mystic religion calls *correspondance*].[135] In "Notes nouvelles sur Edgar Poe," he says that the Imagination (which "n'est pas la fantaisie") "est une faculté quasi divine qui perçoit tout d'abord, en dehors des méthodes philosophiques, les rapports intimes et secrets des choses, les correspondances et les analo-gies" [Imagination, which is not fantasy, is a quasi-divine faculty which perceives right away, without recourse to philosophical methods, the intimate and secret relations between things, their correspondences and analogies].[136]

Later in the same work: "C'est cet admirable, cet immortel instinct du Beau qui nous fait considérer la terre et ses spectacles comme un aperçu, comme une correspondance du Ciel" [It is this admirable, that immortal instinct of Beauty which brings us to consider the earth and its specta-cles as a momentary sighting, as a correspondence of heaven].[137] The tears

133. Charles Baudelaire, "Sur mes contemporains: Victor Hugo," in *Œuvres com-plètes,* 2:133.

134. Baudelaire, "Sur mes contemporains," 2:133.

135. Charles Baudelaire, "Lettre à Alphonse Toussenel du 21 janvier 1856," quoted in Massin, *Baudelaire,* 208.

136. Baudelaire, "Notes nouvelles sur Edgar Poe," 329.

137. Baudelaire, "Notes nouvelles sur Poe," 334.

that come to our eyes in beautiful poetry and music, this is the testimony "d'une nature exilée dans l'imparfait" [of a nature exiled in the imperfect]. These passages might easily mislead us into thinking that Baudelaire is harking back to the original pre-Romantic cosmic theories, where the connections can be captured, if at all, in a fixed code of lexicon; that this is what he is talking about when he speaks of hieroglyphs, universal analogy, and correspondences. Or, "le langage des fleurs et des choses muettes" [the language of flowers and mute things].[138] But in fact he is thinking in the post-Romantic framework.

There are, indeed, particular correspondences which he sometimes draws on: such as animals incarnating vices. The cat = *luxe, propreté, volupté* [luxury, cleanliness, voluptuousness].[139] This is a Swedenborgian idea, expressed by Hugo in *Les Misérables*: "Les animaux ne sont autre chose que les figures de nos vertus et de nos vices, errantes devant nos yeux, les fantômes visibles de nos âmes" [Animals are nothing other than figures of our virtues and vices, wandering before our eyes, the visible phantoms of our souls].[140] And he of course has some images which recur.

But mostly the "symbols" and "allegories" are contextual, and above all enigmatic and incompletely interpretable in their meaning. Take the last four verses of "Correspondances": the perfumes which are "corrompus, riches, et triomphants" [corrupted, rich, and triumphant] "chantent les transports de l'esprit et des sens" [sing the transports of the mind and senses].[141] Baudelaire's poetry uses and sometimes deliberately misuses an inherited vocabulary of connections to make things and situations bespeak something, in ways which can never be explained by such connections.

Perhaps it was something like this that Baudelaire was getting at when he quoted Delacroix: "La nature n'est qu'un dictionnaire" [Nature is but a dictionary].[142] He goes right on to explain what this must mean. Of course,

138. Charles Baudelaire, "III. L'Élévation," in *Œuvres complètes,* 1:10.

139. Jean Pommier, *La Mystique de Baudelaire* (Geneva: Slatkine, 1952), 79.

140. Victor Hugo, *Les Misérables* (Paris: Emile Testard, 1890), 321.

141. Baudelaire, "Correspondances," 11.

142. Charles Baudelaire, "Salon de 1859," in *Œuvres complètes,* 2:624.

Personne n'a jamais considéré le dictionnaire comme une composition dans le sens poétique du mot. Les peintres qui obéis-
sent à l'imagination cherchent dans leur dictionnaire les éléments
qui accordent à leur conception; encore, en les ajustant avec un
certain art, leur donnent-ils une physiognomie toute nouvelle.
Ceux qui n'ont pas d'imagination copient le dictionnaire. Il en
résulte un grand vice, le vice de la banalité.[143]

[No one had ever considered the dictionary as composition in
the poetic sense of the word. Painters who obey their imagination seek in the dictionary the elements which are in accord
with their conception; and then they adjust them with a certain
art, which gives a quite new physiognomy. Those who have no
imagination copy the dictionary; which results in a great vice,
that of banality.]

The distance from the lexicon model is increased if we see the hieroglyphs
as interpreted by the poet through his own resonances, that is, without
being able to prejudice how others may understand them. That is the view
I expounded above. But did Baudelaire share that view? We can't answer
this from his poetry, but it would appear from some of his critical writings that he did. Baudelaire speaks of the poet expressing nature "réfractée
par un tempérament" [refracted by his temperament].[144] "La sensibilité
de chacun, c'est son génie" [The sensibility of each one, is his genius].[145]
"Le Romantisme n'est précisément ni dans le choix des sujets ni dans la
vérité exacte, mais dans la manière de sentir" [Romanticism precisely understood lies neither in the choice of subject, nor in the exact truth, but
in the manner of feeling].[146] The "positiviste" says: "Je veux représenter
les choses telles qu'elles sont, ou bien qu'elles seraient, en supposant que
je n'existe pas. [. . .] L'imaginatif dit: 'Je veux illuminer les choses avec mon
esprit et en projeter le reflet sur les autres.'" [The "positivist" says: I want
to represent things as they are, or better, as they would be, if I didn't

143. Baudelaire, "Salon de 1859," 624–625.
144. Pommier, *Mystique,* 99.
145. Baudelaire, "Fusées," 660.
146. Baudelaire, "Salon de 1846," 420.

exist. . . . The imaginative artist says: I want to illuminate things with my mind, and project this reflection on others.][147]

The sensibility of genius is like that of the child. It makes things over. "Tous les matériaux dont la mémoire s'est encombrée se classent, se rangent, s'harmonisent et subisse cette idéalisation forcée qui est le résultat d'une perception enfantine, c'est-à-dire d'une perception aiguë, magique à force d'ingénuité" [All the materials with which the memory is encumbered classify, order and harmonize themselves, and undergo that forced idealization which is the result of the child's perception, that is an acute perception, magic through its naïveté].[148] "Le génie," he explains earlier, "n'est que l'enfance retrouvée à volonté, puis nettement formulée" [Genius is only childhood recovered at will, and then properly formulated].[149] But perhaps beyond this life, we could read the signs more immediately. "La soif insatiable de tout ce qui est au-delà, et que révèle la vie, est la preuve la plus vivante de notre immortalité" [The insatiable thirst for all that is beyond, and which life reveals, is the most living proof of our immortality].[150]

4

What was the legacy of this many-voiced poet, who above all sought to escape, even overcome spleen? It can be seen to divide into three branches: (1) the first is a disengaged, disabused stance, contenting himself with a view of the whole human condition, as split between the two "postulations," toward God and toward Satan; where the latter seems always capable of neutralizing the former; (2) the second is on the contrary engaged, excited, and energized by the fascination with evil, or even by the bustle and restless novelty of this fallen world; (3) the third is also engaged, but in a movement of sympathy, even compassion, which ultimately would seem to align better with the first postulation. (2) is the charter of the Poète Maudit of the fin de siècle, and ultimately also of certain "decadents"; (3) is the inspiration for poets in the twentieth

147. Baudelaire, "Salon de 1859," 627.
148. Baudelaire, "Le Peintre de la vie moderne," 694.
149. Charles Baudelaire, "Lettres inédits aux siens," in Œuvres complètes, 2:690.
150. Baudelaire, "Études sur Poe," 334.

century who tried to recover meaning in a modern environment often characterized by the meaningless or the sordid (Eliot and others he inspired). (4) But his excitement at novelty, as in his reaction to the work of Guys, was also influential, as can be seen much later in Dada, in futurism, in surrealism. These movements created a poetry of rupture, of incongruous pairings, which opened new and unexplored themes and visions.[151]

But there is a fifth important contribution to his successors. Baudelaire's work is (5) one of the sources of what will later be called "symbolism," which finds full expression at the turn of the century, in such poets as Verlaine, Rimbaud, and most consciously Valéry. Of course, "symbol" was an important word for the pioneers of German Romanticism. We can recall the definition of A. W. Schlegel, where some deeper reality is opened for us through something already visible and in our ken, through a work of art, as Wordsworth makes us sense the force running through all things with his portrayal of the Wye valley, or Hölderlin makes us feel the action of *Vater Aether* through the light which pours down on the valley.

Something like this notion of symbol recurs with Baudelaire, but with important changes. We can see this in a passage of Baudelaire's quoted earlier, where he talks of certain almost supernatural states of the soul, which reveal the depth of life in the spectacle; and he adds: "This spectacle becomes the symbol of that depth."[152] Like in the Schlegel symbol, something is there, ready to be revealed through something else: through the quite ordinary spectacle, "la profondeur de la vie" in its entirety becomes visible. This "depth" only needs formulation by the poet for it to be visible. But this "depth" is given no further formulation. It remains indefinite, what really fills this depth dimension of life. This indefiniteness, this reluctance to define the vision the "symbol" opens for us, becomes a central feature of "symbolism" in the late nineteenth-century sense of the term.

151. This has been brilliantly explored by Humberto Beck in his highly original and suggestive book *The Moment of Rupture*.

152. Baudelaire, "Fusées," 659.

In the prose poem "Le Confiteor de l'artiste," Baudelaire exclaims, "Que les fins de journées d'automne sont pénétrantes! Ah! pénétrantes jusqu'à la douleur! car il est de certaines situations délicieuses dont le vague n'exclut pas l'intensité" [How the end of autumn days penetrate us deeply! penetrate us to the point of pain! because there are certain delicious situations where vagueness doesn't exclude intensity]. And,

> Grand délice que de noyer son regard dans l'immensité du ciel et de la mer! Solitude, silence, incomparable chasteté de l'azur! ... Toutes ces choses pensent par moi, ou je pense par elles, ... elles pensent, dis-je, mais musicalement et pittoresquement, sans arguties, sans syllogismes, sans déductions.[153]

> [The great delight of drowning your vision in the immensity of the sky and the sea! Solitude, silence, incomparable chastity of the blue.... All these things think themselves through me, or I think through them ... they think, I want to say, but musically or in pictures, without syllogisms or deductions.]

Being unable to define further these thoughts becomes so painful, the poet must retreat. "L'étude du beau est un duel où l'artiste crie de frayeur avant d'être vaincu" [Studying the beautiful is a duel where the artist cries out in fright before suffering defeat].[154]

And a bit further on in the prose poems, "Le Fou et la Vénus":

> L'extase universelle des choses ne s'exprime par aucun bruit; les eaux elles-mêmes sont comme endormies. Bien différentes des fêtes humaines, c'est ici une orgie silencieuse. On dirait qu'une lumière toujours croissante fait de plus en plus étinceler les objets; que les fleurs excitées brûlent du désir de rivaliser avec l'azur du ciel par l'énergie de leurs couleurs, et que la chaleur, rendant visibles le parfums, les fait monter vers l'astre comme des fumées.[155]

153. Charles Baudelaire, "Le Confiteor de l'artiste," in Œuvres complètes, 1:278.
154. Baudelaire, "Le Confiteor de l'artiste," 278–279.
155. Charles Baudelaire, "Le Fou et la Vénus," in Œuvres complètes, 1:283.

[The universal ecstasy of things doesn't express itself through anything audible; the waters themselves are as if asleep. Very different from human festivals, we have here a silent orgy. You could say that an ever growing light makes the objects sparkle more and more; that the excited flowers burn with the desire to rival the blue of the sky through the energy of their colors, and that the heat, which makes the perfumes visible, sends them up toward the stars like smoke.]

Something far outside our quotidian experience is suddenly becoming visible, but what it is defies further definition. And the poem ends with a firm refusal to continue this inviting exploration, with the statue of Venus whose eyes of marble stare implacably into the distance.

In this new understanding of the symbol, Baudelaire recognized a kindred spirit in Edgar Allan Poe. The American writer certainly shared his sense that the very perversity of evil exercises a great force of attraction on human beings.[156] For Baudelaire, Poe stands out from other writers for many reasons, but especially "par ce génie tout special, par ce temperament unique qui lui a permis de peind re et d'expliquer, d'une manière impeccable, saisissante, terrible, *l'exception dans l'ordre moral*" [by the unique genius, the unique temperament, which allowed him to paint and explain, in an impeccable, arresting and terrible fashion, *the exception in the moral order*].[157]

But what Baudelaire also greatly admired, and was inspired by, was the power of suggestion in Poe's description of what we usually think of as neutral objects; for instance, the description of the grounds and house of Usher as the narrator arrives there. Poe helped cocreate the new understanding of symbol.

These are five dimensions, undoubtedly among others, in which Baudelaire opened new paths for the poets who followed him.

156. See Poe's short story "The Black Cat."
157. Baudelaire, "Notes nouvelles sur Edgar Poe," 316.

Chapter Eleven

AFTER BAUDELAIRE

I

Lived time and "higher times"   In the early Romantic period, we can speak of attempts to (re)connect through poetry with a continuing cosmic order. It was unclear what (if anything) corresponds in the cosmos, as it objectively is beyond human consciousness, to this experience of connection, but the assumption was that the orders which poetry invokes were like the traditionally accepted cosmic orders, eternal or coeval with the cosmos itself. They were not subject to time, although our contact with them could (and for many, did) go through loss and renewal, occlusion and recovery.

But with Baudelaire, the field in which such loss and recovery occurs is time, and first of all lived time. This has become salient in a new way, because of its distinction from cosmic time, or objective, historical time; and this in turn has become salient for us as we come more and more to inhabit the objectifying scientific-technological stance toward nature and the human world.

The site in which the sense of loss is most unbearable is everyday lived time, in the experience of Spleen, *acēdia*, melancholy in the negative sense of the word, where the succession of moments involves meaningless repetition.

This can just descend on us, uninvited; but we can also be subjected to a time regime which imposes such repetition on us, as in an assembly line; or we can find ourselves pulled into it by some compulsion to repeat, in the context of a gambling establishment; or in that of a cunningly designed computer game.

In the first case, melancholy can be overcome by the agent herself, as we see with Baudelaire's Spleen poetry; but when it is forced on us by others, or our situation, the remedy must involve some transformation of this predicament. But there are other negative ruptures in lived time: where, for instance, we feel acutely some split with the past; where we see ourselves as cut off from a beautiful, rich, and meaningful history, in another country, or another condition, and left in a benighted present.

This kind of feeling can arise in different time perspectives. I may feel this fall from grace as a turn in my own lifetime: say, I am exiled from my home country, where I have family, and friends, and / or played an important role; while now I live in exile, among strangers. Or else, I and many of my contemporaries may feel that at some time in the past, there was a heroic period, where enormously important issues were being decided; and / or people were living in a rich and creative culture, but now that is all over, and we are living in times of cultural dearth and trivial preoccupations.

I invoked this in Chapter 5, where I was commenting on the overwhelming attraction of contemporary tourists toward religious sites (churches, mosques, temples) of great antiquity. The negative that this activity is meant to conjure is, I would argue, this disconnection with our past origins. And this threatened loss also accounts for the anguish that many of us fear before the steady encroachment on and ultimate leveling of great primaeval forests.

But these longings are sometimes met:

First (1) the annual return of the seasons (a kind of "ewige Wiederkunft" [eternal recurrence], if I can steal Nietzsche's expression): like the autumn wind, returning each year; or the wind in the trees rustling the leaves in summer, thinning to a soughing in the pines in winter; the sense of life going on, ever anew, ever the same. Something in us rejoices at the return of spring, and maybe also of other seasons. I mentioned this in Chapter 10, Section V.2, as a paradigm example of what I want to call "deep time." Of course, this joy can be lost; perhaps it must be close to the end of life, because it depends not only on memory of the past, but on anticipation of future repetitions. This joy in repetition can combine well with a sense of cosmic order in the "spatial" or timeless dimension. But the latter doesn't need this kind of "eternal return" to be felt by us.

And there are other examples of "deep" time: for example, (2) the sense of time unfolding a meaningful story, either in our biography, or in history, or in the cosmos—at any of these levels, or all. Time as the site of meaningful action; development; with the thickness and unity of Bergson's durée.

Or we can (3) pick up on a rhythm, a movement in things. Once more, using Bergson's term, we can align our rhythm with what we sense in the surrounding world.[1]

(4) Like Baudelaire's "Le Cygne," time united by solidarity, or other kinship, across the ages.

This is one example of a more general phenomenon: where we have a strongly felt, indeed inspiring, intuition of a pattern in time, exceeding, even transcending the regular moment-flowing-into-moment of ordinary lived time.

Other such experiences: (5) an "eschatological" one, where we have the powerful sense that we are running toward some final reckoning or disaster; or a "rising," aspiring one, where we sense that humans are striving for, coming closer to, a fuller realization of their potential, even destiny. This sense of a rising movement can generate a perception of certain moments as crucial turning points, where the present is experienced as kairos.

Of course, the sense, or theoretical belief, that humans progress in history, which I already invoked under (5) above, doesn't necessarily

---

1. See Souleymane Bachir Diagne, *Bergson Post-colonial: L'élan vital dans la pensée de Léopold Sédar Senghor et de Mohamed Iqbal* (Paris: CNRS Éditions, 2011), ch. 2.

invoke a "higher" time. There is a widespread modern outlook which attributes moral progress to "Enlightenment"; this latter term is understood in many ways, but it can simply mean a progress in "reason": the advances in science, the decay of certain myths, or of religious belief in general, open the way to more rational and moral standards of behavior.

But there are other intuitions about ethical growth in history, which are not grounded in universally recognized trends, like the advance of science, and the decay of certain beliefs: A statement like "The arc of the moral universe is long but it bends toward justice" (Martin Luther King Jr.) or the recognition by Karl Jaspers of an "Axial period," when similar ethical advances came about in the same period, where the convergence cannot be explained by diffusion or mutual influence. These point to forces at work in history which seem to involve some as-yet-unrecognized source; be it a deeper human potentiality, or the action of some higher agency.

But alongside these currents of "deep" time, there have also been moments of exceptional intensity, where the ordinary flow of time is interrupted, and beyond these what we might call "higher times," which go beyond and connect, or gather, moments and phases of ordinary (or secular) time: this latter consists in the ordered succession of one moment after another. Higher times introduce "warps," or unsuspected connections between moments or periods which may be far removed from each other. Premodern forms of such connections are (a) the theological relation between prefiguring events in the Old Testament as "types," and the corresponding events in the New Testament that these types prefigured; or (b) the notion of a "time of origins," which lies in the past, but which we can reapproach periodically through reenactment: an understanding which underlies the liturgical year. As we gather at a pilgrimage site at Easter, we are closer to the original Easter events than we were in the depths of last winter.

This kind of consciousness has deep roots in human history. In many early, small-scale "tribal" societies, or in contemporary societies of the same sort that have not yet been assimilated totally to our globalized "civilization," we find notions of a time of origins which is not confined to the past, but which continues to be operative today, like the Australian aboriginal "dream time," where the original itineraries through the world were laid down by the ancestors, and these "songlines" still shape experience today.[2]

The Koyukon Indians of northwestern Alaska have a similar notion, which translates as "distant time."[3] But the most important of such higher times are often gestured at (c) with the word "eternity," which can designate the theological notion of the *nunc stans,* the way in which all moments of history are somehow present to God. But in the context of some understanding of human moral / ethical advance in history, whether through divine guidance, or some inner potential in humans, the notion of (d) "kairos" becomes crucial, designating the moments at which human history is inflected in a new direction.[4]

The examples just listed (a–d) have roots in our medieval past and are theologically defined. But the connections (re)made by poetry and literature in the past century can also be understood in other terms. Our era has created its own "warps" in time: or more affirmatively put, constellations, where events at a distance from each other take on an intense relation, creating a kind of "force field," which confers on them unexpected powerful meaning. An example is Proust's "temps retrouvé," which brings about a strong and exhilarating connection between noncontiguous events, which may indeed be far distant in ordinary time. I will look in the next section at Proust's vision of time restored, but I want to mention briefly another twentieth-century example in the work of Walter Benjamin.

As Humberto Beck has described this in his book on the "moment of rupture," Benjamin's notion of the "dialectical image" involves such an intense force field, where a recent past which opened a possibility of radical liberating change—a possibility which was not noticed and acted on then—now dawns on us, and provides the basis and inspiration for revolutionary advance, which now begins. In this field, past, present, and

2. W. E. Stanner, *On Aboriginal Religion* (Sydney: Sydney University Press, 2014); Charles Taylor, *A Secular Age* (Cambridge, MA: Belknap Press of Harvard University Press, 2007), 153.

3. See the interesting account by David Abram, *The Spell of the Sensuous* (New York: Vintage, 1997), 145.

4. See Taylor, *Secular Age,* 54–61.

future can no longer be adequately understood in our usual temporal consciousness of the succession of stages, linked perhaps by causal relations. On the contrary, they are closely united in a creative tension, where their unity, and essential relatedness, is seen and lived in this "now of recognition."

We live the succession actively, instead of undergoing it passively, in this dialectic of awakening, where a new legibility of the past grounds a conscious transformation issuing in a higher future. This vision is essentially linked to Benjamin's deep investment in Jewish messianism, and the notion he invoked of "redeeming" the past.[5]

||

Proust and higher time *À la recherche du temps perdu* can be seen as a long attempt to recover, or restore, or rise beyond a time which has been lost, or wasted (*temps perdu* also has this latter sense in French). But what exactly would it mean to restore time? And in the terms of the discussion in this chapter, how to characterize this goal? Does it only consist in a quality of lived time? Or rather, is the goal to accede to what I've been calling a "higher time," one which takes us beyond or outside the succession of moments, the before and after that we understand as time?

Let's look at the peak experiences which Proust thinks are key to this restoration. I want to follow mainly the discussion in the concluding volume of *À la recherche*, entitled *Le Temps retrouvé* [*Time Regained*], with some necessary glances at earlier volumes. Examples of such experiences are: the tasting of the madeleine soaked in tea, which figures in *Du côté de chez Swann*; shifting his weight between the uneven paving stones, evoked in *Le Temps retrouvé*, which called up a similar experience earlier in the Piazza San Marco in Venice; a spoon knocked against a plate, which called up the sound of hammer, heard on an earlier occasion, applied to the wheels of a train; a napkin which a servant gave him,

---

5. I am drawing here on the very interesting discussion of Benjamin in Humberto Beck, *The Moment of Rupture* (Philadelphia: University of Pennsylvania Press, 2019), ch. 5.

invoking an earlier experience of a towel he used to dry himself, looking out a window the day he arrived at Balbec.[6]

In each case the present experience and the past it conjured up were essential; one might say that between the two scenes a kind of force field formed which deeply moved him; these fields "me donnent une joie pareille à une certitude et suffisante sans autres preuves à me rendre la mort indifférente" [give me a joy similar to a certainty and enough, without any other proof, to make me indifferent to death].[7]

Earlier, on the train to Paris, and to the place where the scene of the paving stones just described occurred, the narrator saw a row of trees whose trunks were partly lit up by the setting sun and had the discouraging sense that they should have some meaning for him, but that meaning had fled.

> Arbres, pensai-je, vous n'avez plus rien à me dire, mon cœur refroidi ne vous entend plus. Je suis pourtant ici en pleine nature, eh bien, c'est avec froideur, avec ennui que mes yeux constatent la ligne qui sépare votre front lumineux de votre tronc d'ombre. Si j'ai jamais pu me croire poète, je sais maintenant que je ne le suis plus.[8]

> [Trees, I thought, you have nothing more to tell me, my heart has become cold and I don't hear you any more. But I am nevertheless fully in nature; very well, it's with indifference, with boredom, that my eyes take in the line which separates your luminous façade from your trunks' shadow. If I have ever been able to believe that I'm a poet, now I know that I am no longer one.]

But now, after the paving stones which remind him of the other force fields arising through memory, in particular the noise of a spoon on a plate recalling the sound of a hammer on the wheels of the halted train,

---

6. Marcel Proust, *Le Temps retrouvé*, in *À la recherche du temps perdu* (Paris: Gallimard, 1987), 869–877.

7. Proust, *Le Temps retrouvé*, 867.

8. Proust, *Le Temps retrouvé*, 855.

he remembers the line of trees he saw during that halt, and the joy returns.

So the present experience can't suffice to awaken this joy; there has to be a connection to the past. But not just any connection, or reminiscence, will do. The past event must have the same inspiring vividness as the present one. And this rarely happens, because the past events have many associations, trigger off many disparate thoughts, and these can cover over or drown out the inspiration they could have given us. So in describing the napkin the servant brings to him, and the associated memory of the sea at Balbec, Proust adds the scene was "débarrassé de ce qu'il y a d'imparfait dans la perception extérieure, pur et désincarné," which "me gonflait d'allégresse" [was uncluttered from what is imperfect in exterior, disincarnate perception, and filled me with elation].[9]

If the memory comes through pure and unmixed,

> Il nous fait tout à coup respirer un air nouveau, précisément parce que c'est un air qu'on a respiré autrefois, cet air que les poètes ont vainement essayé de faire régner dans le paradis et qui ne pourrait pas donner cette sensation profonde de renouvellement que s'il avait été respiré déjà, car les vrais paradis sont les paradis perdus.[10]

> [We have suddenly to breathe a new air, precisely because it is air that we breathed in the past, that air which the poets have vainly tried to make reign in paradise and which could only give us that profound feeling of renewal if it had been already breathed before, because the true paradises are the lost ones.]

But this is not an illusion for Proust:

> L'être qui était réné en moi quand, avec un tel frémissement de bonheur, j'avais entendu le bruit commun à la fois à la cuiller qui touche l'assiette et au marteau qui frappe sur la roue, à l'inégalité pour les pas des pavés de la cour Guermantes et du baptistère de Saint Marc, etc., cet être-là ne se nourrit que de l'essence des

9. Proust, *Le Temps retrouvé*, 869.
10. Proust, *Le Temps retrouvé*, 870.

choses, en elle seulement il trouve sa subsistance, ses délices. Il
languit dans l'observation du présent où les sens ne peuvent le
lui apporter, dans la considération du passé que l'intelligence lui
dessèche, dans l'attente d'un avenir que la volonté construit
avec des fragments du présent et du passé auxquelles elle tire encore de leur réalité en ne conservant d'eux ce qui convient à la fin
utilitaire, étroitement humaine, qu'elle leur assigne. Mais qu'un
bruit, qu'une odeur, déjà entendu ou respirée jadis, le soient de
nouveau, à la fois dans le présent et le passé, réels sans être ac-
tuels, idéaux sans être abstraits, aussitôt l'essence permanent et
habituellement cachée des choses se trouve libérée, et notre vrai
moi qui, parfois longtemps, semblait mort s'éveille, s'anime en
recevant la céleste nourriture qui lui est apportée. Une minute
affranchie de l'ordre du temps a recréé en nous pour la sentir
l'homme affranchi de l'ordre du temps. Et celui-là, on comprend
qu'il soit confiant dans sa joie, même si le simple goût d'une madeleine ne semble pas contenir logiquement les raisons de cette
joie, on comprend que le mot "mort" n'ait pas de sens pour lui;
situé hors du temps, que pourrait-t-il craindre de l'avenir?[11]

[The being which was reborn in me when, with such a shudder
of happiness, I heard the sound which was common both to the
spoon touching the plate and the hammer hitting the wheel, or
when I experience the unevenness for my step both in the paving
stones of the Guermantes' courtyard and in the baptistry of San
Marco, etc.—this being only finds nourishment in the essence
of things, in that alone he finds his subsistence, his delight. He
languishes in the observation of present reality where his senses
can't give him this, in considering the past which his intelligence
dries out for him, in the expectation of a future which our will
constructs with fragments of the present or past, all the while
selecting from them only what suits the utilitarian and narrowly
human goals which it assigns to them. But should a noise, an
odor, already heard or breathed in former times, return again,
be met both in the present and the past, be real but not just

11. Proust, *Le Temps retrouvé*, 872.

actually present, ideal without being abstract, immediately the permanent but habitually hidden essence of things finds itself liberated, and our real "I", which seemed dead, often for a long time, comes back to life as it receives the celestial nourishment which has been brought to it. One minute freed from the order of time has recreated in us, so that we can feel it, the human being freed from this order of time. And this person, we can understand that he is confident in his joy, and even if the simple taste of a small madeleine doesn't seem to contain logically good reasons for this joy, we can understand that the word "death" has no more meaning for him: situated outside time, what can he fear for the future?]

We need add here only that this kind of power of vision claimed for poetry can also be reached through (more conventional) novels, visual art, and music, as we can see from the important place in the novel of the writer Bergotte and the artist Elstir, and the composer Vinteuil.

But in whatever medium we try to capture the vision, its object exists at a deeper level than our ordinary consciousness can attain, distracted as this is by all the multiple associations and concerns which obscure it. The task of the artist, whatever the medium, is to find a way to articulate the vision so as to make it accessible to others, and to himself at other times. And this is what Proust has been doing in the passage of *Le Temps retrouvé*, relating example after example of such force fields which have formed in his life. The narrator claims that this is the moment where his vocation as a writer at last became fully clear to him. So "la vraie vie, . . . c'est la littérature" [Real life . . . is literature]. Art is

> la révélation, qui serait impossible par des moyens directs et con-
> scients, de la différence qualitative qu'il y a dans la façon dont
> nous apparaît le monde, différence qui, s'il n'y avait pas l'art, res-
> terait le secret éternel de chacun. Par l'art seulement nous pou-
> vons sortir de nous, savoir ce que voit un autre de cet univers
> qui n'est pas le même que le nôtre et dont les paysages nous se-
> raient restés aussi inconnus que ceux qu'il peut y avoir dans la
> lune.[12]

12. Proust, *Le Temps retrouvé*, 895–896.

[the revelation which would be impossible to attain by direct
and conscious means, of the qualitative difference there is in
the manner that the world appears to us; a difference that, if art
didn't exist, would remain the eternal secret of each particular
human. By art alone, can we escape ourselves, know what
another sees of this universe which is not the same as ours,
and whose landscape would have remained as unknown to us
as those which might exist on the moon.]

But it will not be surprising if these claims leave us puzzled. There is
allegedly a more fundamental reality, at a deeper level than the objects
and people we normally perceive and deal with and relate to. This reality,
the "essence of things," can be grasped only in the interspace between a
past and a present event; it thus is "en dehors du temps" [outside of
time].[13] So not only do we have a problem relating this experience to our
everyday world, but the question about its relation to everyday time is
hard to conceive. In a sense, we might be tempted to say that the interspace in which this experience occurs is no longer unambiguously placed
in time, but rather that the moments it unites come together in us. In
these force fields between present and past, our "lost" time is recovered,
and the years of "wasted" time receive compensation.

I think it fair to say that most readers see these Proustian peak experiences as exceptional moments of lived time, which involve some intense
relation to a past experience; but it seems to me that some kind of notion of higher time is posited here as habitable by us, at least for moments,
where the limitations of time as ordinarily conceived and imagined by
us no longer hold.

We can debate whether the right word to use here is "eternity," but the
expression "higher time" seems unavoidable.

|||

Privileged moments   Benjamin and Proust are representative of a profound shift in the understanding of what cosmic connection consists in,

13. Proust, *Le Temps retrouvé*, 871.

from the "spatial" relation to continuing orders, to the dimension of time. This shift in the very understanding of what reconnection means is only to be expected. If we no longer can credit the notion of a continuing, unchanging order, but only recognize a universe in perpetual change, then what we could aspire to recover contact with are the deeper structures or tendencies or patterns behind our awareness of the moment-to-moment flow of everyday time, which culminate in what I am calling "higher times."

And this contact is what the recovery of these connections across time through poetry and art seems to provide. But this recovery, in what I think of as the period post-Baudelaire, of a connection with such patterns comes not only in and through poetry, or more broadly literature; we can also see it emerging in the context of a number of exceptional experiences, reported by writers and others. Among these are the "privileged moments" of which Jephcott writes in his interesting book on Proust and Rilke.[14] These moments stand out with a kind of eruptive illumination. They are instances of something "breaking in," which I noted earlier in the explanatory note on "wider spaces," in connection with Dostoyevsky's *Brothers Karamazov*.

The descriptions of these experiences are thus very different from the poetic invocations of reconnection which have been central to my discussion in this book so far. Rather, the subject in each case struggles against bafflement to describe what he lived. But they can perhaps serve to put us on the track of the new forms of poetic, or at least literary, invocations which followed them; and this because, in spite of their often confusing and paradoxical nature, they seem to be referring to (re?)connections with a reality beyond our normal conscious awareness.

And, as Jephcott notes, they seem to be reported with greater frequency by writers (and others) from this period onward, that is, the later nineteenth century.

14. E. F. N. Jephcott, *Proust and Rilke: The Literature of Expanded Consciousness* (London: Chatto and Windus, 1972). Jephcott has brought together a number of accounts of exceptional experiences by authors in the late nineteenth century. These are experiences which he calls "privileged moments," and which he claims were drawn upon, in their different ways, by both of these authors.

And perhaps the contrast between the revelations invoked through poetic expression and those which seem to break in unbidden should not be pushed too far. Even the latter call for and receive some description, as we have seen. There is no hard and fast line here, but rather a continuum of intermediate cases between clear extremes.

I want to set out a number of reports of these experiences, and comment on some common features they exhibit. Some of these are drawn from Jephcott's book, and others from different sources; some of them are more recent than others, but all of them have occurred to writers or others during the last century and a half.

Václav Havel:

> All at once, I seemed to rise above all the coordinates of my momentary existence in the world into a kind of state outside time in which all the beautiful things I have ever seen and experienced existed in a total "co-present"; I felt a sense of reconciliation, indeed of an almost gentle assent to the inevitable course of events as revealed to me now, and this combined with a carefree determination to face what had to be faced. A profound amazement at the sovereignty of Being became a dizzy sensation of tumbling endlessly into the abyss of its mystery; an unbounded joy at being alive, at having been given the chance to live through all I have lived through, and at the fact that everything has a deep and obvious meaning.[15]

Bede Griffiths:

> I remember now the feeling of awe which came over me. I felt inclined to kneel on the ground, as though I had been standing in the presence of an angel; and I hardly dared to look on the face of the sky, because it seemed as though it was but a veil before the face of God.[16]

---

15. Václav Havel, "June 19, 1982," in *Letters to Olga: June 1979 to September 1982,* trans. Paul Wilson (New York: Knopf, 1989), 331.

16. Bede Griffiths, *The Golden String* (London: Fount, 1979), 9.

In this case, the sense of fullness came in an experience which unsettles and breaks through our ordinary sense of being in the world, with its familiar objects, activities, and points of reference. These may be moments, as Peter Berger puts it, describing the work of Robert Musil, when "ordinary reality is 'abolished' and something terrifyingly *other* shines through," a state of consciousness which Musil describes as "der andere Zustand" [the other condition].[17] Then there's the text of Hofmannsthal, in his remarkable "Lord Chandos Letter":

> Words fail me once again. For what makes its presence felt to me at such times, filling any mundane object around me with a swelling tide of higher life as if it were a vessel, in fact has no name and is no doubt hardly nameable. I cannot expect you to understand me without an illustration, and I must ask you to forgive the silliness of my examples. A watering can, a harrow left in a field, a dog in the sun, a shabby churchyard, a cripple, a small farmhouse—any of these can become the vessel of my revelation. Any of these things and the thousand similar ones past which the eye ordinarily glides with natural indifference can at any moment—which I am completely unable to elicit—suddenly take on for me a sublime and moving aura which words seem too weak to describe. Even an absent object, clearly imagined, can inexplicably be chosen to be filled to the brim with this smoothly but steeply rising tide of heavenly feeling. . . .
>
> If on some other evening I find under a nut tree a half-full watering can that a gardener's boy has forgotten there, and this watering can and the water in it, dark from the shadow of the tree, and a water beetle sculling on the surface of the water from one dark shore to the other, this confluence of trivialities shoots through me from the roots of my hair to the marrow of my toes with such a presence of the infinite that I want to bring out words, knowing that any words I found would vanquish those cherubim in which I do not believe? . . .

17. Peter Berger, *A Far Glory: The Quest for Faith in an Age of Credulity* (New York: Maxwell Macmillan International, 1992), 128–129.

At those moments an insignificant creature, a dog, a rat, a
beetle, a stunted apple tree, a cart path winding over the hill, a
moss-covered stone mean more to me than the most beautiful,
most abandoned lover ever did on the happiest night. These mute
and sometimes inanimate beings rise up before me with such a
plentitude, such a presence of love that my joyful eye finds
nothing dead anywhere. Everything seems to mean something,
everything that exists, everything I can remember, everything in
the most muddled of my thoughts. Even my own heaviness, the
usual dullness of my brain, seems to mean something: I feel a
blissful and utterly eternal interplay in me and around me, and
amid the to-and-fro there is nothing into which I cannot merge.
Then it is as if my body consisted entirely of coded messages revealing everything to me. Or as if we could enter into a new,
momentous relationship with all of existence if we began to think
with our hearts. But when this strange bewitchment stops, I am
unable to say anything about it; I can no more express in rational
language what made up this harmony permeating me and the
entire world, or how it made itself perceptible to me, than I can
describe with any precision the inner movements of my intes-
tines or the engorgement of my veins.[18]

This letter, purporting to be from Lord Chandos written at the very beginning of the seventeenth century to Francis Bacon, his contemporary,
is a remarkable literary exercise. It announces to Bacon a sudden failure
of Chandos' creative powers, and his inability to carry through on the
projects that he had earlier announced himself to be engaged in. He now
declares that "I have completely lost the ability to think or speak coher-
ently about anything at all."[19] "I tried to rescue myself from this plight
by entering the spiritual world of antiquity"; but both Plato and Cicero
failed to engage him.[20] "Since then I have led an existence which I fear

    18. Hugo von Hofmannsthal, *The Lord Chandos Letter and Other Writings*, trans.
John Banville (New York: New York Review Books, 2005), 123–125.
    19. Hofmannsthal, *Lord Chandos Letter*, 121.
    20. Hofmannsthal, *Lord Chandos Letter*, 122.

you could hardly imagine, so inanely, so unconsciously has it been proceeding."[21] There are good moments, but he can't say what brings them on: "Words fail me once again."[22]

This last remark is often taken as the key to the whole letter; the idea being that Hofmannsthal is pointing to a crisis in the poetry of his age, where older languages of articulation no longer have the power to evoke what they once did. But I would argue that the key to this letter lies in the remarkable passage I have just quoted. It seems to me that he is describing a real experience, overwhelming and baffling, but one charged with deep and powerful meaning, and it is this which made previous ways of articulating human meanings seem radically inadequate. It is not that previous languages failed, but that a new benchmark was raised.

So I would like to place Hofmannsthal's Chandos letter among the records of "privileged moments" that Jephcott enumerates. Does this give some hint to the choice of addressee, Bacon: the champion of the new natural science, whose criterion of success lay in what we would now call technology—that is, in its increasing our ability to control and change our world, so as "to improve the condition of mankind"? This is the science which Scheler would later call *Leistungswissen*—knowledge which gets things done. Not a path to pursue if one wants to recover lost meanings.

IV

Common themes   What seems to emerge from an examination of all these accounts of exceptional intensity, even from the small sample cited in the previous section? In fact, a number of shared themes emerge, which I shall try to describe along with other examples:

21. Hofmannsthal, *Lord Chandos Letter*, 123.

22. Hugo von Hofmannsthal, letter to Lord Chandos, in *Erzählungen: Erfundene Gespräche und Briefe; Reisen* (Berlin: Fischer Taschenbuch, 1979), 471.

1

First of all, with some exceptions, the experience is powerful and inspiring.

Havel's "profound amazement at the sovereignty of being":

Hofmannsthal: "Diese Zusammensetzung von Nichtigkeiten mich mit einer solchen Gegenwart des Unendlichen durchschauert, von den Wurzeln der Haare ins Mark der Fersen mich durchschauert" [This confluence of trivialities shoots through me from the roots of my hair to the marrow of my toes].[23]

Compare Flaubert's "glow of enthusiasm which makes my skin tingle from my heels to the roots of my hair."

Or:

"Often, catching sight of something or other—a drop of water, a shell, a hair—you stopped, stood quite still, your gaze transfixed, your heart opened."[24]

Baudelaire:

> Il est des jours où l'homme s'éveille avec un génie jeune et vigou-reux. Ses paupières à peine déchargées du sommeil qui les scel-lait, le monde extérieur s'offre à lui avec un relief puissant, une netteté de contours, une richesses de couleurs admirables. Le monde moral ouvre ses vastes perspectives, pleines de clartés nouvelles.[25]

> [There are days when you wake up with a young and vigorous inspiration. Your eyelids barely free of the sleep which sealed them, the world offers itself to you: things stand out in relief, with clear contours and wealth of admirable colors. The moral world opens its vast perspectives, full of new clarity.]

23. Hofmannsthal, letter to Lord Chandos, in *Erzählungen*, 469.

24. Gustave Flaubert, *La Tentation de Saint Antoine*, 1849 ed., quoted in Jephcott, *Proust and Rilke*, 16.

25. Charles Baudelaire, "Le Poème du Haschich," in *Œuvres complètes* (Paris: Galli-mard, 1975), 1:401, quoted in Jephcott, *Proust and Rilke*, 15.

Valéry, crossing London Bridge: "My eyes stopped me short; I leant on the balustrade, as if compelled by a vice. The voluptuous pleasure of seeing held me like a thirst, drinking in the rich, delightfully composed light, of which I could not have enough."[26]

2

Objects are not inert; they are live, they appear to enact themselves Valéry: one "falls out of a world made up almost entirely of *signs,* into another world almost entirely formed by *significances.*"[27] We normally get familiar with an object which we can then use or orient ourselves by. Such an object is just a "sign." But the fullness of experience gives us significance. So when in this state, looking at things in a room: "the objects are *active* like the flame of the lamp: the armchair consumes itself where it stands, the table describes itself so quickly that it remains motionless, the curtains flow without end, continuously."[28]

Baudelaire, in "La Chambre double": "Les meubles ont l'air de rêver; on les dirait doués d'une vie somnambulique, comme le végétal et le minéral. Les étoffes parlent une langue muette, comme les fleurs, comme les ciels, comme les soleils couchants." [The furniture seems to be dreaming, you might say it is full of sleepwalking life, parallel to vegetal and mineral life. The fibers of the furniture speak a mute language, like flowers, like skies, like setting suns.][29]

We might ask: Is this the real thing? But in another prose poem: "Le Fou et la Vénus," he says:

> L'extase universelle des choses ne s'exprime par aucun bruit; les eaux elles-mêmes sont comme endormies. Bien différente des fêtes humaines, c'est ici un orgie silencieuse. [...] On dirait qu'une lumière toujours croissante fait de plus en plus étinceler les objets; que les fleurs excitées brûlent du désir de rivaliser avec

---

26. Paul Valéry, *Œuvres* (Paris: Gallimard, 1957), 1:512–513, quoted in Jephcott, *Proust and Rilke,* 17.

27. Valéry, *Œuvres,* 1:514, quoted in Jephcott, *Proust and Rilke,* 17.

28. Valéry, *Œuvres,* 1:1170.

29. Charles Baudelaire, "La Chambre double," in *Œuvres complètes,* 1:280.

l'azur du ciel par l'énergie de leurs couleurs, et que la chaleur, ren-
dant visibles les parfums, les fait monter vers l'astre comme des
fumées.[30]

[The universal ecstasy of things expresses itself without sound;
the waters themselves are as if asleep. But unlike human feasts
the orgy is silent. [. . .] You might say that an ever growing light
makes the objects sparkle more and more; that the excited
flowers are burning to rival the sky with the energy of their
colors, and that the heat, making the perfumes visible, makes
them rise like smoke toward the stars.]

Hofmannsthal: the idea of things as vessels which are filling: "In solchen Augenblicken, irgendeine Erscheinung meiner alltäglichen Umge-
bung mit einer überschwellenden Flut höheres Leben wie ein Gefäß
erfüllenden Flut göttlichen Gefühles bis an den Rand gefüllt zu werden"
[In such moments, some sights of my everyday surroundings can be filled
to the brim by an overflowing flood of life, as if of a sense of the divine].
Later he speaks of a "soft and sudden flood of a sense of the divine" [mit
jener sanft und jäh steigendes Flut göttlichen Gefühles bis an den Rand
gefüllt zu werden].[31]

Valéry: "The objects are *active* like the flame of the lamp: the armchair
consumes itself where it stands, the table describes itself so quickly that
it remains motionless, the curtains flow without end, continuously."

These are momentary experiences which seem to violate basic features
of our perception of our surroundings in space-time. Perception itself
involves activity, sometimes requiring that the perceiver move, change
stance to command a better view. Moreover, the scene perceived will
often involve movement, as when we look down on a flowing river. But
grasping this flow requires a stable background, a sense of the unchanging
context of events, a "monumental" framework for the flow of things.[32]

30. Charles Baudelaire, "Le Fou et Venus," in *Œuvres complètes*, 1:283, quoted in
Jephcott, *Proust and Rilke*, 19.

31. Hofmannsthal, letter to Lord Chandos, in *Erzählungen*, 467.

32. See Paul Ricoeur, *Temps et Récit* (Paris: Seuil, 1984), 2:157–160.

This is the condition which no longer holds when the objects observed seem to be enacting themselves.

3

Things resonate with the subject   The sense is not that we are totally separate from and over against the world, but in vibrant communication with it. Let's look further. The sense I just described, that objects are not inert can go along with the sense that this activity is not just "over there" in the object over against us, but is happening in the interspace between us and the objects.

Baudelaire: "Toutes ces choses pensent par moi; et le 'moi' se perd; elles pensent, mais musicalement et pittoresquement, sans arguties, sans syllogismes, sans déductions" [All things think through me; and the "I" is lost; they think, but musically and pictorially, without arguments, without syllogisms, without deductions].[33]

Hofmannsthal:

> Everything seems to mean something, everything that exists, everything I can remember, everything in the most muddled of my thoughts. Even my own heaviness, the usual dullness of my brain, seems to mean something: I feel a blissful and utterly eternal interplay in me and around me, and amid the to-and-fro there is nothing into which I cannot merge. Then it is as if my body consisted entirely of coded messages revealing everything to me. Or as if we could enter into a new, momentous relationship with all of existence if we began to think with our hearts. But when this strange bewitchment stops, I am unable to say anything about it; I can no more express in rational language what made up this harmony permeating me and the entire world, or how it made itself perceptible to me, than I can describe with any precision the inner movements of my intestines or the engorgement of my veins.[34]

33. Baudelaire, "Le Confiteor de L'Artiste," in *Œuvres complètes*, 1:278.
34. Hofmannsthal, *Lord Chandos Letter*, 125.

Here is another defining condition of human perception which is seemingly negated, the polarity observer-observed.

4

***These experiences carry a fullness which we don't encounter in everyday
life***   And this on two levels: the reality itself enjoys that fullness (Hofmannsthal again: "Some object of my everyday surroundings can be filled
to the brim by an overflowing flood of a sense of the divine"[35]); and our
lives themselves partake of that plenitude.

Even more paradoxically, the roles of perceiver and perceived are no
longer clearly distinguished. We have here a number of experiences in
time, in the sense that there is a before and an after—they are preceded
and followed by ordinary time; but they themselves break out of the basic
conditions of perception in time.

So in addition to our experiencing deep movements or patterns in
time, some writers report moments where the framework of ordinary
temporal experiences breaks down, and the clear separation of subject
and object, of perceiver and perceived, no longer seems to hold. The more
intimate, intense connection with the world seems to relate such moments to the type of reconnection with a cosmic order which Romantic
poets invoked. But the intense interchange with a self-enacting reality has
none of the calm continuing sense of order which the earlier poets
conjured up; and nor does it owe anything to poetic expression. On the
contrary, these experiences "break into" our experience, in the way I described above in the explanatory note on "wider spaces of meaning."

5

***Things happen, but our sense of the time in which they happen is paradoxical in
another way***   And then, in contrast to our experiencing of deep times,
and of a breakdown in the very conditions of temporal experience, we
have a third possibility: things happen, but our sense of the time in which
they happen is paradoxical in another way. There is succession, but also
an apprehension of what I'm calling higher time—even, in a sense, of

35. Hofmannsthal, letter to Lord Chandos, in *Erzählungen*, 467.

eternity. Baudelaire: "Le temps a disparu; c'est l'Éternité qui règne" [Time has disappeared; Eternity reigns].[36]

This is because the time in which these experiences occur is more intensely unified. Our ordinary time experience is of moments which pass and give way to new ones. Certain more intense experiences hold us in what feels like a single act of attention; listening to a piece of music which really moves us, for instance, or engaging in an absorbing conversation with someone we're close to; seeing a powerful theatrical performance. Normal everyday life carries us from one moment to another. But when we listen to a great symphony, or quartet, we are of course aware of passing from one movement to the next, but the whole has a kind of unity which makes of it a single experience. Its parts have a kind of quasi-simultaneity.

It seems that the intense experiences we have been describing have this kind of unity to an even higher degree. What Baudelaire seems to be communicating with his "time has disappeared" is a sense that the events experienced which would ordinarily be spread out in time have this kind of quasi-simultaneity, that they are held together in an extended present, such that the earlier phases are held in being until their end.

The experience seems to be unfolding in a kind of higher time, which we might try to gesture at with the word "eternity," but for the fact that this term turns out to have more than one meaning. What it would indicate in this experience is a kind of duration without succession, a continued coming-to-be without a passing-away.

This seems to resemble Havel's experience that I quoted above: "All at once, I seemed to rise above all the coordinates of my momentary existence in the world into a kind of state outside time in which all the beautiful things I have ever seen and experienced existed in a total 'co-present.'"

As a lived experience, it is an intensified form of what we would all recognize as a most satisfying condition, where our lives as they unfold amount to some meaningful story, which bears some relation to the goals we have been striving to achieve. In Baudelairean terms, this life is at the furthest remove from Spleen, where time is lived as an endless, meaning-

36. Baudelaire, "La Chambre double," 281.

less repetition of the same. So such rare moments when "time disappears" are supercharged; they are beyond the limit of the most meaningful time experience available in everyday life.

This experience, and others which I've described above, carries the suggestion of some "higher times." But this can come about through more than one path, and take more than one form. There is (A) duration without succession; the retaining of the past in the present in a quasi-simultaneity; this can be seen not as the disappearance of time, but as its higher intensification. This is one path to an experience of what we might be tempted to call "eternity."

But we may also use this term when a moment of time (B) seems too full. Events of different layers are crowding into the same instant.

And this brings us back to the twentieth century's invocations of higher times. There is a moment like that in Eliot's "Burnt Norton," where the question of the relation of time and eternity is central. The rose-garden passage in movement 1 of this poem invokes

> The unheard music hidden in the shrubbery,
> And the unseen eyebeam crossed, for the roses
> Had the look of flowers that are looked at. (27–29)

This whole experience of the garden, as we live it, is also figuring in another perspective, that of the "unseen eyebeam." This eerie and powerful sense is maintained, until "a cloud passed, and the pool was empty" (29–30). It had to pass, because "human kind / cannot bear very much reality" (42–43). But the reflection which follows this experience tells us that

> Time past and time future
> What might have been and what has been
> Point to one end, which is always present. (44–46)[37]

It seems that there are here two routes toward recovering a higher time which we might call "eternity": one through the quasi-simultaneity of an intensely lived event; the other when a parallel time seems to break

---

37. T. S. Eliot, "Burnt Norton," in *The Poems of T. S. Eliot,* ed. Christopher Ricks and Jim McCue (Baltimore: Johns Hopkins University Press, 2015), 1:179.

through into the flow of our ordinary existence. Both are short-lived, but they leave a hint of transcendence.

Proust offers a third approach to a higher time, (C) which connects events far apart in sequence so that they touch each other in memory.

All three of these reconnections can be made palpable, like those to the continuing orders discussed earlier, by their formulation in a work of art, poetic or literary.

I have spoken of "reconnection" in this context because I see some continuity with the works of the early Romantics which aimed to recover contact with continuing cosmic orders. Where the cosmos comes to be perceived as undergoing constant change, the analogous sense of distance and recovery will understandably relate to the "higher times" which hold together the visible / tangible flux.

V

I have been discussing three rather different time-related experiences in this chapter: (A) (re)connection to the currents of deep time; (C) in the immediately preceding pages, the connection is to higher times; in between I invoked (B) cases where the very framework of experience, or the boundary between perceiver and perceived, begins to fail.

This crucial role of poetic expression which was evident in the (re)connection to cosmic orders seems equally to hold for (A) and (C), but in the baffling eruptive experiences (B), this sense of connection doesn't seem to arise.

We can note here too that two reactions recur in the reports of these experiences. We see the first, for example, in Hofmannsthal's. "This combination of nothings sends a thrill through me at the presence of the infinite, a thrill which runs from the roots of my hair, to the marrow of my heels."[38] The feeling running from the roots of one's hair to the heels is often a response to the uncanny. But in this case it is accompanied by a kind of spiritual joy: this "thrill at the presence of the infinite" comes also when we sense a contact with eternity.

38. Hofmannsthal, letter to Lord Chandos, in *Erzählungen,* 469.

VI

I will recur to this incursion / evocation of higher times in the chapters which follow; first, controversially, in relation to places in Mallarmé's work (understood, of course, very differently by the poet himself).

Then Eliot's quartets open with a passage of "Burnt Norton," which I cited above, and where the overfullness of the instant points to an eternity, which Eliot understands in traditional terms as that of the *nunc stans*.

And then in Miłosz's work, the overfullness indicates a moment of kairos, where a new, higher departure in human history is both announced and furthered.

Chapter Twelve

MALLARMÉ

I

Mallarmé as a boy, as a teenager, had a love and longing for beauty in a transcendent sense. This is the ideal of a perfect coincidence between Beauty, the Highest goal, and desire. By beauty, I mean what moves us as beautiful in nature and works of art. This is hard to define further, as we saw earlier. But for Mallarmé, it was given obvious and undeniable shape by the example of the great poets of French Romanticism and beyond; in particular, Hugo and Gautier.

The Ideal is when what moves us as beauty is also what gives the highest meaning to life, what is of transcendent value. "Transcendent" I use here in the sense of what transcends the ordinary values of life, prosperity, sexual life, family, not to speak of comfort and self-esteem. This unity usually needs to find its guarantee in a theology, or a notion of a cosmic moral order uniting Good, Beauty, and Truth.

One of the essential threads of Romanticism was precisely to demand recognition of the transcendent in this sense, and to protest against a century which (as they saw it) wanted to reduce everything to utility, to "matter," in the name of "realism."

In the best of all worlds, that of the Ideal fulfilled, this goal of transcendent Beauty would also engage our desires. That is, we would not be split between our ordinary desires and our aspiration toward transcendence, but we would be harmoniously at one, desiring it with all our being. We have seen that for Baudelaire, it was this unity which is lacking. We are fatally flawed by sin, by the "postulation" toward Satan.

This will not be Mallarmé's problem, as we shall see in a minute. But before his twenties, Mallarmé's poems don't seem to reflect a problem, more an unproblematic celebration of the ideal, which for him was validated by his Christian faith.[1] He remains capable of a beautiful evocation of this transcendent Beauty even after he begins to feel a separation from this Ideal, which early takes on the name "Azur."[2] But in his early twenties, he begins to feel a terrible separation. This is not the same as Baudelaire, although he falls under a very Baudelairean influence at this time. Understandably, Gautier and Hugo can't give him a language for this sense of being torn, exiled. But it is not like Baudelaire's sense of sin. The "Azur" is inaccessible for another reason. It is, as the image suggests, way beyond our life, we can't touch it, come close to it.

In "Fenêtres," he invokes in the first five stanzas the image of a dying man in a hospital; ignoring his sordid surroundings, he nevertheless yearns for the beyond:

> Las du triste hôpital, et de l'encens fétide
> Qui monte en la blancheur banale des rideaux
> Vers le grand crucifix ennuyé du mur vide
> Le moribond sournois y redresse un vieux dos,
>
> Se traîne et va, moins pour chauffer sa pourriture
> Que pour voir le soleil sur les pierres, coller

---

1. See Stéphane Mallarmé, "Cantate pour la première communion," in Œuvres complètes (Paris: Gallimard, 1998), 1:170.

2. See the first stanza of "Fleurs" in Mallarmé, Œuvres complètes, 1:10.

Les poils blancs et les os de la maigre figure
Aux fenêtres qu'un beau rayon clair veut hâler.

Et la bouche, fiévreuse et d'azur bleu vorace,
Telle, jeune, elle alla respirer son trésor.
Une peau virginale et de jadis! encrasse
D'un long baiser amer les tièdes carreaux d'or.

Ivre, il vit, Oubliant l'horreur des saintes huiles.
Les tisanes, l'horloge et le lit infligé,
La toux; et quand le soir saigne parmi les tuiles,
Son œil, à l'horizon de lumière gorgé,

Voit des galères d'or, belles comme des cygnes,
Sur un fleuve de pourpre et de parfums dormir
En berçant l'éclair fauve et riche de leurs lignes
Dans un grand nonchaloir chargé de souvenir!³

[Sick of the dreary sickroom and the pall
of stale incense rising from drab white drapes
to the big crucifix tired of the blank wall,
the dying slyboots stiffens his old back, scrapes

along and, less to warm his gangrene than
to see a ray of sunshine on the stones,
presses his white hair and gaunt facial bones
against the glass that bright light longs to tan.

And his mouth, feverish, thirsting for blue skies
as, in its youth, it went to taste its bliss,
some virgin flesh now long gone, putrifies
the warm gold panes with a long bitter kiss.

3. Stéphane Mallarmé, "Fenêtres," in *Œuvres complètes*, 1:9.

Drunk, forgetting the horrible Last Rite,
the clock, the cough, bedrest prescribed, weak teas,
he lives; when dusk bleeds in the tiles, he sees
on the distant horizon gorged with light

some golden galleys beautiful as swans
sleeping on streams of purple redolence
rock their rich fulvid flashing echelons,
in memory-laden vast indifference.][4]

Then, in stanza 6, the poet speaks for himself:

Ainsi, pris du dégoût de l'homme à l'âme dure
Vautré dans le bonheur, où ses seuls appétits
Mangent, et qui s'entête à chercher cette ordure
Pour l'offrir à la femme allaitant ses petits,

Je fuis, et je m'accroche à toutes les croisées
D'où on tourne l'épaule à la vie, et béni,
Dans leurs verre, lavé d'éternelles rosées.
Que dore le matin chaste de l'Infini

Je me mire et me vois ange!! Et je meurs, et j'aime
—Que la vitre soit l'art, soit la mysticité—
À renaître, portant mon rêve en diadème,
Au ciel antérieur où fleurit la Beauté!

Mais, hélas! Ici-bas est maître: sa hantise
Vient m'écoeurer parfois jusqu'en cet abri sûr.
Et le vomissement impur de la Bêtise
Me force à me boucher le nez devant l'azur.

4. Stéphane Mallarmé, "The Windows," in *Collected Poems and Other Verse,* trans. E. H. Blackmore and A. M. Blackmore (Oxford: Oxford University Press, 2006), 11–13.

Est-il moyen, o Moi qui connaît l'amertume,
D'enfoncer le cristal par le monstre insulté
Et de m'enfuir, avec mes deux ailes sans plume
—Au risque de tomber pendant l'éternité.[5]

[So, holding coarse-souled man in detestation—
sprawled in pleasure where his mere appetites
feed; striving to gain that abomination
and give it to the wife suckling his mites—

I flee and cling to every casement through
which we can turn from life, and, blessedly,
in its glass bathed with everlasting dew
gold in the chaste dawn of Infinity

I see myself—an angel!—and I die;
the window may be art or mysticism, yet
I long for rebirth in the former sky
where Beauty blooms, my dream being my coronet!

But, alas, our low World is suzerain!
even in this retreat it can be too
loathsome—till the foul vomit of the Inane
drives me to stop my nose before the blue.

O Self familiar with these bitter things,
can the glass outraged by that monster be
shattered? can I flee with my featherless wings—
and risk falling through all eternity?][6]

5. Mallarmé, "Fenêtres," 9.
6. Mallarmé, "Windows," 13.

But what separates the poet from the Highest is not that he shares some "postulation vers le bas" [aspiration to degrade himself], in the Baudelairean sense of an attraction to evil. Like the dying man, he longs to escape and he can't.

True, in "L'Azur," the poet wants to flee.[7] But first, that's only because he can't reach *l'Azur,* while he desperately wants to. It tortures him with its visible unattainability. And second, he can't flee from it; it continues to haunt him.

What then is the nature of the exile? What makes *l'Azur* out of reach? The first stanza tells us. The poet is "impuissant" [powerless]. He curses his "génie." In other words, *l'Azur* calls for a response. It is in virtue of his genius that the Poet knows this, and feels the call. But he is powerless to answer. What would be the answer? An adequate poetic rendition of *l'Azur,* and what it represents, of the Highest.

It is a poetic failure, not a moral one. Mallarmé complained constantly of his inability to write. His sleepless nights before the white sheet of paper have become well known. There never was a famous poet who wrote so little, and over such long periods seemed incapable of writing anything at all. But what stopped him was not primarily Spleen in Baudelaire's sense—that is, discouragement, demotivation, leading to distraction, wasted time. On the contrary, Mallarmé seems to have put in a tremendous amount of time through those white nights. What stopped him was the inability to say what he felt he had to say.

This sounds hard to credit, when we see what he did write, even, perhaps especially, when we see what he wrote just before and at the time this sense of impotence descended on him. I refer to the passages I mentioned above of lyric celebration of the beauty of flowers, skies, seas, boats. But these weren't what he was getting at. Why?

We have to go back to one of the basic ideas of the Romantic turn to understand this: the notion that the things of this world are a language, and that poets are those who can decipher this. Now by itself, this doesn't have to impose crushing demands on a poet. There is a well-used language of poetic reference which has come down through the ages, which even has some parallels across different cultures.

7. Stéphane Mallarmé, "L'Azur," in *Œuvres complètes,* 1:14.

For instance, traditionally, there is an understanding that flowers, sunsets, mountains, skies, winds have meanings, which can be invoked in poetry, be it about love, or loss, or joy, or sorrow. Before the modern period, the understanding was that what underlay this meaning, what made these realities in a certain sense "emphatic," was their place in the order of being, or in God's plan. That, for instance, these meanings could be explained in an account of the correspondences. Poetry can count on these meanings and be sure to evoke something in portraying these emphatic realities. Moreover, it would seem that, independent of any of these theories of ontic logos, people have always sensed a significance in these realities. And this seems to go beyond our culture, as I mentioned above. So people have always surrounded themselves with flowers, and worshiped mountains; and all these figure in poetry.

The Romantics didn't necessarily change this condition. The old formulations of correspondences were now in doubt; or were thought to be partial, corrupted versions whose integral form has been lost. And the important change in the post-Romantic period is that now poetry is often charged with rediscovery, or as I have been arguing here, with reconnection.

But, of course, poetry in the post-Romantic age, as at any epoch, takes many forms, many of which are not concerned with restoring the links with the cosmos. And many of these are original and take on a new approach. So we can get lyrics like Gautier's in *Émaux et Camées* [*Enamels and Cameos*], where he explores new dimensions of feeling about the world, love, and so on. Like the *précieux* of the seventeenth century, they open new dimensions of refined feeling. Gautier, and in general the milieu which invoked Parnassus, practiced an art analogous to the making of fine jewelry; they concentrated on rendering the beauty of things with exactness.

For after all, this epoch, after the midcentury, was an age of "disenchantment," in the words of Paul Bénichou.[8] However finely constructed the lyrics of Parnassus might be, they had an utterly different aim from that of revealing the deeper (cosmic or theological) meanings in poetry. This turns out to be a crucial distinction for Mallarmé. At the

8. Paul Bénichou, *L'École du désenchantement* (Paris: Gallimard, 1992).

start, there is the sense that his strong feeling about these things, the way they move him, the way he feels called to render them, cannot be articulated in the old ways, the beaten paths. Then even worse, even the best of his new lyrics don't do it.

We could perhaps put it this way. There are certain realities, among them some which belong to the tradition of poetic evocation, like flowers, skies, particularly the crepuscular sky, which figure in Mallarmé's poetry early and late. They strongly move him. It's as though they have a profound and important meaning, which he can't fully articulate. One of the ways which Mallarmé often puts this sounds basically subjective. These things create an "état d'âme" [state of mind, but more literally, a state of the soul] which he is trying to render. (But this turns out to be very complicated, as we will see later.)

What poetry can do is to "évoquer petit à petit un objet pour montrer un état d'âme, ou inversement choisir un objet et en dégager un état d'âme, par une série de déchiffrements" [gradually evoke an object to show a state of mind, or conversely choose an object and extract a state of mind, through a series of decipherings].[9]

At other moments, he speaks of "impressions." In a letter to Henri Cazalis of March 1866, which I'll quote later, he speaks of poetry as "chantant l'Ame et toutes les divines impressions pareilles qui se sont amassées en nous depuis les premiers âges" [singing the soul and all the similar divine impressions which have been piling up since the earliest ages].[10]

This might sound as though the whole drama of poetry simply concerned expressing our own intramental states, however dissociated from reality they might be. But clearly this poetry is not charged with articulating a merely subjective, individual meaning. "La poésie est l'expression, par le langage humain ramené à son rythme essentiel, du sens mystérieux de l'existence: elle doue ainsi d'authenticité notre séjour et constitue la seule tâche spirituelle" [Poetry is the expression, by human language returned to its essential rhythm, of the mysterious meaning of existence;

9. Stéphane Mallarmé, "Réponse à l'enquête de Jules Huret," in *Œuvres complètes*, 1:782.

10. Stéphane Mallarmé, "Lettre à Henri Cazalis, mars 1866," in *Propos sur la poésie* (Monaco: Rocher, 1953), 66.

it thus endows our presence here with authenticity, and constitutes our only spiritual task].[11] And later he will speak of our getting to the "essence" or "notion" behind reality.

But the self-clarification involved in developing these terms of "état d'âme" [state of mind or of the soul] and "impression" allowed Mallarmé to say better why the current modes of poetry on offer weren't adequate. In particular, he was able to distance himself from the Parnassus, from the mainstream of those who wanted to defend the special place and the special beauty of poetry against the assaults of realism and naturalism, Leconte de Lisle and Gautier especially. Not that these weren't important for him. They were and remained so.[12] But just for this reason, he had to clarify why their way of writing poetry—in particular, their focus on the object, on the careful re-creation of the object portrayed—wouldn't do.

Here indeed, we do have a turning away from reality of a certain sort, and this has helped to accredit wrong views of Mallarmé as a poet of subjectivism, a poet of mere dreams. This is made the more tempting in that "Rêve" [Dream] is another of the key words he uses to describe the "impressions" which have to be rendered. But the point is not to turn from the reality out there to a private reaction within. It is rather that for Mallarmé, the deeper meaning of the things concerned gets obscured if we focus on the reality before our eyes. We have somehow to see through it or beyond it. And just accurate portrayal is not going to do this. It will rather distract us from this.

In the "Reply to Enquête of Jules Huret":

> L'enfantillage de la littérature jusqu'ici a été de croire, par exemple, que de choisir un certain nombre de pierres précieuses et en mettre les noms sur le papier, même très bien, c'est faire les pierres précieuses. Eh bien! non! La poésie consistant à créer, il faut prendre dans l'âme humaine des états, des lueurs d'une pureté si absolue que, bien chantés et bien mis en lumière, cela

---

11. Stéphane Mallarmé, "Lettre à Leo Orfer, juin 1884," in *Correspondance* (Paris: Gallimard, 1995), 572.

12. See the moving homage to Gautier in "Toast funèbre" below.

constitue en effet les joyaux de l'homme: là, il y a symbole, il y a création, et le mot poésie a un sens.[13]

[The childishness of literature so far has been to believe, for example, that to choose a certain number of gems and put their names on paper, even very well, is to make gems. Well, no! Since poetry is about creating, we must take from the human soul states and gleams of such absolute purity that, well sung and well brought to light, they are indeed the jewels of man: there, there is symbol, there is creation, and the word poetry has a meaning.]

And a bit earlier:

Les Parnassiens, eux, prennent la chose entièrement et la montrent; par là ils manquent de mystère. . . . Nommer un objet, c'est supprimer les trois quarts de la jouissance du poëme qui est faite de deviner peu à peu: le suggérer, voilà le rêve. C'est le parfait usage de ce mystère qui constitue le symbole.[14]

[The Parnassians, on the other hand, take the thing entirely and show it; in this way they lack mystery. . . . To name an object is to eliminate three-quarters of the poem's enjoyment, which lies in guessing little by little: to suggest it, that is the dream. It is the perfect use of this mystery that constitutes the symbol].

And in "Crise de vers," he talks of an "Idéalisme" which

refuse les matériaux naturels et, comme brutale, une pensée exacte les ordonnant; pour ne garder de rien que la suggestion. Instituer une relation entre les images exactes, et que s'en détache un tiers aspect fusible et clair présenté à la divination. . . . Abolie la prétention, esthétiquement une erreur . . . d'inclure au papier subtil du volume autre chose que par exemple l'horreur de la

13. Mallarmé, "Réponse à l'enquête de Jules Huret," 782.

14. Mallarmé, "Réponse à l'enquête de Jules Huret," 782. The notion of poetry as made of "pierres précieuses" [precious stones] is an idea that Mallarmé took over from Parnassians: Leconte de Lisle, Gautier, Banville. See Albert Thibaudet, *La Poésie de Stéphane Mallarmé: Étude littéraire* (Paris: Gallimard, 1930), 222–224.

forêt, ou le tonnerre muet épars au feuillage, non le bois intrin-sèque et dense des arbres.[15]

[refuses natural materials and, as brutal, an exact thought ordering them; to keep nothing but the suggestion. To institute a relationship between exact images, and that a third, fusible and clear aspect be detached from them, presented to divination. . . . Abolish the pretension, aesthetically an error . . . to include in the subtle paper of a volume something other than, for example, the horror of the forest, or the mute thunder scattered in the foliage, not the intrinsic and dense wood of the trees.]

An important stage on the road to this new stance is captured in an oft-quoted passage from a letter to Cazalis, penned while he was working on "Hérodiade": "Peindre non la chose, mais l'effet qu'elle produit" [Don't paint the thing, but rather the effect it produces].[16] "L'effet" here is a syn-onym of "impression" in quotes like the above, or of "sensation," which he also uses in the same sense.

> Pour moi, me voici résolument à l'Œuvre. J'ai enfin commencé non *Hérodiade*. Avec terreur, car j'invente une langue qui doit nécessairement jaillir d'une poétique nouvelle, que je pourrais définir en deux mots: Peindre, non la chose, mais l'effet qu'elle produit. [. . .]
>
> Le vers ne doit donc pas, là, se composer de mots, mais d'intentions, et toutes les paroles s'effacer devant la sensation.[17]

[Here I am resolutely at work. I have at last started my Herodiade. With terror, I invent a new language, which must arise from a new poetics, that I can define in two words: Peindre non la chose, mais l'effet qu'elle produit. [. . .]

Verse, then, should not be made up of words, but of inten-tions, and all words should give way to sensation.]

15. Stéphane Mallarmé, "Crise de vers," in *Œuvres complètes,* 2:204.

16. Stéphane Mallarmé, "Lettre à Henri Cazalis. 30 octobre 1864," in *Œuvres com-plètes,* 1:664.

17. Mallarmé, "Lettre à Henri Cazalis. 30 octobre 1864," 664.

This needs to be connected back to the description of the Ideal with which I started. The aim is to render something in which Beauty and the Highest come together. Just so, the meaning of things which is inarticulately sensed in our impression or "rêve" [dream] is "le sens mystérieux de l'existence" [the mysterious meaning of existence]. In finding poetic expression it yields both a summit of beauty, and the highest end of life. Of beauty thus understood—the Ideal—we can say: "Il n'y a que la Beauté,—et elle n'a comme expression parfaite, la Poésie. Tout le reste est mensonge—excepté pour ceux qui vivent du corps, l'amour, et cet amour de l'esprit, l'amitié." [There is only beauty—and its only perfect expression is Poetry. All the rest is lies—except for those who live from the body, love, and that love of the spirit, friendship.][18] There is a somewhat uncertain note of taking things back in the last phrase, but this just attenuates, without canceling the bold statement about beauty.

So the shape of and reason for the *impuissance* [incapacity] is beginning to come clearer. Mallarmé is not happy just to invoke the old emphatic realities. He wants to follow the higher Romantic-defined vocation, and give us something of their deeper meaning, why they are emphatic realities. Poets can be original, can explore new facets of feeling and portrayal, without taking this on (Gautier). But this isn't enough for Mallarmé.

So the background to Mallarmé's sense of incapacity can be described this way: certain realities, among them the traditionally emphatic ones of poetic reference, have this status because they carry a deeper meaning, analogous to those attributed to certain levels of the Great Chain of Being, certain terms in the correspondences, certain created things in God's plan. According to the Ideal, articulating this meaning can only properly be done in poetry; and this means that such articulation both would be a summit of beauty, and would reveal the highest, most important goals, purposes, "le sens mystérieux de l'existence."

But, Mallarmé comes to feel, this articulation can't be achieved just by describing these emphatic realities. More, their obtrusive, physical existence blinds us, blocks us, in a certain way. We have to get beyond, or

18. Stéphane Mallarmé, "Lettre à Henri Cazalis. 14 mai 1867," in *Œuvres complètes*, 1:713.

behind, these realities to the meaning. That is why the attitude of those who throw themselves into ordinary life is antithetical to poetry. They are above all concerned with the things which surround us in their physical, fleshly reality. Letter to Cazalis dated June 3, 1863: "O mon Henri, abreuve-toi d'Idéal" [O my Henri, slake your thirst with the Ideal].[19]

But the poet's problem is not that he is irresistibly drawn to "se vautrer dans le bonheur" [wallow in happiness], and therefore can't make the attempt to go beyond. It is much more fundamental than this. The problem is that all we seem to have before us is the fleshly existence of these realities. Hence the image of *l'Azur* as something beyond reach, either too high to reach, or something in an upper level of reality, where we are confined to a lower level. There is a ceiling, or windows, as it were, a skylight, but one that we can't smash through and float beyond, as the protagonist dreams in "Fenêtres."

The distance consists in the fact that we can't find the language; because all that poetry seems to have, even to describe feelings, is a language of emphatic realities. Moreover, the problem is confounded by the fact that we have such a rich lyric language which has cut such gems from these emphatic realities.

(The distance from Baudelaire can be measured by this quote from the same 1863 letter to Cazalis: "La sottise d'un poéte moderne a été jusqu'à se desoler que 'l'Action ne fût pas la soeur du Rêve'" [The foolishness of a modern poet went as far as regretting that "action is not sister of the dream"]; the quote is from Baudelaire's "Reniement de Saint Pierre.")[20]

Baudelaire too, of course, goes beyond just evoking established emphatic realities. Or means to. But he goes beyond this in a different way. Here too, it starts with the old evocations not moving any more, not working. And the exploration is of the condition which brings about this inability, which freezes: ennui; and sin. Plus hints of the way back.

In the course of this, the range of things which have meaning expands considerably. The lowly things, banal things, ugly things enter the canon; they are made to speak.

19. Stéphane Mallarmé, "Lettre à Henri Cazalis. 3 juin 1863," in *Œuvres complètes*, 1:646.

20. Mallarmé, "Lettre à Henri Cazalis. 3 juin 1863," 646.

A crisis. But it got much more critical. In the course of trying to overcome the gap, to forge a language which could evoke the Ideal behind/be-
yond the real, Mallarmé has a crisis of faith. It is not only a crisis of faith
in God. In the mid-1860s what threatens to go under is the Ideal itself,
any deeper meaning. This begins to seem devoid of an ontic underpinning. Mallarmé becomes more and more troubled by a purely materialistic picture of the universe. We don't have many details, but we can
imagine an atoms-and-the-void outlook, which would leave no room for
meaning. There would be nothing but the fleshly, physical reality of
things; we ourselves are matter.

Mallarmé comes through this not by simply denying it, but (it would
seem) by the reflection that this world of matter has after all arisen to
self-consciousness, even to poetry. Ipso facto, there must be something
more to it than atoms and the void; or something more to atoms and the
void than just material reality.

At this point, some second- or thirdhand Hegel came to the rescue.
The basic idea is: we (humans) are the place at which the universe comes
to self-consciousness.

> Je viens de passer une année effrayante: Ma Pensée s'est pensée,
> et est arrivée à une Conception Pure.
>
> Tout ce que, par contre coup, mon être a souffert, pendant
> cette longue agonie, est inénarrable, mais heureusement je suis
> parfaitement mort, et la région la plus impure où mon Esprit
> puisse s'aventurer est l'éternité, mon esprit, ce Solitaire habituel
> de sa propre Pureté, que n'obscurcit plus même le reflet du Temps.
>
> [. . .]
>
> C'est t'apprendre que je suis maintenant impersonnel, et non
> plus Stéphane que tu as connu,—mais une aptitude qu'a l'univers
> spirituel à se voir et à se développer, à travers ce qui fut moi.
>
> Fragile, comme mon apparition terrestre, je ne puis subir que
> les développements absolument nécessaires pour que l'univers
> retrouve, en ce moi, son identité.[21]

21. Mallarmé, "Lettre à Henri Cazalis. 14 mai 1867," 713.

[I have just been through a frightening year. My thought thought itself, and has arrived at a Pure Conception.

Everything that as a reaction my being has suffered, during this long approach to death is impossible to narrate, but happily I am completely dead, and the most impure region where my spirit can venture is eternity; my spirit—this habitual solitary of its own own purity which is not even darkened by the reflection of Time.

[. . .]

This is to inform you that I am now impersonal, and no longer Stéphane whom you've known,—but an aptitude which the spiritual universe has to see itself and develop itself through what was me.

Fragile, in my terrestrial appearance, I can only undergo through the absolutely necessary developments for the universe to recover, in this "I", its identity.]

Again:

Je veux me donner ce spectacle de la matière ayant conscience d'être, et cependant, s'élançant forcément dans le rêve qu'elle sait n'être pas, chantant l'âme et toutes le divines impressions pareilles qui se sont amassées en nous depuis les premiers âges, et proclamant, devant le Rien qui est la vérité, ces glorieux mensonges! Tel est le plan de mon volume lyrique, et tel sera peut-être son titre: *La Gloire du mensonge* ou *Le Glorieux Mensonge.* Je le chanterai en désespéré![22]

[I want to give myself this spectacle of matter, conscious of its being, and nevertheless throwing itself forcefully forward in the dream that it knows it is not, singing the Soul and all the divine impressions of this sort which have accumulated in us for ages, and proclaiming, before the Non-Being which is the truth, those glorious lies! That's the plan of my lyrical volume, and that will be its title: *The Glory of the Lie,* or *The Glorious Lie.* I'll sing it desperately!]

22. Mallarmé, "Lettre à Henri Cazalis, mars 1866," 66.

The slight tone of self-parody in the first quote tells us he's not mad. What it reflects is not only a sense of how weird his developing new outlook may appear to his friend Cazalis, but also his own uncertainty and perplexity about what his new cosmic vision really involves. And I believe that this continues. To the end of his career he is searching, experimenting, trying to find an adequate expression for the poetic program this vision involves. But we should take this program seriously, because Mallarmé did.

Nor should we put too much weight on the expression "mensonges" [lies]. This not only comes from an early stage in the whole crisis and revision, but even as a hyperbolic reference to meaning as something arising in self-consciousness, has to be put in the context of Mallarmé's often-repeated belief that what becomes self-conscious is not primarily the individual, but as he says above, the universe. This was meant seriously. Relative to us individuals, the meanings are not inventions.

The tables are meant to be turned in the following way. The "Rien" [Nothing; Non-Being] is what underlies everything, since all is matter. That means the Non-Being of anything stable; and also of any higher meaning. But once we see that this universe generates self-consciousness, then this Non-Being takes on another aspect. It is that which comes to self-consciousness. But this is more than just the result of a rather shaky syllogism: the Universe is Non-Being (identity statement); the Universe comes to self-consciousness; therefore the Non-Being comes to self-consciousness. On the side of self-consciousness, the Non-Being now means an impersonal consciousness, not mine or yours, but that of the whole which is becoming conscious through you and me.

> Une race, la nôtre, à qui cet honneur de prêter des entrailles à la peur qu'a d'elle-même, autrement que comme conscience humaine, la métaphysique et claustrale éternité.[23]
>
> [A race, our own, to whom this honor falls of lending its entrails to the fear of its own being, other than as human consciousness, but as a metaphysical and claustral eternity.]

23. Stéphane Mallarmé, "Catholicisme," in *Œuvres complètes*, 2:238.

(Hugo Friedrich argues that for Mallarmé the failure of the absolute to come to speech can also be seen as its trying and failing, and not just as our doing so.)[24]

Here Mallarmé is in fact following Hegel. Our finite consciousnesses are emanations, spin-offs of the one great process which is spirit coming to its own self-objectification and self-awareness. It follows that to come to the real meaning of things is to come to their meaning in and for that process of self-awareness. If we are to grasp this meaning, we have in some way to come to coincide with this self-awareness. But this is the negation of any finite consciousness, and so we have to negate ourselves, we have to become one with the Non-Being in this sense.

Does this arid and not very clear metaphysics, hardly worked out in detail by Mallarmé (and even a lot of his detail has not come down to us), help at all with the poetry? No and yes. We're tempted to say "no" because this supposed "materialistic" view seems implausible, and even arguably amounts to a form of "idealism" (as he himself seems to concede: see above). But also yes, because some of the things he's trying to do are justified and made sense of by the metaphysic.

First, there is an effort of negation going on in the poetry, negation in two connected directions. First of the subject; a kind of "disappearance" of the subject, a shift toward impersonality. Second, there is a quasi-disappearance of the object, of the emphatic reality. I use the prefix "quasi" here, because it is still held there, invoked, but as absent. A crucial Mallarmé turn. The flower which is "absente de tous bouquets" [missing from all bouquets]. Just as beyond the finite subject, we are trying to become the impersonal subject, *le Néant* [Non-Being]. So beyond the absent object, we seek the "Notion," the "idea." This is often understood in what sounds more like a Platonic fashion. But this doesn't change anything, because Hegel's use of both "Idée" and "Begriff" owes a lot to Plato.

Then along with both these disappearances, there is a third essential theme. Coinciding with the Non-Being, and grasping the Idea of things, takes us to a kind of eternity. The most important way of describing this

24. Hugo Friedrich, *Die Struktur der modernen Lyrik von Baudelaire bis zur Gegenwart* (Hamburg: Rowohlt, 1965), 101.

step for Mallarmé is that it abolishes chance, *le hasard*. The domain of the merely material is the domain of chance; we could put this also, perhaps even better, in terms of time. Ordinary, secular time, the time of material reality, is submitted to blind contingency. Grasping the notion is overcoming this. Why? Well, presumably, because seen from the standpoint of the Non-Being, of the process of global coming to self-awareness, things don't just hang together contingently, but they have to happen this way, to be connected in this manner, if this self-awareness is to come about. Seeing things from the standpoint of Non-Being brings out the necessity connecting them.

That's a very crucial Hegelian idea, and it seems to have also been Mallarmé's. In any case, overcoming *le hasard* [chance, contingency] is a central theme.

I hope the above quotations and commentary give a sense of his new semi-Hegelian philosophy, where the self is also a locus of Non-Being which underlies and makes possible the appearance of reality.

Fortified with this, let's look at some of the actual poetic practice. But in order to do this, we'll slow down somewhat, and look at some of the creations which arise out of the transition between the two outlooks, which we've just telescoped in its essential points of departure and arrival.

II

In a sense, Mallarmé's is a familiar predicament. That is, familiar for us who have built a picture of the situation of the Romantic poet. It is a question of renewing language. Meaning has been lost, language which used to reveal the meanings of things no longer does so. "Crise de vers": "Les langues imparfaites en cela que plusieurs" [Languages, imperfect, because multiple]. Mallarmé takes the idea of a single, original language perhaps as just a myth; but the notion of imperfection is clearly seriously meant. And it even has a disturbing Cratylus ring to it: "Mon sens regrette que le discours défaille à exprimer les objets par des touches y répondant en coloris ou en allure" [My sense regrets that discourse fails to express objects through touches that correspond to them in color or allure].[25]

Then he goes on right away with the example of "jour" and "nuit." The former sounds somber and closed, the latter sprightly and bright; when it should be the other way around.

(*Les Mots anglais* seems to develop a partly Cratylan program quite seriously, but I don't think this was the crucial issue for Mallarmé, as I explain below.)

But then the paragraph takes a new turn. It is almost as if all this bad state exists (o felix culpa) to require poetry. "Seulement, sachons n'existerait pas le vers: lui, philosophiquement rémunère le défaut des langues, complément supérieur" [Only let's recognize: if verse didn't exist . . . because verse philosophically remedies the defect of languages, brings a higher complement].[26] The point being made here: the "defect" of language mentioned in the previous paragraph is made up by verse, which is superior to ordinary language. Note the importance of the verse here, not just poetry in general. This is an important idea. The verse will combine words musically, so as to bring out their capacity to evoke intrinsically what they say (but not in the Cratylan fashion).

Here is another crucial Romantic idea. There is ordinary language and poetry. The first lamentably fails in this task of rendering the meaning of things; to the second falls this task. This is embroidered on later in the same text with the now-familiar Romantic distinction, that ordinary language is used for utilitarian purposes, just to communicate states of affairs and desires, and so on. It consists of representative tokens. You could in principle substitute money (utility, commerce, money).

So "Crise de vers": "Parler n'a trait à la réalité des choses que commercialement" [Talking is only about the reality of things commercially], while Poetry "donne un sens plus pur aux mots de la tribu" [gives a purer meaning to the words of the tribe].[27] But for Mallarmé the truly adequate

25. Mallarmé, "Crise de vers," 363–364, 364. Cratylus figures in a Platonic dialogue (bearing his name) defending the view that the sound of a word figures its meaning.

26. Mallarmé, "Crise de vers," 364.

27. Mallarmé, "Crise de vers," 366.

form of this language doesn't at present exist. He admires and appreci-
ates many other poets, including his contemporaries: Gautier, Villiers,
Verlaine, Banville. But their language won't do what he wants to do. As
I tried to articulate this lack above: their work is still too much taken up
with describing/evoking emphatic realities, "les pierres précieuses." He
feels that one has to get beyond this to articulate the meanings of these
realities. So although his predicament is in one sense "standard"—the Romantic Predicament—it is in another way unprecedented, and threatens
to lead to an impasse.

But one might reply: How unprecedented really? Didn't all Romantic
poets feel they had to create a new language, or at least a new style, in
some sense? Or at least make a break with poetry as it had become? For
instance, the critique of "classicism." Indeed, this need to make something
new, or restore something old—in either case, to break with the immediate past—has been felt way beyond the confines of Romanticism, by
many generations of poets; by La Pléiade and others.

In Romanticism, there is a particular twist on it. The need for a new
language comes along with the sense that the things they are trying to
say are tremendously difficult—indeed, in a sense impossible—to say adequately. That's because they are moving in a zone where we are close to
being out of our depth. Something about the symbol will always remain
mysterious, not quite fully sayable. (See the quote above concerning
Mallarmé's "idealism" which "refuse les matériaux naturels et, comme
brutale, une pensée exacte les ordonnant; pour ne garder de rien que la
suggestion" [refuses natural materials and, as brutal, an exact thought
ordering them; to keep nothing but the suggestion].)[28]

In this regard, we might want to say that Mallarmé was really back in
the Romantic stream in a sense that Gautier and the Parnassians were
not, with their belief in poems sculpted or carved like jewelry. Although
there is a side of Mallarmé that resembles Parnasse in this, the side that
seems to imply that (in principle) the effect can be exactly calculated. This
is the side that Valéry plays up. But to go too far along this road is to lose
the sense of struggle, of recurrent failure to say it all properly, which is
very much part of Mallarmé's creative life.

28. Mallarmé, "Crise de vers," 204.

So the question still hangs: How unprecedented? Mallarmé is like other poets in what I have called the Romantic stream in his sense that the inherited language won't allow him to articulate the meanings he feels impelled to articulate. He is like them in his sense that this articulation is supremely difficult and will probably always elude us to some degree. He is also like them in holding that the meanings he is trying to articulate bear some relation to what the premoderns believed about the significance of the universe and its contents.

And he is prepared to use some traditional language to describe this task: for example, to speak of discovering the Idea, or the Essence of things, of Eternity or the Infinite; or: "l'explication orphique de la Terre, qui est le seul devoir du poëte et le jeu littéraire par excellence" [the Orphic explanation of the Earth, which is the poet's only duty and the literary exercise par excellence].[29] He even sees this not just as something that poets very much want to do, but as a duty. All this alignment with tradition, of course, is affected by the fact that he has a quite different ontological foundation for it all, a kind of almost-materialistic, atheistic Hegelianism, tinged with Platonism.

What is unprecedented, and which is related to his new ontology, is his notion that there are no more emphatic realities, the description or invoking of which, however debanalized, and in whatever mode of lyric force or freshness, will allow us to articulate the meanings of things. This might be challenged as a way of putting the matter, because we might argue that what Mallarmé ultimately does is devise a new way of invoking these realities, precisely as absent, and that turns out to be a powerful articulation of something, it's hard to say what. This is perfectly true and could be taken as a complement to the negative existential above (there are no more emphatic realities), further clarifying its meaning. His idea is that the path of describing / invoking these realities, trying to render with vividness and force the beauty we spontaneously find in them, and the significance we feel in them (e.g., in flowers, sunsets, the sea, the wind, etc.), moving as this may be, is a dead end, and blocks us from the deeper level of meaning which he wants to unveil, and which it is the poet's

29. Stéphane Mallarmé, "Lettre à Paul Verlaine. 16 novembre 1885," in *Œuvres complètes*, 1:788.

"devoir" [duty] to unveil: "l'explication orphique de la Terre" [the Orphic explanation of the Earth]. Emphatic realities may somehow help us to get to these deeper meanings, but only if we can, as it were, get around them, not have our attention and our admiration captured by them. Just as physical realities, empirical things, phenomena, they are emanations of Nothing. What counts is not themselves, but the process of their emanation; what they are as facets of the self-revealing of Non-Being (*Néant*); what he calls their notion or idea, or essence. Thus: "A quoi bon la merveille de transposer un fait de nature en sa presque disparition vibratoire selon le jeu de la parole, cependant; si ce n'est pour qu'en émane, sans la gêne d'un proche ou concret rappel, la notion pure" [What good is the marvel of transposing a fact of nature into its almost vibratory disappearance according to the play of speech, however; if not for the pure notion—without the embarrassment of a close or concrete reminder—to emanate from it].[30]

This may make Mallarmé appear as a very excarnate poet. And some have compared his basic démarche to that of Descartes, negating the material for what he can discover within (hyperbolic doubt which gives way to the cogito).[31] But this would be a big mistake. "Je crois pour être bien l'homme, la nature en pensant, il faut penser de tout son corps, ce qui donne une pensée pleine et à l'unisson comme des cordes de violon vibrant immédiatement avec sa boîte de bois creux [. . .] il faut cela pour avoir une vue très—une de l'univers" [I believe that to be truly human, nature in thinking, one must think with one's whole body, which gives full thought and unison like the strings vibrating immediately with one's hollow wooden box [. . .] this is necessary to have a very—united view of the universe].[32]

So the "notion pure" is not a description of the object or logically derived from a description. It is transposed by the whole being of the poet, body and mind, following "ces motifs qui composent une logique avec

---

30. Mallarmé, "Crise de vers," 368.

31. See George Poulet, "La Prose de Mallarmé," in *Les Métamorphoses du cercle* (Paris: Flammarion, 1961).

32. Stéphane Mallarmé, "Lettre à Eugène Lefébure. 27 mai 1867," in *Œuvres complètes*, 1:720.

nos fibres" [these motifs which form together a logic with our fibers].[33]
As an example of what this kind of transposition can feed on, take this
passage from one of his letters:

> Je ne connaissais que le grillon anglais, doux et caricaturice: hier
> seulement parmi les jeunes blés j'ai entendue cette voix sacrée
> que celle de l'oiseau de la terre ingénue, moins décomposée
> déjà que celle de l'loiseau, fils des arbres parmi la nuit solaire, et
> qui a quelque chose des étoiles et de la lune, et un peu de mort
> esprit. . . . Tant de bonheur qu'a la terre de ne pas être décom-
> posée en matière et en esprit et en ce son unique du grillon![34]

> [I only knew the English cricket, sweet and caricatured: only
> yesterday among the young wheat I heard this sacred voice,
> that of the bird of the ingenuous earth, less decomposed
> already than that of a bird, son of the trees among the solar
> night, and who has something of the stars and the moon, and a
> little of the spirit of death. . . . So much happiness that the
> earth has not to be decomposed into matter and spirit, and into
> this unique sound of the cricket!]

"Crise de vers" again: "Parler n'a trait à la réalité des choses que commercialement: en littérature, cela se contente d'y faire une allusion ou de
distraire leur qualité qu'incorporera quelque idée" [Talking has to do with
the reality of things only commercially: in literature, it merely alludes to
them and abstracts their quality which some idea will incorporate].[35]

In the first quote this feat of going beyond the object, through its "presque disparition vibratoire" [vibratory near disappearance], to the notion is called "transposition." And immediately after the third quote he
says: "Cette visée, je la dis Transposition" [This take on reality, I call
Transposition].[36] This continues the movement I mentioned above: away
from centering on the object, in order to allow space for the "impression"
or the "état d'âme."

33. Stéphane Mallarmé, *La Musique et les lettres,* in *Œuvres complètes,* 2:62.
34. Stéphane Mallarmé, "Lettre à Lefébure. 17 mai 1867," in *Œuvres complètes,* 1:716.
35. Mallarmé, "Crise de vers," 209.
36. Mallarmé, "Crise de vers," 209.

Also: "La divine transposition, pour l'accomplissement de quoi existe l'homme, va du fait à l'idéal" [This divine transposition, for whose accomplishment the human being exists, moves from the fact to the ideal].[37] Another way in which he often describes his goal is getting beyond the object to the idea:

Je dis: une fleur! Et, hors de l'oubli où ma voix relègue aucun contour, en tant que quelque chose d'autre que les calices sus, musicalement se lève, idée même et suave, l'absente de tous bouquets.[38]

[I say: a flower! And out of the oblivion where my voice relegates any outline, as something other than the known chalices, musically rises, idea even and suave, the absentee of all bouquets.]

What in fact he wants to reveal is not objects, but the connections which constitute objects, as well as the relations between all of them, which hold in virtue of their common source.

"Crise de vers": "En tant que l'ensemble des rapports existant dans tout, la Musique" [As the totality of relationships existing in everything, Music].[39] Le Livre: "L'hymne, harmonie et joie, comme pur ensemble groupé dans quelque circonstance fulgurante, des relations entre tout. L'homme chargé de voir divinement." [The hymn, harmony and joy, as pure ensemble grouped in some dazzling circumstance, of the relations between everything. The human charged with seeing divinely.][40]

"Réponses à des Enquêtes": "Les choses existent, nous n'avons pas à les créer; nous n'avons qu'à en saisir les rapports; et ce sont les fils de ces rapports qui forment les vers et les orchestres" [Things exist, we don't have to create them; we only have to grasp their relationships; and it's the threads of these relationships that form verses and orchestras].[41]

37. Stéphane Mallarmé, "Quelques médaillons et portraits en pied: Théodore de Banville," in Œuvres complètes, 2:144.

38. Mallarmé, "Crise de vers," 210.

39. Mallarmé, "Crise de vers," 210.

40. Stéphane Mallarmé, Le Livre, in Œuvres complètes, 2:224.

41. Stéphane Mallarmé, "Réponses à des Enquêtes," in Œuvres complètes, 2:697.

Another way he famously puts the goal of grasping meaning is negating or abolishing chance (*le hasard*). We can see this as the same under another description. The relations we have to see are ultimately ones of necessity. To see how things all hang together, and must hang together to emerge into the self-awareness of the universe, is to set aside the mere chance relations. The connection between these two descriptions of the goal is made when we see the relations we are seeking to discern as necessary, as of the essence.

> Le vers . . . niant, d'un trait souverain, le hasard demeuré au termes . . . [42]

> [Verse . . . negating with a sovereign stroke, the chance relations which held between the terms . . .]

> Le hasard vaincu mot par mot[43]

> [Chance conquered overcome by word]

The emphasis on relations and overcoming chance explains the importance to Mallarmé of the Book, or *l'Œuvre* (in the singular masculine).[44] The highest artistic creation has to be a revealing of the connections between everything: "comme pur ensemble groupé dans quelque circonstance fulgurante, des relations entre tout" [as a pure whole grouped together in some dazzling circumstance, of the relations between everything].[45] In a famous letter to Paul Verlaine, Mallarmé declares himself

> prêt à y sacrifier toute vanité et toute satisfaction, comme on brulait jadis son mobilier et les poutres de son toit, pour alimenter le fourneau du Grand Œuvre. Quoi? c'est difficile à dire: un livre, tout bonnement. . . . J'irai plus loin, je dirai: le Livre, persuadé qu'au fond in n'y en a qu'un, tenté à son insu par quiconque a

---

42. Mallarmé, "Crise de vers," 210.

43. Stéphane Mallarmé, "Le Mystère dans le lettre," in *Œuvres complètes*, 2:229–234.

44. See Mallarmé, *Propos sur la poésie*, 79.

45. Mallarmé, "Lettre à Paul Verlaine. 16 novembre 1885," 788.

écrit, même les Génies. L'explication orphique de la Terre, qui est le seul devoir du poëte et le jeu littéraire par excellence.[46]

[ready to sacrifice all vanity and satisfaction, just as one once burned one's furniture and the beams of one's roof, to feed the furnace of the Great Work. What? it's hard to say: a book, quite simply. . . . I'll go further, I'll say: the Book, convinced that deep down there's only one, attempted unknowingly by anyone who has written, even the Geniuses. The Orphic explanation of the Earth, which is the poet's sole duty and the literary exercise par excellence.]

The same idea in "Crise de vers": "Même il n'en serait qu'un—au monde, sa loi—bible comme la simulent des nations" [Even it would be only one—to the world, its law—bible which the nations try to copy.][47]

Now the focus on the emphatic realities themselves blocks this vision. And in "Crise de vers," he talks of an "Idéalisme," which

refuse les matériaux naturels et, comme brutale, une pensée exacte les ordonnant; pour ne garder de rien que la suggestion. Instituer une relation entre les images exactes, et que s'en détache un tiers aspect fusible et clair présenté à la divination. [. . .] Abolie la prétention, esthétiquement une erreur [. . .] d'inclure au papier subtil du volume autre chose que par exemple l'horreur de la forêt, ou le tonnerre muet épars au feuillage, non le bois intrinsèque et dense des arbres.[48]

[refuses natural materials and, as brutal, an exact thought ordering them; to keep nothing but the suggestion. To institute a relationship between exact images, and that a third, fusible and clear aspect be detached from them, presented to divination. [. . .] Abolish the pretension, aesthetically an error [. . .] to include in the subtle paper of a volume something other than, for example, the horror of the forest, or the mute

46. Mallarmé, "Lettre à Paul Verlaine. 16 novembre 1885," 788.
47. Mallarmé, "Crise de vers," 211–212.
48. Mallarmé, "Crise de vers," in Œuvres complètes, 365–366.

thunder scattered in the foliage, but not the intrinsic and dense wood of the trees.]

Note: the "presque disparition," because our ordinary awareness of objects remains, even as the poetry adds an insight into a deeper reality. This disappearance is "vibratoire," because poetry (and also music may be included) involves vibrations.

We can perhaps usefully make a contrast with Baudelaire at this point. Both poets upset the traditional way of describing and celebrating emphatic realities. For both this way fails them. For Baudelaire the failure is seen as generated by sin, the drives toward Satan, bringing in the end ennui and paralysis. His creative response was to make paradigmatically nonemphatic realities speak as though they were emphatic, that is, to make their description / evocation revelatory. We could say he enlarges the gamut of emphatic realities; or alternatively that he abolishes the category because it now lacks a clear contrast class. The ordinary, the banal, the ugly can be loci of revelation.

Mallarmé, except for his brief Baudelairean period, leaves the boundary emphatic / nonemphatic more or less untouched. His denial comes at another point, that we can proceed with the emphatic as we have done in the past, that it can offer a route to (what he understands as) revelation of meaning.

So where does this leave us? Arguably in a quandary. How does one get beyond these realities? Isn't the end result of this kind of outlook that one is condemned to silence? That's a conclusion that a number of people have come to, through various routes. One is to pick up on Mallarmé's denial of the place of emphatic realities, in the context of his constatation of the death of God and disenchantment, on the assumption that poetry can only thrive through some kind of recovery of God, or at least reenchantment, Mallarmé's case seems hopeless. Such was Claudel's position, with all the sympathy and admiration he had for Mallarmé.

Or else, more subtly, one can be willing to believe that poetry is possible after disenchantment; or alternatively put, that there is some possible reenchantment consistent with a materialist outlook—for example, a disclosure of the human meanings and resonances of things—but still judge Mallarmé's case hopeless, because one cannot see how poetry can reveal except through description / evocation; in other words, through dealing with things as traditional poetry dealt with the emphatic, even though this category has now undergone a Baudelairean dissolution.

And these pessimistic judgments get a certain color from Mallarmé's massive blockage, his long-lasting inability to write—that is, to write poetry that approached his purpose—and from a reading of the late "Coup de dés" as an avowal of the final impossibility of his task.

III

But it is time to get clearer on what Mallarmé meant by "transposition"; and by the "presque disparition vibratoire" [vibratory near disappearance] which results from it.

In our ordinary human consciousness, the subject observes an object, separate from herself, and registers some description of it. But at the deeper level of Mallarmé's semi-Hegelian theory, the Non-Being which operates through us brings about an appearance, but there is no real question of separation here. The separate subject and object are not the ultimate reality. On the contrary, at the deeper level, everything is connected, and indeed, not just contingently, but by necessity. To reveal this is to lay out the meaning of our existence.

In the everyday world, we live as separate beings among an infinite array of such beings, observers and observed. On a deeper level of Mallarmé's theory, the Non-Being which operates through us brings about the appearance of things, but there is no question of real separation at this level. The separate subject and object are not the ultimate reality. On the contrary, at the deeper level, everything is connected, and indeed, not just contingently, but by necessity.

In the everyday world, we live as separate beings among an array of such beings; on a deeper level, the elements of this array are linked. What the poet can and should do is reveal, bring forth, make evident, this universal connection.

This means that the task of the poet is not limited to showing links between subjects and objects in particular cases, but to reveal the whole system. Hence the reference above to the "Grand Œuvre" or Le Livre. The goal would be to write a book. Mallarmé sometimes uses the term "Gri-moire" (a sacred book, often containing spells). But he often recognizes that this is the ultimate ambition, whose achievement—at least by him—is probably impossible.

But all this talk of failure and impossibility misses an important achievement in Mallarmé. Or achievements, in the plural, because the theory was actually put into practice by him, and in more than one way, and is essential as a key to understanding much of his work.

Let me try to explain what I mean by this, with particular reference to Mallarmé. What emerged from the above discussion could be de-scribed as something like a poetic program, or agenda, or definition of an achievement which had to be attempted. This involved "transposition," meaning in some way bypassing the objects which present themselves as emphatic, and which thus invite us to describe and celebrate them, in order to get to their deeper meaning. This he sometimes referred to as their notion or idea. But it could also be understood as the relations be-tween the objects, or their necessary connections.

Fulfilling this program, even partially, is what I could call the "direct" road; that is, actually writing poems which realized / revealed the deeper connections he postulated.

But there is another way of describing the program which Mallarmé sees as extensionally equivalent. This involves abolishing or getting be-yond not just the object, but the poet. The death of the poet as a particular being, and his rise as the carrier of the self-awareness of the whole.

Let's recall his letter to Cazalis (quoted above):

> This is to inform you that I am now impersonal, and no longer Stéphane whom you've known,—but an aptitude which the spir-itual universe has to see itself and develop itself through what was me.
>
> Fragile, in my terrestrial appearance, I can only undergo through the absolutely necessary developments for the universe to recover, in this "I", its identity.[49]

49. Mallarmé, "Lettre à Henri Cazalis. 14 mai 1867," 713.

This is seen as a kind of death. In spite of the jocular tone, of hyperbolic self-parody, typical of Mallarmé, the idea of in some way transcending his own standpoint, and of this as closely akin to death, approaching death asymptotically, is very seriously meant, and is described, explored, attempted in the poetry.[50] Another quote from the correspondence connects this stepping outside the particular self into death or impersonality with the tracing of the universal and necessary relations:

> J'ai voulu te dire simplement que je venais de jeter le plan de mon Œuvre entier, après avoir trouvé la clef de moi-même, clef de voûte, ou centre, si tu veux, pour ne pas nous brouiller de métaphores, centre de moi-même où je me tiens comme une araignée sacrée, sur les principales fils déjà sortis de mon esprit, et à l'aide desquels je tisserai aux points de rencontre de merveilleuses dentelles, que je devine, et qui existe déjà dans le sein de la Beauté.[51]

> [I wanted to tell you simply that I had just sketched the plan of my entire Work, having found the key to myself, keystone, or center, if you will, so as not to confuse us with metaphors, center of myself where I stand like a sacred spider, on the main threads already leading out of my mind, and with the help of which I will weave at the meeting points of marvelous lace, which I can guess at, and which already exists in the bosom of Beauty.]

But does this whole vision leave us with an utterly inoperable program? It depends what one is looking for here. It might mean: write a poem which itself realizes a "transposition"—that is, the "presque disparition vibratoire" [vibratory near disappearance] of some object; this would be a direct, practical realization of the doctrine. In fact, I think there are a few poems in which Mallarmé comes close to doing this.

But there are other ways that the theory informs the poetry. It gives us the background against which the poems were written and thus makes them more comprehensible for us, the readers. These are the interpre-

---

50. See particularly, but not only, "La Cantique de Saint Jean"; also "Tel qu'en Lui-même l'Éternité le change" in "Le Tombeau d'Edgar Poe."

51. Stéphane Mallarmé, "Lettre à Théodore Aubanel. 28 juillet 1866," in *Œuvres complètes,* 1:204.

tive applications, showing how the theory inspired the poet. I want to discuss some of his works in what follows, with this theory in mind. But these poems fall short of what I am calling direct practical achievements of what the theory adumbrates.

But this not to disparage these latter. In fact, we are now on very familiar terrain. Poetry in general, and Romantic poetry in particular, is full of evocations of the absent. The very common theme of exile offers endless variations on one form of this. One makes more vivid and palpable what it would be like to have arrived at the fullness of being by painting one's distance from it. By the waters of Babylon, we laid down our harps and wept. Jerusalem if I forget thee. We bring back into the soul's vision what we long for, the home which defines our present estate as exile.

This can be a vital necessity, essential that is, for the life of the soul. We saw this with Baudelaire. The crushing weight of ennui, its creeping glacial paralysis, threatens to rob us even of a sense of what our heart really desires. The vivid portrayal of the condition of Spleen, of pain and exile, shakes off this lethargy, allows the soul once again the fullness of longing. The comparison with the depictions of human depravity, and its punishments in Hell, among hyper-Augustinians, is evident enough, and was made above.

Now early Mallarmé contains a classic example of this; of how structuring our condition around images of exile can give definition and vividness to what we long for. "Les Fenêtres" and "L'Azur" offer a similar structure to our spiritual universe. They see it as divided, between inside / outside, which is also below / above. Inside and below is the world bereft of beauty and meaning, the life of mere appetite "où ses seuls appétits mangent" [where only his appetites eat]. Above and outside is the world of fullness, beauty, higher meaning. Drawing the distinction, making the partition, allows the outside-upper world to stand forth in the fullness of its beauty and purity.

The object of vague longing is given shape; it finds defining images. More, we can say that the master images of this partition identify and endow with power certain emphatic realities, which could be the center of premature-Mallarméan poetics. Two key ones acquire this kind of power in early Mallarmé: the blue sky, and the window. The first bears the recurring name "azur." The second is named in a number of different ways: "carreaux d'or" (stanza 3), "croisées," "verre" (stanza 7), "vitre" (stanza 8), "cristal" (stanza 10). The recurring theme is the window as both boundary and opening: an opening to see a further world, but one which can't be gone through. To say that they become emphatic realities for early Mallarmé is to say that in evoking / describing them, he brings closer and makes more vivid what he longs for.

But the mature Mallarmé is not as concerned with longing; his later poems rather give readings of his (or the human) situation as read through his mature vision.

Early Mallarmé was a most eloquent poet of exile. But this didn't satisfy him. It rather increased his dissatisfaction. His situation was the opposite of Baudelaire's. Where the elder poet won a victory over ennui in recovering the object of longing, the younger found the longing unbearable without some satisfaction of it. Writing as he still does in very Baudelairean terms, he even calls ennui to his aid against the unbearable beauty of l'Azur: "Cher Ennui, pour boucher d'une main jamais lasse / Les grands trous bleus que font méchamment les oiseaux" [Dear Ennui, to plug with a never-weary hand / The big blue holes that birds wickedly make].[52]

What emerges first from the mutation in outlook is the attempts at "Hérodiade," which he was working on during the period of his dramatic letters to Cazalis.[53] This involves an important change. L'Azur was defined in opposition to life, ordinary life. "Je fuis et je m'accroche à toutes les croisées / D'où l'on tourne l'épaule à la vie" [I flee and cling to all the crossroads / From which one turns one's shoulder to life].[54] This turning from life is a constant in Mallarmé, as we can see with the place of death / impersonality in his mature conception. But what it involves changes rather radically.

For the early Mallarmé of "Les Fenêtres," l'Azur was still connected to the innocence of childhood. It was what one had possessed and lost. So

52. Mallarmé, "L'Azur," 14.

53. It has been suggested that "Hérodiade" owes something to Les Fleurs du Mal XXVIII.

54. Mallarmé, "Fenêtres," 9.

stanza 7 goes on: "et béni, / Dans leur verre, lavé d'éternelles rosées, / Que dore le matin chaste de l'Infini" [and blessed, / In their glass, washed with eternal dews, / That gild the chaste morning of the Infinite]. And stanza 8 wants to be reborn "au ciel antérieur où fleurit la Beauté" [to the former heaven where Beauty flourishes].[55] The "innocence" of childhood means, for the adult, life before elemental sexual desire, and before the pulsations of self-affirming, self-glorifying power, which come with maturity (or manhood, if one thinks the second are exclusively male).

(Of course, Freud denied that either are exclusively connected to maturity; but the importance of the images of innocence in childhood is attested by the shock with which his theories were greeted.)

The speaker in stanzas 7 and 8 of "Les Fenêtres" is looking backward to this innocence. (Indeed, in some ways the present text was altered from the original form: verse 28 used to read "et je songe, et j'aime" [and I dream, I love].) Turning your shoulder to life means taking one's stance in this innocence. "Hérodiade" changes this utterly. Sex and power are there, and turning away from life doesn't mean just turning one's shoulder on them, escaping their power.

But there still is a turning away from life. There is an aspiration, descended from the Romantics, which takes on board sex and power, and wants to unite them in a harmonious synthesis with the love of the highest. The kind of thing which is captured in Schiller's idea of beauty. Its contemporary influence is in a certain thread of Frankfurt School thought, or Marcuse. Such is not Mallarmé's way. "Hérodiade" also turns from life. But this means turning all the energy of sex and power into a refusal of sexual life; or into a purely narcissistic mode of this. It's not clear what to say here, because there are a number of versions; the piece was not completed, and even the published version of the part we have leaves one baffled. But in any case, what is clear is that this being feels the stirrings of sex and power, and wants to channel them, mainly into an affirmation of power.

How did this work serve Mallarmé's quest for poetic articulation? Because it situates the poet in quite a new predicament. What he is trying to articulate is not what was once lived, in a purer past, before the desires

55. Mallarmé, "L'Azur," 14.

and cares of adulthood supervened. Beauty is still linked to purity. But now the purity is not that of innocence, but one of sacrifice and denial. It is a purity won through power, rather than given in the absence of temptation.

Consequently, (1) the beauty is not one of effortless innocence, but of power. It is a beauty not of flowers, but of glaciers ("je te dirai que je suis depuis un mois dans les plus purs glaciers de l'Esthétique" [I tell you that I am for a month in the purest glaciers of the Aesthetic]).[56] Glaciers are not only pure, but they make everything in their vicinity pure; they freeze it. They have power. Or: not the kind of power that flowers have; more like that of metals, stones. "Oui, c'est pour moi, pour moi, que je fleuris, déserte!" [Yes, it's for me, for me that I bloom, alone!]; and she speaks of "ors ignorés, pierres, bijoux, nuits blanches de glaçons et de neige cruelle!" [unknown golds, stones, jewels, icicles and of sleepless snow-covered nights!].

(2) The stones also suggest that this beauty is made, formed. It is a beauty not found in what preexisted, but shaped. The poetic of "Hérodiade" is explicitly a new one. "Peindre, non la chose, mais l'effet qu'elle produit."[57] He has moved explicitly away from describing emphatic objects. We are already in mature Mallarmé, with the surprising, even tortured syntax, building a complex effect out of words combined in a stunning new way.

(3) The "ciel antérieur" [original sky] is no longer the benchmark. We are not trying to re-create what was there before. This cannot be our model, the pole of our longing.

(4) This purity exists in counterpoint to violence, menace, desire. It can only be maintained against desire, which is a constant threat; and / or through a violence done against desire: the beheading of St. John, because (allegedly, according to the story Mallarmé wanted to follow) his gaze was too unsettling. The glacier is alongside a volcano.

(3) and (4) are admirably rendered already in the "Ouverture." The sky at dawn is now powerless. "Caprice Solitaire d'aurore au vain plumage

---

56. Stéphane Mallarmé, "Lettre à Henri Cazalis. 13 juillet, 1866," in *Œuvres complètes,* 1:701–702.

57. Mallarmé, "Lettre à Henri Cazalis. 30 octobre 1864," 664.

noir" [Lonely caprice of dawn in vain black plumage], "l'eau reflète l'abandon de l'automne éteignant en elle son brandon" [the water reflects the abandonment of autumn extinguishing its torch]. And the swan's head is "désolée / Par le diamant pur de quelque étoile, mais / Antérieur, qui ne scintilla jamais" [desolate, by the pure diamond of some star / but Anterior, which never shone].[58]

(How's that for taking it back? But obviously related to "les diamants élus / D'une étoile, mourante, et qui ne brille plus!" [the elect diamonds / of a star, dying, and which no longer shines!] at the very end.)[59]

Later, "le vieux Ciel brûle" [the old sky burns]. It is a "triste crépuscule" [sad twilight]; but this is taken back almost at once. "De crépuscule, non, mais de rouge lever, / Lever du jour dernier qui vient tout achever" [No, not a twilight, but a red dawn, / dawn of a last day which comes to finish it all off].[60] We move from a sky without power to one which menaces.

And Hérodiade is an enemy of *l'Azur:*

> Prophétise que si le tiède azur d'été,
> Vers lui nativement la femme se dévoile,
> Me voit dans ma pudeur grelottante d'étoile,
> Je meurs![61]

> [Prophetise if the tepid azure of summer
> toward him the woman unveils herself naïvely
> sees me in my shivering star-like modesty
> I die!]

And later: "Mais avant, si tu veux, clos les volets: l'azur / Séraphique sourit dans les vitres profondes, / Et je déteste, moi, le bel azur!" [But first,

---

58. Stéphane Mallarmé, "Ouverture d' 'Hérodiade,'" État corrigé puis abandonné, 1866–1898, in *Œuvres complètes*, 1:137–138.

59. Mallarmé, "Ouverture d' 'Hérodiade,'" État corrigé puis abandonné, 1866–1898, 138.

60. Mallarmé, "Ouverture d' 'Hérodiade,'" État corrigé puis abandonné, 1866–1898, 139.

61. Stéphane Mallarmé, "Hérodiade," in *Œuvres complètes*, 1:21.

if you want, close the shutters;/the seraphic azure smiles in the deep windows/and, myself I hate the beautiful azure!].[62]

There is just a moment of hesitation: "Du reste, je ne veux rien d'humain, et, sculptée,/Si tu me vois les yeux perdus aux paradis,/C'est quand je me souviens de ton lait bu jadis" [Besides, I want nothing human, and sculpted as I am/if you see my eyes lost in paradise/It's when I remember your milk which I drank of yore].[63] Note she is "sculptée" [sculpted].

And the "Ouverture" is full of menace: "Crime! bûcher! aurore ancienne! supplice!/Pourpre d'un ciel! Étang de la pourpre complice!" [Crime! Funeral pyre! Ancient dawn! Torture!/heavenly purple!/Pond of complicit purple!][64]

This connection of sunset (or here rise, but there's some confusion) with sacrifice, blood, death, becomes very important in later Mallarmé, as we'll see. Also the wonderful passage about her father: "Son père ne sait pas cela" [Her father doesn't know that].[65] Here also an invocation of glacier.

"Hérodiade" starts at the beginning of the evolution which will take him from "Fenêtres" through the crisis to the vision of *Néant*. But he went on working on it. He began again shortly before his death. (Lots of problems, including that it couldn't be performed.) So we can't just assign it one meaning. In relation to the mature position, we can't count it as a direct attempt to apply it, but rather as another indirect route, this one being an allegory of the poet or of poetry. Another not uncommon form, especially in the post-Romantic period. It offers an image of what it is to turn from Life to Beauty, alternative to and quite different from breaking through the window to *l'Azur* of the early poems.

But things could have turned out differently. We can only call this indirect in the context of the mature position which sets the program of "l'explication orphique de la Terre," of *le Livre*. The original move to "Hérodiade" could have turned out quite differently in another artist. That is, the deserting of emphatic realities, the turn to a poetics of construction, of careful assembly of effect, almost *orfèvrerie* [the goldsmith's

62. Mallarmé, "Hérodiade," in *Œuvres complètes*, 1:48.

63. Mallarmé, "Hérodiade," 20.

64. Mallarmé, "Ouverture d' 'Hérodiade,'" État corrigé puis abandonné, 1866–1898, 138.

65. Mallarmé, "Ouverture d' 'Hérodiade,'" État corrigé puis abandonné, 1866–1898, 137.

art], could have led to an abandonment altogether of the idea that there is some deep meaning out there to capture. It could have led to a new basis for a practice with affinities to that of Gautier and Parnassus, a construction of poems as beautiful objects.

It is perhaps, in fact, this propensity for constructivism to pose the ontological question of whether there is anything there, which helped to bring on the crisis which coincides with the writing of the first "Hérodiade" (letter to Cazalis announcing that he's started, with the device "Peindre non la chose," October 1864).[66]

So we can imagine "Hérodiade" playing a role in a different evolution. But even so, there are problems with this. Poetry is here in a kind of dialectic with violence and temptation which is quite unsettling. Indeed, it seems to require violence to affirm itself ("la décollation de Saint Jean" [the beheading of Saint John]). In fact, part of the "Hérodiade" complex is "Le cantique de Saint Jean," the event seen from St. John's side as it were. And here we have the kind of unity between death and elevation that the mature position calls for. Another route to the glaciers, even beyond:

> Là-haut où la froidure
> Éternelle n'endure
> Que vous le surpassiez
> Tous ô glaciers.[67]

> [Up there where the eternal
> cold can't endure
> that you surpass it
> all of you glaciers].

66. Mallarmé, Lettres à Henri Cazalis, 30 octobre 1864, 13 juillet 1866, 14 mai 1867, in *Œuvres complètes*, 1:663, 701, 713; Mallarmé, "Lettre à Henri Cazalis, mars 1866," in *Propos sur la poésie*, 66. His letters to Cazalis in this period give an idea of what he went through: "J'ai rencontré deux abîmes" [I've come across two abysses], March 1866; "purs glaciers de l'Esthétique" [pure glaciers of the Aesthetic], July 1866; "Je viens de passer une année effrayante" [I have just passed a frightening year], May 1867; ("Hérodiade" occupied these three winters).

67. Stéphane Mallarmé, "Les Noces d'Hérodiade: Cantique de Saint Jean," in *Œuvres complètes*, 1:148.

But, of course, this is the version he ultimately published. And, for what it's worth, it seems that Hérodiade herself is portrayed as incapable of holding her position, in the last lines. Though that is contested. But this by itself is not a problem. It is possible for a failed attempt at adequate expression to offer an allegory for the poet, as we shall see in a minute with "the Faun."

The move to the constructed effect, which was a definitive one for Mallarmé, and is central to his poetics in the mature position, went along with blockage, uncertainty, doubt, which plagued him for the rest of his life. When he speaks in the autobiography of the sacrifices he made—like burning the furniture in the stove—there was something behind it. He could have been a great and prolific lyric poet in his first Azure-windows-exile mode. "Qu'est une immortalité relative, et se passant souvent dans l'esprit d'imbéciles, à côté de la joie de contempler l'Éternité, et d'en jouir, vivant, en soi?" [What is relative immortality, and what often happens in the minds of fools, next to the joy of contemplating Eternity, and enjoying it, alive, in oneself?][68]

And whenever he relaxed and did something else than his most exigent attempts at articulation, he still had great ease (occasional pieces). But he was often dried up and paralyzed by the demands of his program.

I mention this because, perhaps strangely, he gives Hérodiade a speech reflecting this. "O miroir!" Here is a kind of glaciation which isn't one of power, but of confusion and incapacity, even despair. The mirror, as against the window; not giving out on anything, but rather reflecting, reflexive, intensifying the self. ("J'ai besoin, . . . , de me regarder dans cette glace pour penser, et que si elle n'était pas devant la table où je t'écris cette lettre, je redeviendrais le Néant" [I need, . . . , to look at myself in this mirror to think, and (I fear) that if it weren't in front of the table where I'm writing you this letter, I'd become Nothingness again].)[69]

Not the statement of a self-sufficient, happy, self-affirming constructor, but rather of one seeking a meaning he's never quite sure he has found; and may even doubt altogether in moments of severe questioning. "Mais

68. Mallarmé, "Lettre à Théodore Aubanel. 28 juillet 1866," 204.
69. Mallarmé, "Lettre à Henri Cazalis. 14 mai 1867," 1:713.

horreur! des soirs, dans ta sévère fontaine, / J'ai de mon rêve épars connu la nudité!" [But horror! of evenings, in your severe fountain, / I have known the nakedness of my scattered dream!][70]

"Hérodiade" is an allegory of poetry, and of the poet, at the moment where the writer himself is undergoing a metamorphosis, which carries him from being the author of "Les Fenêtres" to the visionary of the creative power of Non-Being, from the aspiration to rise to "le ciel antérieur où fleurit la Beauté" [the original sky where beauty blossoms], to the Author of the Book of the noncontingent events.[71]

But so is the Faun allegorical, in a different way. Mallarmé works *pari passu* on the Faun in these years, "Hérodiade" in the winter, the Faun in the summer. As is fitting, since Hérodiade is the dweller in glaciers; while the Faun is the seat of sexual desire par excellence.

But as well as allegory, "the Faun" represents another possibility: a failed attempt can point beyond itself to what it doesn't quite encapsulate.

"The Faun" allows us to explore desire and art, but in a different way. Or ways. In part, because the Faun himself is an artist, and he exhibits something of what this involves. First, his playing is a consolation and sublimation of frustrated desire. It comes in the place of desire which can't be fulfilled. "Évanouir du songe ordinaire de dos / Ou de flanc pur suivis avec mes regards clos, / Une sonore, vaine et monotone ligne" [Make Faint from the ordinary dream of my back / Or pure flank followed with my closed eyes, / A sound, vain and monotonous line].[72]

Then looking through the grape skins, he creates his own roseate reality. (But this is also a window, and perhaps it's not that unreal.) But finally, his failure in the entanglement with the nymphs reveals something—not to the Faun, now, but to us. Something not entirely clear and ambiguous perhaps. The crux of his error, more than error perhaps, his sin, blasphemy, was the separation of the two nymphs. That's what blew it. Perhaps we can see this as an error, the error of a Hamlet figure who

---

70. Mallarmé, "Hérodiade," 21.

71. Mallarmé, "Fenêtres," 10.

72. Stéphane Mallarmé, "L'Après-midi d'vn favne," in *Œuvres complètes*, 1:25.

couldn't decide; that is, just opt for one and let the other go. And in this case, we have a figure emblematic of the artist, in Mallarmé's view.

Or else we have a "crime" "d'avoir . . . divisé la touffe échevelée / De baisers que les dieux gardaient si bien mêlée" [to have . . . divided the disheveled tuft / Of kisses that the gods kept so well mingled].[73]

Sexual love is the crime of destroying, or rather obscuring and losing the connections between things, which it is the duty of poetry to make evident again. The Faun, as lover-poet, seeking to realize together both sides of his nature, cannot but fail. Moreover, his doomed attempt itself has no real substance, and easily falls into uncertainty, confused with a dream.

But as the Faun falls asleep, drowsy and bemused, promising in his unwisdom to try again, we catch a glimpse of this truth; just a glimpse, as one can feel on a hot summer's day in the forest, under the bright sun, that a revelation is about to break.

IV

I have looked at three "indirect routes," potential ways to bring us closer to Mallarmé's poetic program: paintings of exile (which he abandons in his mature position), allegories of the poet / poetry, and failed attempts, which can somehow point beyond themselves. Besides the ones I've mentioned here, "Igitur" seems to be such an allegory, and "Un Coup de dés," like "the Faun," perhaps combines the two latter categories.

There is one other relatively indirect route which I want to deal with, prior to looking at the nearest thing to a direct realization of his theory in his writing which Mallarmé seems to have tried. This is an attempt not to allegorize but to describe two poets, their experience, what they achieved. Their achievement is read through his theory. In a sense, this should perhaps not be called "indirect." But I see an important reason to class it with the others I've just dealt with. If Mallarmé's central aim is "transposition," then these descriptive poems still don't realize it. They

73. Mallarmé, "L'Après-midi d'vn favne," 25.

attempt to give a sense of what it is like, but they don't constitute actual examples of it.

I want to look at two poems in this category. Two "homages" to dead poets: "Toast Funèbre" to Gautier, and "Le Tombeau d'Edgar Poe."

TOAST FUNÈBRE

O de notre bonheur, toi, le fatal emblème!

Salut de la démence et libation blême,
Ne crois pas qu'au magique espoir du corridor
J'offre ma coupe vide où souffre un monstre d'or!
Ton apparition ne va pas me suffire:
Car je t'ai mis, moi-même, en un lieu de porphyre.
Le rite est pour les mains d'éteindre le flambeau
Contre le fer épais des portes du tombeau:
Et l'on ignore mal, élu pour notre fête
Très-simple de chanter l'absence du poëte,
Que ce beau monument l'enferme tout entier:
Si ce n'est que la gloire ardente du métier,
Jusqu'à l'heure commune et vile de la cendre,
Par le carreau qu'allume un soir fier d'y descendre,
Retourne vers les feux du pur soleil mortel!

Magnifique, total et solitaire, tel
Tremble de s'exhaler le faux orgueil des hommes.
Cette foule hagarde! elle annonce: Nous sommes
La triste opacité de nos spectres futurs.
Mais le blason des deuils épars sur de vains murs,
J'ai méprisé l'horreur lucide d'une larme,
Quand, sourd même à mon vers sacré qui ne l'alarme,
Quelqu'un de ces passants, fier, aveugle et muet,
Hôte de son linceul vague, se transmuait
En le vierge héros de l'attente posthume.

Vaste gouffre apporté dans l'amas de la brume
Par l'irascible vent des mots qu'il n'a pas dits,
Le néant à cet Homme aboli de jadis:
"Souvenir d'horizons, qu'est-ce, ô toi, que la Terre?"
Hurle ce songe; et, voix dont la clarté s'altère,
L'espace a pour jouet le cri: "Je ne sais pas!"

Le Maître, par un œil profond, a, sur ses pas,
Apaisé de l'éden l'inquiète merveille
Dont le frisson final, dans sa voix seule, éveille,
Pour la Rose et le Lys, le mystère d'un nom.
Est-il de ce destin rien qui demeure, non?
O vous tous! oubliez une croyance sombre.
Le splendide génie éternel n'a pas d'ombre.
Moi, de votre désir soucieux, je veux voir,
A qui s'évanouit, hier, dans le devoir,
Idéal que nous font les jardins de cet astre,
Survivre pour l'honneur du tranquille désastre
Une agitation solennelle par l'air
De paroles, pourpre ivre et grand calice clair,
Que, pluie et diamant, le regard diaphane
Resté là sur ces fleurs dont nulle ne se fane,
Isole parmi l'heure et le rayon du jour!

C'est de nos vrais bosquets déjà tout le séjour,
Où le poëte pur a pour geste humble et large
De l'interdire au rêve, ennemi de sa charge:
Afin que le matin de son repos altier,
Quand la mort ancienne est comme pour Gautier
De n'ouvrir pas les yeux sacrés et de se taire,
Surgisse, de l'allée ornement tributaire,
Le sépulcre solide où gît tout ce qui nuit,
Et l'avare silence et la massive nuit.[74]

74. Stéphane Mallarmé, "Toast funèbre," in *Œuvres complètes*, 1:27.

[FUNERARY TOAST

You fatal emblem of our happiness!

A toast of lunacy, a wan libation,
not to the passage's magic aspiration
I raise my void cup bearing a gold monster in distress!
Your apparition is not enough for me:
I myself set you in the porphyry.
The rite requires that hands should quench the torch
against the strong iron gates at the tomb's porch:
chosen for our feast simply to declare
the poet's absence, we must be aware
that this fair monument holds all of him.
Unless the bright fame of what he has done,
until the ashes' hour so common and so grim,
through glass lit by a dusk proud to fall there
returns toward the fires of the pure mortal sun!

Sublime, total and solitary, then
he fears to breathe out the false pride of men.
"We are", declare these haggard teeming hosts,
"the sad opaque forms of our future ghosts".
But with blazons of woe strewn across each vain wall
I scorn the lucid horror of a tear,
when, proud, mute, blind, the guest of his vague graveyard shawl,
one of those passers-by, failing to stir or hear
even my sacred verse, goes through a transformation
into the virgin hero of posthumous expectation.
That dream the void, a massive chasm hurled
by the fierce wind of words he did not say
into the mist, howls at this Man dead long ago:
"Recalled horizons, speak, what is the World?"
and space, a voice whose clarity fades away,
toys with this cry: "I do not know!"

The Master's keen eye, as he went, brought ease
to Eden's restless wonder, whose last throes
in his unique voice wake the mysteries
of a name for the Lily and the Rose.
Is none of this destiny enduring? none?
Forget so dark a credo, everyone.
Radiant eternal genius leaves no shade.
Mindful of your desires, I wish to see
in our task, the ideal that our star's parks have laid
upon us, for this man who vanished recently,
a solemn stir of words stay alive in the air
in honour of the calm catastrophe—
a huge clear bloom, a purple ecstasy,
which his diaphanous gaze remaining there,
rain and diamond, on these flowers that never fade away,
isolates in the hour and radiance of day!

Already within these true groves we stay,
where the true poet's broad and humble gesture must
keep them from dreams, those enemies of his trust:
so when he rests in pride at break of day,
when ancient death is as for Gautier
not to speak nor to open his consecrated eyes,
an ornamental tribute of the path may rise,
the solid tomb bedding all forms of blight,
and grudging silence and the massive night.][75]

This was his homage to Gautier: it states clearly his mature position, against the Christian and traditional ideas of an afterlife. The first two sections bring this home. There is great play with sunset light on the windowpanes at the end of the first section. The second contains some very controverted matter. But the message of nonsurvival is very clear "ce beau monument l'enferme tout entier" [this fair monument holds all of him].

---

75. Stéphane Mallarmé, "Funerary Toast," in *Collected Poems*, 49–51.

In the third section, we define the poet's achievement: "de l'éden l'inquiète merveille" [to Eden's restless wonder]—things trembling on the brink of meaning, they deeply disturb us, they seem to demand to be articulated. The poet appeases this; through his voice, giving these (emphatic) realities a name. Their name, reminiscence of the original names?

Now this is what remains. It won't die, as the person did. What survives of the one who did the duty which "les jardins de cet astre" [our star's parks] lay on us is precisely his speech, "une agitation solennelle par l'air / De paroles" [a solemn stir of words stay alive in the air]; like a calice, holding, presenting (this word goes way back; see "Fleurs," verse 3). But this *parole* [word] is also a regard (an act of observing). What a poet needs is sight and then speech to articulate it. By keeping the latter, we regain and hold on to the former. This "diaphanous" look sees through the particular, to the Idea; these flowers don't fade; they are in a sense separated from the real changeable gardens (see "lucide contour" of "Prose").

This is the *séjour* of our real *bosquets;* this must be *interdit au rêve.* Strange and wonderful ending. The poet is sight and speech. Death means that both of these go: "De n'ouvrir pas les yeux sacrés et de se taire" [Not to speak nor to open his consecrated eyes]. But we can keep both of these going. The complement of this survival of his poetry in us is that all of the forgetfulness, all of the blinding and silencing of Gautier, is relegated to the tomb.

The tomb "l'enferme tout entier," in a sense; the whole mortal being. There is no exception for a shade or whatever. But the counterpart is that all the mortality, his now blindness and silence, is contained in the tomb, and doesn't spill out into our world, eroding his speech and vision among us. So in the "sépulcre solide" [solid tomb] there must lie "tout ce qui nuit, / Et l'avare silence et la massive nuit" [all forms of blight, / and grudging silence and the massive night].

Note that survival is not reputation, glory, as in the ancient notion; but the work as living *parole* / vision. This is his eternity. Because it lasts, but also because it is from the standpoint of eternity. Death consummates his unity with eternity, because he is now nothing but this standpoint from Eternity.

(I must pause here to note the extraordinary generosity of Mallarmé. Of course, Gautier agreed with him in his rejection of Christianity, but his poetic aspirations and practice were very different; and Mallarmé frequently pointed this out. Nevertheless he treated his contemporary poets not as rivals but as colleagues in the same enterprise.)

LE TOMBEAU D'EDGAR POE

Tel qu'en Lui-même enfin l'éternité le change,
Le Poëte suscite avec un glaive nu
Son siècle épouvanté de n'avoir pas connu
Que la mort triomphait dans cette voix étrange!

Eux, comme un vil sursaut d'hydre oyant jadis l'ange
Donner un sens plus pur aux mots de la tribu
Proclamèrent très haut le sortilège bu
Dans le flot sans honneur de quelque noir mélange.

Du sol et de la nue hostiles, ô grief!
Si notre idée avec ne sculpte un bas-relief
Dont la tombe de Poe éblouissante s'orne

Calme bloc ici-bas chu d'un désastre obscur
Que ce granit du moins montre à jamais sa borne
Aux noirs vols du Blasphème épars dans le futur.[76]

[THE TOMB OF EDGAR ALLAN POE

Changed to Himself at last by eternity,
with a bare sword the Poet has bestirred
his age terrified that it failed to see
how death was glorying in that strange word.

76. Stéphane Mallarmé, "Le Tombeau d'Edgar Poe," in *Œuvres complètes*, 1:38.

The spell was drunk, so they proclaimed aloud
(as vile freaks writhe when seraphim bestow
purer sense on the phrases of the crowd),
in some black brew's dishonourable flow.

If our idea can carve no bas-relief
from hostile clod and cloud, O struggling grief,
for the adornment of Poe's dazzling tomb,

at least this block dropped by an occult doom,
this calm granite, may limit all the glum
Blasphemy-flights dispersed in days to come.][77]

Here again he invokes something of the power of monuments. But in another way; somehow summing up the force of Poe's work with the image of an aerolith: "désastre" [disaster] suggests "astre" [star].

"Tel qu'en Lui-même l'éternité le change" [Changed to Himself at last by eternity]. Poe too is now just this voice from eternity. It changes him, because there is no longer the particular Poe, but it is "en Lui-même," because this is essential, intimate to Poe, his voice / vision. And this voice had as aim and effect to "donner un sens plus pur aux mots de la tribu" [bestow / purer sense on the phrases of the crowd]. But his terrified century was incapable of recognizing that Death (the Non-Being which inhabits the human) triumphed in this strange voice.

Then we can cite a poem which seems to describe the poet's own experience:

PROSE
(POUR DES ESSEINTES)

Hyperbole! de ma mémoire
Triomphalement ne sais-tu
Te lever, aujourd'hui grimoire
Dans un livre de fer vêtu:

77. Stéphane Mallarmé, "The Tomb of Edgar Allan Poe," in *Collected Poems*, 71.

Car j'installe, par la science,
L'hymne des cœurs spirituels
En l'Œuvre de ma patience,
Atlas, herbiers et rituels.

Nous promenions notre visage
(Nous fûmes deux, je le maintiens)
Sur maints charmes de paysage,
O sœur, y comparant les tiens.

L'ère d'autorité se trouble
Lorsque, sans nul motif, on dit
De ce midi que notre double
Inconscience approfondit

Que, sol des cent iris, son site,
Ils savent s'il a bien été,
Ne porte pas de nom que cite
L'or de la trompette d'Été.

Oui, dans une île que l'air charge
De vue et non de visions
Toute fleur s'étalait plus large
Sans que nous en devisions.

Telles, immenses, que chacune
Ordinairement se para
D'un lucide contour, lacune
Qui des jardins la sépara.

Gloire du long désir, Idées
Tout en moi s'exaltait de voir
La famille des iridées
Surgir à ce nouveau devoir,

Mais cette sœur sensée et tendre
Ne porta son regard plus loin
Que sourire et, comme à l'entendre
J'occupe mon antique soin.

Oh! sache l'Esprit de litige,
A cette heure où nous nous taisons,
Que de lis multiples la tige
Grandissait trop pour nos raisons

Et non comme pleure la rive,
Quand son jeu monotone ment
A vouloir que l'ampleur arrive
Parmi mon jeune étonnement

D'ouïr tout le ciel et la carte
Sans fin attestés sur mes pas,
Par le flot même qui s'écarte,
Que ce pays n'exista pas.

L'enfant abdique son extase
Et docte déjà par chemins
Elle dit le mot: Anastase!
Né pour d'éternels parchemins,

Avant qu'un sépulcre ne rie
Sous aucun climat, son aïeul,
De porter ce nom: Pulchérie!
Caché par le trop grand glaïeul.[78]

78. Stéphane Mallarmé, "Prose (Pour des Esseintes)," in *Œuvres complètes*, 1:28.

[PROSE
(FOR DES ESSEINTES)

Hyperbole! can you not rise
from my memory triumph-crowned,
today a magic scrawl which lies
in a book that is iron-bound:

for by my science I instil
the hymn of spiritual hearts
in the work of my patient will,
atlases, herbals, sacred arts.

Sister, we strolled and set our faces
(we were two, so my mind declares)
toward various scenic places,
comparing your own charms with theirs.

The reign of confidence grows troubled
when, for no reason, it is stated
of this noon region, which our doubled
unconsciousness has penetrated,

that its site, soil of hundredfold
irises (was it real? how well
they know) bears no name that the gold
trumpet of Summertime can tell.

Yes, in an isle the air had charged
not with mere visions but with sight
every flower spread out enlarged
at no word that we could recite.

And so immense they were, that each
was usually garlanded
with a clear contour, and this breach
parted it from the garden bed.

Ideas, glory of long desire,
all within me rejoiced to see
the irid family aspire
to this new responsibility,

but Sister, a wise comforter,
carried her glance no further than
a smile and, as if heeding her,
I labour on my ancient plan.

Let the litigious Spirit know,
as we are silent at this season,
the manifold lilies' stem would grow
to a size far beyond our reason

not as the shore in drearisome
sport weeps when it is fraudulent,
claiming abundance should have come
in my initial wonderment

hearing the heavens and map that gave
endless evidence close at hand,
by the very receding wave,
that there was never such a land.

The child, already dexterous
in the ways, sheds her ecstasy

and utters "Anastasius!"
born for scrolls of eternity

before a sepulchre chuckles "Ha!"
beneath its forebear any sky
to bear the name "Pulcheria!"
veiled by too tall gladioli.][79]

This, I believe, plainly refers to an original vision—although this conclusion is contested. There was a moment or moments when he seemed to see the meaning, the connection, behind these emphatic realities. It seemed to be there in them, larger than life.

The first two quatrains state again the ambition to create through "science" the "grimoire" [spell book], the volume which will encompass all reality. But first, this reality would need to be patiently captured in the craft of poetry. The reference to "science" reflects Mallarmé's belief that to write this volume he had to draw on all the wisdom of the ages. He needed to study history and mythology. And this because there was some wisdom there, even if not properly understood. So he studied and wrote *Les Dieux antiques.* But this study was also important, because the "grimoire" has in a sense to sum up not just what the poet has identified, but what everybody has seen. The impersonal point of view summates all personal experience.

But as Paul Bénichou points out, "hyperbole" refers to a description which is in excess of the reality described, whereas here it indicates the experience which is somehow an excessive reality. He senses in this a recognition that capturing this in a "grimoire," or in "Atlas, herbiers, rituels" [atlases, herbaria, rituals], must involve some recognition of a loss in relation to the original lived reality.[80]

Starting with the third quatrain, we have an account, I would claim, of the poet's own experience: "Nous fûmes deux, je le maintiens" [We were two, so my mind declares]. There is inevitably controversy about what this parenthetical remark means. I opt for it meaning his Muse, his

79. Stéphane Mallarmé, "Prose (for des Esseintes)," in *Collected Poems,* 53–55.
80. Paul Bénichou, *Selon Mallarmé* (Paris: Gallimard, 1995), 219–220.

alter ego, restraining him; but this function was probably embodied in a real person.

I skip the detail of stanzas 4–5; obviously, they refer to the unavoidable controversy which can be raised about the experience: that it is purely subjective. And the same issue is raised in stanzas 10–12, which terminate with the lapidary phrase "que ce pays n'exista pas" [that there was never such a land].

The experience itself is captured in the three stanzas of the vision:

> Oui, dans une île que l'air charge
> De vue et non de visions
> Toute fleur s'étalait plus large
> Sans que nous en devisions,

> [Yes, in an isle the air had charged
> not with mere visions but with sight
> every flower spread out enlarged
> at no word that we could recite.]

The second line is telling us that what I (or perhaps we) saw, in the charged atmosphere of the island, came across as really there, not a purely subjective vision. The flowers were larger than life, and we didn't talk each other into this (line 4). Moreover, they stood out from their surroundings, surrounded by a "lucide contour, lacune / Qui des jardins la sépara" [clear contour, and this breach / parted it from the garden bed]. In this, the flowers were answering to a "duty":

> Gloire du long désir, Idées
> Tout en moi s'exaltait de voir
> La famille des iridées
> Surgir à ce nouveau devoir.

> [Ideas, glory of long desire,
> all within me rejoiced to see
> the irid family aspire
> to this new responsibility.]

Then my "sœur sensée et tendre" [Sister, a wise comforter], my muse and companion, seems to restrain me. She smiles, and calls me back to "mon antique soin" [my ancient plan]. This I take to mean my task of transposition, to which the poet has to return. It isn't enough to have had this experience. There must be a slow and laborious forming of the language you need. The vision has to be captured in adequate language, which has to be a language which takes us beyond the brute reality there. It has to be a language of dusk, or midnight, not noon: "De ce midi que notre double / Inconscience approfondit" [Of this noon region, which our doubled / unconsciousness has penetrated].

Then the "Esprit de litige" [litigious Spirit] enters. The issue is that "nous nous taisons" [now that we are silent], and have emerged from the trance, it should be clear that we haven't in fact grasped what we claim to have seen. One explanation is that it went way beyond our reason; so it takes time. The other is that the whole thing was a mirage: "Que ce pays n'exista pas" [That there was never such a land].

Then the last two verses are (to me) very obscure. Perhaps my wise muse or feminine principle is telling me to get on with putting this experience into the *parchemins:* that is, articulating it in a poem, which should last eternally. But to do this, she had to "abdicate from her own experience of ecstasy," and tell me: "Anastase," that is, Rise up! But why did the poet use these two strange names? Byzantine? Des Esseintes? This has all the signs of an in-joke.

If this hunch is right, then the last verse means that otherwise the grave will take me down without this being said. It will be lost. Beauty will still remain hidden in the larger-than-life flower, which hasn't been articulated. "Sous aucun climat, son aïeul" [Under a climate, his ancestor] remains still really enigmatic.

But what still is to be retained from this is that: he seems to have had a vision. The content is similar to the poem on Gautier, who left behind him

> Une agitation solennelle par l'air
> De paroles, pourpre ivre et grand calice clair.
> Que, pluie et diamant, le regard diaphane

Resté là sur ces fleurs dont nulle ne se fane,
Isole parmi l'heure et le rayon du jour![81]

[the calm catastrophe—
a huge clear bloom, a purple ecstasy,
which his diaphanous gaze remaining there,
rain and diamond, on these flowers that never fade away,
isolates in the hour and radiance of day!][82]

Because we are all conscious of the "materialist," or at least anti-transcendent, view of Mallarmé, it is tempting to resist the interpretation that he took this experience seriously. But it seems more plausible to hold that he didn't himself take the debunking standpoint of "la rive" [the riverbank]: there was a reality here, but one that needed to be captured in a poetry of transposition. It needed this, not just to be handed on, but even to be properly possessed by the seer, agreeing with the Gautier poem.

(The description of his experience in "Prose" resembles the moments of illumination which I described in the coda on Rilke, what Jephcott called "privileged" moments. And the same can be said for "le regard diaphane" [diaphanous gaze] of the Gautier poem: which "isole [le grand calice clair] parmi l'heure et le rayon du jour" [isolates [the grand bright chalice] between the hour and the radiance of the day]. This seems similar to the lines of "Prose": "Chacune / Ordinairement se para / D'un lucide contour, lacunae / Qui des jardins la sépara" [each / was usually garlanded / with a clear contour, and this breach / parted it from the garden bed].

But these experiences are often understood in terms of the eruption of something higher. Or else, understood in the perspective of lived time, this place-time is felt too full, as overflowing, as marking the eruption of some higher time, even of eternity. So in the first movement of Eliot's "Burnt Norton," which owes a debt to Mallarmé, "the roses / had the look

81. Mallarmé, "Toast funèbre," 27.
82. Mallarmé, "Funerary Toast," lines 49–51.

of flowers that are looked at."[83] The main theme of this, Eliot's first quartet, is the relation of time and eternity. This is one of the two experiences of a "higher time," which I distinguished in Chapter 11, "After Baudelaire," which can be seen as an intimation of "eternity," in some sense. The other is a sense of the quasi-simultaneity of an extended moment (see, for example, Havel's quote in Chapter 11). This also figures in Mallarmé's work, as we shall see later.)

But before going on to look at the poems which seem to realize a "transposition," there is one more poem which casts some indirect light on his work. This is the sonnet about his "vieux Rêve." Clearly the "Rêve" here is his earlier belief in God, or later a religion of Beauty as the Highest. And the first quatrain recounts the crushing of this early dream.

> Quand l'ombre menaça de la fatale loi
> Tel vieux Rêve, désir et mal de mes vertèbres,
> Affligé de périr sous les plafonds funèbres
> Il a ployé son aile indubitable en moi.

> Luxe, ô salle d'ébène où, pour séduire un roi
> Se tordent dans leur mort des guirlandes célèbres,
> Vous n'êtes qu'un orgueil menti par les ténèbres
> Aux yeux du solitaire ébloui de sa foi.

> Oui, je sais qu'au lointain de cette nuit, la Terre
> Jette d'un grand éclat l'insolite mystère,
> Sous les siècles hideux qui l'obscurcissent moins.

> L'espace à soi pareil qu'il s'accroisse ou se nie
> Roule dans cet ennui des feux vils pour témoins
> Que s'est d'un astre en fête allumé le génie.[84]

83. T. S. Eliot, "Burnt Norton," in *The Poems of T. S. Eliot*, ed. Christopher Ricks and Jim McCue (Baltimore: Johns Hopkins University Press, 2015), 1:179.

84. Stéphane Mallarmé, "Sonnet (Quand l'ombre menaça)," in *Œuvres complètes*, 1:36.

[When the shade threatened with the fatal decree
that old Dream, my bones' craving and their blight,
pained to die under the funereal height
it bowed its doubt-less plumage deep in me.

Splendour—ebony hall where, to allure
a king, illustrious wreaths writhe in their doom—
you are merely a pride lied by the gloom
to the faith-dazzled solitary viewer.

Yes, Earth has cast into this night afar
the startling mystery of sheer dazzlingness
beneath dread aeons darkening it less.

Space, its own peer, whether it fail or grow
rolls in this tedium trivial fires to show
the genius kindled by a festive star.][85]

The first two lines of the second quatrain I take to be describing the immediate fallback position of a poet who has lost this early faith (this is the *vieux Rêve*): celebrate imposing and beautiful realities in the courts of the powerful through a fine and elevating description of them—in short, something like the practice of Gautier and Parnassus. But the next two lines record the end of the illusion; and the second quatrain as a whole is devastating. The greatness here is illusory, shown to be so by the darkness that in fact surrounds it: that is, the blindness to the true vocation of poetry. The illusion is supported by a false pride (*orgueil*) which is dazzling to its solitary devotees.

I take it that the two tercets declare what follows from the renunciation of this false pride: the light of a new poetic practice breaks through the darkness of limitless space-time, for "s'est d'un astre en fête allumé le génie" [the genius kindled by a festive star].

85. Stéphane Mallarmé, "Sonnet (When the shade threatened)," in *Collected Poems*, 67.

V

But now let's try the direct route. Let's look at the poems which really seem to try some kind of direct realization of the theory in their conception. That is, they are loci of transposition in Mallarmé's sense. In some kind of "presque disparition vibratoire" [vibratory near disappearance], something comes through, even if not the whole Orphic explanation.[86]

Mallarmé talks of transposition in terms of the "disparition" of the object. But a fuller account of the program, as I mentioned above, would include the "disappearance" of the subject. Not in the sense of the recent trend of "poststructuralism" which reached its height a decade or two ago. But in the sense that the poet undergoes a kind of death, and returns as impersonal, as an "aptitude qu'a l'univers spirituel" [aptitude of the spiritual universe].

And indeed, in some of his poetry, there is a way of negating the objects which brings about a negation of the subject. There is an account of the demise or absence or uncertainty of objects, in particular but not only emphatic ones, which carries us into a region of death, where the finite particular subject is no longer—but where something like vision subsists.

One of the most important of these themes—the negation of an emphatic reality leading us into the region of death—involves the sun. Sunsets are important for Mallarmé. Of course, the sunset, and not just the sun, has always figured as an emphatic reality. The splendor of the sight, the poignancy of the sun's decline, the foreboding—or anticipation—of the night, the fear of the sun's nonreturn, the nostalgia for the day which is ending, the sense of passing time and life—all this and more is there in the sunset. Mallarmé was also moved by the valetudinarian, dying moment, full of sadness, beauty, and memory. "Ainsi, dans l'année, ma saison favorite, ce sont les derniers jours alanguis de l'été, qui précèdent immédiatement l'automne et, dans la journée, l'heure où je me promène est quand le soleil se repose avant de s'évanouir, avec des rayons de cuivre jaune sur les murs gris et de cuivre rouge sur les carreaux" [Thus, in the

86. Mallarmé, "Crise de vers," 209.

year, my favorite season is the last languid days of summer, which immediately precede autumn, and, in the daytime, the time when I walk is when the sun is resting before fading, with rays of yellow copper on the gray walls and red copper on the tiles].[87]

Also, now is the time that the sun itself can at last be looked upon, as it cannot be when at its zenith. In a sense, this is an emblem of human experience, whose full meaning we often miss, or cannot encompass, in the heat of the moment, but only when "recollected in tranquility." This reflection, very commonly felt (it was also central to Proust's recovery of time), seems to confirm Mallarmé's crucial tenet, that emphatic realities, taken head on as it were, obstruct our grasp of their meaning; they have to be taken *de biais* [sideways], coming or going, at dawn or dusk, not in the fullness of here, or the great midday. ("De ce midi que notre double / Inconscience approfondit" [Of this noon region, which our doubled / unconsciousness has penetrated].)

Mallarmé enriches further this rich set of resonances, with the idea of death, sacrifice, fire, and blood. We see this in "Ouverture": "Crime! bûcher! aurore ancienne! supplice!" [Crime! Funeral pyre! Ancient dawn! Torture!].[88] And it was undoubtedly further enriched by his reading in ancient mythology, as we can see in *Les Dieux antiques*.[89] The sunset as a kind of battle (for example, the struggle with the clouds in *Les Dieux antiques*), a scene of heroism, thus a kind of triumph, even in defeat— because the sun offers a display of its most stunning beauty just at this moment of passing; like the procession of a royal burial. In particular, as the defeat, the going under of the clear blue sky, Mallarmé's early most emphatic reality, the sunset captures his move away from this to a new understanding of the absolute as *Néant* [Nothing].

(By a parity of symbolic reasoning, dawn means the return of *l'Azur*: and the sense of despair connected to the fact that all the work of the night, all the "digging," has left him still unprepared, not yet in possession of the language of transposition, confronted with unmediated azure.)

87. Stéphane Mallarmé, "Plainte d'automne," in *Œuvres complètes*, 2:84.

88. Mallarmé, "Ouverture d' 'Hérodiade,'" État corrigé puis abandonné, 1866–1898, 138.

89. Stéphane Mallarmé, *Les Dieux antiques*, in *Œuvres complètes*, 2:1446–1567.

In "Las de l'amer repos . . ."; "Que dire à cette Aurore, ô Rêves . . . ?"; and
also "Une dentelle s'abolit . . .".

And so Mallarmé can take the sunset as a path of negation, a triumphal way into darkness, the eclipse of all emphatic realities, and hence a
kind of darkness of meaning for the subject who yearns for this meaning,
a kind of death, therefore, of this yearning, particular subject.

This is the "death." What is the "resurrection"? Or perhaps, a better
image: Wwhen this subject and his emphatic reality disappears, does
some new vision (in both senses, verbal and substantive, both a power
of seeing and things seen) emerge? Or, changing the modality, in the
stillness is something nevertheless heard? This is the wager, that from
the "presque disparition vibratoire" will emerge something, "la notion
pure."

In a sense, the challenge of this poetry is that it not just tell you that
this happens, but allow you to see (hear) it. And the remarkable thing
about some of these poems is that as they unfold, the reader feels how
much the issue is still in hazard, uncertain; how much the poet is still in
the way of searching, convincing himself.

Now I want to take the "Sonnet en -X," and its sister, its early 1868 version "Sonnet allégorique de lui-même."

SONNET EN -X

Ses purs ongles très haut dédiant leur onyx,
L'Angoisse ce minuit, soutient, lampadophore
Maint rêve vespéral brûlé par le Phénix
Que ne recueille pas de cinéraire amphore

Sur les crédences, au salon vide: nul ptyx,
Aboli bibelot d'inanité sonore,
(Car le Maître est allé puiser des pleurs au Styx
Avec ce seul objet dont le Néant s'honore).

Mais proche la croisée au nord vacante, un or
Agonise selon peut-être le décor
Des licornes ruant du feu contre une nixe,

Elle, défunte nue en le miroir, encor
Que, dans l'oubli fermé par le cadre, se fixe
De scintillations sitôt le septuor.[90]

[With her pure nails offering their onyx high,
lampbearer Agony tonight sustains
many a vesperal fantasy burned by
the Phœnix, which no funerary urn contains

on the empty room's credences: no ptyx,
abolished bauble, sonorous inanity
(Master has gone to draw tears from the Styx
with that one thing, the Void's sole source of vanity).

Yet near the vacant northward casement dies
a gold possibly from the decorations
of unicorns lashing a nymph with flame;

dead, naked in the looking-glass she lies
though the oblivion bounded by that frame now spans
a fixed septet of scintillations.][91]

SONNET ALLÉGORIQUE DE LUI-MÊME

La Nuit approbatrice allume les onyx
De ses ongles au pur Crime, lampadophore,
Du Soir aboli par le vespéral Phœnix
De qui la cendre n'a de cinéraire amphore.[92]

[Approving Night brightly begins to burn
her onyx nails at pure lampbearing Crime

---

90. Stéphane Mallarmé, "[Sonnet en X]," in *Collected Poems,* 68–70.

91. Stéphane Mallarmé, "[-X Sonnet]," in *Collected Poems,* 69–71.

92. Stéphane Mallarmé, "Sonnet allégorique de lui-même," in *Œuvres complètes,* 1:131.

of Dusk abolished by the vesper-time
Phoenix whose ashes have no funerary urn.][93]

These are, at least in origin, sunset poems. The allegorical one talks in the first quatrain about the "pur Crime . . . Du Soir aboli par le vespéral Phœnix" [pure Crime . . . Of evening abolished by the vesperal Phœnix]. This recurs in the "Sonnet en -X" as "Maint rêve vespéral brûlé par le Phénix" [Many vesperal dreams burnt by the Phoenix].

Perhaps the reference to a crime in the first one needs some explaining: it is certainly a poem of going into night, even though it now starts at midnight, because there is a kind of handing over of light, becoming ever weaker. But why "crime"?

We are thinking of an allegorical night, lifting its arms to the setting sun, with its nails reflecting the light. "Le Crime du soir" figures in tragic mode through a shedding of blood, the blazing red which often accompanies the sun at this moment.[94] Anguish is "lampadophore," [lamp-bearing], then there is "un or qui agonise" [a dying gold], then just the mirror and the Big Dipper. So there are in a sense four stages.

Imagine a room, or an apartment; first the sunset occurs (this is already over, just remembered), then anguish arising with the passing of the day with its "lamp," meaning the momentary flashing of light around the cadre of the mirror as the sunset occurs, and then darkness falls, and a constellation (the *septuor*, the "big dipper") shines through a window and is reflected in a mirror.

There is progressive loss, stages of an extinction of light. The sun has gone, leaving not even ashes in an amphora. The triumphal burial has itself disappeared without trace. And emptiness: the amphora, if it exists, is empty. The "ptyx," which could itself be an amphora—or perhaps a shell—anyway it is doubly insubstantial; it is empty and gone: "Aboli bibelot d'inanité sonore" [Abolished trinket of sonic inanity]. And this is the moment where all this disappearance carries away with it the finite subject, "le Maître" [the Master].

93. Stéphane Mallarmé, "Sonnet Allegorical of Itself," in *Collected Poems*, 252n14.
94. I owe this account to Bénichou, *Selon Mallarmé*, 138–139.

This is the moment where Anguish goes as well, with the Master, and hence the lamp it was holding continuing the sunset. In the "Sonnet en -X," the first two quatrains place us in the immediate aftermath of the sunset, still vividly remembered, and the first tercet gives us the last flashing of the light reflected in a mirror, a *glace de Venise,* a mirror surrounded by a cadre in gold, with a unicorn motif.[95] There is a flickering here, as though a transaction between frame and mirror, unicorns against the nymph of the lake. Then nothing. But in the second tercet when the constellation arises, it is reflected in the mirror.

So emptiness, darkness, absence. But nevertheless, the emergence of vision, presence. This emergence is that of a constellation in the mirror; treated in both versions not as something which was already there, but which now happens. It is the emergence which is the counterpart to all the negation.

What emerges? A sense of place, or perhaps a scene, but in each case with a temporal depth. The dwelling in which the oncoming night took place is in one sense empty, but as evoked in the poem, it also carries a memory of the negations and departures which brought this about. In the real world, what remains at midnight is an empty apartment with the Big Dipper in the window, reflected in a mirror. But what is invoked in the poem is an emptiness which is full of its past.

It is a place; and places, as against the post-Newtonian notion of "space," are identified by the things that figure in them. Human beings live and orient themselves in places. But in the objectifying language of natural science, things are identified by their coordinates in a space-time that might just as well be occupied by other objects. The constellation in the mirror defines a place. But with a difference: this place holds within it, as it were, the time of its coming about, the march of negations which occupy the quatrains and first tercet. It has a temporal dimension, and this too is not just a part of empty space-time, but embraces the process, the negations which engender it. We can speak of it as a "place-time." "Rien n'aura eu lieu que le lieu, excepté peut-être une

95. A lot of sleuthing here; but fortunately, we have the description to Cazalis (Mallarmé, "Lettre à Henri Cazalis, mars 1866," 99), and also in Stéphane Mallarmé, "Frisson d'hiver," in *Œuvres complètes,* 2:85.

constellation" [Nothing will have taken place but the place, except perhaps a constellation].[96]

Let me try to fill out a little more this novel notion of a place-time. At the end of the sonnet we are left with the image of the constellation in the window and mirror of the now-emptied apartment; emptied both of its contents and even of an observer. This image is not one of empty space, but of a definite place. But this place holds the process of its becoming within it; this process involved a series of negations, of objects and events which have disappeared—one might even say, died. It has an emptiness, but haunted by a retrospective "memory" of what was there.

This death / emptiness answers to *le Néant* which we are, which consciousness is. It takes what we experience as a series of objects and events and holds them in a kind of frozen stasis. This stasis reflects the real nature of what for the ordinary observer is an event in time; its "Notion Pure." The event in time is usually seen as contingent, but in the place-time as gathered stasis, as the negation of this contingent process, its features are essentially related to each other. "Le hasard" [chance, contingency] is overcome, which means that its constituent elements no longer hold together just contingently.

Of course, we couldn't *live* in this kind of unchanging stasis, but we can, through poetry, have an inkling of an underlying reality, which constitutes the real nature of things, "le secret orphique de la Terre." Thanks to the power of *le Néant,* which defines the real nature of consciousness, we can have this (at least momentary) access to this basic reality.

(This refers us back to the discussion in Section IV of the chapter. Seen in the perspective of lived time, these place-times have the same quality of being temporally "overfull," of holding too much, of compressing time. What relation does this kind of temporal thickness have to the experience of a moment as "overflowing," which seemed to arise from reading "Prose"? Or perhaps even to the experience of an eruption of some higher time, à la "Burnt Norton"? Referring back again to the distinction I made in Chapter 11, "After Baudelaire," between two kinds of "higher time," it seems to me that these strongly suggest the eruption of a higher time,

---

96. Stéphane Mallarmé, "Un Coup de dés n'abolira jamais l'hasard," in *Œuvres complètes*, 1:371–387.

whereas the Mallarméan place-time which overcomes "le hazard" gathers the past of its becoming into a kind of enlarged present; it realizes a kind of simultaneity of the extended moment.

This is an issue we shall have to take up later, partly in this book, but also as an object of further reflection.)

What is the background of thought which makes sense of Mallarmé's claim here (on this reading, which I admit may very well be wrong)? Human beings define their world through language. But there are different kinds, or levels, of language. There is the speech in which we define the objects which surround us, and on which we rely to produce the things we need and avoid the dangers which threaten us. This level reaches its highest point when we take up the Cartesian-Baconian stance of objectification and develop sciences which enable us to control things (what Scheler called "Leistungswissen" [a science which helps to get things done]).

Mallarmé is referring to this level when he says: "Parler n'a trait à la réalité des choses que commercialement" [Talk only has to do with the reality of things commercially].

But there is another deeper, creative level of language, to which poetry belongs. This can take us beneath the things which figure in Cartesian-Baconian space-time; through the "presque disparition vibratoire" of these objects we come to a more fundamental level, that of "la Notion pure." I am proposing to read the "Sonnet en -X" as an attempt to bring about a transfer of this kind to a deeper level, a move that Mallarmé designates "transposition."

Transposition invokes or "suggests" beyond and beneath the process which could have occurred in space-time, the fuller notion of an eventfully rich place. Can this allow us to discern the formula of a Mallarméan "transposition"? Maybe something like this: out of an emptiness, it brings about fullness; out of absence, presence; perhaps also: out of distance, proximity (thinking of "Sainte," which I'll discuss later).

Except that: as I already said above, Mallarmé is continually exploring, feeling his way; so there wasn't any final, fixed formula. The whole oeuvre was work-in-process.

In the following paragraphs I want to check this reading against certain key features of transposition which the poet himself identifies.

First (1), what we are trying to bring out is this: "Je veux me donner ce spectacle de la matière, ayant conscience d'être" [I want to give myself this spectacle of matter, conscious of being].[97] The consciousness we are trying to recover, or channel, is that of the *Néant* [Non-Being] itself. It is beyond that of the finite human subject and involves the "disparition vibratoire" of objects.

(2) This consciousness doesn't focus on objects, but on the relations between them: "Les choses existent, nous n'avons pas à les créer; nous n'avons qu'à en saisir les rapports; et ce sont les fils de ces rapports qui forment les vers et les orchestres" [Things exist, we don't have to create them; we only have to grasp their relationships; and it's the threads of these relationships that form verses and orchestras].[98] This same point is put in another way, when Mallarmé says that his goal is to negate or abolish chance (*le hazard*). "Le vers [...] niant, d'un trait souverain, le hasard demeuré au termes" [The verse [...] denying, with a sovereign stroke, the chance left in its [constituent] terms].[99] "Le hasard vaincu mot par mot" [Chance overcome word for word].[100]

How does a poem like the "Sonnet en -X" meet this requirement? It does because the temporally extended vision of place includes the particular negations which brought it into being. They are all essential to its being *this* place. There is no merely contingent connection here.

This helps answer a question which arises here: Why does he speak of a "presque disparition 'vibratoire'"? Because the negations which help constitute the time-extended space don't disappear completely but go on reverberating within it.

In fact the phenomena which are assembled in the process of making the poem don't disappear at all, but along with their negation, "la réminiscence de l'objet baigne dans une neuve atmosphère" [the reminiscence of the object is bathed in a new atmosphere].[101]

97. Mallarmé, "Lettre à Henri Cazalis, mars 1866," 66.
98. Mallarmé, "Réponses à des Enquêtes," 697.
99. Mallarmé, "Crise de vers," 204–213.
100. Mallarmé, "Le Mystère dans les Lettre," 229–234.
101. Mallarmé, "Crise de vers," 213.

In fact, (3) "le vers qui de plusieurs vocables refait un mot total, neuf, étranger à la langue et comme incantatoire, achève cet isolement de la parole: niant d'un trait souverain, le hasard demeuré aux termes malgré l'artifice de leur retrempe alternée en le sens" [the verse that remakes several vocables into a total, new word, foreign to the language and as if incantatory, completes this isolation of the word: denying with a sovereign stroke, the randomness that has remained in the terms despite the artifice of their alternating re-embedding in meaning].[102] This new "total" word figures in the deeper level of language, by which we can grasp the deeper reality. Its constituents are the ordinary surface-level terms, which recur in our ordinary speech again and again in different combinations. But the unpredictable hazard of these multiple combinations doesn't negate the invariant specificity of the combined "total" poem-word. This is indissolubly tied to the particular place-time it evokes and reveals.

As we discussed in Chapter 1, the Renaissance postulated various perfect languages, in which words evoked the realities they designated, and there was no contingent association of word and thing. Such were the languages thought to be implicit in the Kabbalah, and the supposedly perfect Adamic language, born when he followed God's invitation to name the animals. Notions of this kind go back to ancient philosophy, and Cratylus, in the Platonic dialogue of that name, proposed to explain the meanings of existing words based on their constituent sounds. But this has never worked very convincingly, and Mallarmé rejects it as true for French, or any other natural language. (But he seems to relapse partly into Cratylism in *Les Mots anglais*.)

> Les langues imparfaites en cela que plusieurs . . . la diversité, sur terre, des idiomes empêche personne de proférer les mots qui, sinon se trouveraient, par une frappe unique, elle-même matériellement la vérité. . . . La perversité conférant à *jour* et *nuit* contradictoirement, des timbres obscur ici, là clair.[103]

> [Languages imperfect from the fact that there are several of them . . . the diversity on earth prevents anyone from putting

102. Mallarmé, "Crise de vers," 213.
103. Mallarmé, "Crise de vers," 210.

forward the words which otherwise would by their single
creation materially find the truth. . . . The perversity of
conferring on "jour" and "nuit" in contradictory fashion
sounds which are here clear, there obscure.]

But the Renaissance's perfect languages didn't depend on Cratylus-type
theories, and nor does Mallarmé suggest one for the deeper-level language which poetry can provide. Rather it is clear that the "total" words
of poetry each evoke only one time-extended place.

Each successful poem like the "Sonnet en -X" gives a partial glimpse
into the underlying reality. One can extrapolate from this and imagine a
whole book, which would reveal the whole of it. This would amount
to the "explication orphique de la Terre" [the Orphic explanation of
the Earth].

But this would be a purely notional goal, to be perhaps approached
but never fully attained. It would be something analogous to what Kant
called an "Idea of Reason"; an "Idea of Prosody," perhaps. The difficulties seem even greater when we reflect that to vanquish chance fully, we
need something more than a plurality of poem-words. The relations between what these "words" designate must also be shown to be necessary.
And so the ultimate goal which Mallarmé projects (perhaps not for
himself but for humanity) is a work—which he doesn't by any means
propose to write alone himself—which he describes as "l'hymne, harmonie et joie, comme pur ensemble groupé dans quelque circonstance
fulgurante, des relations entre tout. L'homme chargé de voir divinement" [the hymn, harmony and joy, as pure ensemble grouped in some
dazzling circumstance, of the relations between everything. The man
charged with seeing divinely].[104]

How does this new vision help to "donner un sens plus pur aux mots
de la tribu" [to give a purer meaning to the words of the tribe], something he attributes to Poe? Undoubtedly in part because they free this
search for a deeper, truer language from (what Mallarmé considered to
be) the erroneous spiritual beliefs concerning God and immortality
which he had earlier held. That's why he felt he had to say in his "Tombeau"
for the American poet, "Son siècle épouvanté [n'avait] pas connu / Que

104. Mallarmé, *Le Livre*, 224.

la mort triomphait dans cette voix étrange" [His frightened century [had] not known / That death triumphed in that strange voice].[105]

Let's look at the expression "baigne dans une neuve atmosphère" [bathes in a new atmosphere]: undoubtedly, the object appears in a new light; but is this same light also invoked in some of the language of the Gautier poem: "le regard diaphane" which "isole [le grand calice clair] parmi l'heure et le rayon du jour" [the diaphanous gaze which isolates [the great clear chalice] among the hour and the ray of daylight]? And of "Prose": "Chacune / Ordinairement se para / D'un lucide contour, lacunae / Qui des jardins la sépara" [each / was usually garlanded / with a clear contour, and this breach / parted it from the garden bed]?

We can understand this presence-in-absence from another standpoint too, that of time. Something richer than Newtonian time seems to surround these objects, to be part of the atmosphere in which they "baignent" [bathe]. It is the time which reverberates in the aftermath; everything is over; we are at a standpoint looking back; a kind of final, absolute endpoint. The objects are taken up in a sort of retrospective stance.

We can feel this quite palpably in another poem-transposition of Mallarmé, "Sainte." The object supposedly evoked here is a stained-glass window portraying St. Cecilia, the patron of music. The saint is represented holding an old sandalwood viola which is already losing its gilding, and an unfolding book containing the Magnificat which was sung at vespers and compline. The window is like a monstrance (*ostensoir*) which not only represents the saint, but also suggests an angel about to take flight in the evening. The whole poem evokes a remote past which is captured and summed up in the last line: "musicienne du silence" [musician of silence]. (See my tentative parenthetic remark above.)

Sainte

A la fenêtre recélant
Le santal vieux qui se dédore
De sa viole étincelant
Jadis avec flûte ou mandore,

---

105. Mallarmé, "Le Tombeau d'Edgar Poe," 38.

Est la Sainte pâle, étalant
Le livre vieux qui se déplie
Du Magnificat ruisselant
Jadis selon vêpre et complie:

A ce vitrage d'ostensoir
Que frôle une harpe par l'Ange
Formée avec son vol du soir
Pour la délicate phalange

Du doigt que, sans le vieux santal
Ni le vieux livre, elle balance
Sur le plumage instrumental,
Musicienne du silence.[106]

[At the window that veils her old
sandalwood viol voiding gold
which used to cast its glitter in
the past with flute or mandolin

is the pale Saint displaying that
old volume the Magnificat
unfolded, from which compline or
vespersong used to stream before:

at this ostensory pane draped
by a harp that the Angel shaped
in his flight through the evening shade
for the delicate finger-blade

as she is poising to caress,
neither old wood nor old edition,

106. Stéphane Mallarmé, "Sainte," in *Œuvres complètes*, 1:26.

but instrumental featheriness—
being the silence's musician.][107]

(Hugo Friedrich picks up on the retrospective nature of Mallarmé's notion of place-time. He speaks of the "absolute Spätes" [absolute lateness], "absolute Abendlichkeit" [absolute afternoon-nature], "das absolute Späte schlechthin, die angemessene Zeitkategorie des Versinkens und Vernichtens" [simply the absolute lateness, the appropriate category for what sinks and disappears], "das absolut zu verstehende Spätsein" [the absolutely understood lateness].)[108]

This notion, that the meaning of things appears from the end looking back, is also evident in his way of thinking of the oeuvre of dead poets. Gautier, Poe: "Tel qu'en Lui-même l'éternité le change" [Changed to Himself at last by eternity]. Once they are free from the struggle, stress, confusion, and impurities of life, their vision and voice stand out clear. Also "Igitur" and "Un Coup de dés." Eternity as the future perfect subjunctive.

It is this, as well as the drama of the death of the poet, which is very much at work in the famous triptych of sonnets, published in 1887, but perhaps written much earlier, at least in earlier drafts. They have a lot in common with the "Sonnet en -X." The death of light, and of the poet; but here, at the antipodes from "Quand l'ombre menaça," with its triumphal declaration; and different also from the "Sonnet en -X" which seems to bring it off, and know that it has; in this case, the issue seems in doubt. Indeed, death and nonexistence seem to be having things all their own way, until the tercets of the third sonnet. And even then, the turnaround is very hesitatingly put forward, with a conditional.

I

Tout Orgueil fume-t-il du soir,
Torche dans un branle étouffée
Sans que l'immortelle bouffée
Ne puisse à l'abandon surseoir!

107. Stéphane Mallarmé, "Saint," in *Collected Poems,* 47–49.
108. Friedrich, *Die Struktur,* 76.

La chambre ancienne de l'hoir
De maint riche mais chu trophée
Ne serait pas même chauffée
S'il survenait par le couloir.

Affres du passé nécessaires
Agrippant comme avec des serres
Le sépulcre de désaveu,

Sous un marbre lourd qu'elle isole
Ne s'allume pas d'autre feu
Que la fulgurante console.[109]

                              [I

Does every Pride in the evening smoke,
a torch quenched by some sudden stroke
without the divine pre-eminent
cloud halting its abandonment!

The ancient chamber of the heir
to precious but outmoded ware
would surely not be warmed at all
if he should enter through the hall.

Destined agonies of the past
holding denial's tombstone fast
as if in eagles' claws, below

a heavy marble slab that it
isolates, not one fire is lit
except the console's lightning glow.][110]

109. Stéphane Mallarmé, "Sonnet I," in *Œuvres complètes,* 1:41.
110. Stéphane Mallarmé, "Sonnet I," in *Collected Poems,* 73–75.

First line: Tout Orgueil fume-t-il du soir.

I: Quatrain 1 has strong sunset imagery. "Orgueil" invokes "Quand l'ombre menaça," verse 7.

Tercet 1: we have to imagine the scene. There is a console, a platform with support coming out from the wall, and gripping a marble top, maybe with claws. Like trying to hold on to the tomb to keep the person from slipping away. These *affres* [torments] are unavoidable (*nécessaires*); we have to go through them. Then tercet 2: the fulguration. The light for a minute, and then it goes out. Not the stopping place of the "Sonnet en -X," where we have an emblem of the pure clearing. But another step along the way of retreat, which we saw in that poem in all stages save the last. The end statement is a negation of fire, linking up with the end of quatrain 2. The sun is dead, and there is no fire more. Abandon. Night. Death.

II

Surgi de la croupe et du bond
D'une verrerie éphémère
Sans fleurir la veillée amère
Le col ignoré s'interrompt.

Je crois bien que deux bouches n'ont
Bu, ni son amant ni ma mère,
Jamais à la même Chimère,
Moi, sylphe de ce froid plafond!

Le pur vase d'aucun breuvage
Que l'inexhaustible veuvage
Agonise mais ne consent,

Naïf baiser des plus funèbres!
A rien expirer annonçant
Une rose dans les ténèbres.[111]

111. Stéphane Mallarmé, "Sonnet II," in *Œuvres complètes*, 1:42.

[II

Arisen from the rump and bound
of fleeting glassware, the distraught
vigil is never flower-crowned,
the unknown neck merely stops short.

I feel sure two mouths never fed,
neither her lover nor my mother,
on the same Fantasy as each other,
I, sylph with cold eaves overhead!

The vase pure of any drink save
widowhood inexhaustibly
suffers death but does not agree,

a kiss naive and O how grave!
to breathe out any final mark
that heralds some rose in the dark.][112]

Here some have seen a vase. But others, a chandelier, reminding of a vase, and thus the same object throughout. The theme here is incompleteness. The vase has no flower, no water or drink. Sterility; because this turns to the impossible meeting of love, its nonmeeting. And beyond this of the procreation which springs from love. If it is sundown and after, this might be thought to be the sterile night thoughts which follow. We are in a "veillée" [wake]; "ténèbres" [darkness].

So the nonexistence of the flower in quatrain 1. Then the sylph (perhaps suggested by the chandelier) also doesn't exist, his speech tells us: his parents never could meet; and we sense the impossibility of meeting. So he is "sylphe de ce froid plafond" [the sylph of this cold ceiling].

112. Stéphane Mallarmé, "Sonnet II," in *Collected Poems,* 75.

Then the tercets: back to the vase. It is empty of drink, and although itself close to death, it does not consent even to announce a rose completing it. We are kept in the farthest regions of nonexistence, coldness, nonfecundity, absence of the promise of any birth. And yet the tercets are written so as irresistibly to suggest such an emergence of a rose in the dark. The vase is not just pure of any drink; it is pure; it offers a kiss; and the refused possibility is laid out at the very end with the feel of a positive statement, in spite of the *rien* which precedes it. "Agonise mais . . ." [Is dying but . . .]. It trembles on the brink.

This absence brings the denied object out and makes it "baigne dans une neuve atmosphère."

III

Une dentelle s'abolit
Dans le doute du Jeu suprême
A n'entr'ouvrir comme un blasphème
Qu'absence éternelle de lit.

Cet unanime blanc conflit
D'une guirlande avec la même,
Enfui contre la vitre blême
Flotte plus qu'il n'ensevelit.

Mais, chez qui du rêve se dore
Tristement dort une mandore
Au creux néant musicien

Telle que vers quelque fenêtre
Selon nul ventre que le sien,
Filial on aurait pu naître.[113]

113. Stéphane Mallarmé, "Sonnet III," in *Œuvres complètes*, 1:42–43.

[III

A lace vanishes utterly
in doubt of the last Game, to spread
out only like a blasphemy
eternal absence of a bed.

This unanimous white affray
fought by the garland with the same,
fled to the pallid window-frame,
rather floats than buries away.

But in one gilded by his dreams
there sleeps a mandolin forlorn
musician of the void unknown

so that toward some pane it seems
one might filial have been born
due to no belly but its own.][114]

III: This seems to be dawn. One of those anxious, despairing times for Mallarmé, after a sleepless night in which nothing was accomplished.[115] Lace curtains floating before the window. The *vitre* [vitrine] is "blême" [pale], a weak dawn. "Jeu suprême" [supreme game]? Of day and night? Of life and procreation?

Anyway, the curtains suggest those around a bed, a place of procreation. And the blasphemy against the "Jeu suprême" [supreme game] is that there is no bed, even eternally. There is no more difference, the curtain merely fights with itself, wind against the pale window. It "flotte plus qu'il n'ensevelit" [floats more than it enfolds]. So it doesn't cover anything. But perhaps there also is a sign of hope in that it doesn't bury anything.

114. Stéphane Mallarmé, "Sonnet III," in *Collected Poems*, 77.
115. See Stéphane Mallarmé, "Le Don du poème," in *Œuvres complètes*, 1:17.

At last, in the tercets, we have the faint beginnings of hope, of a possible turnaround. The golden dream; but the mandora sleeps. And *tristement* [sadly]. It is that of emptiness and *Néant;* but this can turn into a "ventre de procréation" [a womb of procreation], on its own. "On aurait pu naître" [one could have been born] . . . the result is very uncertain.

Note that window has again come back to its early meaning. Out of the most absolute deprivation the hope springs of something quite different. A music of nothing.

(Note that in the 1880s, some of this imagery gets used in a different way. There is a new, more positive place of love in the wake of his relation with Méry Laurent. So "Victorieusement fui" starts with great sunset imagery; but what then "relaye" [relays] the sun is her blond head. Light mood of love banter, drawing on triumphal imagery of the sun.)[116]

This tryptic of sonnets is difficult to read. In the light of the paradigm I tried to define through the "Sonnet en -X" they are less convincing, and in addition can be interpreted in other ways. Paul Bénichou interprets the first simply as a statement of his metaphysical rejection of immortality. But I don't see Mallarmé writing a poem just to state this. He founds his argument partly on the reference to "orgueil" [pride] in the first quatrain, but I would relate this rather to the *orgueil* invoked in "Quand l'ombre menaça." The invocation of "La chambre ancienne de l'hoir [archaic for "héritier"] / De maint riche mais chu trophée" [The old room of the heir / of many rich and fallen trophies] speaks perhaps more to the wrong way to fill the void created by the discredit of his earlier search for transcendent beauty. At the end, the only fire lighting "le sépulcre de désaveu" [the sepulcher of disavowal] is "la fulgurante console" [the flaming console]. This seems to me a much less effective attempt to invoke the sense of place than the "Sonnet en -X."

I would say the same of II, "Surgi de la croupe et du bond" [Arisen from the rump and bound]. But of the third, "Une dentelle s'abolit" [A lace vanishes utterly], I would want to say that the interpretation in terms of the difficulty of writing, experienced in the vain attempts through sleepless nights, seems to take over as a major theme. Certainly it

116. See also Stéphane Mallarmé, "M'introduire dans ton histoire," in *Œuvres complètes,* 1:43.

dominates the two quatrains. But the two tercets introduce a new line of hope: "Mais, chez qui du rêve se dore / Tristement dort une mandore / Au creux néant musicien" [But in one gilded by his dreams / there sleeps a mandolin forlorn / musician in the void unknown]. This resonates perhaps with the "musicienne du silence" of "Sainte." And the poem finishes with an invocation, in the conditional, of a possible new birth.

"Presque disparition vibratoire": this new program demands a new poetics, a very different way of writing. It aims for a disappearance of the poet as finite being. But does this mean simply an abolition of the subject, as recent trends have seen it? This seems to find support in the famous line from "Crise de vers." Let's read the whole paragraph:

> L'Œuvre pure implique la disparition élocutoire du poëte, qui cède l'initiative aux mots, par le heurt de leurs inégalité mobilisés; ils s'allument de reflets réciproques comme une virtuelle traînée de feux sur des pierreries, remplaçant la respiration perceptible en l'ancien souffle lyrique ou la direction personnelle enthousiaste de la phrase.[117]

> [The pure work implies the elocutionary disappearance of the poet, who cedes the initiative to the words, through the clash of their mobilized inequalities; they light up with reciprocal reflections like a virtual trail of fire on jewels, replacing the breathing perceptible in the ancient lyrical breath or the enthusiastic personal direction of the sentence.]

But what this means is what Mallarmé called a "disparition élocutoire." It is not that the poet just cedes initiative to the words: he isn't trying to build them together to make an effect which he already has in mind. Mallarmé surely made clear that this couldn't have been his procedure. Nor does it mean that in so fitting them together, their semantic meanings have no importance. This too would be impossible to square with his practice—although semantic combinations are so interwoven into musical ones that one cannot trace anything like a separate effect of each.

---

117. Mallarmé, "Crise de vers," 212.

(This is the place perhaps to note how Mallarmé continues another important tradition of some French poetry, that of the *précieux*. *Précieux*-type periphrasis is one of the ways of contributing to the "presque disparition vibratoire." And for reasons which are not without continuity with the original invocations of periphrasis, which Friedrich describes as "eine Sache von ihrer brutalen Stofflichkeit, aber auch von der Verbrauchtheit ihres üblichen Wortes zu entlasten" [to liberate some matter from its brutal materiality, but also from the worn-out nature of a much-used word].)[118]

What Mallarmé is perhaps also driving at here is the putting aside of the whole tradition of eloquence. The French poetic tradition was deeply rhetorical, from the Grand Siècle, Corneille, and Racine, through to Hugo and Baudelaire. Poems were declarations, built like speeches, declaiming something. This is what Mallarmé breaks with. The words are going to affect each other, build something out of their mutual "shock"; they will "reciprocally reflect" on each other, like a powder chain on the stones; but that means that the way they are combined has to be liberated from combinations subordinated to the end of the lyric declaration ("ancien souffle lyrique" [ancient lyrical breath]), or the rhetorical demands of enthusiastic statement.

The liberation from eloquence is what we do find in Mallarmé's later poetry, and it is part of what made it so disconcerting and perplexing. Or rather, it is directly what made it sound strange to French ears, and as a consequence it could seem incomprehensible. Because the fact is not that his poems don't make statements. They still do, and puzzling them out is crucial to feeling the full effect of the poems (however much he may have joked to the contrary)—although sometimes there is a certain willed, studied vagueness, but that is a different matter (see his uses of *selon,* for instance).[119]

The consequence is rather that the way they are put together isn't concerned with the "normal" or most rhetorically effective syntax of the declarative statement. On the contrary, this normal syntax is often tortured, word order changed (often adjective before noun, which some

118. Friedrich, *Die Struktur,* 94.

119. For an account of the *disparition élocutoire,* see Thibaudet, *La Poésie,* 122.

people have attributed to his familiarity with English), verbs which come
far away from their subjects or complements, lots of intercalated matter,
modes of negation which aren't intuitively obvious at first blush, and so
forth. Then the move away from the statement also meant a lesser emphasis on the verb. Mallarmé has a penchant for putting verbs in the in-
finitive. Of nouns, he frequently avoids the plural—often getting around
it by using the term *maint,* for instance. It's as though he wanted maxi-
mally to liberate his words from the statement-integrating forces binding
them, in order to free them to combine in other ways.

The underlying idea seems to be that normal declarative syntax is essential to normal, utilitarian, descriptive "commercial" speech; and that
the break with this requires another type of combination.[120]

What is the goal of these combinations? The goal is to have the "words,"
the different terms and expressions, work on each other, to produce a
total effect which no statement could capture, like the absence-in-
presence discussed above, or the sense of a time-extended place. As
with the normal rhetoric of declaration, the order of terms matters; but
unlike this normal rhetoric, and quite disconcerting, one can't just grasp
the meaning of any normal-sized chunk at the beginning before one goes
on. Some essential term, for instance, will still have to come, many verses
later; or it is unclear without further examination what a pronoun refers
to; and so on.[121] So that Mallarmé's poems only yield themselves on re-
reading. Hence while the order matters, there also has to be an awareness of what comes after. Temporality and simultaneity are superimposed.
The "Sonnet en -X" has a progression of light-bearers, but it is also held
together by the eternity (or at least transtemporal existence) of the vision which emerges.

The effect is the final cause, one might say, of the construction. But
what in fact organizes the poetry as it is constructed, the organizing
principle replacing rhetoric, is the verse and rhyme. Mallarmé, in some
ways the most innovative poet of the nineteenth century, never warmed
up to blank verse.[122] The forms of alexandrine, of sonnet, especially, were

---

120. Mallarmé, *La Musique et les lettres,* in *Œuvres complètes,* 2:62.

121. See "Prose (Pour des Esseintes)," stanzas 10–12.

122. See Mallarmé, *La Musique et les lettres,* 62.

crucial to him. They set, as it were, the force fields within which his "words" interacted, mutually reflected. In this interaction, which was indivisibly musical and semantical, they set the rhythm, the periods, the points of recurrence (such as rhymes) of the music.

There is something magical, unanalyzable, about the way meaning and music combine. They make together the vibration of Mallarmé's poetry (the "disparition vibratoire"), the incantatory force of it. "Le vers qui de plusieurs vocables refait un mot total, neuf, étranger à la langue et comme incantatoire" [The verse that remakes a total, new word from several vocables, foreign to the language and as if incantatory].[123] Or from his essay on Villiers de l'Isle-Adam: "Le vers n'étant autre qu'un mot parfait, vaste, natif" [Verse being nothing other than a perfect, vast, native word].[124]

There is something bewitching about the "-x" sonnet. The importance of the music, of the rhyme, is attested by the anecdote we have about this sonnet. Mallarmé asks Cazalis to find the meaning of "ptyx" for him. He wanted to make an "-x" sonnet, and needed the rhyme. Indeed, the whole thing is a tour de force, because there are only four rhymes, and these can be reduced to two if you ignore the masculine / feminine distinction. In the letter to Cazalis, where he jokes about the possible lack of meaning, he says: "Le sens, s'il en a un (mais je me consolerais du contraire grâce à la dose de poésie qu'il renferme, ce me semble) est évoqué par un mirage interne des mots mêmes. En se laissant aller à le murmurer plusieurs fois, on éprouve une sensation assez cabalistique." [The meaning, if it has one (but I'd console myself with the contrary thanks to the dose of poetry it contains, it seems to me) is evoked by an internal mirage of the words themselves. If you let yourself whisper it a few times, you get a rather cabalistic sensation.][125]

It is of these musical-semantic combinations that Mallarmé makes the seemingly strong claim, that they "[refont] un mot total, neuf, étranger

123. Mallarmé, "Crise de vers," 213.

124. Stéphane Mallarmé, "Quelques médaillons et portraits en pied: Villiers de l'Isle-Adam," in *Œuvres complètes*, 2:113–118.

125. Stéphane Mallarmé, "Lettre à Henri Cazalis. 18 juillet 1868," in *Propos sur la poésie*, 98.

à la langue" [[make up] a total, new foreign word in the language].[126] The truth behind this is that some of Mallarmé's expressions, like "Aboli bibelot d'inanité sonore" or "creux néant musicien," take on a meaning, and work in our memory as new arresting units, which one couldn't have imagined from one's antecedent familiarity with their component words. Any new coinage semantically innovates, for instance: "circuit breaker." But we see how the compound came about, and can't feel surprised by it. Whereas there are resonances around these Mallarmé lines which remain arresting and unanalyzable back into the component terms.

In a sense a whole poem by Mallarmé can be considered a limiting case of such a new expression (of course, not a longer poem, like "Hérodiade," or even the "Toast funèbre" for Gautier, but his sonnets, the one in "Sonnet en -X," for instance). It is built through the connection, and mutual shock or reflection of all the key terms. "La totale arabesque," as he refers to it in *La Musique et les lettres:*

> Qui les [quelques figures belles] relie, a de vertigineuses sautes en un effroi que reconnue; et d'anxieux accords. [. . .] Chiffration mélodique tue, de ces motifs qui composent une logique, avec nos fibres. [. . .] Nulle torsion vaincue ne fausse ni ne transgresse l'omniprésente Ligne espacée de tout point à toute autre pour instituer l'idée.[127]

> [The total arabesque which connects [some beautiful figures] has vertiginous jumps in a dread that we recognize and anxious chords. [. . .] Melodic ciphering kills, with our fibers, those motifs that compose a logic. [. . .] No defeated twist distorts or transgresses the omnipresent Line running from any point to any other to institute the idea].

The liberating of words from the syntax of declarative, "commercial," utilitarian speech, with its "logic," into the verse and poem which realizes their potential to evoke the idea is certainly also part of what he meant, in relation to Poe, by "donner un sens plus pur aux mots de la tribu."

---

126. Mallarmé, "Crise de vers," 213.
127. Mallarmé, *La Musique et les lettres,* 62.

And we can see now the point (a possible point) of the strange Cratylan remarks of "Crise de vers." Something is wrong as things stand. Words do not musically evoke what they are about. But the new "words," combining the original inadequate ones in new musical-semantic combinations, have recovered their power to evoke what they describe (albeit not in Cratylan fashion, as I argued in the previous section). "Aboli bibelot d'inanité sonore."

The musical-semantic does what music does, only in superior way: "reprendre notre bien" [recover our property].[128]

It remains to say a word about silence; a word which constantly recurs in Mallarmé. There are indications that, for Mallarmé, transposition was (perhaps essentially) a silent operation (hence purely intramental?).

> Évoquer, dans une ombre exprès, l'objet tu, par des mots allusifs, jamais directs, se réduisant à du silence égal, comporte tentative proche de créer: vraisemblable dans la limite de l'idée uniquement mise en jeu par l'enchanteur de lettres jusqu'à ce que, certes, scintille, quelque illusion égale au regard. Le vers, trait incantatoire![129]

> [Evoking, in an express shadow, the unnamed object, in allusive words, never direct, reducing to equal silence; this involves a close attempt to create: believable within the limit of the idea only brought into play by the enchanter of letters until, certainly, there sparkles, some illusion equal to the gaze. Verse, an incantatory power!]

What should temper this reading is that the poem is also "incantatoire." So our silent reading of it borrows from its properties when cited aloud.

> Le vers et tout écrit au fond par cela issu de la parole doit se montrer à même de subir l'épreuve orale ou d'affronter la diction comme un mode de présentation extérieur pour trouver haut et dans la foule son écho plausible, au lieu qu'effectivement il a lieu

---

128. Mallarmé, "Crise de vers," 213. Mallarmé speaks of these two as "face presentations" of the same phenomenon, l'Idée. Mallarmé, *La Musique et les lettres,* 62.

129. Stéphane Mallarmé, "Magie," in *Œuvres complètes,* 2:250.

au-delà du silence que traverse se rarifiant en musiques mentales
ses éléments, at affecte notre sens subtil ou de rêve.[130]

[Verse and all writing that is basically derived from the spoken
word must be able to stand the oral test or face diction as an
external mode of presentation in order to find its plausible echo
high up and in the crowd, even though it actually takes place beyond
the silence that its elements cross while rarifying its elements
into mental music, and affects our subtle or dream sense.]

You can't just neglect the voice. But in the end, the transposition happens in "le silence profonde, divin, gisant dans l'âme des lecteurs" [in profound silence, divine, lying in the souls of the readers].[131]

L'armature intellectuelle du poème se dissimule et tient—a lieu—
dans l'espace qui isole les strophes et paermi le blanc du papier:
significatif silence qu'il n'est pas moins beau de composer, que le
vers.[132]

[The intellectual framework of the poem is concealed and
held—takes place—in the space that seems to isolate the
stanzas in the white of the paper: a significant silence that is no
less beautiful to compose, than the verse.]

In "Quant au Livre," Mallarmé speaks of "le hasard vaincu mot par
mot."[133] In "Sur Poe," "significatif silence"; "L'opulent silence entre les mots
purement nourrit l'esprit" [The opulent silence between the words nourishes the mind].[134] "[L'art suprême] consiste . . . à ne jamais en les chantant, dépouiller les objets, subtils ou regardés du voile justement de
silence sous quoi ils nous séduisirent et transparaît maintenant le secret
de leur signifiance" [[The supreme art] consists . . . in never as we sing

130. Stéphane Mallarmé, "Sur le vers," in Œuvres complètes, 2:474, quoted in Henri
Meschonnic, Stéphane Mallarmé: Écrits sur le Livre (Arles: Éditions de l'Éclat, 1985),
54–55.

131. Mallarmé, "Sur le vers," 474.

132. Mallarmé, "Réponses à des Enquêtes," 659, quoted in Meschonnic, Mallarmé, 31.

133. Mallarmé, "Quant au Livre," in Œuvres complètes, 387.

134. Stéphane Mallarmé, "Sue Poe," in Œuvres complètes, 872.

them, stripping the objects, subtle or directly looked at, of the veil precisely of silence under which they seduced us and the secret of their significance becomes evident].[135]

There is a double point to this image of silence. One is the negation of the declaratory, eloquence, rhetoric. There is no one talking, in the sense of declaiming, in Mallarmé's poems. And beyond this, silence is an image which captures the absence-in-presence of the things in the world of this poem. The time-extended place which the poem calls up for us is a kind of silence underneath the noisy, obtrusive presence which things normally have. "Le sens est un second silence au sein du silence; il est la négation du mot-chose" [Meaning is a second silence within silence; it is the negation of the word-thing].[136]

VI

Already Mallarmé's program seems very difficult. This difficulty is magnified many times, when we remember that the ultimate goal was not the poetic creation of a certain number of new "words" revealing the real nature of certain things or situations, but rather the writing of a total oeuvre, or "grimoire," containing a system of such "words" covering all reality. We have to understand this latter goal as a possibility in principle, toward which we can make a few halting steps, rather than a viable object of poetic ambition. The point is to remind ourselves that the ultimately real is what a complete network of transposed "words" would describe.

Why do we (including me) strive so hard to unravel the mystery, and understand the goals that Mallarmé sought in his mature poetry? It is

135. Stéphane Mallarmé, "Lettre à Georges Rodenbach. 25 mars 1888," quoted in Jean Paul Sartre, *Mallarmé: La lucidité et sa face d'ombre* (Paris: Gallimard, 1986), 161–162.

136. Sartre, *Mallarmé*, 160. This work by Sartre is an extraordinary combination of insight and reductive crudity; Mallarmé turning from things is seen as a flight from life, the need to recover the protective regard of his mother; this is interesting, but wrong, but not totally reductive. What is the account of the Wertherism of Mallarmé's milieu in class terms? See Sartre, *Mallarmé*, 40–45.

partly because of the amazingly high quality of his lyric poetry. There is no better measure than this: that phrases of his, even (maybe especially) those that we ill understand, remain in our memory like fires which illuminate a starless night: each one a source of renewed joy.

The hope recurs that we can come to understand better why this poetry so seizes us by digging deeper into the metaphysic of *Néant* that Mallarmé espoused. But alas, for me this hope has yet to realize its promise.

NOTE ON
"Symbolism"

This is the word used to designate a certain school of thought about the nature of poetry, as well as the practice of certain poets during the later nineteenth century, and into the twentieth. The poets concerned were predominantly French, such as Verlaine and Rimbaud; though there were also others in Europe (Verhaeren, Maeterlinck), and England (Swinburne), and Quebec (Saint-Denys Garneau, Émile Nelligan); and the school of thought flourished in these countries (Valéry, Symons). One important influence was Baudelaire, whose use of the term "symbol" identified a crucial feature of what emerged as the Symbolist movement.

As I argued at the end of Chapter 10 on Baudelaire, his use of the term represented what one can call an "epistemic retreat" from the early Romantic one, represented, for instance, by A. W. Schlegel (see Chapter 1). On Schlegel's view, we can talk of a "symbol" where some deeper reality is opened for us through something already visible and in our ken, paradigmatically through a work of art, as Wordsworth makes us sense the force running through all things through his portrayal of the Wye valley, or Hölderlin makes us feel the action of *Vater Aether* through the light which pours down on the valley.

(In these cases, the operation of the symbol can also be understood as a triad: the poem opens a deeper dimension, whereby the mountainside in "Heimkunft" is made to reveal for us the action of *Vater Aether*.)

Something like this notion of symbol recurs with Baudelaire, but with important changes, as we can see from the passage I quoted earlier. Or:

Il y a des moments de l'existence où le temps et l'étendue sont plus profonds, et le sentiment de l'existence immensément augmenté. [. . .] Dans certains états de l'âme presque surnaturels, la profondeur de la vie se révèle toute entière dans le spectacle, si ordinaire qu'il soit, qu'on a sous les yeux. Il en devient le symbole.[1]

[There are moments in one's existence when time and space are deeper, and the feeling of existence immensely increased. [. . .] In certain states of one's soul which are almost supernatural, the depth of life is revealed totally in the spectacle, however ordinary, before one's eyes. This spectacle becomes the symbol of that depth.]

Here, like in the Schlegel symbol, something is there, ready to be revealed through something else: through the quite ordinary spectacle, "la profondeur de la vie" [the profundity of life] in its entirety becomes visible. This "depth" only needs formulation by the poet for it to be visible. But this "depth" is given no further formulation. It remains indefinite, what really fills this depth dimension of life. This indefiniteness, this reluctance to define the vision the "symbol" opens for us, becomes a central feature of "Symbolism" in the late nineteenth-century sense of the term. Mallarmé was another important influence on the Symbolists.

La poésie consistant à créer, il faut prendre dans l'âme humaine des états, des lueurs d'une pureté si absolue que, bien chantés et bien mis en lumière, cela constitue en effet les joyaux de l'homme: là, il y a symbole, il y a création, et le mot poésie a un sens. Nommer un objet, c'est supprimer les trois quarts de la jouissance du poème qui est faite de deviner peu à peu: le suggérer, voilà le rêve. C'est le parfait usage de ce mystère qui constitue le symbole.[2]

[Since poetry is about creating, we must take from the human soul states and gleams of such absolute purity that, well sung

---

1. Charles Baudelaire, "Fusées," in *Œuvres complètes* (Paris: Gallimard, 1975), 1:658–659.
2. Stéphane Mallarmé, "Réponse à l'enquête de Jules Hure," in *Œuvres complètes* (Paris: Gallimard, 1998), 1:782.

and well brought to light, they are indeed the jewels of man: there, there is symbol, there is creation, and the word poetry has a meaning. To name an object is to supplant three quarters of the pleasure of the poem, which is made to divine it little by little: to suggest it, that is the dream. This is the perfect usage of the mystery that we call the symbol.][3]

Of course, he thought of his poetry as revealing an underlying reality, that of the cosmos as it truly appears to *le Néant* [Non-Being]. But this was sketched in such a tentative and enigmatic manner that it didn't often take the reader farther than Baudelaire had. The epistemic retreat in relation to the Schlegel symbol remained palpable.

But if the symbol remained indefinite, how did Symbolists define their position, and what other schools of art provided the contrast which enabled them to draw the line? The main enemy was often identified as "realism" or "naturalism." On the French scene, paradigm examples were, among others, Flaubert, Taine, Zola. As Arthur Symons, one of the major English theorists of Symbolism, put it: "Zola has tried to build in brick and mortar inside the covers of a book."[4] Works that attempt to see the world through science, and seek exact representations of reality, are condemned.

But another contrasting quality they wanted to ban was rhetoric; literature which makes a plea for one or another course of action, and which thus seeks eloquence, persuasiveness, was considered strictly inferior. Even such poetic giants as Hugo and Lamartine were condemned for this fault. But this negative movement was carried further. A true Symbolist work should not seek some ulterior purpose, apart from beauty itself. As Verlaine put it:

> Le Poète, l'amour du Beau, voilà sa foi,
> L'Azur son étendard, et l'idéal, sa loi.[5]

> [For the poet, the love of the beautiful, that's his faith
> The Azure his standard, and the Ideal, his law.]

3. Translation by Thom K. Sliwowski.

4. Arthur Symons, *The Symbolist Movement in Literature* (New York: Dutton, 1919), 5.

5. Paul Verlaine, "Prologue," in *Œuvres complètes de Paul Verlaine* (Paris: L. Vanier, 1907), 6.

In this he was influenced by Baudelaire:

> Oui, le but de la poésie, c'est le Beau, le Beau seul, le Beau
> sûr, sans alliage d'Utile, de Vrai ou de Juste.[6]
>
> [Yes, the goal of poetry is the Beautiful, only the Beautiful,
> the Beautiful alone, without alloy from the Useful. The True,
> the Just.]

Over against these false paths, indefiniteness was seen as a virtue; exact description was banned in order to open the way for suggestion, evocation. As Symons saw it, mystery was not to be feared; literature should make the soul of things visible. Literature in a sense replaces religion: "Art returns to the one path leading through beautiful things to eternal beauty."[7] Of course, not all Symbolists shared Symons' spiritual views, but they concurred in his condemnations.

How was this indefiniteness of the symbol understood? There were two big models, which were sometimes associated with different thinkers, although it could also occur that a thinker would oscillate between them; for example Walter Pater. The difference turned on the dimension of intentionality, in the sense that phenomenology gives to this expression; this concerns what an expression is about, or what it says: Is it essential to the work of art which moves us that it reveal something, however hard to pin down exactly, about us and / or the cosmos in which we exist, and / or a transcendent reality?

Some thinkers, at least some of the time, were willing to give up altogether on the intentional dimension: the crucial quality of a work of art consists in the feeling that it arouses. This can be simply defined as pleasure; or it can call for stronger terms: its function is to give "the highest quality to your moments as they pass, and simply for those moments' sake." Intensity is the key. The "supreme value is not form but force, energy, the flow of mind among phenomena."[8] "To burn always with this hard gem-like flame, to maintain this ecstasy, is success in life."[9]

---

6. Paul Verlaine, "Charles Baudelaire," in *Œuvres posthumes* (Paris: Messein, 1913), 18.

7. Symons, *Symbolist Movement*, 2.

8. Denis Donoghue, *Walter Pater: Lover of Strange Souls* (New York: Knopf, 1995), 52–53.

9. Donoghue, *Walter Pater*, 14.

Edgar Allan Poe, who had a considerable influence on the Symbolists, through Baudelaire and Mallarmé, seemed to take an even flatter
version of this anti-intentionalist position: "A poem in my opinion is
opposed to a work of science by having, for its *immediate* object,
pleasure, not truth: to romance, by having for its object an *indefinite*
instead of a *definite* pleasure."[10]

The other way of understanding the indefiniteness of the symbol
invoked music as the key paradigm. And Pater, famously, also used this
comparison. But the analogy with music shows how Symbolist poetry
can also have an intentional dimension.

How to understand the intentionality that can accompany, in fact define, how we are moved by music? I say "can accompany" because, in
some cases, a gay tune can cheer us up; somber music may depress our
spirits, without conveying any view of things. But music which more
deeply moves us does have an intentional dimension. One way to see
this is to look at how operas (certain operas, such as Mozart's) come
about. First there is a libretto, written, for example, by Da Ponte; then
Mozart writes the score; and brilliantly, capturing the spirit of the libretto,
while carrying it in a certain direction. There are obviously affinities between a certain unfolding dramatic action, and certain ways in which it
can be set to music.

But the point can also be made if one looks only at instrumental
music. We can see this if we recur to the discussion in Chapter 2 on the
work of Roger Scruton.[11]

I will put this in my own terms: I would say of the music which really
moves me that it puts me in a kind of "space" (in an analogous sense of
this term), in which the appropriate intentional objects for certain strong,
deep, often morally tinged, but not fully defined emotions are embedded, or better still, find expression. I said in that earlier discussion
that Chopin's *Fantaisie-Impromptu* in C sharp minor, opus 66, gives expression for me to a profound longing—for I don't know quite what. I
would add the finale of Mozart's *Jupiter* Symphony. I feel in this a striving
upwards, an expression of praise and thanks, straining to reach some
higher addressee (for me, this would be God, but I can imagine that

10. Peter Ackroyd, *Poe: A Life Cut Short* (New York: Nan Talese / Doubleday, 2009), 54.
11. Roger Scruton, *The Aesthetic of Music* (Oxford: Clarendon, 1997), 354–356.

someone else, feeling the ascending movement, would imagine another destination).

Scruton's discussion of Beethoven's Ninth Symphony shows how this kind of embedding makes us experience the succession of the movements in terms of contrasting and conflicting emotions, and their ultimate resolution in the choral finale. And of course, this finale is given more defined meaning by the Schiller poem it contains.

So music can contain and evoke its own emotional "space," but this cannot properly be defined in words. Words can make it more precise, take it in a certain direction; or to use another image, words may anchor it. Gregorian chant is immediately recognized as prayer, even when you don't understand the Latin. And something similar can be said for operatic music, as we saw above in connection with Mozart. In these cases, there is a kind of fusion of meaning between words and music, which has an effect on both; on one side, the libretto anchors the music; on the other, the music gives its own "reading" of the story. A story first created by the playwright Beaumarchais is differently "read" by Mozart (*The Marriage of Figaro*) and Rossini (*The Barber of Seville*).

In the light of this discussion of musical meaning, what does it tell us about "Symbolist" poetry to liken it to music, as both Pater and Valéry do? ("Il faut reprendre à la musique son bien" [We have to take back its essential property from music]).[12] I would conclude that what is being asserted here is that the ultimate (and probably intended) effect of the poem is to put us, unanchored, in a certain emotional "space." But how can this be, when a poem will undoubtedly be made up of statements? It must be that these statements are contradictory or enigmatic, either individually ("Je est un autre") or in combination.

But obviously, being contradictory and/or enigmatic is not a sufficient condition of being a poem, let alone one which introduces us to such a "space." The poem must have a strong suggestive power, as indeed the works of Rimbaud, Verlaine, and Valéry possess.

Perhaps we might use this term "suggest," in contradistinction to "state," as the term for the way that "Symbolist" poetry communicates

---

12. Mallarmé, *Œuvres complètes*, 367–368.

to and moves us. But T. S. Eliot puts the difference in other, perhaps less complimentary, terms.

In *The Sacred Wood*, discussing a poem by Swinburne, Eliot claims, in connection with the lines, "Time with a gift of tears / Grief with a glass that ran," that the object has ceased to exist, because the meaning is merely the hallucination of meaning, because language, uprooted, has adapted itself to an independent life of atmospheric nourishment.[13]

But I see the expression "nourishing an atmosphere" as another attempt to get at what I'm calling "suggesting an emotional 'space.'" All poetry does this, if it rises above the level of flat doggerel. The crucial distinction concerns whether the space / atmosphere arises out of the way its statements are made (or "objects" presented), or out of contradiction and the enigma they generate.

Explanations of "Symbolist" poetry move between two poles: one is to deny altogether that it communicates any "message," anything that one can approve of as true or reject as false; or, as I put it above, this poetry would have no dimension of intentionality. (Poe: a poem has "for its *immediate* object, pleasure.")

The other pole emerges with the affirmation that poetry, while making no *statement*, nevertheless can powerfully suggest something (Mallarmé: "Suggérer [l'objet], voilà le rêve" [To suggest [the object], that is the dream]).

The analogy with music can serve to illustrate either pole: on one hand, music makes no statement; on the other, it can induct us into a space saturated with powerful suggestion. And the suggestions felt by the hearer / reader may not be those which moved the writer / composer, but some practitioners of "Symbolism" can reconcile themselves to this disparity.

We can see here that to speak of "pleasure" is much too flat. There can be pleasures, like that of drinking a cool beer on a hot day, or of leaving a hot room to enjoy a cool breeze, which for Poe's account above would not make the grade. And Poe would certainly agree. These

13. T. S. Eliot, *The Sacred Wood: Essays on Poetry and Criticism* (London: Methuen, 1957), 148–149.

pleasures would be judged by him too "definite." But does a term like "indefinite" really capture what we respond to in poetry which moves us?

On the other hand, approaching the issue from another angle, Pater was right about music: the meaning is so closely embedded in the form that there is no question of a paraphrase in verbal language. So perhaps we can capture the point he was driving at by looking at the possibility of paraphrase or translation into another medium, say, from music to poetry.

I discussed this issue in Chapter 1. There is obviously such a thing as an affinity between certain poetic works and a specific musical setting. We can argue that a certain libretto was brilliantly set to music by a given composer: for example, Mozart with the libretti of Da Ponte. But a different composer would have carried these words in another direction. So "translation" cannot be the right term here. Any more than there can be (unambiguously adequate) translation of descriptions between different natural languages when one goes beyond bald statements of physical fact to touch on deeper human meanings.

We can make something like the same point in another way, if we examine what it might mean to explain the power we feel in a given piece of music. If we compare this task with the way we explain the meaning of an obviously "factual sentence" about some physical reality to someone who doesn't fully understand some of the terms used, the difference in our resources stands out. In the latter case, we clarify the semantic force of certain words, perhaps translating some into a more familiar idiom, and our end is achieved (but a crash course in a certain scientific domain might also be needed).

It is clear that no resources exist for this kind of explanation when someone asks us why we are moved by a powerful piece of music, why it resonates deeply in us, and might in them. We might have recourse to different ranges of metaphor with "suggestive" power, in the hopes of communicating something of the "force" and "depth" we feel. (And the appropriate metaphors might vary with the interlocutor.) But there is no recourse to the literally correct descriptions that we relied on when explaining our factually correct proposition.

Words cannot explain music. But words and meaning can magnificently combine in a higher, fuller Music, as Mallarmé claimed: "Je pose ... cette conclusion ... que la Musique et les Lettres sont la face alternative ici élargie vers l'obscur: scintillante là, avec certitude, d'un phénomène, le seul, je l'appelai, l'Idée" [I draw ... this conclusion ... that Music and Letters are alternative faces of the same, single phenomenon—in the latter case [meaning, Letters], stretched toward the obscure, in the former [Music], sparkling there, with certainty; this phenomenon, the only crucial one, I called the Idea].[14] What Mallarmé is naming "Idée" here is the powerful, arresting human meaning, into whose presence (or "space" in my language) the work puts us. Perhaps Eliot's complaint against Symons could have been rephrased: not that through suggestion it places us in an atmosphere, but that this atmosphere suggests no powerful, arresting human meaning. (I don't say that this would be entirely fair.)

Symbolism has to be recognized for what it is, because Eliot's work, and indeed modernism in general, drew on it; in fact, it is hard to understand the modernist era without it, whatever transformations the writers of this age wrought in it. (I will return to this point in connection with Eliot.) And, indeed, Yeats, a figure in the modernist canon, is often described as a Symbolist.

14. Stéphane Mallarmé, *La Musique et les lettres*, in *Œuvres complètes*, 2:62.

PART V

THE MODERNIST TURN

Chapter Thirteen

T. S. ELIOT

I

After the flowering of symbolism, and the full-scale epistemic retreat it involves, Eliot finds an original way to create a picture of a believable cosmic order, theologically centered, which is light-years away from the invocations of order of the early Romantics (which remain underappreciated by Eliot).

Even more surprising, the path which will eventually lead him to this discovery begins with the inspiration he took from the poetry of Jules Laforgue, usually seen as a writer of the "decadent" wing of symbolism.

Many of Laforgue's poems follow a similar trajectory:

Take the highest aspirations—to love, to beauty, to some transcendent fulfillment—and take them down, through ridicule, through the banal, through linking them with the flattest, everyday reality: this is a recurring staple of much of Laforgue's poetry.

For instance, this parody of "Au clair de la lune" from "Complainte de Lord Pierrot" (the aristocratic title accorded to a clown already conveys the message):

Au clair de la lune,
Mon ami Pierrot,
Filons en costume,
Présider là-haut!
Ma cervelle est morte.
Que le Christ l'emporte!
Béons à la Lune,
La bouche en zéro.[1]

[*Au claire de la lune,*
Mon ami Pierrot,
Up there, in costume,
We'll direct the show!
Now my brain's quite dead
To Christ be it sped!
Let's bay at the moon,
Our mouths shaped like O.][2]

Further on:

En costume blanc, je ferai le cygne,
Après nous le Déluge, ô ma Léda!
Jusqu'à ce que tournent tes yeux vitreux,
Que tu grelottes en rires affreux,
Hop! Enlevons sur les horizons fades
Les menuets de nos pantalonnades!
    Tiens! L'Univers
    Est à l'envers . . . [3]

[In my white costume, the swan part's mine,
O my Leda, after us the deluge!

1. Jules Laforgue, "Complainte de Lord Pierrot," in *Œuvres Complètes de Jules Laforgue* (Paris: Mercure de France, 1904), 128–129.

2. Jules Laforgue, "Complaint of Lord Pierrot," trans. Patricia Terry, in *Poems of Jules Laforgue* (Berkeley: University of California Press, 1958), 39.

3. Laforgue, "Complainte de Lord Pierrot," 129.

Until, turning your vitreous eyes,
Your shiver in horrible laughing cascades,
Up! Let's plant against colorless skies
The minutes of our masquerades!
   Oh, look! The universe
   Is in reverse . . .][4]

And in "Autre Complainte," the poet responds to the woman's declarations of love, where she says: "Mes claviers ont du Coeur, tu seras mon seul theme" [My keys have feeling, you'll be my only theme].[5]

Moi: "Tout est relatif."[6]

[Me: "Everything is relative."]

The poems pull in two directions: aspiration, undercut by banalizing takedown. But we can perhaps discern a third, half-hidden longing: Lord Pierrot's smile is bitter; he renounces these aspirations with a wrench: if only the world, the way things inevitably are, allowed for them to be genuinely realized.

Read this way, the movement is threefold: naïve aspiration, takedown, then longing for a world where the takedown wasn't called for.

What would this world look like? We have no positive description of it; but we have a negative characterization, because we see the hole, the lack it would fill. We have, as it were, a *dessein en creux,* the shape of the space it would fill.

I'll try here to give an explanation of expressions like *dessein en creux,* or *marque en creux.* Let's say someone has been sitting or lying on a soft cushion; and then they get up. They often leave the shape of the cushion unchanged, and the empty hollow tells us their shape, the form of its emptiness. I want to use the expression "empty marker" to indicate this phenomenon in English.

To read Laforgue through this lens, we can distinguish three stages in poems like the above: (1) inhabiting fully the innocent beauty of the nursery rhyme "Au clair de la lune"; then (2) realizing that this is absurd

4. Laforgue, "Complaint of Lord Pierrot," 39.
5. Translated by Thom K. Sliwowski.
6. Jules Laforgue, "Autre Complainte," in *Œuvres Complètes,* 132.

and ridiculous in the existing world; but (3) there is just a hint toward a third possibility, a higher world where a higher version of our spontaneous aspirations could be fulfilled. The existing poem is an empty marker, hinting at the shape of that alternative aspiration and world.

I would claim that this three-direction reading of Laforgue offers the model for Eliot's "Prufrock."

I I

"Prufrock" "Prufrock" begins with a very Baudelairean passage, as I mentioned above in Chapter 10: it describes while transfiguring a passage through an urban landscape. The details in this landscape are of the flat, uninspiring, even sordid kind—"one-night cheap hotels," "streets that follow like a tedious argument / Of insidious intent"—which depress the spirit, and threaten to slow down time to a meaningless repetition of the same; in short to bring on "Spleen." But the music of the verse gathers them up into a movement which promises to carry them to a meaningful consummation. And in fact, the first stanza ends with the promise that all this is bringing us to an "overwhelming question."[7]

But at this point the movement stops; we get a reference to women in a room, talking of Michelangelo, and an arresting description of fog descending on the scene, via a strange conceit which sees the fog as an agent, in fact, like a cat.

> The yellow fog that rubs its back upon the window panes.
> The yellow smoke that rubs its muzzle on the window panes,
> Licked its tongue into the corners of the evening,
> Lingered upon the pools that stand in drains,
> Let fall upon its back the soot which falls from chimneys,
> Slipped by the terrace, made a sudden leap,
> And seeing that it was a soft October night,
> Curled once about the house, and fell asleep. (15–22)[8]

7. T. S. Eliot, "The Love Song of J. Alfred Prufrock," in *Collected Poems, 1909–1962* (London: Faber and Faber, 1963), 13.

8. Eliot, "Prufrock," 5.

And after this stanza, we do indeed return to the flow of time, only to discover that we are far from the moment of decision about our "over-whelming question." On the contrary, our time opens the possibility for "a hundred indecisions, / And for a hundred visions and revisions / Before the taking of a toast and tea" (32–34).[9]

But what is this "overwhelming question"? Here comes the Laforguian moment, his second movement, in which the initial crucial aspiration turns out to be tawdry and / or slightly ridiculous; in short the moment of takedown.

> And I have known the eyes already, known them all—
> The eyes that fix you in a formulated phrase,
> And when I am formulated, sprawling on a pin,
> When I am pinned and wriggling on a wall,
> Then how should I begin (55–59)[10]

The fear is of humiliation; and the issue filling this seemingly endless time is "Do I dare?"

> And indeed, there will be time
> [. . .]
> Time to turn back and descend the stair,
> With a bald spot in the middle of my hair—
> (They will say: "How his hair is growing thin!")
> My morning coat, my collar mounting firmly to the chin,
> My neck-tie rich and modest, but asserted by a single pin—
> (They will say: "But how his arms and legs are thin!")
> Do I dare
> Disturb the universe? (37–46)[11]

The Laforguian takedown is consummated in this passage, in the ridicu-lous contrast between the grandiose description of the last two lines, and the fearful ruminations which precede them.

Prufrock yearns to work up the courage to declare his love to a lady he wants to woo, but he is intimidated by the fear that he will make a

9. Eliot, "Prufrock," 6.
10. Eliot, "Prufrock," 7.
11. Eliot, "Prufrock," 6.

fool of himself, that he might turn out to have misread her (seemingly encouraging) response to him, and might humiliate him, saying, "That's not what I meant at all."

And this drama takes place in intimate indoor settings in which people indulge in somewhat pretentious but not very meaningful conversation.

> In the room the women come and go
> Talking of Michelangelo. (35–36)

Against this background, time stretches before him:

> And indeed, there will be time
> [. . .]
> Time for you and time for me,
> And time yet for a hundred indecisions,
> And for a hundred visions and revisions, (24, 31–33)

Faced with the moment of possible decision, he thinks of all the reasons to back off, "to turn back and descend the stair." How can he presume? He gradually comes to the conclusion:

> I have seen the moment of my greatness flicker,
> And I have seen the eternal Footman hold my coat and snicker,
> And in short, I was afraid. (84–86)

"Would it have been worth it after all," if after the immense effort of a declaration, she,

> Settling a pillow, or throwing off a shawl,
> And turning towards a window, should say:
> "That is not it at all,
> That is not what I meant at all".

> No, I am not prince Hamlet, nor was meant to be. (107–111)[12]

The seemingly endlessly extensible time slides toward the meaningless repetition of the same, which is central to the Baudelairean experi-

---

12. Eliot, "Prufrock," 8–9.

ence of Spleen. The protagonist sees this as ultimately to be redeemed by the moment of decision, but in fact he is wallowing in indecision—and not only on the main issue, Does he fail to make his declaration? but on a series of ancillary questions, Do I dare eat a peach? and so on.

The combination of pusillanimity and futility cannot but raise the question: Is there not something more significant in life outside this hot-house? Properly understood, his only liberation would be to step out of the humiliating predicament where the whole point of his life depends on the capricious, momentary acceptance of a society queen.

But what lies outside? I would argue that the poem hints at this beyond. It happens first of all about halfway through, when a two-line interjection interrupts the anguish of indecision amid the sordid urban scenes:

> I should have been a pair of ragged claws
> Scuttling across the floors of silent seas. (73–74)

One might argue that the ragged claws represent menace, but what I feel in these lines is the relief which would attend this escape. The image of the engulfing ocean carries the hesitant promise of a fuller life outside.

I think this interpretation is strengthened by the last lines of the poem:

> I shall wear white flannel trousers, and walk along the beach.
> I have heard the mermaids singing, each to each.

> I do not think that they will sing to me.

> I have seen them riding on the waves
> Combing the white hair of the waves blown back
> When the wind blows the water white and black.

> We have lingered in the chambers of the sea
> By sea-girls wreathed with seaweed red and brown
> Till human voices wake us, and we drown. (123–131)[13]

13. Eliot, "Prufrock," 9.

One might object to this interpretation that our liberation from this narrow social world involves a kind of death. But coming from Eliot, this equivalence should not surprise us. (Think of the purification in *The Waste Land* IV: "Death by Water.") I think that what we have here is a repetition of the Laforguian three-step movement: There is (1) the aspiration to be accepted as the lover of the lady, which is (2) perpetually defeated by Prufrock's sense that this involves a ridiculous presumption, which would almost certainly be rebuffed. But (3) this aspiration is described in absurdly hyperbolic terms, granted its shallowness as a human goal: the issue of whether he dares declare his love is described as an "overwhelming question"; does he dare "disturb the universe"? As with Laforgue, the standard itself ends up looking not all that impressive, in fact, rather pathetic.

The body of the poem, apart from the two brief "sea" passages, could be read as embodying Laforgue's first two movements, and the shuddering collision they generate; and this very impasse could be a marker of a deeper aspiration: to be engulfed in the chambers of the sea.

III

The Waste Land *commented*   *The Waste Land* assembles "fragments," some of them first-person statements (like "Prufrock"), some of them reporting conversations and other events; some are citations of paradigmatic works of literature, in more than one language; the whole in combination has an immense power of suggestion, and in this way resembles a symbolist work. Otherwise put, it works on us like music.

And clearly what we might call Eliot's poetic music (combining the music of sound and that of thoughts and ideas) reaches heights that are rarely equaled. It is not surprising that the impact of this work was immense, and remains so.

It has been understood as a profound and devastating critique of our Western civilization at the moment of its creation, in the early 1920s. And it is certainly true that this civilization at that time was in a state of confusion and disarray, in the aftermath of the massive slaughter of the "Great War," as it was known; a gigantic sacrifice of young lives, which seemed to have resolved none of the problems which had triggered it. In fact, smaller regional wars continued with dangerous intensity in Europe and the Middle East until well into the 1920s.[14]

It is not surprising that many younger people saw the poem as a portrait of their time. The crucial controlling intuition of this critique: that we suffer (in our civilization) from an inability to recognize or even imagine properly what the fullness of life would be like, and thus what the sources are, contact with which would bring this fullness; and this often means that we are unable even to pine after contact with these sources.

The Waste Land can be read as an attempt to portray, invoke, this lack of or distance from fullness, in order to trigger the insight into what it would be like, and the sources which could make it flourish. The poem is—or at least could be taken as—an empty marker of what this life and its sources could be. The hope would be that a powerfully evocative portrayal of the life lacking fullness will help us see what this fullness would consist in.

This is analogous to a Laforguian exercise, but with a difference. Where "Prufrock" is fully Laforguian, because what the protagonist aims to achieve suggests its own inadequacy, here there is not one protagonist, and one standard, but rather a portrait of modern life through a series of different agents and situations which exhibit their joint impoverishment, interrupted by flashes of insight into what a fuller life might be.

And secondly, the empty marker doesn't depend on the incongruity between passionate longing and slightly ridiculous aspiration. It is painted directly in powerful images of deprivation which in themselves should indicate what we lack.

Later we will see that the poem for Eliot had also a deeper goal: without ceasing to be a critique of his time, it was also the beginning of an exploration of the conditions, if any, of a nondestructive, nondegenerative love.

This enterprise, of offering an empty marker, is also different from a simple evocation / statement of the emptiness of contemporary life, such as "The Hollow Men" seemed to be, at first blush, in that its powerful

14. See Robert Gerwarth, *The Vanquished: Why the First World War Failed to End, 1917–1923* (London: Penguin, 2017).

negative images tend to occlude the hints it offers of what could be a way
out from this predicament.

One master trope of *The Waste Land* is drought, a land deprived of
water; and this means also deprived of fertility, and hence of the fullness
of a flourishing which fertility can bring. To the point where what fullness of life could mean comes to be hard to imagine, and the power to
recover the vision seems to flag.

But on another, metaphorical level, the absence of fertility can be seen
in a world where sexual love, the source of human fertility, suffers from
an absence of all intensity; of real, self-transforming desire; and from a
surfeit of boredom, mutual manipulation, even violence (the reference
to the rape of Philomel in "A Game of Chess").

(In an earlier version, the poem had an exergue from Conrad's *Heart
of Darkness:* Kurtz's cry: "The horror!")

What is given first is the dismay of the poet-narrator, but this is expressed in a vision of civilization today. The personal is transmuted. The
crisis in civilization is shown through a crisis in the self, as illustrated
through many protagonists. The path to a cure might emerge (the reader
hopes) from this poem; the poetry of an empty marker which will reveal and connect us to the sources of renewal.

A pause to look at where we have arrived. My master trope in this book
is (re)connection; this was originally framed as recovering contact with
a continuing cosmic order. But that is not at all what is at stake in Eliot's
The Waste Land: what the poem strives for is contact with the sources of
a fuller life. Now this may turn out to require connection to a standing
cosmic order—and it does turn out to involve this for Eliot, as will become evident in his later work. But in the first instance, this is not how
the issue seems to be defined for this work.

The Burial of the Dead

The Waste Land starts:

> April is the cruellest month, breeding
> Lilacs out of the dead land, mixing
> memory and desire, stirring
> Dull roots with spring rain. (1–4)

This starting point reflects Eliot's belief about the role that fertility rites play in the early stages of human culture and religion. But fertility is ambivalent: brings life, but also desire—"memory and desire"—and desire shakes us. We don't yet know how to live the fullness of desire and fertility, and so both memory and anticipation arouse fear.

> Winter kept us warm, covering
> Earth in forgetful snow, feeding
> A little life with dried tubers. (5–7)[15]

And then another voice enters, Marie; it seems she is one of the dispossessed, fleeing in the aftermath of the First World War: "Bin gar keine Russin, stamm' aus Litauen, echt Deutsch." She takes up the same theme: "Summer surprised us, coming over the Starnbergersee / With a shower of rain." In a few lines, Eliot invokes a whole human existence, with its nostalgic memories: a recent one about that moment in the sunlit Hofgarten, and more remote childhood ones about sledding at the archduke's. In the winter mountains "you feel free."[16]

There follows another voice, not necessarily human, addressing us under the appellation "Son of Man," telling us that we live in a rocky terrain, in fact a desert:

> you know only
> A heap of broken images, where the sun beats,
> And the dead tree gives no shelter, the cricket no relief
> And the dry stone no sound of water. (21–24)

We may look for shade, and "there is shadow under this red rock."[17] But what the voice shows us there, in a frightening reversal of Blake's eschatological vision, is not eternity in a grain of sand, but "fear in a handful of dust."

In this short opening page of the first movement, Eliot has set out the three master images which help define *The Waste Land*. First, it is (1) a dry land, a land in drought; then, not unconnected, this land is (2) infertile.

---

15. T. S. Eliot, *The Waste Land*, in *Poems*, 1:55.

16. Eliot, *Waste Land*, 55.

17. Eliot, *Waste Land*, 55.

But the infertility is not only due to drought; there is also a fear of and incapacity for a fully affirmed sexual love which can bring fertility across its whole range.

But just at this point there breaks through a declaration, on the part of the presumed protagonist, of what this full love might mean. His companion says: "You gave me hyacinths first a year ago; / They called me the hyacinth girl." To which the man replies:

> Yet when we came back, late, from the hyacinth garden,
> Your arms full, and your hair wet, I could not
> Speak, and my eyes failed, I was neither
> Living or dead, and I knew nothing.
> Looking into the heart of light, the silence. (37–41)[18]

But in a typical Eliot move, this inspiring vision is not allowed to stand uncommented. Both immediately before and right after, it is framed by quotes from *Tristan and Isolde,* the first from the exciting early days of their love, the second from the bleak waiting for its end: "*öd' und leer das Meer.*" Then, at the close of this movement, another important Eliot theme is introduced, that of the "Unreal City":

> Under the brown fog of a winter dawn,
> A crowd flowed over London Bridge, so many,
> I had not thought death had undone so many. (61–63)[19]

The obvious borrowing of the third line from Dante's *Inferno* says everything about the spectral, unreal lives attributed to this mass of undiscriminated beings. The movement ends with another reference to early fertility cults, in which burial of the dead figured; rites which are obviously no more accessible for us.

A Game of Chess

This movement opens in a beautiful and richly furnished room; it could be the boudoir of a queen. This is lovingly described, its furnishings, and its décor. This latter includes a sylvan scene, in which a horrifying act of

---

18. Eliot, *Waste Land,* 56.
19. Eliot, *Waste Land,* 56–57.

sexual violence, the rape of Philomela by Tereus, is portrayed. The passage segues into a conversation between a nervous and frightened woman who seeks reassurance from her spouse/lover, and is met with a brutal refusal. At the climax of the conversation, she asks: "What shall we do tomorrow? What shall we ever do?" To which the reply is:

> The hot water at ten.
> And if it rains, a closed car at four.
> And we shall play a game of chess,
> Pressing lidless eyes and waiting for a knock on the door.
>   (135–138)[20]

There follows one side of a conversation overheard, as it were, in a pub, in which the female speaker advises another woman how to hold her husband who has just returned from the war. The manipulative nature of the advice shows how much the relationship has shriveled.

The Fire Sermon

This section is oddly named, because the Buddha in his sermon speaks of desire, especially sexual desire, as "burning," and Enlightenment as a way of dousing the fire, but the issue in *The Waste Land* is much more the mechanical, loveless, even passion-free nature of sexual relations.

This movement has an antiphonal character, in which citations from the Bible and great works of literature alternate with (generally deflating) contemporary scenes or events. It is about the Thames; but the nymphs have departed, and the river is enjoined, "Sweet Thames, run softly, till I end my song."[21] Despite the jarring juxtaposition of beauty from the literary tradition with often sordid contemporary reality, the movement as a whole flows musically, and carries us with it: "But at my back in a cold blast I hear / The rattle of the bones, and chuckle spread from ear to ear"; or:

> A rat crept slowly through the vegetation
> Dragging its slimy belly on the bank

---

20. Eliot, *Waste Land,* 59–60.
21. Eliot, *Waste Land,* 62.

> While I was fishing in the dull canal
> On a winter evening round behind the gashouse (187–190)

And:

> Musing upon the king my brother's wreck
> And on the king my father's death before him. (191–192)[22]

The movement also incorporates an "unreal city" passage in which the old, hermaphroditic, disabused observer of human life describes a mechanical, passion-free seduction. Afterward

> She turns and looks a moment in the glass,
> Hardly aware of her departed lover;
> Her brain allows one half-formed thought to pass:
> "Well now that's done; and I'm glad it's over".
>
>
> When lovely woman stoops to folly and
> Paces about her room again, alone,
> She smooths her hair with automatic hand,
> And puts a record on the gramophone.
> "This music crept by me on the waters". (249–257)[23]

Shortly after this point, the river takes over and carries us along toward the sea:

> The river sweats
> Oil and tar
> The barges drift
> With the turning tide
> Red sails
> Wide
> To leeward, swing on the heavy spar. (266–272)[24]

22. Eliot, *Waste Land*, 62.
23. Eliot, *Waste Land*, 64.
24. Eliot, *Waste Land*, 65.

And we are carried forward, punctuated by the song of the Rhine maidens, by Elizabeth and Leicester carried downstream on this same river, by references to other passionless seductions, finally to Augustine, quoting "To Carthage then I came," where the saint learned what it was to burn, in the full Buddhist sense of the term. And finally to the sea which is the scene of the next movement.

Death by Water

> Phlebas the Phoenician, a fortnight dead,
> Forgot the cry of gulls, and the deep swell,
> And the profit and loss.

>   A current under sea
> Picked his bones in whispers. As he rose and fell
> He passed the ages of his age and youth
> Entering the whirlpool

>   Gentile or Jew
> O you who turn the wheel and look to windward,
> Consider Phlebas, who was once handsome and tall as you.
>   (312–321)[25]

There is a catharsis here, entering the element where all differences, between profit and loss, age and youth, Gentile or Jew, are wiped clean. The ocean seems to have returned to its place in "Prufrock," where (as I believe) it represents this rising to a higher realm, beyond the fruitless and demeaning search for amorous conquests. And the fact that this also means death will not have been seen by Eliot as a drawback, then and later.

But that doesn't seem to represent the end of the search that the poem undertakes, the search for the sources of a fuller life, beyond drought and sterility. And so we have:

25. Eliot, *Waste Land,* 67.

IV

What the Thunder Said   The search for these now starts on a new basis. We have undergone a kind of death. "He who was living is now dead / We who were living are now dying." We start the search as new people, but we have to start from the beginning, making our way from the heart of *The Waste Land,* where there is rock and no water. "There is not even silence in the mountains / But dry sterile thunder without rain."

"Who is the third who walks always beside you?"[26] We learn from this that we are two, but from time to time there seems to be a third companion, hooded. (A hint in Eliot's notes seems to say that this is a reference to Christ who accompanied the disciples on the road to Emmaus.) Over the mountains, the unreal cities have disappeared from view:

> And upside down in air were towers
> Tolling reminiscent bells, that kept the hours
> And voices singing out of empty cisterns and exhausted wells.
>   (382–384)[27]

We now find only an empty chapel, only the wind's home

> Only a cock stood on the roof tree
> Co co rico co co rico
> In a flash of lightning. Then a damp gust
> Bringing rain.

> Ganga was sunken, and the limp leaves
> Waited for rain, while the black clouds
> Gathered far distant, over Himavant.
> The jungle crouched, humped in silence.
> Then spoke the thunder. (391–399)[28]

We think: surely we have come to the end of our quest. The dry land has found rain. The empty marker has generated what it lacked. And the thunder which accompanies the rain speaks to us in three Sanskrit

26. Eliot, *Waste Land,* 69.
27. Eliot, *Waste Land,* 68.
28. Eliot, *Waste Land,* 69–70.

words: *Datta, Dayadhvam, Damyata*—Give, Sympathize, Control. And the explanation of the first command seems to be the answer to our question:

> . . . What have we given?
> My friend, blood shaking my heart
> The awful daring of a moment's surrender
> Which an age of prudence can never retract
> By this and this only, we have existed
> Which is not to be found in our obituaries
> Or in the memories draped by the beneficent spider
> Or under seals broken by the lean solicitor
> In our empty rooms. (401–409)[29]

This daring surrender seems to realize the promise of our love of the hyacinth girl. The vision of the heart of light, the silence has become the center of our lives. Is this the idea? But when we come to the second command, "sympathize," the explanation of what this involves seems a stark repudiation: "We think of the key, each in his prison / Thinking of the key, each confirms a prison."[30]

Dayadhvam may be the formula by which to live, but we have manifestly not been given the power to live by it. But surely that is what we were looking for?

Damyata, by contrast, is spelled out with the image of the expert sailor. "The sea was calm, your heart would have responded / Gaily, when invited, beating obedient / To controlling hands." (Moving swiftly over water is always something which excited Eliot.)

Where does this leave Eliot? He seems to be perplexed. The last stanza seems to be in his own voice:

> I sat upon the shore
> Fishing, with the arid plain behind me
> Shall I at least set my lands in order? (423–425)[31]

---

29. Eliot, *Waste Land*, 70.
30. Eliot, *Waste Land*, 70.
31. Eliot, *Waste Land*, 71.

This is followed by a number of short lines, a number of even smaller "fragments"; some seem positive, some much more negative. All he says about them is: "These fragments I have shored against my ruins."

What are we to think? That the poem fails in what it set out to do? Perhaps not. Perhaps we can still see the work as a whole as attempting the kind of empty marker that I described, but not as a simple failure. It makes some headway toward defining the direction in which one must search but leaves more to be done. In the meanwhile, he offers a beautiful and compelling description of his world: the aftermath of the Great War, which slaughtered young men in their millions, and which left behind the bewildering and troubling question: What was it all for? And deeper, in the difficulty of answering this convincingly, the more fundamental question, What is human life for? became all the harder to answer.

The Waste Land articulated in unparalleled fashion this mood of searching among the younger generation, and all the more effectively in not jumping in with ready-made answers. I would bet that it is the most read and cited poem Eliot ever wrote.

Later, he does attempt to answer these questions, in a Christian, rather than Upanishadic, frame. And those works were brilliant, but perhaps less widely appreciated.

But even without the answer to its defining question, the poem helps define its epoch, and to orient those who lived through it. And they were looking for orientation, for a "way of controlling, of ordering, of giving a shape and a significance to the immense panorama of futility and anarchy which is contemporary history"; what Joyce tried to do through myth, and Pound through his ordering of the literary tradition.[32]

But the unsatisfactory "solution" to the condition so powerfully described in the first three movements forces us to see the poem in the light of the work that followed, and particularly in that of "Ash Wednesday."

The dry land finds water—in fact two kinds of water: the salt-water sea, reminding us of the target of "Prufrock," read as an empty marker; but also the torrents of rain following the thunder. But the fertility brought

---

32. T. S. Eliot, "Ulysses, Order, and Myth," in *Selected Prose of T. S. Eliot,* ed. Frank Kermode (New York: Harcourt Brace, 1975), 177.

by rain does nothing to address infertility on the metaphorical level. The question posed by the intense hyacinth passage of section I can be phrased: how to live out a fulfilled, nondestructive, nondegenerating sequel to this moment. The answer will be: only through renunciation of sexual union, and its sublimation into the love of God. Eliot's model will be Dante, whose ultimate fulfillment comes when his beloved Beatrice guides him into Paradise. And this will be a hard transformation, requiring both suffering and insight. Seen as describing the starting point for this long and arduous journey, section V of *The Waste Land* makes more sense than it could as the answer to the drought and desolation its first three sections explore.

V

Eliot's order   In both "Prufrock" and *The Waste Land,* Eliot gives us a picture of an unlivable predicament—that is, one which renders impossible the fullness of life—and the way in which this predicament denies us and our fulfillment gives some hint of what a full life might be. But in neither case does this negation of life provide enough of a hint to allow us to define the context in which we can live fully and creatively, and more specifically as truly creative poets and writers.

But Eliot was not only a great poet; he was also a philosopher (his Harvard doctoral thesis was on Bradley); and the combination of these two capacities made him a formidable critic.

If *The Waste Land* can be placed in the stream of (what I've been calling) post-Romantic attempts to invoke and thus reconnect with a cosmic order occluded through disenchantment, then this is a path which Eliot abandons.

Instead, he sets out as a thinker to develop a very clear idea of what such a context of full and creative life must be. It is a very traditional notion of order: first in being Christian, even (in a nonpapal sense) Catholic, underpinned by an Aristotelian-Thomistic philosophy of Being. But the demonstration of this order as both good and inescapable didn't come from the empty marker of *The Waste Land,* nor a fortiori from that of "Prufrock." It came through his understanding of literature, in particular

European literature. The writer must place himself within the tradition he belongs to. This doesn't mean that we should follow "the ways of the immediate generation before us in a blind or timid adherence to its successes":

> Tradition is a matter of much wider significance. It cannot be inherited, and if you want it you must obtain it by great labour. It involves, in the first place, the historical sense . . . and the historical sense involves a perception, not only of the pastness of the past, but of its presence. The historical sense compels a man to write not only with his own generation in his bones, but with a feeling that the whole of the literature of Europe from Homer and within it the whole literature of his own country has a simultaneous existence and composes a simultaneous order. This historical sense, which is a sense of the timeless as well as the temporal and of the timeless and the temporal together, is what makes a writer traditional. And it is at the same time what makes a writer most acutely conscious of his place in time, of his own contemporaneity.[33]

The value of each poetic creation can only be judged in relation to the whole tradition, but this does not mean slavishly following past writers. For the tradition is also altered to some degree by each valid addition to it. So something "happens simultaneously to all the works of art which preceded it."[34]

But should new writers not express themselves? This for Eliot was the most dangerous heresy.

Giving vent to one's personality is emphatically not the goal. The poet must engage in "a continual surrender of himself as he is at the moment to something which is more valuable. The progress of the artist is a continual self-sacrifice, a continual extinction of personality."[35]

33. T. S. Eliot, "Tradition and the Individual Talent," in *Selected Prose,* 38.
34. Eliot, "Tradition," 38.
35. Eliot, "Tradition," 40.

"The more perfect the artist, the more completely separate in him will be the man who suffers and the mind which creates."[36]

As he puts it a little later: "Poetry is not a turning loose of emotion, but an escape from emotion; it is not the expression of personality, but an escape from personality. But, of course, only those who have personality and emotions know what it means to want to escape from these."[37]

(This last statement is followed by a quote in Greek from Aristotle's *De Anima* [1.4], which translates: "The intellect is doubtless more divine and less subject to passion" [than the passions].)

Impersonality in the above sense is one of Eliot's fundamental doctrines. The contrast case, art which seeks to express the self and his / her feelings, is branded as "Romantic"; in this Eliot was at one with other members of his generation in England during and after the First World War, such as T. E. Hulme and Wyndham Lewis.

(It goes without saying that I find this definition of "Romanticism" absurdly oversimple and one-sided, but "classicism," as the negation of "Romanticism," became one of Eliot's defining allegiances. Unfortunately, more was at stake here than simply an issue of nomenclature. Eliot's famous self-definition in three terms—"classicist in literature, [Anglo]-Catholic in religion, and monarchist in politics"—was clearly modeled on Maurras' similar declaration, which had various sinister connotations of which Eliot should have been aware. In particular, "monarchist in politics" is utterly uninformative in England [where were / are the republicans?], whereas in France it was a declaration of war on the Republic, involving virulent anti-Semitism and other repulsive traits.)

(For Hulme and his modernist successors, "Romanticism" was defined by the impulse toward subjective expression of feeling. But I think this, absurdly dismissive as it was, does reflect, even if distortively, a real difference between "Romantics" and "modernists," which I tried to account for in an earlier work: considering the "epiphanic" power of poetry, I distinguished the "expressive epiphanies" of Romantic authors from the

36. Eliot, "Tradition," 41.
37. Eliot, "Tradition," 43.

"interspatial" or "framing epiphanies" of modernist writers [Eliot, but especially Pound, Vorticism, Wyndham Lewis].[38])

In any case, this affirmation of classicism was Eliot's way into a conception of a created cosmic order, as defined philosophically by Aristotle and Thomas. The "simultaneous order" of European literature was grounded in Latin poetry which had already taken on board classical Greek literature. The defining figure of the Latin tradition was Virgil, and the paradigmatic work of the medieval continuation of this tradition was Dante's *Divine Comedy:* Dante, who was guided (in the poem itself) by Virgil, and (in philosophy) by Thomas.

This order was embraced by Eliot, and he set out to give it new expression in contemporary terms, which would endow it with a new dimension of interpretation, following his doctrine of tradition as an ever-changing simultaneous order.

(We might pause here to note the distance we have traveled from the invocations of order among the early Romantics and through the nineteenth century. The emerging primacy of time that I noted in Chapter 11 is reflected in Eliot's having to extract and distill his order from a history, that of European literature.)

In thus defining an order within a literary tradition and making this the key to finding an order in contemporary history, Eliot made a step unprecedented in the past, but he wasn't alone in his time in this. Pound did something similar, although he took his literary order in a very different direction. And we can argue the case for similar moves among other contemporaries. Joyce in *Ulysses* did something similar in taking the myth of Ulysses as his guiding thread as Stephen Dedalus moves through Dublin. One can argue that a similar malaise prompted many writers to find in literature, broadly conceived, "a way of controlling, or ordering, of giving a shape and a significance to the immense panorama of futility and anarchy which is contemporary history."[39]

38. See Charles Taylor, *Sources of the Self: The Making of Modern Identity* (Cambridge, MA: Harvard University Press, 1989), ch. 24.

39. Eliot, "Ulysses," 177.

I said above that Eliot gave a new expression to the traditional order; he used the means that contemporary poetry had created to give us a new angle of approach to a long-standing doctrine.

To sum up in one term what this new approach was, I would say that Eliot's poetry is "postsymbolist." Earlier, in the "Note on 'Symbolism,'" I tried to explain the distinction in terms of the distinction between "state" and "suggest." Presymbolist poetry made statements with powerful suggestive force; but the statements in "symbolist" poetry are either contradictory ("Je est un autre") in the extreme case, or so enigmatic in their combination that we are left mainly if not entirely with the suggestive force that they jointly yield.

On this criterion, an argument could be made that some of Eliot's early poetry is "symbolist"—for instance, "Rhapsody on a Windy Night." But I would like to describe *The Waste Land* as "postsymbolist," or symbolist on a wider scale.

In describing *The Waste Land* earlier, I spoke of the fragments of which it was composed. For instance, in the first movement, "The Burial of the Dead," there is a first fragment (1) starting "April is the cruellest month"; then a second (2) around the memories of Marie, then (3) one about dry rock and shadow, which reverses Blake; then (4) the "hyacinth girl," followed by the declaration about "the heart of light, the silence." This last one is surrounded fore and aft by short quotations from *Tristan*. Now each of these fragments is not symbolist by the above criterion. It is clear what statements are being made, even if some of them tread on enigmatic territory. But when it comes to what they (and the following fragments) are meant to communicate jointly, this is left entirely in the realm of suggestion. (Of course, we cannot but feel that the quotes from *Tristan* surrounding the statement about the heart of life are meant to fragilize it as a declaration of love.)

We are left in a zone resembling where music puts us. In this case, the powerful poetic music of Eliot. I call this postsymbolist because it draws on potentialities of poetry explored by symbolists, albeit to other ends. But the prefix "post" is meant to mark another difference from standard "symbolism." If what the fragments together point to is not entirely clear, the fragments themselves often carry an undeniable force; they not only convey an emotion, but make us feel it, as clear and definite as, in a garden, we recognize the smell of a rose.[40]

Now something of this recurs in Eliot's most mature statements of his position, in, say, *Four Quartets*. The analogy with music is invoked in this term, and the fragments of the earlier long poems are replaced by "movements." Here, indeed, it is clearer how the movements relate, how they together contribute to the same vision, because the movements, much more clearly than the earlier fragments, occupy each a different standpoint.

V

Four Quartets   I want to look at the first quartet, "Burnt Norton," in order to see how Eliot has created out of contemporary means a new avenue of approach to a traditional doctrine. Doctrinally, this poem explores what I called "God's eternity," the way in which Christian faith conceives God as present to all times, in the *nunc stans*.

The first movement invokes for us the way in which this can be indirectly experienced in a moment which is acutely felt as "overfull." He is drawing here on some of the explorations of exceptional "higher times," which occurred in the nineteenth century, and continue into the twentieth. In particular, there seems to be a debt to Mallarmé.

> Footfalls echo in the memory
> Down the passage which we did not take
> Towards the door we never opened
> Into the rose garden. (11–14)[41]

Some parallel reality was powerfully present. "Quick, said the bird," who summons us into that "first world," where things are there in their invisibility with unheard music, undeniably sounding.

40. See F. O. Matthiessen, *The Achievement of T. S. Eliot: An Essay on the Nature of Poetry* (Oxford: Oxford University Press, 1935).

41. T. S. Eliot, "Four Quartets: Burnt Norton," in *Poems*, 179.

> And the unseen eyebeam crossed, for the roses
> Had the look of flowers that are looked at.
> There they were as our guests, accepted and accepting. (28–30)[42]

Too much is happening. Alongside our ordinary lived time, we feel another, fuller presence is sharing this moment with us:

> And the pool was filled with water out of sunlight,
> And the lotus rose, quietly, quietly
> The surface glittered out of heart of light,
> And they were behind us, reflected in the pool
> Then a cloud passed, and the pool was empty.
> Go, said the bird, for the leaves were full of children,
> Hidden excitedly, containing laughter.
> Go, go, go, said the bird: human kind
> Cannot bear very much reality. (35–43)[43]

These overfull moments that we fleetingly share with a higher time are too much for us. The second movement starts:

> Garlic and sapphires in the mud
> Clot the bedded axle-tree. (1–2)[44]

(Another invocation of Mallarmé.) There are cyclical movements, repeated *corso e ricorso,* and these cycles happen on the highest as well as the lowest levels; and these levels are linked as the image of the axle-tree tells us; there is strife and its appeasement, and all these are linked together and come to ultimate repose above:

> We move above the moving tree
> In light upon the figured leaf
> And hear upon the sodden floor
> Below, the boarhound and the boar
> Pursue their pattern as before
> But reconciled among the stars. (10–15)[45]

---

42. Eliot, "Burnt Norton," 180.
43. Eliot, "Burnt Norton," 180.
44. Eliot, "Burnt Norton," 180.
45. Eliot, "Burnt Norton," 180–181.

The movement continues with an invocation of a "still point," an unavoidable image after the portrayal of continuing cyclical movement, and a powerful suggestion of the eternity of the *nunc stans*.

> At the still point of the turning world. Neither flesh nor fleshless;
> Neither from nor towards; at the still point, there the dance is,
> But neither arrest nor movement. And do not call it fixity,
> Where past and future are gathered. Neither movement from nor
>   towards,
> Neither ascent nor decline. Except for the point, the still point,
> There would be no dance, and there is only the dance.
> I can only say, *there* we have been: but I cannot say where.
> And I cannot say, how long, for that is to place it in time. (16–23)[46]

Even to get close to grasping this still point, we have to take the path of renunciation. It is not just that we time dwellers can't grasp eternity. We are also spiritually unprepared to receive it.

> Yet the enchainment of past and future,
> Woven in the weakness of the changing body,
> Protects mankind from heaven and damnation
> Which flesh cannot endure. (33–36)[47]

But what is possible are the moments when time seems overfull, when some higher time seems about to break in:

> But only in time can the moment in the rose-garden,
> The moment in the arbour where the rain beat,
> The moment in the draughty church at smokefall
> Be remembered; involved with past and future.
> Only through time is time conquered. (39–43)[48]

The third movement forces this on our fickle attention:

> Neither plenitude nor vacancy. Only a flicker
> Over the strained time-ridden faces

46. Eliot, "Burnt Norton," 181.
47. Eliot, "Burnt Norton," 181.
48. Eliot, "Burnt Norton," 181.

> Distracted from distraction by distraction
> Filled with fancies and empty of meaning
> Timid apathy with no concentration
> Men and bits of paper, whirled by the cold wind
> That blows before and after time,
> Wind in and out of unwholesome lungs
> Time before and time after.
> Eructation of unhealthy souls
> Into the fetid air, the torpid
> Driven on the wind that sweeps the hills of London,
> Hampstead and Clerkenwell, Camden and Putney,
> Highgate, Primrose and Ludgate. Not here
> Not here the darkness, in this twittering world. (10–24)[49]

We have to descend lower:

> Desiccation of the world of sense,
> Evacuation of the world of fancy
> Inoperancy of the world of spirit; (30–32)[50]

And the fifth movement shows how inadequate and treacherous the words we want to use to invoke this still point are.

> Desire itself is movement
> Not in itself desirable;
> Love is itself unmoving,
> Only the cause and end of movement,
> Timeless, and undesiring
> Except in the aspect of time
> Caught in the form of limitation
> Between un-being and being.
> Sudden in a shaft of sunlight
> Even when the dust moves
> There rises the hidden laughter
> Of children in the foliage
> Quick now, here, now always—

---

49. Eliot, "Burnt Norton," 182.
50. Eliot, "Burnt Norton," 182–183.

Ridiculous the waste sad time
Stretching before and after. (25–39)[51]

The second quartet, "East Coker," contains a splendid passage in movement III, reminiscent of the "Unreal City" passages in *The Waste Land*. It ends with another call for renunciation, even of hope and love.

But the faith and the love and the hope are all in the waiting.
Wait without thought, for you are not ready for thought:
So the darkness shall be light, and the stillness the dancing.

Whisper of running streams, and winter lightning.
The wild thyme unseen and the wild strawberry,
The laughter in the garden, echoed ecstasy
Not lost, but requiring, pointing to the agony
Of death and birth. (26–33)[52]

The last movement of "The Dry Salvages" softens the point a little:

But to apprehend
The point of intersection of the timeless
With time, is an occupation for the saint—
No occupation either, but something given
And taken, in a lifetime's death in love,
Ardour and selflessness and self-surrender.
For most of us, there is only the unattended
Moment, the moment in and out of time,
The distraction fit, lost in a shaft of sunlight,
The wild thyme unseen, or the winter lightning
Or the waterfall, or music heard so deeply
That it is not heard at all, but you are the music
While the music lasts. These are only hints and guesses,
Hints followed by guesses; and the rest

51. Eliot, "Burnt Norton," 184.
52. T. S. Eliot, "Four Quartets: East Coker," in *Poems*, 188.

Is prayer, observance, discipline, thought and action.
The hint half guessed, the gift half understood, is Incarnation.
(17–32)[53]

I hope these quoted passages make plain how much Eliot's renewal of what he sees as the age-old tradition owes to the poetry of his time, among other things, to symbolism. But his abandoning the earlier approach, where the order is hinted at by a powerful description of a world in which the contact with it has been lost, has opened the way for a new kind of work, fusing poetry and philosophy, which comes to full expression in the quartets. In these Eliot has found a way of formulating his vision which reflects fully the duality of his take on things, both as poet and as thinker.

Eliot's poetic music is present throughout these works, but the different "movements" in each quartet have as it were different "tempi," and above all different themes.

The background assumption, or we might say truth, of the whole work is that, as creatures living in time, we cannot ever grasp the eternity of *nunc stans*. We can only be nudged toward some indirect sense of it and offered some considerations which might induce us to put our faith in it as our ultimate destination. Poet and philosopher operate together in this double enterprise.

The indirect sense comes through the powerful experience of a higher time erupting into our everyday world. These are epiphanic moments when something like higher time breaks through: the experience in the rose garden of "Burnt Norton" I. And we return to this, as we noticed above, at luminous moments in the next two quartets: at the end of "Burnt Norton" II, and of "Burnt Norton" V; near the end of "East Coker" III; and in the last movement of "The Dry Salvages" ("hints and guesses").

The considerations which might edge us toward a reasonable, if never certain, belief in this eternity are of several kinds.

There is (1) the suggestion of a still point at the center of the world's cycles, which we saw above in "Burnt Norton" II—and perhaps something similar in the first lines of "East Coker" II.

53. T. S. Eliot, "Four Quartets: The Dry Salvages," in *Poems*, 199–200.

There are (2) self-discrediting descriptions of our full immersion in time with no higher perspective, like the beginning of "East Coker" III:

> O Dark, dark, dark. They all go into the dark
> The vacant interstellar spaces, the vacant into the vacant,
> The captains, merchant bankers, eminent men of letters
> The generous patrons of art, the statesmen and the rulers (1–4)[54]

And "Burnt Norton" III:

> Here is a place of disaffection
> Time before and time after (1–2)[55]

Then there is (3) the insistence that radical renunciation is the only way to this final destination:

"Burnt Norton" III at the end:

> Descend lower, descend only
> Into the world of perpetual solitude,
> World not our world, but that which is not world,
> Internal darkness, deprivation . . . (124–127)[56]

"East Coker" III, at the end:

> I said to my soul, be still, and wait without hope (23)[57]

And then there are (4) second-order comments on his own, on the incapacity of our language to deal adequately with the relation of time to eternity:

"Burnt Norton" V: "words strain / Crack and sometimes break, under the burden" (13–14).[58]

"East Coker" II: "That was a way of putting it—not very satisfactory" (18).[59]

---

54. Eliot, "East Coker," 188.
55. Eliot, "Burnt Norton," 182.
56. Eliot, "Burnt Norton," 182.
57. Eliot, "East Coker," 189.
58. Eliot, "Burnt Norton," 183–184.
59. Eliot, "East Coker," 187.

And all of "East Coker" V:

> And so each venture
> Is a new beginning, a raid on the inarticulate
> With shabby equipment always deteriorating,
> In the general mess of imprecision of feeling,
> Undisciplined squads of emotion.[60]

The inadequacy of our words to express our deepest intuitions about life has rarely found such a striking image.

And, of course, the summing up of the last quartet, "Little Gidding" V.

Then there are (5) explorations of other times, attempts to see the past, or the *longue durée,* as the source of valuable insight:

"East Coker" I has particular weight here. East Coker was the village from which Eliot's ancestor departed for New England. His choice of this place cannot have been thoroughly disconnected from this biographical fact. But he has a sense of

> their living in the living seasons
> The time of the seasons and the constellations
> The time of milking and of harvest
> The time of the coupling of man and woman
> And that of beasts. Feet rising and falling.
> Eating and drinking. Dung and death. (41–46)[61]

The last three words say it all. The wisdom of experience, the supposed wisdom of the ages, doesn't give us what we are looking for. What to think of the "wisdom of age"?

> Had they deceived us
> Or deceived themselves, the quiet-voiced elders,
> Bequeathing us merely a recipe for deceit?
> The serenity only a deliberate hebetude,
> The wisdom only the knowledge of dead secrets

---

60. Eliot, "East Coker," 188.
61. Eliot, "East Coker," 186.

> Useless in the darkness into which they peered
> Or from which they turned their eyes. (25–31)[62]

"The Dry Salvages" opens another door into an endless past, that of a great river; here is another draught on Eliot's early American roots, life by the Mississippi. Here too, it seems at first that there is no lesson for us:

> There is no end of it, the voiceless wailing,
> No end to the withering of withered flowers,
> To the movement of pain that is painless and motionless,
> To the drift of the sea and the drifting wreckage,
> The bone's prayer to Death its God. Only the hardly, barely prayable
> Prayer of the one Annunciation. (31–36)[63]

With this ending comes a sudden reversal, which has been prepared by the whole six stanzas which open "The Dry Salvages" II, a kind of poem within the greater poem, in the form of a sestina. The reversal comes from the fact that the moment of extreme suffering and deprivation can also be the moment of turning, of receiving the annunciation of a higher, fuller life.

The insight is worked out in the longer, more discursive passage which completes "The Dry Salvages" II. There is a single, constant message here, which we can grasp in moments of sudden illumination, where we see that "we had the experience but missed the meaning":

> People change, and smile: but the agony abides.
> Time the destroyer is time the preserver,
> Like the river with its cargo of dead negroes, cows and chicken
>   coops,
> The bitter apple and the bite in the apple,
> And the ragged rock in the restless waters,
> Waves wash over it, fogs conceal it;
> On a halcyon day it is merely a monument,
> In navigable weather it is always a seamark

---

62. Eliot, "East Coker," 187.
63. Eliot, "Dry Salvages," 195.

To lay a course by: but in the sombre season
Or the sudden fury, is what it always was. (66–75)[64]

The only adequate response to this endlessly repeated suffering is prayer; our prayer to the virgin to pray for the sailors and their wives ("The Dry Salvages" IV).

"The Dry Salvages" III invokes Krishna and the Bhagavad Gita to deliver the same message in a different form. One might say, the moment when suffering or distress and uncertainty turn us to the eternal can be any moment. As "Little Gidding" V will put it: history is a pattern of timeless moments.

"The Dry Salvages" V:

But to apprehend
The point of intersection of the timeless
With time, is an occupation for the saint—(17–19)[65]

And the passage continues as quoted above.

All these reminders:

- the occasional epiphanic hints and guesses pointing to a higher time

- the suggestion of a still point to the turning world

- the reminders of the emptiness and lack of meaning we often encounter (which in their very lack can work like empty markers)

- the hope placed in radical renunciation

- the sense that no deeper insight can be found in the repetitive movements of history, unless it be the invitation to turn

All these could combine to help us see God's eternity, ontically, as the source of everything, and, eschatologically, as our final destination.

Indeed, the very difficulty—even impossibility—of formulating this conclusion could tell in its favor: the realities here are by definition beyond our powers to grasp.

64. Eliot, "Dry Salvages," 196–197.
65. Eliot, "Dry Salvages," 199.

I come now to "Little Gidding," the last quartet, written some time after the first three, which in a sense takes up the argument / invocation afresh—to the extent that it is really the same argument. "Little Gidding" I tells us:

> If you came this way,
> Taking any route, starting from anywhere,
> At any time or at any season,
> It would always be the same: you would have to put off
> Sense and notion. You are here not to verify,
> Instruct yourself, or inform curiosity
> Or carry report. You are here to kneel
> Where prayer has been valid. And prayer is more
> Than an order of words, the conscious occupation
> Of the praying mind, or the sound of the voice praying.
> And what the dead had speech for, when living,
> They can tell you, being dead: the communication
> Of the dead is tongued with fire beyond the language of the living.
> Here, the intersection of the timeless moment
> In England and nowhere. Never and always. (39–53)[66]

Little Gidding was the site of a community devoted to prayer which was dissolved in the run-up to the Civil War and the Puritan victory. It is their intense prayer which Eliot is pointing to here.

What is remarkable about this passage is that it doesn't call on us to repeat their words; rather, it calls for a new language. It calls on us to find the sense, the inner direction of the prayers of those who came before us, and to find a new formulation, which would be "tongued with fire." We are still in the predicament described in the earlier three quartets, in the sense that we are seeking the "intersection of the timeless moment," but we need a new language to approach this.

One is tempted to speculate that Eliot is responding here to the massive destruction wrought by the bombing of London, and beyond this, the war in general. Certainly, the next section, "Little Gidding" II, is full of images of destruction:

66. T. S. Eliot, "Four Quartets: Little Gidding," in *Poems,* 202.

> Water and fire succeed
> The town, the pasture and the weed
> Water and fire deride
> The sacrifice that we denied.
> Water and fire shall rot
> The marred foundations we forgot,
> Of sanctuary and choir.
>   This is the death of water and fire. (17–24)[67]

This too calls for a new language.

> For last year's words belong to last year's language
> And next year's await another voice. (65–66)[68]

We are impelled

> To purify the dialect of the tribe (74)[69]

(Eliot's debt to Mallarmé emerges again here, as it did at the very beginning of "Burnt Norton," even though their stands on religion were diametrically opposed.) At this point, Eliot's companion in this section of the poem speaks:

> Let me disclose the gifts reserved for age (76)[70]

His offer turns out to be highly ironical, or seems so, in that the list of "gifts" turns out to enumerate the multiple ways in which the old begin to fall apart. But it turns out that these setbacks end up generating the truly fruitful response:

> From wrong to wrong the exasperated spirit
> Proceeds, unless restored by the refining fire,
> Where you must move in measure, like a dancer. (91–93)[71]

67. Eliot, "Little Gidding," 203.
68. Eliot, "Little Gidding," 204.
69. Eliot, "Little Gidding," 205.
70. Eliot, "Little Gidding," 205.
71. Eliot, "Little Gidding," 205.

With this refining fire, we return to the askesis, the kenosis, the self-denial which was the crucial road of access to eternity in the earlier quartets. As "Little Gidding" IV puts it,

> The dove descending breaks the air
> With flame of incandescent terror
> Of which the tongues declare
> The one discharge from sin and error
> The only hope, or else despair
>   Lies in the choice of pyre or pyre
>   To be redeemed from fire by fire.
>
> Who then designed the torment? Love.
> Love is the familiar Name
> Behind the hands that wove
> The intolerable shirt of flame
> Which human power cannot remove.
>   We only live, only suspire
>   Consumed by either fire or fire. (1–14)[72]

But there is also another path we have to tread: of liberation ("Little Gidding" III).

>   —not less of love but expanding
> Of love beyond desire, and so liberation
> From the future as well as the past. Thus, love of a country
> Begins as attachment to our own field of action
> And comes to find that action of little importance
> Though never indifferent. History may be servitude,
> History may be freedom. See, now they vanish,
> The faces and places, with the self which, as it could, loved them,
> To become renewed, transfigured, in another pattern. (8–16)[73]

---

72. Eliot, "Little Gidding," 207–208.
73. Eliot, "Little Gidding," 205–206.

Our sympathy must widen, to take in everyone, to rise above the party strife of the past. And following on this path, another voice makes itself heard. Julian of Norwich:

> Sin is behovely (17)[74]

(I take this to mean here: inevitable, can't be avoided)

> but
> All shall be well, and
> All manner of thing shall be well. (17–19)[75]

As we look back our sympathy should take in both parties in the struggles which make up our history.

> We have taken from the defeated
> What they have left us—a symbol:
> A symbol perfected in death.
> And all shall be well and
> All manner of thing shall be well
> By the purification of the motive
> In the ground of our beseeching. (44–50)[76]

So the considerations which illuminate our path (I could say "argument," but this seems too strong) are not quite the same in "Little Gidding" as in the first three quartets. There is the need for a new language, to "purify the dialect of the tribe." What would this be like? This is the first question. And the path to the *nunc stans* passes not only through askesis, renunciation (the pyre), but also through a widening affirmation. How so? This is the second question. Perhaps the beginnings of an answer to these questions is to be found in "Little Gidding" V. To the first:

> And every phrase
> And sentence that is right [. . .]

---

74. Eliot, "Little Gidding," 206.
75. Eliot, "Little Gidding," 206.
76. Eliot, "Little Gidding," 207.

> is an end and a beginning.
> Every poem an epitaph. (3–4, 11–12)[77]

But what does that mean? Perhaps the answer to this question can be illuminated by the answer to the second; and this can be seen below in the same movement:

> A people without history
> Is not redeemed from time, for history is a pattern
> Of timeless moments. So while the light fails
> On a winter's afternoon, in a secluded chapel
> History is now and England. (20–24)[78]

And what could this mean? Fully immersed in time, we are cut off from, cannot grasp, the eternity of *nunc stans*. But by the same token, if we can break through to some intuitions about eternity, this can happen at any moment. Eternity stands immediately to every moment (a distant analogy here to Leopold von Ranke's claim that all ages are "unmittelbar zu Gott" [immediate to God]). And this is what gives its sense to the last passage of the work:

> We shall not cease from exploration
> And the end of our exploring
> Will be to arrive where we started
> And know the place for the first time.
> Through the unknown, remembered gate
> When the last of earth left to discover
> Is that which was the beginning;
> And the source of the longest river
> The voice of the hidden waterfall
> And the children in the apple-tree
> Not known, because not looked for
> > But heard, half-heard, in the stillness
> > Between two waves of the sea.
> > Quick now, here, now, always—

77. Eliot, "Little Gidding," 208.
78. Eliot, "Little Gidding," 208.

> A condition of complete simplicity
> (Costing not less than everything)
> And all shall be well
> When the tongues of flame are in-folded
> Into the crowned knot of fire
> And the fire and the rose are one. (239–258)[79]

I'm not sure I have grasped everything in this passage, particularly toward the end, but I welcome the return of the children, last heard laughing in the foliage ("Burnt Norton" V). And it is also worth remarking that his reconnection to an older notion of cosmic order invokes an understanding of lived time that was developed and became important only in the last half of the nineteenth century. Before that, attempts at (re) connection were concerned only with continuing cosmic orders.

VI

The whole lineage of understandings of the cosmos as order, grasping which quickens and arouses our ethical nature or dimension, as this moves from premodern forms up to Rilke, tends to be repressed into neutrality and indifference by the objectifying scientific-technological stance. But if our science of nature goes deeply enough, and comes to grasp the complexity and beauty of nature's orders, another kind of ethical aspiration is awakened, moving us to act like stewards who will protect and preserve this order. This may come through a strong sense of how destructive we have been to ecological orders, so we sense that we are failing our vocation.

But this doesn't necessarily replace earlier modes of quickening through (re)connection. The truth seems to be that we relate in multiple ways to nature and the cosmos: on the Hopkins axis, the Rilke axis. We may not fully understand the feeling of earlier modes of relation: of cosmic orders, or of Hölderlin. But we can recognize that other, earlier human beings did so. Just as with early tribal people, we can't understand

79. Eliot, "Little Gidding," 208–209.

spirits and gods, but we see that something analogous was going on there to what we can experience. The cosmos always registers with us, even in mutually noncombinable forms. (I will return to this in Chapter 16.) But the big shift in the last two centuries brings forward (re)connection through time. And this too involves the recovery of something which existed before in another form.

In hindsight, in the light of "Burnt Norton" and "East Coker," the "hyacinth girl" passage in *The Waste Land* sounds like the record of an experience of higher time; but (in the terms of Chapter 11) more like the quasi-simultaneity, the duration without succession, than like the incursion of higher time we feel in "Burnt Norton."

The Buried Life

I

A number of the poets that I have been looking at in the foregoing chapters are, at least implicitly, concerned with an issue which can be put in a variety of ways: What is human life all about? Or what are the ends of life? Or what is the good life for humans? Or what is the meaning of life?

And in the nineteenth century, it came to be that this question could be put on two levels: On one hand, what is the good life for humans in general? On the other hand, one can ask: What is a good and fulfilling life for me, this individual being which I am? A few reflections on this period can help explain why the question arose on this second level.

A new "middle class," neither part of the common people, nor gentry, develops in the nineteenth century, with the opening of new occupations; industrial, commercial, administrative-managerial. Their children are much more educated than those of the "people." But it is not clear to any of them that they should follow their fathers / mothers, unlike aristos, who are often in the army. But just "trade" or manufacturing doesn't necessarily seem meaningful enough to lots of them.

Many of them are drawn precisely to the creative vocations which have been so validated by the Romantic turn. For many, the "bourgeois" life lacks something, some higher purpose. Adventure abroad, imperial military-administrative "service," but not just minding the store.

The questioning here is made more intense by the spread of the ethic of authenticity closely linked to creative vocations, which stress the importance of originality.

But issues of the meaningful life become more acute at this time, because of the accelerating growth in the force and influence of instrumental rationality in this whole period (and indeed, over a longer period, as we shall see). In economic terms, the value concerned is "rationalization."

Already in the novels of Jane Austen, we can see the tug-of-war among the landed gentry between the values of "stewardship," preserving the land and those who live on it (each according to his station), on one hand, and the potential rewards of economic rationalization, on the other. But, of course, this is a centuries-long process, beginning in the fifteenth century with enclosures (which continue right up into the eighteenth and nineteenth centuries in Scotland, with the cruel reinvention of Highland clan leaders as outright owners, expelling their followers to Nova Scotia in order to run sheep on their now-empty lands). And the issue remains alive into the twentieth century (as reflected in fiction by the series *Downton Abbey*); and continues to this day with the purblind single-minded extension of crop land at the expense of hedgerows, swamps, and other "useless" areas, the source of ecological disaster, and in the end even declining yields.

So the conditions come together to make issues of meaning more and more central and urgent: not only the new "middle-class" population, for whom issues of identity remain undecided; not only the decline in prestige which comes with the challenge to certain traditional class identities; but now as well the need to defend the intrinsic worth of any identity against the demands of an instrumental rationality which offers higher and higher payoffs.

Which is not to say that the great achievers in fields of instrumental reason, captains of industry, or creators of new technologies find that their lives lack meaning. This thought is as unlikely to have occurred to Carnegie or Rockefeller in their day as to Jobs and Bezos in ours. My point is just that it doesn't go without saying that one can find meaning in this way, and that for many in other walks of life, cultural creators for instance, such successful producers can be classed in the gray category of "bourgeois."

And so, we enter an age in which questions of a meaningful life become more open and more widely felt. These questions arise on two levels. The first level touches the source of ultimate and most important meaning, hitherto defined by religion. This has been contested since the Reformation; but now the issues are more radical. There are now antireligious, even atheist currents; and then there are issues of religion which are not simply to do with which confession is the truly Christian one, but which bring forth different kinds of spirituality, more or less in congruence with Christian faith. And then there are figures like Arnold, who wants to replace Christianity with high culture.

But then there is a second level, which hasn't to do with the source of meaning *überhaupt,* but rather with what my life is all about. It is often easy for someone to miss this, within the social confines of conformism. This is a main theme in the novels of Henry James, for instance, *Portrait of a Lady* and *The Ambassadors.* James' work was an important reference point for the "generation of 1914," the writers of early modernism, like Eliot and Pound.

And Arnold articulated the issue in its individual form in his poem on the "buried life."

> But often, in the world's most crowded streets,
> But often, in the din of strife,
> There rises an unspeakable desire
> After a knowledge of our buried life;
> A thirst to spend our fire and restless force
> In tracking out our true, original course;
> A longing to enquire
> Into the mystery of this heart which beats
> So wild, so deep in us—to know
> Whence our lives come and where they go.[1]

And this against the background of the new urban built environment, which is often sordid, chaotic, given over to instrumental purposes, and expressive neither of some overall meaning (as earlier cities were), nor of a propitious surrounding for the discovery of one's own path.

1. Matthew Arnold, "The Buried Life," in *The Essential Matthew Arnold* (London: Chatto and Windus, 1969), 126.

II

With Eliot and Pound, but also with James and Conrad, we are in the epoch of what has often been called "modernism." Earlier novelists of the nineteenth century, like Jane Austen and Dickens, were grounded in a clear ethic, one which would have been recognizable to the majority of people in their time, and approved of by most (but, of course, not necessarily lived up to, which gives the novels of these authors their bite). Their ethic provided a steadying framework for the stories they told.

This kind of framework was missing in the works of the modernists. Their background assumption was that it was not so clear what life was all about, and that many people were deluded and confused on this score. And as a consequence, the answers given by the modernist authors to their own questions are not easy to discern.

And we today are living a continuation of the shift they brought about. I think this comes to the surface in the widespread use of the term "identity" in our period—the period which starts in the aftermath of the Second World War. Our contemporaries demand that their identity be recognized and respected.

And what is meant by my "identity" is something like: my fundamental commitments, the landmarks in my moral horizon which guide me in my important choices, be these my religion, or national identity, or my sexual orientation, or my vocation, and so on.

But the puzzling question is: Why do we speak of "identity" rather than simply invoking these fundamental commitments?

One part of the answer comes from our wanting to speak of "my" identity. Our fundamental commitments, as in the examples above, are shared by lots of coreligionists, fellow members of my nation, fellow gay people, and so forth. But today we want to speak of the identity of individuals, aware as we are that each person may have their own particular combination of such widely shared commitments; but we are also aware of how individuals may have their particular take on being, say, Lutheran, German, a historian, or whatever.

And this brings us to the crucial point of continuity with the modernist era. "My particular take" on some widely shared commitment could be described as my interpretation of what it means to be Catholic, Canadian, and so on. My appropriation of one of these poles of belonging will often involve my working out what it means for me. And this is what puts us back in continuity with the modernists of the early twentieth century. If these crucial dimensions of belonging are not to remain "buried," merely implicit, without full recognition of what they amount to, they need an act of appropriation, which brings a fuller consciousness of what they mean for me.

This marks the basic difference between an unreflecting, inherited fundamental commitment, and something I "identify with." And this is why we speak today of "identities," and not just basic commitments.

III

Of course, those two great anglophone modernist poets, Pound and Eliot, were far from indefinite and hesitant in the advice they offered and the positions they took. But their work survives in a world of ever-greater political, moral, and religious diversity, where even those who appreciate them most are ready to challenge their most cherished convictions.

Chapter Fourteen

MIŁOSZ

I

The twentieth century saw some terrible horrors, but one of the really unfortunate places to live was Poland, which spent half the century (1939–1989) under first Hitler, and then Stalin, followed by Stalinism. For a poet, there might be an understandable temptation to ignore history, and write about beautiful things; nature, gardens, flowers, finer feelings. But for Czesław Miłosz, this was impermissible.[1] From "Dedication": "What is poetry which does not save / nations or people?"[2]

I will start from his *Treatise on Poetry* (1957): We have to be, and act, in history. But the Spirit of History, at least in the 1940s and 1950s, seems

1. This chapter owes a great deal to the work of Peter Dale Scott and to the illuminating writings of Łukasz Tischner. See Peter Dale Scott, *Ecstatic Pessimist: Czesław Miłosz, Poet of Catastrophe and Hope* (New York: Rowman and Littlefield, 2023). See also Łukasz Tischner, *Miłosz and the Problem of Evil*, trans. Stanlez Bill (Evanston, IL: Northwestern University Press, 2015).

2. Czesław Miłosz, "Dedication," in *New and Collected Poems: 1931–2001*, trans. Czesław Miłosz et al. (New York: HarperCollins, 2001), 77.

one of wild destruction; a blind necessity which destroys everything valuable in human life. And the responses, both Communist and Romantic nationalist, are dead ends. We can speak of blind necessity, because the political forces that are (or seem) dominant in the world espouse theories of history as ruled by iron laws; and action guided by these leads us into a "heart of darkness" (Miłosz quotes here his famous compatriot). The two such outlooks which dominated Poland in succession in this terrible half century were the struggle for dominance between higher and lower people of the Nazis, on one hand, and the dialectical materialism of Soviet Leninism, on the other. Neither could allow for a meaningful, humane outcome of "history."

This was obvious in the case of Nazism, but may seem unfair to Marxism, which at least sought and predicted the spontaneous self-rule of liberated workers, without a coercive state. But in its Leninist variant which counted on state violence, endless purges, and elimination of whole categories of "enemies," the heart of darkness was clearly unavoidable.

So necessity in this world came to seem unbeatable, not only because of the might of the Wehrmacht and Red Army, but also metaphysically. Underlying both these inhumane theories stood the prestige of the reductive Enlightenment, whose basic epistemic principle was that humans can only be understood in language modeled on natural science. So there was no place there for talk about a higher destiny, or a goal for humans to reach in order to realize themselves fully. Both metaphysics, Nazi and Marxist, give Darwinism the last, crucial word.

In addition to rejecting these two foreign ideologies, Miłosz couldn't accept the dominant form of Polish nationalism, which put a high value on rebellion against foreign rule, even in the face of hopeless odds, on the grounds that glorious defeat leaves a model and a legend which can inspire future generations. It was this which inspired the Warsaw uprising against the Nazis on the eve of their retreat in 1944. Miłosz refused to join this. In addition, this stream of nationalism often included a streak of anti-Semitism. But it was the twin ideological visions of the degrading and imprisoning unfolding of events that Miłosz invokes in the phrase "the spirit of history."

Where wind carries the smell of the crematorium
And a bell in the village tolls the Angelus,
The spirit of history is out walking.[3]

This is a realm of necessity: the necessity of struggle between races, where the winner takes all; or the necessity of the laws of *diamat*.[4] It is no use struggling.

"King of the centuries, ungraspable Movement
You who fill the grottoes of the ocean
With a roiling silence, who dwell in the blood
Of the gored shark devoured by other sharks,
In the whistle of a half-bird, half-fish,
In the thundering sea, in the iron gurgling
Of the rocks when archipelagoes surge up.
[. . .]
You in whom cause is married to effect,
Draw us from the depth as you draw a wave,
For one instant, limitless, of transformation.
You have shown us the agony of the age
So that we could ascend to those heights
Where your hand commands the instruments.
Spare us, do not punish us. Our offense
Was grave: we forgot the power of your law.
Save us from ignorance. Accept now our devotion."

So they foreswore. But every one of them
Kept hidden a hope that the possessions of time
Were assigned a limit. That they would one day
Be able to look at a cherry tree in blossom,
For a moment, unique among the moments,
Put the ocean to sleep, close the hourglass,
And listen to how the clocks stop ticking.[5]

3. Czesław Miłosz, "Treatise on Poetry," in *New and Collected Poems*, 128.
4. Dialectical materialism, the Stalinist incarnation of Marxism-Leninism.
5. Czesław Miłosz, "III. The Spirit of History," in *Collected Poems*, 132–133.

This was the voice of cowardice, for those who "didn't want to die without a reason." They entered the heart of darkness, but they couldn't stifle the question: Where / how to escape? Where to exercise freedom?

> With what word to reach into the future,
> With what word to defend human happiness—
> It has the smell of freshly baked bread—
> If the language of poets cannot search out
> Standards of use to later generations?
> We have not been taught. We do not know at all
> How to unite Freedom and Necessity.[6]

But if history as it is unfolding is, to use Joyce's expression, a nightmare from which we are trying to awake, can nature provide a refuge? This is what Miłosz explores in the next section of the *Treatise on Poetry* after "The Spirit of History." This draws on his experience of wilderness areas in North America shortly after the war. After the Red Army expelled the Nazis, Stalin set up a puppet regime in Poland. But it was not immediately evident to non-Communist Leftists like Miłosz how total the control from Moscow would be on the new government. Many agreed to work in the rebuilding of Poland, in the hopes that they could inflect the new structures in a more humane direction, which would reflect more adequately Polish culture and aspirations. Miłosz joined the diplomatic corps and was posted to New York, and later to Washington. It is then that he had his first experience of the wilder parts of the continent.

Later, when he saw how relentless the Soviet control of the new government would be, he defected and, after a short but eventful period in Paris, he rejoined his wife in the United States and eventually took up a post teaching Slavic literature at Berkeley, where he remained for some decades. The work I have been quoting from, the *Treatise on Poetry*, was written early in this second phase in America.

Section IV of this work is entitled "Natura." I would like to follow this passage more closely, because it seems to me especially powerful and moving. It explores the possibility of an escape from history into nature. This resonated with the experience of his childhood in rural Lithuania;

6. Miłosz, "III. The Spirit of History," 130.

a land where human cultivation existed alongside untamed forests; and where age-old pagan-derived customs were woven into Catholic faith and practice. This was not only the world of his childhood, but also that of the great national poet Mickiewicz, an inspiration and model for many Polish writers, including Miłosz.

In a crucial passage of this section, he is paddling a canoe, trying to get close to a beaver; an effort which must fail, because the beaver can smell him and dive under the surface to escape. This opens the path to a deep reflection on our relation to nature. We belong to it, and yet we don't. We are both animals, and he can smell me, and flee; and we are both mortal (which is why he reacts to my proximity by fleeing), but I am aware of mortality, and he is not.

The awareness of this difference throws him back into a vivid memory of an event which epitomizes what human life is like: a wedding in Basel. Human life is social, lived among others; at times festive with ritual; moments lived among friends, sometimes tinged with a hint of sexual attraction; the polar opposite of the lonely approach to the elusive beaver.

The two memories, both powerful (the beaver scene grows larger than life), jostle together; the beaver's splash exhibits the unconscious necessities of animal life; but does the human festive occasion take us beyond this? The next stanza suggests doubt:

> Peace to the princesses under the tamarisks,
> [...]
> Before the body was wrapped in bandelettes
> [...]
> Before stone fell silent, and there was only pity.[7]

This awareness forces choice on me: How to live my life, what to seek?

The insight breaks in on the poet by the sight of a dead snake on the highway, crushed by the wheels of a passing car. Two kinds of time meet here: blank necessity, and necessity interwoven with freedom. The snake on one hand, and the human instrument, the wheel, on the other; we are inexorably involved in this juncture:

---

7. Czesław Miłosz, "IV. Natura," in *Collected Poems,* 143.

> There are two dimensions. Here is the unattainable
> Truth of being, here at the edge of lasting
> and not lasting. Where the parallel lines intersect,
> Time lifted above time by time.[8]

There is an obvious reference here to Eliot's "Burnt Norton." But, as we'll see later, there will be a big difference. Whether I want to or not, I belong in the history where such moments of juncture occur. But can I inflect its course, however minimally? The two answers to this question vie for our consent:

> The kingdom, you say. We do not belong to it,
> And still, in the same instant, we belong.[9]

A part of us always holds back, but we can break out beyond all the self-proclaimed "iron laws." Moreover, it is poets who can best articulate this open path.

> I want not poetry, but a new diction,
> Because only it might allow us to express
> A new tenderness and save us from a law
> That is not our law, from necessity
> Which is not ours, even if we take its name.[10]

The need is

> [. . .] to gather in an image
> The furriness of the beaver, the smell of rushes,
> And the wrinkles of a hand holding a pitcher
> From which wine trickles. Why cry out
> That a sense of history destroys our substance
> If it, precisely, is offered to our powers,
> A muse of our gray-haired father, Herodotus,
> As our arm and our instrument, though
> It is not easy to use it, to strengthen it

8. Miłosz, "IV. Natura," 143.
9. Miłosz, "IV. Natura," 143.
10. Miłosz, "IV. Natura," 144.

So that, like a plumb with a pure gold center,
It will serve again to rescue human beings.
[. . .]
Aware at this moment I—and not only I—
keep, as in a seed, the unnamed future.[11]

The poet says: "not poetry, but a new diction," but this new medium is a higher form of poetry, the kind that can "save nations and people." It can reveal a new dimension of history, open to transformation. It can break open the sense of imprisonment in the iron necessity of what he called earlier the "spirit of history." But this seems to involve a vision which lifts us beyond ordinary time, a sense of an "eternal moment" (*moment wieczny*).

Such moments when we are touched by a "time lifted above time" can open vistas of human transformation. A powerful image of this figures in the ode "O City, O Society, O Capital," which comes immediately after the passage from the "Natura" section I've been quoting. The city, the capital, stands for all the structures of our civilization which keep us bound by the spirit of history.

Steel, cement, lime, law, ordinance
We have worshipped you too long,
You were for us a goal and a defense,
Ours was your glory and your shame.
[. . .]
From stucco and mirrors, glass and paintings.
Tearing aside curtains of silver and cotton,
Comes man, naked and mortal,
Ready for truth, for speech, for wings.[12]

Something of the same force comes in a later poem of Miłosz: "Throughout Our Lands" (Po Ziemi Naszej).

The human mind is splendid, lips, powerful,
And the summons so great, it must open paradise.

11. Miłosz, "IV. Natura," 144.
12. Miłosz, "IV. Natura," 145.

Umysł ludzki jest wyspianały, usta potężne
I wezwanie tak wielke, żę musi otworzyć się Raj.[13]

[They are so persistent, that give them a few stones
And edible roots, and they will build the world.][14]

This can liberate from presumed historical necessity and determinism. A new stance to time starts with Vico: history as time remembered is different from nature, to which we both belong and don't. In nature, necessity is the only god. Miłosz amends the vision of his former mentor Kronski, who drew inspiration from Hegel.[15] It is poetry, not philosophy, which can tell the deep truth of our age.

One clear stanza can take more weight
Than a whole wagon of elaborate prose.[16]

II

Many of the powerful themes that emerge from Miłosz's work come together here: first, to try to flee from history into nature is not to escape necessity, but to enter into an even more iron form of it, that of killing and being killed. In his semiautobiographical novel about his childhood, *Issa Valley,* the protagonist Thomas seeks a kind of communion with the natural world around him; and at first he seems to find it when he joins some older hunters in their forays into the forest. He is validated by their acceptance of him, until the moment when he is humiliated by his failure to pull the trigger at a target right in front of him. But even before this expulsion, he is troubled by the fact that this mode of communion involves killing. He shoots a squirrel and is immediately cast down and troubled by the sight of the lifeless animal.

13. Czesław Miłosz, *Wiersze* (Kraków: Wydawnictwo Znak, 2002), 2:316–323.

14. Czesław Miłosz, *New and Collected Poems* (New York: ECCO, 2003), 184.

15. Czesław Miłosz, "Tiger 2," in *Native Realm* (Garden City, NY: Doubleday, 1968), 285–300.

16. Czesław Miłosz, "Preface," in *Collected Poems,* 109.

The real escape for a poet from both kinds of necessity would be to write about flowers, gardens, sunsets, the wind in the trees, what Miłosz calls "living inside the rose." Here you are really sheltered from death inflicted and suffered. But as I remarked above, this is an escape from reality which a poet should not, cannot, permit himself. "What is poetry which does not save / nations or people?" (Czym jest poezja, która nie ocala / narodów ani ludzi?).[17]

There is in the end no alternative to this; the poet has to find a way of inflecting the iron, inhuman necessity of the spirit of history, find the chink in its armor, which will allow us to see the path to a truly human future. There is a supreme, at times almost unbearable, tension in much of Miłosz's poetry between an acute sense of the destructive, antihuman force of historical necessity, on one hand, and the longed-for, hoped-for, not always visible path outward and upward. This is what he often describes as his "Manichean" temptation. As though our ordinary, everyday experience of life in history was dominated by the necessity which closes all paths to transformation, and an utterly different power must break in, if these paths are to open.

In this, he felt very close to Simone Weil, who became one of his major sources. Her emphasis on "la distance entre le nécessaire et le bien" [the distance between the necessary and the good] became one of his axioms. But an utterly stark opposition could lead to a kind of paralysis in the face of a universal causal necessity. And on some level, Weil seems to have accepted this: "God consigned all phenomena without exception to the mechanism of the world"; "necessity / mechanism is the veil of God." It is the domain of what she called "la pesanteur" [weight].[18] But that is not the whole story. There is also the realm of grace; hidden by a veil, but nevertheless there.

Only it is hard to see how these two realities, these two thrusts in history, that of mechanism and that of grace, can relate, or articulate into each other. Where would the second thrust, that powered by grace, originate? "Only from the past, if we love it," is Weil's response. And Miłosz

---

17. Miłosz, "Dedication," 77.

18. Czesław Miłosz, *The Witness of Poetry* (Cambridge, MA: Harvard University Press, 1983), 53–54.

continues to quote from her: "Two things cannot be reduced to any rationalism: Time and Beauty. We should start from them"; and "distance is the soul of beauty." "The past is woven with time the colour of eternity." Only a distance allows us to see reality without coloring it with our passions. And reality seen that way is beautiful. "The sense of reality is pure in it. Here is pure joy. Here is pure beauty. Proust."[19] We can be saved by beauty. This vision greatly moved, and influenced, Miłosz. And he saw something of the same doctrine of salvation through beauty in Dostoyevsky and also Mickiewicz.

> When quoting Simone Weil I think of what made me personally so receptive to her theory of purification. It was probably not the work of Marcel Proust, so dear to her, but a work I read much earlier, in childhood, and my constant companion ever since—*Pan Tadeusz* by Adam Mickiewicz, a poem in which the most ordinary incidents of everyday life change into the web of a fairy tale, for they are described as occurring long ago, and suffering is absent because suffering only affects us, the living, not characters invoked by all-forgiving memory.[20]

Reality is thus purified by the "color of eternity"; and Miłosz invokes Dostoyevsky's similar belief that the world will be saved by beauty: "This means that our growing despair because of the discrepancy between reality and the desire of our hearts would be healed, and the world which exists objectively—perhaps as it appears in the eyes of God, not as it is perceived by us, desiring and suffering—will be accepted with all its good and evil."[21]

Weil's mention of Proust also hints that the reversal of necessity, in history and nature, comes through contact with a higher time, as was already hinted above in the invocation of "Burnt Norton." Miłosz seems to have found a way to integrate the two thrusts in history in the more systematic vision of Blake. Blake's Urizen, the power of the analytic, reductive, objectifying stance to the world, engenders and perpetuates the

19. Miłosz, *Witness of Poetry,* 114–115.
20. Miłosz, *Witness of Poetry,* 115.
21. Miłosz, *Witness of Poetry,* 115.

divided human being who lives subject to the spirit of history. But Blake holds out the hope that the whole human being, integrating intellect and emotions, analysis and participation, can and will emerge, and this will transform the human condition, and will open paths of creativity which seem inaccessible at the moment.

The Blakean side of Miłosz seems to lead toward an apocalyptic perspective, one which awaits a new and total transformation. And this reflects perhaps the influence of his distant cousin, Oscar Miłosz, which certainly had an important impact on his thinking. But I think it would be a mistake to define Miłosz purely in terms of this global transformation. His poetry seems to me to speak also of privileged moments, when the web of necessity is broken through by a new spirit of compassion— like the "time lifted above time" mentioned above.[22]

III

But what is the power underlying the breakout? It has to be an ethical purpose, a higher goal, or a religious faith. For Miłosz it is catholic faith, but one in dynamic struggle with doubts. While growing up, he had lots of bad experiences of a narrow, antimodernist, rule-dominated, antiflesh, punitive Catholicism (e.g., from Father Chomski, one of his high school teachers); while at the same time and later he responded positively to some open, humanist liberals. He was also very averse to the narrow patriotic form of the faith, which was frequently anti-Semitic. So his Catholicism was different from the standard form, and also in some sense embattled. It occupied a space of struggle: both to maintain it, and to keep at bay the deviations he encountered in his world.

So to touch this power, he had to navigate around not only the fixed, closed form of modern society ("O City, O Society, O Capital"), but also the rigid forms of the faith. One way into this passed through his experience of childhood, in a Lithuania where the faith could coexist without tension with folk customs, some of which stemmed from pagan times. Another way is opened when he is struck by the boundless mercy of God.

22. I have found Scott's book on Miłosz very useful in my discussion of Miłosz's *Treatise on Poetry*; see Scott, *Ecstatic Pessimist*.

And certainly the work of Weil was a great help in bringing him to this intuition.

In Chapter 9, I spoke of the shift of dimension in the aspiration toward reconnection, from that toward continuing orders to that toward higher times. There I saw this in the context of the growing scientific understanding of the cosmos as the site of overwhelmingly transformative evolution. But with Miłosz, we see another context pressing this change: our modern consciousness of the transformations in history, leading us repeatedly into uncharted territory, which we vainly try to foresee "scientifically."

We are forced to recognize that we no longer live in a history with a clear beginning and ending, one such as the Bible can be read as offering us, or which the philosophies of secular Enlightenment have developed, of which the Marxism dominating postwar Poland offered a particularly rigid variant. It is this latter which Miłosz shows in all its inhumanity and horror in his *Treatise on Poetry,* posing immediately the crucial question: How can this all-encompassing steamroller be opposed? From what other standpoint can it be combatted?

One answer can be found in religion, in Miłosz's case his open and human variant of Catholicism, very different from the cramped, self-enclosed, and backward-looking Catholicism which Father Chomski tried to convince him to adopt (and which, alas, has returned with great force to Poland today).

But this is obviously not enough. The new predicament where we are conscious of living in a history in which change is both inevitable and, with the collapse of confident "scientific" theories, very hard to predict requires us nevertheless to project some notion of what the major features of our contemporary world are. We can only do this if we combine both these facets: both the continuing essential truths about humans as free, conscious, and spiritual beings and an insight into the moral conundrums and choices which our time faces us with. Just having insight into the first will no longer suffice:

> Amid Thunder, the golden house of *is*
> Collapses, and the word *becoming* ascends.[23]

---

23. Miłosz, "III. The Spirit of History," 132.

In his essay on Weil, Miłosz points to the gap between orthodox Thomism and the kinds of accounts we need to understand history. He quotes a Thomist philosopher, Father Gaston Féssard, to the effect that the order of reason = order of nature: "If the historical plays a capital role in Hegel, in Marx, and in many philosophers of existence, in the opinion of good judges it is . . . completely absent from the Thomist doctrine."[24]

Miłosz, for all his admiration for Eliot, and without rejecting Thomas, wants to make us aware of something else—namely, a call from God to make history in a new way, outside the framework of "necessity." He is not rejecting a search for the essence of things. Among the "words of the prophets" cited in *From the Rising of the Sun* are these:

> "Whatever can be Created can be Annihilated. Forms cannot.
> The Oak is cut down by the Ax, the Lamb falls by the Knife,
> But their Forms eternal Exist forever. Amen. Hallelujah!"[25]

But the *esse* of reality is only one dimension; we also have to give an account of its becoming; as he puts it, we have to relate *esse* to *devenir*.[26] The vision of history has to be shot through with a sense of the spiritual being who must live it.

In ages past, we often thought that religiously inspired philosophers were best suited to define this latter element (for Catholics, the work of Aquinas). In the contemporary world, we look to political scientists or historians to discern the trends. The daring idea that Miłosz puts forward is that a poet can do that; and a poet with the means of a poet: that is, not the study of learned documents, works of Plato and Aristotle, or the works of social science; but the poet's way of articulating the deepest intuitions that come to him / her as a spiritual being contemplating our

24. Czesław Miłosz, "The Importance of Simone Weil," in *To Begin Where I Am* (New York: Farrar, Straus and Giroux, 2001), 248.

25. Czesław Miłosz, "From the Rising of the Sun: VII. Bells in Winter," in *Collected Poems,* 331. Here, Miłosz is quoting from William Blake, "Milton, a Poem," in *William Blake: The Complete Illuminated Books* (New York: Thames and Hudson, 2000), 442.

26. "How to combine 'transcendence' and 'devenir' has always been my main question." *Striving towards Being: The Letters of Thomas Merton and Czeslaw Miłosz,* ed. Robert Faggen (New York: Farrar, Straus and Giroux, 1997), 9.

present condition. This would mean articulating a powerful and inspiring intuition—here about a possible way forward—by sensing and then rendering its thrust and rhythm.

This, he thinks, would be the "poetry which can save nations and people." A shocking thought for our usual way of thinking. But he came close to proving himself right.

If faith in God's mercy can open a channel beyond the "necessity" of history, what insight flows back to us through this channel? What guidance do we receive through it?

I will try to answer this by referring back to the passage from *Treatise on Poetry* I quoted above, where Miłosz speaks of "time lifted above time by time." "There are two dimensions," he affirms: there is the ordinary time we live in every day, and then there is a higher time which breaks through here.[27] This seems an implicit reference to Eliot's first quartet, "Burnt Norton." This work starts with a riveting evocation of such a breakthrough:

> And the bird called, in response to
> The unheard music hidden in the shrubbery,
> And the unseen eyebeam crossed, for the roses
> Had the look of flowers that are looked at.
> [...]
> Dry the pool, dry concrete, brown edged,
> And the pool was filled with water out of sunlight,
> And the lotus rose, quietly, quietly
> The surface glittered out of the heart of light,
> And they were behind us, reflected in the pool.
> Then a cloud passed, and the pool was empty.[28]

We know this is no ordinary moment; too much is happening; too much is being experienced. The roses are being looked at, not just by us in ordinary time; and the heart of light in the pool is an experience of fullness unwarranted by the dry concrete. Ordinary time is being

---

27. Miłosz, *Collected Poems*, 143.

28. T. S. Eliot, "Burnt Norton," in *The Poems of T. S. Eliot,* ed. Christopher Ricks and Jim McCue (Baltimore: Johns Hopkins University Press, 2015), 1:183.

crossed by a higher time. And in this respect Miłosz's experience of "time lifted above time" seems strongly analogous. We have to connect two times: that of ordinary one thing after another, and a higher time. But there is a difference between the two authors in their invocations of a higher time. For Miłosz, grasping the essence of the cosmos is no longer enough.

What this experience hints at for Eliot is the eternity surrounding God, the eternity of the *nunc stans,* where everything, at every time, is present to God. This is "the still point of the turning world."[29] But for Miłosz, eternity touches us in a different way: it shows us the significance of the moment, of the challenge, and of how we should go forward. So the contact with a higher time is seen very differently by the two poets. For Eliot, its point is to bring us in contact with an unchanging order, moving via Dante, and Dante's Thomist outlook, to a vision of the very essence of creation.

This shows us that the "higher time" invoked by Miłosz is not the same as that Eliot points us toward in the *Four Quartets.* What, then, is it?

Although the instant when we grasp it is called a *moment wieczny* [an eternal moment], it is the time of a movement in human history, which Peter Dale Scott has named "ethogeny," the slow growth of ethical vision, which starts (if not earlier) with the breakthrough insights of what Karl Jaspers called the "Axial period" (roughly the middle of the last millennium BCE), when different but related formulations arose about universal human standards.[30] The movement has continued since.

Miłosz's claim seems to be that the poet—not just any poet but the one who is capable of a "new diction"—can sense the potential move upward and give expression to it. And this is not a simple foretelling;

---

29. Eliot, "Burnt Norton," 183.

30. See the remarkable book of Peter Dale Scott, *Reading the Dream: A Post-secular History of Enmindment* (Lanham, MD: Rowman and Littlefield, 2024). Scott sets out his notion and detailed unfolding of "ethology" as the multimillennial history of human ethical growth. See also Scott, *Ecstatic Pessimist,* on Miłosz, which deals in a very illuminating fashion with Miłosz's relation to Eliot.

formulating the vision helps to bring it about. Or as Miłosz himself put it: "The poetic act both anticipates the future and speeds its coming."[31]

This foretelling / furthering bespeaks a sense of another kind of higher time than the passage in "Burnt Norton" points to; it is a sense of what is afoot in history, and of the potential turning points. Eliot's quartet gives us a hint of what we can call "eternity"; Miłosz's sense of the new possible departure yields a sense of time as kairos.

In Chapter 15, I will give at somewhat greater length my account of this deep movement of ethical growth, which is not carried by any one spiritual or religious tradition, but has somehow been furthered and elaborated between them, although their explanations of why this has happened differ. (From a Christian point of view, this has been attributed to a divine "pedagogy," following the lead of St. Irenaeus.)

IV

Miłosz's Catholic faith was both a deep source of inspiration, and the sire of much contestation and doubt.

In a late work, *From the Rising of the Sun,* we can see these two intertwined in the last section. The immediately preceding section, VI, titled "The Accuser," lets us hear the voices of accusation that must have assailed him; and all the other obstacles that stood in his way.

> Who will free me
> From everything that my age will bequeath?
> From infinity plus. From infinity minus.
> From a void lifting itself up to the stars?

> Throats.
> Choking.
> Fingers sinking.
> Into flesh.
> Which in an instant will cease to live.

31. Miłosz, *Witness of Poetry,* 109.

> A naked heap.
> Quivering.
> Without sound.
> Behind thick glass.

And what if that was you, that observer behind thick glass?[32]

Then comes section VII, "Bells in Winter." "Returning from far Transylvania," begins the account. The one telling the story recounts that he fell asleep during a halt in the journey. In a dream he meets a young man in Greek raiment, who was chastised by St. Paul for living with his father's wife and was excommunicated by Paul.

> But my Lord and my God, whom I knew not,
> Tore me from the ashes with his lightning,
> In his eyes your truths count for nothing,
> His mercy saves all living flesh.[33]

And the teller of the tale continues:

> Awake under a huge starry sky
> Having received help unhoped for,
> Absolved of care about our paltry life,
> I wiped my eyes wet with tears.[34]

Later the poet tells us, "Yet I belong to those who believe in *apokatastasis*"— that is, the restoration of everyone, all the lost, all the condemned.[35]

> . . . So believed: Gregory of Nyssa,
> . . . and William Blake
> For me, therefore, everything has a double existence.
> Both in time and when time shall be no more.[36]

32. Miłosz, "From the Rising of the Sun: VI. The Accuser," in *Collected Poems*, 324.
33. Miłosz, "VII. Bells in Winter," 326.
34. Miłosz, "VII. Bells in Winter," 326–327.
35. Miłosz, "VII. Bells in Winter," 328.
36. Miłosz, "VII. Bells in Winter," 328.

And then the scene shifts to the Lithuania of his childhood. And he sees Lisabeth wrapped up in her cape, going to morning Mass.

"Our sister Lisabeth in the communion of saints": and this includes

> witches ducked and broken on the wheel
> Under the image of the cloud enfolded Trinity
> Until they confess that they turn into magpies at night;
> Of wenches used for their masters' pleasure;
> Of wives who received a letter of divorce;
> Of mothers with a package under a prison wall.[37]

In other words, so many people are ignored, betrayed, even persecuted by the Church; they are present while the officiant begins the Mass: "*Introibo ad altare Dei*," and the server replies: "*Ad Deum qui laetificat juventutum meum*." And this last line is repeated in Lithuanian.

> As long as I perform the rite
> And sway the censer and the smoke of my words
> Rises here.[38]

What is the poet saying here? It can only be that, in spite of all the imperfections, shortcomings, and even downright betrayal of the humans serving here, the smoke of their words is heard by God. "His mercy saves all . . . but we fall short." "And always the same consciousness unwilling to forgive"; that is, our consciousness, yours and mine. And then the seeming non sequitur: "Perhaps only my reverence will save me."[39] But this reverence at least allows me to say, along with the prophets:

> "For God himself enters Death's door always with those that enter
> And lies down in the grave with them, in Visions of Eternity
> Till they awake and see Jesus and the Linen Clothes lying
> That the Females had woven for them and the Gates of their
> Father's House."[40]

---

37. Miłosz, "VII. Bells in Winter," 329.
38. Miłosz, "VII. Bells in Winter," 329.
39. Miłosz, "VII. Bells in Winter," 330.
40. Miłosz, "VII. Bells in Winter," 331.

The poem finishes with an announcement of the Last Judgment:

> It shall come to completion in the sixth millennium, or next
>   Tuesday.
> The demiurge's workshop shall suddenly be stilled. Unimaginable
>   silence
> And the form of every grain will be restored in glory.
> I was judged for my despair because I was unable to understand
>   this.[41]

Here we have the whole complex, contradictory picture. His Lithuanian childhood, in one way, and a sense of the boundless mercy of God, in another, nourish a faith that the forces of necessity can be overcome, and yet . . . at other moments, or even simultaneously, boundless mercy strains belief to even beyond the limits of possibility, and despair beckons.[42]

V

As well as his inner struggle around his Catholic faith, described above, there was another source of tension in his thought; he was very aware of how far his vision of time and ethical growth in history was from the "official story" of secular modernity. He was tempted to affirm that our human species is divided between those who know and do not speak, and those who speak but do not know. And that this had always been the case. In the medieval period, serious thought was in Latin, a language incomprehensible to peasants in their sheepskin coats, or to Lisabeth, going to Mass, wrapped up in her cape.

Miłosz aspired to close this gap, to give expression to the deep aspiration to a more human world, felt by many inarticulate contemporaries. But then his work was traversed by repeated attempts to get beyond widely felt oppositions between stances which urgently needed to be combined: between the poetry of Blake and Eliot, between Romanticism and classicism; between his "Manichaeism" and the shape of a new de-

41. Miłosz, "VII. Bells in Winter," 331.
42. Miłosz, "VII. Bells in Winter," 320–331.

parture in history; and crucially, between faith and its denial, which the bleakness of the world seems to confirm. He continually affirmed the positive, while always feeling the backlash of doubt at the temerity of such affirmations.

And what often triggered a returning flood of confidence after uncertainty and doubt was some particular perception, often of light. Łukasz Tischner in his very perceptive book sees a parallel with Gerard Manley Hopkins, who lived moments of great despair toward the end of his life, but whose faith found inspiration in discovering the "inscape" of particular beings, like the kestrel caught in midflight in his "Windhover" (see the discussion in Chapter 7). Tischner sees the parallel between the two poets as particularly strong in Miłosz's last two collections of poems. ("Not soon, as late as the approach of my ninetieth year / I felt a door opening and I entered the clarity of the early morning."[43]) What for Hopkins was "inscape," for Miłosz was flashes of light. Tischner on the last page of his book quotes the lines:

> Czy nie było zawsze naszym
> największym pragnieniem
> żyć i na wieki zamieszkać w jasności?[44]

> [Wasn't it always our
> greatest wish
> to live and to dwell for ages in brightness?][45]

V I

I cannot close this chapter without noting that Miłosz, with his critical Catholicism, and his skepticism about spectacular rebellion, wrote poetry that helped inspire that union of the Church and the Left in Poland

43. Tischner, *Problem of Evil*, 217.

44. Tischner, *Problem of Evil*, 221. The poem quoted here is "Obróceni twarzami ku Niemu," in Miłosz, *Wiersze Wszystkie* (Krakow: Znak, 2021), 1351.

45. Czesław Miłosz, "Turning Our Faces to Him," in *Selected and Last Poems, 1931–2004* (New York: HarperCollins, 2011), 322.

which brought about the nonviolent resistance movement Solidarność; which in turn played an important role in overturning the Soviet empire in Eastern Europe. Adam Michnik, who took a leadership role in the dialogue with the Church, was a great admirer of Miłosz and his poetry, as were many in Poland in opposition to the regime. Miłosz's poetry helped in the charting of a new way forward, which was eventually taken, and which changed history.[46]

46. Scott, *Ecstatic Pessimist,* 20.

PART VI

RELATION TO HISTORY
AND THE PRESENT

Chapter Fifteen

HISTORY OF ETHICAL GROWTH

This chapter follows Chapter 14, which takes up the basic issue raised by Miłosz's work, in particular his (for many, startling) claim: "The poetic act both anticipates the future and speeds its coming."[1] The future must contain potentially something better for this claim to make moral sense; so something like Martin Luther King Jr.'s quote "The arc of the moral universe is long but it bends toward justice" must be true. But is it?

I

Is there something like ethical or moral growth in history? When we look at the standards we now recognize, and try to hold one another to, the answer seems clearly affirmative. But if we ask, Are we better behaved than our remote ancestors? doubt begins to creep in. Were there, in the

1. Czesław Miłosz, *The Witness of Poetry* (Cambridge, MA: Harvard University Press, 1983), 109.

remote past, such acts of large-scale savage and senseless killings like those we witnessed in the twentieth century? The issue needs some sorting out, and I'll try to say something about this toward the end of this chapter. But first let's look at some of the evidence for growth in standards, always recognizing that these norms were never integrally lived up to.

In fact, there was always a lot of failure; there even was such failure in earlier stages of history where the demands were not that severe. And these demands increase with time. And then new forms, while in some respects an advance, often have costs, entailing some loss of earlier features which were in conformity with the telos: a good example of this is the growth of larger societies, incorporating and dwarfing early tribal societies, and their religions. These smaller societies had a degree of equality and solidarity which the big civilizations tend to lose and leave behind them, developing as they do relations of exploitation, and breeding harshness and a shocking lack of concern.[2] And yet the larger societies make possible facets of human culture, of art, of writing and thought, of higher visions of the human condition; and these are plainly in the line of development toward what I described as the human telos.

For clearly to understand this ethical growth we have to suppose an Aristotle-type theory of the human Form, a set of innate goals which demand fulfillment. (I will return to this understanding of the ethical as defined by a mode of life, and its contrast with the sphere of what we usually call "morality," in Sections IX and XV below.)

And, if we follow Teilhard, we can posit the telos as more than the human goal; the notion of Form has to be seen as of wider application than merely to humans. And we could say that the whole planet, the entire ecosystem, is striving, is groaning and travailing to some end: to live up to the demands of the space of agape (or of *karuna*, or *salaam*, or . . .). But I am not proposing to go this far in this chapter.

---

2. David Graeber and David Wengrow, *The Dawn of Everything: A New History of Humanity* (Toronto: McClelland and Stewart, 2021), remind us that these deleterious consequences of large scale are not inevitable, but large scale seems to be a necessary condition of class alienation.

But the process of realizing this goal is not smooth and continuous. It has rather a dialectical form; but not in the Hegelian sense where each move resolves a tension and thereby creates a new one; and this new one is at a higher level, so that the whole process can be understood retrospectively as a progress of Reason. In fact, things are messier and more chaotic than this.

So the first big step forward, the creation of higher civilizations, inevitably brings a terrible loss, inequality, what we now recognize as a huge departure from the goal. This calls for an answer. Perhaps we can see the changes of the Axial period as the beginnings of such an answer. Not that they recovered equality, but they offered new ideals of the human which were genuinely universal, no longer simply dictated by the civilizational or social ethos.

||

The "Axial" turn   The notion of an "Axial period" was proposed by Karl Jaspers, who noted that around the middle of the last millennium BCE, important changes occurred in four cultural zones which were as yet not really in contact: ancient Greek philosophy; the prophets of Israel; the rise of Upanishadic and Buddhist religion in India; and the thought of Confucius and Mencius in China.[3]

Taking the innovations of the Axial period as an important step in mankind's ethical growth, we should note the feature that struck Jaspers: for all their differences, there is a strong analogy between the new doctrines which arose at close to the same time in very different civilizations, between which there was little or no contact. We can see here the germ of what we now recognize as the ecumenical sources of ethical growth: this is not sustained and furthered alone by any one spiritual source.

The common feature of these new doctrines was that the good they were trying to define was seen as universal—that is, it offered a standpoint

---

3. See the important discussion of the Axial period in Robert Bellah, *Religion in Human Evolution: From the Paleolithic to the Axial Age* (Cambridge, MA: Harvard University Press, 2017).

outside the existing society from which it could be criticized, even condemned as inadequate or defective. So Plato severely condemned the
existing poleis, the Hebrew prophets denounced the actual practices of
the people and kingdom of Israel, Confucius set a standard which contemporary Chinese society fell short of, and Buddhism, for instance, at
least implicitly, showed up contemporary powers as in various ways
deviant. The force of the Buddhist critique appears clearly a couple of
centuries later in the attempts at reform of the ruler of the Mauryan
Empire, Ashoka, and find expression in his famous "Rock Edicts."[4]

This eruption of radical criticism into human history has been noted
by a number of thinkers in recent decades. Robert Bellah enumerates several formulations of this: Arnaldo Momigliano's "criticism," Yehuda El-
kana's "second-order thinking," Merlin Donald's "theoretic culture" and
"metacognitive oversight." Each of these notes the identification in the
Axial Age of conceptions of truth against which the invalidity of contemporary norms could be shown, conceptions which claimed to be universal, not simply local.[5]

Moreover, this calling-to-account opened the possibility that the standard of criticism might evolve: markers are laid down which will serve
later to criticize and alter the standards we now accept. So the prophets
can question what previously was accepted as good practice: in Israel,
ritual correctness is no longer enough; one must also deal justly with one's
fellows; in Greece, Plato and Aristotle will question ongoing practice in
the polis; Buddhist doctrine was, at least implicitly, critical of caste discrimination in Indian society; and a Buddhist king, Ashoka, will call on
his subjects to refrain from the rivalrous mutual denigration practiced
by many sects.[6]

Now this process of critique is potentially open-ended: the crucial
standards—Plato's justice, the prophets' justice and compassion,
Buddhist-Upanishadic *moksha,* Confucius' *ren*—all are potentially open

4. See the very interesting account of Ashokan reforms in Rajeev Bhargava, "The
Roots of Indian Pluralism: A Reading of Asokan Edicts," *Philosophy and Social Criticism*
41, no. 4–5 (2015): 367–381.

5. Bellah, *Religion in Human Evolution,* 268–282.

6. See Bhargava, "Roots of Indian Pluralism."

to new definitions. A new philosophical insight; a deeper judgment of a prophet; a more rigorous definition of what Buddhism or Confucianism requires; these will move critique forward and raise more stringent standards.

Of course, these sources of critique were often—even usually—at odds with power: Ashoka was an exceptional case. Effective power resisted. And the result was that the carriers of critique were often in a sense marginal figures; sometimes rejected, even persecuted; but even when they didn't suffer at the hands of rulers, they could be outsiders, what Louis Dumont called "individus hors du monde"; figures whose role and importance (as we now understand it) went unrecognized by society as a whole.[7] We need only think of what the average bien-pensant Athenian thought of Socrates, even before his condemnation; or what King Ahab and his entourage thought of Elijah and the prophets who criticized him and his wife.[8]

But if rulers, and even society as a whole, often looked askance at, and mistrusted and marginalized, these "extra-worldly" individuals, these had their own reasons to live on the margins; they often felt that they had to drop out of normal social life to fulfill their vocation: Indian "renouncers," Jewish prophets, Hellenist "cynics."

Jaspers found this convergence-in-difference between the four civilizations remarkable, and others have been similarly impressed (including the thinkers Bellah lists above). Apart from the important step outside the ethos of established societies or civilizations, which allowed for their critical stance, these "Axial" moves had much in common. They called for an undiscriminating benevolence toward human beings—even, in some cases, living beings as such—regardless of rank or status. This would be the basis later on for more radical, egalitarian notions of justice.

The similarities seem greater than can be accounted for by diffusion through contact, and this could suggest one of three possible explanations: (1) the existence of a human milieu, in which ideas and intuitions might pass between societies very far removed from each other; or

7. Louis Dumont, *Essais sur l'individualisme* (Paris: Seuil, 1983).

8. Kings 1:17–24 (New Revised Standard Version, Catholic Edition, National Council of Churches).

(2) some divine pedagogy, on the lines proposed by St. Irenaeus; or (3) the telos implanted in each one of us that unfolds according to a similar time scheme; or some combination of these (my guess would be that (1) and (2) come together here).

For the majorities in these civilizations, these high demands were seen as binding on the marginal-critical individuals, but impractical for whole societies. Such institutions and practices as slavery, social hierarchy, law enforcement through violence, war; these were understood as regrettable necessities. They perhaps should not exist in an ideal world, but in the really existent one, they are unavoidable; we can't do without them. This gap between individual ethos and the "normal" way societies function is what Dumont was getting at when he described the faithful followers of these exceptional visionaries as individuals "hors du monde."

The relation of these exceptional individuals to the majority living a less stringent code seems similar to the distinction in pre-Axial religions between shamans or priests, on one hand, and the majority of ordinary folk, on the other. The shaman lives a more demanding form of life, in virtue of his office, but there is no sense that ideally others should do likewise. There is a complementarity between the ordinary everyday life of the majority and the more demanding one of the special vocation. Something of this complementarity will long survive in the aftermath of the Axial period: think of the different codes of clergy and laity in the medieval Christian church. For instance, clergy were not supposed to engage in war, while the lay nobility had no higher vocation than fighting. But the special character of post-Axial society resides in the fact that in some sense the belligerent laity were understood to be living less close to the essential universal ideals of the faith which all shared. The *imitatio Christi* is ultimately addressed to everyone.

In the wake of these exceptional individuals, new forms of group life begin to form: the Buddhist sangha, Greek philosophical schools, Talmudic schools, Christian religious orders.[9] But the gap between the

9. Peter Dale Scott, *Reading the Dream: A Post-secular History of Enmindment* (Lanham, MD: Rowman and Littlefield, 2024). I have drawn a great deal from this very fertile work, whose thesis is similar to mine, and is much richer in its detailed account of developments.

standards they upheld and the institutions and practices of whole societies remained (and still remains) very great.

David Martin has introduced a useful term to speak of the relation
between these ideal forms of life and the effective ethos of the societies
that really exist. The ideal forms "transcend" the regnant ethos, but some
exist at a more "acute angle of transcendence" than others. For instance,
Buddhism and Christianity stand at a more acute angle to the societies
which nominally embrace these faiths than Confucianism does.[10]

But the story of ethical growth brings about changes in the demands
made on ordinary people. In what follows, I want to single out and look
at three important passages or transitions which have transformed our
moral standards in recent centuries, and which together cast some light
on the conflictual and often chaotic process involved.

III

Passage no. 1: Toward human rights   Over the centuries, we can discern
two lines of development: (1) In virtue of the tendency mentioned above
to seek more adequate, more radical definitions of the key critical
concepts—justice, *moksha, ren,* and so on—new demands are seen as implicit in, or emerging from, the faiths or philosophies which descend
from the Axial period. These by themselves increase the angle of transcendence with the existing social world. An area in which these have
emerged in recent centuries concerns the needs and rights of individuals.
Individual human beings come to be endowed in the regnant ethic with
rights: to freedom, to recognition of and respect for their "identity," to
new levels of help and concern on the part of society and government.
And along with these grows the demand for equality, and nondiscrimination *between* individuals. These generate the French Revolutionary
trilogy of *liberté, égalité, fraternité.* All of these reach one important culminating formulation in the Universal Declaration of Human Rights
adopted by the United Nations in 1948.

10. David Martin, *Ruin and Restoration: On Violence, Liturgy, and Restoration* (London: Routledge, 2018).

These demands of themselves increase the angle of transcendence of the reigning moral-political outlook to really existing societies, even though they are far from reflecting the full range of human aspirations, as we see them formulated in the different religions and spiritualities.

As a result, moves have been made to realize effectively in societies standards which have long been considered just impractical ideals. An example is the imperative demand growing in the late eighteenth century effectively to abolish slavery—something which, at least as a legal facade, has been realized planetwide.

Hans Joas has argued that this was part of a broader change in the eighteenth century, which he calls the "sacralisation of the human person."[11] By this he means the spread of the idea that the human person by its very nature commands respect: for his / her bodily integrity, freedom, needs, and goals; even though this respect would undercut and invalidate many of the ways in which criminals, rebels, heretics, subversives, and deniers of legitimate authority—and, of course, slaves—were routinely treated in the name of good social order.

In other words, the limitations of the Axial ethic in the name of practicality to exceptional individuals came to be gradually lifted, and the harmful consequences for slaves, and many categories of prisoners, denounced. Of course, in certain of these cases—for example, criminals—some retribution and confinement was right and necessary, but this should never take the form of "cruel and unusual" punishment.

Joas describes this immunity of the human subject as a "sacralisation," following the use of Durkheim, who famously defended his pro-Dreyfus position with this term, which led to his denunciation by the anti-Dreyfusards as an "individualist," uninterested in the general good.[12] But Durkheim was precisely not defending the individualism of unlimited freedom, of a general license to follow my own way (cf. US Republicans today), but exactly the opposite: there are limits to what a majority can force on defenseless individuals.

11. Hans Joas, *The Sacredness of the Human Person: A New Genealogy of Human Rights* (Washington, DC: Georgetown University Press, 2013).

12. Joas, *Sacredness of the Human Person.*

During the eighteenth century, belief in the supposed necessity of slavery for the production of sugar, and of harsh punishment for heretics, subversives, and other undesirables, gave way before the mounting sense of desecration. This immunity of the human subject has been described as "untouchability"—*Unantastbarkeit,* in the words of the contemporary German constitution.

This shift in the perceived moral status of the human person lies behind, in Joas' view, the two great charters of human rights, generated respectively by the American and French Revolutions which cap the eighteenth century, and set us on the path toward the Universal Declaration of 1948. (Of course, many of those who were ready to sign on enthusiastically to declarations of the "rights of man" also held to hierarchical views on race, class, civilization, and gender logically incompatible with these—with what degree of hypocrisy or unconsciousness we can never know. I will return to this issue below—especially in Section XI.)

What was (or were) the motive forces behind this shift? A common explanation here points to the "Enlightenment" as a rational, secularizing force. But it is clear that religious motivations also played a big role. In fact from the beginning, Axial-driven reforms have been driven by more than one outlook. Think of the evangelicals driving abolitionism, on one hand; and the roles of Beccaria and Voltaire in pushing legal reforms, on the other.

(2) Over against this raising of standards, we see in history another kind of innovation, which has the effect of bringing these standards within reach. A good example is the practice of nonviolent rebellion, started by Gandhi in the early twentieth century, and then followed by the civil rights movement in the United States, then practiced in the Philippine insurgency against Marcos, and then in the uprisings which ousted Communist governments at the end of the century, and attempted in the "color" revolutions since, most recently and not yet successfully in Belarus.

These in some ways startling and unpredictable developments have the opposite effect from those under (1): they decrease the angle of transcendence, not by lowering expectations, but by raising the repertory of effective historical action to new ethical heights. But there is an important difference between these two examples [(1) and (2)]: violence tends to breed violence, and the aftermath of abolition, won through civil war, illustrates this very clearly. Jim Crow, and white supremacy, continue to wrack American society.

The immense ethical advantage of (2) nonviolent resistance, as well as institutions such as Truth and Reconciliation Commissions after the handover of power (e.g., in South Africa), is that they offer a hope of reducing the legitimacy, and hence also the frequency, of acts of violence—in strong contrast to the pioneering revolutions of modern democracy, the French and the Russian, which unleashed paroxysms of "Terror."

I will return to this issue in Sections XII and XIV.

IV

We can see something of the shape of what I have been supposing is a drive to ethical ascent in human history. It has a dialectical form, messy and thus non-Hegelian, in which attempted steps forward can generate other evils—as the founding revolutions against French and Russian autocracies bred spectacular violence; and these evils can in turn call forth remedies: in this case practices of nonviolent disobedience or protest. But there are other ways in which steps forward, as measured by the demands of the Universal Declaration, can generate very bad consequences which worsen or degrade the lives of the many while improving the lot of elites. The Industrial Revolution as enabler of the rapid development of capitalism certainly increased the well-being of capitalists as well as many landholders, but at the cost of impoverishment of the many, both in terms of living standards, and in those of living conditions: ugly, overcrowded, polluted surroundings in the new cities, until democratic action by nonelites succeeded in winning some economic gains for workers; and until the social-democratic institutions and policies which tamed early capitalism were undermined by globalization and neoliberalism in the late twentieth century, which laid the conditions in which the present wave of xenophobic populism is now sweeping the democratic world.

And another condition of this wave is also the perverse consequence of another valuable development, that of the creation of democratic political identities. Later, in Section XI, I will return to the crucial role these identities play in modern democracies, as well as the deviations they are prone to.

V

Apart from these side effects of what at least appear to be ethical steps forward, we have to reckon with the fascination with evil which humans can easily fall into: the kind of thing we see breaking out in situations of conflict, when people—and especially men—can launch into orgies of destruction: killing, raping, laying waste to the land. The very horror of this, its utterly forbidden nature, is what renders it exciting, lived as liberation, the headiest wine of all.

There is a joy at breaking the rules which we can all experience, the adolescent moment when we escape the supervision of tutors and guardians, but this usually remains safely within bounds. It takes a giant step from there to the massacres of Daesh, and we can only dimly sense the deprivation of meaning which these are meant to assuage, or the relief offered by the utter self-forgetfulness in the group which opens the path to mindless violence. Orgiastic violence often finds a springboard in calculated strategic killing, undertaken in cold blood; as we can see with the case of Nazism, and Bolshevism.

Reforming minorities can revel in their own power, often serving a good end (e.g., the Chinese Communist Party "lifting" many millions out of abject poverty), but crushing many human beings in the process, in total disrespect of their freedom, integrity, culture, and religion.

Then their righteous sense of their power and efficacy can come to be enjoyed for its own sake. There is a kind of excitement which comes from herding people, which can slide into a perverse enjoyment of domination and destruction for its own sake. The self-satisfaction of a Xi Jinping can call forth, or become, the reveling in destruction of a Pol Pot, or in rape of a Beria. Or the justified self-defense of the Red Army against

Nazi invasion can generate the orgy of rape after the victory over conquered Germany.

These excesses are often intensified by the excitement that humans
can feel at transgression. As Simone Weil puts it: "License has always
entranced men, and that is why, throughout history, cities have been
sacked."[13]

VI

From all this, it should be clear that human ethical growth is not simply
linear, or additive, with higher stages building on earlier, lower ones. Advances in one respect trigger (often unsuspected) evils: civilization engenders hierarchy and exploitation; economic growth can do something
similar, besides devastating the environment. Violence in defense of the
good against evil can generate orgiastic destruction. So we witness a dialectical process in which new forces have to arise to deal with the evils
generated by past efforts at improvement, even where these were well in-
tentioned and benignly motivated. And this process is chaotic; it is not
teleologically directed upward à la Hegel, so that each successful outcome
of struggle is guaranteed to take us higher than the previous ones. History seems to offer no guarantee that the forces of light will always
prevail.

The result can be evil on an unprecedented scale. The violence of the
twentieth century: the Holocaust, Gulag, and Killing Fields puts the massacres of previous centuries in the shade. In the face of this, we could
easily be tempted to speak of history as the site of a monstrous growth
of evil.

VII

Another reason to abandon the model of history as steady growth of ethical performance toward a model like the Universal Declaration is that

13. Quoted in Miłosz, *Witness of Poetry*, 33.

this entirely ignores the range of human aspirations which go beyond the widely accepted conceptions of human flourishing in our contemporary civilization (or indeed, in any previous civilization).

These include religious aspirations, but they are also given expression in literature, art, and music. (In the latter category, we could cite Beethoven's late quartets, Bach's Mass in B Minor, and a host of other works.) These aspirations stand outside widely agreed-on formulae of the good life because they call for much more far-reaching transformations of human life—for example, toward self-emptying agape, or Buddhist *karuna*—or they call for a perception of the particular potentiality of each human being, which can easily be lost to view in some generalized conception of well-being supposedly applicable to everyone.

The failure to appreciate, even to perceive, the person in the Citizen or Worker, with his or her deep aspirations, has been one reason why revolutionary attempts to realize the (highly valid) triple democratic norms of Liberty, Equality, and Fraternity have often gone so terribly awry in modern history. One of the most horrifying contemporary examples is Xi Jinping's attempt to submit Muslim Uighurs to cultural genocide in order to make them happy, lobotomized members of a socialist society "with Chinese characteristics."

The same screening out of our depth aspirations underlies the "transhumanist" dream of Yuval Harari, dubbed "Homo Deus." This foresees a world in which humans remake themselves through their control of the human genome, by means of a nonbiological intelligence which the advances of AI will provide us with.

It should be obvious that this path, if it can be followed at all, is a road to horror rather than divinity. You don't have to be a person of faith to appreciate this, as Jürgen Habermas has shown. Or as Leszek Kolakowski put it: "Culture, when it loses its sacred sense, loses all sense."[14]

14. Leszek Kolakowski, "On the Dilemmas of the Christian Legacy," in *Modernity on Endless Trial* (Chicago: University of Chicago Press, 1997).

VIII

But then why talk of ethical "growth"? Because in fact, along two axes
there does seem to be movement forward. One is the raising of ethical
standards, through steps like the adoption of the Universal Declaration
of 1948; or the growing demand since the eighteenth century to abolish
slavery altogether. Why cite this when these standards are so widely and
flagrantly violated in practice? The striking fact here is that those who
violate them so often feel called upon to pretend that they are observing
them. The present Chinese government feels it has to say that reports of
its cultural genocide in Xinjiang are malicious lies originating in the
United States. Continued bad practice has to be accompanied by ever
greater waves of hypocrisy. One might ask: Is this progress?

Maybe not. But there is another axis where advances are being made,
and this involves what I called above raising the repertory of effective historical action to new ethical heights. I invoked a striking example of this
in Section III, when Gandhi succeeded in transposing the fight against
foreign rule in India into nonviolent form, and further when King and
the civil rights movement did something analogous in their battle against
racism and for equality. The genuine ethical growth involved can be seen
if we examine more closely what is involved in these changes.

IX

The role of "Enlightenment"   The modern period sees a gigantic catch-up,
whereby the full demands of the Axial ethic cease to be the achievement
of a small marginal group of saints and *bhikkhus,* and become realized in
the society as a whole. One of the most dramatic incidents in this process
was the relatively sudden spread of the movement to abolish, first, the
slave trade, then slavery itself, which I described in Section III.

We often attribute this whole process to what is referred to as the Enlightenment: the move toward a more rational, scientific view of the
world. This was held to have undermined the old myths and is often seen
as having undercut religious beliefs as well. In the process it undermined
the old idea of legitimate authority, and rightful obedience to this au-

thority; and proposed a new kind of carte blanche of traditions, which opened the way to reform of institutions guided by science and instrumental rationality.

As I argued in Section III, the case of abolitionism shows that this scientific reason was not the only inspiration of moral advance, but it is undoubtedly part of the story of how our present democratic rights-based societies, with their faith in law, due process, and negotiations over difference, came to be.

An interesting question to examine would be the properties of the two motivations for this advance, the scientific-rational one, and the often religiously driven advance of the "sacralization" of the human subject.

We can perhaps approach this question if we reflect on the degree to which modern natural science was bound up with, and confirmed by, the new technologies it made possible. Scientific enlightenment as a source of moral progress makes sense if we acknowledge the ways in which this progress was realized (or at least meant to be realized) through different forms of what we might call "social engineering," in the broadest sense of the term, including constitution making and legal reform.

That this is not the whole story behind modern ethical growth we know not just through examples like abolitionism, but also through the blind spots and limitation of modern attempts to achieve progress through altering social and political arrangements. "Enlightenment"-guided reform has two glaring limitations: one is the weakness for "invisible hand" arrangements, whereby ordinary, reliable human motivations can be channeled toward beneficial social results. Adam Smith, who first coined this expression, was keenly aware of the limitations of this kind of arrangement, which needed to be complemented by state action to yield the benefits it promised. But the subsequent history has seen repeated lapses into forgetfulness of such limiting conditions, until we find ourselves with the disastrous ravages of Hayek-inspired neoliberalism which threaten our democracies today.

The other great failure of Enlightenment social engineering emerges in its tendency to overreach and to limit and even repress human freedom, the fundamental condition of all ethical growth. This reaches its apogee in Bolshevik Leninism, in a disordered paroxysm of "liquidation" under Stalin and Mao, and a horrifying invasive systematicity under Xi.

These failures are part of a more general pattern of self-congratulatory modern theories of "progress." These often fail to see how pursuing an advance along one line of moral advance can produce perverse and damaging results unless accompanied by complementary advances on other dimensions. Thus just enlarging the freedom of the individual, unconnected to a deepening of human solidarity, can produce the self-satisfied outlook of neoliberalism and meritocracy which is threatening the very existence of modern democracy.

And similarly, rejoicing in the increasing control that humans can exercise over their natural environment, uncomplemented by a lively sense of what our planetary natural surroundings mean to us, can land us in the ecological crisis we are living today.

There is a third limitation from which this "Enlightenment" tradition suffers. It acknowledges the importance in the broad stream of ethical growth of what we called above the "moral," the rules which should govern our treatment of each other, but has little place for the issues we called "ethical," which concern the ends of human life, and the nature of human fulfillment.

This relative neglect of the ethical in much contemporary philosophy perhaps calls for a further account of what this involves. Perhaps the crucial concept which can help us grasp this is that of "fulfillment." In some respects, our fulfillments may differ from person to person: A has great musical talents and is drawn to a career as a pianist; B is similarly drawn to be a painter; C has great organizational skills and an ambition to improve the conditions of youth in his city, and founds a new organization promoting football in the inner city; D is a good doctor who is not satisfied with ordinary practice in her rich country, and joins Médecins sans frontières.

In all these cases, we would say that whatever frustrated these vocations, whether it be parents who insist that A should train as a lawyer, or a heavy family debt that stops D going to Africa, would rob these lives of their fullness.

What ethical theory in my sense would add to these is fulfillments which all humans have as humans, which would enrich all human lives, such as living in the truth about oneself, or reaching out to others in need. We will see other examples toward the end of this chapter.

Perhaps the relative neglect of the ethical is bound up with the belief that moral rules can be established by reason alone, once one concedes with Kant their universal applicability as a necessary feature of these rules, whereas defining the ends of life requires a hermeneutic inquiry, which must grope toward an adequate language in which these ends can be fully brought to light—a quest which is never fully completed.

I will return to this distinction in Section XV. But first we should examine certain historical developments which may be seen as advances in human ethical life.

X

Passage no. 2: A history of legitimate authority In early modern Europe, up to the revolutions of the late eighteenth century, American and French, authority was conceived as residing in established orders. The monarch belonging to the reigning dynasty possessed legitimate power, in virtue of ancient right (which involved covering over some pretty shocking acts of usurpation). Even the English rebellion against Charles I was justified in terms of a traditional right, that of Parliament in virtue of an "ancient constitution," which had existed since "time out of mind."

The big change which comes about in the next century and a half is a move from established orders and the rights they contain to the notion of natural rights, conceived not just as an ideal which might not be fully realizable in the real world, as with the traditional notion of natural law, but as the basis of political legitimacy itself. This notion covered not only individuals and their legitimate demands, but also by extension political authority.

So the American Declaration of Independence spoke of "inalienable" rights, rights which couldn't be given up, which made any political arrangements which overrode them automatically illegitimate. And a similar authoritative status was implicit in the French declaration adopted in 1789.

Both moves made all claims to historical legitimacy conditional, and therefore made rebellion against historical structures of authority allowable, even mandatory, in certain circumstances; and the bulk of argument in the American declaration deals with the issue of the conditions under which a people can rise against established forms of sovereignty.

Once the consent of the governed moved from being a right of Englishmen to the status of a natural right (as in the French declaration), the stage was set for a new kind of regime. The dominant regime in Europe was, until 1815 and even beyond, what would be understood later as an empire, fruit of an accretion of power over history which ended up including many peoples of diverse cultures and even religions. This is not to say that all political entities had this form, but many strove for it, and the Great Powers in the European scene were of this type.

In 1815, six imperial powers dominated Europe. Four of these—those in the east (Germany, Austria-Hungary, Russia, and the Ottomans)—were mainly geographically contiguous, while two (Britain and France) were "overseas." This division is too neat, however: Germany aspired to have overseas colonies; and France had just been deprived of a vast contiguous empire under Napoleon and was just about to start its "overseas" career with the invasion of Algeria in 1830.

And apart from the "Great" powers, smaller nations had overseas possessions, like the Netherlands and Belgium, whereas Spain and Portugal had been among the first to build "sea-borne" empires. And the memory was still there of peoples who had tried to conquer their surroundings and build shorter-lived contiguous empires, like Poland and Sweden.

But the nineteenth century saw the slow growth of another concept of legitimate order, that based on the right of peoples to self-government. Part of what drove this movement was what we can see as the logic of the demand for self-government, or otherwise put, the right to live under governments to which its subjects have consented. This kind of government is hard to establish in an empire: self-rule, through common deliberation and democratic decision, requires a degree of common identity, as I will argue below in Section XI, such that citizens can trust each other as partners in deliberation to be concerned with the common good of all, and to have the mutual commitment which motivates them to aid one another in the face of threats from nature or other powers. It is rare that this kind of trust and mutual concern can hold between the different peoples who composed the great empires, even when we ignore the difference of interest between those in the ruling core and their subject nations.

The kind of common identity which can support self-rule is generally that which unites what we call nations or ethnically unified peoples. And so the nineteenth century, the period between 1815 and 1919, sees the slow assertion of the new force, pushing for national self-assertion against the great empires, breaking out in Poland, even before the start of this period in 1791; then in 1830 and 1863; breaking out elsewhere in 1848, in the various staging posts of Italian unification; in 1871 with the unification of Germany under Prussia; and so on.

One can argue that the movement starts with the Greek uprising in 1831. The consensus among the Great Powers at the Congress of Vienna cemented a Holy Alliance of the Continental powers to uphold traditional authority against the subversion of revolutionary movements. But the Greeks managed to gain European support in spite of this, because of the cultural force of Philhellenism, and in the Russian case solidarity with fellow Orthodox Christians. Metternich had to stand by powerless while Britain, France, and Russia liberated Greece.[15]

The period ends with the consecration of the principle of self-determination of peoples, but applied only to Europe. After a fierce reaction denying this principle by the Axis powers, the period post-1945 starts off codifying human rights in the Universal Declaration of Human Rights of 1948, and the ensuing decades see the dissolution of the big overseas empires. Self-determination comes to seem more and more axiomatically justified.

What kind of movement is this which we've been following from the late eighteenth century to our present place in the twenty-first century? There have been ups and downs, lurches forward and back, but over the whole period there is a continuing trend advancing certain legitimacy ideas—advances in two dimensions, both in a wider and wider spread of people holding them and in a radicalization of their inner logic, so that

---

15. See Mark Mazower, *The Greek Revolution* (New York: Penguin, 2021). For the movement from empire to nation-state, see Timothy Snyder, *The Reconstruction of Nations: Poland, Ukraine, Lithuania, Belarus, 1569–1999* (New Haven, CT: Yale University Press, 2004).

they are understood to undercut more and more features of the traditional scene and to apply to more and more areas (e.g., from winning the
independence of Iberian colonies in the Americas, to liberating small
countries in Central Europe, to dissolving European empires in Asia and
Africa).

What lies behind this kind of movement? In the end, no one can be
sure, but it is at least not implausible to see in it a working out through
long periods of history of certain core ethical insights common to human
beings as such, of whatever culture and tradition.

That's the happy story. The unhappy face of it all is that the struggles
and battles to win through to effective progress often greatly increase
mutual hostility and violence. Take the liberation of Greece and the dissolution of the empire that held it down for so many centuries. The
Philhellene in me (and so many other Westerners) cannot refrain from
applauding, but we must also follow the story out to the ultimate stages
of Izmir in 1923, the mutual massacres, finally resolving the issue in
massive ethnic cleansings of Anatolia, on one hand, and Thrace, on the
other. Greeks whose ancestors had lived in Asia Minor since before the
Persian invasions were expelled, as well as Turkish peasants and other
Muslims from the Balkans. Populations which had lived together hier-
archically, but in peace, for centuries were now self-governing but engaged in mutual killing.

The biggest error is to think of the history of ethical growth as linear:
on this understanding, we would just have to keep moving ahead,
bringing more and more people to Enlightenment, liberalism, and
freedom. Rather, the whole process should be seen more "dialectically,"
in a sense that even Hegel couldn't conceive, as I stated above. Our
greater grasp of the human good has unleashed a lot of hostility and
violence; or, to think of another dialectic at work: we have won through
in certain societies to some important insights, but these have bred
egregious self-images of superiority over other peoples and civilizations, which have in turn legitimized much injustice. And then there is
the "populist" backlash in many democracies where the demands to
overcome certain historical discriminations have been pressed most
urgently (see Section XI). The road ahead is not just more of the same.
It requires that we respond to these hostilities and injustices and

resistances with measures of reparation and mutual recognition which can bring about reconciliation.

In the light of all this, the above account of the steadily advancing application of the principle of self-determination, while descriptively true, turns out to be highly misleading. What it leaves out is, for example, the way in which highly "progressive" figures in the nineteenth century, like John Stuart Mill and Marx, could justify British rule in India, on the grounds that it was bringing the fruits of advanced civilization to a backward society.

What is the balance sheet of positive versus negative in this two-centuries-old movement? We have ethical advances in both standards and real action (the latter rather spotty, but real), to be weighed against legacies of violence, hatreds, resentments, and stances of unmerited superiority. But through all this is a measure of perhaps irreversible advance: it is not likely, short of a civilizational collapse (but this is becoming a real possibility in the wake of our failure to act against climate change), that we revert to justifying political power by immemorial tradition (of which there are still vestiges in our world, like *Russky mir*!).

Dialectic, not linear, advance is virtually inevitable, because the measures which realize steps upward provoke resistance, and moreover involve methods which intensify this resistance, while the resultant conflict can easily give space for the all-too-human fascination with transgressive violence.

The crucial insight here is that advances in justice have to be accompanied by forward steps in reconciliation. A vital part of the ethical growth in the twentieth century has been a perception of this truth and the growth of insight into paths of reconciliation and healing, which we see with Gandhi, King, Desmond Tutu, and many others.

XI

The spotty, uneven advance of forms of democratic self-rule can be better understood if we look at the basic requirements of these forms. The inauguration of any such form requires (1) that the people concerned develop viable institutions of self-government. To take the two such cases which have served widely as models for others, the American and French Revolutions, this step was more easily and quickly taken in the first case than in the second; partly because the American colonies already had institutions of self-government. But success in this area also requires (2) changes in political culture, in sensibility, in the appropriate virtues. It demands a high degree of solidarity, which is where the new national identities come in, which I discussed in Section IV—with all their dangers and difficulties. Just liberating a group of individuals from foreign rule and then relying on various invisible-hand mechanisms to determine their economic relations (as with contemporary neoliberalism) is a formula for democratic decay (see Section IX).

Why do democratic republics require a very definite sense of common identity: Americans, Canadians, Quebecois, German, French, and so on? Well, because the very nature of democracy, for several reasons, requires this strong commitment: it requires participation in voting, participation in paying taxes, participation in going to war, if there is conscription. If there is to be redistribution, there has to be a very profound solidarity to motivate these transfers from more to less fortunate. Democracy therefore requires a strong common identity.

Finally, and very importantly, if we are in a deliberative community— we are talking together, deciding among ourselves, voting, and making decisions—we have to trust that the other members of the group are really concerned with our common good.

You see a situation arising where independentist movements start very easily—and I happen to know a case like that, coming from Quebec—in which the minority says, "Well when they're talking about the good of our society, they're not talking about us; they're talking just about them. We're not part of their horizon." When that kind of trust breaks down, democracy is in very big trouble. It can even end up splitting into two. So we need a powerful common identity.[16]

But these powerful identities can slip very easily in a negative and exclusionary direction. A very good book by the Yale sociologist Jeffrey Alexander, *The Civic Sphere*, makes this point: the common properties

---

16. See Craig Calhoun, *Nations Matter: Culture, History, and the Cosmopolitan Dream* (London: Routledge, 2007).

that make up this identity are very strongly morally charged; they're good.[17] As a matter of fact, in most contemporary democratic societies, there are two sides to this identity: one facet defines certain principles—that we believe in representative democracy, human rights, equality—but they also have a particular side: as a citizen, I am engaged in a particular historical project aimed at realizing these principles. Canadians, Americans, French, Germans, we each believe in our national project which is meant to embody these values. This is what Habermas is referring to with the term "constitutional patriotism."

It's easy to see how the principles side can generate exclusion. Take the infamous speech by Mitt Romney in the 2012 US presidential election, which cost him defeat at the hands of Barack Obama. This contained the "47 percent" remark: 47 percent of the people are just passengers, they are being given what they need, they are not really producing. They are taking from the common stock without adding to it. The underlying moral idea is that the real American is productive, enterprising, self-reliant. The allegation is that 47 percent of the people are not living up to the stringent requirement of this idea. So these people are not behaving like real Americans.

A little reflection would show how false this particular moralization is: many of the people who receive state aid—welfare, say, or food stamps—are clearly doing their best to take care of themselves and their families; while many of those whom this calculation includes in the other 53 percent owe their prosperity to luck or their parents or some form of inherited wealth.

But this false moralization is not innocent. It provides the justification for a lot of measures adopted by the American Right—things like vote-suppressing legislation, which many American states are making even tighter in the wake of Trump's defeat. This could be a totally cynical move, but it is one that is probably justified in the perpetrators' minds by the sense that the people excluded fail to live up to the moral

17. Jeffrey C. Alexander, *The Civic Sphere* (Oxford: Oxford University Press, 2008). See also Michael Mann, *The Dark Side of Democracy* (Cambridge: Cambridge University Press, 2005); and Bellah, *Religion in Human Evolution*.

requirements of citizenship as we (good, upstanding, self-reliant citizens; or good "conservatives" of the American way) define them.

Or, you can get another kind of exclusion: basically ethnic or historical, which provides the criteria. There are the people who really belong to the ethnicity which defines "our" identity, and then there are the people who came along later. There are the people who have always been here, in contrast to the immigrants who came later. What is operative here is basically an ethnic coding. And here, this slide to exclusion can occur.

Take Quebec: What's behind the identity expressed in "Je suis Québécois"? In one sense, there is a very powerful ethnic story behind that: seventy thousand French speakers were left on the banks of the St. Lawrence when the British conquest occurred, ratified by the Treaty of Paris in 1763. And they've now built this vibrant French-speaking society of eight million. This is the result of a highly successful fight for survival. It's a very easy slide from a definition of *Québécois* as a citizen of Quebec today, to a narrower concept including only what we call *Québécois de souche*—old-stock Quebecois. The memory of the struggle to survive, and the fears surrounding this, can encourage that narrowing.

In the United States, there are more, stranger, sometimes horrifying notions of precedence. I invoked some of these in Section III: the unacknowledged hierarchical reservations in the minds of many who declared support for human rights.

In a very interesting book by Arlie Hochschild, *Strangers in Their Own Land,* the author describes an instance of this outlook.[18] In the imaginary of certain "old-stock" populations, there is a kind of order of precedence: the natives (but, of course, these don't include the indigenous populations, who are conveniently forgotten) come first, the people who arrived later come second; or, in an even more damaging version: whites come first, and Blacks, Hispanics, and so on come after. Or: men are the "normal" candidates for certain positions or careers, and women only qualify in special circumstances.

These—rarely explicitly avowed—assumptions of precedence provide the basis for campaigns against "liberal" governments that are allegedly

---

18. Arlie Russell Hochschild, *Strangers in Their Own Land: Anger and Mourning on the American Right* (New York: New Press, 2016).

helping all these people with second priority and at the expense of those with first priority. That was a very powerful part of the Trump campaign. You get this slide, from all Americans are equal, to: some are more fully, really core Americans, and we shouldn't lose sight of this.

And in all "settler" societies, including my own, there is a widespread sense that indigenous people are backward and need to be brought under tutelage, which legitimizes grievous forms of exploitation.

This slide is a catastrophe for various reasons. It's a catastrophe because it deeply divides, hampers, and paralyzes the democratic society, dividing us into first- and second-class citizens. But it is also a catastrophe in another way because it builds on the deprivations imposed on nonelites by the spread of a Romney-type moralistic outlook among the rich and powerful. In many Western democracies, this has brought about a frustration caused by a Great Downgrade in the living standards of workers, who, as a result, feel that the system is stacked against them, that they can't affect it, and that their citizen efficacy is virtually nonexistent. They are ready for a program which would liberate the demos or give the demos power again, against the elites.

Only the demos has now been redescribed—either in a moralist, or ethnic, or historical-precedence way that excludes many people—which has the double disadvantage that it deeply divides the society, and this second disadvantage, that it does not at all meet the actual problems and challenges of the Downgrade.

XII

Passage no. 3: Battles over equality and nondiscrimination　We have just been looking in Section XI at the assumptions of privilege and precedence that have gone, often unremarked, into the building of modern democratic political identities. It is therefore not surprising if, following on from our potted history of legitimate authority, we note the more recent coda to this: in the aftermath of the Second World War there has been a remarkable move in certain democracies to overcome certain historical inequalities and discriminations, some of which I outlined in Section XI: "assumptions of precedence," deeply embedded in the consciousness

of many citizens—men before women, whites before Blacks, settlers before indigenous, and so on. In former imperial powers, like France and
Britain, immigrants from the former colonies are often silently deemed
to be quasi-outsiders.

After about 1960, we see a steady growth of movements to challenge
these assumptions, and right the discrimination and injustices they underpin: feminist movements, battles for gay rights, Black Lives Matter
campaigns, and the like.

Normally these battles are seen by those engaged in them as fights over
privileges enjoyed—for example, by whites, deservedly in the eyes of
many whites, but clearly undeservedly by Blacks and most uninvolved
bystanders. To resolve these disputes in a satisfactory way, whites would
have to lose something. Instinctively, many of those in the privileged
categories respond in self-defense. Very often their sense of identity is
bound up with their privileged situation: a man seems to lose dignity if
women can do the same job; or the culture and self-respect of whites may
be inseparable in their minds from their higher position.

Without seeing it clearly in these terms, they are struggling to defend
their identity. They condemn their challengers as indulging in gratuitous
"identity politics," but when liberal elites dismiss them contemptuously
as "rednecks" or "deplorables," they react with all the fury of an offended
identity.

The politics which ensues has all the appearance of a zero-sum game.
But the discourse of civil rights has another take on the situation. From
this standpoint, the defense of privilege here exacts huge costs. It involves
inhabiting a cage which inhibits, even crushes, ethical growth. (1) Whites
have to cling to a deep untruth, that of their superiority over Blacks; (2)
at some deep level, whites are aware of what they have inflicted on Blacks,
and they fear retaliation; and this even when they refuse conscious
acknowledgment of this. A factor in many cases of white police officers
shooting Black men is that fear, which pushes them to shoot first and ask
questions afterward. So racist whites have to live with an untruth (1), and
a fear (2). But there is a third deprivation: (3) this privilege is an obstacle
to the kinds of collective achievements that a more equal society could
enable whites and Blacks to realize together.

The first (1) goes against the human telos to live in the truth; factor
(2) subjects racists to live in fear, and (3) deprives them of the positive

achievements of democratic self-rule, provided they could come to see the person in each other. And perhaps most important of all, (4) the continued division deprives them of the mutual enrichment, the enlarging and deepening of their humanity which comes from open exchange between people of widely different backgrounds and cultures.

This is what John Lewis was talking about when he called on his fellow citizens to "lay down the burden of hatred." To identify this as a burden requires ethical discernment. To build this insight into a democratic society's self-understanding takes this insight further, beyond the enlightened views of some individuals, into the collective awareness of the community. This would be something new in human history.

Of course, for believers in white superiority, whether self-admitted or denied, this message of liberation is seen as another gratuitous insult heaped on them by "liberal elites": Are you saying we live in untruth and fear? How dare you? It can only be delivered by people who understand their sense of identity and the many admirable features it contains. Ideally, it should come from insiders who have come to see the limitations of the traditional self-understanding.

But even coming from the victims of discrimination (as was the case with Lewis), it can unlock a situation of seemingly unbridgeable mutual hostility. Within the zero-sum mentality, both sides are filled with hatred and fear. The very suggestion that we could move to another plane, could deliberate together how to work positively on a common project of reconciliation, may have the power to overcome the impasse.

Will this deeper insight win through in the polarized exchange of insult and accusation which politics has become in many Western democracies? There is certainly no guarantee. But the very fact that such spaces of reconciliation can be conceived, and the possible repertory of creative and humane social life enlarged, needs to be taken into account. There is a more humane space beyond and above our present bitter divisions.

We should also note that those who are most effective in communicating these new insights are people in whom the satisfactions of winning the contest, and / or of venting their anger on agents of destruction, are overcome by a recognition of the human potential of their adversaries and the desire to establish a new relation of mutual recognition and collaboration with them. In fact, those who are capable of this are people who are deeply rooted in their spiritual sources, often religious.

And indeed, the gains (1)–(4) above only become stable and secure where this new understanding of them becomes widespread, and the sense that we are fighting a zero-sum game, where the gains of the former underprivileged entail a corresponding loss by those who used to be on top, begins to fade. The actual *experience* of mutual enrichment is what enables us to go beyond the crippling inequalities of history.

And here we can take hope from the fact that many younger people have already learned from their own experience how enriching this contact across cultures and life conditions can be.

Ethical growth comes as a result of battles; but only if these are followed with a peace grounded in mutual recognition.

XIII

An ecumenical sense is growing over the last decades which inspires attempts to elaborate this common human ethic, and to take interfaith action to promote it. Some recent encyclicals of Pope Francis—I am thinking of *Laudato si* and *Fratelli Tutti*—are obviously not addressed only to the faithful, but amount to a contribution to this world exchange aimed at elaborating a common ethic. Take, for instance, this remarkable passage from *Fratelli Tutti:*

> Our relationships, if healthy and authentic, open us to others who expand and enrich us. Nowadays, our noblest social instincts can easily be thwarted by self-centred chats that give the impression of being deep relationships. On the contrary, authentic and mature love and true friendship can only take root in hearts open to growth through relationships with others. As couples or friends, we find that our hearts expand as we step out of ourselves and embrace others. Closed groups and self-absorbed couples that define themselves in opposition to others tend to be expressions of selfishness and mere self-preservation.[19]

19. Francis, "*Fratelli Tutti*: Encyclical Letter of the Holy Father Francis on Fraternity and Social Friendship," Holy See, October 3, 2020, paragraph 89, https://www.vatican.va

There is a lot of (good) moral advice in Francis' encyclical, but there is also another (ethical) dimension: a philosophical anthropology which sees us as realizing more fully our humanity through contact and exchange with people and cultures beyond our original comfort zone. Through these exchanges new creative human possibilities are disclosed, and human life is enriched. This is how I understand what Francis calls in this encyclical the "law of extasis" operative in human life.

This takes us a step beyond the injunction to lay down the burden of hatred. This first step would liberate us from the shackles of fear and negativity. Francis takes us further with the promise of a richer form of life.

Our common ethic is in fact being enriched in the exchanges which are happening today. This is actually a source of optimism in our present crisis of divided democracies. So many young people today have had the living experience of growth and a sense of a fuller meaning to life through cross-cultural exchange, that they welcome the end to discriminations not just as a gain in justice, but as a source of deep fulfillment. But this comes about not only through greater justice, but in the reconciliation of friendship.

XIV

The example I just invoked—the insight of Francis about plurality, exchange, and the human telos—is an example of the way in which new, deeper insights into human ethical life can open new ways out of the impasses which the dialectic between ethical advances and the backlashes they release are repeatedly creating for us. They do not by themselves overcome the impasse; they have to be turned into political demands and seek a path of reconciliation with their opponents. But they chart a new course for us.

/content/francesco/en/encyclicals/documents/papa-francesco_20201003_enciclica -fratelli-tutti.html.

The profound polarization of our contemporary democracies is not only depriving many of our compatriots of the potential mutual enrichment of exchange; it also stands in the way of another important ethical fulfillment, which we can only achieve together, or not at all. This is the one invoked by Hannah Arendt: the creation of a common space of deliberation and exchange, where we can reason together and receive the recognition that our contribution merits.

In very recent years, we have witnessed the new creation of such a common social space, in the remarkable elaboration of a new common national identity in Ukraine, a process which gathered momentum from the Maidan demonstrations of 2014 and has produced the extraordinary feats of solidarity and courage we now witness in the resistance to Russian aggression. This has been the birth of a new democratic nation, superseding old divisions and suspicions.[20]

XV

At this point I'd like to reflect further on what I'm calling the dialectic between advance and resistance that I've been trying to describe in these pages. That it is not Hegelian is obvious: each stage of opposition doesn't end with a resolution which serves as the starting point for the struggle in the next stage. But nor does this story resemble the standard Enlightenment progress account. What we cannot but see as steps forward awaken great resistance, which can continue for a long time. But they also provoke and / or encourage other kinds of destructive developments.

Take the example above of the abolition of slavery, most dramatically in the United States. This only came about as the result of a very bloody civil war. And violence on this scale breeds more violence, and not only on the part of the losers. Violence in this kind of case receives a certain legitimation, which makes it easier to justify in other causes, whether good or bad. The same reflection holds for the massive level of violence and destructive control wrought by Leninist regimes, up to and including the present rule of the Chinese Communist Party.

20. See Snyder, *Reconstruction of Nations.*

We saw in Section IX how the struggle for democracy and self-determination not only (very understandably) provoked armed resistance, but also was all-too-easily combined with empire building and thus fed assumptions of civilizational superiority, justifying the subordination of others. This generated new struggles by the colonized; and hence more violence; not to speak of the legacy of hierarchical assumptions among the colonizers, which continue (although much weakened) to this day and go on perpetuating division and hostility.

A great step forward comes with Gandhi and the forms of nonviolent struggle for liberation, which promise to end the destructive chain of violence breeding further violence into an indefinite future. And this has not only inspired others to follow—from King and the civil rights movement, to the overturning of the Marcos regime in the Philippines, and the peaceful overthrow of Communist regimes with the fall of the Berlin Wall in the 1980s—it has also inspired other measures, like Truth and Reconciliation Commissions, which aim to promote reconciliation between former enemies.

One might speculate that this new form of nonthreatening struggle might be adopted for purely instrumental reasons, because of its positive consequences for moral behavior: in the long run it can bring about a world with less killing, maiming, attacking. Undoubtedly, some supporters of Gandhi and King must have backed them with these consequences in mind. But clearly, these inspiring figures, and those they persuaded to put their bodies in the line of *lathi* attacks, police dogs, water cannons, and so on, saw what was at stake here in ethical terms, as deeper and more human ways of carrying out the unavoidable struggle for a better world. Their inspiration was spiritual in nature, and from the Axial age onward, spiritual visionaries have been sources of fresh ethical insight.

And indeed, the way they recognize each other across great differences of theological or metaphysical belief—the Dalai Lama and Tutu, for instance (and there are many other examples)—manifests a deep and powerful spiritual affinity.

But these new insights don't simply inaugurate a new era in which they become universally accepted. They remain contested, denied, fought against. The age of Gandhi also saw Hitler, and the massive killing of the

Second World War. True, this inspired a new departure, under the slogan "never again," which saw the Universal Declaration of Human Rights and the determination to end aggression against weaker states. But here we are in 2024 facing the aggressive war on the part of a would-be hegemonic Russia.

We can also look at another great push to establish real equality and nondiscrimination in modern democracies, starting in the 1960s, which I discussed in Section XII. This has generated a massive backlash of threatened hegemonic identities, and in many countries the issue remains in the balance.

But this battle between the felt need to discriminate and the demands of equality is the occasion of a new ethical insight, which I articulated above in Pope Francis' terms: that difference embraced can be a source of great human enrichment.

What does this say about human ethical advance? That it can bring about new and higher ethical insights; these for a long time will remain confined to minorities, but they can at some point become part of a widely accepted obligation to live up to them. But this doesn't mean that the human race as a whole embraces them; they are contested, and their very radicality provokes fierce resistance. Over time, some of them will become more widely accepted, like the legitimacy principle of self-determination, but they remain hotly contested, and arouse the hostility of older dreams of hegemony, like that of *Russky mir,* or the imperial realms of the Middle Kingdom, reinforced by the ruthless vision of Leninism.

The "dialectic" in this history lies in the fact that higher moral demands provoke more bitter struggles, and that no visible end to this process can be discerned on the historical horizon. That's the bad news; the encouraging message is that these struggles can provoke further, deeper, fuller ethical visions. This is the "good" side of the dialectic.

But perhaps we are being unfair to the Enlightenment visions of continued progress, which come to the surface again, for instance, in the work of Steven Pinker. Surely we would agree that such practices as Aztec priests ripping the hearts out of prisoners of war to sacrifice to the God in the sky don't exist today, and couldn't return? I concede; *these* practices not, but we moderns have our own gruesome moments: the Holocaust, the Killing Fields, the killing and rape of innocent civilians by "peacekeeping" forces, the attempted remaking by force of the identity of Uighurs, and so on.

XVI

Perhaps we can get a better idea of the kind of noncumulative and non-Hegelian dialectic we see in our history, if we see it in the light of the distinction often made between two kinds of ethical-moral demands. (I invoke this distinction in Section II and characterize it more fully in Section IX.) One of these concerns the demands we make on each other in the name of justice, equality, mutual concern; we might think of these as "what we owe to each other," to borrow the title of T. M. Scanlon's excellent and influential book.[21] This is often referred to as morality, as distinguished from the "ethical," and one of its most influential definitions is found in the philosophy of Kant.

The other concerns what forms of life would most fully realize the human potential, and its complete description would define the good life. Plato and Aristotle are the most influential thinkers in this stream of the Western tradition.

The history of ethical growth I have been trying to sketch here involves advances on these two lines. The contemporary demands to overcome historical modes of inequality and discrimination would draw us forward on the moral dimension. But the attempts to meet these demands provoke resistance, backlash, open up new divisions and new lines of hostility; so that we find ourselves stymied, unable to agree, or even recover some sense of common purpose in society. This seems to be our situation today in a number of democratic societies.

But taking a step forward in the ethical dimension would transform our situation. The step forward would be the realization that dialogue and exchange with people of other cultures and spiritual traditions could open the path to a deeper human fulfillment, the insight that I identified

---

21. T. M. Scanlon, *What We Owe to Each Other* (Cambridge, MA: Harvard University Press, 2000).

above in Pope Francis' recent encyclical (Section XIII). Moral demands which, though undeniable, remain unrealizable on one ethical level become possible on a higher, fuller level.

Similarly, liberation from colonial rule, or from the rule of a self-ascribed "superior" race, as in South Africa, which can so easily unleash hostilities, resentments, the desire for revenge, can hope to escape these consequences to the extent that the parties concerned recognize nonviolent action as a more fully human way of being.

This is not to reveal a panacea for moral strife. Ethical growth cannot be produced or engineered on demand. It just points to a human possibility, which we may someday come to desire, enough to grow into it.

XVII

Perhaps I might suggest a way of summing up some of the arguments I have been making in the course of this chapter, if we imagine what we might say in response to the question I raised at the beginning: Have humans made moral progress through their long evolution and history? Some answer emphatically "yes": for instance, Pinker.[22] Others, appalled by the massacres of the twentieth century (which seem set to continue into the twenty-first), reply emphatically in the negative.

My reply would be to split the question into three parts: (1) Do we on the whole act more morally than our ancestors? (2) Do we profess higher standards than our forebears?

Let me pause here to give my answers to these first two queries: to (1) I say no; to (2) I say yes. But this might not be considered a great advance. It just means that more people and governments will lie about the atrocities they commit; it may just mean that the level of hypocrisy has risen.

A third question (3) would be: Have we managed to come up with deeper ethical insights which might eventually help us to do better on (1)? Here my answer would be strongly positive. We have come some dis-

---

22. See Steven Pinker, *The Better Angels of Our Nature: Why Violence Has Declined* (London: Penguin, 2012).

tance from the Axial Age, when the full ethic of exceptional individuals was not demanded of ordinary mortals. There has in this sense been ethical growth, which might someday make it possible for us to act more humanly. But we have still a long way to go.

XVIII

I have been looking here at a gradual growth through history, a movement toward and convergence on a common human morality and ethic. But if we are converging on a common ethic, must it follow that we are heading for a single universal spirituality or religion? Obviously not. Think of how different, for example, Christian faith and Buddhist spirituality are. (As the Dalai Lama once put it, "You can't put a sheep's head on a yak's body.")

Will these spiritualities then fall away as irrelevant? Even more obviously not. They each offer paths of transformation—through liturgy, prayer, meditation, disciplines—without which our ethic will be forever a dead letter. It seems that the paths are irreversibly plural.

Chapter Sixteen

COSMIC CONNECTION
TODAY—AND PERENNIALLY

I

Where does the concern for cosmic connection go in the later twentieth century, and beyond into the new millennium?

There are traces in poetry—for instance, in the work of Wallace Stevens. But the most prominent strand is a continuation of the Goethe-Humboldt response to the discoveries of science, and the more and more detailed grasp of the intricate orders, both macroscopic and microscopic, in which we live. There are no more higher and lower levels in this cosmology, but the whole structure and its evolution over eons inspires awe, and (in us conscious animals) a sense of gratitude for its having enabled and nurtured life. This latter reaction has become especially prominent as we come to realize with horror how we have recklessly disabled this nurturing function, perhaps (as we humans are concerned) irreversibly.

These interwoven orders are not revealed in poetry, but as Humboldt repeatedly affirmed, they inspire us in somewhat the way poetry does.

And new avenues open up: there are certain writers in this Humboldtian vein who incorporate in their scientifically informed descriptions fragments of poetically enabled insight reminiscent of the early Romantics. A striking example is to be found in the work of Annie Dillard; in her reflections on our experiences in nature, informed by science.

As we pay close attention to what is happening around us, we are often taken aback, even appalled (at pain and suffering); but then we are surprised by beauty, "an inrush of power and light."[1] Dillard records and communicates an intense experience, an occurrence in the "interspace" between human observer and world which carries a force of conviction similar to the sense of cosmic order of the early Romantics, but which is momentary, a flash of depth perception.

Perception of what? Words occur, "beauty," "wonder"; but what she communicates is an exceptional openness, a readiness to resonate with the creation; or better put, with the natural world seen and experienced as God's creation. The readiness is a steady condition, but the moments of resonance are punctual.

What she records here are moments of deep and resonant (re)connection which powerfully move us. We the readers can recognize that the author has experienced a connection which has an unmistakable resemblance to what Wordsworth or Hölderlin had; with two important differences: Dillard's connection is punctual; it doesn't link her to a cosmic order; and it is *her* experience: reading her doesn't of itself make us share it—although it does awaken the hope that we can achieve something similar, and her descriptions can trigger off a recognition of something similar in our experience.

More than this: she tries as hard as she can to tell us how to share her vision. She shows how we are blinded by light, blinded by habit, by the familiarity of things, and the usual concerns they arouse in us. "But there is another kind of seeing which involves letting go."[2] What is this like? She tells us: "Something broke and something opened. I filled up like a new wineskin. I breathed an air like light; I saw light like water. I was the

1. Annie Dillard, *Pilgrim at Tinker Creek* (New York: Harper Perennial, 2013), 9.
2. Dillard, *Pilgrim at Tinker Creek*, 33.

lip of a fountain the creek filled forever; I was ether, the leaf in the zephyr; I was flesh-flake, feather, bone."[3]

Then another, I presume deeper, moment of revelation or connection. Only this one is not described. It can't be, because the self-consciousness you need in order to find the right words puts an end to the experience. "*Self*-consciousness . . . hinder[s] the experience of the present."[4] These moments of deep connection are already over when you can say, or struggle to say, what they were like. And Dillard invokes a passage in Goethe's *Faust,* where the protagonist says of a supreme moment (*Augenblick*), "Verweile doch, du bist so schön" [Stay, you are so beautiful].[5] But it can't.

There are, however, fragments of space-time when one can almost extend this presence, bathe in it: in *Tinker Creek,* "I never merited this grace, that when I face upstream I see the light on the water careening towards me, inevitably, freely, down a graded series of terraces like the balanced winged platforms on an infinite, inexhaustible font. . . . This is the present, at last."[6]

Dillard gives voice to what striving toward cosmic connection has become for most of us in the twentieth (and twenty-first) century: tentative and indirect; we who now see that the complexity, generosity, exuberance of Nature also brings mass death.[7] We are shaken.

We recover our true direction in autumn, the moment of decline:

> I have gutted on richness and welcome hyssop. The distant silver November sky, these sere branches of trees, shed and bearing their pure and secret colours—this is the real world, not the world gilded and pearled. I stand under wiped skies directly, naked, without intercessors. Frost winds have lofted my body's bones with all their restless spirits to an airborne raven's glide. I am buoyed by a calm and effortless longing, and angled pitch of

3. Dillard, *Pilgrim at Tinker Creek,* 34.
4. Dillard, *Pilgrim at Tinker Creek,* 82.
5. Dillard, *Pilgrim at Tinker Creek,* 84.
6. Dillard, *Pilgrim at Tinker Creek,* 103.
7. Dillard, *Pilgrim at Tinker Creek,* 163.

the will, like the set of the wings of the monarch which climbed
a hill by falling still.[8]

This is what corresponds in our time to the reconnection through poetry of the early Romantics.

| |

These reflections open onto a broader question. One could argue that
cosmic connection has always been a human aspiration. But it has taken
so many forms in history—from the earliest indigenous religions (many
of which are still alive today), through various philosophical-theological
theories of cosmic order, including in our time theories of the earth as
Gaia; and also to the attempts of the last two centuries in Western literature that I have been dealing with (a small parochial corner of a much
broader canvas). And an eloquent recent book by Karen Armstrong
shows how a deep concern for the whole of creation lies at the heart of
all the great spiritual traditions of humanity.[9]

Can one map the common features and the differences? Would such
a map yield new insights into our place and interest in the cosmos? I
would like here to try to sketch some features of what I just referred to
as "indigenous" religions, in order to see what relation they have, if any,
to the forms of cosmic connectedness I've been examining in this book.

First, I would like to explain what the word "indigenous" was meant
to convey. Perhaps something like "local community" would do better.
The point is to single out forms of religious life which are not understood
as local enactments of a wider religious community, in which case the
local rituals are seen, as it were, as those of a "parish"; but the indigenous
forms are rather essentially and only those of this local community. They
are religions of a tribe, or group of tribes. This local spirituality has not
yet been incorporated within a larger international, or even "world,"
religion.

8. Dillard, *Pilgrim at Tinker Creek,* 263.

9. Karen Armstrong, *Sacred Nature: Restoring Our Ancient Bond with the Natural
World* (New York: Bodley Head, 2022).

Such local religions must have been at one time the only forms of spiritual life in human society, but some survive today, continuing with difficulty and under pressure in "indigenous" communities within polities where the majority belong to world religions or to none.

They obviously incorporate a strong form of cosmic connectedness, but with specific features which differ from those invoked in the poetic traditions dealt with earlier in this work.

First (1) the connection is primarily to a place, a particular local geography, a mountain, a valley, a plain. "World" religions also have sacred centers—Jerusalem, Mecca, Varanasi—but their religious life radiates beyond these.

Then second (2) these emphatically "located" religious forms harbor a powerful sense of relatedness to their surroundings; they see human life as essentially and intimately connected to life-forms, seasons, sun, moon, sky. We might say that the identity of the people is formed by, or consists in, these relations. The people involved stand in polar opposition to what has become modern civilization, which values and celebrates a stance of distance to nature, enabling manipulation and control.

The point is well made by Rupert Ross:

> This relationship [that is, to place] is predicated on the fact that all Indigenous tribes—their philosophies, cultural ways of life, customs, language, all aspects of their cultural being in one way or another—are ultimately tied to the relationships that they have established and applied during their history with regard to certain places and to the earth as a whole. . . . Native people interacted with the places in which they lived for such a long time that their landscapes become reflections of their very souls.[10]

The identity here is that of an "embedded, enfolded, socio-centric self."[11]

Third (3): many of the accounts of these "located" religions translate the word for a creator or guiding being with the term "spirit." I want to

---

10. Rupert Ross, *Indigenous Healing: Exploring Traditional Paths* (Toronto: Penguin Canada, 2014), 45.

11. Ross, *Indigenous Healing*, 25.

take off from this to build some (I admit contestable) view on spirituality.

I see it as inseparably connected with the ethical in the widest and deepest sense—that is, with the full good life, realized life, fulfilled life; life as it was "meant to be"; where that expression can be used literally, with reference to some creator god or spirit, or else as a placeholder for whatever the full good life is—what our nature or being calls on us to be.

In this context, I see the "spiritual" as what gives us the wisdom and the strength to realize this full life. Once again, this term will have a different referent for people with different views: for Christians it invokes the third person of the Trinity; but for atheists, it will be whatever, inner or outer, resources they have to call on to live the full life. What I'm trying to get at here, I referred to in another work as our "moral sources."[12]

Now for many of these "located" religions, these sources are found in the deeply interdependent relation to the cosmos, as refracted to them through their place. They regain the strength to realize their full potential by reconnecting, through ritual, story, ceremony, solemn assembly, to this place.

As Aaron Mills puts it in his interesting and instructive paper on the crucial place of kinship in defining mutual obligations in (Canada's) First Nations:

> There is no nature / culture cleavage within Anishinaabe legal and political thought. Anishinaabeg[13] understand that we are immanently and inextricably part of Earth's inherent order, and as such, we have developed our legal system to function as a logical extension of it, reconcilable to it. Order within Anishinaabe kinship therefore reflects our understanding of Earth's inherent order through what we might call ecological mimesis in respect of the ethological path to understanding, or family resemblance in respect of the cultural one. . . . Many Anishinaabeg have not

12. See Charles Taylor, *Sources of the Self: The Making of Modern Identity* (Cambridge, MA: Harvard University Press, 1989).

13. The ethnonym for an Algonquian-speaking indigenous people of North America.

forgotten the specific way in which law connects us to Earth's implicit normativity, and second, our desire to sustain that connection today.[14]

The kinship model means that our obligations to others are not uniformly
reciprocal, as are those of rights-bearing citizens in a standard republican
democracy. The duties of parents to children cannot be the same as those
of the children to their parents. But over the whole life span there is a
"circular" reciprocity, whereby all members receive their due.[15]

III

All this raises an interesting question—or perhaps better, a field of
questions—which I briefly invoked at the beginning of Section II. Something like what I have been calling "cosmic connection" seems to be a
goal, or a need, of at least some human beings throughout our history.
But it takes very different forms, and this book has already rehearsed
some of them.

This seems to invite us to an exploration of this domain, one which
seems crucial to our self-understanding. What is the nature of this
continuing desire, or aspiration? What are the different forms it can
take? And what changes in human history underlie these variations?
Any adequate philosophical anthropology must give an account of
this dimension.

The objectifying, even instrumental stance to our world which has
dominated the modern world sees this as a nonquestion; or perhaps one
which calls for a psychological etiology of human delusion. The dismissive stance toward indigenous religions and cosmologies, the joint result
of objectifying dismissal of all religions, and the narrower forms of
historical religions (mainly, in the West, Christianity) has—beyond its
devastating consequences for indigenous communities—produced an

14. Aaron Mills, "First Nations' Citizenship and Kinship Compared: Belonging's
Stake in Legality," *American Journal of Comparative Law* (forthcoming).

15. Mills, "First Nations' Citizenship."

obtuseness, a blindness, which prevents us from asking questions whose answers are crucial to our self-understanding as humans.

IV

Perhaps I can add some considerations in favor of this hypothesis that there has indeed been a perennial human goal which I've been calling "cosmic connectedness," which has taken different forms in different ages, and that this book covers some representative forms of this aspiration in our age.

I return to the concept of an "interspace," which I introduced in Chapter 2. This was intended to define the locus—one might say the epistemic status—of that strong sense of cosmic order, and of our connection to it, which early Romantic poetry generated; this sense stopped short of a conviction about the underlying explanation which might demonstrate that this connection was founded in objective reality, beyond the subject.

Now it seems clear that other strong feelings of connection to cosmic forces, and/or patterns in time and higher times, which I have invoked and tried to characterize, all find their epistemic locus in such an interspace. I would include here the response of Humboldt to the new, scientifically discovered orders in nature that he helped lay bare, orders which he judged "poetic"; as well as the sense, which he helped inspire, of Wilderness as making a claim on us which forbids desecration, and calls on us to preserve its pristine power (as seen with Muir, for instance—but also Thoreau). And a similar point can be made of the aperçus of something higher which occur in the flashes of insight that arrest us in the writings of Dillard.

But this sympathetic reading of the claims advanced here meets with strong resistance in contemporary culture. The great advances of the natural sciences over the last three centuries, which in recent decades have accelerated, have (understandably but wrongly) helped create a mindset which refuses to take any knowledge claim seriously which cannot meet the validation conditions of these sciences—unless they be about everyday observable realities (How many chairs are in this room? How many people attended the meeting?). This outlook has led many of our contemporaries to dismiss the experiences of connection I've been describing here as purely "subjective," exclusively in the domain of individual psychology.

But my sense throughout this book has been that this reductive stance is mistaken, and that these historically evolving intuitions correspond to something real and important in our relation to our natural environment, something that we need to understand better, appreciate more fully, and in the end cherish more strongly—if this relation is not to turn terminally lethal.

V

I am proposing that the need / desire for cosmic connection has been a perennial feature of human life. But this book has only examined a small portion of human history: Western civilization in the last few centuries, from Renaissance beliefs in cosmic orders, through early Romantic invocations of orders in nature, to the contemporary Humboldtian sense of wonder at and spiritual nourishment by our natural environment. Not a very wide basis, one might say, for a vast and general thesis about humans' relations to their planetary home.

But what is striking in this context has been the way in which the decline in one mode of such connection (Renaissance orders) through disenchantment calls forth another: ritual invocation through poetry of the experience of connection to such orders; and then how a dawning sense of the vast and cataclysmic history of our universe, undercutting any sense of continuing (spatial) orders, calls forth the sense of deeper connections through time: to patterns in deep time, and to higher times. The fact that the loss of one channel seems to open another bespeaks a continuing, perennial need or aspiration.

VI

It might help to place this evolving sense of cosmic connection in a wider context, that of the last phase of the evolution of our species, from hominid to full human. Merlin Donald has convincingly argued that one essential feature of human life is the creation of a common understanding (of course, endlessly contested) of human society, the ancestor to what we might now call a "social imaginary."[16] Of course, under today's conditions, and for millennia, this common understanding has been partly constituted of established facts: measurement or other definitions of territory, census counts of populations, the recording of sociological facts, patterns of political power, and so on. And then later, we have books of law, written constitutions, and the like. These are creations of what Donald describes as the (relatively late) "theoretic" phase of evolving human culture.

But this phase, Donald argues, must have been preceded by what he calls a "Mythical" one, in which the original sense of the common life was expressed in story (myth), and periodic ritual reconnections to the gods, spirits, forces which figure in the story.

Ritual reconnection: we who are far advanced into the theoretic age can look back in condescension at our ancestors; and many of us (mistakenly) do. But there is no reason why we should have totally lost the need, and the skills, including those of ritual invocation, we had in the earlier phase. They seem, indeed, to still survive among our poets, writers, painters, composers, some of whom have been invoked in this book.

VII

Finally, I want to return to the beginning, indeed, before the beginning, and remind myself and readers that this book was conceived as a companion study to my *The Language Animal*.[17] The point of origin for both is the theory of language which developed in the Romantic period, which

16. Merlin Donald, "An Evolutionary Approach to Culture," in *The Axial Age and Its Consequences*, ed. Robert N. Bellah and Hans Joas (Cambridge, MA: Harvard University Press, 2012), 47–76. See also Merlin Donald, *A Mind So Rare: The Evolution of Human Consciousness* (New York: Norton, 2001); and Merlin Donald, *Origins of the Modern Mind: Three Stages in the Evolution of Culture and Cognition* (Cambridge, MA: Harvard University Press, 1991).

17. Charles Taylor, *The Language Animal: The Full Shape of the Human Linguistic Capacity* (Cambridge, MA: Belknap Press of Harvard University Press, 2016).

I associate most closely with three thinkers of that time: Hamann, Herder, and Humboldt (hence the appellation "HHH," by which I refer to it). The view of language which I develop in *The Language Animal* was built around this theory, which was elaborated in the milieu which came together in the 1790s in Germany (to a large degree in Jena). This milieu nourished the ambition to overcome the divisions, even opposition, between reason and emotion in humans, and between humans and the nature they live in and from. I have traced in this book some of the crucial stages of this aspiration to reconnect. And I am now, at the very end of this book, looking speculatively beyond its time frame of a scant two and a half centuries, to posit the idea of a perennial longing to invoke and renew this sense of connection.

As I said in that book, the "landscapes" of meaning we live by are never fully explicable by features of the world beyond our experience but have to be explained and justified hermeneutically.[18] Many of the crucial meanings that our world has for us are only identifiable in what I have called here the "interspace."

In fact, the understanding implicit in the HHH theory ramifies in two directions: On one side, theoretically, it makes visible the many ways in which language is crucial to human life, not just as enabling description and theory, but also as constituting the spaces of shared awareness, and the footings we stand on with each other, and the ways we navigate what is not fully decidable, objectively, "scientifically"—through art, music, poetry—and makes these realities palpable for us. On the other side, it invites us to engage in this navigation, this attempt to articulate what is really of ultimate importance to us, in the full gamut of media available to us, including the poetry which has been central to our discussion in this book.

18. Taylor, *Language Animal*, 195–197.

ACKNOWLEDGMENTS

CREDITS

INDEX

ACKNOWLEDGMENTS

My intellectual debts in writing this book are too many to relate here, and they are reflected in the footnotes.

But this work has been accompanied from the very beginning by a lot of uncertainty and self-doubt, and I want to thank especially those whose encouragement has kept me going.

First, my wife, Aube Billard. I have been working on this book, with some interruptions, during the three decades that we have been together. Her affinity for this project, and her belief in it, have kept me on this path in spite of everything. This book is dedicated to her.

I also thank Paolo Costa, who understood the nature of the book I should write and helped me see this.

Finally, I want to express my gratitude to two colleagues in the Centre for Transcultural Studies: Craig Calhoun and Dilip Gaonkar, who helped me overcome my doubts and keep moving. I especially want to thank Craig for his help in organizing the full manuscript and orchestrating the production of the book, as well as Carolyn Forbes and Thomas Sliwowski for their invaluable help in preparing the final manuscript.

CREDITS

INDEX